An Introduction to Cognitive Psychology: Processes and Disorders is a comprehensive introductory textbook for undergraduate students. It covers all the key areas of cognition, including perception, attention, long-term memory, working memory, thinking and language. Uniquely, alongside the chapters on normal cognitive function, there are also chapters on the related clinical disorders - agnosia, amnesia, thought disorder and aphasia, which helps to provide a thorough insight into the nature of cognition.

Key features:

* This new edition has been carefully revised throughout to provide a comprehensive overview of current thinking in the field
* Includes greater coverage of neuropsychological disorders, with additional material from the latest research using brain imaging
* Accessibly written, by authors at the cutting edge of their subject areas
* Specially designed textbook features such as chapter summaries, further reading, and a glossary of key terms

Written to cover all levels of ability using helpful figures and illustrations, this book has sufficient depth to appeal to the most able students while the clear and accessible text, written by experienced teachers, will help students who find the material difficult. It will appeal to any student on an undergraduate psychology degree, and also to those working in related clinical professions such as nursing.

David Groome is Senior Academic in the Psychology Department at the University of Westminster. He has published three previous text books, together with many journal articles and conference presentations. His two main research areas at present are memory and mood disorders.

An Introduction to Cognitive Psychology

■ Processes and disorders

Second edition

David Groome

with Nicola Brace, Hazel Dewart, Graham Edgar,
Helen Edgar, Anthony Esgate, Richard Kemp
Graham Pike and Tom Stafford

Psychology Press
Taylor & Francis Group
HOVE AND NEW YORK

First published 2006
by Psychology Press
27 Church Road, Hove, East Sussex BN3 2FA

Simultaneously published in the USA and
Canada
by Psychology Press
270 Madison Avenue, New York, NY 10016

*Psychology Press is an imprint of the Taylor &
Francis Group, an informa business*

Typeset in Century Old Style and Futura by
Keystroke, 28 High Street, Tettenhall,
Wolverhampton

Printed and bound in Great Britain by
TJ International Ltd, Padstow, Cornwall

Cover design by Anú Design

This publication has been produced with paper
manufactured to strict environmental
standards and with pulp derived from
sustainable forests.

British Library Cataloguing in Publication Data
A catalogue record for this book is available
from the British Library

*Library of Congress Cataloging in Publication
Data*
Groome, David, 1946–
    An introduction to cognitive psychology:
processes and disorders/David Groome
with Nicola Brace . . . [*et al.*].– 2nd ed.
    p. cm.
Includes bibliographical references and
index.
Cognitive psychology – Textbooks.
2. Cognition disorders – Textbooks.
I. Brace, Nicola.   II. Title.
BF201.G76 2006
153–dc22   2006008909

ISBN13: 978–1–84169–543–3 (hbk)
ISBN13: 978–1–84169–544–0 (pbk)

ISBN10: 1–84169–543–2 (hbk)
ISBN10: 1–84169–544–0 (pbk)

Contents at a glance

*Chapter 12 was based on a chapter in the first edition by Kevin Gurney

Contents

CONTENTS

CONTENTS

8   Thinking: problem-solving and reasoning   235

9   Disorders of thinking: executive functions and the frontal lobes   263

Figures

Sources for figures are given below the captions on the pages where they appear in the book. All reasonable efforts have been made to contact copyright holders but in some cases this was not possible. Any omissions brought to the attention of Psychology Press will be remedied in future editions.

Preface

This book is aimed primarily at undergraduate students of psychology and other related disciplines, who should find sufficient depth and range of content to carry them right through to the completion of their degree courses. Whilst this inevitably means that much of the content is pitched at a fairly advanced level, the opening chapter has been deliberately written for the absolute beginner, offering a very simple introduction to the theories and terminology which are dealt with in the subsequent chapters.

We wrote this book because we felt that it filled an important gap. As far as we know, it is the first textbook to cover all of the main aspects of cognitive psychology and all of their associated disorders too. We believe that an understanding of the disorders of cognition is an essential requirement for understanding the processes of normal cognition, and in fact the two approaches are so obviously complementary that we are quite surprised that nobody had put them together in one book before. There are books about normal cognition, and there are books about cognitive disorders (usually referred to as 'cognitive neuropsychology'), but there do not seem to be any other books which cover both topics in full. We feel that this combined approach offers a number of advantages. In the first place, combining normal and abnormal cognition in one book makes it possible to take an integrated approach to these two related fields. References can be made directly between the normal and abnormal chapters, and theories which are introduced in the normal chapters can be reconsidered later from a clinical perspective. We chose to keep the normal and abnormal aspects in separate chapters, as this seemed clearer and also made it more straightforward for those teaching separate normal and abnormal cognitive psychology courses. There is possibly one further advantage of a combined textbook, which is that students can use the same textbook for two different courses of study, thus saving the cost of buying an extra book.

Another reason for writing this book was that we found the other available cognitive psychology texts were rather difficult to read. Our students found these books were heavy going, and so did we. So we set about writing a more interesting and accessible book, by making more connections with real life and everyday experience. We also cut out some of the unnecessary detail that we found in rival texts. For example, most neuropsychology books include a large amount of detail about the anatomical structure of the brain, but most psychology students do not really need this. So we decided to concentrate instead on the psychological aspects of cognitive disorders rather than the anatomical details. And finally, we decided to put in lots of illustrations, because we think it makes the book clearer and more fun to read. And also we just happen to like books which have lots of pictures.

So here then is our textbook of cognitive psychology and cognitive disorders, made as simple as possible, and with lots of pictures. We enjoyed writing it, and we hope you will enjoy reading it.

David Groome

Authors' affiliations

Nicola Brace: Open University (UK)

Hazel Dewart: University of Westminster (UK)

Graham Edgar: University of Gloucestershire (UK)

Helen Edgar: Chartered Psychologist (UK)

Anthony Esgate: Kingston University (UK)

David Groome: University of Westminster (UK)

Richard Kemp: University of New South Wales (Australia)

Graham Pike: Open University (UK)

Tom Stafford: University of Sheffield (UK)

Acknowledgements and thanks

We would like to offer our thanks to a number of people who helped us to produce this book. Firstly, thanks to Kevin Gurney whose chapter in the first edition of this book provided the basis for chapter 12. Many thanks also to Wido La Heij, who provided many helpful comments and suggestions, and who also assisted with some of the figures for chapter 3. Thanks also to Diane Catherwood for some additional figures. Others who gave us advice and help include Gezinus Wolters, Mark Williams, Kevin Brooks, and Kevin Coulson. Finally we would like to thank the staff at Psychology Press, and in particular Tara Stebnicky, Imogen Burch, and Sue Dickinson (freelance copyeditor), for turning our ideas into a book.

Chapter 1

Introduction to cognitive psychology

1.1 Cognitive processes

A definition of cognitive psychology

Cognitive psychology has been defined as the psychology of mental processes. More specifically it has also been described as the study of understanding and knowing. However, these are rather vague terms, and whilst they do provide an indication of what cognition involves they leave us asking exactly what is meant by 'knowing', 'understanding' and 'mental processes'. A more precise definition of cognitive psychology is that it is the study of the way in which the brain processes information. It concerns the way we take in information from the outside world, how we make sense of that information, and what use we make of it. Cognition is thus a rather broad umbrella term, which includes many component processes, and this possibly explains why psychologists have found it so difficult to come up with a simple and unified definition of cognitive psychology. Clearly cognition involves various different kinds of information processing which occur at different stages.

Stages of cognitive processing

The main stages of cognitive processing are shown in Figure 1.1, arranged in the sequential order in which they would typically be applied to a new piece of incoming sensory input.

Information taken in by the sense organs goes through an initial stage of **perception**, which involves the analysis of its content. Even at this early stage of processing the brain is already extracting meaning from the input, in an effort to make sense of the information it contains. The process of perception will often lead to the making of some kind of record of the input received, and this involves *learning* and *memory storage*. Once a memory has been created for some item of information it can be retained for later use, to assist the individual in some other setting. This will normally require the *retrieval* of the information. Retrieval is sometimes carried out for its own sake, merely to access some information stored in the past. On the other hand, we sometimes retrieve information to provide the basis for further mental activities such as *thinking*. Retrieval is often used to assist the thought process, as for example when we use previous experience to help us deal with some new problem or situation. Sometimes this involves the rearrangement and manipulation of stored information to make it fit in with a new problem or task. Thought is thus rather more than just retrieval of old memories.

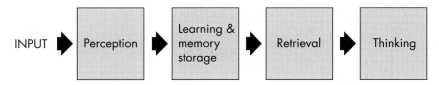

Figure 1.1 The main stages of cognitive processing

The cognitive processes shown in Figure 1.1 are in reality a good deal more complex and interactive than this simple diagram implies. The diagram suggests that the various stages of cognitive processing are clearly distinct from one another, each one in its own box. This is a drastic oversimplification, and it would be more accurate to show the different stages as merging and overlapping with one another. For example, it is impossible to establish the exact point at which perception ceases and memory storage begins, because the process of perception brings about learning and memory storage and thus in a sense these processes are continuous. In fact all of the stages of cognition shown in the diagram overlap and interact with one another, but a diagram which attempted to show all these complex interactions would be far too confusing, and in any case a lot of the interactions would be speculative. Figure 1.1 should therefore be regarded as a much-simplified representation of the general sequential order of the cognitive processes which typically occur, but it would be better to think of cognition as a continuous flow of information from the input stage through to the output stage, undergoing different forms of processing along the way.

Approaches to the study of cognition

There have been four main approaches to the study of cognitive psychology (see Figure 1.2). In the first place there is the approach known as **experimental cognitive psychology**, which involves the use of psychological experiments on human subjects to investigate the ways in which they perceive, learn, remember, or think. A second approach to cognitive psychology is the use of **computer modelling** of cognitive processes. Typically this approach involves the simulation of certain aspects of human cognitive function by writing computer programs, in order to test out the feasibility of a model of possible brain function. The third approach is known as **cognitive neuroscience**, which involves the use of techniques such as brain imaging (i.e. brain scans) to investigate the brain activities that underlie cognitive processing. The fourth main approach is known as cognitive

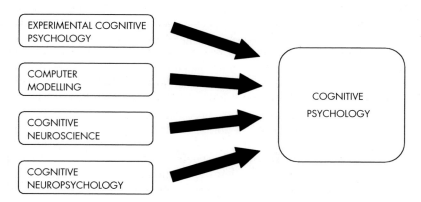

Figure 1.2 The four main approaches to studying cognitive psychology

neuropsychology, which involves the study of individuals who have suffered some form of brain injury. We can discover a great deal about the working of the normal brain by studying the types of cognitive impairment which result from lesions (i.e. damage) in certain regions of the brain. Brain damage can impair information processing by disrupting one or more stages of cognition, or perhaps by breaking the links between stages.

These four approaches have all proved to be valuable, especially when it has been possible to combine different approaches to the same cognitive process. The rest of this chapter deals with these approaches to cognitive psychology, starting with experimental cognitive psychology (Section 1.2), then computer modelling (Section 1.3), and finally cognitive neuroscience and neuropsychology (Section 1.4). Subsequent chapters of the book will continue to apply the same basic approaches in a more detailed study of each of the main areas of cognition.

1.2 Experimental cognitive psychology

The first cognitive psychologists

The scientific study of psychology began towards the end of the nineteenth century. Wilhelm Wundt set up the first psychology laboratory at Leipzig in 1879, where he carried out research on perception, including some of the earliest studies of visual illusions. In 1885 Hermann Ebbinghaus published the first experimental research on memory, and many subsequent researchers were to adopt his methods over the years that followed. Perhaps the most lasting work of this early period was a remarkable book written by William James in 1890, entitled *Principles of Psychology*. In that book James proposed a number of theories which remain acceptable today, including (to give just one example) a theory distinguishing between short-term and long-term memory.

The rise and fall of behaviourism

Cognitive psychology made slow progress in the early years due to the growing influence of **behaviourism**, an approach which constrained psychologists to the investigation of externally observable behaviour. The behaviourist position was clearly stated by Watson (1913), who maintained that psychologists should consider only events that were observable, such as the stimulus presented and any consequent response to that stimulus. Watson argued that psychologists should not concern themselves with processes such as thought and other inner mental processes which could not be observed in a scientific manner. The behaviourists were essentially trying to establish psychology as a true science, comparable in status with other sciences such as physics or chemistry. This was a worthy aim, but like many worthy aims it was taken too far. The refusal to consider inner mental processes had the effect of restricting experimental psychology to the recording of observable responses, which were often of a rather trivial nature. Indeed, some behaviourists were so keen to eliminate inner mental processes from their studies that they preferred to work on rats rather than on human subjects. A human being brings a whole lifetime of personal experience to the laboratory, which cannot be observed or controlled by the experimenter. A rat presents rather fewer of these unknown and uncontrolled variables. A good example of the behaviourist approach is the classic work carried out on learning by B.F. Skinner (1938), who trained rats to press a lever in order to obtain a food pellet as a reward (or 'reinforcement'). The work of Skinner and other behaviourists undoubtedly generated some important findings, but they completely disregarded the cognitive processes underlying the responses they were studying.

Despite these restrictions on mainstream psychological research, some psychologists began to realise that a proper understanding of human cognition could only be achieved by investigating the mental processes which the behaviourists were so determined to eliminate from their studies. Among the first of these pioneers were the **Gestalt** psychologists in Germany and the British psychologist Frederick Bartlett, who between them helped to lay the foundations of modern cognitive psychology.

Gestalt and schema theories

It is very easy to demonstrate the importance of inner mental processes in human cognition. For example, a glance at Figure 1.3 will evoke the same clear response in almost any observer. It is a human face. However, a more objective analysis of the components of the figure reveals that it actually consists of a circle and two straight lines. There is really no 'face' as such in the figure itself. If you see a face in this simple figure, then it is you, the observer, who has ADDED the face from your own store of knowledge.

The idea that we contribute something to our perceptual input from our own knowledge and experience was actually proposed by a number of early theorists, notably the Gestalt group (Gestalt is German for 'shape' or 'form'). They suggested that we add something to what we perceive, so that the perception of a whole object will therefore be something more than just the sum of its component parts

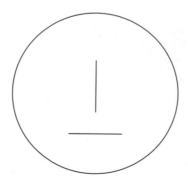

Figure 1.3 A shape recognised by most observers

(Wertheimer, 1912; Köhler, 1925). They argued that the perception of a figure depended on its 'pragnanz' (i.e. its meaningful content), which favoured the selection of the simplest and best interpretation available (Koffka, 1935). These theories were perhaps rather vague, but they did at least represent an attempt to explain the perception of complex figures such as faces. The behaviourist approach, which refused to consider any influence other than the stimulus itself, could not offer any explanation at all for such phenomena.

The **schema** theory proposed by Bartlett (1932) was another early attempt to provide a plausible explanation for our ability to make sense of perceptual input. The schema theory proposes that all new perceptual input is analysed by comparing it with items which are already in our memory store, such as shapes and sounds which are familiar from past experience. These items are referred to as 'schemas', and they include a huge variety of sensory patterns and concepts. Figure 1.4 illustrates the process of selection of an appropriate schema to match the incoming stimulus (NB: This is purely diagrammatic. In reality there are probably millions of schemas available, but there was not enough space for me to draw the rest of them).

The schema theory has some interesting implications, because it suggests that our perception and subsequent memory of an input may be changed and distorted to fit our existing schemas. It also suggests that we make sense of our perceptual input in terms of our knowledge and past experience, which will differ from person to person. Different people will therefore perceive the same input in different ways, depending on their own unique backlog of experience. Both of these phenomena were demonstrated by Bartlett's experiments (see Chapter 5 for more details), so the schema theory can be seen to have considerable explanatory value.

The schema approach has much in common with the old saying that 'beauty lies in the eye of the beholder'. Perhaps we could adapt that saying to fit the more general requirements of schema theory, by suggesting that 'perception lies in the brain of the perceiver'. As a summary of schema theory this is possibly an improvement, but I would concede that it possibly lacks the poetry of the original.

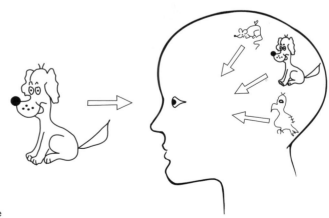

Figure 1.4
Schemas generated for comparison with new input
Source: Drawing by David Groome

Schema and Gestalt theory had a major influence on the development of cognitive psychology, by emphasising the role played by inner mental processes and stored knowledge, rather than considering only the stimulus and the response to it.

Top-down and bottom-up processing

Inspired by the schema theory, Neisser (1967) identified two main types of input processing known as **top-down** and **bottom-up processing**. Top-down processing involves the generation of schemas by the higher cortical structures, and these schemas are sent down the nervous system for comparison with the incoming stimulus. Top-down processing is also sometimes referred to as **schema-driven** or conceptually-driven processing.

Bottom-up processing is initiated by stimulation at the 'bottom end' of the nervous system (i.e. the sense organs), which then progresses up towards the higher cortical areas. Bottom-up processing is also known as **stimulus-driven** or data-driven processing, because it is the incoming stimulus which sets off some appropriate form of processing. One obvious difference between 'top-down' and 'bottom-up' processing is that their information flows in opposite directions, as shown in Figure 1.5.

Bottom-up processing theories can help to explain the fact that processing is often determined by the nature of the stimulus (Gibson, 1979). However, bottom-up theories have difficulty explaining the perception of complex stimuli, which can be more easily explained by top-down theories.

Schemas

Top-down processing

Bottom-up processing

Stimulus

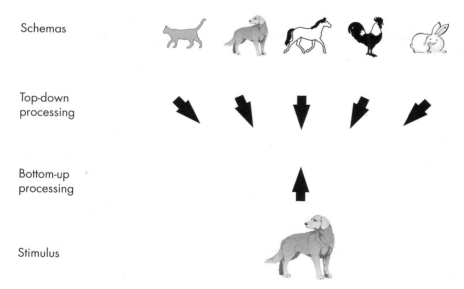

Figure 1.5 Top-down and bottom-up processing

7

Although there have been disputes in the past about the relative importance of 'top-down' and 'bottom-up' processing, Neisser (1967) argues that both types of processing probably play a part in the analysis of perceptual input and that in most cases information processing will involve a combination of the two. We can thus think of input processing in terms of stimulus information coming up the system, where it meets and interacts with schemas travelling down in the opposite direction.

1.3 Computer models of information processing

Computer analogies and computer modelling of brain functions

A major shift towards the cognitive approach began in the 1950s, when the introduction of the electronic computer provided a new source of inspiration for cognitive psychologists. Computer systems offered some completely new ideas about information processing, providing a helpful analogy with possible brain mechanisms. Furthermore, computers could be used as a 'test-bed' for modelling possible human brain functions, providing a means of testing the feasibility of a particular processing mechanism. By separating out the various component stages of a cognitive process, it is possible to devise a sequential flow chart which can be written as a computer program and actually put to the test, to see whether it can process information as the brain would. Of course, such experiments cannot prove that the programs and mechanisms operating within the computer are the same as the mechanisms which occur in the brain, but they can at least establish the basic feasibility of a processing system.

Among the first to apply computers in this way were Newell *et al.* (1958), who developed computer programs which were able to solve simple problems, suggesting a possible comparison with human problem-solving and thought. More recently, programs have been developed which can tackle far more complex problems, such as playing a game of chess.

Subsequently computer programs were developed which could carry out perceptual processes, such as the recognition of complex stimuli. These programs made use of feature detector systems, which are explained in the next section.

Feature detectors

Selfridge and Neisser (1960) devised a computer system which could identify shapes and patterns by means of **feature detectors**, tuned to distinguish certain specific components of the stimulus such as vertical or horizontal lines. This was achieved by wiring light sensors together in such a way that all those lying in a straight line at a particular angle converged on the same feature detector, as illustrated in Figure 1.6.

This system of convergent wiring will ensure that the feature detector will be automatically activated whenever a line at that particular angle is encountered.

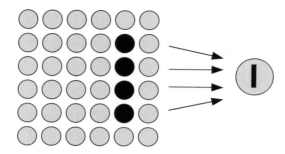

Figure 1.6 Wiring to a simple feature detector

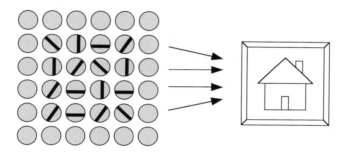

Figure 1.7 Wiring to a complex feature detector

Simple feature detectors of this kind could be further combined higher up the system to activate complex feature detectors, capable of detecting more complicated shapes and patterns made up out of these simple components (see Figure 1.7).

A hierarchy of feature detectors continuing through many levels of increasing complexity could, at least in theory, identify very complex shapes such as faces. Selfridge and Neisser demonstrated that such a system of simple and complex feature detectors could be made to work very effectively on a computer, which suggests that it does provide a feasible mechanism for the identification of shapes and patterns. This raised the possibility that human perception could involve similar feature-detecting systems, and indeed such feature detectors have been found in the brain. Hubel and Weisel (1959) found simple feature detector cells when carrying out microelectrode recordings in the brain of a cat, and recently Haynes and Rees (2005) have found similar feature detector cells in the human brain by means of functional imaging techniques.

The discovery of feature detectors can be regarded as an example of different approaches to cognition being combined, with contributions from both neuroscience and computer modelling. The concept has also had a major influence on cognitive psychology because feature detectors are thought to operate as 'mini-schemas' which detect specific shapes and patterns. This approach paved the way towards more advanced theories of perception and pattern recognition based on computer models, such as those of Marr (1982) and McClelland and Rumelhart (1986). These theories are considered in more detail in Chapter 12.

The limited-capacity processor model

Broadbent (1958) carried out experiments on divided attention, which showed that people have difficulty in attending to two separate inputs at the same time. Broadbent analysed his findings in terms of a sequence of processing stages which could be represented as a series of stages in a flow chart. Certain crucial stages were identified which acted as a 'bottleneck' to information flow because of their limited processing capacity (see Figure 1.8).

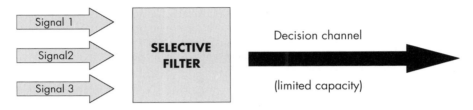

Figure 1.8 Broadbent's model of selective attention

This was an approach to information processing which owed its inspiration to computing and telecommunications technology. There is a clear parallel between the human brain faced with a large array of incoming information and a telephone exchange faced with a large number of incoming calls, or alternatively a computer whose input has exceeded its processing capacity. In each case many inputs are competing with one another for limited processing resources, and the inputs must be prioritised and selectively processed if an information overload is to be avoided. Broadbent referred to this process as 'selective attention', and his theoretical model of the 'limited-capacity processor' provided cognitive psychology with an important new concept.

This work on selective attention will be considered in more detail in Chapter 3, and the general approach of computer modelling is fully covered in Chapter 12. But for the moment these approaches are of interest chiefly for their role in the early development of cognitive psychology.

1.4 Cognitive neuroscience and neuropsychology

The structure and function of the brain

Cognitive neuroscience is concerned with the relationship between brain function and cognition, and normally makes use of brain imaging techniques. Cognitive

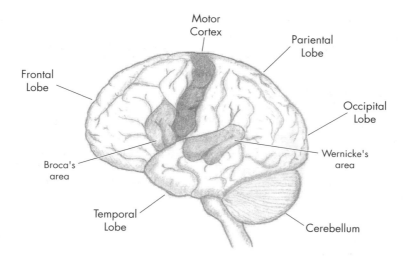

Figure 1.9 A side view of the human brain, showing the main lobes
Source: Drawing by David Groome

neuropsychology is also concerned with the brain mechanisms underlying cognition, by studying individuals who have suffered brain damage. Both of these related approaches are now accepted as important components of cognitive psychology.This is not a textbook of neurology, so it would not be appropriate here to deal with brain anatomy and function in any great depth. However, there will be references throughout this book to various regions of the brain, so there is a need for a very basic working map of the brain. Figure 1.9 presents a side view of the human brain, showing the position of its main structures.

The outer shell of the brain is known as the cerebral cortex, and it is responsible for most of the higher cognitive processes. The various lobes of the cortex are extensively interconnected, so that a single cognitive process may involve many different cortical areas. However, the brain is to some extent 'modular' in that certain brain areas do perform specific functions. We know this largely from the study of brain lesions, since damage to a certain part of the brain can often cause quite specific impairments. In recent years the introduction of brain scanning equipment has provided an additional source of knowledge to supplement the findings of brain lesion studies.

Taking a general overview of the whole brain, it has been established that the left and right hemispheres have particular specialisations. In right-handed people the left hemisphere of the brain is normally dominant (the nerves from the brain cross over to control the opposite side of the body), and the left hemisphere also tends to be particularly involved with language and speech. The right hemisphere seems to be more concerned with the processing of non-verbal input, such as the perception of patterns or faces. These functions may be reversed in left-handed people, though most have left hemisphere specialisation for language.

It would appear then (to borrow a football cliché) that it is a brain of two halves. But in addition to these specialisations of the right and left hemispheres, it can be argued that the front and the rear halves of the brain also have broadly different functions. Luria (1973) points out that the front half of the brain (in fact the area corresponding to the frontal lobes) is primarily concerned with output, for example the control of movements and speech. In contrast the rear half of the brain (the parietal, temporal and occipital lobes) tend to be more concerned with the processing of input, as for example in the analysis of visual and auditory perception.

The *frontal lobes* include the *motor region* of the cortex, which controls movement. Damage to this area is likely to cause problems with the control of movement, or even paralysis. Also in the frontal lobes is **Broca's area**, which controls the production of speech, and is normally in the left hemisphere of the brain. It was Broca (1861) who first noted that damage to this region caused an impairment of speech production. Other parts of the frontal lobes seem to have less specific functions, but the frontal cortex does seem to be involved in the **central executive** system which controls conscious mental processes such as the making of conscious decisions.

The *occipital lobes* at the back of the brain are mainly concerned with the processing of visual input, and damage to the occipital lobes may severely impair visual perception. The *parietal lobes* are also largely concerned with perception. They contain the *somatic sensory cortex*, which receives tactile input from the skin as well as feedback from the muscles and internal organs. This region is also important in the perception of pain, and other parts of the parietal lobes may be involved in some aspects of short-term memory.

The *temporal lobes* are so called because they lie beneath the temples, and they are known to be particularly concerned with memory. Temporal lobe lesions are often associated with severe amnesia. For example, Milner (1966) reported that a patient called HM, whose temporal lobes had been partly removed by surgery, was unable to register any new memories. The temporal lobes also include the main auditory area of the cortex, and a language centre known as **Wernicke's area** (again usually in the left hemisphere), which is particularly concerned with memory for language and the understanding of speech (Wernicke, 1874).

The study of brain and cognition obviously overlap, and in recent years cognitive psychologists and neuropsychologists have been able to learn a lot from one another. A deliberate attempt has been made in this book to bring normal cognitive psychology and cognitive neuropsychology together, to take full advantage of this relationship.

Information storage in the brain

In order to operate as an information-processing system, the brain must obviously have some way of representing information, for both processing and storage purposes. Information must be encoded in some representational or symbolic form, which may bear no direct resemblance to the material being encoded.

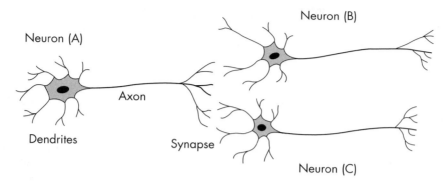

Figure 1.10 Neurons and their connecting synapses

Will neuron (A) succeed in firing neuron (B), or neuron (C)? Whichever neuron is fired, this will strengthen the synaptic connection between the two neurons involved

Source: Drawing by David Groome

Consider, for example, how music may be encoded and stored as digital information on a silicon chip, laser-readable pits on a CD, as electromagnetic fields on a tape, as grooves on a vinyl disc (remember them?), or even as notes written on a piece of paper. It does not matter what form of storage is used, so long as you have the equipment to encode and decode the information.

There have been many theories about the way information might be represented and stored in the brain, including early suggestions that information could be stored in magnetic form (Lashley, 1950) or in chemical form (Hyden, 1967). However, neither of these theories was very plausible because such mechanisms would be unable to offer the necessary storage capacity, accessibility, or durability over time. The most plausible explanation currently available for the neural basis of information storage is the proposal by Donald Hebb (1949) that memories are stored by creating new connections between neurons (see Figure 1.10).

The entire nervous system, including the brain, is composed of millions of neurons, which can activate one another by transmitting chemical substances called **neurotransmitters** across the gap separating them, which is known as the **synapse**. All forms of neural activity, including perception, speech, or even thought, work by transmitting a signal along a series of neurons in this way. These cognitive processes are therefore dependent on the ability of one neuron to activate another. Hebb's theory postulated that if two adjacent neurons (i.e. nerve cells) are fired off simultaneously, then the connection between them will be strengthened. Thus a synapse which has been frequently crossed in the past will be more easily crossed by future signals. It is as though a path is being worn through the nervous system, much as you would wear a path through a field of corn by repeatedly walking through it. In both cases, a path is left behind which can be more easily crossed in future.

Hebb argued that this mechanism of synaptic strengthening would make it possible to build up a network of interconnected neurons, which could represent a particular pattern of input. Hebb called this a **cell assembly**. Figure 1.11 shows

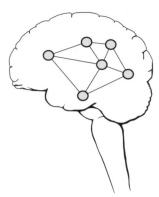

Figure 1.11 A cell assembly

a diagrammatic representation of such a cell assembly, though in practice there would probably be thousands of neurons involved in each cell assembly rather than half a dozen as shown here.

Hebb argued that a cell assembly such as this could come to represent a particular stimulus, such as an object or a face. If the stimulus had caused this particular group of neurons to fire simultaneously, then the neurons would become connected to one another more and more strongly with repeated exposure to the stimulus. Eventually the cell assembly would become a permanent structure, readily activated by any similar stimulation in the future.

Hebb's theory has considerable explanatory value. In the first place it can explain how thoughts and memories may come to be associated with one another in memory. If two cell assemblies are activated simultaneously then some of the neurons in one assembly are likely to become connected to neurons in the other assembly, so that in future the activation of either one will activate the other.

Hebb's theory can also explain the difference between short-term and long-term memory. Hebb speculated that the temporary activation of a cell assembly by active neural firing could be the mechanism underlying short-term memory, which is known to be fragile and short-lived. However, after repeated firing the synaptic connections between the neurons in the assembly eventually become permanent, and this provides the basis of long-term memory storage. The creation of a lasting memory is thus seen as depending upon permanent changes to the synapse.

When Donald Hebb first proposed this theory in 1949, it was still largely speculative. However, since that time a great deal of evidence has been gathered to confirm that the synapse does indeed change as a result of frequent firing of the neuron. Perhaps the most convincing evidence is the discovery that when electrical stimulation is applied to living tissue taken from the brain of a rat, the neurons do actually change in a lasting way, with their threshold of firing becoming much lower so they can be more easily activated by subsequent stimuli (Bliss and Lomo, 1973). This phenomenon is known as **long-term potentiation (LTP)**. It has also been found that rats reared in a stimulating and enriched environment, with plenty of sensory input, develop more synaptic connections in their brains than rats reared in an impoverished environment where there is little to stimulate them (Greenough, 1987). More recent research has shown that short-term storage involves the strengthening of pre-existing synaptic connections, whereas long-term storage involves the growth of new synaptic connections between the neurons (Bailey and Kandel, 2004).

Brain imaging techniques such as PET scans have recently confirmed that memory storage and retrieval do in fact coincide with the activation of large-scale neural networks spread diffusely through the brain (Habib *et al.*, 2003). Reviewing all this research, Bailey and Kandel (2004) conclude that activity-dependent modification of synaptic strength has now been established as the probable mechanism of memory storage in the brain. It has taken over half a century to collect the evidence, but it begins to look as if Donald Hebb got it right.

1.5 Unconscious and automatic processing

Automatic and controlled processing

Schneider and Shiffrin (1977) made a distinction between **controlled** cognitive processes, which are carried out consciously and intentionally, and **automatic** cognitive processes, which are not under conscious control. They suggested that because controlled processes require conscious attention they are subject to limitations in processing capacity, whereas automatic processes do not require attention and are not subject to such processing limits. Automatic processing will therefore take place far more rapidly than controlled processing, and will be relatively unaffected by distraction from a second task taking up attention. Another feature of automatic processing is that it is not a voluntary process, and it will take place regardless of the wishes and intentions of the individual.

For a simple demonstration of automatic processing in a cognitive task, try looking at the words in Figure 1.12, taking care *not* to read them. You will undoubtedly have found it impossible to obey the instruction not to read the message in Figure 1.12. Reading is a largely automatic process (at least for practised readers) and you will therefore find that if you attend to the message you cannot prevent yourself from reading it. Schneider and Shiffrin suggested that cognitive processes

DO NOT READ THIS MESSAGE

Figure 1.12 A demonstration of automatic processing

become automatic as a result of frequent practice, as for example the skills involved in driving a car, in playing a piano, or in reading words from a page. However, we have the ability to override these automatic sequences when we need to, for example when we come across an unusual traffic situation while driving.

The automatic processing of words was first clearly demonstrated by Stroop (1935), who presented his subjects with colour words (e.g. red, blue, green) printed in different coloured inks. Subjects were instructed to name the ink colours as rapidly as possible, but they were not required to read the words. Stroop found that subjects could name the ink colour far more rapidly if it matched the word itself (e.g. the word 'red' printed in red ink) than if it did not (e.g. the word 'red' printed in blue ink). Since the words had a marked interfering effect on the colour-naming task despite the fact that subjects were not required to read them, it was assumed that they must have been read automatically. More recent theories about the stroop effect are discussed in McLeod (1998).

The distinction between controlled and automatic processing has been useful in many areas of cognitive psychology. One example is face familiarity. When you meet someone you have met before, you instantly and automatically recognise their face as familiar, but remembering where and when you have met them before requires conscious effort (Mandler, 1980).

Automatic processing has also been used to explain the occurrence of everyday 'action slips', which are basically examples of absentmindedness. For example, the author found during a recent car journey that instead of driving to his present house as he had intended, he had in fact driven to his previous address by force of habit. This was quite disturbing for the author, but considerably more disturbing for the owner of the house. Another of the author's recent action slips involved absentmindedly adding instant coffee to a mug which already contained a teabag, thus creating a hybrid beverage of a highly unpalatable nature. Action slips of this kind have been extensively documented and in most cases can be explained by the activation or perseveration of automatic process which are not appropriate (Reason, 1979).

Norman and Shallice (1986) suggest that automatic processes can provide adequate control of our neural functions in most routine situations without needing to use up our attention, but they must be overridden by the supervisory attention system when more complex or novel tasks require the flexibility of conscious control (see Figure 1.13). Crick and Koch (1990) argue that the flexibility of the conscious control system stems largely from its capacity for binding together many different mental activities, such as thoughts and perceptions. Baddeley (1997) suggests that conscious control may reside in the central executive component of the working memory (see Chapter 6), which is largely associated with frontal lobe function.

Johnson-Laird (1983) compares conscious control with the operating system that controls a computer. He suggests that consciousness is essentially a system which monitors a large number of hierarchically organised parallel processors. On occasion these processors may reach a state of deadlock, either because the instructions they generate conflict with one another, or possibly because they are mutually dependent on output from one another. Such

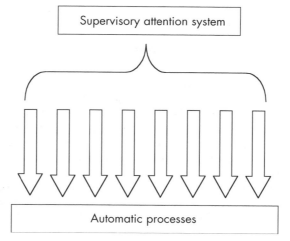

Figure 1.13
The supervisory attention system model

Source: From Norman and Shallice (1986)

'pathological configurations' need to be overridden by some form of control system, and this may be the role of consciousness.

Such theories add an interesting perspective to our view of automatic processing. Automatic processes are obviously of great value to us, as they allow us to carry out routine tasks rapidly and without using up our limited attentional capacity. However, automatic processes lack flexibility, and when they fail to provide appropriate behaviour they need to be overridden by consciously controlled processing. There is some evidence that this override system may be located in the frontal lobes of the brain, since patients with frontal lesions are often found to exhibit perseveration of automatic behaviour and a lack of flexibility of response (Shallice and Burgess, 1991; Parkin, 1997). Frontal lobe functions will be examined further in Chapters 8 and 9.

Conscious awareness

We all have consciousness, but none of us really know what it is. I am quite certain that I am conscious because I experience things consciously, and you probably feel the same. We can all understand what is meant by the term consciousness as a subjective experience, but no one has yet been able to provide an explanation of what conscious awareness actually is, or how it might arise from neural activity. Indeed the very assumption that conscious awareness must somehow arise from the mere firing of neural circuits seems remarkable in itself. Crick (1994) calls it 'the astonishing hypothesis', yet it remains the only plausible hypothesis.

Consciousness remains the last unexplored frontier of psychology, and arguably one of the greatest mysteries of life itself. Although we do not understand what consciousness is, we are beginning to learn something about what consciousness does, and the part it plays in cognitive processes. As explained in the previous section, psychologists have recently devised methods of distinguishing between processes which are consciously controlled and those which are unconscious and automatic. For example, judging whether a person's face is familiar seems to occur automatically and unconsciously, but if we need to remember actual occasions when we have previously met them, then a conscious recollection process is required (Mandler, 1980). This distinction will be considered in more detail in Chapter 5.

The study of patients with certain types of brain lesion has provided particularly valuable insights into the nature of conscious and unconscious cognitive processes. For example, some patients with occipital lobe lesions can detect visual stimuli at an unconscious level, despite having no conscious awareness of seeing them (Weiskrantz, 1986). This phenomenon is known as **blindsight**, and it will be examined in more detail in Chapter 4. A similar phenomenon has been observed in amnesic patients, who often reveal evidence of previous learning of which they have no conscious recollection whatsoever. Mandler (1989) has argued that it is usually not the memory trace which is lost, but the patient's ability to bring it into consciousness. These studies of amnesia will also be discussed further in Chapter 7.

Autism is another disorder which has shed light on the nature of consciousness, because autistic individuals appear to lack some of the characteristics of conscious processing. Their behaviour tends to be highly inflexible and repetitious, and they usually lack the ability to form plans or generate new ideas spontaneously. Autistic individuals also tend to lack the ability to develop a rapport with others, and often disregard other people as though they were merely objects. Observations of such symptoms have led Baron-Cohen (1992) to suggest that autistic people may lack a 'theory of mind', meaning that they are unable to understand the existence of mental processes in others. This may provide a clue about some of the possible benefits of having consciousness. An awareness of other peoples' thoughts and feelings is crucial if we are to understand their behaviour, and it is also an essential requirement for normal social interaction.

Figure 1.14 Does your dog have conscious awareness? And is he wondering the same thing about you?

Source: Drawing by David Groome

One interesting finding from an EEG study (Libet, 1985) is that when we make a conscious decision to act in some way, the conscious awareness of the decision appears to follow the actual decision, rather than preceding it. From such findings Wegner and Wheatley (1999) have suggested that decisions may actually be made at an unconscious level, and the conscious awareness of the decision only follows later when we observe its outcome. This is an interesting view, as it reverses the usual assumption that decisions arise from a conscious process. Indeed it is a view that questions the very existence of free will, suggesting that the impression we have of making conscious decisions may be illusory.

The studies discussed above appear to shed some light on the nature of consciousness, but this too may be illusory. They may tell us a little about what consciousness does, or which parts of the brain are involved, but we are no nearer to knowing what consciousness actually is, or how it arises from neural activity. As philosopher David Chalmers (1995) puts it, we are addressing 'the easy questions' about consciousness, but making no progress at all with 'the hard question'. Sutherland (1989) put it even more strongly when he remarked of consciousness that 'nothing worth reading has ever been written on it'. McGinn (1999) suggests that human beings will never fully understand the nature of consciousness, because it may be beyond the capability of the human brain to do so. Blackmore (2001) takes a somewhat more optimistic view. She believes that understanding consciousness will one day be possible, but only if we can find a totally different way of thinking about consciousness, since there is apparently something fundamentally wrong with our present approach. For the moment I tend to side with the pessimists, if only because the best brains in the known universe have been working on the problem of consciousness for many centuries without making any worthwhile progress. I hope that someone will one day prove me wrong.

1.6 Minds, brains and computers

Integrating the main approaches to cognition

It has been argued in this chapter that our present understanding of cognitive psychology has arisen from the interaction between experimental cognitive psychology, cognitive neuroscience, cognitive neuropsychology and computer modelling. These different approaches were first brought together in Ulric Neisser's (1967) book *Cognitive Psychology*, which was an important turning-point in the study of human cognition.

The same four approaches provide the subject matter of the rest of this book, and they will be applied to each of the main areas of cognitive processing in turn. These areas are perception, attention, memory, thinking and language, and there will be a separate chapter on each of these processes. A unique feature of this book is that each chapter (or pair of chapters) on a particular cognitive process is followed by a chapter dealing with its associated disorders. In this way it is intended that the relationship between normal cognition and cognitive disorders can be fully explored and understood.

Summary

- Cognitive psychology is the study of how information is processed by the brain. It includes the study of perception, learning, memory, thinking, and language.
- Historically there have been four main strands of research which have all contributed to our present understanding of cognitive psychology. They are experimental cognitive psychology, cognitive neuroscience, cognitive neuro-psychology, and computer modelling of cognitive processes.
- Experimental cognitive psychology has provided theories to explain how the brain interprets incoming information, such as the schema theory which postulates that past experience is used to analyse new perceptual input.
- Computer modelling has provided models of human cognition based on information processing principles, and introduced important new concepts such as feature detector systems and processors of limited channel capacity.
- Cognitive neuroscience makes use of brain imaging techniques to investigate the relationship between brain mechanisms and cognition.
- Cognitive neuropsychology provides knowledge about brain function based on the study of people who have suffered cognitive impairment as a result of brain lesions.
- The science of cognitive psychology has generated new concepts and theories, such as the distinction between top-down and bottom-up processing, and the distinction between automatic and controlled processing.
- The study of consciousness has yielded some interesting findings but at present we have no real understanding of what consciousness is, or how it arises from neural activity.

Further reading

Neisser, U. (1967). *Cognitive Psychology*. New York: Appleton-Century-Crofts. This was the book which provided the main starting-point for modern cognitive psychology. Of course it is well out of date now, but still of historical interest.

Blackmore, S. (2003). *Consciousness: An Introduction*. London: Hodder Arnold. Susan Blackmore embarks on a search for human consciousness. She doesn't find it, but the search is interesting.

Esgate, A. and Groome D. *et al.* (2005). *Introduction to Applied Cognitive Psychology*. Hove: Psychology Press. This book is about the application of cognitive psychology to real-life settings. There are very few books on this topic at present, so if you are interested in the practical applications of cognitive psychology you have little choice but to get this one. I cannot praise this text highly enough, though this is possibly because I am one of the authors.

Perception

2.1 Introduction

Our perception of the world is something that we often tend to take for granted. We detect the sights, sounds, smells, etc. of things around us, and (sometimes) recognise objects and make decisions about how we are going to interact with them. It all seems so simple – until you try and work out how the process of perception operates. There are many theories of perception and they can appear to be quite different and, indeed, sometimes contradictory. It *is* possible that some of the theories are right and any contradictory theories are wrong, but it is more likely that the various theories are just looking at different aspects of a very complicated process. As an analogy, imagine trying to produce a theory of how a car works. One theory could be based on which pedals need to be pressed to make the car go, another could present the theory of the internal combustion engine. Both theories would provide valuable insight into how the car works, but would appear to be quite different. This chapter will thus provide an overview of a number of theories and will attempt to reconcile the different theories to give an impression of how perception 'works'.

2.2 Visual perception

Theories of perception – schemas and template matching

The Grimm's fairy tale of 'Little Red Riding Hood' (Grimm and Grimm, 1909; first published 1812), illustrated in Figure 2.1, is an excellent illustration of a problem that lies at the very heart of the process of perception. Little Red Riding Hood is fooled, and ultimately eaten (although there *is* a happy ending) by a wolf that tricks her, masquerading as her grandmother. So a key issue for perception (and

Figure 2.1 'But, Grandmother, what big teeth you've got.'
Source: Drawing by David Groome

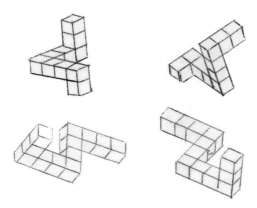

Figure 2.2 Stimuli of the kind used by Shepard and Metzler (1971)

The participants' task was to judge whether or not the figure on the right was a rotated version of the one on the left (as in the top pair above) – or a different figure (as in the bottom pair).

Source: Adapted from Shepard and Metzler (1971)

for Little Red Riding Hood!) is how *do* we recognise an object such as a chair or our grandmother? Just as importantly, how do we recognise when an object has changed and granny has, for instance, been replaced by a scheming and very hungry wolf? Well, one way to recognise your grandmother would be to have an internal schema or 'template' that could be compared with incoming sensory information. If the incoming sensory information matches the grandmother template then she is recognised. The template theory is essentially a development of the schema theory introduced in Chapter 1, as it is a system which uses information from past experience to make sense of a new stimulus.

There is some evidence for the existence of internal **templates**. For instance, Shepard and Metzler (1971) did experiments that required people to say whether two shapes (such as those shown in Figure 2.2) were the same or different (e.g. mirror images). The more the picture of one shape was rotated from the other, the longer it took people to make a decision. This suggests that people could be rotating a **template** of one shape to see if the second shape fits it. Template matching can only occur (if it occurs at all), however, after information from the outside world has been encoded in some way by the visual system. This, in itself, is not a trivial problem. For instance, in the Shepard and Metzler task, how do we pick the shape out from the background and work out just what we are going to compare with our template?

The Gestalt approach

The issue of how objects are defined was central to the theories developed by the Gestalt approach (Rubin, 1915; Wertheimer, 1923), which was introduced in

Figure 2.3 A reversible figure

If you concentrate on the white area as the figure then you will see a vase; if you concentrate on the black areas then you will see two faces. Adapted from Rubin (1915).

Chapter 1. A key issue addressed by the Gestalt psychologists was the way that we might segregate the world into figures and the background against which they appear. This may sound trivial but is crucial as, if we are to recognise objects, we need to be able to tell them apart from everything else. The importance of figure and ground can be illustrated by one of the well-known 'reversible figures' shown in Figure 2.3. If you consider the white area to be the 'figure' and the black area the 'ground' then you see a vase. If you consider the black area to be the figure and the white area to be the ground then you see two faces. The picture is the same, but it can be segregated into figure and ground in different ways and demonstrates the influence on perception that organising things into figure and ground can have. Before deciding which part of the scene is the figure and which parts are ground it is necessary to decide which parts of a visual scene constitute a single object. Gestalt psychologists proposed a number of laws of perceptual organisation that could be used to group parts of a visual scene into objects. Two of these laws are illustrated in Figure 2.4.

While appealing, however, the Gestalt approach only covers a small part of the process of visual perception. For instance, using Gestalt laws we could work out which parts of the visual scene are objects that we might be interested in, and compare them to a template to decide what they are. Both the Gestalt and template-matching theories are, however, rather vague in specifying how we might get information into the 'system' in the first place, although a possible mechanism is provided by feature-extraction theories.

Feature-extraction theories

Feature detectors were introduced in Chapter 1 as a possible mechanism for extracting the features contained in an incoming stimulus. In many ways, feature-extraction theories are simply a variation on template theories; it is just the nature of the template that is different. Rather than trying to match an entire object (such as a grandmother) to a template, feature-extraction theories look to break objects down into their component features. The process is basically still

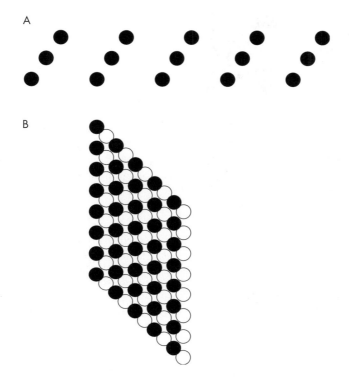

Figure 2.4 Examples of Gestalt laws of perceptual organisation

(A) Demonstrates the law of proximity. Items that are grouped close together tend to be considered as part of the same object and so (A) is usually perceived as five slanted lines of dots rather than three horizontal lines. (B) Demonstrates the law of similarity. Although the circles can be 'grouped' in many different ways it appears to be natural to group them on the basis of common colour.

template matching, but with *features* of the object rather than the whole thing at once. A key issue, of course, is just what constitutes a feature? Little Red Riding Hood appears (unsuccessfully) to have been applying a form of feature extraction in order to recognise her grandmother (picking out ears, eyes, hands and, finally, teeth). Perhaps one of the nicest conceptualisations of the feature-extraction approach was Selfridge's Pandemonium model (Selfridge, 1959) which is illustrated in Figure 2.5. The way that the model works is that there are layers of 'demons'. Demons at the lowest level in the system (remember this is essentially a bottom-up approach) look for very simple features (such as lines or angles). Each demon looks for only one feature. If they 'see' it, they shout. Demons at the next level up listen and only respond if certain combinations of demons shout. If this happens, then they have detected a more complex feature (such as a line-junction), and they will shout about that. So each level of demons detects more

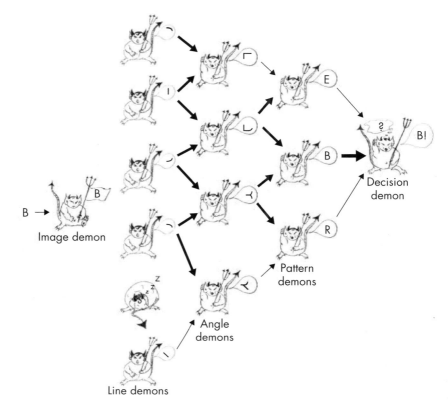

Figure 2.5 Pandemonium (Selfridge, 1959)

The heavier arrows illustrate which demons are shouting the loudest!

Source: Adapted from Lindsay and Norman (1972); demon artwork by Helen Edgar

and more complex features, until the object is recognised. Of course, as many demons are likely to be shouting at once it will be pandemonium, hence the name.

Most people would probably not believe that we have little demons in our brain, but the feature-extracting computer model of Selfridge and Neisser (1960) discussed in Chapter 1 suggests that the general approach is workable. Furthermore, there has long been evidence to suggest that, at least at the lower levels of the visual system, there are cells that do the job of Selfridge's demons. For instance Kuffler (1953) demonstrated that cells in the cat retina (ganglion cells) responded to a spot of light at a particular position in the visual field. Hubel and Wiesel (1959) found cells in the cat's brain (in the visual cortex) that responded to edges and lines. These cells receive inputs arising from ganglion cells and, of course, you can construct relatively complex features such as edges and lines from simple features such as spots. Modern brain imaging techniques also support the existence of 'feature detectors' in the human brain (Haynes and Rees, 2005).

Thus there is a physiological basis for feature-extraction theories, at least at the 'lower' levels of the visual system.

Breaking an image down into its component features is a useful way of coding information within the visual system, but the difficult part is working out how the different features can be interpreted and used to recognise an object. Essentially, they have to be put back together again.

Marr's computational theory

Marr (1982) developed an approach that concentrated on the implementation of some of the processes discussed above, progressing through a number of stages until an internal representation of the viewed object is achieved. The first stage is called the *raw primal sketch* when features such as circles and lines are extracted from the image. In particular, Marr proposed that the visual system can use *natural constraints* to work out which features form the borders of an object. For instance, a border that is created by the edge of an object tends to have a greater and more sharply defined change in luminance than an edge caused by, for instance, a shadow. Once the features have been identified, they can be grouped according to Gestalt principles and these groups of features then define the surface of the object. This is referred to as the *2 1/2-D sketch*. This sketch is only 2 1/2-D and not 3-D as it is a representation of an object – but only from the viewpoint of the person looking at it. From this 2 1/2-D sketch a 3-D sketch can be constructed (although Marr was a little vague about the details of how this might be done) to give a 'full' representation of the object that is independent of the viewer (that is, there may be a representation of parts that the viewer cannot see directly). Marr and Nishihara (1978) suggest that this 3-D representation can then be compared against previously stored representations, and the object can be recognised. This approach thus rather nicely combines feature extraction and template matching into a plausible theory.

Biederman's recognition-by-components approach

There have been many developments of Marr's general approach such as the theories developed by Biederman (1987) which, again, are based on feature extraction. In this case, however, the features are three-dimensional and are referred to as **geons**. Biederman devised a system using 36 basic geons such as cones, cylinders and blocks that could be used to construct a vast range of objects. The basic principle of Biederman's theory was that if we can identify the geons that make up an object, then we can recognise that object. One problem with this (and other feature-extraction theories) is that it is relatively easy to imagine that very different objects (such as a car and a tree) can be recognised and discriminated quite easily, but it is more difficult to imagine how the process might deal with more subtle distinctions (such as discriminating two different faces).

As well as the problem of discriminating between different objects, there is also the problem of how to recognise changes in the *same* object. This issue presents a particular difficulty for template-matching approaches. To illustrate this, let us return to the problem of recognising your grandmother. It is plausible that you could recognise her by comparing the incoming visual input to an internal 'grandmother template', and perhaps there is even one special cell, a 'grandmother cell' (for a discussion of the origin of this term see Rose, 1996), in your brain that fires when (and only when) you see your grandmother. The problem occurs if there is some change in your grandmother (such as being replaced by a wolf for instance). Would the template still work? What happens if she is facing away from you? Would you need a 'grandmother facing the other way' template as well? You may end up with the impossible situation of requiring a template for every possible view and orientation of your grandmother; and all other objects as well. While there are many neurons in the brain, this is still rather impractical.

Parallel distributed processing (PDP) approaches

One way of getting around the problem of needing an almost infinite number of 'grandmother cells' in the brain is provided by PDP models (Rumelhart and McClelland, 1986) that were discussed in Chapter 1. PDP models are also sometimes referred to as connectionist or neural network models and these models, while implemented on computers, attempt to model the way in which the brain may work. In some ways, PDP approaches are still template approaches but the templates are much more flexible and, given that they represent stored knowledge, they are another conceptualisation of the schema described in Chapter 1. Crucially, any object can be represented not by the activation of a single neuron, but by the activation of many cells forming a *network*. Thus an object is represented not by the activity of a single cell, but by a *pattern* of activity across many cells. Initially, this may seem to make the problems discussed above worse. Now you need not just one cell to represent an object but many. The key point, however, is that any one cell can form a part of many *different* networks (as exemplified by the work of Hebb discussed in Chapter 1). It is the connections between cells that are important as much as the cells themselves.

Neural networks also have the ability to make the object recognition process much more 'fuzzy'. If the object doesn't quite match the template, not all the cells in the network may be activated, but many of them may be. Thus, the system can make a 'best guess' at what the object is *most likely* to be. Given feedback on whether the guess is right or wrong (this can be done in the real world by simply gathering more information) the system can *learn* and the networks can change and adapt. If your grandmother is replaced by a wolf, *some* parts of a grandmother network may be activated (by the clothes and bonnet, etc.) but, hopefully, so will some parts of a 'wolf network'. Given further feedback as to what the object is (getting eaten in Little Red Riding Hood's case – feedback in the truest sense) you will *learn* to recognise the wolf more easily.

The notion that the object recognition process can learn is an important one. Apart from anything else, without learning it would be impossible to recognise any new objects. Learning implies stored knowledge (whether as templates, within neural networks, or in some other form) and this is something that most of the theories discussed above do not address in detail. This is not a criticism of the theories but reflects the fact that the theories discussed so far mostly concentrate on bottom-up processing. They are thus attempting to explain how sensory information gets into the visual system to be processed further. All the theories do, however, have some aspect of top-down schema-driven processing incorporated into them (e.g. templates or neural networks). This reflects the fact that perception is essentially the interface between the physical world and our interpretation of it (more in the next section). Thus, at different levels of perception there is a changing balance, moving from simply encoding and transmitting information from the outside world to interpreting and making sense of it. It is often hard to appreciate the difference between these different aspects of perception, however, until something goes wrong. When something *does* go wrong with our perceptual system and what we perceive does not truly represent the outside world we usually refer to this as an **illusion**, and the study of such illusions provides valuable insights into how perception operates at different levels.

Visual illusions

Richard Gregory (1997) has attempted a classification of illusions. One of the dimensions of this classification is essentially the contribution of bottom-up and/or top-down processes to the generation of the illusion. This then gives a rather satisfying continuum running from those illusions that arise from the physical properties of the world to those that arise largely from the cognitive processes of the mind. For instance, at the 'lowest' level are illusions that are really nothing to do with the sensory processes at all, and these illusions would include such things as rainbows and mirages. They arise from physics, not perception. At the next level are the illusions that *do* arise from basic properties of the perceptual system but are really not influenced by cognitive processes. An example of an illusion of this type is provided by the Hermann grid, named after L. Hermann in 1870, and shown in Figure 2.6. The illusory spots at the intersections are supposedly due to the lateral connections between cells in the retina with no top-down influences evident.

Perhaps the most interesting illusions, however, are those that are generated as a result of top-down influences on perception. These illusions provide strong evidence for the notion that what we know affects what we perceive. One of the most well-known illusions of this type is shown in Figure 2.7. This is the Müller-Lyer illusion, first reported by Franz Müller-Lyer in 1889. The illusion is that, although the two vertical lines are actually the same length, the one on the left is perceived as being longer. The theories discussed so far cannot easily explain such an effect without reference to top-down influences. For instance, a simple feature-extraction approach should not be biased by the precise arrangement of the features (the left and right figures are both made up of the same features) so that this suggests that something beyond what is present in the image is influencing our perception of it. Richard Gregory (1966) (whose theories we will discuss in more detail later) suggested that, although the figure is just a two-dimensional arrangement of lines, we *interpret* them using our knowledge and

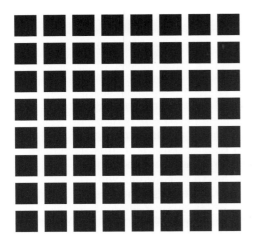

Figure 2.6 The Hermann grid

Illusory grey spots should be visible at the intersections of the white lines. Interestingly, the spot is usually not so obvious at the junction that you are visually fixating

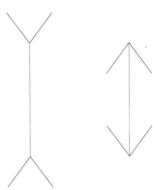

Figure 2.7 The Müller-Lyer illusion

The vertical line on the left appears to be longer than the one on the right, even though they are actually the same length

experience of a three-dimensional world. Thus, Gregory suggests that we see the illusion as two corners (as shown in Figure 2.8) with one corner going away from us (and so appearing more distant) and the other coming towards us (and so appearing closer). To explain the illusion, we have to accept that we also 'know' that things that are further away give rise to a smaller image on our retina and we scale them up to make allowances for this (we don't perceive people as shrinking in size as they walk away from us). This is an example of *size constancy*. In the illusion the two lines are actually the same length, but one *appears* to be further away and so is scaled up by our visual system, giving the impression that it is longer.

Support for the role of knowledge and experience in the interpretation of the Müller-Lyer illusion also comes from a study of the Bete people (Segall *et al.*, 1963) who live in a dense jungle environment with relatively few corners. The Bete people do not perceive the Müller-Lyer illusion as strongly, providing support for the role of knowledge and experience in the interpretation of the figure. It is possible to get an idea of the influence of our 'square world' on perception by considering another illusion, the Ames room (invented by one Adelbert Ames), which is shown in Figure 2.9. The two figures in the room appear to be of vastly different size even though they are, in fact, identical in size. The explanation becomes clear when we see the shape of the room. The room is distorted so that from one viewpoint only (shown by the arrow in the figure) it *appears* to be a 'normal' square room. In actual fact, one corner is much further away than the other. Thus, although it appears that both the little figures are the same distance away from us (so we *do not* do any scaling up as we do in the Müller-Lyer illusion) one is actually much further away, giving rise to a much smaller image. The illusion works because

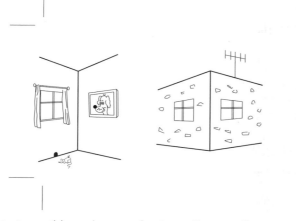

Figure 2.8 A possible explanation for the Müller-Lyer illusion.

The figures are perceived in three-dimensions as illustrated here and this leads to distortions of perceived size

Source: Drawing by David Groome

we *know* that rooms are usually square (certainly we rarely encounter rooms shaped like the Ames room) and so we do not challenge that, preferring instead to perceive figures in the room as being of radically different sizes.

There is still some debate as to how much top-down influences are responsible for illusions. For instance, there are explanations of the Müller-Lyer illusion that do not rely on top-down processing (e.g. Day, 1989) and it is possible to get the Ames room illusion without the room! It is, however, hard to explain all

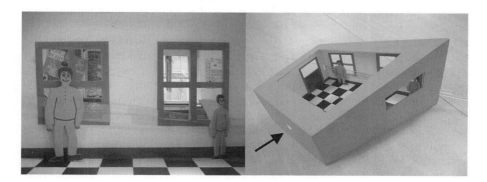

Figure 2.9 The Ames room

Two identical figures (shown in the panel on the left) appear to be of very different sizes. This is due to the unusual shape of the room (show in the right-hand panel)

Source: Photographs by Graham Edgar

illusions without at least some reference to the influence of what we know on what we perceive.

Visual illusions demonstrate that we certainly need to consider the role of top-down processing and the role of knowledge in visual perception. Before doing that, perhaps we should think carefully about what we mean by 'knowledge'. Pure bottom-up processes rely only on information gleaned from incoming sensory information, whereas top-down processes use information that is not present within the sensory information, things such as knowledge of the way the world usually is. Thus our working definition of 'knowledge' in the rest of this chapter will be:

'Information that is not contained within the sensory stimulus.'

Thus the Gestalt laws could be considered to be a form of implicit knowledge, likewise the precise configuration of neural networks. They represent information present within the individual, and not the stimulus.

The use of knowledge as a part of top-down processing allows us to *interpret* incoming sensory information, rather than just encoding it. It also means that our final perception of the sensory information may (as we have already seen) be strongly influenced by what we already know. The rest of this section on visual perception will consider in more detail the role of knowledge in perception, particularly when considering perception in the 'real world' (as opposed to the laboratory). Crucially, the distinction between sensation and perception will be considered and two further theories of perception will be discussed that differ markedly in the importance they place on the role of knowledge in perception.

The difference between sensation and perception

Imagine that you are in a car driving along a road that you do not know. The road disappears around a bend. What do you do? If it were not for your top-down processing, you would probably have to get out of the car and peer around the corner to check that the road does, in fact, continue and that there are no other unexpected occurrences such as that in Figure 2.10. In 'real life', however, you will almost certainly proceed round the bend, secure in the *knowledge* that roads tend to continue and do not simply terminate without warning. An example such as this, while superficially rather silly, emphasises just how much we rely on what we *know* to influence almost everything that we do.

It is now worth defining what we mean by sensation and perception. **Sensation** will be considered to be the 'raw' bottom-up input from the senses and *perception* will be considered to be the subjective experience of that sensation. Perception and sensation may well be quite different. Not only is it likely that what we know will influence what we perceive, but it is possible that not all the information that is sensed will be perceived. Some of the sensory information may be filtered out by our attentional processes (discussed briefly in Chapter 1, and in detail in Chapter 3) and not form a part of our perception. A simple diagram of the route from sensation to perception is presented in Figure 2.11. Only a

Figure 2.10 'Well I never expected that!'
Source: Drawn by Dianne Catherwood

certain proportion of the information available in the world is detected by the senses. Of the huge amount of sensory information that *is* detected, some may be filtered out by our attentional processes presumably to reduce the cognitive load. What we know may also influence the way that the attentional filtering operates, *and* our final perception of the sensory information. It should be noted, however, that the process described above is a very simplified version of what really appears to be happening.

The philosopher Immanuel Kant refers to the objects or events that exist independently of the senses as 'numena' and our experience of those objects and

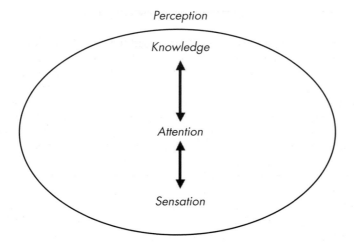

Figure 2.11 The components of perception
Raw sensory information is filtered and combined with knowledge to form the overall percept. Note that information is seen as flowing top-down as well as bottom-up at all stages

events as 'phenomena'. Kant argued that we can never truly access the numena, only the phenomena. That is, we can never know the world as it truly is, only our perception of it after it has been filtered and modified by our senses and cognitive processes. There is a saying that is often attributed to Kant which sums up perception, and which runs, 'We see things not as they are, but as we are.'

To illustrate the difference between sensation and perception, we will return to the discussion about driving and, in particular, accidents that occur while driving. Generally, those individuals who are most likely to have an accident while driving lie at the ends of the age range for drivers (Claret *et al.*, 2003). Young drivers (under 25) and older drivers (75+) tend to have an increased risk of accidents, whereas those drivers in between have a lower risk of being involved in an accident. This is the case for most types of accident, with one notable exception. These are accidents that are usually referred to as 'looked but failed to see' (LBFS) accidents (Sabey and Staughton, 1975).

Looked but failed to see (LBFS) accidents

Looked but failed to see accidents refer to occasions when drivers have crashed into something and claimed subsequently that they simply 'did not see it', even though the object they have just hit should be easily visible (see Figure 2.12). This is where the distinction between sensation and perception becomes particularly important. Undoubtedly, many LBFS accidents *are* due to a failure of sensation. The driver's senses simply do not register the article they crash into. This would explain why these accidents are particularly common at road junctions (where there is often a limited time to detect other road users), and cyclists and motorcyclists are far more likely to be victims of LBFS accidents as they are smaller and harder to see. The term used to describe how easily an item can be detected by the senses is **sensory conspicuity**, and refers to the intrinsic properties of an object (such as shape, colour, brightness, amount of noise that it is making) that are likely to be registered by the senses.

Research by Cole and Hughes (1984) has, however, suggested that sensory conspicuity, although necessary for the detection of objects, may not always be sufficient. Cole and Hughes suggest that in order to be able to consciously perceive (and react to) an object, it should also have high **attention conspicuity**. This term refers to the fact that to perceive something, the individual needs not only to detect that it is there, but also has to *attend* to that information. The discussion of attention above, and that in Chapter 3, suggests that much information that we sense is not attended to. There is an interesting distinction that can be made between sensory and attention conspicuity. Sensory conspicuity relates mainly to aspects of the object being perceived (brightness, etc.), whereas attention conspicuity is more likely to be influenced by aspects of the individual doing the observing (previous experience, expectations, etc.). Broadly speaking, sensory conspicuity relies primarily on bottom-up processing whereas attention conspicuity is more heavily influenced by top-down processes. Thus if, for instance, a driver is not expecting a motorcyclist at a particular location they may drive into them, even if the motorcyclist has high sensory conspicuity.

Figure 2.12 High sensory conspicuity does not guarantee accurate perception . . .
Source: Photograph courtesy of Gloucestershire Constabulary

Is there any evidence that accidents of this kind occur? Martin Langham and his co-workers (Langham *et al.*, 2002) looked at accidents involving vehicles that have perhaps the highest sensory conspicuity of any on the road – police cars. Despite having a full range of conspicuity enhancers (reflective and retro-reflective materials, flashing lights, cones) stationary police cars have been hit by drivers who subsequently claimed that they did not see them. In these cases it is hard to believe that the individuals' senses failed to register the police car, but something has gone wrong after the initial registration. The police car, while having high sensory conspicuity, has low attention conspicuity *for those individuals*.

Langham *et al.* were interested in establishing just what factors of the situation or the individual (or the interaction between them) would be likely to lead to LBFS accidents. To do this, they gathered survey data from a variety of sources, obtaining details of 29 vehicle accidents. This survey identified a number of interesting aspects of LBFS accidents that will now be considered in relation to the discussion above on the role of knowledge in perception. The factors that seemed to be important in LBFS accidents were:

1 *There were more accidents when the police vehicle was parked 'in-line' (stopped in a lane and facing in the same direction as the prevailing traffic flow) than*

when it was parked 'in echelon' (parked diagonally across a lane). It is easy to speculate that the orientation of the car may influence the perception of that car. Experience tells us that most cars that we see on a road have the same orientation as the other cars and, crucially, that they are moving. Thus a car parked in-line may well be perceived as a moving car – until it is too late. There is much less ambiguity with a car that is parked in echelon; it is an unusual (or even impossible!) orientation for a moving car, and so it is perhaps much more likely to be perceived as stationary.

2   *Deployment of warning signs and cones did not guarantee detection.* The deployment of such aids would almost certainly raise the sensory conspicuity of the police car still further, but not enough to prevent an accident.

3   *Although the accidents usually occur on motorways and dual carriageways, 62 per cent of the accidents were close (within 15 km) to the perpetrators' homes.* Again, it is possible that this finding is the result of experience. Drivers are familiar with the environment and the roads around their home. They may have driven the same route every day for years – and never seen a police car parked in the road. Thus, when they do see a stationary police car, they assume it is moving, with disastrous consequences.

4   *The offenders were all, except one, over the age of 25.* As discussed above, this is highly unusual as it is usually the younger drivers that are more likely to be involved in accidents. The finding emphasises the likely role

Figure 2.13 Vehicles that had earlier been carrying members of a TV team, hit by 'friendly fire' from an aircraft in the 2003 Iraq war.

The pilot apparently believed that he was attacking enemy forces that were nearby. Note the clear markings on the side of the vehicle (and the top of the vehicle was also marked)

that knowledge and experience are likely to play in these accidents. More experienced drivers have learnt that cars on the motorway are nearly always moving, and so do not pay sufficient attention to cars that are not moving. It seems highly likely that they detect them, but they do not perceive them appropriately.

It would thus appear that one explanation for LBFS accidents is that more experienced drivers are placing more reliance on what they already know and this is affecting what they perceive. Edgar *et al.* (2003) have also demonstrated that an overemphasis on using prior knowledge to drive perception may underlie serious accidents referred to as 'friendly fire' in which the military open fire on their own side (or on civilians) believing them to be the enemy, even though there are plenty of sensory cues to suggest that they are not (as illustrated in Figure 2.13).

The influence of top-down processing: an example

There appear to be numerous, not to mention dramatic, examples of what we know influencing what we perceive. To try and drive (excuse the pun) the message home and to allow you to experience a clear example of knowledge influencing perception, have a look at Figure 2.14. What do you see? It is most interesting if you just see a pattern of light and dark blobs. Does it change your perception of the picture if you are told that it is, in fact, a picture of a cow? If you could not see the cow initially but now can after being provided with extra information about the picture, then this is a clear example of knowledge influencing perception. The sensory aspects of the picture have not changed *at all*. It is still a collection of light and dark blobs. What has changed is what you know about the picture, and this has changed your perception of it. Even if you did see the cow immediately, your perception of it will be forever changed (hopefully) by knowing that it has been used as an illustration in a textbook.

The constructivist approach: perception for recognition

From the examples discussed above, and from your own experience, it should now be clear that what we know has huge (and sometimes detrimental) effects on what we perceive, even sometimes overruling apparently clear sensory information that may be telling us something different. Truly, 'We see things not as they are but as we are.' The next issue to consider is just why we make so much use of stored knowledge. Given that the consequences of using what we know can sometimes be somewhat detrimental, perhaps it would be better not to use it to such an extent. So why does stored knowledge appear to have such an influence on perception?

One of the theories of the way in which perception operates and which deals explicitly with why we make so much use of stored knowledge is the constructivist theory which was initially proposed by Irvin Rock (1977, 1983) and Richard

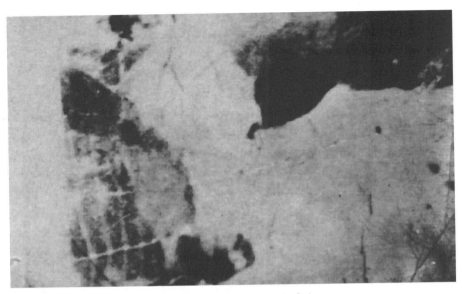

Figure 2.14 What do you see? (for answer see end of chapter)

Source: K.M. Dallenbach (1951) from *American Journal of Psychology.* © 1951 by the Board of Trustees of the University of Illinois. Used with permission of the University of Illinois Press

Gregory (1980). It is called a constructivist theory because it is based on the notion that it is necessary for us to 'construct' our perception of what we see from *incomplete* sensory information. Thus we use what we already know to fill in the gaps and interpret the sensory information coming in. In order to do this Gregory suggests that we act as 'scientists', generating perceptual hypotheses (predictions) about what we may be seeing and testing those hypotheses against the sensory information coming in. The cow picture used previously can be used again to give an idea of how this works. The picture is not at all clear and may be difficult, at first, to resolve into anything that makes sense. You might thus generate a range of hypotheses about what it may be (horse, cow, battleship, chair, duck) which you can then check against the sensory information, 'It looks as though it has ears, so the hypothesis that it is a battleship is probably wrong.' Of course the process is not seen as occurring that consciously or that explicitly, but that is the general idea. Once the hypothesis fits the sensory information, the image is then recognised, hopefully correctly. The constructivist theories thus emphasise a strong interaction between sensory information moving 'bottom-up' (see Chapter 1) and knowledge moving 'top-down'. The interaction of the two determines what is perceived.

As we have already seen in this chapter, however, the end result of the perceptual process may be wrong (as with the Müller-Lyer illusion). Gregory, in particular, has demonstrated that we can perhaps learn as much about the perceptual processes when things go wrong as when they go right. Once again, when things go wrong, it seems to be previous knowledge that is to blame. Gregory uses a nice demonstration that illustrates this point (Gregory, 1970, 1997). Look at the faces in Figure 2.15. The figure is a hollow mask of Einstein with the view from the 'normal' (convex) side on the left of the figure and the view from the (concave) back on the right. Under certain viewing conditions, whichever view of the mask we take, it still *looks* like a solid face – *not* a hollow face. Gregory suggests that this is because we are very familiar with faces as visual stimuli and we are used to seeing 'normal' faces with the nose sticking out towards us. A hollow face is a very unusual visual stimulus and we appear very resistant to accepting the hypothesis that what we are viewing is a face that is essentially the spatial 'negative' (the bits that normally stick out now go in) of those that we normally see.

If what we know seems to have so much impact on what we perceive and, apparently, lead to so many errors (as discussed above), then the obvious question is, 'Why do we make so much use of what we already know in driving our perception of the world?' It only seems to lead to trouble, so why not ignore what we already know? Apart from the obvious answer that we would never be able to recognise our own grandmother, there are other reasons for involving knowledge in the process of perception. We have already touched on a possible answer when we first considered the constructivist theory. This is the notion that the sensory input is rather impoverished, and we need to 'construct' our perception aided by what we already know to make best use of the rather limited information coming in. The incoming information is limited in two ways. One way has been considered in Chapter 1 (and will be covered in much more detail in Chapter 3) and this is that our cognitive resources can only cope with a certain amount of incoming information, so that a proportion of it is filtered out by our attentional processes. Another factor limiting the completeness of the sensory information

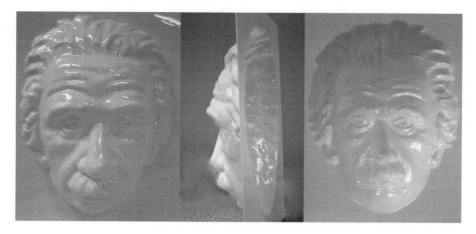

Figure 2.15 The faces of Einstein

The left-hand view of the mask is from the front showing a 'normal' convex face. Even though the right-hand panel shows a 'hollow' face (with the nose going away from you) the percept is of a normal face.

Source: Photographs courtesy of Graham Edgar

Figure 2.16 Demonstrating what we really see (lower picture) as opposed to what we feel we see (upper picture)

Source: Original concept Anstis (1998)

coming in is (as already mentioned) that our senses may not provide a full picture in the first place.

This is illustrated by the lower part of Figure 2.16. Our visual acuity is not constant across our field of view and the scene in the upper picture has been progressively blurred in the lower picture to represent the effect of the reducing acuity of the eye with increasing distance from the high acuity centre (the fovea). What this means is that much of the visual information coming in is actually of quite poor quality. Thus the constructivist theory seems to be making a reasonable assumption in proposing that we need to use prior knowledge to help us to interpret the rather blurry image that we receive from our retina.

Evidence for the constructivist approach: masking and re-entrant processing

Although using stored knowledge to aid in the interpretation of incoming information is likely to make object recognition better and faster, the iterative process of generating hypotheses and testing them is going to take a certain amount of time. This is not a problem if the incoming sensory information remains constant (or if the observer is, at least, continuing to look at different bits of the same object), but what happens if it changes? The hypothesis testing constructivist approach would predict that a sudden change in the visual input would disrupt processing and make it more difficult to recognise an object, and this appears to be exactly what happens. Di Lollo *et al.* (2000) demonstrated that changing one stimulus rapidly for another, disrupted processing of the first stimulus, a process referred to as 'masking'. A typical target stimulus and mask are shown in Figure 2.17. In a masking paradigm, a second stimulus can prevent recognition of an earlier stimulus if the mask follows very soon after presentation of the stimulus. It is not even necessary for the stimulus and mask to be at the same position in the visual field (i.e. not spatially coincident). A mask that surrounds the stimulus (as in Figure 2.17) but does not appear in the same place can be effective in blocking recognition of a target (Enns and Di Lollo, 2000).

Enns and co-workers (Enns and Di Lollo, 2000; Di Lollo *et al.*, 2000) suggest that the mask is effective because it disrupts *re-entrant processing*. Re-entrant processing is a term used to describe the finding in neuroscience research that communication between different areas of the brain is never in one direction only. If a signal goes from one area to another, then there is sure to be one coming back the other way (Felleman and Van Essen, 1991). Thus the flow of information diagrammed in Figure 2.11 could conceivably be a high-level representation of hypothesis testing using re-entrant processing. Indeed, masking could be conceptualised as drawing attention away from the initial target stimulus so that cognitive resources are no longer allocated to processing it. Certainly, masking provides support for the constructivist approach. Hupe *et al.* (1998) suggest that

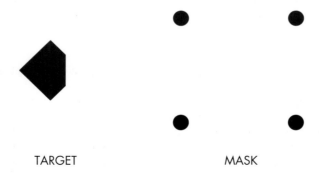

TARGET   MASK

Figure 2.17 A target and mask of the type used by Enns and Di Lollo (2000)
Source: Adapted from Enns and Di Lollo (2000)

re-entrant processing could be the basis of the hypothesis testing postulated by Gregory. Incoming sensory information (flowing bottom-up) is used to generate an initial hypothesis. The accuracy of this hypothesis is then checked against the continuing sensory input using re-entrant pathways (flowing top-down) and the hypothesis can then be modified and re-checked.

The constructivist theory of vision is thus very appealing, elegantly combining bottom-up and top-down processing. One slight puzzle remains, however. If this approach is so good, why does it make so many mistakes? Much of the evidence used to support the constructivist approach, as already discussed, comes from examples of where it goes wrong and visual illusions such as the Müller-Lyer are good examples. Given that it seems to be so easy to 'fool' the perceptual system, why aren't such things as LBFS accidents far more common? They are, thankfully, quite rare. One criticism of the constructivist approach is that previous knowledge appears to be so important due to the kinds of methods and stimuli used to test perception. Many investigations of perception are done in the laboratory using deliberately simple, and often static, stimuli. Thus, the sensory input is a very impoverished version of what an individual would normally be exposed to in the real world. Some of the stimuli used to illustrate the use of knowledge are even deliberately difficult to recognise, such as the dog picture in Figure 2.14. Thus, it could be argued that if you ask people to view a static two-dimensional, impoverished, image under laboratory conditions, you will force them to use knowledge to try and make sense of it. If you allow people to move around in the world, with a rich flow of sensory information coming in and changing as the individual moves and looks around (and as objects in the world move around them), then it is possible that far less top-down information will be needed – or perhaps none at all! Thus the lower picture in Figure 2.16 only looks so poor because it represents what the world would look like if we were unable to move our eyes, or ourselves.

The Gibsonian view of perception: perception for action

The notion that studying perception in artificial conditions in a laboratory will give rise to false conclusions of how the system works was a notion championed vigorously by J.J. Gibson (1950, 1966). Gibson, rather than considering *how* perception operates, was much more concerned with what perception is *for*. That is, Gibson considered that perception should be considered in terms of how it allows us to interact with the world we live in. Gibson's approach may be summed up by the term 'perception for action'. In the theories of Gibson there is a strong link between perception and action with perception being referred to as 'direct'. The basis of direct perception is that the sensory information available in the environment is so rich that it provides sufficient information to allow a person to move around, and interact with, the environment without the need for any top-down processing. Gibson would claim that the results obtained in laboratory studies are misleading in that they are studying *indirect* perception of static

2-D representations of the world. That is, laboratory studies do not demonstrate how we interact with the world, merely how we react to impoverished representations of it.

For Gibson, moving within the environment and interacting with the environment are crucial aspects of perception. As Gibson (1979) put it, 'perceiving is an act, not a response'. One problem, of course, with denying the use of stored knowledge in perception is that it becomes rather difficult to work out how we can interact with objects in the world without recognising them in the way that would be proposed by the constructivist approach. Gibson (1979) developed his theories by suggesting that we are able to interact with objects in the world because they *afford* their use. For instance, consider Figure 2.18. It is a picture of a hammer and Gibson would suggest that a hammer would afford hitting things. If you think this is an unreasonable assumption, try giving a hammer to a two-year-old who has never seen a hammer before, and see what they do with it. Actually *do not* try that, although it would almost certainly be a good example of objects affording their use.

Evidence for the Gibsonian approach

Although Gibson's theories may seem a little unreasonable there is evidence that at least some part of the perceptual process may act in a 'Gibsonian' manner.

Figure 2.18 What do you do with this?
Source: Photograph courtesy of Graham Edgar

Handy *et al.* (2003) presented participants with pictures of two task-irrelevant objects while they were waiting for a target to be presented. One of the pictures was of a tool and the other was of a non-tool. Objects that could be grasped (such as hammers) drew attention and functional magnetic resonance imaging (fMRI) of brain function indicated activity in dorsal regions of premotor and prefrontal cortices. Also, as suggested by Bruce *et al.* (1996), direct perception would make sense in terms of instinctive, visually-guided behaviour. For example, if a frog were trying to snare a fly with its tongue, it is not necessary for the frog to 'know' anything about flies, or even to recognise the small buzzing object *as* a fly. All it needs to do is to sense the small flying object and use that sensory information to guide its tongue to allow it to snare it (although it could be a nasty surprise if it is not a fly).

Thus the constructivist and Gibsonian theories seem to conflict, one emphasising the centrality of stored knowledge in the perceptual process, the other denying that it is necessary at all. The question, of course, is which one is right? Well, it is not giving too much away to say that it looks as though both theories could be right and that both types of processing could be occurring in perception. To illustrate this, we shall have a look at the structure of the visual system.

The structure of the visual system

Even very early in the visual system there appear to be (at least) two distinct streams of information flowing back from the retina (Shapley, 1995). These streams are referred to as the parvocellular and magnocellular pathways (e.g. Shapley, 1995), the names deriving from the relative sizes of the cells in the two pathways. These pathways carry information back to the primary visual cortex. You may already have an idea of where your visual cortex is if you have ever been hit on the back of the head (where the visual cortex is) and 'seen stars'. A blow to the back of the head can lead to spontaneous firings within the visual cortex – and the impression of 'stars'. After the visual cortex, the visual information is still maintained in two distinct streams (see Figure 2.19). One stream is termed the **ventral stream** and leads to inferotemporal cortex and the other, leading to parietal cortex, is known as the **dorsal stream**.

The dorsal and ventral streams

While heavily interconnected and apparently converging in prefrontal cortex (Rao *et al.*, 1997), the dorsal and ventral streams seem to be specialised for different functions and to have different characteristics. For instance:

1   The ventral stream is primarily concerned with recognition and identification of visual input whereas the dorsal stream provides information to drive visually guided behaviour such as pointing, grasping, etc. (Ungerleider and Mishkin, 1982; Goodale and Milner, 1992).

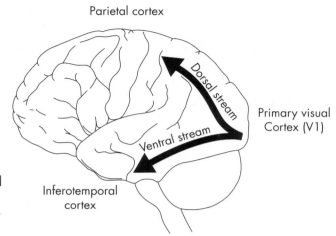

Figure 2.19
The dorsal and ventral systems
Source: Drawing courtesy of David Groome

2   The ventral system is better at processing fine detail (Baizer *et al.*, 1991) whereas the dorsal system is better at processing motion (Logothesis, 1994), although the differences are only relative as, for example, the ventral system can still carry motion information.

3   The ventral system appears to be knowledge-based using stored representations to recognise objects whilst the dorsal system appears to have only very short-term storage available (Milner and Goodale, 1995; Bridgeman *et al.*, 1997; Creem and Proffitt, 1998).

4   The dorsal system is faster (Bullier and Nowak, 1995).

5   We appear to be more conscious of ventral stream functioning than dorsal. For instance individuals may report awareness of ventral processing, while manifesting different dorsal processing (Ho, 1998).

6   The ventral system aims to recognise and identify objects and is thus object-centred. The dorsal system is driving some action in relation to an object and thus uses a viewer-centred frame of reference (Goodale and Milner, 1992; Milner and Goodale, 1995).

These characteristics support earlier research (Schneider, 1967, 1969) which suggested that the ventral stream is concerned with the question, 'What is it?' whereas the dorsal stream is concerned with the question, 'Where is it?' Thus, the ventral pathway is often known as a 'what' system, and the dorsal pathway a 'where' system (Ungerleider and Mishkin, 1982).

Norman (2001, 2002), following on from similar suggestions by Bridgeman (1992) and Neisser (1994), has suggested a dual-process approach based on the characteristics of the two streams outlined above. In this approach, it is suggested that the dorsal and ventral streams act synergistically, with the dorsal stream largely concerned with *perception for action*, and the ventral stream with *perception for recognition*.

The function and characteristics of the two streams thus seem to fit rather nicely with the two theories of perception outlined above, with the dorsal stream appearing rather Gibsonian in the way that it operates, and the ventral stream rather constructivist. Thus, we appear to have a fast system ideally suited for driving action, but which makes relatively little use of stored information (the Gibsonian dorsal stream) combined with another slower system that uses stored knowledge to analyse fine detail and recognise objects (the constructivist ventral stream).

The interaction of the dorsal and ventral streams: perception for recognition and action

It is interesting to speculate, as we finish this discussion of visual perception, just *how* these two types of processing may act together to allow us to perceive our world. To do this, it is worth considering our experience and consciousness of what we are perceiving, i.e. our **phenomenological experience**. The founder of the phenomenological tradition was a German philosopher-mathematician called Edmund Husserl (1931) who suggested the concept of *intentionality*, whereby the mind reaches out to the stimuli that make up the world and interprets them in terms of our own personal experience, which is a theme that has been developed throughout this chapter. As an example of this, consider once more the pictures in Figure 2.16. At any one moment the sensory information coming in from the world gives us a view of the world rather like that in the lower picture. Our phenomenological experience of the world, however, is more like that of the upper picture. We have the impression that we have a clear and accurate perception of the world surrounding us at any one time. An analogy for this is the light in your refrigerator (Thomas, 1999). It always appears to be on because whenever you go to the fridge and open the door, the light *is* on (the irreverent magazine *Viz* once suggested that it would be a good idea to drill a hole in the door of your refrigerator so you can really be sure that the light *does* go off when you close the door!). The experience of the real world is much the same. Whenever you look at any object in the real world it appears clear and sharp (assuming your eyesight is good) because as soon as you become interested in some part of the visual world, you tend to move your eyes so that the image of that part falls on the high acuity central region of the retina. Thus, you tend not to be aware that the rest of the time that part of the world is just a blur (in the same way that you never see the refrigerator light off).

Stored knowledge allows us to maintain this phenomenological percept that the world is sharp and clear. Having looked at something, we can remember it as sharp and clear, even when we look away and the sensory information coming from that information is actually blurred. Essentially, we could build up an internal 'model' of the world around us at any time using our knowledge. This is not to suggest that we do have a little 'model' of the world inside our heads. We don't really need it as we can use our environment as an 'external memory' (O'Regan, 1992) that we can recall at any time just by looking around. The constructivist ventral stream would seem to be ideal for building up and maintaining our representation of the world, recognising objects as they appear in central vision and generating stored representations of those objects for when we are looking elsewhere. As long as everything remains unchanged, our perception of the world should be fairly accurate. To maintain that accuracy, however, we need a system that will warn us if some part of the visual world changes. This is one of the functions that the dorsal stream could serve.

Just as the ventral stream appears to be ideally suited for recognising objects, so the dorsal stream appears to be well suited to detecting change in the visual world (e.g. Zeki, 2003). Indeed, Beck *et al.* (2001) used a change blindness paradigm (asking participants to detect a change made to an image) to look at regions of the brain that were involved in detecting change to the visual stimulus. They found enhanced activity in the parietal lobe (an element of the dorsal stream) when subjects were conscious of a change, but not when the change went unnoticed. Of course, fMRI studies of the sort conducted by Beck only reveal an *association* between a region of brain activity and some behaviour on the part of the individual. Beck *et al.* (2005), however, used repetitive transcranial magnetic stimulation to disrupt activity in the right parietal cortex and found that the ability to detect changes in a visual stimulus was disrupted (no effect if the left parietal cortex was disrupted). There thus appears to be evidence that the dorsal stream is, indeed, well suited to a role of detecting change in the environment, so that the ventral stream can then be brought into play to see what has changed and how.

This is, of course, a simplification of the way in which the visual system may operate, but there certainly appears to be plenty of evidence to suggest that there are (at least) two distinct streams involved in processing the visual input and that they work synergistically to allow us to maintain a phenomenological impression of a clear and sharp visual world all around us. Thus, to return to the question earlier in this chapter, it may not be necessary to get out of your car every time you come to a sharp bend. If there is something unexpected around the corner, your visual system will probably be able to cope with it – most of the time.

2.3 Auditory perception

So far we have only considered one of the senses – vision. As we shall see (or hear!), there are many others, although perhaps the most researched sense after vision is that of hearing. Our sense of hearing serves many functions, not least in allowing us to hear speech. There is, however, not space to consider the complexities of speech perception in this chapter and good introductions to speech perception are provided in Banich (2004) and Goldstein (2002). This section will therefore consider the role of hearing in an area that we have already discussed: detecting change in the environment. Any sound occurring in the environment will, by definition, be the result of some change. To produce the transient changes in air pressure that form sound waves, something must have changed, even if only by a small amount. Thus one of the functions of our auditory system is to detect sounds resulting from changes in the environment and to give some indication of *where* those sounds are occurring.

A discussion of auditory localisation is useful here, in that it emphasises particularly strongly that the senses do not operate independently, but act *synergistically* to allow us to perceive the world around us.

Auditory localisation

Auditory localisation is usually described using the following three coordinate systems:

1   **Azimuth** (horizontal), determined primarily by **binaural cues**, specifically *time* and *intensity* differences between stimuli reaching the left and right ears (see Figure 2.20). *Interaural intensity differences* are largely due to the **shadowing** effect of the head that keeps high frequency sounds from reaching the far ear. Long wavelengths (low frequency sounds) are unaffected by the head, but shorter wavelengths (high frequency sounds) are reflected back. This feature has been shown to be surprisingly useful in an evolutionary perspective. As a general rule, animals with smaller heads are sensitive to higher frequencies. Pheasant chicks have evolved a chirp that exploits this feature. The chicks emit chirps at roughly the same wavelength as a fox's head width, thus making it very difficult for their main predator to locate them by sound, whereas, the chicks' mother (having a smaller head than a fox) can locate them easily (Naish, 2005).

2   **Elevation** (vertical), determined mainly by **spectral cues** which are generated by the way in which the head and outer ears (pinnae) affect the

Figure 2.20 Sound localisation in the horizontal plane

Sounds to one side of the head will reach the nearest ear sooner and tend to sound louder in that ear. Individuals can use these cues to localise a sound and so orient towards it.

Source: Photographs courtesy of Graham Edgar

frequencies in the stimulus. Sound can also be reflected back off the torso ('shoulder bounce') (Gardner and Gardner, 1973).

3 **Distance coordinate** (how far a sound source is from the listener). Generally, judgements of distance for sounds within an arm's length are good (interaural level difference (ILD) is large), but as sounds get further away then distance judgement is much more difficult, and distance to far away sounds is generally underestimated. There are several mechanisms for auditory far-distance judgement, which are used together to determine perception of a sound's distance (much as with visual distance cues); they include:

- **Sound level** – (Doubling distance of the source can reduce sound pressure level (SPL) by around 6 dB outside in the open with no echoes.) It is difficult, however, to make a judgement of distance based on sound pressure intensity without some *prior knowledge* of how loud the source should appear at different distances. Therefore the listener needs to be familiar with the sound source (e.g. a voice) or making a comparative judgement of the distance of two identical sources.
- **Frequency** – High frequencies undergo more attenuation by the atmosphere than low frequencies. Sounds that are further away, therefore, become more dull and muffled.
- **Motion parallax** – See Figure 2.21. Nearby sounds appear to shift location faster than sounds that are further away. This is analogous to the visual depth cue of motion parallax.
- **Reflection** – Sound can reach the ears in two ways:
  - **direct sound**: an uninterrupted path from source to ear;
  - **indirect sound**: sound that is bounced off (reflected by) objects e.g. walls or ground.

  As distance increases so does the ratio of indirect to direct sound and the change in sound quality provides a distance cue.

The differences in auditory processing result in differences in the accuracy with which the human listener can place sounds along these axes. Localisation accuracy is generally lower for elevation sources than for sources that differ in azimuth (Middlebrooks, 1992). Listeners can localise sounds directly in front of them most accurately (errors average 2–3.5°) and sounds that are off to the side and behind the head least accurately (errors up to 20°). For further discussion of auditory localisation acuity see Oldfield and Parker (1984a, 1984b).

Much of the work on auditory localisation has concentrated on how a listener (often with fixed head position in a quiet room or an anechoic chamber) can hear sounds. And some interesting problems have been highlighted, for instance, for auditory stimuli that are equidistant from the two ears, confusion can occur as to whether the source is in front of or behind the observer. For most situations in the real world, however, the listener will be able to move freely and will have visual cues available that can be used to resolve any ambiguity. Under real-world conditions the visual system and the auditory system work together and accurate predictions of real-world responses are difficult to measure or gener-

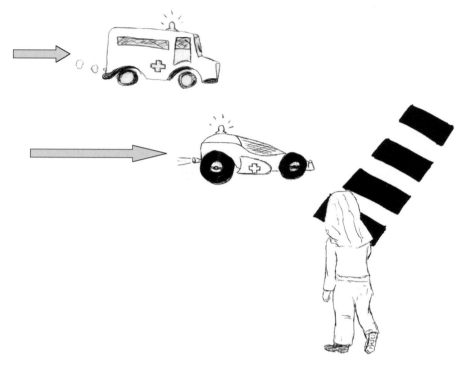

Figure 2.21 Motion parallax

Moving sound stimuli that are closer will tend to shift location *with respect to the listener* faster than those that are further away. The same is true for visual stimuli.

Source: Drawn by Helen Edgar

alise when considering the auditory system in isolation. In fact, the auditory and visual systems interact in many ways that influence our final percept. For example, Vroomen and DeGelder (2000) demonstrated that the perceptual organisation of sound affects visual scene analysis. Links between auditory and visual systems can occur at the low-level bottom-up stages (Vroomen *et al.*, 2001), or through the influence of higher cognitive processes (top-down) such as the prior expectations of a participant (Egeth and Yantis, 1997). When considering the cognitive psychology of auditory perception, it is therefore advisable to remember that, although a single aspect may be studied in order to isolate factors for investigation, these factors rarely act alone in the real world. Interactions can lead to rather different results to those found in the laboratory, for example improved auditory localisation with visual cues.

Cross-modal studies of auditory localisation have demonstrated that visual cues can improve the accuracy of auditory localisation both in azimuth and elevation, provided that the visual cues are congruent with the auditory stimulus (an inconsistent or mismatched visual cue is worse than no cue). The McGurk effect, where a listener hears a completely new sound 'da' when viewing mismatched lip movements 'ga' and sound 'ba' from a monitor, could be considered as an extreme example of incongruent auditory and visual stimuli.

In addition the *type* of visual stimulus will affect the degree of improvement. If the visual stimulus strongly matches the auditory stimulus, then participants perform more accurately. Thus if the visual stimuli are speaker icons, then performance is better than if a simple card marks the possible sound sources. Also, visual facilitation of auditory localisation is better if the source locations are marked with objects placed in actual 3-D positions, rather than represented on a 2-D grid. *Thus, auditory localisation performance is improved if an auditory stimulus is accompanied with a meaningful (congruent) visual cue* (Saliba, 2001).

These findings demonstrate once again the influence of knowledge on perception. For instance, we *know* that there has to be a source for a sound – such as a loudspeaker.

Auditory attention

Unlike our eyes, our ears cannot be directed to avoid registering material that we wish to ignore. In a busy setting we are swamped with simultaneous sounds. Principles of auditory grouping analogous to the Gestalt laws of visual perception can be utilised to solve this problem and help *direct* auditory attention to differentiate 'signal' from 'noise' and separate superimposed sounds:

- **Location:** Sounds created by a particular source usually come from one position in space or move in a slowly changing and/or continuous way (e.g. a passing car).
- **Similarity of timbre:** Sounds that have the same timbre are often produced by the same source, i.e. similar sounding stimuli are grouped together.
- Sounds with similar frequencies are often from the same source.
- **Temporal proximity:** Sounds that occur in rapid progression tend to be produced by the same source.

Treisman and Gelade (1980) suggest people must focus attention on a stimulus before they can synthesise its features into a pattern. This applies not only for visual stimuli, but also for auditory stimuli . . . *you must focus your attention on complex incoming information in order to synthesize it into a meaningful pattern.* Thus, *meaning* is also important for deciding where an auditory stimulus is and whether it will be processed to the level of perception.

Interactions and real-world examples

There is an important distinction between reductionist laboratory-based research and more applied areas such as auditory display research (Walker and Kramer, 2004). Psychophysical experiments that isolate particular aspects of a stimulus provide fundamental background information (from a carefully controlled environment) about how sound reaches the ears and how it is sensed. This approach, however, is just a starting-point for the study of auditory perception. Concentrating upon individual aspects of the (auditory) system and *not* the interactions that lead to the final percept can lead to some interesting (and expensive) problems.

Example, concert theatre design: The optimum reverberation time for a concert hall is considered to be 2 seconds. The New York Philharmonic Hall, which opened in 1962, was designed to replicate this single factor of '*ideal reverberation*'. Despite achieving a reverberation figure very close to the 'ideal', the musicians could not hear each other and the acoustics were obviously not as expected. This culminated in a complete re-build of the interior. Current practice uses *multiple measures*, e.g. intimacy, spaciousness, timbre, and tone colour (Beranek, 1996).

The current approach recognises what has been termed a more *ecological* approach and attempts to consider the effects of sound as it is heard in the real world (natural sound). This is more akin to the approach of Gibson, discussed earlier in this chapter.

Top-down influences on auditory perception

A listener's experience and frame of mind can influence how a message is perceived. Diana Deutsch (2003) demonstrated, with 'phantom word' illusions, that people often report 'hearing words related to what is on their minds'. The demonstration used simple words, e.g. 'Boris', 'Go back', 'Harvey' played repeatedly and continuously. Listeners reported hearing new words and phrases that were not present in the original recording. As with vision, there is an interaction of top-down and bottom-up processing.

A real-world example of how different individuals may extract very different meanings from the same stimulus is given by the following summary adapted from a report in the confidential human factors incident reporting (CHIRP) aviation bulletin of 2005.

Public announcement (PA) overload – a personal perspective?

- An early afternoon flight was slightly delayed due to maintenance.
- During boarding the cabin crew twice announced a welcome, apologised for a short maintenance delay and offered the opportunity to purchase scratch cards.
- Those on board tended to ignore the PA and continue to chat or read.
- When all were on board, the Captain made a PA (at a low volume) apologising for the delay. He gave a few details about the trip and asked passengers to pay attention to the safety brief.
- The safety brief was preceded by an announcement about the in-flight magazine, gift items and scratch cards.
- The aircraft pushed back and the safety brief commenced.
- Most people continued to chat or read and some revellers in the rear [of the cabin] continued to make a noise.
- The aircraft commenced take off; at the point of rotation (aircraft still on the ground but starting to pitch up) the aircraft lurched quite markedly.

- The aircraft became airborne and all seemed normal again.
- During the climb the cabin crew broadcast a PA about the imminent scratch-card sale.
- After the scratch-card sale was over, another PA informed passengers that snacks, drinks and gift items featured in the magazine would be offered for sale.
- The next PA was from the Captain, again at low volume. He announced details of the weather at the destination, the expected arrival time and a couple of features of interest visible from the left-hand side of the aircraft.
- Again most people were reading, chatting or being noisy. Most were not listening to the Captain's PA, which had by this stage been on air for a minute or so.
- The Captain then proceeded to quietly inform the passengers: 'Oh by the way, some of you may have noticed a roll on take off, we may have a problem with the aircraft so just as a precaution we are going to prepare the cabin for an emergency landing.'
- The emergency brief was delivered by the cabin crew very quickly, but included a demonstration of the brace position (the position that passengers are advised to sit in for an emergency landing).
- There were still a significant number of passengers who were unaware that anything out of the ordinary was going on.
- The cabin crew hurriedly secured the cabin.
- The aircraft descended and there were no further PAs.
- The writer [of the report] was unsure whether or not to adopt brace position.
- The aircraft touched down normally and taxied onto the stand, followed by emergency vehicles.
- The next PA (low volume) came from the Captain, apologising for the emergency preparation and saying, 'Better safe than sorry.'
- Almost immediately a cabin crew PA thanked passengers for choosing their airline. After a brief pause the PA continued with information about car hire, bus tickets and hotel offers.
- In the baggage hall, one woman was openly crying, some people were excitedly talking about the incident whilst some seemed unaware that anything untoward had happened.

The writer concluded that the constant bombardment of PAs caused people to 'switch off' and not listen. 'If there had been a problem on landing and we did thump and skid across the airfield, there would have been a significant number of passengers who were not prepared for it.'

What is clear from this incident report is that different people came away from the same flight with widely different ideas about what was going on. Some passengers were so upset by the emergency landing, and what they considered to be a narrow escape, that they were reduced to tears, whereas others were totally unaware that there had been an emergency landing. So, how could this happen since they were all *'listening'* to more-or-less the same auditory stimuli (messages) in the same environment (the aircraft cabin)? To answer this question, it is necessary to consider the aspects of *both* the *stimulus* and the *listener* that might lead to different percepts in different individuals:

- Each individual will not have received exactly the same auditory stimuli. There will have been variations in the level of sound due to the cabin *environment*.
- The individuals' **mental model** of what is going on or likely to happen could influence what they attended to.
- **Sensory overload**: A listener can be 'overloaded' with auditory messages or warnings (Meredith and Edworthy, 1994). In this example there were eleven public announcements (PAs) and two safety briefings containing information on at least twenty different topics.
- *Confusion*: Critical information embedded in messages with lots of trivial/irrelevant information (Edworthy *et al.*, 2003).

This example highlights the fact that, just because a stimulus is above threshold and is capable of being 'heard' does not mean that the listener will attend to the stimulus or that the information content can be extracted and assimilated into a meaningful percept ready for action. In effect, this is the auditory equivalent of the looked but failed to see problem (listened but failed to hear?).

In order to study how a listener will respond to a particular auditory stimulus in the real world, be it music in a concert hall or an auditory warning display in a cockpit, it is essential that *multiple factors and interactions* are considered. After all, humans are not passive listeners in their environment, hearing has a function and that function is usually linked to action. For instance, if a person hears a loud bang, they will have some idea from their auditory system about where that bang has originated, they will probably orientate towards the bang in order to gather additional visual information to improve the accuracy (with which they can localise the source); if they have any previous knowledge of that type of sound, they may move towards the sound (if the mental model is of a four-year-old falling off a chair) or away from the sound (if the mental model is of a runaway truck approaching).

The example of a runaway vehicle highlights another important aspect of how auditory stimuli are perceived in the real world, that is the stimuli are by nature dynamic, transient (e.g. a clap) or changing (the source could be moving, or varying as in speech or music). In many cases the listener will also be moving, for example walking, travelling in a car, or simply turning or nodding the head. Thus, there are a myriad of links between action, vision, hearing and other senses, some of which will be discussed in the next section.

2.4 Haptic perception

More than five senses?

It is usual to think of humans as having five senses: these being vision, hearing, smell, taste and touch. However, can we not also sense whether we are standing upright or leaning forward, and if so, which sense is this? Similarly, if I close my eyes I can sense quite precisely where my arms and legs are, at least with respect to my body and to one another; but what sense am I using? When I touch an object I can discern whether it is smooth or rough, large or small and also whether it is hot or cold, but are all of these worked out using my sense of touch? If so, how is it I can sense the heat from a hot cup of tea as I move my hand above it or that I feel cold as I walk along the freezer aisle at my local supermarket, even though I'm not touching either the tea or the freezers? What about pain; is that the same thing as touch? If it is, am I somehow touching my intestines when I have indigestion? In addition, I can somehow sense, for example, whether I am thirsty or hungry and whether my lungs are inflated.

From the above, it should be clear that five senses are not nearly enough to encompass the entire spectrum of information that we can detect. So, how many senses do we actually possess? Even excluding such phenomena as a sense of disappointment, a sense of achievement or a sense of belonging, and restricting the definition of a sense to detection of a specific form of information by a specific type of sensory cell which in turn is processed by a particular part of the brain, Durie (2005) suggests that there are at least 21 senses, possibly a lot more (see Figure 2.22). It should also be apparent that we have some senses, such as hearing and smell, that are primarily concerned with sensing information coming from our environment, and some senses, such as our sense of pain (we call this 'nociception') and senses such as thirst and hunger (which involve specific types of interoceptors) that provide information about the state of our own bodies.

Importantly, we can combine cues from these two broad categories of senses (i.e. internal and external senses) to provide more detailed information about the environment around us. For example, even without using my eyes I can determine where objects are and how large they are simply by moving my hands over their surface. In doing this I'm combining information about the relative position of my hands (where they are with respect to each other and my body) with information from the touch receptors in my fingers, that let me know when they are in contact with a surface, to determine exactly where my hands are when they come in contact with the surface. In the rest of this section we will be exploring in more depth how we can perceive the environment using senses such as 'touch' and looking at how we combine information from more than one sense.

Sensory Modality	Conservative	Accepted	Radical	Sensory Modality	Conservative	Accepted	Radical
Vision	✓			Hearing	✓	✓	✓
Light		✓	✓				
Colour		✓		Mechanoreception	✓		
Red			✓	Balance	✓	✓	
Green			✓	Rotational acceleration			✓
Blue			✓	Linear acceleration			✓
				Proprioception - joint position		✓	✓
Smell	✓	✓		Kinesthesis		✓	
2000 or more receptor types			✓	Muscle strength - Golgi tendon organs			✓
Taste	✓			Muscle stretch - muscle spindles			✓
Sweet		✓	✓				
Salt		✓	✓	Interoceptors			
Sour		✓	✓	Blood pressure	✓	✓	
Bitter		✓	✓	Arterial blood pressure			✓
Umami			✓	Central venous blood pressure			✓
				Head blood temperature			✓
Touch	✓	✓		Blood oxygen content		✓	✓
Light touch			✓	Cerebrospinal fluid pH		✓	✓
Pressure			✓	Plasma osmotic pressure (thirst?)		✓	✓
Pain	✓	✓		Artery-vein blood glucose difference (hunger?)		✓	✓
Cutaneous			✓	Lung inflation		✓	✓
Somatic			✓	Bladder stretch			✓
Visceral			✓	Full stomach			✓
Temperature	✓			Total	10	21	33
Heat		✓	✓				
Cold		✓	✓				

Figure 2.22 How many senses do we have?

Source: Adapted from Durie (2005)

Proprioception, kinesthesis and haptic information

The sense that keeps track of the position of our body, limbs, fingers, etc. is known as **proprioception** and it operates through a system of nerve cell receptors (known as proprioceptors) that allow us to ascertain the angle of our various joints. A related sense, known as kinesthesis, allows us to discern how our body and limbs are moving and is a key element in such things as hand–eye coordination, and as such is a sense that can be improved through training and practice. Unfortunately there is considerable variability in exactly what the terms kinesthesis and proprioception are taken to mean (Owen, 1990). For example, Riccio and McDonald (1998) define kinesthesis as the perception of the change in the location of the whole body compared to the environment (thus movement of the whole body is necessary to generate kinesthetic information) and proprioception to mean the perception of where our body parts are in relation to each other and the environment. Proprioception is also sometimes used as a collective term encompassing all the information regarding the position of the body, including kinesthesis and our sense of balance. We will not concern ourselves with debating a precise definition here, but instead will stick to the key point, which is that we are able to sense the position and movement of our bodies and limbs without resorting to looking to see where they are.

If you try reaching out (with your eyes closed of course) and feeling an unknown object in front of you, you will quickly realise that to obtain any information that might be useful in recognising what the object is, you need to be able to sense when your fingers touch the object (through the touch receptors in your skin) and also where your fingers are when they touch it. As you move your fingers to explore the object, you need to sense whether or not they are still in contact with the object and also how far they are moving. Thus in exploring the environment we need to combine our sense of touch with proprioception and kinesthesis, and in so doing we produce what is referred to as **haptic information**.

Our ability to judge the position and movement of our hands seems to be quite accurate and compares well with the acuity of our visual system (Henriques and Soechting, 2003). There are some elementary judgements that are more accurately performed using visual rather than haptic information; we tend to mistake an inwardly spiralling movement as describing a circle for instance, but on the whole we can judge the geometry of any surface we touch very accurately without recourse to vision (Henriques and Soechting, 2003).

As you might expect, given how similar our hands are and also our brains, there appears to be great similarity in how people explore the environment in order to generate haptic information. Klatzky *et al.* (1987) reported that their participants tended to employ a consistent series of exploratory procedures when asked to explore an object using their hands. Lederman and Klatzky (1990) found that each particular exploratory procedure seemed to be used in order to determine a specific aspect of the object, so that unsupported holding was used to ascertain the object's weight, whilst enclosing the object with one or both hands was used to tell what the overall shape of the object might be.

The use of the term 'exploratory procedure' suggests that the way we obtain haptic information has a lot in common with 'active perception' and the ideas of Gibson that were discussed previously; in fact it was Gibson who first coined the phrase 'haptic information' (Gibson, 1966). If we just sat still and did not attempt to explore our environment using our hands, we would not gain very much new information at all. Instead, on most occasions we have to interact with the environment actively to generate haptic information that will be of use. It is also the case that we can think about our sense of touch (and kinesthesis) in terms of 'bottom-up' and 'top-down' processing. A lot of haptic information is likely to be processed in a very bottom-up manner: for example the information about the texture and resistance of my keyboard keys and the relative position of my fingers can be said to flow from my senses upward through the perceptual system. However, haptic information can also have a top-down element and one excellent example of this is the parlour game where blindfolded people are asked to guess what object has been placed in their hand. Although this task involves considerable bottom-up processing, it is likely that the person would use their prior knowledge regarding the size, shape, weight and texture of objects to form and test hypotheses as to what the object might be.

Using illusions to explore haptic information

One of the key approaches to distinguishing between top-down and bottom-up processing is based on illusions. You may remember that the Müller-Lyer illusion provides evidence of top-down processing, as we use existing knowledge to interpret the lines and mistakenly decide that one is longer than the other. Interestingly, there is evidence that the Müller-Lyer illusion works for haptic as well as visual information. Heller *et al.* (2002) produced a version of the illusion in which the lines were 'raised' (in a similar fashion to Braille) to allow them to be felt and participants estimated the size of the key lines using a sliding ruler. Blindfolded-sighted, late-blind, congenitally blind, and low-vision participants completed the task and all were influenced by the illusion, i.e. they estimated the 'wings-in' line to be shorter than the 'wings-out' line. Not only does this experiment demonstrate that the Müller-Lyer illusion is not reliant on either visual imagery or experience, it also suggests that there is an element of top-down processing with haptic information, just as there is with visual information.

Previously, the concept was introduced that haptic information was generated by combining information from our sense of touch with proprioception and kinesthesis, but as we reach to feel or pick up an object we also need to take account of the information picked up by other senses, most notably vision. That both vision and haptic information are used to explore or pick up an object with our hands is obvious, otherwise it would be just as easy to pick something up with our eyes closed as it would with them open. As well as demonstrating visual top-down processing, illusion studies can also show the extent to which visual and haptic information is integrated.

Gallace and Spence (2005) constructed a task that involved participants looking at the Müller-Lyer illusion whilst at the same time attempting to tell which of two sticks hidden from view was the longest. The sticks were placed directly behind the Müller-Lyer illusion (see Figure 2.23), which was presented in a horizontal '< > <' configuration with just the 'wings' and not the lines themselves drawn (this is known as the Brentano version of the illusion). This meant that the Müller-Lyer illusion was being presented visually, and at the same time as they were viewing it participants were performing a task utilising haptic information. The results of this experiment revealed that the visual illusion did interfere with the participant's ability to 'feel' the correct length of the line, so that the length of the sticks were either over- or underestimated as a result of the participant seeing the illusion. Thus, visual information was affecting the processing of haptic information.

Another distinction that was introduced earlier when discussing visual perception is that of perception for recognition and perception for action, and this distinction is particularly relevant to the processing of haptic information. If you remember, the idea is that the information from our retinas is processed through two separate, but interconnected, visual pathways in the brain: the ventral pathway

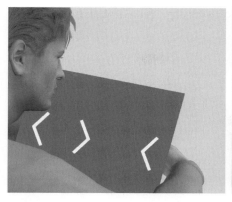

Figure 2.23 A (CGI) recreation of the task from the Gallace and Spence (2005) study in which a participant feels the length of two unseen sticks placed behind the Müller-Lyer illusion
Source: Adapted from Gallace and Spence

appears to be used for processing information that is used to recognise objects, whilst the dorsal pathway is used for processing information used to guide the visual control of action (Milner and Goodale, 1995). Above, studies by Klatzky *et al.* (1987) and Lederman and Klatzky (1990) were described that examined how we can use our hands to generate haptic information in order to recognise objects. However, unless there is no light available or the person concerned has impaired vision, most of the time we rely very heavily on vision in order to recognise objects. Instead, we tend to make use of haptic information to interact with the environment around us in precise ways, i.e. haptic information is probably more useful in terms of guiding action than in recognising objects.

A key question, therefore, is whether there is a divide between perception for recognition and perception for action in the processing of haptic information? In attempting to answer this question, it is possible to make further use of evidence from studies that have utilised illusions. The Ebbinghaus illusion is an example of a size-contrast illusion (see Figure 2.24) in which two circles of equal size appear to be of different sizes due to the presence of surrounding circles. If you look at Figure 2.24 and compare the two circles in the centre of the others (we call these the 'target' objects), the one on the right will appear to be larger than the one on the left even though both are exactly the same size. In judging the size of the two target circles your perceptual system is taking into account the contrast between their size and the size of the circles surrounding them (we call these 'flanker' objects). Thus a target object will appear smaller when placed next to flanker objects that are larger than it and will appear larger when placed next to flanker objects that are smaller than it.

Aglioti *et al.* (1995) found evidence to support the dissociation between ventral and dorsal processing by conducting an experiment in which participants were asked either to estimate the size (ventral processing) of the central circle in the size-contrast illusion described above or to reach out and pick it up (dorsal

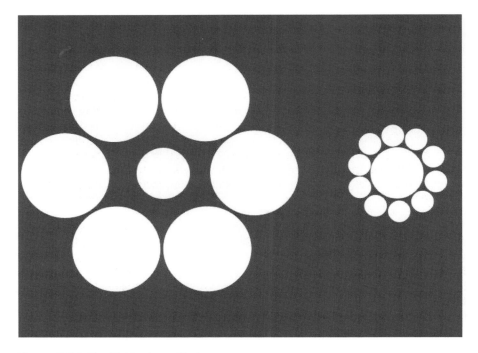

Figure 2.24 The Ebbinghaus illusion

processing). When estimating the size of the circle the participants' judgements were affected by the illusion, but analysis of the size of their grip revealed that the action of picking-up the circle did not appear to be affected.

Hu and Goodale (2000) conducted a series of studies utilising a different version of the size-contrast illusion in which participants were presented with two objects (the objects were actually 'virtual' as they were presented by reflecting a video image onto a mirror placed in front of the participant) and were asked either to pick up the target object or to indicate its size using a manual estimate (i.e. by separating their finger and thumb). These two tasks were both performed either immediately or after a five-second delay. The results showed that when performed immediately, the manual estimates were influenced by the size of the flanker object. However, analysis of the recording of the participants' hand movement in the 'pick-up' condition revealed that the size of their grip was not influenced (statistically significantly) by the size of the flanker. When providing the manual estimate, the participants must have been utilising 'perception for recognition' processing, as they would have had to generate a mental description of the object in order to estimate its size. When picking the target object up, the processing required would have been 'perception for action'. Further evidence that this task demonstrates dissociation between perception for action and recognition was provided by asking participants to perform both the manual estimate and pick-up tasks from memory. Here, both tasks necessitate the use of perception for recognition, as the participant has to create a mental description of the object in their memory. Analysis of this experiment did indeed show that both tasks were influenced by the size-contrast illusion, i.e. the size of the flanker influenced the perceived size of the target.

The Hu and Goodale (2000) study involved the processing of haptic information, as proprioception and kinesthesis were used in moving the participants' arm and fingers, and their touch receptors were used for detecting when the fingers came in contact with the target object. However, the actual illusion employed (the size-contrast illusion) was presented visually and therefore it was visual information and not haptic information that was responsible for the participants misjudging the size of the target object. So, whilst the study provides evidence that visual information is processed in a dissociated manner, through either perception for recognition or action, it does not tell us whether haptic information is also processed in this way.

To explore this issue further, Westwood and Goodale (2003) conducted a similar study to that of Hu and Goodale (2000), except that they replaced the visual size-contrast illusion with a haptic version. Participants were asked first to feel an unseen flanker object and then to feel an unseen target object using their left hand. When they had done this they were asked to use their right hand either to provide a manual estimate (again using finger and thumb) of the size of the target object or to reach out and pick up an object placed in front of them (which

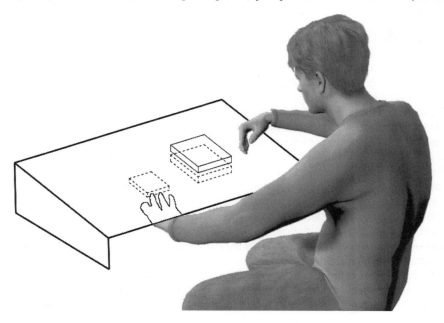

Figure 2.25 A (CGI) recreation of the task from the Westwood and Goodale (2003) study in which a participant feels unseen flanker and target objects with their left hand and indicates the size of the target with their right

Source: Adapted from Westwood and Goodale (2003)

was also not in view, as they were asked to keep their eyes closed) that was matched in size to the target (see Figure 2.25). The results of this experiment showed that the manual estimate task was affected by the illusion, in that participants tended to overestimate the size of the target when it was paired with a smaller flanker object and to underestimate the size of the target when it was paired with a larger flanker object. However, when the data from the pick-up task was analysed, the size of the participants' grip as they reached for the object did not appear to have been affected by the illusion, i.e. their grip was the same regardless of the size of the flanker object. This is evidence suggesting that haptic information is processed in a similarly dissociated manner as that of visual information, or indeed (as the authors themselves suggest) that all sensory processing might be organised according to a general principle.

In summary, the common notion that there are five human senses is somewhat inaccurate (to the tune of at least sixteen!) and we usually confuse several different senses (particularly kinesthesis and proprioception) when we talk about touch. Our ability to explore the environment with our hands is very well developed and by combining haptic and visual information we can interact with objects very accurately. In addition, the way in which we process haptic information seems very similar to visual information, in that both bottom-up and top-down processing are employed and there appears to be a dissociation between perception for recognition and perception for action.

2.5 Conclusion

There are a number of points made throughout this chapter that will be drawn together here. One of the major themes running through this chapter is the distinction between perception for recognition and perception for action. How these two systems interact (or not) is an issue that runs throughout the chapter. The section on vision concluded with the supposition that the two perceptual systems operate synergistically to allow us to perceive the world. The final section of the chapter on haptic perception ends with the proposition that there can be a dissociation between perception for action and perception for recognition. These apparently contradictory conclusions can be reconciled by appealing to the argument that is made particularly clearly in the section on auditory perception. It is possible to use sophisticated experimental techniques to study, for instance, the perception for action and perception for recognition systems in isolation. This approach is invaluable in that it gives an indication of how these systems operate. It does not, however, give a complete picture of how these systems operate in 'real life'. If this issue is considered, then there is evidence that the two systems are heavily interconnected and that perception results from an interaction of these two (and possibly other) systems. So, perception for recognition and perception for action *can* work together, but whether they do or not will depend upon the circumstances.

One theme that runs through the discussion of all the senses considered in this chapter is the notion that perception consists of far more than the simple collection of sensory information. Perception involves building up a model of the world around us and the objects and people in it. We certainly use sensory information to do this but we also use our knowledge, experience and expectations to build up our percept. This chapter could best be summed up by re-wording a phrase that has already been used, namely: 'We *perceive* things not as they are, but as we are.'

Summary

- There are a number of theories that attempt to explain how we encode incoming sensory information.
- Perception is not the same as sensation. We may detect something but not perceive it.
- Knowledge is crucial in our influencing our perception of the world – according to constructivist theories.
- Knowledge is unnecessary in our perception of the world – according to direct perception theories.
- Both approaches may operate in vision with the ventral stream operating primarily for perception for recognition and the dorsal stream operating primarily for perception for action.
- Knowledge is also crucial in auditory perception.
- There are strong interactions between auditory and visual perception.
- There may be at least twenty-one senses (not just five!).
- Knowledge also influences haptic perception.
- We sense things not as they are, but as we are.

Further reading

Goldstein, E.B. (2002). *Sensation and Perception*. Pacific Grove, CA: Wadsworth. A highly readable and comprehensive discussion of aspects of perception.

Banich, M.T. (2004). *Cognitive Neuroscience and Neuropsychology*. Boston, MA: Houghton Mifflin. If you like the squishy stuff, then this is for you. An excellent introduction to the workings of the brain.

Mannoni, L., Nekes, W. and Warner, M. (2004). *Eyes, Lies and Illusions*, London and Aldershot: Hayward Gallery Publising/Lund Humphries. If you are interested in illusions then this is the book for you. An entertaining read that covers the history of illusions rather than the explanations for them. Basically, all the bits that this chapter did not cover.

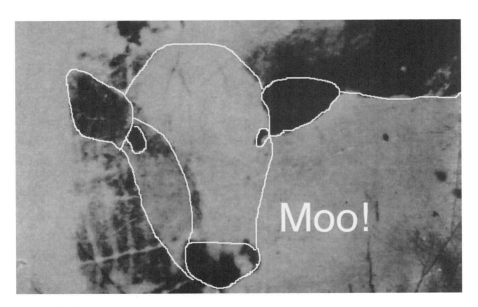

Figure 2.14 Answer

Attention

3.1 Introduction

Attention

Attention was defined first by William James in 1890. He saw it as involving the holding of something before the mind to the exclusion of all else. This is what would today be called **focused**, or **selective**, attention. Selective attention implies conscious awareness of, and concentration upon, a particular source of stimulation or information. That source of stimulation or information could be sensory stimulation in any of the sensory modalities or could be an internal state implicated in an activity such as mental arithmetic. As well as focusing on a single source of stimulation, we are also capable of dividing ourselves between multiple activities. This is the issue of **divided attention**. Divided attention is concerned with how attention may be distributed over a range of competing inputs or internal states so that all of them receive some processing. Divided attention is thus typical of most tasks in the real world. Some of the assumptions implicit in James' definition remain controversial, for example the issue of whether or not we can process stimuli without becoming consciously aware of them. Processing of stimuli without awareness is what is termed **subliminal perception**, or non-conscious processing.

Real-world tasks only very rarely involve attending to a single input. An example is the **vigilance task**. In this task an operator of, for example, a radar screen monitors the screen in order to detect rare occurrences such as an encroaching 'enemy' aircraft. Studies have shown that people have considerable difficulty in maintaining attentional vigilance under such circumstances and need regular breaks to help them keep focused on the (very boring) task in hand. The radar screen monitoring task is an example of one in which attention is directed primarily to a stimulus in the visual modality. Other tasks may involve attending selectively to heard stimuli or even to stimuli in one of the other sensory modalities. If the radar screen operator also needs to monitor conversations between aircrew or to give instructions then he or she may be engaged in a divided attention task. The result would be a much more interesting task than one of simply monitoring the screen and likely to be one in which the operator's attention could more readily remain engaged.

In this chapter we consider focused auditory and focused visual attention before going on to look at the issue of automaticity. We then consider divided attention. Finally, we look at problems such as slips and lapses that are associated with aspects of attention, and also at some issues surrounding subliminal perception.

3.2 Focused auditory attention

Listening to one thing

Attention is a classic issue within experimental psychology and was one of the first topics to be addressed from within the cognitive perspective (Cherry, 1953;

Broadbent, 1958; Moray, 1959). Whilst much of the discussion of issues in perception has relied on examples and experiments from visual perception, most of the early studies of attention have in contrast involved hearing. This may have been largely because of the ease with which the two ears can be provided with separate inputs via headphones. These early studies were also seen as having some ecological validity since competing auditory input appeared to be a reasonable simulation of situations that arose in the operation of complex systems. Much of the impetus for the study of such systems arose in turn from military developments during World War II. For example, in vehicles such as tanks, commanders may need to communicate with gunners and other crew simultaneously via separate headphones due to the noisy environment.

The cocktail-party phenomenon

It is not necessary to consider communication between members of tank crews to find examples of issues relating to the focusing of attention. One of the first attentional phenomena to be studied (Cherry, 1953) was the '**cocktail-party phenomenon**'. This refers to the ability of normal people to attend to a single conversation against a background of numerous conversations that all take place at the same time. In addition to maintaining their attentional focus on a particular conversation, most people also retain the ability to switch their attention either at will, or seemingly involuntarily, to another source. This may occur upon hearing, for example, one's own name or some other personally important word being spoken in another conversation.

Shadowing

A situation in which competing sources of auditory input are available to subjects, whether in noisy military vehicles or in the more civilised environs of a cocktail-party, can be **simulated**, or modelled, experimentally by means of the 'shadowing' technique. Shadowing depends upon **dichotic listening**. This entails having subjects listen to two competing sources of auditory stimulation each coming simultaneously via separate headphones to each of each subject's ears. Dichotic listening has been extensively used within experimental psychology. As well as being a tool for the investigation of attention, it has also been employed within neuropsychology. Here it offers a window upon the differences in functioning (or lateral differences) between the two cerebral hemispheres of the brain since under dichotic conditions the cerebral hemispheres are stimulated selectively.

Dichotic listening directly enables the study of divided attention and is a ready laboratory simulation of the tank crew or cocktail-party scenarios outlined above. In studies one would simply have to see how much input from the two competing sources (often referred to as **channels**) the subject can process under dichotic conditions. Dependent variables would include, for example, how much can be remembered from each of the two inputs (often referred to as **messages**). It may be noted that good experimental design needs to counterbalance for the laterality effects mentioned above. In most people, linguistic material presented to the right ear will be better processed than that presented to the left (since the right ear, under dichotic conditions, stimulates the linguistic left hemisphere of the brain).

In order to study focused attention, one more thing needs to be added to dichotic listening. This is **shadowing**. Shadowing involves the subject attending to one of the two competing channels and repeating the material presented on that channel back aloud. The task is actually surprisingly difficult to accomplish and requires much effort on the part of the subject, especially if they are not practised at it.

The fate of the unattended message

When the subject is required to shadow the input to one ear in the dichotic situation, a natural question that arises concerns how much of the input to the other ear is perceived. Early experiments (Broadbent, 1958) suggested that virtually nothing is registered from the non-attended ear. The fate of the unattended message appeared therefore to be to rapidly decay away to nothing, at least to nothing that the subject could subsequently retrieve. However, the simplest aspects of the stimulus *were* noticed. These included such aspects as whether the unattended message consisted of speech or music. If the unattended message was linguistic then the sex of the speaker would be noticed, possibly inferred from pitch of voice, even though the semantic content of the message was lost.

Broadbent (1958) filter model

Broadbent (1958) put forward a filter concept of attention to account for these early findings. This is represented diagrammatically in Figure 3.1. Functionally, the role of attention was to control entry into consciousness, depicted here as short-term memory, in order to prevent cognitive overload by irrelevant material. The assumption that attention implies conscious awareness is implicit here. On this model, selection takes place at an early stage, on the basis of physical characteristics. The most obvious of these is a channel which corresponds in an obvious way to physical location. Thus, where the cocktail-party is concerned, the factors that enable us to maintain our focus on the person with whom we are conversing include that person's physical location as well as other physical characteristics, such as those connected with their voice. A complete account of focused attention must include both the ability to maintain attention and the ability to switch attention to something else. The filter model was less successful in trying to account for the second of these.

For switching to take place in a way that is dependent upon the **semantic** content, or meaning, of the stimulus to which attention is to be switched, then at least some processing of the latter input must have occurred. Overhearing one's own name being spoken would have no significance if we did not know that it is *our* name and not just some random word that is being spoken. This would be

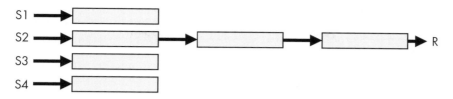

Figure 3.1 Broadbent's filter model

precisely the situation if selection takes place solely at the physical level before meaning has been apprehended. Clearly, however, we can switch attention to significant stimuli like our own name very easily and readily. Thus, there is a basic paradox within attentional switching which the Broadbent filter model does not resolve. Filtering on the basis of physical characteristics cannot be the whole story since attention can readily be switched to a source of input that is being selected out and which therefore should not be in a position to serve as the basis for that switching. Some writers have taken this ability as evidence for subliminal perception, i.e. processing of material taking place outside awareness. A challenge for models of attention is to try to account for the phenomenon of attentional switching in a more parsimonious way than by positing a large amount of processing outside awareness.

Other problems

Further problems with the filter model include the finding that the amount of material registered on the unattended channel greatly increases with practice of shadowing (Underwood, 1974). In addition, if a message alternates between the two ears, subjects follow it back and forth rather than continuing to shadow the ear receiving only part of the whole message. This can also be shown in the divided attention situation when subjects recall messages in coherent forms. For example, instead of presenting 'A B C' and '1 2 3' simultaneously, the 'message', in the sense of one being alphabetic and one numeric, alternates between the ears so that '1 B 3' and 'A 2 C' are presented. However, subjects will chunk their recall by message as 'A B C' and '1 2 3' rather than chunking by ear as '1 B 3' and 'A 2 C' (see Figure 3.2). Although structuring may take place at the time of recall, the possibility cannot be eliminated that subjects are selecting on the basis of semantics rather than location

Another difficulty for the filter model is the phenomenon of subliminal perception. This may involve subjects' behaviour being influenced by an input despite their lack of any conscious awareness of that input. The occurrence of subliminal perception questions the view that the role of attention is to control entry into consciousness in order to prevent cognitive overload by irrelevant material since, in principle, there may be no limit upon the amount of processing taking place outside awareness. A typical subliminal perception paradigm involves conditioning subjects to produce galvanic skin responses (GSRs) in response to

Left Ear	Right Ear
1	A
B	2
3	C
Recall 'ABC123'	

Figure 3.2 Evidence for processing of unattended message

certain stimuli. This can be readily accomplished by, for example, associating the stimuli with mild electric shocks. Subjects will continue to exhibit a GSR indicative of anticipation of the shock for some time after the conditioning session. Experiments by Von Wright *et al.* (1975) and others have clearly demonstrated the occurrence of GSR responses to words presented on the unattended channel even when the subjects were not consciously aware of those words having been spoken.

Govier and Pitts (1982) found that subjects were capable of discriminating between alternative meanings of an unattended, shock-conditioned word. They presented 'polysemous' words (that is, words having multiple meanings, such as 'bank', which could refer to either a money bank or a river bank), and conditioned subjects to expect shocks in response to the presentation of one of the two meanings. In a subsequent dichotic shadowing task subjects displayed the same pattern of selective GSRs to particular meanings of the polysemous word on the unattended channel, where this meaning was determined by the context provided by the message on that channel.

Early or late selection

Demonstrations such as the above clearly indicate that there is far more processing of unattended material than the filter model would predict. Broadbent's filter model is an **early selection** model, in which filtering takes place at the earliest opportunity in perception, usually on the basis of physical attributes and before any significant amount of semantic processing can occur. In contrast, experiments such as that by Govier and Pitts (1982) suggest that processing of the unattended message may reach the very highest levels of semantic processing, involving the extraction of specific meanings of ambiguous words, without conscious awareness and therefore before any filtering operations controlling entry into consciousness.

One way out of this dilemma is to propose a **late selection** model in which all stimuli are processed, albeit most of them outside awareness, to the highest level possible, usually the semantic level, before any filtering operations take place.

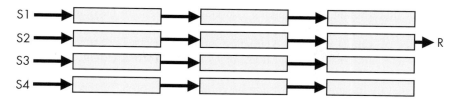

Figure 3.3 Deutsch and Deutsch's late selection model

This view is associated with the work of Deutsch and Deutsch. They postulated (Deutsch and Deutsch, 1967) that selection actually takes place at the level of response. Stimuli not responded to in some way are therefore less likely to enter consciousness or to be forgotten than are those associated with a response. The main objections to this view are that (i) it is not parsimonious, and (ii) it is not cognitively economical. That is, (i) simpler models may account equally well for the data, and (ii) it is intuitively very unlikely that evolution would equip us to process all stimuli to the highest level possible when virtually all of those stimuli are quite irrelevant to our survival, particularly when having the large brain needed to carry out that processing may impose certain physiological costs. The model is depicted in Figure 3.3.

Attenuation model

Probably the most satisfactory model of attention is the **attenuation** model proposed by Treisman (1964), which proposes that the non-attended channel is not completely shut down but merely attenuated, or adjusted, much as one might turn down the volume knob on a radio. On this account incoming stimuli undergo three different types of analysis. The first analysis is concerned with physical characteristics. The second analysis is concerned with determining whether or not stimuli are linguistic and, if so, grouping them into syllables and words. The final stage is concerned with the allocation of meanings. This is the highest level of processing and is referred to as semantic-level processing. The approach has much in common with the influential levels-of-processing model of memory (described in Chapter 5) and is represented in Figure 3.4.

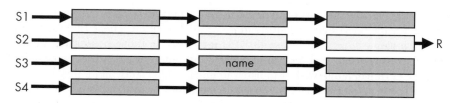

Figure 3.4 Treisman's attenuation model

On this account, disentangling two competing stimuli becomes difficult if both require the same level of processing. The cocktail-party situation is accounted for readily by simply rejecting competing input on the basis of physical characteristics (sex and position of speaker, for example). To that extent the model is similar to Broadbent's but, unlike that model, the attenuation account does not require that the unattended message be completely ignored. Instead it is merely attenuated to a lower level. Processing of the unattended message may, therefore, be much more complex and may occur at any level up to and including the semantic level. The model assumes that inputs are attenuated differently and flexibly, so the setting for a personally relevant item, such as one's name, reflects much greater sensitivity for such material. Moreover, the flexibility of settings allows for attention to be paid to other aspects of the environment under conditions that require this. The model therefore deals with the switching of attention much more readily than did Broadbent's and is more parsimonious and cognitively economical than that of Deutsch and Deutsch (1967).

Experimental evidence has tended to favour Treisman's view (Broadbent, 1982). In one such study, the effects of response were compared. It will be recalled that on the late selection view a response is predicted to result in a greater likelihood of that item entering consciousness. Using tapping in response to word stimuli presented under dichotic shadowing conditions, many more taps were generated in response to occurrences on the attended ear as compared with the unattended ear. In order to eliminate the possibility that shadowing itself may be increasing the likelihood of recognition, as it could be regarded as a second response to the stimulus on the attended channel, the experiment was repeated with subjects instructed to stop shadowing when the target occurred on either ear. Although this reduced the difference between the numbers of detections on either ear, that difference was still large (Treisman and Geffen, 1967).

Streaming

An alternative view, termed the '**streaming**' hypothesis (Jones *et al.*, 1999) suggests that the ability to segment two competing sources of input into separate streams and keep these in memory as distinct, temporally-ordered sequences is key to focusing attention upon a single source of stimulation. A competing stimulus will only intrude if it possesses sufficient variation to prevent its maintenance as a separately streamed sequence. Stimuli that form a coherent stream are easier to keep separate than those that do not. Evidence in favour of this assertion comes from studies in which short-term memory (STM) performance is affected by background sounds possessing relatively more or less variation. Those that vary least, such as a single tone, interfere with STM less than do those possessing greater amounts of variation. It is possible to draw out some practical inferences from this. For example, if one wishes to listen to music whilst studying, it may be advisable to listen to music that contains little variation, or few surprises, since this may be predicted to intrude less than music containing many variations in, for example, tempo, pitch or volume.

Capacity and resources

As well as being the best able to account for the maintenance and switching of attention, Treisman's model also acknowledges that mental resources are limited. That is, it acknowledges the need for cognitive economy. The failure to acknowledge this was a key criticism of the late selection approach since semantic-level processing of all incoming stimuli would make unrealistic demands upon available processing resources. In Treisman's model there is a flexible 'bottleneck' in processing. The bottleneck is seen as a limited **capacity** processor whose available capacity depends in turn upon task demands. Task demands would reflect either the complexity of a task or the need to carry out a concurrent (i.e. simultaneous) task. Stimuli will be attenuated, i.e. processed to a lower level, when there is insufficient capacity to process them further or when other stimuli must take priority. Johnston and Heinz (1978) take a similar view, arguing that early selection imposes fewer demands on available capacity and that selection will then to some extent depend upon task demands, including whether or not concurrent tasks must be undertaken.

The concept of processing capacity may be made more specific by consideration of the types of processing required by particular tasks. These are likely to differ between, for example, verbal memory and mental arithmetic tasks. The concept of specific processing resources, as relatively discrete information-processing **modules**, is an important one that is relevant to consideration of divided attention and multi-task performance. Under these circumstances, tasks combine readily to the extent that they do not demand the same specific processing resources. This enables us to make a further recommendation selection of musical background to study. The streaming hypothesis suggests that music with minimal variation will intrude less than other sorts. In addition, one would want to select music that did not make demands upon the same processing modules as those needed for the (hopefully) main task of study. Since study mainly involves words, it would make sense to have instrumental rather than vocal selections for background music to minimise interference and intrusion. The best selections then are those that are both instrumental and relatively unvarying, such as the work of contemporary minimalist composers.

3.3 Focused visual attention

Selective attending at the global or local level

Experiments by Navon (1977) suggest that it may be the norm to process the **global** attributes of a stimulus before the **local** detail. Navon presented stimuli to subjects in which large letters were made up of many smaller ones (see Figure 3.5). Subjects' attention was then directed to the global or local level by having them report either the large or small letters presented. It was found that conflicting information at the global level impaired report of local features but not vice versa. Thus, in an echo of the Gestaltist view that the 'whole is greater than the sum of the parts', global-level attending appears to take priority over local-level attending.

```
H     H        O      O        S      S
H     H        O      O        S      S
H     H        O      O        S      S
HHHHHH        OOOOOO        SSSSSS
H     H        O      O        S      S
H     H        O      O        S      S
H     H        O      O        S      S

HHHHHH        OOOOOO        SSSSSS
H     H        O      O        S      S
H     H        O      O        S      S
H     H        O      O        S      S
H     H        O      O        S      S
H     H        O      O        S      S
HHHHHH        OOOOOO        SSSSSS

 HHHHH        OOOOO        SSSS
H     H      O     O      S     S
H            O            S
HHHHHH      OOOOO        SSSSS
     H            O            S
HHHHH        OOOOO        SSSS
```

Figure 3.5 Stimuli of the type used by Navon (1977)

Other studies of selective attention in vision have required subjects to attend to a physical property such as colour or spatial location. The Stroop task is an example of the former and the Eriksen interference paradigm an example of the latter. The Stroop effect (explained briefly in Chapter 1) depends upon subjects trying to do something other than read a word that they are presented with. In the classic study, colour words are written in variously coloured inks, for example the word 'green' in blue ink. Subjects are instructed to call out the colour of the ink rather than the word written in that ink. Most subjects show a considerable interference effect (that is, slower responding and more errors) when there is an inconsistency between the word and the colour of the ink. Under such conditions semantic or identity information from unattended elements affects performance indicating that it may be difficult to divert attention away from reading the word. Boucart and Humphreys (1992, 1994) further investigated whether access to high-level information could be prevented when the task only requires the processing of a physical property. They found that semantic content affects performance even though the task only required attention to a physical property of the stimulus. However, this held when subjects attended to the global shape of the stimulus, but not when they attended to other physical features such as colour or luminance.

Visual search

One of the most used procedures in the area of visual attention is the **visual search** task. This requires detection of a particular stimulus, called the '**target**' against a background of other items collectively referred to as '**distracters**'. Various features of the relationship between targets and background distracters can be altered, such as the similarity between and within sets of targets and distracters. Visual search was first investigated by Neisser (1964, 1967) who wished to investigate the considerable variation in the ease with which we can identify a given object from other objects. One example quoted by Neisser concerns the ease with which a familiar face can be identified in a crowd. In support of everyday intuitions, Neisser found that his US subjects could easily identify the face of the late President Kennedy from amongst many thousands of others in a photograph of a crowd at a baseball match. This contrasts with other visual search situations, such as identifying objects on the ground or sea from the air, which can be extremely difficult. A goal of visual attention research is then to identify under what circumstances a visual object attracts the attention of the visual system very easily and under what circumstances it does not. Neisser modelled the visual search task by having subjects search among an array of letters presented on paper or on a computer screen for a specified target. The relationship between targets and distracters could then be manipulated.

Simple visual search – target and distracters different

In one experiment (Neisser, 1967), subjects tried to locate a letter defined by angular or by round features (Z or Q respectively) in a field of predominantly angular or round distracters. Neisser found a very considerable advantage for identification of targets against a dissimilar background (see Figure 3.6).

The advantage of a dissimilar background may be readily explained in terms of **feature analysis**. Here we are using the term 'feature' to refer to constituent components of letters. These correspond to orientations of lines and curves and their combinations. Since there are no features in common between the target and distracters when the background is dissimilar to the target, distracters may be readily rejected on the basis of the most preliminary analysis of one such discrepant feature. This is the so-called *pop-out* effect. Pop-out appears to be what happened when Neisser's subjects rapidly identified President Kennedy against a background of other faces, as well as what happens when we identify a familiar face in a crowded place such as a railway station. Subjects in Neisser's studies often reported that the background distracters were merely a 'blur'. This may now be explained. Since the target pops out there is therefore no need to fully process, or recognise, all or indeed any of the distracters.

Search time in milliseconds:

		Background	
		Angular	Round
Target	Q	80	580
	Z	240	110

Figure 3.6 Results of Neisser's (1967) visual search study

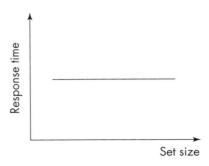

Figure 3.7 Set-size function for simple search

Further experiments (for example Treisman and Gelade, 1980) suggest that feature analysis is a **parallel process**. If a single target is to be located against a background of distracters that are dissimilar to the target, then the total number of distracters present has little or no effect on the response time and the set size function is flat. The **set-size function** is the graph of search time against the total size of the array displayed. If the targets are randomly embedded within the array of distracters across trials then the total search time should increase with set size if the distracters are being processed serially. The fact that this does not happen and the function is flat indicates that all of the elements of the display are processed in parallel and that additional distracters require no extra processing (see Figure 3.7).

Conjoint search – target and distracters similar

Where many features are common to target and distracters, much more process-ing is required in order to reject distracters. Such a situation is provided by the **conjoint search** (or conjunction search) in which a target is defined by a combi-nation of features, for example a white circle against a background that includes circles that are not white and white items that are not circles. Stimuli of this sort are illustrated in Figure 3.8. There is thus some similarity between targets and distracters. The set-size function in this case shows a linear increase indicative of **serial processing** (see Figure 3.9). That is, with conjoint search each distracter imposes a requirement for additional processing since it has some similarity with the target and so must be checked for the presence of the target's other features. It does not appear to be possible for this checking to be accomplished in parallel across the whole field of distracters.

Illusory conjunctions

In the conjoint visual search task, subjects occasionally report seeing examples of **illusory conjunctions**. These are cases when features are combined in such

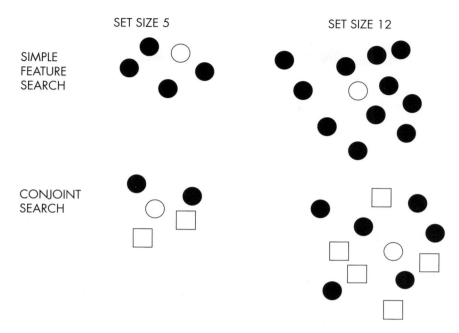

Figure 3.8 Examples of simple and conjoint searches

Note: Target is white circle in all cases

a way that people believe they have seen items that were not actually presented. For example, they may report seeing a red O against a background that contains only blue Os and red Xs. Thus two features present in the array have been combined in a way that does not resemble any of the items actually present within the array. A theoretical model developed by Treisman and colleagues to explain performance on the simple and conjoint visual search tasks appears capable of explaining this type of error and this theory is now outlined (Treisman, 1988).

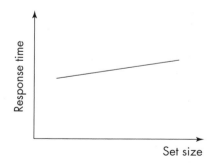

Figure 3.9 Set-size function for conjoint search

Feature integration theory (FIT)

Treisman's (1988) **feature integration theory (FIT)** was developed in order to explain performance on visual search tasks of the kind described above. FIT assumes a two-stage process in visual search. The first stage is feature analysis. This is a parallel process in which all of the features present in the display are processed simultaneously and distracters rapidly rejected on the basis of possession of discrepant features. The second stage involves feature combination. Visual attention, on this account, is the **visual glue** that enables features which may have been processed separately to be put back together to form coherent percepts of objects in mental space. This is the stage that requires attention-dependent, serial processing. Stimuli must be processed one at a time since feature combination requires attention to re-bind the features together. Stored, top-down, knowledge of possible objects may well also contribute to this stage.

Evidence for the serial nature of the second stage is available from visual search tasks involving conjoint searches. Recall that a conjoint search is one in which, for example, a white circle is sought against a background that includes circles that are not white and white items that are not circles. When a distracter contains one or other feature it cannot be rejected on the basis of simple parallel feature processing. Instead, the presence or absence of the second feature must be checked. Studies involving conjoint searches give rise to a set-size effect. That is, the more elements that are present in the display the longer on average (assuming that the position of the targets varies randomly across trials) it takes to detect the target. This is clear evidence of serial processing since each additional element imposes a requirement for additional processing and contrasts with the flat set-size function evident with single-feature searches (see Figures 3.7, 3.9).

The FIT approach appears also to be capable of explaining illusory conjunctions. These, it is argued, occur because insufficient attention is available. For example, attention is not focused upon a single spatial location. It may also occur when top-down knowledge is insufficient to resolve ambiguities. This may occur in real-life cases. For example, someone unfamiliar with a pack of playing cards after being shown a selection of cards may report having seen a red ace-of-clubs when they have not actually seen this card but have instead seen red cards and black aces-of-clubs separately. The concept of illusory conjunction has also been taken up in social psychology where it is used to explain prejudice on the basis that people believe that certain groups and certain attributes co-occur when in reality they co-occur much less often than is believed.

Attentional engagement theory (AET)

Duncan and Humphreys (1992) modified Treisman's approach in their **attentional engagement theory (AET)**. They proposed that visual search times depend on the degree of similarity between target and distracter, as in Treisman (1988), but in addition proposed that the degree of similarity between distracters themselves is important. As before, processing starts with a parallel, feature analysis stage. However, on their model there is then a competition for entry of stimuli into visual

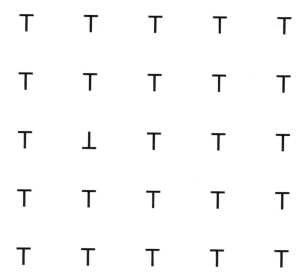

Figure 3.10 The upside-down T-task

short-term memory (VSTM). Selective attention is a product of this competition phase. Unique targets enter VSTM unimpeded but those that resemble distracters have to compete for entry. The competition for entry is easier if the distracters are all the same than it is when they are different. People are slow at conjoint searches because the distracters share features with the target and the distracters also differ among themselves.

The upside-down T-task is an example of a visual task search that ought to be relatively hard, according to feature integration theory, but which most normal subjects can accomplish very easily and rapidly. The task involves detecting an upside-down T against a background of right-way-up Ts (see Figure 3.10). Since target and distracters share features, serial processing should be required, on the FIT view, to detect the upside-down T. In reality the task is in fact very easy. AET claims that this is because all of the distracters are identical. Whilst the task is easy for normal subjects, however, some agnosic patients with deficits relatively early in visual processing have been shown to have particular difficulties with it (Humphreys and Riddoch, 1987).

Flanker effect

The **flanker effect** concerns the fact that the time taken to understand the meaning of a printed word may be affected by the presence of other nearby words. Priming effects are well known, for example the word 'nurse' can prime the word 'doctor', i.e. makes recognition of the latter word faster and more accurate. However, Shaffer and LaBerge (1979) presented words in a way that should have

Figure 3.11 Stimuli of the type used to demonstrate the flanker effect

eliminated priming but which nonetheless demonstrated it. For their experiment words were presented on a screen and subjects had to decide, as quickly and as accurately as possible, which category the word belonged to, indicating this by pressing appropriate buttons. However, the target was not presented in isolation. Other words were written above and below the target. The target was always at the centre and the surrounding words, termed 'flankers', occurred, for example, above and below. Shaffer and LaBerge found that it was harder to categorise a word if it was surrounded by words from other semantic categories than was the case when it was surrounded by words from the same semantic category (see Figure 3.11). Thus, details about the flankers were being processed in parallel with the target, creating conflict not unlike that present in the Stroop task. However, categorisation involves access to the semantic representation of the word. This finding created some difficulty for the feature integration approach since categorisation must initially involve focused attention to the target and it should not be possible for focused attention to both targets and flankers to be achieved simultaneously.

Models of visual attention: spotlight model

Treisman's concept of attentional glue offers an explanation for the functional role of visual attention. It is required to re-bind in internal space the visual features identified through feature analysis. A question that arises in connection with visual selective attention is whether its focus is on objects, for example letters in an array used for visual search, or on the spatial locations at which those objects occur. Posner (1980) believed that attention was to locations in space rather than to objects. He developed a somewhat metaphorical account of visual attention termed the **spotlight** model (see Figure 3.12). The spotlight, or visual attention, ranges over internal representations of the visual world and can be focused on a particular spatial location to enhance the processing of stimuli within its beam. Eriksen (1990) proposed a 'zoom-lens' modification of the original spotlight metaphor. This has the advantage of being more flexible since the size of the beam may be altered in response to task demands. It may be regarded as simply a variable beam spotlight. LaBerge (1983) produced some data supporting this modification. He asked subjects to judge either an entire word or the central letter

Figure 3.12 Spotlight model of visual attention

of a word. There were thus two attention conditions: a globally-directed attention condition (entire word) and a locally-directed attention condition (central letter). When subjects, presented with a surprise probe indicating a location within the word, had to recall a particular letter, no effect of letter position was found for the subjects in the word condition whilst subjects in the letter condition were as fast in response as the globally-directed attention group on the central letter only but slower for all other letters. In the locally-directed attention condition, letters falling outside the main focus of attention received less processing than did the central letters. This appears to confirm that the size of the attentional spotlight is indeed modifiable by task requirements.

Posner (1980) used dot-probe studies to provide evidence for the contention that attention was to locations in space rather than objects. He asked subjects to fixate their gaze on a point in the centre of a screen and to respond when a dot appeared on either side of fixation. In some trials arrows preceded the dots. The arrows predicted the position of the dots in ways that were either correct or misleading. Response times were faster when the arrow correctly predicted the location of the subsequent dot, relative to control, and was slower if the arrow pointed in the wrong direction. However, response times overall were too fast for it to be possible for eye movements to account for these **facilitatory** or **inhibitory** effects. Instead, Posner concluded that subjects engaged in **covert attending** (or covert visual **orienting**). That is, they altered their focus of visual attention, or spotlight, without moving their eyes. Altering the focus of attention in ways that involved eye movements or head movements were termed *overt* attending (or overt visual orienting).

Posner's (1980) contention that visual attention is to locations rather than objects is somewhat controversial. Neisser and Becklen (1975) asked subjects to report a moving scene that was superimposed over another and found subjects could do this relatively effortlessly. Subjects were thus attending to the scenes themselves rather than to the locations at which they occurred, evidence for object-based attending. Further evidence for object-based models of visual attention comes from Juola *et al.* (1991) who presented stimuli in concentric rings to subjects. If subjects were cued to expect stimuli in a particular ring then detection in that ring was facilitated, consistently with the findings of Posner. However, if an outer ring were facilitated then the stimuli occurring at the centre of the ring should also be responded to quicker since this is the centre of the area illuminated by the spotlight. But this was not found to be the case. Subjects could selectively attend to the outer ring whilst selectively ignoring surrounding stimuli. In order to account for this the spotlight model would have to allow that the shape as well as the width of the spotlight's beam could be altered as a result of priming with the target's location. Further evidence concerning location-based and object-based aspects of visual attending is available from studies concerning neurological impairments in orienting and concerning negative priming, and these are considered next.

Neurological aspects of orienting

A number of distinct processes in visual orienting have been identified. These include general alerting, disengaging attention from the currently attended stimulus, shifting attention to a new target, and engaging attention to that new target. Neurological impairments of perception and attention have been found in which some of the processing elements (alerting, disengaging, shifting, or engaging) appear to have been disturbed. One such condition, unilateral visual neglect (UVN), is described more fully in Chapter 4. Posner *et al.* (1984) found that UVN patients performed very badly on the standard Posner task when the cue was presented to the unimpaired visual field and the target to the impaired field. UVN is characterised by the tendency to ignore objects on one side of space, usually the left side following right-hemispheric brain damage to the parietal region. Posner *et al.* (1984) suggested that some UVN patients have difficulty in disengaging attention from the unimpaired side of space. Similar studies of patients with midbrain damage, such as supranuclear palsy or Balint's syndrome (Posner *et al.*, 1985) have shown that these patients experience problems with the shifting of attention. Finally, studies of patients with damage to the pulvinar nucleus of the thalamus (Rafal and Posner, 1987) have shown that these patients have difficulty in engaging attention to a new target. Posner and Petersen (1990) conclude that the parietal lobe is responsible for disengaging attention from its present focus, midbrain areas act to shift attention to a new focus, whilst the pulvinar nucleus is involved in reading out information from the newly selected location.

Data from clinical patients bears upon the issue of whether visual attention is directed towards spatial locations or towards objects. Tipper and Behrmann (1996) asked UVN patients to respond to targets appearing on either side of a computer screen or on either side of a dumb-bell-shaped object portrayed on the same screen. Patients failed to detect targets on the left-hand side in either case. However, they also failed to notice targets appearing on the left-hand side of a slowly rotating object presented on the screen. That is, they neglected such targets even when it had rotated through 180° to be on the right-hand side of the computer screen. Tipper and Behrmann used this finding to argue that attention is both object- and location-based since the patients' attention had followed the objects originally presented on the right-hand side of the screen, even when it had been transferred to the previously neglected left-hand side.

Negative priming

Negative priming studies (Tipper, 1985) provide further evidence that attention may be directed to both objects and locations. Tipper suggested that selective attention involves inhibition of unwanted information as well as selection of wanted information and also showed that unattended items are processed to quite a high level, including the semantic level, even though they are ultimately ignored. In a typical negative priming study, a given trial involves attending to one stimulus whilst ignoring another stimulus presented at the same time and location. If the ignored stimulus becomes the target of the next trial, typically about three seconds later, participants respond more slowly than when a completely new stimulus is used. This slowing occurs even if the ignored stimulus is presented in a new location. In another experiment, Tipper and Driver (1988) found that having a picture as the unattended stimulus on one trial slowed the processing of the corresponding word on the next trial. This is illustrated in Figure 3.13. This strongly suggests that visual attention is to objects rather than to the locations at which they occur. However, processing of a new stimulus occurring in the location of the previously ignored stimulus is also impaired. This shows that visual attention may be simultaneously location-based and object-based.

Locations or objects?

Efficient attention-directed visual search for an object requires attention be prevented from returning to recently examined environmental locations. This is

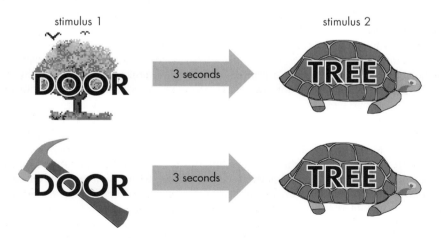

Figure 3.13 Stimuli of the type used to demonstrate negative priming

termed inhibition of return (IOR). Posner and Cohen (1984) proposed that IOR is a search mechanism that prevents attentional perseveration, or wasteful re-examination of empty or previously checked locations, in visual search and other tasks. The internal representations upon which IOR operates were examined by Tipper *et al.* (1994). They found that IOR mechanisms have access to both object-based and environment-based representations. Environment-based inhibition can be associated with a featureless environment whereas the object-based mechanism requires that attention be oriented to a visible object. Once a target has been engaged in an environment, the object-based system ensures that attention moves with that target rather than become fixed to locations in space previously occupied by that object. Tipper and Behrmann's (1996) finding with UVN patients suggests that the object-based system may be engaged even in patients whose environment-based system leads them habitually to fail to interrogate one side of space. Other evidence suggests that failures in the environment-based system in UVN patients can be countered, for example, by linking the attended object in the right-hand side of space with the neglected object in the left-hand side of space to form a single 'object'. Ward *et al.* (1994) did this using circle shapes on a computer screen. When left- and right-hand circles were lined up to form a single dumb-bell-shaped object, patients were more likely to be able to respond to it appropriately.

From his work on negative priming, Tipper (Tipper *et al.*, 1994) has developed a theory of inhibitory processes in attention. These processes complement the excitatory processes applied to representations of desired information. Excitatory processing enhances and maintains representations of selected objects whereas other representations merely decay passively. A mechanism that actively inhibits unwanted representations increases the rate and level of this differentiation. Tipper argues that these inhibitory mechanisms may be flexible enough to operate at the level of individual features, as well as whole objects, and that their role is to facilitate action. This led Tipper *et al.* (1994) to conclude that the main reason for the existence of selective attention is to link perception to action. This approach has echoes in the emphasis on response found in the late-selection theory of Deutsch and Deutsch (1967), as well as in the more recent work of Goodale and Milner (1992).

Kanwisher and Driver (1992) argue that covert attention may be directed to grouped objects rather than regions of space illuminated by the spotlight. An initial problem that occurs for the visual system on this account is then how to group those parts of the complex image that belong together from those that belong to separate objects. The Gestaltist approach identified several basic principles for doing this. Objects so grouped are then likely to be part of the same object in the real world. On this view, grouping precedes the allocation of attention with the result that coherent objects tend to be attended as a whole. In one experiment designed to test this, Driver and Baylis (1989) asked subjects to judge a central target while ignoring flanking letters. The flankers impaired performance more when they were grouped with the target by various factors, such as good continuation, common colour or common motion, then when they were not so grouped. This indicates that grouping affects the spatial distribution of attention and suggests that it can indeed precede selection. Driver and Baylis (1989) also found that distant distracters produced more interference than did distracters lying between the target and those distant distracters but which were not grouped with them. This finding is problematic for a strict spotlight view since the spotlight would have to specifically exclude certain areas within the attended region of space, as in Juola *et al.* (1991). Driver (1996) concludes that such results 'show unequivocally that attention can select a spatially dispersed group to the exclusion of a separate but spatially intermingled group'.

3.4 Automaticity

Shiffrin and Schneider's theory

This section will consider evidence that some forms of perceptual processing, following extensive practice, become effectively 'automatic'. This issue was introduced in Chapter 1. The possibility of automatic processing was investigated by Shiffrin and Schneider (1977) who defined automatic processing as processing which is not capacity-limited, that is, not affected by the limitations of short-term or working memory, and not dependent upon attention. As a result of this lack of capacity limitations, automatic processing of a number of stimuli may occur in parallel. They also argued that **automatic** processes are difficult to change once learned. They defined **controlled** processes as being exactly the opposite, that is, processing that is capacity-limited, attention-dependent and therefore almost inevitably serial. The main advantage of controlled processing is that it is under much more conscious control than is automatic processing, enabling it to be used flexibly and adaptively.

An adequate definition of the term 'automatic' would also include that automatic processing is inevitable, that it will always occur when an appropriate stimulus is presented and also that, once activated, it will run to its completion. For most adult readers, reading a word is an example of an automatic process. It is virtually impossible to not read a word of one's native language. Here, reading may be defined as accessing the phonology (sound), semantics (meaning), and orthography (spelling) when the perceived word is (automatically) matched to an internal representation of that word in our memory store of word knowledge (referred to as the internal lexicon). The effect is readily demonstrated in the classic Stroop effect as described in the previous section and in Chapter 1. In this case, the controlled task of naming colours suffers a decrement as a result of the automatic activation of the reading task that has become automatic through practice. The definitions of automatic and controlled processing would not allow for interference in the reverse direction, i.e. for the controlled task to interfere with the automatic one.

Shiffrin and Schneider (1977) made use of the visual search paradigm to investigate automaticity. Subjects memorised a memory set comprising one, two, three, or four letters and had to decide, as quickly but also as accurately as possible, whether any of those targets were present in a visual display comprising a sequence of arrays of letters and numbers. Two experimental conditions will be considered. In one, called **consistent mapping**, only consonants were used as

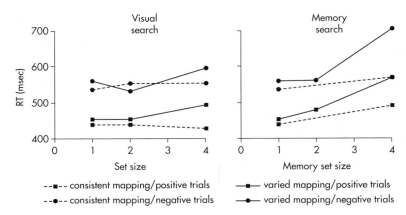

Figure 3.14 Results of Shiffrin and Schneider's results of processing demands on response time (1977)

Source: Esgate and Groome *et al.* (2005) reproduced by permission of Psychology Press

memory set elements and numbers were used as distracters, or vice versa. In the **varied mapping** condition a mixture of consonants and numbers were used as elements of both the memory and distracter sets. Two main effects were found (see Figure 3.14, memory search). First, negative trials, in which the targets did not occur in any of the arrays examined, took longer than positive trials in which targets did occur. This is not surprising and is readily explainable since on average targets will occur half-way through arrays, and once the target has been located no further processing is required. This is an example of a **self-terminating search**. In contrast, in a negative trial processing can stop only when all of the array elements have been processed, an example of an **exhaustive search**. Clearly an exhaustive search will always take longer than a self-terminating one. Secondly, Shiffrin and Schneider (1977) found no set-size effects under consistent mapping conditions for positive or negative trials but found linearly increasing functions for both under varied mapping conditions. They interpreted this as implying that subjects in the consistent mapping condition employed automatic, parallel processing based upon many years of discriminating letters from numbers. Since there does not appear to be any hard-wired basis in the brain for such discrimination, this ability therefore represents a clear example of the acquisition of perceptual skills by learning from experience.

Automatic processes in memory

Hasher and Zacks (1979) used Schneider and Shiffrin's (1977) distinction between controlled and automatic processes to explain the differences in memory for different types of information. They argued that whereas some processes become automatic through practice others are innately automatic. Included among the latter are those that encode information about context, such as spatial location, timing and frequency. The automatic encoding of frequency information is consistent with early behavouristic accounts of learning. Repeated presentation of stimuli strengthens the links between those stimuli and responses regardless of intention to learn and is readily demonstrated with lower species, such as rats and pigeons, in which such intention is unlikely.

Hasher and Zacks (1979) offer the following criteria for automaticity in memory. Automatic processes are unaffected by intention to learn, practice, concurrent task demands, age, arousal, or individual differences. Tests for Hasher and Zacks' (1979) framework for classifying memory phenomena have investigated the effects of these six variables on memory for context. For example, Andrade and Meudell (1993) asked subjects to count aloud whilst words appeared in different locations on a computer screen. Counting by sevens impaired memory for the words more than counting by ones but had no effect on memory for the locations in which the words had appeared. Such spatial locations may therefore be encoded automatically. Reason (1990) argues that automatic encoding of frequency information may underlie aspects of human error (see Section 3.6) since errors typically take the form of highly practised but inappropriate responses. Many examples from his collected human error 'corpus' support this conclusion.

3.5 Divided attention

Dual task performance

A useful approach was provided by Wickens (1992) who observed that any task could be described in broad terms as involving four stages in a processing sequence. Initially, registration of task-relevant stimuli needs to be accomplished such that those stimuli are encoded from sensory buffer storage into working memory. Thus, in the case of the very simple piece of skilled behaviour involving computing the answer to the sum '2 + 2', the sum must first enter the subject's awareness, or working memory, as a result of focused attention to a visual or auditory presentation of the problem. Then, processes need to be carried out in order to compute the answer to the sum. These processes are not unique and could involve either direct look-up of the answer in memory or computation involving some arithmetic rule. With a simple problem and/or an individual skilled in mental arithmetic direct look-up may be favoured whilst a harder problem or less skilled individual may favour some explicit procedure of calculation. Finally a response needs to be output, in this case '4', which may be written, spoken, or typed. This scheme is illustrated in Figure 3.15. Three factors have been identified that influence the ease with which two (or more) tasks can be combined. These are how similar the tasks are, how practised the operator is at performing them, and how difficult the tasks are. These will now be considered in turn.

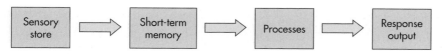

Figure 3.15 Stages in a typical task

Source: Esgate and Groome *et al.* (2005) reproduced by permission of Psychology Press

Task similarity

Wickens' (1992) analysis is useful since it enables loci for interference between two ongoing tasks to be identified at each of the four stages within the processing sequence. Thus, two tasks or subtasks may compete with one another at the level of input modality if both employ, for example, verbal or visual stimuli. At the level of memory coding within working memory tasks may compete if both require, for example, verbal or imaginal coding. At the level of processing resources, competition for the same processing modules implicated in, for example, mental arithmetic may also give rise to interference. Finally, at the level of output, response competition may occur if both tasks require, for example, verbal or manual output. In considering task combination the emphasis is on complete tasks rather than just the perceptual elements that are the main consideration when focused attention is discussed. Divided attention tasks may involve attending to multiple sources of perceptual input but more usually combinations of complete tasks forming part of a repertoire of skilled behaviour are considered. Whilst this analysis assumes two ongoing tasks, it may be noted that a single task may involve simultaneous demands at more than one of the stages in Figure 3.14.

Allport *et al.* (1972) in a classic experiment explored the possibility of interference between two tasks at the input stage. They employed the shadowing paradigm described above. This involves presentation of two simultaneous auditory messages to subjects via headphones. Each headphone presents different material that could be, for example, speech, music, or tones. In order to ensure focused attention to one of these messages, or channels, shadowing requires repeating back the input, usually speech, heard on that channel. Allport *et al.* examined the combination of shadowing with learning of words presented on the unattended channel. In keeping with other studies of shadowing, only a chance level of performance was exhibited in a subsequent recognition test of words presented on the unattended channel. However, when the experiment was repeated using the same to-be-learned words but now presented visually whilst subjects shadowed the attended message, subsequent recognition of those words was greatly improved. Thus, there appears to be an advantage in using different sensory modalities in two tasks if those tasks are to be combined. Allport *et al.* (1972) extended this finding to examine memory codes by comparing visually presented words with visually presented pictorial representations of those words. It is reasonable to assume that these will foster verbal and imaginal representations in memory respectively. Pictorial representations resulted in a further gain in recognition performance consistent with the view that using different memory codes also confers an advantage if two tasks requiring those memory codes are to be combined.

Competition for processing resources in dual-task performance has been examined in a number of situations. One such is driving while using a mobile phone, which has been shown in some studies to be as disruptive of performance as ingestion of small amounts of alcohol. Simulator studies have indicated an increase in response times and reduced ability to detect deceleration of a car in front (Lamble *et al.*, 1999; Garcia-Larrea *et al.*, 2001). Garcia-Larrea *et al.* (2001)

found that maintaining a phone conversation was associated with a decrease in attention to sensory inputs where this was evident from recordings of event related potentials taken from the subjects' heads. This is a technique from psycho-physiology which enables brain activity to be monitored. They argued that this decrease in attention to sensory inputs is characteristic of dual-task situations and is unlikely to be affected by whether conventional or hands-free telephones are used. Data from Alm and Nilsson (1994) are consistent with the view that use of hands-free equipment has little benefit in terms of reducing performance decrements due to concurrent phone use.

As well as creating competition for processing resource, driving whilst simultaneously holding a mobile phone in order to input a telephone number or hold a conversation will also result in competition at the output level since the same hand cannot both operate the steering wheel and hold the mobile phone. Whilst this competition could be resolved by the use of hands-free devices, this does little to limit more central disruption of sensory uptake. It may also affect the assembly of motor programs in the brain. These enable the brain to issue muscles with instructions for movement. In a relevant experiment, McLeod (1977) had subjects carry out a manual tracking task involving the following of a con-tour in combination with identification of tones. Pitch of tones could be indicated either verbally or manually, the latter by pointing at response alternatives. It was found that the manual tracking task suffered more interference when responses to the tone identification task were made manually. The fact that different hands were used to carry out the tracking task and to make the pointing response indicates that response competition is not just a matter of one hand being unable to do two things at once. Rather, more central interference appears to occur, where this may concern competition for the cognitive resources involved in assembling motor programs prior to manual output.

Practice

Successful task combination is influenced by factors other than the amount of similarity between the tasks in terms of the demands that they make on cognitive resources. The ability to combine two tasks is greatly increased by the development of skill via practice. The difficulty of the two tasks is also relevant, easier tasks being more readily combined than hard ones, though it should be noted that difficulty is a somewhat subjective concept since the difficulty of a task diminishes with increased expertise in that task.

Spelke *et al.* (1976) in another classic study had two volunteers train extensively on an unfamiliar combination of tasks. The tasks were reading for comprehension and writing to dictation. Given that these tasks have shared requirements for processing codes (linguistic) as well as for processing resources, a high level of interference between the two tasks would be predicted, to the detriment of both tasks. Initially this was the case, with reading speed, handwriting, and recall of comprehension passages all adversely affected. The study, however, involved intensive daily practice and after six weeks of this, handwriting, reading speed and recall were all greatly improved. After four months the subjects could carry out an additional activity, categorising dictated words, at the same time as understanding the dictated passages. Similar studies included examination of the ability of expert musicians' ability to sight-read at the piano whilst shadowing speech (Allport *et al.*, 1972) and the ability of expert touch typists to type whilst shadowing speech (Shaffer, 1975). In all cases practice resulting in expertise at the tasks produced highly successful task combination without apparent interference.

Whilst it is tempting, on the basis of such studies, to conclude that performance on sufficiently practised dual tasks may be such as to suggest that absolute limits on our ability to combine tasks may not exist, a careful analysis by Broadbent (1982) indicated that this is probably not so since some, often quite subtle, interference may be demonstrated statistically in many cases. This is consistent with earlier studies of the **psychological refractory period** (Welford, 1952) or *response selection bottleneck* (Pashler, 1990). These refer to a delay in responding when a second stimulus is presented shortly after an initial one. Thus, it may not be possible to produce two responses simultaneously. What is acquired through practice may then be the ability to rapidly interleave, or **time-share**, attention between concurrent tasks rather than truly carry them out at the same time. This is an example of a strategy for the effective 'running off' of motor programs in ways that make minimal demands upon attention. Practice may also result in an increase in the implicit knowledge underlying motor programs and motor schemas. Clearly a task that has become largely automatic through extensive practice (see Section 3.4) will suffer the least interference from a secondary task.

Task difficulty

Task difficulty also contributes to the ease or difficulty with which two tasks can be combined. Clearly a difficult task is likely to be more demanding of attentional resources or capacity (together referred to here as 'assets') than is a simple one and will limit the cognitive assets that can be devoted to a secondary task. However, task difficulty is itself difficult to define. Flying an aircraft is difficult, but not particularly so if you are a pilot. Difficulty is therefore not independent of practice. Generally, difficulty diminishes as practice increases. However, some tasks will always be intrinsically more difficult than others owing to the requirement to process greater amounts of information in the former.

Navon and Gopher (1979) proposed a framework that sheds some light on the task difficulty notion. On this view, tasks can be difficult because they are either **data-limited** or **resource-limited**. A data-limited task is one made difficult by the nature of the information provided. Solving a murder mystery may be an example. Resource-limited tasks, on the other hand, are ones that are made difficult as a result of the cognitive demands that they make. The difference is that performance of the latter can be improved by investing more cognitive assets into a task, for example by concentrating upon it to the detriment of a concurrent task. We do this whilst driving a car when we decide, usually unconsciously, to stop talking to a passenger and concentrate on driving when the latter becomes tricky for some reason. Then, since only resource-limited tasks are able to benefit from juggling assets between multiple tasks, these must be the ones that can be combined with varying degrees of success with secondary tasks. Data-limited tasks are largely unaffected by a secondary activity; the detective can get on with other things whilst waiting for a vital clue to the murder mystery to emerge. However, this may be an oversimplification. Data limitations may impose some resource demands since reducing the quality of auditory stimulation (data limitation) has been shown to affect performance on a concurrent, resource-limited visual task (Payne *et al.*, 1994).

Theoretical interpretations: capacity and resources revisited

Kahneman (1973) proposed a single capacity model in which a single pool of cognitive assets (capacity or resources) is shared amongst competing tasks. The assets available at any time depend upon arousal and individual differences, and allocation of those resources is to some extent under voluntary control. Competition in dual-task performance occurs, to the detriment of one or both tasks, when the pool of assets is too small, the demands if the task(s) exceeds what is available, or both. Johnston and Heinz (1978) made similar assumptions in their account of selective attention. They proposed that assets are allocated flexibly. If the main task makes comparatively few demands, non-selected stimuli need not be attenuated to as low a level as would be the case if the main task was highly demanding cognitively.

The literature on task similarity effects in dual-task performance creates problems for models of this kind, however, since even two quite demanding tasks can be combined if they are sufficiently dissimilar. Such findings may be accounted for in models that posit that cognitive assets are organised into relatively discrete processing units, or modules. Tasks can then be combined to the extent that they do not make excessive demands upon the same modules. Those modules are then controlled and coordinated by a **central executive**, closely resembling that proposed in the **working memory** model (see Chapter 6). Such an approach is, then, a promising way of linking attention with memory research.

3.6 Slips and lapses

Human error: the price of automaticity

A basic distinction may be made between errors and mistakes. Broadly speaking an error is an appropriate action that has gone awry somewhere in its execution. A mistake, on the other hand, is a completely inappropriate action based upon, for example, faulty understanding of a situation, or faulty inferences and judgements (Kahneman *et al.*, 1982). Here we are mainly concerned with errors. Errors can be further subdivided into two classes. As well as errors *per se* (such as putting coffee into the teapot) which may be termed a **slip**, there are also what Reason (1984) terms **lapses**. These are failures to remember something such as a word, a person's name, or failure to remember to carry out an action such as taking medicines at regular intervals. Laboratory-based studies have been devised to simulate lapses, such as those involved in the tip-of-the-tongue (TOT) state (Brown and McNeill, 1966). The study of error has mainly employed ecologically valid methodologies that include the keeping of diaries, naturalistic observation, or the *post hoc* study of accidents and disasters. In addition, laboratory studies have been carried out in order to model the conditions giving rise to error.

A taxonomy of error types based on the study of 1,000 action slips gathered as part of a diary study was provided by Norman (1981). A similar diary study was carried out by Reason (1979) and Reason and Mycielska (1982) and involved subjects keeping diaries of known errors over an extended period. They found that slips of action were most likely to occur in highly familiar surroundings during the performance of frequently and/or recently executed tasks in which a considerable degree of automaticity had been achieved. As such, Reason (1979) regards error as the price we pay for automaticity. In Reason's error corpus, occurrence of errors was commonly associated with states of attentional capture. Such capture could be by some pressing internal preoccupation or by some external distraction. A large proportion of the slips (40 per cent) took the form of intact well-organised action sequences that were judged as recognisably belonging to some other task or activity that was frequently and/or recently executed. These they referred to as strong habit intrusions. These included place-losing errors, blends, and reversals. Place-losing errors most commonly involved omissions or repetitions. These typically resulted from a wrong assessment of the current stage of the action sequence or from an interruption and are apparent in everyday activities, as when one is interrupted when counting items such as sheets of paper. Blends and reversals appeared to result from crosstalk between two current activities, either verbal or behavioural, such that the objects to which they were applied became partially or completely transposed. This is evident in everyday slips of the tongue such as spoonerisms. Famously, the Reverend Spooner once said to a student 'you have tasted the whole worm' instead of 'you have wasted the whole term'. In this case syllables blend to form words that were not intended. To give a more mundane example, a social worker thinking about a personal appointment may say 'hair care' when he or she means 'home care'.

Reason (1990) went on to propose two primitives of the cognitive system that he termed frequency gambling and similarity matching. Frequency gambling may result in frequently or recently executed behaviour taking precedence over correct responses. For example, a frequently-dialled telephone number, such as that of a friend, may be input instead of the one that was intended. Similarity matching occurs in situations in which attention is captured by a few salient features of a stimulus, resulting in the activation of incorrect schemas. For example, one might try to open one's office door with a car key. Hay and Jacoby (1996) argued that action slips are most likely to occur when the correct response is not the strongest or most habitual one, and attention is not fully applied to the task of selecting the correct response. They tested this prediction by having subjects complete paired associates of the form knee: b_n_. Based on previous pairing trials, the correct response could be either the strongest response (e.g. bend) or not the strongest response (e.g. bone). Subjects had one or three seconds

1	What do you call the tree that grows from an acorn?	(oak)
2	What do you call a funny story?	(joke)
3	What sound does a frog make?	(crack)
4	What is Pepsi's major competitor?	(Coke)
5	What is another word for cape?	(cloak)
6	What do you call the white of an egg?	?

Figure 3.16 The oak-yolk task

Source: Reason (1992) reproduced by permission of Psychology Press

to respond. Error was more likely when responses were both not the strongest associate, and the response had to be made quickly.

An experimental task that readily demonstrates laboratory-induced error is the oak-yolk task (Reason, 1992). The subject is asked questions as presented in Figure 3.16. Many subjects respond to the final questions with the word 'yolk'. The correct answer is, of course, albumin. The effect of the preceding questions is to build up a response set such that subjects are responding on the basis of rhyming rather than meaning. 'Yolk' is a common and easily retrieved word, in contrast to 'albumin', and the former was given as the answer by some 85 per cent of subjects.

3.7 Subliminal perception

A look at the 'new looks'

Greenwald (1992) claimed that 'unconscious cognition is now solidly established in empirical research'. However, the unconscious so revealed appears to be 'intellectually much simpler than the sophisticated agency portrayed in psychoanalytic theory'. This telling remark reveals the lengthy history of the issue of unconscious processes which can in large measure be traced back to Freud and the psychoanalytic school of psychology, for whom unconscious psychic forces were the main determining influences on thought and behaviour. Bruner and Postman (1947) introduced an empirical approach to the role of unconscious processes in cognition, a development that was termed the 'New Look' at unconscious mechanisms. A number of further 'New Looks' have been taken at the issue of unconscious cognitive processing, known as New Look 2 (Erdelyi, 1974; Dixon and Henley, 1974), and New Look 3 (Greenwald, 1992; Loftus and Klinger, 1992). In these studies unconscious cognition was demonstrated using experimental paradigms such as subliminal perception, in which behaviour or physiological responses were influenced by stimuli that fell below the subject's threshold of conscious awareness. This is achieved by presenting stimuli of very low intensity, or very short duration, or at frequencies beyond the range for conscious perception, by visual or auditory masking, or by the use of unattended channels as in dichotic listening. The sorts of behavioural or physiological responses that have been elicited in response to subliminal stimuli have included GSRs, evoked EEG potentials, verbal behaviour, and conscious perception of above-threshold stimuli, all of which have been shown to be influenced by subliminal stimuli.

Automaticity can provide other examples of non-conscious processing. When a task becomes automated it makes minimal demands on attention. For example, when driving a car under routine conditions, highly practised procedural (or implicit) knowledge is employed with conscious control available as a back-up strategy under difficult conditions. How then does the operator know when such conditions pertain? In order to switch from automatic to conscious control the subject must be monitoring the environment unconsciously. This consideration harks back to the cocktail-party scenario in which background conversations are unconsciously monitored for mention of a salient word such as one's own name.

Dixon (1981) argues that subliminal perception implies that the processes responsible for conscious perceptual experience are not the same as those which mediate the transmission of information through the brain from receptors to effectors since the former also require a coincident excitation from the ascending reticular activating system of the brain (which controls the brain's level of arousal or alertness) in order to produce that awareness. Subliminal stimuli may be subjected to extensive preconscious processing involving long-term memory and emotional responses. This is particularly evident in the phenomenon of perceptual defence, in which the perception of disturbing or embarrassing material is selectively inhibited. Groeger (1984) has effectively dismissed the possibility that subliminal perception may be based on the conscious perception of fragments of the stimulus since greater semantic influences were found following a subliminal stimulus than were found following a supraliminal one.

A further technique that has been used for the study of subliminal effects is priming. This refers to the effect of prior exposure to a priming stimulus on the recognition of a subsequent stimulus. A considerable literature exists on the 'costs' and 'benefits' of priming on subsequent performance in terms of impairments or facilitation of that performance. Cheesman and Merikle (1986) have demonstrated that priming effects may occur even if the primes are presented too briefly for conscious identification. This technique has been used on brain-damaged patients who may be primed by stimuli that they fail to identify explicitly. Neuropsychological syndromes such as blindsight (see Chapter 4) may also involve the processing of stimuli of which subjects are not consciously aware.

Marcel (1983) conducted some studies using **visual masking** that in many ways are among the most convincing, as well as the most controversial, examples of semantic-level processing in the absence of conscious awareness. He adapted an associative priming paradigm first used by Meyer and Shavaneveldt (1971). Subjects were presented with a masked prime and the time taken to make a lexical decision (such as word/non-word) was measured. Under normal conditions, a prime such as 'bread' facilitates the lexical judgement of a related word such as 'butter' but not of unrelated words such as 'nurse'. Marcel applied masking such that the priming word could not be detected on more than 60 per cent of trials (see Figure 3.17). However, when the primes were masked by a pattern there was clear evidence of priming. This did not occur with a random noise mask, consistent with the suggestion that priming may operate via two different

prime	mask	target	response
CAT	$$$	DOG	'DOG'
PEN	$$$	DOG	'DOG'

Figure 3.17 Stimuli of the type used in visual masking studies

mechanisms of interruption and interference (Turvey, 1973). Marcel proposed that the pattern mask did not prevent automatic, unconscious access to stored semantic knowledge but that it did disrupt perceptual integration and hence entry to consciousness. Similar suggestions were made by Allport (1977) and also by Coltheart (1980b).

Greenwald (1992) distinguishes two senses of the term 'unconscious'. First, material is unconscious if it falls outside the spotlight of attention. Secondly, the term unconscious may be used to imply failure to access or report material via introspection. According to Greenwald the two senses of unconscious cognition are explicable within a network representation. In the first sense of conscious attention, consciousness is defined as corresponding to network operation that boosts activation to a sufficiently high level. Secondly, in the sense of introspection, Greenwald argues that by virtue of having verbal outputs the network can report on its own internal network status. However, such introspection is not guaranteed to be valid.

The connectionist approach overcomes the basic paradoxes of serial-stage accounts. These include, for example, the seemingly paradoxical operation of a late stage in processing (semantic analysis) when an earlier stage (feature analysis) is not complete. In contrast, by permitting semantic and feature analysis to occur in parallel rather than in series, the network paradigm can account non-paradoxically for semantic analysis without the need for absence/presence discrimination of the unattended object. However, Greenwald (1992) argues that unconscious cognition has been demonstrated to achieve nothing more cognitively sophisticated than the analysis of part of the meaning of single words. Although unconscious perceptual processing is clearly possible, the extent of its sophistication appears on this view to be considerably less than psychoanalytic theory gave it credit for.

Summary

- Attention helps guide processing to important objects.
- Focused auditory attention appears to attenuate input to an appropriate level of processing in a flexible manner.
- The role of attention in visual perception may be to 'glue' features together in a coherent form or to appropriately direct perception-behaviour linkages.

- Visual attention can be directed to spatial locations but convincing evidence also exists for the direction of attention to objects or to both locations and objects.
- Automaticity may build up through extensive practice.
- Multi-task performance is influenced by the similarity of the tasks, the expertise of the performer, and the difficulty of the tasks involved.
- Effects observed in multi-task performance suggest a modular organisation of processing resources with overall executive control as suggested by the working memory model.
- Slips and lapses may be the price that we pay for the convenience of automatic processing.
- Awareness of an object may not be a necessary condition for the activation of semantic-level representations of that object.

Further reading

The neuroscience of perception and attention is covered in considerably more detail in: Gazzaniga, M.S., Ivry, R.B. and Mangun, G.R. (1998). *Cognitive Neuroscience: The Biology of the Mind.* New York: W.W. Norton.

There is a distinct lack of introductory textbooks devoted solely to attention. Probably the best is: Styles, E.A. (1997). *The Psychology of Attention.* Hove: Psychology Press.

Applied aspects of attention are covered in considerably more detail in: Esgate, A., and Groome D. *et al.* (2005). *An Introduction to Applied Cognitive Psychology.* Hove: Psychology Press (especially ch. 6).

Note: The assistance of Dr Wido la Heij in the preparation of illustrations for this chapter is gratefully acknowledged.

Chapter 4

Disorders of perception and attention

4.1 Introduction

In the previous chapters we described the processes involved in perception and attention, and learned how we construct an internal representation of the world around us. Given the complexity of these processes, it is not surprising that brain damage can disrupt perception and attention. However, what is surprising is the range and nature of the deficits that are observed. By systematically studying these deficits, we are able to learn much about the processes that occur in the intact brain. The emphasis in this chapter is to study the pattern of disorders, and relatively little attempt has been made to locate functions within particular brain regions. I have taken the view that we are interested in *how* we perceive not *where* we perceive.

Most of the disorders discussed in this chapter result from brain injury which leaves the affected individual with a noticeable deficit. However, the first condition we will consider is a little different in that many of those affected regard the condition as a special gift rather than a disability – this is the extraordinary case of synaesthesia. For the remainder of the chapter we will study syndromes which have an increasingly specific impact on perception and attention. We will first consider disorders which prevent conscious perception or distort attention, we will then consider disorders which affect the ability to recognise objects, and finally we will discuss disorders which appear to affect the ability to recognise one particular category of object or the ability to encode one particular type of information.

4.2 Synaesthesia: what colour is Monday?

What colour is Monday? How about the number 7? What does blue taste like? For most people these are incomprehensible questions, but a small proportion of the people reading this chapter will have no difficulty with these strange questions – these individuals are likely to have a fascinating perceptual condition called **synaesthesia**. The word synaesthesia literally means 'to perceive together'. When presented with sensory input of one modality, an individual with synaesthesia will consistently and automatically experience a sensory event in a different modality. In the most common form of synaesthesia an individual will experience particular colours when they hear or see words or letters of the alphabet. Hence, for some people Monday might be yellow, and blue may have a metallic taste.

Synaesthesia was first described by Galton in the last years of the nineteenth century (Galton, 1883) but with the rise of behaviourism during the twentieth century the study of synaesthesia fell out of favour until a landmark paper by Baron-Cohen *et al.* (1987) provided us with a test of the 'genuineness' of the condition. Baron-Cohen responded to an advertisement placed in the *Bulletin* of the British Psychological Society by a synaesthete called EP who described herself as 'an artist who has experienced the life-long condition of hearing words and sounds in colour'. Baron-Cohen's first task was to establish whether EP's reports of hearing in colour were genuine – after all, this could have been nothing but the vivid imagination of an artistically inclined individual rather than a genuine neurological condition. After ruling out other possible causes, Baron-Cohen *et al.* (1987) tested the reliability of EP's reports of her synaesthetic experiences. They reasoned that if this was a genuine condition then EP's sensory experience would be stable over time whereas someone who was faking the condition would probably not be able to report the same experience when tested with the same materials on two different occasions. The results of these investigations were very clear-cut. EP was asked to describe the sensory experience associated with a list of over 100 aurally-presented words, letters, names and numbers, and a selection of non-words. Ten weeks later and without warning EP was retested on the same list of items, and in every case the description provided on the second test was judged to match that given on the first test. This 100 per cent test-retest consistency after a ten-week delay was compared with the performance of a young female non-synaesthete who served as a control participant and was tested using the same procedure. This control participant managed a test-retest consistency of only 17 per cent after an interval of just two weeks. EP's remarkable consistency was achieved despite the fact that the descriptions she provided were much more detailed and elaborate than those offered by the control participant (see Figure 4.1). Baron-Cohen also noted that the perceptual experience EP reported for pseudo-words was dependent on the letters making up the non-word. For EP each letter is associated with a particular colour and the shade experienced in response to non-words was determined by the mix of the colours induced by each letter.

The nature of synaesthesia

This high level of consistency over time is not unique to EP. Mattingley *et al.* (2001) found a similar level of consistency for fifteen **synaesthetes** who were compared to fifteen non-synaesthete controls. The synaesthetes' reports of the colours associated with a variety of items were significantly more consistent over a three-month test-retest interval than were the controls after a delay of just one month. For some classes of items, such as Arabic numerals, the synaesthetes achieved a mean consistency of more than 90 per cent compared to less than 30 per cent consistency in the control participants.

EP experiences colours on hearing words or numbers – one of the most common forms of the condition. Other forms include synaesthetes who feel sounds, see tastes, see musical notes or musical intervals, and see colours for familiar faces (Carpenter, 2001; Baron-Cohen *et al.*, 1996). Many synaesthetes also report that sequenced items such as letters of the alphabet, days of the week or months of the year are experienced in a particular arrangement in perceptual space (see Figure 4.1).

Synaesthesia is usually a unidirectional process, so for a letter-colour synaesthete the letter A may give rise to the perception of red, but seeing red does not induce the perception of the letter A. For most synaesthetes the synaesthetic percept can be induced by imagining the inducing stimulus as well as the presence of the inducer, so thinking about the letter A may be enough to trigger the experience of the colour red. Synaesthetic experiences are limited to fairly low-level percepts such as colour or spatial location rather than the appearance of a

Inducing Item	Description of the induced synaesthetic experience
Moscow	darkish grey with spinach-green, and a pale blue in places
Fear	Mottled light grey, with a touch of soft green and purple
Daniel	deep purple, blue and red, and is shiny
Maria	deep violet blue
Huk (non-word)	The combination of the colours of the component letters; dark red (H), yellow (U), and purple (K)
H	Dark red
M	Blue-black
Q	Greeny yellow

Part (a)
Some examples of the very consistent colour descriptions offered by synaesthete EP in response to the sound of words, names, non-words and letters.

Part (b) The spatial arrangement of the letters of the alphabet as perceived by EP

Figure 4.1 Baron-Cohen's investigation of EP's synaesthesia
Source: After Baron-Cohen *et al.* (1987)

face or an object (Grossenbacher and Lovelace, 2001). Most synaesthetes regard their condition as a blessing, and would not wish to be free of it (Carpenter, 2001), but Baron-Cohen *et al.* (1996) describe one individual, JR, who experiences particularly strong colour and sound associations working in both directions, so when she looks at a scene each colour is experienced with a different musical note, and as she hears sounds each triggers its own colour experience. Understandably, JR experiences considerable fatigue and restricts her lifestyle to avoid excessive stimulation.

Steven and Blakemore (2004) reported the details of six synaesthetes who experienced seeing colours on hearing or thinking about letters or numbers despite being blind for many years. All had experienced letter-colour synaesthesia for as long as they could remember and the condition persisted after they became blind. One of the six had been blind for thirty-five years, and another, experienced colour when he touched the raised dots of Braille characters even though he had been without colour vision for ten years. As Steven and Blakemore comment, this suggests that synaesthesia 'persists for very long periods with little or no natural experience in the referred modality' (2004: 855).

There is a great deal of commonality to the subjective reports provided by synaesthetes. Almost all report that they have had the condition for as long as they can remember (Baron-Cohen *et al.*, 1993) and many have strong memories of the moment at which they discovered that they were different to other people (see Box 4.1). However, Dixon *et al.* (2004) distinguish two forms of synaesthetic experience – they differentiate between 'projectors' who experience the colour as if it were 'out there' in the physical world and 'associators' who see the colour in their 'mind's eye'. Dixon *et al.* report that about 90 per cent of synaesthetes in their sample were associators. I will return to this distinction later.

Box 4.1 Discovering one is a synaesthete: a case history

Synaesthete Patricia Duffy provides a vivid account of the moment she first realised that her experience of coloured letters was unusual. Duffy recounts a conversation she had at age 16 in which she reminisced with her father about learning to write the letters of the alphabet (Duffy, 2001).

> I said to my father, 'I realized that to make an "R" all I had to do was first write a "P" and then draw a line down from its loop. And I was so surprised that I could turn a yellow letter into an orange letter just by adding a line.'
> 'Yellow letter? Orange letter?' my father said. 'What do you mean?'
> 'Well, you know,' I said. '"P" is a yellow letter, but "R" is an orange letter. You know – the colors of the letters.'
> 'The colors of the letters?' my father said.
> It had never come up in any conversation before. I had never thought to mention it to anyone. For as long as I could remember, each letter of the alphabet had a different color. Each word had a different color too (generally, the same color as the first letter) and so did each number. The colors of letters, words and numbers were as intrinsic a part of them as their shapes, and like the shapes, the colors never changed. They appeared automatically whenever I saw or thought about letters or words, and I couldn't alter them.
> I had taken it for granted that the whole world shared these perceptions with me, so my father's perplexed reaction was totally unexpected. From my point of view, I felt as if I'd made a statement as ordinary as 'apples are red' and 'leaves are green' and had elicited a thoroughly bewildered response.

```
2 2 2 2 2 2 2 2 2 2 2 2 2 2 2 2        2 2 2 2 2 2 2 2 2 2 2 2 2 2 2 2
2 2 2 2 2 2 2 2 2 2 2 2 2 2 2 2        2 2 2 2 2 2 2 2 2 2 2 2 2 2 2 2
2 2 2 2 2 2 2 2 2 2 2 2 2 2 2 2        2 2 2 2 2 2 2 2 2 2 2 2 2 2 2 2
2 2 2 2 2 2 2 2 5 2 2 2 2 2 2 2        2 2 2 2 2 2 2 2 5 2 2 2 2 2 2 2
2 2 2 2 2 2 2 5 2 5 2 2 2 2 2 2        2 2 2 2 2 2 2 5 2 5 2 2 2 2 2 2
2 2 2 2 2 2 5 2 2 2 5 2 2 2 2 2        2 2 2 2 2 2 5 2 2 2 5 2 2 2 2 2
2 2 2 2 2 5 2 2 2 2 2 5 2 2 2 2        2 2 2 2 2 5 2 2 2 2 2 5 2 2 2 2
2 2 2 2 5 5 5 5 5 5 5 5 5 2 2 2        2 2 2 2 5 5 5 5 5 5 5 5 5 2 2 2
2 2 2 2 2 2 2 2 2 2 2 2 2 2 2 2        2 2 2 2 2 2 2 2 2 2 2 2 2 2 2 2
2 2 2 2 2 2 2 2 2 2 2 2 2 2 2 2        2 2 2 2 2 2 2 2 2 2 2 2 2 2 2 2
2 2 2 2 2 2 2 2 2 2 2 2 2 2 2 2        2 2 2 2 2 2 2 2 2 2 2 2 2 2 2 2
```

Part (a)   Part (b)

Figure 4.2 A test for genuine synaesthesia

First look at the block of digits in part (a) of the figure. Can you see the hidden shape? It will probably take you some time to find the triangular pattern made by the series of 5s in among the block of 2s. Now look at part (b) of the figure which is identical to part (a) except that the two digits are reproduced in different shades of grey. The difference in shade (or colour) makes the triangle 'pop-out'. Ramachandran and Hubbard (2001) used stimuli like part (a) of this figure as a test of genuineness with synaesthetes who reported experiencing colour when they saw numbers. The synaesthetes were significantly better at detecting the hidden shape than non-synaesthetes.

Source: After Ramachandran and Hubbard (2001)

Incidence and familiarity

Based on response rates to newspaper adverts, Baron-Cohen *et al.* (1996) esti-mated the incidence of synaesthesia was about 1 in 2,000, with about 80 per cent being female. All of Baron-Cohen's respondents experienced seeing colours on hearing words and many also reported other forms of synaesthesia. About one third had a close relative with the condition, suggesting a strong genetic component to the condition, and interviews with the families of synaesthetes revealed a prevalence of about 50 per cent among first-degree relatives. Mothers and daughters who were both synaesthetes usually reported different word-colour associations, suggesting that although the condition may be genetically deter-mined, the precise perceptual experiences probably are not. Baron-Cohen pro-posed that the condition is 'sex-linked dominant with lethality', suggesting that 50 per cent of males born to a mother with the condition will die *in utero*. However, some more recent findings are incompatible with this account. Smilek *et al.* (2005) report a pair of monozygotic (i.e. genetically 'identical') twin boys only one of whom is a synaesthete – an observation which is incompatible with Baron-Cohen's model. Smilek *et al.* (2005) also cite several recent surveys which suggest that the incidence of synaesthesia may be much higher than proposed by Baron-Cohen (possibly as high as 1 in 20 of the population) and that the incidence is roughly equal for men and women. If true then this would also undermine the notion of an X-linked dominant trait.

Experimental investigations of synaesthesia

Several researchers (e.g. Mills *et al.*, 1999; Mattingley *et al.*, 2001) have used versions of the Stroop test (Stroop, 1935) to investigate the nature of synaesthesia. In these investigations synaesthetes who experience colour on seeing a word or letter were asked to identify the colour of the ink used to print letters or words (or the colour of the video used to display the words on a computer screen). When the colour of the ink matches the synaesthetic colour induced by the word, then the time taken to name the ink colour is reduced relative to the neutral condition which does not induce a synaesthetic experience. However, when the ink colour is inconsistent with the synaesthetic experience then synaesthetes, unlike controls, take significantly longer to name the ink colour. It appears that synaesthetes cannot 'switch-off' their synaesthesia even when it interferes with the colour-naming task.

Mattingley *et al.* (2001) modified this technique to investigate whether conscious processing of the inducing stimulus is necessary to give rise to the synaesthetic perception. Participants were shown very brief presentations of a letter or number (the inducing stimulus) followed by a visual mask. This procedure prevents conscious processing of the stimulus but is sufficient to allow some unconscious processing, and as a result neither synaesthetes nor control participants could name the inducing stimulus but both groups demonstrated some unconscious processing of the items. Under these conditions the synaes-thetes performed like the control participants and showed no evidence of Stroop interference when asked to name the colour of a patch which was incongruent with the synaesthetic colour normally induced by the stimulus. The researchers concluded that 'overt recognition of inducing stimuli is crucial ... Synaesthesia is elicited by selectively attended stimuli that are available for conscious report' (Mattingley *et al.*, 2001: 582).

Dixon *et al.* (2000) used the Stroop procedure to demonstrate that the actual perception of the inducing stimulus is not necessary to induce the synaesthetic percept. Dixon and colleagues worked with a synaesthete called C for whom numbers induced colours; for C the number 7 was yellow. What would happen, Dixon and colleagues asked, if C was required to add the numbers 2 and 5. In a series of trials C was sequentially presented with first one digit, then an arith-metic operator (+, – etc.), then a second digit and finally a colour patch. Synaesthete C was asked to name the colour of the patch as quickly as possible. The colour patch was either congruent with the colour induced by the result of the arithmetic operation (e.g. 2; +; 5; yellow) or incongruent with it (e.g. 10; –; 3; blue). C took longer to name the colour patch in the incongruent trials than the congruent trials, demonstrating that the external inducing stimulus induces (e.g. the digit 7) is not necessary to trigger the synaesthetic experience. Merely activating the concept of the number through mental arithmetic was enough to give rise to the synaesthetic experience. A similar conclusion follows from other research by Dixon and colleagues (Myles *et al.*, 2003), who used ambiguous graphemes to demonstrate that the speed with which a synaesthete, PD, could name the colour of an alphanumeric character on a computer screen depended on the interpretation of the character rather than its physical appearance.

Ambiguous graphemes are interpreted in light of their context, so the same grapheme will be interpreted as the digit 2 when presented as part of a sequence of numbers, but as a letter Z when in a sequence of other letters. This enabled the researchers to use the same stimulus in both congruent and incongruent trials in a Stroop task. The results demonstrated that it is the synaesthete's interpretation of a stimulus rather than its physical properties which predict the synaesthetic experience and hence task performance. Together, these results suggest that the synaesthetic experience is triggered only after some interpretation of the stimulus has occurred.

As described earlier, Dixon *et al.* (2004) differentiated between 'projectors' who report that their synaesthetic experience is 'out there' and 'associators' who report that the experience is in their 'mind's eye'. Dixon *et al.* used the Stroop paradigm to assess the degree of automaticity in the perception of synaesthetic colours and real colours in projectors and associators. Dixon measured the degree of Stroop interference caused by the perception of incongruent synaesthetic colours on the naming of real colours and compared this with the degree of interference caused by the perception of real colours on the naming of synaesthetic colours. In the case of projectors the synaesthetic colours were more disruptive to real colour-naming than real colours were to the naming of synaesthetic colours. This suggests that for the projectors the perception of the synaesthetic colour was more automatic than the perception of the real colour. For the associators, the degree of Stroop interference induced by the synaesthetic colour was not so great, suggesting that the synaesthetic perception was more under conscious control and less automatic than for the projectors. These results suggest that the distinction between projectors and associators is useful and may reflect real differences in the nature and causes of the synaesthesia in these individuals.

The experience of synaesthesia

You might agree that a saxophone makes a 'cool' sound, whereas a violin makes a 'sharp' sound. Of course, neither of these statements is literally true, but the metaphor between the sensations of sound, temperature and touch seems to reflect something which is true in a physical sense and as a result you would probably be reluctant to accept the reverse pairings – that is, you would not accept that a violin makes a cool sound and a saxophone makes a sharp sound. Despite the apparent validity of the metaphor between sound and touch, you never confuse the experience of the sound made by a violin with the experience of a pinprick, yet the two seem to have something in common which makes the association seem unbreakable and obvious. Some associations are so strong they affect our perceptions. For example, for most people the association between the word 'blood' and the colour red is so strong that they are quicker to name the colour of the ink in which the word 'blood' is printed when the ink is red than when it is some other colour such as green (i.e. they demonstrate a Stroop effect for the word-colour association). This is not to suggest that synaesthetic experiences are merely associations or elaborate metaphors – the research reviewed here demonstrates they are much more than that, but this is probably the closest a non-synaesthete can come to understanding the experience. Ramachandran and Hubbard (2001) suggest we can think of metaphors as involving cross-activation of conceptual maps in a manner analogous to cross-activation of perceptual maps in synaesthesia.

Brain imaging studies of synaesthesia

One of the most significant advances in cognitive neuroscience in recent decades has been the refinement of imaging techniques which allow scientists to identify which areas of the brain are active during different types of mental activity. In the last few years psychologists have applied these imaging techniques to the study of synaesthesia, and the general finding has been that the pattern of activity observed when an individual reports a synaesthetic experience is similar to that associated with actual perception in non-synaesthetes. For example, when listening to words which induce synaesthetic colours, the brain of a synaesthete will show patterns of activity similar to those seen when looking at colours. Paulesu *et al.* (1995) used Positron Emission Tomography (**PET**) to study the blood flow in the brain in a group of synaesthetes who experience colour on hearing words. The pattern of activation seen in the synaesthetes when listening to words suggested that the synaesthetic experience resulted from partial activation of sections of the visual pathway. However, we should note that in normal individuals the act of forming a mental image also results in patterns of brain activity similar to those observed when perceiving the imagined object (e.g. Kosslyn *et al.*, 1995). PET has rather limited resolution so it is difficult to determine precisely which areas of the visual cortex are active and which are not. Nunn *et al.* (2002) used **fMRI** (functional magnetic resonance imaging – a technique with better spatial resolution than PET) to study the brain activity of synaesthetes who experienced colour on hearing words. In normal individuals, perception of colour is associated with activity in the 'colour area' of the visual cortex know as V4. The synaesthetes showed activity in V4 when listening to words. To exclude the possibility that this activation was simply the result of associative memory or mental imagery of the associated colour, Nunn and colleagues also trained a group of control subjects to associate colours with the words and asked them to imagine these colours when hearing the words while being scanned. These control individuals did not show the same pattern of activity in V4 displayed by the synaesthetes. Thus, the greater resolution afforded by fMRI leads us to the same conclusion drawn from the experimental investigations, namely that synaesthesia involves more than learned associations or mental imagery.

The processes underlying synaesthesia

In non-synaesthetes the perception of spoken words and colours takes place in separate 'modules'. This 'modularity' within the brain is seen as an important evolutionary step in the development of complex and efficient information processing systems. In such a modular system there are no interconnections between, for example, the pathways involved in the perception of spoken words and colours. Baron-Cohen (1993) suggests that synaesthesia results from a breakdown of this modularity caused either by abnormal interconnections which develop between modules, or because the connections which exist in normal infant brains fail to 'die out' during early development. Thus one possibility is that we were all synaesthetes once, but have lost the interconnections between the different sensory modalities which underlie this condition.

Ramachandran and Hubbard (2002) note that anatomical, physiological and imaging studies of the brains of humans and monkeys reveal that the area of the brain responsible for colour perception (V4 in the fusiform gyrus) are immediately adjacent to the area shown to be responsible for the reading of visually presented letters (also in the fusiform). 'Can it be a coincidence', they comment, 'that the most common form of synaesthesia involves graphemes and colours and the brain areas corresponding to these are right next to each other? We propose, therefore, that synaesthesia is caused by cross-wiring between these two areas' (2002: 9).

Grossenbacher and Lovelace (2001) point out that it is not necessary to posit the existence of unusual connections between sensory pathways. In their 'disinhibited-feedback' theory, they suggest that connections between sensory pathways exist in 'normal' brains, but that the activity of these pathways is usually inhibited to prevent cross-talk between sensory modalities. Synaesthesia, they suggest, results from the failure to inhibit these pathways. They point out that certain hallucinogenic drugs such as LSD can induce temporary synaesthetic experiences in non-synaesthetes, suggesting that the pathways connecting the different sensory modules exist in normal brains. The action of LSD could plausibly involve the **disinhibition** of existing pathways but is not likely to induce the 'growth' of new pathways.

It is clear that the study of synaesthesia is likely to enhance our understanding of the mechanisms involved in normal perception and that the study of normal perception will help us better understand this fascinating condition. As Ramachandran and Hubbard (2001) observe, 'Far from being a mere curiosity, synaesthesia may provide a window into perception, thought and language' (2001: 3).

Conclusions

Because most synaesthetes regard the condition as a gift, I have been careful to avoid terms such as 'disorder' or 'patient' when discussing synaesthesia. For the remainder of this chapter we will turn our attention to a variety of conditions which result in considerable loss of ability, and for which terms such as these are more useful. However, what the following conditions have in common with synaesthesia is that careful study of the nature of the deficit has increased our understanding of perception and attention in the normal brain. We will first consider the result of damage to areas of the visual cortex.

4.3 Blindsight

As we have seen the striate cortex, or area V1 as it is now known, is central to visual perception. Damage to the left striate cortex will result in blindness in the right *visual field* of both eyes and damage to the right striate cortex will result in blindness in the left visual field of both eyes. These areas of blindness are called *scotomata* (plural of **scotoma**). In order to imagine the effect of such damage, look straight ahead, and cover the left half of each eye. The very restricted visual field you now experience is similar to that which you would experience following damage to your right striate cortex. To see anything to your left side you need to turn your head (the patient would be able to turn their eyes).

Now imagine that you were asked to point to a flash of light that had occurred somewhere to your 'blind' left side. If persuaded to take part in this puzzling experiment you would expect to perform at chance levels, sometimes guessing the correct location but more often being wrong. Poppel *et al.* (1973) studied a group of ex-servicemen who suffered visual field deficits as a result of gun-shot wounds to the striate cortex, and asked his participants to make just such judgements. Lights were flashed in the defective area of the visual field of each participant. Because the servicemen could not see the flashes, the light was paired with the sound of a buzzer, and on hearing the buzzer the servicemen were asked to move their eyes in the direction of the light source. The servicemen found this a difficult task, but to their surprise, all were able to direct their gaze towards the light which they could not see.

In the following year, Weiskrantz *et al.* (1974) described a patient DB who seemed to demonstrate the same remarkable ability. DB was blind in his lower-left visual field following surgery to remove part of his right striate cortex to relieve very severe migraine headaches. What was remarkable about DB was the extent to which he could report details of objects appearing in the blind areas of his visual field despite no conscious experience of seeing them. Weiskrantz coined the term '**blindsight**' to describe this phenomenon.

In a series of experiments covering many years (see Weiskrantz, 1986), Weiskrantz and colleagues were able to systematically investigate the perceptual abilities preserved in the 'blind' areas of DB's visual field. DB was able to detect the presence of an object, and indicate its location in space by pointing. He could discriminate between moving and stationary objects, and between horizontal and vertical lines, and he could distinguish the letter X from the letter O. However, he was unable to distinguish between X and a triangle, suggesting that the ability to distinguish between X and O was dependent on some low-level characteristic of these stimuli rather than any residual ability to discriminate form. DB's inability to discriminate form is further demonstrated by his failure to distinguish between rectangles of various sizes or between straight- and curved-sided triangles.

Blindsight – a sceptical perspective

Some scientists have questioned the existence of blindsight, arguing that there are several possible explanations which need to be considered carefully. Cowey

(2004) summarised the arguments put forward by sceptics such as Campion *et al.* (1983). Three of these arguments are summarised below.

The stray light hypothesis

Campion *et al.* (1983) favoured the stray light explanation of blindsight, suggesting that blindsight patients were responding to light which was reflected from the object onto the functioning areas of the visual field (remember, that patients such as DB are only partially blind, and can see normally in large areas of their visual field). Campion *et al.* described one patient who reported that he was using such a strategy to distinguish between vertical and horizontal bars presented to the blind areas of his visual field. This patient claimed that he could see a faint glow in the preserved areas of his visual field and used this cue to undertake the task. Campion *et al.* also demonstrated that such a strategy could lead to the accurate localisation of a light in a 'blind' area of the visual field of normal subjects whose vision had been masked. However, it is difficult to see how this stray light could explain DB's ability to distinguish letters such as X and O or two different spatial frequency gratings with the same average brightness. In addition, DB could locate objects even against a bright background, whereas Campion *et al.*'s normal subjects could only locate a light source against a low level of background illumination.

Paradoxically, the best evidence against the stray light explanation came from DB's *inability* to respond accurately to objects whose image fell onto his blindspot. The blindspot, where the optic nerve passes through the retina, is devoid of receptor cells so we are blind to images falling on this part of the retina. If DB's blindsight was explained by stray light, then we would expect him to perform equally well whether the image of the object fell on the blindspot or in the scotoma. In fact, DB showed no evidence of being able to detect the presence of objects or lights presented at his blindspot, yet could accurately detect objects or events occurring within the scotoma immediately adjacent to the blindspot (see Figure 4.3).

More recently, some evidence has emerged to suggest that one form of the 'stray light' hypothesis might help to account for some reports of unexpected abilities in blindsight patients. Cowey (2004) noted that most research with blindsight patients uses 'raster displays' (television screens or computer monitors) to present the visual stimuli. Cowey demonstrated that a pattern displayed on one side of such a screen will often give rise to a faint 'ghost' image on the other side of the screen. Cowey and Azzopardi (2001) showed that in a display that included this artefact a normal participant could determine whether a grating presented in the masked area of the visual field was drifting up or down. However, once the display was modified to remove the artefact, this ability disappeared. Similarly, when the unmodified display was used, three blindsight patients could detect both the presence of a moving pattern and the direction of movement, but once the artefact was removed they were sensitive to the presence of movement but not its direction. Thus, it seems that some, but not all of the apparent abilities of blindsight patients might be attributed to the presence of these artefacts.

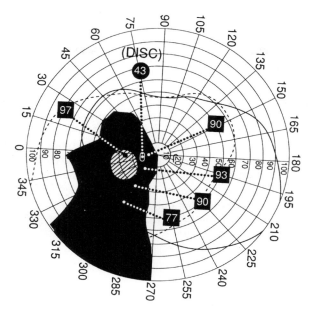

Figure 4.3 Weiskrantz's investigation of DB's blindsight

Note: The dark area indicates the 'blind' area of DB's visual field. The hashed area indicates that region in which DB had some partial awareness of the presence of the light. When the light occurred at his blindspot (marked DISC) DB performed at chance level, correctly reporting the presence of the light on less than 50 per cent of occasions. However, performance at all other locations was well above chance. The stray light hypothesis would predict that performance at the blindspot should be well above chance.

Source: Weiskrantz (1986), reproduced by permission of Oxford University Press

Spared islands of residual vision

Wessinger *et al.* (1997) suggested that blindsight was attributable to small areas or 'islands' in the scotoma within which vision is spared and that blindsight may be mediated by what is left of the primary visual pathway rather than other secondary pathways. This suggestion was tested by Kentridge *et al.* (1997) who looked for scattered regions of spared vision in one patient using a procedure which ensured that the effects of eye-movements were abolished. Under these stringent testing conditions Kentridge *et al.* noted blindsight did not extend across the whole of the area of the scotoma, but that blindsight was evident in some areas even after eye-movements had been eliminated, leading to the conclusion that although there may be some spared islands within the scotoma, these cannot account for all blindsight. Furthermore, Cowey (2004) notes that the results of MRI scanning of several blindsight patients has shown 'not a shred of evidence' of any sparing of the striate cortex in the area of the scotoma.

A change in criterion to report the presence of the stimulus?

Another explanation offered by sceptics is that blindsight represents a change in response criterion but not in sensitivity, such that blindsight patients are equally sensitive to the presence of a stimulus but less willing to report conscious awareness than a normal subject. Cowey and Azzopardi (2001) employed a signal detection approach to determine whether performance in a two-alternative-forced-choice task (such as determining in which of two time intervals a stimulus has been presented) was determined by a change in sensitivity or a change in criterion. The results suggest that the performance of blindsight patients tested was characterised not only by a change in response criterion, but also by a different mode of processing. That is, blindsight is qualitatively and not just quantitatively different from normal vision. However, Cowey (2004) notes that we should not ignore the possibility that changes in response criteria might partially account for some aspects of the performance of blindsight patients. This is an area of continuing research interest.

The sensation of blindsight

It is very difficult to imagine what a patient such as DB experiences when a stimulus is presented within the 'blind' regions of his visual field. It is clear that the experience is very different from that of normal vision. Weiskrantz records DB as saying that he 'felt' movement rather than saw it. As far as we can tell, blindsight patients are learning to respond to very subtle experiences which have little in common with the normal perceptual experience. As Cowey (2004) observes, it is important not to think of blindsight as 'normal vision stripped of conscious visual experience' (588). Blindsight is a very poor substitute for normal vision with very significantly reduced sensitivity to fundamental aspects of the scene.

So how can we imagine the experience of blindsight? Suppose you are sitting reading this book when suddenly, in your peripheral vision ('out of the corner of your eye'), a spider scuttles across the floor. Before you are conscious of the motion, you move your head and eyes towards the spider. You did not 'see' the spider but your visual system was able to guide you towards it. Perhaps this is a reasonable analogy to the experience of blindsight. Patients such as DB do not have any conscious experience of perception, yet, at some level below that accessible to introspection, the visual system does have access to information about the outside world.

The implications of blindsight: one visual system or two?

The most widely accepted explanation for blindsight is that we have two separate visual systems, one primitive non-striate system and a more advanced striate system. The primitive non-striate system might be sensitive to movement, speed, and other potentially important characteristics of a stimulus without giving rise to conscious perception. A frog can catch a fly because it can locate its position in space very accurately, but we do not imagine that the frog consciously perceives the fly. Perhaps blindsight represents the working of this primitive visual system whose functioning is normally masked by the conscious perception which results from the action of the striate visual system.

A slightly different explanation would be to see the striate and non-striate systems as having evolved to fulfil different roles. One possibility would be that the striate system has evolved to allow the identification of an object whereas the non-striate system has evolved to allow the localisation of that object in space. There is some evidence from non-human animal studies to support this view. Based on a series of lesion studies in hamsters, Schneider (1969) suggested that there were two separate visual pathways: one responsible for the identification of objects, and the other for the location of objects in space.

Goodale and Milner (1992, 2004) suggested that the distinction might be between a system responsible for the recognition of objects and one responsible for the control of actions such as picking up an object. Goodale and Milner (1992) suggested that object recognition and the control of action might be mediated by different and mutually incompatible types of representation. In this case, they reasoned, it might be *necessary* to separate these two pathways and only allow one of them to have access to consciousness.

4.4 Unilateral spatial neglect

As we saw in the previous section, patients with blindsight are able to respond to a stimulus they cannot see. In unilateral spatial neglect the opposite seems to be true – patients fail to respond to stimuli which they can see. The patient with unilateral neglect has normal visual acuity, but fails to react to objects or events to one side of their body. Neglect occurs following damage to the contralateral hemisphere, most commonly damage to the right hemisphere results in left spatial neglect. A typical patient with left neglect will fail to notice objects to the left side of space, for example only eating the food on the right-hand side of their plate or only drawing the right-hand side of an object.

A classic demonstration of spatial neglect is to ask a patient to draw a clock face. Neglect patients will either omit the numbers between 7 and 11, or will try to squeeze these numbers onto the right side of the clock (see Figure 4.4).

A disorder of attention?

At first sight unilateral spatial neglect seems to be a failure of attention. The patient is failing to attend to any object which appears in the left half of their visual field. However, there are several reasons to reject this description of the problem. First, there is the phenomenon of extinction where patients are able to respond to a stimulus in their neglected field when presented on its own, but fail to respond to a stimulus in the neglected field when it is paired with an identical stimulus occurring in the preserved field. Baylis *et al.* (1993) demonstrated that an object would be recognised in the left visual field if it was paired with a different object

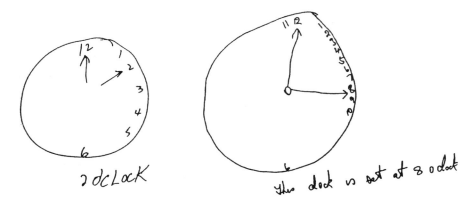

Figure 4.4 Examples of drawings of clock faces produced by patients with unilateral visual neglect

Source: Halligan and Marshall (1993), by permission of Psychology Press Limited, Hove, UK

appearing in the right visual field. However, if the objects in the left and right visual fields were identical then the patient would only report the existence of the object in the right visual field.

Secondly, it is clear that some patients with left spatial neglect are not simply failing to report objects to the left of fixation, but rather are failing to report the left side of an object, regardless of where this falls. For example, Marshall and Halligan (1993) asked patients with left neglect to copy pictures of plants. They found that patients would fail to draw stems or leaves on the left side of the plant, but would also fail to draw the petals on the left-hand side of a flower even if that flower was on the right-hand side of the plant. Thus, the neglect seems to be at the level of the object or part of the object (flower) rather than simply in terms of space relative to the patient.

Thirdly, recent studies have observed a dissociation between peri-personal space (areas of space within reach of the patient) and extra-personal space (space which is beyond reach). Halligan and Marshall (1991) demonstrated that their patient showed left unilateral neglect for peri-personal but not extra-personal space. Cowey *et al.* (1994) demonstrated the reverse pattern, showing that in some patients left neglect was worse in extra-personal than in peri-personal space.

In addition, spatial neglect has been shown to occur for stimuli that are imagined rather than observed. Bisiach and Luzzatti (1978) asked neglect patients to describe a piazza (square) in Milan from memory. The patients were asked to describe the piazza from two different perspectives. Buildings which were neglected from one perspective were described from the other perspective as the patients only described buildings which would appear to their left.

Finally, there is some evidence that patients show insight into aspects of a neglected stimulus. Marshall and Halligan (1988) showed a patient pairs of drawings of a house. The patient failed to notice when the house on the left was on fire, but when asked which house they would prefer to live in they indicated the non-burning house. Berti and Rizzolatti (1992) required neglect patients to press one of two keys to indicate whether a briefly presented picture was of a fruit or an animal. The target stimuli were presented to the right of fixation, but were preceded by a priming stimulus presented to the left of fixation which was from either the same or a different category as the target stimulus. Patients denied any awareness of the priming stimulus, yet were significantly faster to categorise the target when it was preceded by a congruent rather than an incongruent prime, suggesting that some fairly high-level processing of the neglected stimuli was occurring and that this processing was sufficient to allow the patient to distinguish between pictures of fruit and animals. Berti (2002) reviewed the evidence for unconscious processing in neglect and compared this phenomenon to that of blindsight (see above). In both cases, Berti commented, the patient denies any awareness of the stimulus presented contralateral to the brain damage, but in both of these conditions it is possible to show that some unconscious processing of the stimulus is occurring. However, as Berti noted, one very significant difference is that the blindsight patient acknowledges being blind whereas the neglect patient typically reports no problem with their vision. In blindsight the puzzle is how patients have knowledge of stimuli they cannot 'see', whereas in neglect the critical question is why patients do not report stimuli which are falling in intact areas of the visual field.

Explaining spatial neglect

It is becoming clear that unilateral spatial neglect may be a group of deficits rather than a single unitary disorder. The explanations offered for the syndrome can be broadly categorised as emphasising either perceptual or motor factors (e.g. Milner and McIntosh, 2002). While perceptual hypotheses propose that the patient fails to perceive the stimulus because of a failure of perceptual attention, motor hypotheses propose that the patient perceives this stimulus but is unwilling or unable to respond to it.

It is also increasingly apparent that the neglect syndrome can take a variety of forms. Patients demonstrate a range of different deficits, and in the future it may be possible to classify these deficits in some systematic manner which will aid our understanding of attention and perception (see Heliman et al., 2002). In the following section we will consider a disorder for which attempts to classify the deficits observed have been rather more successful, leading to a better understanding of the processes involved in normal perception.

4.5 Visual agnosia

A patient suffering from visual **agnosia** is unable to recognise everyday objects despite having apparently normal visual acuity, memory, language function and intelligence. An agnosic patient can move around without bumping into things, and can reach for and pick up objects which they are unable to recognise. Farah (1990) defined the condition as 'an impairment in the higher visual processes necessary for object recognition, with relative preservation of elementary visual functions'. Farah's use of the word 'relative' is important. As we shall see, the question of whether it is possible to observe a 'pure' agnosia in which there is no degradation of basic perceptual function is unresolved.

At first sight, this inability to recognise an object might appear to be a failure of language or of memory. However, visual agnosia differs from these memory or language disorders in that agnosic patients retain their knowledge about objects, and so can, for example, name an object when allowed to touch it, or describe an object when told its name.

The word 'agnosia' roughly translates as 'not knowing', so visual agnosia is 'not knowing through vision'. In tactile agnosia a patient cannot recognise objects by touch, and in auditory agnosia a patient is unable to recognise an object by its sound (such as a bell ringing). In this chapter we will only consider cases of visual agnosia.

Apperceptive and associative agnosia

Lissauer (1890), one of the first people to study this condition systematically, identified two different patterns of deficit: apperceptive agnosia and associative agnosia. In apperceptive agnosia the failure to recognise an object appears to be due to an inability to perceive form. Patients suffering from apperceptive agnosia cannot draw an object (see Figure 4.5), match similar objects, or even describe the component parts of the object despite normal visual acuity. The patient can form an image of the object but not build a representation based on that image.

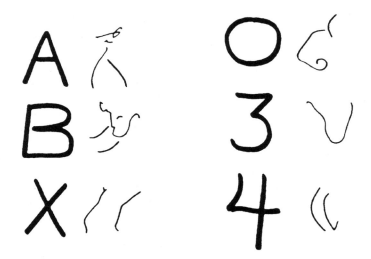

Figure 4.5 The attempts of a patient with apperceptive agnosia to copy six simple figures

Source: Farah (1990), reproduced by permission of MIT Press

Associative agnosia is thought to result from a failure at a later stage in the object recognition process. A patient suffering from this condition is able to draw an object, match similar objects and describe the component parts of an object, yet is unable to recognise the object. In associative agnosia, the perceptual process results in a stable representation, but the patient then fails to use this representation to access stored knowledge about the object. Teuber (1968) described this condition as 'a percept stripped of its meaning'.

Although first proposed over 100 years ago, Lissauer's distinction between individuals who cannot form a stable representation of an object, and individuals who can achieve a stable representation but cannot then link this representation to their semantic knowledge about the object, is still regarded as a useful one. The distinction relates well to David Marr's (Marr, 1982) description of visual perception in the normal brain. Adopting Marr's terminology, apperceptive agnosia would result from an inability to form a stable 3-D representation of the object. This failure to achieve a 3-D representation could be either due to a failure to achieve an adequate viewer-centred 2.5-D sketch or because of an inability to progress from the 2.5-D sketch to a full 3-D sketch. By contrast, an individual with associative agnosia might be able to form a stable 3-D representation but be unable to link this representation to stored knowledge about the object – the very last stage of the perceptual process.

In practical terms, the decision to categorise a patient as apperceptive or associative often is based on their ability to copy a drawing. Apperceptive patients cannot copy a drawing due to their inability to perceive a picture accurately. Associative patients, on the other hand, can accurately copy a drawing despite being unable to recognise either the object or their drawing of it.

The nature of the impairment in apperceptive and associative agnosia

Apperceptive agnosia appears to result from bilateral lesions, and as a result is much less common than associative agnosia. Carbon monoxide poisoning seems to be a particularly common cause of apperceptive agnosia (for example patient 'Dee' described by Goodale and Milner, 2004). Carbon monoxide poisoning can result in a large number of widely-spread small **lesions**, sometimes called 'peppery' lesions. Campion and Latto (1985) suggested that these lesions might result in tiny scotomata scattered across the entire visual field which would make it difficult for the patient to discern the contours of an object. However, as Farah (2004) notes, it is difficult to see why the perception of simple geometric shapes should be disrupted by such a 'peppery mask'. Farah (1990, 2004) favours the 'grouping hypothesis' as an explanation of apperceptive agnosia and describes how the perception of characteristics such as depth, velocity, acuity and colour must give rise to a 'kind of rich but formless visual goo' (Farah, 2004: 19) which then must be grouped together before we can represent an object. It is the failure of these grouping processes which are thought to give rise to apperceptive visual agnosia.

In the case of associative agnosia, the deficit seems to result from a failure to access a stored visual memory about the object being perceived. Farah (2004) notes that the problem could lie either with a failure to form a high-level visual representation, thus preventing access to an otherwise intact memory, or with damage to the stored memory itself. Thus, we can ask whether associative agnosia is a deficit of perception or memory. In support of the former, Farah notes that although patients thought to have associative visual agnosia may be able to reproduce line drawings, they usually achieve this by an unnatural and slavish line-by-line copying, suggesting a significant perceptual component to the disorder.

Concerns over the validity of visual agnosia

Just like blindsight and synaesthesia, visual agnosia has not always been recognised as a 'real' condition. The diagnosis of agnosia came under particularly strong attack from Bay (1953) who argued that patients who were thought to be suffering from visual agnosia had not been adequately screened for deficits of visual acuity. Bay was also worried by the inconsistent behaviour exhibited by agnosic patients who recognised some objects but not others and failed to recognise an object on one occasion yet correctly identified it on another. He considered this to be evidence that agnosia was actually a mild form of dementia. Although some patients with dementia can show symptoms which are similar to those of agnosia (Mendez *et al.*, 1990), many agnosic patients are highly intelligent and motivated and show no evidence of intellectual impairment (e.g. patient HJA described by Humphreys and Riddoch, 1987; or 'Dee' described by Goodale and Milner, 2004).

Warrington (1982, 1985) has been particularly careful to rule out the possibility that patients may be suffering from sensory deficits which could account for their difficulties in object recognition. Warrington has argued that an inability to discriminate colour, shape or orientation suggests a sensory deficit which may be sufficient to explain the apparent agnosia, and patients showing one or more of these deficits are classified as pseudo-agnosic. However, this very clear distinction between sensory and perceptual disorders is not widely supported. For example, patient HJA described by Humphreys and Riddoch became completely colour-blind following his stroke. This is a very common condition in patients with object recognition difficulties, but Humphreys and Riddoch would not describe their patient as suffering from a pseudo-agnosia. Although there is little doubt that on occasions the inability to perceive colour did hamper HJA's attempts to name objects, this deficit cannot fully account for his problems, and most colour-blind people show no evidence of visual agnosia.

The experience of visual agnosia

Goodale and Milner (2004) provide a powerful description of the problems faced by one patient, Dee, who suffers from apperceptive agnosia following carbon monoxide poisoning. Goodale and Milner note the many ways in which Dee is impaired, but it is important to note the surprising extent to which Dee can cope with everyday life. Dee can move around freely and in her own home can under-

Box 4.2 HJA A case history in visual agnosia

Humphreys and Riddoch's research on visual agnosia has been greatly influenced by their work with one famous patient, HJA. In a fascinating account of their work with HJA, Humphreys and Riddoch (1987) provide a valuable insight into the life of an individual with visual agnosia.

HJA suffered damage to both occipital lobes following a post-operative stroke which affected his posterior cerebral artery. On waking in hospital HJA was faced with a confusing and unfamiliar world. HJA described how he felt that his inability to recognise his surroundings must be due to some 'hangover' or 'bang on the head'. Despite some improvement over the next few weeks, HJA remained unable to recognise many familiar objects. When formally assessed, it was found that he was blind in the top half of both visual fields, but this alone could not account for his problems in recognising objects as simple movements of his eyes or head would have been sufficient to reveal those aspects of his environment previously hidden by this visual field deficit. HJA could move around without bumping into objects and could reach out and pick things up, but had considerable difficulty in naming objects on the basis of their appearance alone. Although he could recognise some objects, many were a mystery to him and he had particular difficulty in differentiating between members of a class of object with common characteristics (such as animals or plants). This problem is illustrated by the fact that HJA was capable of successfully trimming the garden hedge with shears, but would fail to notice the difference between the hedge and the roses, which he would decapitate.

It appears that HJA's difficulty in naming objects was not due to a memory deficit as he was able to give detailed definitions of named objects, demonstrating that his memory for both the function and the appearance of objects was intact. However, when shown these very same objects HJA failed to recognise them (see Figure 4.6).

It is clear that HJA could form a stable representation of the major components of the image and could deduce form and texture from a simple line drawing. However, he appeared to be unable to integrate these parts into a single representation which he could relate to his memory of common objects. Critically, when blindfolded and asked to identify objects by touch he was able to name many objects which he could not identify by sight alone, demonstrating that his problem was not some form of anomia (loss of memory for the names of objects).

HJA was able to describe a favourite etching of London which had hung on his living room wall for many years, and was still able to pick out some characteristic aspects of objects in the picture (such as the dome of St Paul's cathedral), but he commented poignantly:

> But now it does not 'fit' my memory of the picture nor of the reality. Knowing that I should be able to identify the general design of the dome-headed, high circular central tower covering a particularly cruciform

building, I can point out the expected detail but cannot recognise the whole structure. On the other hand, I am sure I could draw a reasonable copy of the picture.

(Humphreys and Riddoch, 1987: 33)

HJA also described a visit to an aircraft museum. During the war he had served in the RAF and at the museum he was able to describe the shape of his bomber to his friends, and was able to recount various stories and describe technical aspects of the aircraft. It is clear that he had a detailed memory for the aircraft and its appearance; however, HJA stated that 'in all honesty, I did not recognise the "whole"'.

When asked to copy a picture, such as the etching of London described above, HJA could produce a reasonable likeness (see Figure 4.7), but this image took six hours to complete by a laborious process of line-by-line reproduction which did not seem to be guided by any knowledge of the form of the object. It was as if he was being set the task of copying a complex pattern of random lines. However, when drawing from memory rather than attempting to copy, HJA produced very recognisable and detailed drawings (see Figure 4.8) indicating that he retained a good visual memory for the objects which he could no longer recognise. He stated:

I don't find [drawing from memory] too difficult, bearing in mind that I never had much drawing ability . . . My mind knows very clearly what I should like to draw and I can comprehend enough of my own handiwork to know if it is a reasonable representation of what I had in mind.

HJA offered the following definition of a carrot:

'A carrot is a root vegetable cultivated and eaten as human consumption world wide. Grown from seed as an annual crop, the carrot produces long thin leaves growing from a root head; this is deep growing and large in comparison with the leaf growth, some times gaining a length of 12 inches under a leaf top of similar height when grown in good soil. Carrots may be eaten raw or cooked and can be harvested during any size or state of growth. The general shape of a carrot root is an elongated cone and its colour ranges between red and yellow.' (p. 64)

However, HJA was unable to identify a line drawing of a carrot, saying:

'I have not even the glimmerings of an idea. The bottom point seems solid, and the other bits are feathery. It does not seem to be logical unless it is some sort of a brush.' (p. 59)

Figure 4.6 HJA's definition of the word 'carrot' and his attempt to recognise a line drawing of a carrot (as recorded by Humphreys and Riddoch, 1987)

Figure 4.7 HJA's copy of his favourite etching showing St Paul's Cathedral, London which took six hours to complete by a laborious process of line-by-line reproduction
Source: Humphreys and Riddoch (1987), reproduced by permission of Psychology Press Limited, Hove, UK

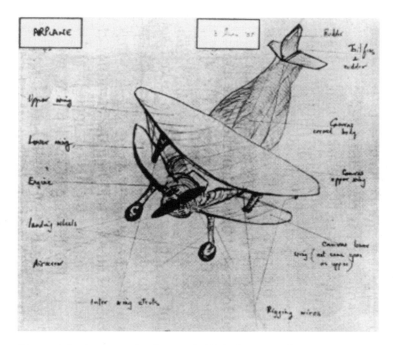

Figure 4.8 An example of one of HJA's drawings from memory
Source: Humphreys and Riddoch (1987), reproduced by permission of Psychology Press Limited, Hove, UK

take tasks such as making a cup of tea without assistance. It is very difficult to guess just what it is like to suffer from a visual agnosia, and the experience must vary greatly with the type of agnosia. Apperceptive agnosics clearly experience a very confused and distorted visual world in which almost nothing seems familiar and even basic forms are indistinguishable from each other. Perhaps the best analogy would be to imagine looking at the world through a very powerful microscope. To look at an object you would have to scan the microscope around trying to remember what each view of the object has revealed. To form a representation of the object to allow recognition you would have to assemble a mental picture of the overall structure of the object by piecing together the independent microscopic views. In this way, despite being able to see the component details of the object accurately you would find it very difficult to recognise the whole, and the more complex the local detail the harder the recognition task would become.

Recognising living and non-living objects

Warrington and Shallice (1984) caused considerable interest when they reported that the ability of one of their patients, JBR, to name drawings varied depending upon the category of object that the drawing depicted. In particular Warrington and Shallice had noticed that although JBR could name drawings of many non-living objects (such as spade or hairbrush), he couldn't name drawings of living things (such as dog or fly), or musical instruments (e.g. trumpet). Several other authors have since reported other patients with particular difficulty in naming living things (for example, Farah *et al.*, 1989 reporting the case of LH; Farah *et al.*, 1991 reporting the case of MB; Stewart *et al.*, 1992 reporting the case of HO). This may suggest different processes and/or different parts of the brain are involved in the recognition of living and non-living objects. However, caution should be exercised here. The distinction between living and non-living is not perfect – typically these patients show some impairment for non-living things and greater impairment for living things. This suggests the possibility of some other explanation. In particular the fact that JBR also had difficulty naming musical instruments (as did HO) suggests that the critical distinction may be something other than living/non-living. One possibility is that the living and non-living things used to demonstrate this effect may also differ in other characteristics.

Stewart *et al.* (1992) pointed out that, although the living and non-living pictures used to demonstrate this effect were matched for the familiarity of the object names, they were not matched for the familiarity of the pictures themselves. Furthermore they observed that there is a tendency for line drawings of living things to be more complex than drawings of non-living things. When Stewart *et al.* retested their patient HO with a new set of materials which were matched for familiarity of both name and picture as well as image complexity, they found that he no longer demonstrated a category-specific agnosia, and when Funnell and Sheridan (1992) retested Warrington and Shallice's patient JBR using materials which controlled for item familiarity, there was no evidence of the category-specific naming deficit that Warrington and Shallice had originally observed.

Rather than construct a very tightly controlled set of stimuli in which all these different factors were matched, Farah *et al.* (1991) used a statistical (regression) approach to adjust for the impact of these confounding variables. Even after accounting for the effect of image complexity, familiarity and other factors, Farah *et al.* still found a difference in performance between living and non-living items. Farah (2004) attributes these contradictory findings to differences in statistical power. She notes that the approach taken by Stewart *et al.* and Funnell and Sheridan results in a smaller set of stimuli and a reduced number of trials. This has the effect of reducing the ability to detect a difference in performance, should one exist. Farah (2004) also notes that there have been some reports of patients who per-form better with living than non-living objects, suggesting that the effect cannot be attributed to an artefact of the stimulus materials. Research in this area continues.

Perception and action

As noted earlier, even severely agnosic patients frequently retain the ability to interact with objects they are unable to recognise. Most agnosic patients are perfectly capable of navigating themselves around their immediate environment without bumping into things. Goodale and Milner (1992, 2004) suggested that the visual recognition of an object and the control of actions directed towards an object might be mediated by separate areas of the brain. When we move to pick up an object we direct our actions towards the appropriate position in space and adjust our grip ready to grasp the object. We are unaware of these actions, which normally are not under conscious control. Goodale and Milner (2004) describe their work with patient Dee who was unable to recognise an object or describe its size, shape or orientation. However, by attaching small infrared light sources to the tip of Dee's index finger and thumb, Goodale and colleagues were able to monitor the shape of her grasp as she reached to pick up the blocks and demonstrated that Dee accurately adjusted the shape of her grasp to suit the size of the block she was reaching for. Thus, although unable to describe the size or orientation of an object, Dee was able to use this information to control her movements.

Goodale and Milner (1992) concluded that, while areas of the parietal cortex provide information about the structure and orientation of objects required to control action, the temporal lobe provides the visual information, which mediates conscious perceptual experience. They suggested that these separate channels of information might be giving rise to different types of representation – they noted that the information required to control actions is likely to be viewer-centred, whereas object recognition requires an object-centred representation. Goodale and Milner suggest that the separation of these two channels might even be necessary to prevent the viewer-centred description used to drive action from interfering with the object-centred description which results in conscious perceptual experience.

4.6 Disorders of face processing – prosopagnosia and related conditions

Face recognition is probably one of the most demanding tasks undertaken by our visual system. Each of us can recognise thousands of different faces, a remarkable feat when we consider how similar all human faces are. The face is a thin layer of tissue stretched over the skull, and the structure of the skull is very tightly constrained by the position of the eyes, nose and mouth and mechanical considerations such as the requirement to maintain clear air passages. As if to make identification even harder, we also distort our faces into various facial expressions to signal our emotions. Given all this, it is not surprising that brain damage can result in deficits in face processing. However, the pattern and nature of these deficits tells us a great deal about both face processing and perception in general.

Bruce and Young (1986) incorporated the knowledge gained from studying individuals with a variety of face processing deficits with information gleaned from experimental studies of normal individuals into a successful model of normal face processing (see Figure 4.9). This model suggests that the recognition of identity, expression and lip-reading (facial speech analysis) are independent processes, and, as we shall see, evidence from brain-damaged patients largely supports this view. However, the model is neutral on the question of whether face processing is dependent on 'special' perceptual processes that are qualitatively different from those involved in the recognition of other non-face objects. This has become a central issue in the field of face processing research, with evidence from experimental studies of normal subjects, developmental studies of neonates and neuropsychological studies of brain-injured patients all being considered. However, it is neuropsychological studies of patients suffering from conditions such as **prosopagnosia** which are seen as providing the most direct test of this question.

Prosopagnosia

Prosopagnosia is an inability to recognise faces that cannot be explained by sensory impairment. Severely prosopagnosic individuals are unable to recognise members of their immediate family and sometimes do not recognise their own reflection. It is not that they have forgotten who these people are; once they hear the voice of a friend or relative they recognise them and interact normally. Prosopagnosic patients know that a face is a face, and many can identify facial expressions such as anger and happiness, but these individuals are unable to identify someone they know on the basis of their facial appearance.

The term prosopagnosia was first used by Bodamer (1947). Bodamer reported three patients who he believed showed a face-specific deficit, apparently being able to recognise non-face objects normally. However, in recent years this claim that prosopagnosia can be observed in a 'pure' form and is face-specific has come under close examination (see Bruce and Humphreys, 1994).

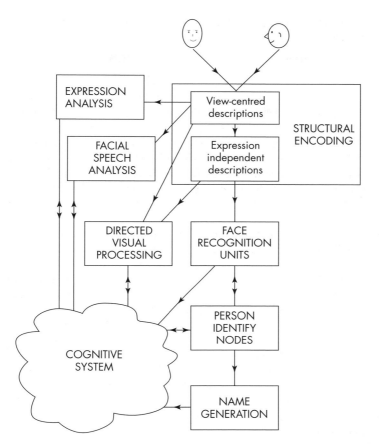

Figure 4.9 Bruce and Young's model of face processing showing independent pathways for face recognition, expression analysis and speech analysis

Source: Bruce and Young (1986), reproduced by permission of the British Psychological Society

Prosopagnosia – a face-specific disorder?

Face recognition places unusual demands upon the visual system. We have to be able to recognise a chair as a chair, but do not normally need to recognise a particular chair amongst other chairs, that is, we do not need to **individuate** chairs. Face recognition is all about individuation – to function successfully in society we must accurately recognise many different individuals. In deciding whether prosopagnosia is a face-specific disorder we need to establish whether prosopagnosic patients retain the ability to distinguish between members of a perceptually similar class of objects. The challenge for researchers working in this area is to find a set of non-face stimuli which are as similar to one another as faces are to each other. Some researchers have used sets of similar manufactured items such as eyeglasses or cars (De Renzi *et al.*, 1991; Sergent and Signoret, 1992; Farah *et al.*, 1995; Tippett *et al.*, 2000), and on the whole these studies find that prosopagnosic patients are significantly more impaired with faces than these other non-face items. However, unlike faces, cars or eyeglasses are not natural biological objects and for this reason some researchers have also attempted to study performance on tasks which require patients to identify individual members of non-human species including cows and sheep. Bruyer *et al.* (1983) reported that Mr W, a prosopagnosic farmer, was still able to recognise his cows. This is in contrast to the report by Bornstein, Sroka and Munitz (1969) who described a prosopagnosic farmer who could not recognise either humans or his cows and Assal *et al.* (1984) who describe a farmer who was initially unable to recognise either humans or cows but after six months recovered the ability to recognise human faces but not to individuate cows. Thus, almost unbelievably, we have evidence of a double dissociation between the ability to individuate humans and animals following brain injury. McNeil and Warrington (1993) described the case of WJ, who took up farming *after* becoming prosopagnosic (see below). This is an important case because it demonstrates that it is possible to *learn* to distinguish between very similar biological forms (sheep) despite being prosopagnosic and unable to identify even highly familiar human faces. This is in contrast to the patient described by Tippett *et al.* (2000) who could recognise faces and non-faces he had learned prior to his injury, and could learn new non-face objects but could not learn to identify new faces.

It is still not clear what conclusions should be drawn concerning the degree of face specificity in prosopagnosia. In part the problem lies with the fact that faces are, in one sense at least, special – it is difficult to find suitable non-face control stimuli which can be individuated as well as faces by normal subjects. Tests of the ability to individuate non-human animals are interesting but it might be unwise to place too much emphasis on results from a few people who have either preserved or lost the very rare ability to name large numbers of similar farm animals.

Developmental prosopagnosia

Until recently, almost all reported cases of prosopagnosia involved an acquired or adult-onset disorder. In the last few years there have been reports of cases of developmental prosopagnosia – individuals who report being aware from an early age that they were unable to recognise faces. Developmental prosopagnosia appears to have a genetic component as sufferers often share their condition with other members of their immediate family (De Hann, 1999). One significant difference between the developmental and acquired forms of the condition is that in developmental prosopagnosia there is no evidence of brain lesions (Barton *et al.*, 2003). As with acquired prosopagnosia, there has been debate regarding the extent to which developmental prosopagnosics also suffer other perceptual deficits. Barton *et al.* (2003) and Duchaine and Nakayama (2004) have both tested groups of individuals with developmental prosopagnosia using the Benton Facial Recognition Test, which requires participants to match different views of unfamiliar faces. While some of the participants showed evidence of impairment using this test, others performed normally. It seems likely that developmental prosopagnosia and the differences between the developmental and acquired forms of the condition will be a significant area of research in coming years.

Covert recognition in prosopagnosia

Some, but not all prosopagnosic patients have been found to show some covert recognition of faces (Bruyer, 1991). Some of these patients demonstrate covert familiarity – for example showing differences in the evoked potentials produced by viewing familiar and unfamiliar faces (Renault et al., 1989). In other cases it has been possible to demonstrate some retained knowledge about the person shown in a photograph, such as occupation or name. Bruyer et al. (1983) found it was easier to teach a prosopagnosic patient to associate faces with their real names than randomly assigned names, and de Haan et al. (1987) showed this was true even for people their patient had met after he had become prosopagnosic, suggesting that he continued to learn the names and faces of people he met despite having no conscious awareness of recognition.

Barton et al. (2001) looked for evidence of covert recognition in patients with acquired and developmental prosopagnosia. There was evidence of covert recognition in all five of the patients with acquired prosopagnosia, but no indication of covert recognition was observed in any of the three patients with developmental prosopagnosia.

Facial expression, lip-reading and face recognition

Faces are not only used to signal identity; we also use facial expressions to indicate our emotional state and there is evidence that we all tend to lip-read when listening to someone speak. Thus the face provides us with several independent channels of information, and models of face recognition, such as that proposed by Bruce and Young (1986), assume independent processing of these various channels. In support of this model, some prosopagnosic patients are able to identify the expressions posed by faces they couldn't recognise (e.g. Bruyer et al., 1983) while other patients are unable to identify the expression on a face that they could recognise (e.g. Kurucz et al., 1979). Young et al. (1993) used a standardised set of tests with a group of ex-servicemen who had suffered head injuries during World War II. Even after adopting very stringent criteria they found evidence of the dissociation between the ability to identify facial expression and to recognise identity. The dissociation between expression analysis and person identification makes good sense. We need to be able to recognise a face regardless of which expression it is displaying (although I am reminded of a particularly miserable student who I failed to recognise on the day of her graduation – the only time I had seen her smile!).

Box 4.3 *The case of the unknown sheep: a case study in prosopagnosia*

McNeil and Warrington (1993) described the case of WJ, a 51-year-old man who suffered a series of strokes causing profound prosopagnosia. When shown a set of three photographs of one famous and two unfamiliar faces, WJ was not able to pick out the famous face. However, when this task was modified by giving WJ the name of the famous person in the trial ('which one is ...?'), performance improved significantly, indicating some covert recognition for famous faces. Following the onset of his prosopagnosia, WJ acquired a flock of sheep which he photographed for McNeil and Warrington. WJ knew his sheep by number, and McNeil and Warrington were able to determine that he could recognise at least eight out of sixteen of the pictures of these 'known sheep' (this is probably an underestimate – McNeil and Warrington report that on several trials WJ could recognise the sheep but not remember its number, making comments such as: 'This sheep had three lambs this year'). This is remarkable evidence of an ability to learn to recognise individual sheep while still being profoundly prosopagnosic for human faces. In order to ensure that this ability was not attributable to some characteristic specific to WJ's own sheep, McNeil and Warrington obtained photographs of 'unknown sheep' and managed to recruit two control subjects who had also acquired flocks of sheep after retiring, together with a number of age- and profession-matched non-sheep-owning subjects. These subjects were all shown photos of eight of the sheep and then shown these eight randomly mixed with eight 'distractor' sheep. The subjects were required to say whether each picture was of one of the original eight or was a distractor sheep. Understandably, the control subjects, both sheep-owning and 'normal', found this a difficult task and their performance was poor compared with that with human faces. WJ showed the opposite pattern of results, performing rather well on the sheep task (correctly recognising 81 per cent of unknown and 87 per cent of the known sheep – better than any other subject), and performing very badly with human faces. McNeil and Warrington conclude that WJ provides 'further evidence that prosopagnosia can occur as a face-specific deficit' (445).

Figure 4.10 (*opposite*) The computer-manipulated images used by Calder *et al.* (1996)

Source: Reproduced by permission of Psychology Press Limited, Hove, UK

Note: These images were produced by manipulating the original images that Ekman and Friesen (1976) produced to illustrate prototypical facial expressions. In this sequence each image is a mixture of two of different prototypical expressions. As we move from left to right across the images in the top row, we progress from happiness to surprise. The leftmost image is made up of 90 per cent of the happiness image and 10 per cent of the surprise image. The next image is 70 per cent happiness and 30 per cent surprise, and the middle image in the row is made up of equal proportions of happiness and surprise. The fourth image shows 30 per cent happiness and 70 per cent surprise and the final image in this row shows 10 per cent happiness and 90 per cent surprise. The images in the other rows show the same proportions of surprise-fear (second row), fear-sadness (third row), sadness-disgust (fourth row), disgust-anger (fifth row) and anger-happiness (sixth row). Most people see these images as illustrating one expression or another rather than a mixture of two expressions.

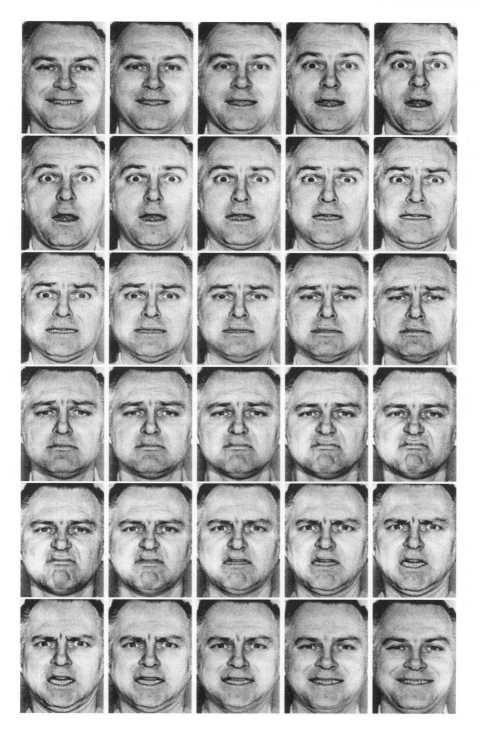

There is also evidence of a double dissociation between facial speech analysis, or lip-reading, and face recognition. Our reliance on facial speech analysis is best demonstrated by McGurk and MacDonald (1976) who showed that if we hear one phoneme, such as 'ba', while watching the speaker make the mouth movements normally associated with the production of a different sound, such as 'ga', then we tend to perceive a sound which is a combination of the phoneme heard and that predicted by the mouth movements, in this case 'da'. This effect is known as the McGurk illusion, and is of interest to us because some prosopagnosics have been shown to be susceptible to the illusion (and hence can be assumed to be lip-reading normally), while other patients have been identified who are immune to the McGurk illusion (and hence are not lip-reading) yet can recognise faces normally (Campbell *et al.*, 1986).

Deficits in the perception of specific facial expressions

In recent years psychologists have investigated whether brain damage can result in a deficit in expression analysis specific to one particular expression. For example, can we lose the ability to recognise fear while retaining the ability to recognise other expressions? To investigate this possibility, Calder *et al.* (1996) produced a series of images based on photographs of six facial expressions (happiness, surprise, fear, sadness, disgust and anger) originally photographed by Ekman and Friesen (1976). Calder computer-manipulated the Ekman images to produce a sequence which included interpolated images bridging the gap between one expression and another. For example, a sequence could be produced which started with the standard fear response and over a number of images changed into the standard sadness image. These images are reproduced in Figure 4.10. Using these images Calder *et al.* (1996) found that two patients with amygdala damage showed a deficit in the recognition of the expressions of fear or anger, tending to identify the images from these parts of the sequence as showing some other expression. This is in line with several other findings which have suggested that the amygdala might be particularly involved in the recognition of fear and anger.

Adolphs *et al.* (1994) described one individual who, following bilateral damage to the amygdala, had particular difficulty in recognising or drawing a face showing fear, and Morris *et al.* (1996) have shown that the pattern of blood flow in amygdala is related to the degree to which a facial stimulus shows a fearful expression. In addition, Sprengelmeyer *et al.* (1996) have demonstrated a deficit in the ability to recognise expressions of disgust in a group of people with Huntington's disease, a degenerative neurological disorder which has various symptoms including emotional disturbance. Sprengelmeyer *et al.* (2006) compared non-symptomatic carriers of the Huntington's disease gene with non-carriers. They found that the Huntington's group were significantly impaired in their ability to recognise the facial expression of disgust. Thus, we have some evidence that neurological disorders can result in a loss of sensitivity to one particular facial expression while preserving the ability to recognise other expressions.

Summary

With the exception of synaesthesia, the disorders we have considered in this chapter are debilitating and distressing conditions which severely disable the individuals who suffer them. However, for psychologists these individuals afford an invaluable opportunity to glimpse the inner workings of the processes of perception and attention.

- Damage to different brain regions can result in a variety of perceptual and attention disorders which display a surprising degree of specificity.
- The pattern of disorders observed suggests a highly modular system in which a series of independent processes each contribute towards the goal of perception. This point is best illustrated by the case of face perception where the recognition of expression is separate from that of identity, and by synaesthesia which seems to result from a breakdown in this modularity.
- The study of disorders of perception and attention has also provided evidence of a dissociation between conscious experience and the ability to respond appropriately to a stimulus. This dissociation, which characterises the condition of blindsight, was also seen in prosopagnosia, where it is called covert recognition, and in unilateral neglect, where some patients show evidence of partial insight into the nature of neglected objects.
- Finally, there is some evidence that the nature of the representation formed might be dependent on the task to be performed, and in particular there may be an important distinction between the perceptual processes that mediate action and those which result in recognition.

Further reading

Harrison, J (2001). *Synaesthesia: The Strangest Thing*. Oxford: Oxford University Press. This book provides a very accessible account of synaesthesia.

Karnath, H.O., Milner, A.D. and Vallar, G. (2002). *The Cognitive and Neural Bases of Spatial Neglect*. Oxford: Oxford University Press. This edited volume brings together some of the leading researchers in the field.

Farah, M.J. (2004). *Visual Agnosia*. (2nd edn). Cambridge, MA: MIT Press. A very readable account of disorders of object recognition written by one of the leading researchers in the field.

Goodale, M. and Milner, D. (2004). *Sight Unseen*. Oxford: Oxford University Press. In this book Goodale and Milner provide a fascinating account of their work with patient 'Dee'.

De Gelder, B., De Hann, E.H.F. and Heywood, C.A. (2001). *Out of Mind: Varieties of Unconscious Processes*. Oxford: Oxford University Press. This edited collection of papers examine the nature of blindsight and related conditions.

Young, A.W. (ed.) (1998) *Face and Mind*. Oxford: Oxford University Press. Provides a fuller description of prosopagnosia, and related conditions including some not covered in this chapter.

Chapter 5

Long-term memory

5.1 The nature and function of memory

Memory and its importance in everyday life

Memory is the process of storing information and experiences for possible retrieval at some point in the future. This ability to create and retrieve memories is fundamental to all aspects of cognition, and in a broader sense it is essential to our ability to function properly as human beings. Our memories allow us to store information about the world so that we can understand and deal with future situations on the basis of past experience. The process of thinking and problem-solving relies heavily on the use of previous experience, and memory also makes it possible for us to acquire language and to communicate with others. Memory also plays a very basic part in the process of perception, since we can only make sense of our perceptual input by making reference to our store of previous experiences. Even our social interactions with others are dependent upon what we remember. In a sense it can be said that our very identity relies on an intact memory, and the ability to remember who we are and the things that we have done. Almost everything we ever do depends on our ability to remember the past.

Encoding, storage and retrieval of memory

The memory process can be divided into three main stages (see Figure 5.1). First of all there is the *input* stage, where newly perceived information is being learned or encoded. Next comes the *storage* stage, where the information is held in preparation for some future occasion. Finally there is the *output* stage, where the information is retrieved from storage.

Those who have had any experience of using a computer will probably be able to see clear parallels between these three stages of human memory and the input/storage/output processes involved in storing a computer file onto disk. Perhaps the most important reason for distinguishing between these three stages is that each stage will need to be successfully completed before we can retrieve a memory. This means that when we find we are unable to recall some item, the cause could be either a failure at the input stage (i.e. faulty learning), a failure at the output stage (i.e. faulty retrieval), or even a failure of the storage mechanism. In practice storage failures probably do not occur unless there is damage to the brain, so it is probable that most forgetting is caused by either learning failure or retrieval failure.

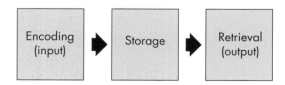

Figure 5.1 The encoding, storage and retrieval stages of memory

5.2 The first memory experiments

Ebbinghaus and the forgetting curve

The scientific study of memory began with the work of Hermann Ebbinghaus (1885), whose methods were to have a huge influence on memory research for many years. Using himself as the experimental subject, Ebbinghaus carried out a number of classic experiments in which he attempted to measure memory performance in a scientific and quantified manner, making an effort to control all unwanted variables out of his experimental design. For example, Ebbinghaus realised that the use of verbal items in a memory test would add an uncontrolled variable to the design, since the words used would vary in their meaningfulness and familiarity. He therefore decided to eliminate this variable by using nonsense material instead of meaningful words in his experiments. Ebbinghaus compiled lists of test items known as 'nonsense syllables', so called because they are pronounceable syllables but have no meaning, such as VOP or TUV. Ebbinghaus considered that all nonsense syllables were roughly equivalent in their memorability, since they were meaningless.

Having devised lists of nonsense syllables, Ebbinghaus used them to investigate the way that forgetting took place with the passage of time. A list of syllables would be learned and then retested after a certain retention interval, and scores were plotted as a 'forgetting curve', as shown in Figure 5.2.

As the graph shows, forgetting was extremely rapid at first, but as the retention interval increased, the rate of forgetting gradually levelled off. This same basic forgetting curve has been confirmed in many subsequent experimental studies. In fact Rubin and Wenzel (1996) reviewed no less than 210 studies of

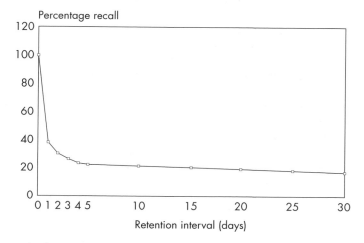

Figure 5.2 The forgetting curve
Source: Ebbinghaus (1885)

forgetting carried out over the years, all of which reported forgetting curves which were generally similar to that found by Ebbinghaus.

Interference and decay

The forgetting curve demonstrates that memories tend to dissipate over a period of time, and Ebbinghaus suggested two main theories to explain why this might occur:

1   **Decay** – memories deteriorate with the passage of time, regardless of other input.
2   **Interference** – memories are actively disrupted by the influence of some other input.

Ebbinghaus was able to demonstrate experimentally that interference did indeed have a significant effect on memory. He showed that memory scores for the learning of one list were considerably reduced by the subsequent learning of a second list, a phenomenon known as retroactive interference. Another experiment showed that the memory for a list was also subject to interference from a previously learned list, a phenomenon known as proactive interference. In summary, the interference effect could be caused by any additional input occurring either before or after the target list. Many subsequent studies have confirmed the effects of interference, which have been shown to depend largely on the degree of similarity between the target item and the items interfering with it (McGeoch, 1932; Underwood and Postman, 1960).

Producing evidence for the occurrence of spontaneous decay has proved to be rather more problematic because of the difficulty of separating its effects from those of other forms of forgetting (including interference) which also inevitably take place over time. However, the interference and decay theories both remain plausible.

Thorndike (1914) suggested that decay only affects memory traces which are left undisturbed for a long period, an idea known as the 'decay with disuse' theory. This theory has recently been revived and updated by Bjork and Bjork (1992), who suggest that access to a memory trace is strengthened by frequent retrieval, whereas access to unretrieved memories becomes more and more difficult as time passes. Bjork and Bjork call this the 'New Theory of Disuse'. Recent research has shown that there are inhibitory mechanisms at work in the brain, which actively suppress unretrieved memories (Anderson, 2003). This phenomenon is known as 'retrieval-induced forgetting', and it may provide the explanation for the occurrence of memory decay over time. If so, then this puts the whole concept of forgetting into a totally new perspective, because it suggests that forgetting may be caused by an inhibition system built into the brain rather than by some failing or inadequacy of the memory system. The new theory of disuse and the retrieval-induced forgetting phenomenon will both be considered in more detail in Section 5.7.

The serial position effect

Ebbinghaus also demonstrated that memory performance was affected by the serial position of an item in a list. Items at the end of the list are particularly well remembered (the 'recency effect'), and to a lesser extent items at the start of the list also tend to be remembered (the 'primacy effect'). However, items in the middle of the list are more likely to be forgotten. This serial position effect is illustrated in Figure 5.3.

Ebbinghaus suggested that the serial position effect could be explained in terms of interference theory. Items in the middle of the list are subjected to the greatest interference, as they suffer from both proactive and retroactive interference. However, items at either end of the list are subjected to only one kind of interference, and thus suffer less interference overall. This explanation of the recency effect seemed to be quite plausible at the time, but subsequent research has shown that there is a more likely explanation. Following the discovery of separate short-term and long-term components of memory, it has been shown that items at the end of a list are probably remembered because they are still held in the conscious short-term memory store (Glanzer and Cunitz, 1966). This evidence will be considered in more detail in Chapter 6.

A number of different explanations have been suggested for the primacy effect, but there is some evidence (Oberauer, 2003) that items at the beginning of the list benefit from greater attention than those later in the sequence. It is also possible that the retrieval of the first items on the list may inhibit the retrieval of subsequent items, a phenomenon known as output interference.

The experiments carried out by Ebbinghaus over a century ago had a tremendous influence on subsequent memory research. However, although his basic findings (such as the forgetting curve and the serial position effect) are still generally accepted, the theories he proposed to explain them have been superseded by new theories derived from the results of subsequent research. One aspect of Ebbinghaus' approach which has been particularly criticised is his

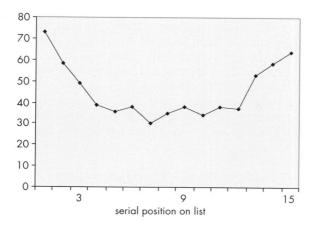

Figure 5.3 The serial position curve

use of nonsense material, since meaning is a central factor in memory processing. This will be considered in the next section.

5.3 Meaning, knowledge and schemas

Bartlett's story recall experiments and the schema theory

The early memory experiments of Ebbinghaus influenced memory research for many years, but psychologists eventually came to question one very central feature of his research, namely his use of nonsense items as test material. By controlling out the effects of meaning and knowledge, Ebbinghaus had eliminated what was possibly the most important single feature of memory function.

The first clear experimental demonstration of the important effect of meaning and knowledge on memory was provided by Bartlett (1932), in a classic study regarded by many as the first step towards the modern cognitive approach to memory. Bartlett investigated the way that his subjects remembered a short story. In order to make the experiment more interesting Bartlett used slightly unusual stories such as the one below, which is a Native American folk tale called 'The war of the ghosts'. If you wish to try the experiment on yourself you should read through the story once, then cover it over and write down as much of it as you can remember.

The war of the ghosts

One night two young men from Egulac went down to the river to hunt seals, and while they were there it became foggy and calm. Then they heard war-cries, and they thought, 'maybe this is a war party'. They escaped to the shore, and hid behind a log. Now canoes came up, and they heard the noise of paddles, and saw one canoe coming up to them. There were five men in the canoe, and they said, 'What do you think? We are going up the river to make war on the people.' One of the young men said, 'I have no arrows.' 'Arrows are in the canoe,' they said.

'I will not go along. I might be killed. My relatives do not know where I have gone. But you,' he said, turning to the other, 'may go with them.' So one of the young men went, but the other returned home. And the warriors went up the river to a town on the other side of Kalama. The people came down to the river, and they began to fight, and many were killed. But presently the young man heard one of the warriors say: 'Quick, let us go home: that Indian has been hit.' Now he thought, 'Oh, they are ghosts.' He did not feel sick, but they said he had been shot. So the canoes went back to Egulac and the young man went ashore to his house, and made a fire.

And he told everybody and said: 'Behold I accompanied the ghosts, and we went to fight. Many of our fellows were killed, and many of those who attacked us were killed. They said I was hit, and I did not feel sick.' He told it all, and then he became quiet. When the sun rose he fell down. Something black came out of his mouth. His face became contorted. The people jumped up and cried. He was dead.

This story is rather strange to the average person from a Western cultural background because it contains references to various supernatural entities such as ghosts, magic, and states of invulnerability, all concepts which are rather unfamiliar to most of us. Bartlett's most important finding was that his subjects tended to recall a changed and distorted version of the story. However, the changes noted by Bartlett were not random, but were systematically directed towards the creation of a more rational and sensible story. Bartlett concluded that subjects tended to rationalise the story to make it fit in with their expectations, based on their own past experience and understanding of the world. Typically the story recalled by Bartlett's (British) subjects would be a far more straightforward account of an expedition which was relatively free from ghostly or magical interventions. Some of the more unfamiliar parts of the story tended to be left out altogether, whilst others would be distorted and changed to fit in with a more conventional and British view of the world.

Bartlett explained these findings in terms of his schema theory (see Chapter 1), which proposes that we perceive and encode information into our memories in terms of our past experience. Schemas are the mental representations that we have built up from all that we have experienced in the past, and according to Bartlett we compare our new perceptual input with these schemas in an effort to find something meaningful and familiar. Any input which does not match up with existing schemas will either have to be distorted until it does match up, or else it will not be retained at all.

These findings have quite important implications for a variety of real-life situations, as they raise questions about whether we can rely on the accuracy of eyewitness testimony. We should expect, for example, that witnesses presenting evidence in a court of law will be likely to produce a distorted and rationalised version of events they have witnessed. We should also question the accuracy of any eyewitness account such as news reports, and accounts of historical events. Indeed we should even question the accuracy of our own memories of the past, since much of what we think has happened in our lives has in fact been subject to distortion of which we are completely unaware. On those rare occasions where we do actually get a chance to check the accuracy of our memories, as for example when chatting with a friend about some shared experience from the past, we often discover quite major discrepancies between two people's accounts of the same event. Bartlett's experiments showed that we should never expect memory to be entirely accurate, since it will tend to reflect our own efforts to make sense of its content. Bartlett also gave us an insight into the way that memory actually works. He showed us that memory appears to be stored in terms of its meaningful content, and thus depends on the extent to which the subject's knowledge can be used to make sense of the incoming information.

The effect of meaning and knowledge on memory

Bartlett's theories were not widely accepted at first, partly because they concerned inner mental processes (such as schemas), which were unacceptable to the behaviourists who dominated mainstream psychology at that time. Moreover, Bartlett's experiments were not very scientifically designed. For example, the main variable in his story recall experiments was the meaningfulness of the story content, but as this was determined purely on the basis of subjective opinion it is perhaps not surprising that it met with some criticism.

In recent years a number of studies have provided a more scientific basis for Bartlett's theories, providing an objective means of varying the meaningfulness of the narrative. For example, Bransford and Johnson (1972) tested their subjects' ability to recall a short passage, which made relatively little sense unless the subject was provided with some kind of explanatory context, which in this case was provided by a picture (see Figure 5.4). Two groups of subjects were used in this experiment. One group was shown the helpful picture, but the other group was not. The group who had seen the picture were subsequently able to recall far more of the passage than the other group, probably because the picture helped them to make sense of the passage. The passage is reproduced below, and you may wish to try out the experiment on yourself.

The balloons passage

If the balloons popped the sound wouldn't be able to carry since then everything would be too far away from the correct floor. A closed window would also prevent the sound from carrying, since most buildings tend to be well insulated. Since the whole operation depends on the steady flow of electricity, a break in the middle of the wire would also cause problems. Of course, the fellow could shout, but the human voice is not loud enough to carry that far. An additional problem is that the string could break on the instrument. Then there would be no accompaniment to the message. It is clear that the best situation would involve less distance. Then there would be fewer potential problems. With face-to-face contact, the least number of things could go wrong.

In this experiment the subject's ability to find meaning in the passage was scientifically controlled by giving helpful information to one group but not to the other. This method of controlling the variable of meaningfulness was thus quite objective and did not rely at all on the subjective opinion of the experimenter as was the case in Bartlett's story recall experiments. Since the two groups of subjects were read exactly the same passage in exactly the same conditions, the only major variable was the degree of meaningfulness, which was systematically controlled by the experimenter.

These experiments on story recall suggest that a passage is more memorable if we can make use of our knowledge and experience to increase its meaningfulness. Other studies have shown that subjects who possess a great deal of expert knowledge about a subject are particularly good at remembering material which relates to their field of expertise. Chase and Simon (1973) found that expert chess players were able to remember the positions of the pieces in an uncompleted chess game with great accuracy, whereas chess novices produced far less accurate recall. However, the chess experts only achieved superior recall when

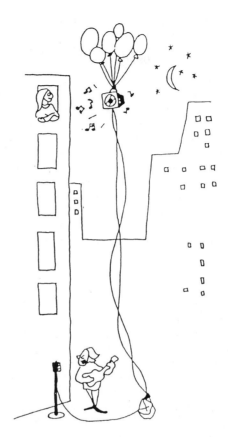

Figure 5.4
The picture used to make the
balloons' passage meaningful
Source: Bransford and Johnson (1972)

the test material consisted of real or plausible chess games, but not when the chess pieces were placed in random positions. This suggests that the real games were probably more memorable to the chess experts because they held more meaning and significance for the expert player, full of implications for the subsequent development of the game. Similar benefits of expert knowledge have been reported for the memories of experts on football (Morris *et al.*, 1981) and experts on TV soap operas (Reeve and Aggleton, 1998).

Schemas and scripts

Schank and Abelson (1977) proposed a form of schema called a script, which combines a sequence of events that might normally be expected in a particular situation. Scripts can therefore guide our behaviour by enabling us to anticipate what will happen next. For example, a visit to a restaurant typically involves the following sequence of events and actions:

Enter restaurant / Find table / Choose seat / Sit down /
Get menu / Choose food / Order from waiter / Wait for food /
Food arrives / Eat food / Waiter brings bill / Pay bill / Leave restaurant.

This sequence provides us with a general idea of what to expect when we go to a restaurant. It will therefore come as no great surprise when a bill is presented after the meal (though the size of the bill may well be a surprise). Scripts may help us to organise our plans and our actions, by providing us with a general framework with which to organise them. They also help us to understand events and the behaviour of others.

Of course events in real life do not always follow a script in a precise and invariant manner, so it is better to think of scripts as a set of 'default' options which may be liable to alteration or even substitution. Schank (1982) recognised this point by suggesting that scripts contain various sub-components which are to some extent interchangeable. This version of script theory makes allowances for the variable nature of real-life experience and thus allows script theory to explain how people manage to deal with unusual or even quite novel situations.

Schemas and distortion

Although there have been many studies demonstrating the effect of knowledge and schemas on memory, the phenomenon of distortion has not been so extensively studied. However, there have been a few such studies, and some of these have extended the study of distortion into real-life settings. For example, Hastorf and Cantril (1954) found that fans watching an American football match subsequently recalled a highly distorted and biased version of the game, with the supporters of each team somewhat predictably recalling more fouls being committed by the opposing team.

Distortion of eyewitness testimony by previous schemas has also been investigated. Tuckey and Brewer (2003) discovered that eyewitnesses were able to provide far more accurate information about events that were consistent with their existing schemas, such as a robbery involving masked criminals carrying guns and escaping in a getaway car. However, their memory was likely to be distorted for any events they had witnessed which were inconsistent with their previous knowledge and schemas. A number of other studies have shown that eyewitness testimony for a crime or accident can also be distorted by subsequent events as well as by previously existing schemas, and these findings will be considered in Section 5.8.

Apart from the studies mentioned above, there have been relatively few studies of memory distortion since Bartlett's pioneering work. Koriat *et al.* (2001) suggest that the main reason for this is the fact that distortion cannot easily be quantified, so investigators are forced to find some qualitative means of assessment (i.e. observing the type of forgetting rather than the amount). Now that qualitative research methods are becoming more accepted it is likely that memory distortion will be studied more extensively.

Meaning and mnemonics

As Bartlett showed, people are very bad at learning things which they find meaningless. The human brain does not appear to be well suited to rote-learning, or 'parrot learning' as it is sometimes called. However, this point was understood long before Bartlett's studies, and in fact for centuries people have made use of **mnemonic** techniques which depend on adding meaning to an item. For example, if you read the number 1984747365 just once, there is very little chance that you will still remember it in ten minutes' time. In fact you have probably forgotten it already. However, try looking at the number again and this time try to imagine George Orwell (1984) sitting on a jumbo jet (747) for one year (365). By adding these associations to the numbers they become more meaningful and thus more memorable. Consequently you are not only likely to remember these numbers in ten minutes' time, but it is entirely possible that you will still remember them in ten years' time (I offer my apologies if this turns out to be the case). Essentially what we have done here is to make use of knowledge that is (probably) already in your long-term memory (LTM) store, to add meaning to a list of otherwise meaningless digits. Many techniques and tricks have been devised over the years to enable us to add some meaning to an otherwise meaningless list of numbers or words. These techniques are known as mnemonics, and you probably already know and use several. One good example is the use of mnemonics to assist with the recall of the sequential order of the colours of the spectrum, by turning it into a sentence such as 'Richard Of York Gave Battle In Vain'. The first letters of these seven words may help the retrieval of the colours of the spectrum in their correct order (red, orange, yellow, green, blue, indigo, and violet). It will be noticed that in this case the colours themselves are not devoid of meaning but their sequential order is. There are other popular mnemonics for remembering the notes on the musical scale, the number of days in each calendar month, the twelve cranial nerves, and many other items which are either meaningless or else occur in a meaningless sequence. A number of books have been written about the use of mnemonic strategies to enhance memory performance (e.g. Lorayne and Lucas, 1974; Herrmann *et al.*, 2002), and there is a section on mnemonics in Esgate and Groome (2005). Mnemonics usually work by adding meaning to items which are otherwise fairly meaningless, and their effectiveness provides evidence for the view that people are much better at memorising meaningful information which makes sense to them in terms of their previous knowledge.

5.4 Input processing and encoding

Levels of processing theory

Craik and Lockhart (1972) proposed a theory to explain the role of knowledge and meaning in memory, which in some ways borrows from schema theory in that it stresses the importance of extracting meaning from the perceptual input. Their 'levels of processing' (LOP) theory suggests that the processing of new perceptual input involves the extraction of information at a series of levels of

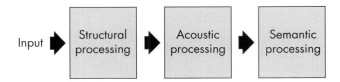

Figure 5.5 The levels of processing model
Source: Adapted from Craik and Lockhart (1972)

increasing depth of analysis, with more information being extracted at each new level (see Figure 5.5). Thus initial processing will be shallow, extracting only the more superficial features of the input such as the shape of an object (structural processing) or the sound of a word (acoustic processing). However, the input may subsequently be processed at a deeper level where more complex features are analysed, such as the meaningful content of a word (semantic processing).

The main prediction of the LOP theory is that the retention of a memory trace will depend on the depth to which it has been processed during the encoding stage. It is therefore a theory that emphasises the importance of input processing, and in fact Craik and Lockhart suggest that the memory trace is essentially a by-product of perceptual processing. Like schema theory, the LOP theory is able to explain the well-established finding that meaningful material is more memorable than non-meaningful material, by postulating that meaningful material can be more deeply processed. However, unlike schema theory, the levels of processing theory specify a number of distinct stages in the processing sequence, and then make a firm prediction that memory performance will depend on the level to which processing has progressed.

Possibly the most important aspect of the LOP theory is that it emphasises the need to carry out processing on incoming information in order to store it. Previously it had been widely assumed that information could gain entry into the long-term storage memory by merely being repeated or held for a period of time in consciousness. Craik and Lockhart argued that this is not enough, and that long-term storage can only be achieved by active processing of the input. They provided evidence in support of the levels of processing theory, based on the use of orienting tasks.

Orienting tasks

An **orienting task** is essentially a set of instructions which are intended to direct the subject towards a certain type of processing. For example, Craik and Tulving (1975) presented the same list of 60 words to three different groups of subjects, but gave each group a different orienting task to carry out. The orienting tasks were as follows:

1   **structural** (e.g. is word in block capitals?)
2   **acoustic** (e.g. does word rhyme with 'bat'?)
3   **semantic** (e.g. does word fit the sentence 'the cat sat on the ...'?)

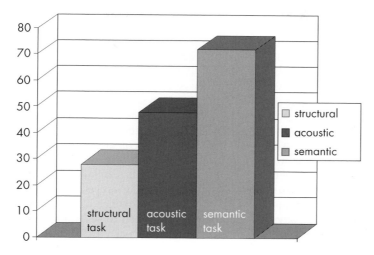

Figure 5.6 The effect of orienting task on retrieval
Source: Craik and Tulving (1975)

Craik and Tulving's results are shown in Figure 5.6. They show that tasks which require deep processing tend to produce better retrieval than do tasks which involve shallower processing, and this general finding has been confirmed by other orienting task studies (e.g. Hyde and Jenkins, 1973; Craik, 1977; Parkin, 1983). The effect of processing depth is not limited to verbal test items. For example, Winograd (1976) showed that face recognition scores were higher for subjects rating the pleasantness of each face than for subjects who were required to report on a more superficial structural feature of each face, such as whether or not it had curly hair.

The design used by Craik and Tulving for their orienting task experiment required the subjects to read through the wordlist without realising that their memory of it would later be tested. In other words it was a test of incidental learning rather than intentional learning. This technique was used in order to prevent subjects from deliberately trying to learn the wordlist, since subjects motivated to learn the words might tend to disregard the instructions to carry out a particular orienting task. It is interesting to note that when Craik (1977) instructed a group of subjects to try to learn the list deliberately, their recall scores were no better than those of the group performing a semantic orienting task. This suggests that even when we are deliberately trying to learn something we cannot do better than employ semantic processing, and this is more important than making a general effort to learn. This latter point is entirely consistent with our experience of learning in real life. You can probably remember in considerable detail many of the things you did earlier today, despite the fact that you did not at any point say to yourself, 'I must try hard to remember this.' You are likely to remember the events which you thought about, and which held some meaning or significance for you.

Levels theory revised

In its original form the LOP theory proposed a strict sequential order of processing, beginning with structural processing and then proceeding to acoustic and finally semantic processing. However, this processing sequence is not entirely plausible, since the three types of processing are qualitatively different and thus discontinuous with one another. It is difficult to see how structural, acoustic and semantic processing might somehow blend into one another. Furthermore there is some evidence (e.g. the Stroop effect) that semantic processing can sometimes take place before the 'shallower' structural and acoustic stages are complete. It was partly in answer to these criticisms that the original sequential model of processing depth was replaced by a revised version (Craik and Tulving, 1975), in which structural, acoustic and semantic processing are assumed to take place in parallel (i.e. simultaneously) rather than in sequence (see Figure 5.7). This theory assumes that any new input will be subjected to several different types of processing at the same time, though semantic processing apparently creates a more effective and lasting memory trace than the non-semantic forms of process. Craik and Tulving explained this by arguing that semantic processing offers more opportunity for elaborative encoding.

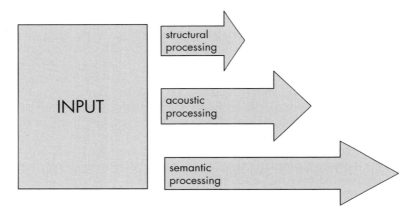

Figure 5.7 The revised levels of processing model

Elaborative encoding

Elaborative encoding refers to the formation of associative connections with other memory traces, and this occurs most effectively where meaningful associations can be found. A number of studies have confirmed that semantic elaboration does indeed create a stronger and more lasting trace (Craik and Tulving, 1975; Cherry *et al.*, 1993). The elaborative encoding theory thus proposes that semantic processing creates a large number of associative links with other items in the memory store, so that the new trace becomes incorporated into an extensive

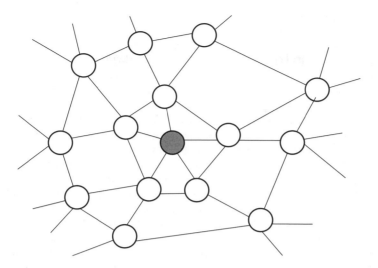

Figure 5.8 Elaborative connections between memory traces

network of interconnected memory traces, as illustrated in Figure 5.8. Since each of these associative links can serve as a potential retrieval route, the trace will be more easily retrieved because there are so many possible pathways back to it. Recent versions of the theory have therefore tended to place emphasis on the strengthening of inter-item associations and the consequent creation of additional retrieval routes which are brought about by elaborative processing (Lockhart and Craik, 1990).

An alternative view was proposed by Eysenck (1979), who provided evidence that in some cases the value of extensive input processing was that it produced a more distinctive and unique memory trace, which could be more easily retrieved because it stood out clearly from other items in storage. At the present time both the 'elaboration' and 'distinctiveness' accounts of processing depth remain plausible, and it is possible that both mechanisms may operate together.

Elaborative and maintenance rehearsal

Rehearsal is commonly employed as a method of retaining a piece of information, as for example repeating a telephone number over and over to yourself until you have the chance to write it down. Craik and Lockhart (1972) made a clear distinction between 'maintenance rehearsal', in which the input is merely repeated without further processing, and 'elaborative rehearsal', in which elaborative processing is carried out on the input. They argued that only elaborative rehearsal would lead to long-term retention of the information, and that maintenance rehearsal served only to hold it temporarily in conscious awareness and did not help to strengthen the trace.

Whilst it has certainly been found that elaborative rehearsal tends to be more effective than maintenance rehearsal, research suggests that both forms of rehearsal can improve memory, but in different ways. According to Hunt and McDaniel (1993), elaborative rehearsal assists with *relational processing* (i.e. forming new associative connections with other items), whereas maintenance rehearsal assists *item-specific processing* (i.e. strengthening the trace itself). This would explain the finding (Glenberg *et al.*, 1977) that recall tests benefit mainly from elaborative rehearsal (since associative connections are required for recall), whereas recognition tests benefit from maintenance rehearsal (since a stronger and more distinctive trace is easier to recognise).

Several studies have shown that recall scores are particularly high for test items which the subjects have used in reference to themselves (Rogers *et al.*, 1977), as for example when an orienting task requires subjects to decide whether adjectives can be used to describe them personally. This is known as the self-reference effect. It has also been found that subjects are more likely to remember items which they have generated themselves in a word association test, a phenomenon known as the generation effect (Slamecka and Graf, 1978; Smith and Healy, 1998).

Levels of processing theory today

The LOP theory has been subjected to much criticism over the years, but research has generally supported the basic underlying principle that semantic processing is more effective than non-semantic processing (Craik, 2002). There is also recent evidence from PET scans which show that semantic and non-semantic processing involve different areas of the brain (Otten and Rugg, 2001), with semantic processing mainly activating the left prefrontal cortex whilst non-semantic processing mainly activates the posterior sensory cortex. Furthermore Nyberg (2002) found that the same sensory areas of the brain which were activated during encoding were once again activated during retrieval, which is consistent with the hypothesis that a memory is a by-product of the processing it underwent at the encoding stage.

In summary, the LOP theory remains credible, and it has been very influential in recent memory research. However, the current version of LOP theory has been greatly modified since its original formulation. Perhaps the most important development has been the realisation that input processing interacts with retrieval, since elaboration of the trace at input creates a large number of potential retrieval cues.

5.5 Retrieval and retrieval cues

The effectiveness of retrieval cues

Tulving (1972) argued that the retrieval of a memory is largely cue-dependent. In other words, whether we can retrieve a memory or not will depend on the presence of suitable retrieval cues which act as reminders that help reactivate the original memory trace. There is a considerable body of evidence confirming that retrieval success is closely related to the number and quality of the retrieval cues available (Tulving, 1972; Mantyla, 1986; Hunt and Smith, 1996).

In fact memory performance can be surprisingly good when suitable cues are provided. Mantyla (1986) asked people to read a list of 600 words, and to think of three things they knew about each word. When these three self-generated cues were employed in a subsequent recall test, the average retrieval score obtained was over 90 per cent. To recall about 550 words from a list of 600 words is actually quite an impressive performance, and this finding demonstrates how good the human memory can be when given the right retrieval cues.

You can demonstrate the benefits of retrieval cues for yourself by trying to recall the names of as many British prime ministers (or US presidents) as you can. You will probably find it easy to recall a very well-known prime minister such as Winston Churchill, because the trace for Churchill will have been elaborated with a large number of associations, any of which can provide a potential connection with your memory trace for Churchill. Thus any mention of the war, spitfires, cigars, bowler hats, or vee-for-victory signs might be expected to provide direct access to the 'Churchill' memory trace. However, a less well-known prime minister such as Stanley Baldwin will be far harder to recall, since there are probably very few things that you associate with him and thus very few potential retrieval routes.

Feature overlap and the encoding specificity principle

Tulving (1972) proposed that the retrieval of an item from memory depends on the availability of retrieval cues that match up with specific aspects of the stored memory trace. Tulving called this the **encoding specificity principle** (often abbreviated to 'ESP'), since it proposes that retrieval cues will only be successful if they contain some of the same specific information which was encoded with the original input. Of course it is not necessary for *all* of the stored features of the item to be available in the retrieval cues too, but some of them must be if retrieval is to be successful. Tulving suggested that the chance of retrieving a memory trace depends on the amount of **feature overlap** between input and retrieval information, which is the extent to which features of the trace stored at input match those available at retrieval. The principle of feature overlap is illustrated in Figure 5.9.

The crucial aspect of Tulving's ESP theory is that successful retrieval depends on the interaction between encoding and retrieval information, rather than depending on either one alone. A useful analogy is the way in which a key fits a lock. Opening a locked door does not depend on either the key or the lock alone, but on whether they fit one another.

A number of studies have provided support for the ESP theory, by showing that retrieval of target items is far better when retrieval cues coincide with information encoded with the original trace (Tulving and Thomson, 1971; Klein and Murphy, 2001). For example, Tulving and Thomson (1971) showed that retrieval scores were dramatically increased when the retrieval cue was an item which had

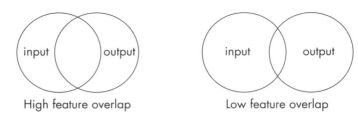

Figure 5.9 The overlap between features of the stimulus encoded at input and the features available in the retrieval cue at output

been present at the encoding stage. Their subjects were required to learn paired associates such as 'fast-river', word pairs that were deliberately chosen for their relatively weak association strength. When retrieval was tested later for the second word in each pair (e.g. river), cueing with the word presented at encoding (fast) proved to be far more effective than cueing with a stronger associate (e.g. lake) which had not been present at encoding.

In addition to these experimental studies, ESP theory also gains much credibility from the fact that it can provide a convincing explanation for many of the observed phenomena of memory function. For example, ESP theory can provide an explanation of the effects of processing depth and elaboration on retrieval (see Section 5.4). Elaborative encoding of a memory trace creates associative connections with other traces, each of which can serve as a potential retrieval route in the future (see Figure 5.10). Thus the use of elaborative processing increases the chance of feature overlap between input and output information. Feature overlap and ESP theory can also explain many other memory phenomena, including transfer-appropriate processing and context-dependent memory, which will be considered in the sections that follow.

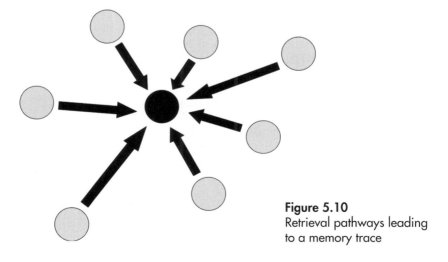

Figure 5.10
Retrieval pathways leading to a memory trace

Transfer-appropriate processing

Transfer-appropriate processing (TAP) refers to the finding that the most effective type of input processing will be whatever offers the closest match with the available retrieval cues (i.e. processing transfers from input to output stage). TAP has been demonstrated in a number of studies (e.g. Morris *et al.*, 1977; Fisher and Craik, 1977), which show that when the retrieval cues are acoustic in nature (as for example when the subject is asked to recall a word similar in sound to a cue word), then acoustic orienting tasks are found to produce superior retrieval. On the other hand, when the retrieval cues are semantic, then a semantic orienting task will produce the best retrieval (see Figure 5.11). The most effective type of input processing is thus found to be that which best matches up with the processing at the retrieval stage. This finding was originally considered to provide evidence against the levels of processing theory, since it shows that semantic processing does not always prove to be superior to non-semantic forms of processing. However, Craik (2002) points out that when the overall total number of retrieved items is considered, semantic processing still produces better recall than non-semantic processing. Thus the TAP data actually offer support for both the ESP theory and the levels of processing theory. It has also been argued that deep and elaborative processing would increase the chances of a matching of encoding data with retrieval cues, so the TAP findings are entirely consistent with the elaborative encoding version of LOP theory (Lockhart, 2002).

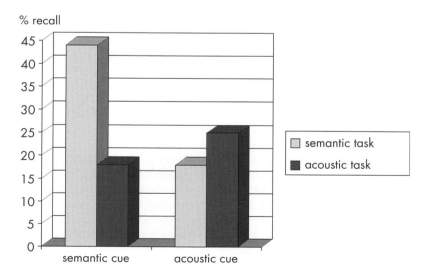

Figure 5.11 Transfer-appropriate processing
Source: Fisher and Craik (1977)

Recall and recognition

Recall and recognition are two different forms of retrieval, which are commonly employed not only in experiments but also in everyday life. The main difference between them is that in recognition the test material is presented again at the retrieval stage, and the subject merely has to decide whether or not they were presented earlier, whereas in a spontaneous recall test the subject is required to generate the test items without assistance. Between these two extremes lies cued recall, where the subject is given cues (i.e. reminders) of the target items but not the actual items themselves. There are thus three main ways of testing memory performance, which are as follows:

1 **Spontaneous recall**: requires the generation of items from memory without any help.
2 **Cued recall**: retrieval cues are provided to remind us of the items to be recalled.
3 **Recognition**: the original test items are re-presented at the retrieval stage.

It is generally found that people can recognise far more items than they can recall. For example, Mandler *et al.* (1969) presented their subjects with a list of 100 words, which were repeated 5 times. The average recall score obtained was only 38 per cent, whereas the average recognition score was 96 per cent. It is worth noting that cued recall performance usually tends to fall somewhere in between recall and recognition performance (Tulving, 1976), though the actual score will depend on the quality of the retrieval cues.

The apparent superiority of recognition performance over recall performance is so striking that clearly any theory of retrieval must provide an explanation for it. The encoding specificity principal (ESP) model of memory explains the superiority of recognition over recall by suggesting that recognition tests offer more feature overlap between input and output, since a recognition test provides more retrieval information than does a recall test (Tulving, 1976).

An alternative approach is the 'generate and recognise' (GR) theory (Kintsch, 1968; Anderson and Bower, 1972), which suggests that recall and recognition are fundamentally different processes. According to GR theory, during recall the subject must first generate possible target items spontaneously, after which the items generated are subjected to a recognition test in order to discriminate between correct and incorrect items. In a recognition test, however, there is no need for the subject to generate possible test items since the items are already in front of them. Thus recall is seen as having two stages (i.e. generate and recognise), whilst recognition has only one (i.e. recognise). This could explain why recall is more difficult than recognition.

An important feature of the GR theory is that it makes the assumption that recognition is actually one of the sub-processes of recall. This means that in theory any item that can be recalled should also be recognisable. However, it has been shown that in certain situations subjects are unable to recognise items which they can recall (Tulving and Thomson, 1973). This phenomenon is known as 'recognition failure' (short for 'recognition failure of recallable items'), and it provides strong evidence against the GR theory. Recognition failure is most easily demonstrated with a design in which strong retrieval cues are provided for recall but not for recognition. It has now been demonstrated with a number of different experimental designs (for a review see Nilsson and Gardiner, 1993), and it is one of the main reasons why GR theory is no longer widely accepted. Although not entirely discredited, the GR theory cannot rival the explanatory power of ESP theory.

Context and retrieval

It is a common observation in everyday life that returning to some earlier contextual setting can serve as a powerful cue for the retrieval of memories. You may have noticed that when you revisit some place where you spent part of your earlier life, old memories from that period tend to come flooding back, cued by the sight of a street or a building that you have not seen for many years. Sometimes a particular piece of music may bring back old memories. Even a smell or a taste can help to revive memories from the past. These are all examples of context-dependent memory, and they rely on revisiting or reinstating an earlier context which then serves as a retrieval cue.

In one of the first experimental studies of the effect of context on retrieval, Greenspoon and Ranyard (1957) tested the recall of two groups of children who had learned the same test material in the same room. However, for the retrieval test one group returned to the room where they had carried out the learning, whereas the other group were tested in a different room. It was found that the group whose learning and retrieval took place in the same room showed better retrieval than those who were tested in a different room. This finding has been confirmed by subsequent studies (e.g. Smith, 1986), and it has been shown that merely imagining the original room and its contents can assist the recall of what was learned in that room (Jerabek and Standing, 1992).

One experiment which demonstrated the phenomenon of context-dependent memory in a particularly clear manner was that of Godden and Baddeley (1975), who carried out their research on divers. The divers were required to learn a list of 40 words, either in a 'wet' context (i.e. under the sea) or in a 'dry' context (i.e. on the seashore). Similarly, recall of the list of words could be tested in either the 'wet' or 'dry' settings (see Figure 5.12). In comparison with previous studies, the two contexts used by Godden and Baddeley are very distinct and contrasting. One of the possible reasons why previous studies had produced a fairly modest context-dependent learning effect was that the contexts employed were rather similar (e.g. moving from one room to another similar room). On the other hand there are very obvious differences between sitting under the sea in full diving equipment and sitting on the seashore without it.

The recall scores obtained by Godden and Baddeley are shown in Figure 5.13. It is clear from these findings that divers who learned the wordlist underwater recalled it best when they were also tested underwater, and those who learned on dry land also produced the best recall when they were tested on dry land. The main conclusion of this experiment was that recall of the wordlist was

Figure 5.12 The 'wet' and 'dry' contexts used by Godden and Baddeley (1975)
Source: Drawing by David Groome

maximised when the context of learning (i.e. wet or dry) was reinstated for the recall test. However, a subsequent experiment suggested that context reinstatement tended to assist recall but not recognition (Godden and Baddeley, 1980), possibly because contextual features act as retrieval cues, which are particularly scarce in a recall test.

The context reinstated in the above experiments was predominantly visual in nature, though clearly other sense modalities might also have made a contribution. Subsequent studies have shown that retrieval can be enhanced by the reinstatement of cues relating to specific odours. Chu and Downes (2000) found that odours could also act as strong cues to the retrieval of events from early life, a finding which has been referred to as the 'Proust phenomenon' as it parallels the observations of Marcel Proust about the evocative nature of odours.

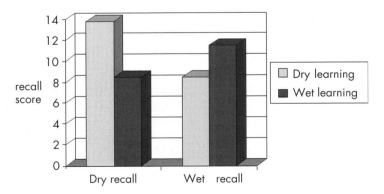

Figure 5.13 The recall of words by divers under 'wet' and 'dry' learning and retrieval conditions
Source: Godden and Baddeley (1975)

The phenomenon of context-dependent learning has now been convincingly demonstrated by a large number of studies. Davies and Thomson (1988) reviewed twenty-nine context reinstatement studies, and they reported that twenty-seven of them had confirmed the occurrence of improved recall with context reinstatement, and only two studies failed to find such an improvement. Eich (1985) suggested that such negative findings might reflect a failure of the test item to become strongly connected to its learning context, and he demonstrated that the effect of context reinstatement was increased when subjects were instructed to form images of the test items in their context rather than alone. Smith and Vela (2001) found that context reinstatement has a greater effect when the subject is actually paying attention to their surroundings rather than engaging in introspective thought.

In some cases the effect of context reinstatement may be masked by distraction or stress caused by the context. Thompson et al. (2001) compared wordlist recall for subjects who were either on the ground or skydiving during their learning and recall trials. In this case no significant context reinstatement effect was found, but this was probably due to the relatively poor memory performance of subjects during skydiving. Most of us would probably find it difficult to concentrate on a wordlist whilst falling freely from an aircraft at high altitude, so it is perhaps not surprising that recall scores were low and that context reinstatement did not significantly improve them. Interestingly, Thompson et al. did succeed in finding context effects when subjects merely watched a video of skydiving during learning and recall trials, rather than actually jumping out of an aircraft.

The occurrence of context-dependent memory clearly fits in very well with ESP theory, which predicts that retrieval depends on the amount of feature overlap, including feature overlap for contextual information.

State-dependent and mood-dependent memory

A phenomenon related to context-dependent learning is the finding that retrieval can be assisted by the reinstatement of a particular mental state at the retrieval stage which was also present at the learning stage. For example, several studies have shown that subjects who were in a state of alcoholic intoxication at the learning stage of the experiment would recall the test items more readily if they were again intoxicated during the recall test (e.g. Goodwin et al., 1969). Apparently the experience of being drunk constitutes a form of inner context which can help to cue memories. This phenomenon is known as 'state-dependent memory', and it has also been reported with other variations in mental state, such as depression. Bower et al. (1978) found that retrieval of a wordlist was slightly better if the subject was in the same depressed mood at retrieval as they had been in at the learning stage. In this experiment depressed mood states were induced by the use of hypnosis. Another study (Bower, 1981) showed that when asked to recall events from earlier in their lives, subjects in a depressed mood tended to recall a disproportionate number of sad and depressing events, whereas non-depressed subjects tended to recall rather more of their happier experiences. This phenomenon is more accurately referred to as mood-congruent memory rather than mood-dependent memory, since the subject retrieves words which are congruent with their present depressed mood but which are not actually known to have been present during a previous depressed phase.

The finding that memory can be mood-dependent has significance not only for theories of memory and retrieval but also for theories of depression. It has been suggested that some people are prone to depression because they have a cognitive bias to perceiving the more depressing aspects of their experience and not to noticing the more positive aspects (Beck *et al.*, 1979). Mood-dependent retrieval might perpetuate this selective cognition, by making a depressed person more likely to recall experiences from previous periods of depression, thus trapping them in a cycle of selective cognition leading to further depression. The phenomenon of mood-dependent retrieval is not a particularly strong or reliable effect (Bower and Mayer, 1989), but it has important implications.

The effect of context reinstatement has been clearly established in many lab experiments, but it has also proved to be of great practical value in helping eyewitnesses to improve their retrieval of events such as crimes they have witnessed. This finding has led to the development of the cognitive interview, which is considered in more detail in Section 5.8.

5.6 Memory systems

Episodic and semantic memory

Some theorists have argued that the LTM contains a number of separate memory systems. For example, Tulving (1972) has made a distinction between **episodic memory**, which is our memory for events and episodes in our own lives, and **semantic memory**, which is essentially our general knowledge store. Perhaps the most important difference between these two memory systems is that episodic memory involves the retrieval of a personal experience associated with a particular context (i.e. the place and time when it occurred), whereas semantic memory involves the retrieval of facts and information (such as the meanings of words), which are not attached to any particular context.

Tulving pointed out that most memory retrieval in everyday life and in psychology experiments tends to involve episodic memory. For example, in a typical experiment on the retrieval of a list of words, you might be asked if the word 'dog' was on the list. In fact you are not being asked to recall any information about dogs, or even what the word 'dog' means. You are being asked whether the word 'dog' was on that particular wordlist, presented in a particular place and time. In other words, you are being asked to recall the *context* in which you heard the word 'dog'. In contrast, there are occasions where we are required to retrieve general knowledge about some item, without reference to any specific context or event, as for example if you were asked to explain what a 'dog' is, or whether it has four legs and a tail. This type of retrieval involves semantic memory, and it is essentially context-free. Other psychologists have come up with their own terms for episodic and semantic memory, notably Warrington (1986) who refers to 'memory for events' and 'memory for facts'.

Tulving points out that a semantic memory represents an item which has been experienced many times (e.g. eating food), so its retrieval may depend on repetition and the consequent increase of associative strength. However, an episodic memory involves a specific event which has occurred only once (e.g. eating dinner last night), so its retrieval is likely to be entirely dependent on feature overlap since a single event offers no opportunity to strengthen associative connections.

The distinction between semantic and episodic memory received some initial support from reports that patients suffering from organic amnesia appeared to be selectively impaired in their ability to recall specific episodes and events, whilst showing little impairment in their ability to recall semantic knowledge (Tulving, 1983; Warrington, 1986). These conclusions have been questioned in recent years because most amnesics tend to show some impairment of semantic memory too, but certainly there are some amnesics who show episodic impairment with a relatively intact semantic memory (Tulving, 2001; Rosenbaum et al., 2005). This issue will be considered in more detail in Chapter 7.

Rather more convincing evidence for a dissociation between episodic and semantic memories has come from brain scan studies, which have shown that episodic and semantic recall tasks produce activation in quite different areas of the brain. It has been found that the recall of semantic knowledge produces activation primarily in the left temporal lobe, whereas the recall of contextual episodes causes activation of the right prefrontal area (Buckner, 2000).

The exact relationship between semantic and episodic memory remains uncertain. Tulving (1972) originally regarded them as two quite separate memory stores, but more recently (Tulving, 1987) he has suggested that semantic and episodic memories probably represent different processes within essentially the same memory storage system, with each semantic memory being derived from the occurrence of a series of memories for related episodic events.

Tulving (2001) argues that episodic memory involves a higher level of consciousness than semantic memory, and probably represents a more recently evolved memory process than semantic memory. Indeed Tulving suggests that episodic memory may be unique to humans. He speculates that non-human mammals (such as cats and dogs) may be restricted to recalling the more general kind of knowledge available from semantic memory, and are probably unable to consciously recollect specific events from their past experience. Of course this hypothesis is entirely speculative since we cannot ask a dog to describe its experiences.

Familiarity and recollection

Another theory distinguishing between two memory sytems is that of Mandler (1980), who argues that recognition involves two different retrieval processes. The first is a judgement of **familiarity**, which simply involves deciding whether or not an item has ever been encountered before. The second is the **recollection** of when and where the item was encountered (i.e. recollection of context). Mandler's main evidence for making this distinction is the fact that it is possible

Figure 5.14 Familiar faces – but who are they? (You can find their names at the end of this chapter.)

Source: © BARIL PASCAL/CORBIS KIPA; © Rune Hellestad/CORBIS; © Reuters/Corbis; © Focus Features/ZUMA/Corbis

to find someone's face familiar and yet be unable to recall the context in which we have met them before. This is actually a common experience in everyday life and all of us will have experienced it at some time, especially when we meet an acquaintance outside their usual context. For example, if you happen to meet your local greengrocer on the bus, you may find, at least for a moment, that although his face is very familiar you cannot remember who he is. At this stage the person's familiarity has been established but the setting from which they are familiar cannot be recollected. This may come to us later, but recollecting actual occasions when we have previously met the person usually requires some thought. The crucial point here is that it is evidently possible to have familiarity without context recollection, demonstrating that they must be separate retrieval processes (see Figure 5.14).

The main distinction between familiarity and recollection is that one involves context retrieval and the other does not. There is therefore some overlap here with the episodic/semantic distinction, though in the case of familiarity/recollection the systems are essentially mechanisms of retrieval. Mandler suggests that familiarity and recollection probably operate as two independent retrieval routes, which may be used either separately or in combination.

Mandler (1980) pointed out that a familiarity judgement seems to be an automatic process, something which occurs without any conscious effort or volition (see Chapter 1 for the differences between automatic and controlled processes). When you recognise someone's face in a crowd, their familiarity seems to jump out at you automatically. No effort is required, and you cannot prevent yourself from making this familiarity judgement. Recollection, on the other hand, seems to be a controlled process, and one which requires some degree of volition, conscious attention and effort. This theory receives further support from the finding (Parkin *et al.*, 1995; Jenkins *et al.*, 2002) that performing a second task during presentation of the faces has no effect on the accuracy of face familiarity judgements, whereas recollection scores are significantly reduced.

Another interesting recent finding is that sleeping directly after a learning session leads to an improvement in contextual recollection but does not assist familiarity judgements (Drosopoulos *et al.*, 2005). It has also been found that amnesic patients appear to show relatively unimpaired familiarity judgements but severely impaired context recollection (Huppert and Piercy, 1976; King *et al.*, 2004). This finding will be discussed further in Chapter 7.

The R & K ('remember and know') procedure

The 'Remember and Know' (R & K) procedure was introduced by Tulving (1985), and it involves asking subjects to indicate whether their recognition responses are based on consciously remembering the presentation of a test item (the 'R' score), or on simply knowing that the item appeared without a specific memory of seeing it (the 'K' score). Thus the R & K distinction in some ways resembles that between familiarity and recollection.

Using the R & K procedure, Gardiner and Parkin (1990) found that 'remember' (R) scores for verbal items were significantly reduced when the subject was distracted by a second task during the learning of the list, but divided attention had no discernible effect on the 'know' (K) scores. Similar results were obtained by Parkin *et al.* (1995) using face recognition rather than verbal items. These findings suggest that 'remember' scores depend on full and undivided conscious attention at the learning stage, whereas 'know' scores do not. Another difference between 'R' and 'K' scores is that semantic orientic tasks produce higher 'R' scores than do non-semantic tasks, whereas 'K' scores are unaffected by processing depth (Gardiner and Java, 1993).

Based on such findings, Gardiner (2002) argues that R & K scores reflect two different underlying memory processes. However, there is some doubt as to the exact nature of these two factors. Tulving (1985) regarded the R & K scores as a measure of episodic and semantic memory respectively. However, Parkin (2000) suggests that R & K scores may correspond more closely with Mandler's distinction between familiarity and recollection.

Implicit and explicit memory

Most tests of memory involve the direct testing of what the subject is able to consciously remember and report, which is known as **explicit memory**. Tests of recall and recognition are both examples of explicit memory, and for many years this was the only type of memory to be studied. However, recently there has been an increasing interest in the use of more indirect memory tests detecting

implicit memory, which is a memory for which the individual has no conscious awareness. Although such memories cannot be deliberately and consciously retrieved, their existence is implicit in the behaviour of the individual (hence the term 'implicit memory') because it affects their performance on certain tasks.

Jacoby and Dallas (1981) demonstrated the existence of implicit memory by showing that subjects who had studied a list of words subsequently found those words easier to identify than unstudied words, even when they had lost any conscious memory of the words on the list. In another key experiment, Tulving *et al.* (1982) presented their subjects with a list of words, then later on (when the wordlist had been largely forgotten), they asked their subjects to produce the first word they could think of to complete a fragmented word. For example, if the original target word was 'telephone' then the fragmented word might be '-el-p-o-e'. Half of the words in the test had been studied earlier, but the other half had not. Most subjects were able to complete far more of the fragmented words which had been previously studied, even for words which they were unable to identify in a recognition test. Indeed, subjects were found to be equally likely to complete a fragmented word with the previously primed target word regardless of whether that word could be recognised or not. The initial presentation of the wordlist in these experiments was carried out in a way that involved presenting the words as part of some other task, so that the subject was not required to learn the words and was quite unaware that they would be tested later. This kind of presentation is known as 'priming', and it is a useful technique in an implicit memory experiment because although the subject is exposed to the words they do not attempt to learn them and thus tend to have no explicit memory of them later.

The significance of these experiments is that they demonstrated that priming a word could influence subsequent performance on a test of implicit memory, even when the word could not be recognised explicitly. Similar effects have been obtained with a variety of implicit memory tests, including word-stem completion (e.g. complete the word 'tel—') and anagram solution (e.g. solve the anagram 'leopetneh'). Such tasks are used to guide recall towards the primed items, but subjects are not actually required to recall the primed words. They are simply asked to produce the first suitable word that comes into their head.

Parkin *et al.* (1990) investigated the effect of divided attention on implicit and explicit memory by priming subjects with a list of target words whilst distracting them with a second task. They found that divided attention during priming caused a marked deterioration in a subsequent test of explicit memory (word recognition), but had no effect on the performance of an implicit task (fragment completion). These findings suggest that implicit memory does not require full conscious attention. Graf *et al.* (1984) found that implicit memory is also unaffected by the level of input processing carried out, whereas explicit memory benefits from semantic processing rather than non-semantic processing.

These studies suggest that explicit memory requires full attention and deep semantic processing, but implicit memory does not. This finding is consistent with the suggestion that implicit memory draws mainly on data-driven processing (such as the identification of perceptual features of the target item), whilst explicit memory may depend more on schema-driven processing (Hayman and Tulving, 1989).

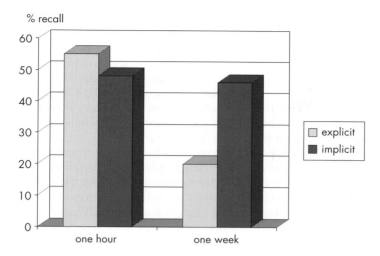

Figure 5.15 Scores for recognition (explicit) and fragment completion (implicit) after retention intervals of one hour and one week

Source: Tulving *et al.* (1982)

Further evidence for the distinction between implicit and explicit memory arises from the finding that implicit memories seem to be more durable and lasting than explicit memories. Tulving *et al.* (1982) showed that implicit memory tends to survive for very long periods of time, often continuing to influence responses long after the subject has lost any ability to retrieve the target items explicitly. Their results are shown in Figure 5.15. It seems that memories can remain in store at an unconscious level for very long periods, but that people may gradually lose the ability to access them consciously.

The distinction between implicit and explicit memory has received further support from the finding that organic amnesic patients show impaired explicit memory but relatively intact implicit memory (Graf *et al.*, 1984; Conroy *et al.*, 2005). These findings will be examined in Chapter 7.

Implicit memory in everyday life

The existence of implicit memory has led to speculation about its possible influence in everyday life. For example, Claxton (1998) suggests that implicit memory may be the mechanism underlying intuition, or 'hunches'. Sometimes we may not be sure of the answer to a question, but we have a hunch that a certain answer is probably correct. This probably reflects the retrieval of an implicit memory. It has also been suggested that implicit memory may be the mechanism underlying the phenomenon of 'conversational plagiarism' (Parkin, 1993), where someone unwittingly repeats a word they have just heard without being aware of having heard it. You have probably noticed this yourself at some time. One person happens to use an unusual word during a conversation, such as 'exquisite' or 'fortuitous', and shortly afterwards a different person will use that same word, without being aware of having copied it. Hearing the word has apparently heightened its level of activation in the memory of the listener, so that they are more likely to use the word themselves despite having no conscious recollection of hearing it spoken. This phenomenon occurs frequently in everyday life, but it has also been demonstrated in experimental studies (Brown and Murphy, 1989). In fact it was first noted by Taylor (1965), who referred to it as 'cryptomnesia'.

Brown (2004) suggests that implicit memory may also explain the occurrence of 'déjà vu', which is the feeling that you have experienced something before when in fact you have not. This is basically a mistaken judgement of familiarity, and although it is a rare occurrence most people will probably have experienced it a few times. Brown considers that the déjà vu experience occurs when some new situation triggers an implicit memory for some similar experience in the past, which can no longer be recalled in a conscious and explicit manner.

It has also been suggested that implicit memory may help to explain the occurrence of distressing intrusive memories in patients suffering from PTSD (Post-Traumatic Stress Disorder), and possibly also the repressed traumatic memories which trouble many neurotic patients. Implicit memory shares certain characteristics with repressed traumatic memories, in that both are unconscious, largely unprocessed, cue-dependent, and essentially physical in nature. However, there are ways in which implicit memory differs from repressed memories so there is some disagreement over whether or not they share a common underlying mechanism (Milchmann, 2003).

Automaticity and the process dissociation procedure

Jacoby (1991) argues that both implicit memory and familiarity judgements reflect the same underlying mechanism, which is unconscious automatic processing. Explicit memory and recollection are thought to reflect conscious effortful processing. However, Jacoby points out that the test procedures used to measure implicit memory and familiarity do not measure automatic and effortful processing in a pure and uncontaminated form. For example, scores obtained on an explicit recognition task are likely to reflect a combination of automatic and effortful retrieval. Jacoby claims that tests of explicit and implicit memory provide *task* distinctions rather than *process* distinctions, since the tasks employed do not directly correspond with underlying cognitive processes.

Jacoby devised a method known as 'process dissociation procedure', which is intended to distinguish between pure retrieval processes rather than merely between tasks. A wordlist is presented which is later subjected to two different types of retrieval test, known as the 'inclusion' and 'exclusion' tasks, as follows:

Inclusion task: subjects are instructed to respond to retrieval cues by making deliberate use of the previously primed words where possible.

Exclusion task: subjects are instructed to respond to the retrieval cues deliberately *avoiding* the use of the previously primed words if possible.

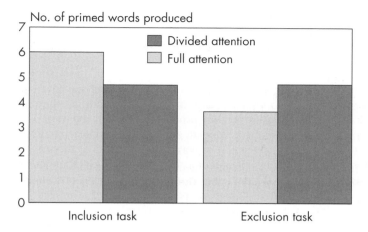

Figure 5.16 Scores obtained on inclusion and exclusion tasks following encoding under conditions of full or divided attention
Source: Jacoby *et al.* (1993)

Jacoby argued that the 'inclusion' condition measures the combined efforts of conscious and unconscious retrieval. However, in the 'exclusion' condition, conscious and unconscious retrieval are working in opposite directions (i.e. the subject is consciously excluding primed words but is unconsciously including them). Thus any primed words generated by the exclusion task will be words that were not consciously recalled. This rather complex manipulation is intended to allow the contributions of conscious and unconscious retrieval to be calculated in a reasonably pure form.

Jacoby *et al.* (1993) made use of the process dissociation procedure to confirm that divided attention during priming has different effects on the conscious and unconscious components of retrieval. Their results are shown in Figure 5.16. Under full attention learning conditions the inclusion task produced far higher scores than did the exclusion task, presumably because conscious recollection helps the former but hinders the latter. However, with divided attention the influence of conscious recollection is reduced, so inclusion scores and exclusion scores are virtually the same now that both are reduced to a largely unconscious response.

The process dissociation procedure has been widely used in recent years, but some of its basic assumptions have been questioned. For example, Graf and Komatsu (1994) have cast doubt on the claim that it can isolate pure measures of the conscious and unconscious components of memory. Richardson-Klavehn and Gardiner (1995) have also found evidence for an involuntary effect of conscious memory in a process dissociation task, thus disputing the previous assumption that conscious memory was always voluntary and that unconscious memory was always involuntary. The original authors, however, maintain that process dissociation procedure still provides the best available means of separating automatic and effortful retrieval processes (Toth *et al.*, 1995; Yonelinas, 2002).

Processes underlying different memory systems

It is interesting to note that the dissociations found between implicit/explicit memory closely resemble those found between familiarity/recollection. In each case there are differential effects of divided attention, processing depth, and impairment in amnesic patients. One might therefore speculate that implicit memory and familiarity may be related in some way, and that they may possibly reflect the same underlying memory processes. Implicit memory and familiarity judgements appear to share a dependence on unconscious automatic retrieval processes, involving the activation of perceptual features of the trace rather than associative and contextual connections. In contrast, explicit memory and recollection seem to share a dependence on controlled effortful processes, and make use of associative inter-item links. One possible view is that implicit memory and familiarity judgements both involve the retrieval of automatically processed perceptual features of a trace, but whereas familiarity involves the recognition of that trace, implicit memory corresponds with the equivalent recall process.

Some theorists have argued that the episodic/semantic distinction also relates to these systems. Schacter *et al.* (2000) argue that semantic memory is essentially a form of implicit memory whilst episodic memory is explicit. Their classification of memory systems is illustrated in Figure 5.17. Although this classification of memory systems is fairly widely accepted, alternative classification systems have been put forward, especially by those who work on amnesic patients. These views will be considered in more detail in Chapter 7.

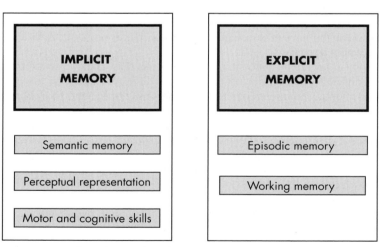

Figure 5.17 Types of implicit and explicit memory
Source: Based on Schacter *et al.* (2000)

5.7 Decay, disuse and retrieval inhibition

Decay with disuse

As explained in Section 5.2, memories tend to fade away with the passage of time, a phenomenon originally recorded by Ebbinghaus (1885). Whereas Ebbinghaus suggested that memories might decay spontaneously with time, Thorndike (1914) argued that decay only occurs when a memory is left unused for a long period. This theory was known as the 'decay with disuse' theory, and an updated version of this theory has recently been proposed by Bjork and Bjork (1992). They argue that a memory trace which is not retrieved will eventually become inaccessible, whereas a frequently retrieved memory trace will be strengthened and becomes easier to retrieve in the future. They call this theory the New Theory of Disuse (NTD), and there is a good deal of evidence supporting it. The most important feature of the New Theory of Disuse is the assumption that retrieving an item strengthens its subsequent retrievability, and many studies have confirmed that this does indeed occur (Landauer and Bjork, 1978; Payne, 1987; Macrae and MacLeod, 1999). Thus the act of retrieval is in itself a learning event, and this finding has important implications for real-life learning such as exam revision. These findings suggest that learning and revision techniques will be more effective if they involve active retrieval of the target items rather than merely reading them in a passive way. So if you are revising for an exam, you should try to find ways of practising and testing your retrieval of the material rather than just reading it through.

A further implication of the NTD is that retrieving one item successfully will inhibit the retrieval of other unretrieved items. Recently a great deal of evidence has accumulated in support of this hypothesis, most notably the discovery of **retrieval-induced forgetting**.

Retrieval-induced forgetting (RIF)

It has recently been discovered (Anderson *et al.*, 1994) that the successful retrieval of a memory trace inhibits the retrieval of rival memory traces. For example, if you practise the retrieval of a particular word, you will subsequently find it harder to retrieve other related or similar words. This phenomenon is known as retrieval-induced forgetting (RIF).

Anderson *et al.* demonstrated the RIF effect by presenting their subjects with a series of word pairs, each consisting of a category word and an example of an item from that category (e.g. fruit-banana). The list contained further items from the same category (e.g. fruit-apple), and others from different categories (e.g. drink-whisky). Half of the items from certain categories (e.g. fruit) were subjected to retrieval practice. A subsequent recall test, using the category word as a cue, showed that retrieval of these practised items was greatly improved, as you would expect. But the unpractised items from the same category proved to be very difficult to recall, more difficult in fact than items from a completely unpractised category. So, for example, retrieving 'banana' inhibited the recall

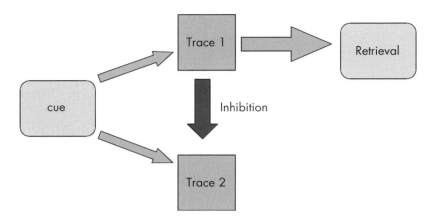

Figure 5.18 Retrieval-inducing forgetting

of 'apple', because it belongs to the same (tested) category. But retrieving 'banana' did not inhibit 'whisky' because it belongs to an unrelated (and untested) category. Anderson *et al.*, concluded that the retrieval of an item from a particular category somehow inhibits the retrieval of other items from the same category (see Figure 5.18).

The RIF phenomenon has now been confirmed by a large number of studies (e.g. Anderson *et al.*, 2000; MacLeod and Macrae, 2001; Groome and Grant, 2005). It has been shown that RIF only occurs as a consequence of retrieval, and is not brought about by passive study such as re-reading test items (Anderson *et al.*, 2000). Furthermore a retrieved item only generates inhibition in a rival item which interferes with it, and it does not apparently inhibit other unrelated items (Anderson *et al.* 1994). For example, Anderson *et al.* (1994) reported that frequently encountered items (e.g. banana) produced a strong RIF effect on other items from the same category (i.e. fruit), whereas less frequently occurring items (e.g. guava) produced very little RIF. This finding probably reflects the fact that frequently paired items create more interference with one another, so that inhibition is required in order that one item can be retrieved while the other is suppressed.

Studies of RIF inhibition arising from a single retrieval event suggest that the effect lasts for only about a day or so (MacLeod, 2002). However, it is possible that RIF could lead to more lasting memory inhibition if an item was subjected to repeated RIF inhibitions over a long period of time. This raises the possibility that RIF could explain the long-term forgetting which occurs in disused memory traces, as hypothesised in the New Theory of Disuse (Bjork and Bjork, 1992).

RIF in real life

The discovery of retrieval-induced forgetting raises an obvious question – what is this mechanism for? Anderson (2003) suggests that the purpose of RIF is to suppress unwanted memories, so that we can retrieve the items we actually require. RIF thus serves the function of helping memory to be more selective, by reducing interference from rival items.

It is easy to see how such an inhibitory mechanism might have evolved, because selective retrieval of this kind would offer benefits in many real-life situations. For example, remembering where you left your car in a large car park would be extremely difficult if you had equally strong memories for every previous occasion on which you had ever parked your car (see Figure 5.19). A mechanism that activated the most recent memory of parking your car, whilst inhibiting the memories of all previous occasions, would be extremely helpful (Anderson and Neely, 1996).

If the RIF mechanism really has evolved in order to facilitate selective retrieval, then we might expect RIF to produce benefits in real-life settings. Such benefits have in fact now been found. In a recent study (Groome and Grant, 2005) we investigated the relationship between RIF and everyday forgetting as measured by the Cognitive Failures Questionnaire (CFQ). The CFQ, devised by Broadbent *et al.* (1982), is a standard measure of everyday forgetting, and it includes items such as 'Do you forget where you put something like a newspaper or a book?' and 'Do you forget why you went from one part of the house to another?' We found that the susceptibility of individual subjects to RIF was inversely correlated with CFQ scores, meaning that participants with a relatively strong RIF mechanism tended to report fewer cognitive failures in everyday life. Our data therefore support the hypothesis that individuals who lack an effective memory inhibition mechanism will be more forgetful in real-life settings.

Macrae and MacLeod (1999) showed that retrieval-induced forgetting affects exam revision. Their subjects were required to sit a mock geography exam, which

Figure 5.19 Where did you leave your car?

involved learning twenty facts about two fictitious islands. One group of subjects practised the retrieval of ten of these facts intensively whilst the other group did not. Subsequent testing revealed that the first group achieved excellent recall for the ten facts they had practised (as you might expect), but their recall of the ten unpractised facts was far worse than that achieved by the control group who had not carried out any additional practice. These findings confirm the occurrence of RIF in an examination setting, but they also hold possible implications for exam revision techniques. Macrae and MacLeod suggest that last-minute cramming before an examination may sometimes do more harm than good, because it helps the recall of a few practised items only at the expense of poorer recall for all of the others.

Shaw, Bjork and Handal (1995) have also demonstrated the occurrence of RIF in an experiment on eyewitness testimony. Their subjects watched a slide show about a crime, after which they were tested for their recall of what they had just seen. It was found that the successful retrieval of some details of the crime inhibited the retrieval of other items. Shaw *et al.* concluded that in real crime investigations there was a risk that police questioning of a witness could lead to the subsequent inhibition of any information not retrieved during the initial interview. However, MacLeod (2002) reported that these inhibitory effects tended to subside about 24 hours after the initial questioning, so a second interview with the same eyewitness might produce further retrieval so long as the two interviews were separated by at least 24 hours.

Perhaps the most intriguing implication of the RIF phenomenon is that it suggests that forgetting may have a purpose. For centuries it has been assumed that forgetting is caused by a failure or inadequacy of the memory system, but RIF research suggests that forgetting may be caused by an inhibitory mechanism whose purpose is to discard unwanted memories in order to facilitate selective retrieval.

Retrieval inhibition and psychiatric disorders

Retrieval-induced forgetting and the New Theory of Disuse may have implications for the understanding and treatment of neurotic disorders. Although neuroses have not traditionally been regarded as disorders of memory as such, it is clear that neuroses often do involve memories, so it is possible that memory mechanisms could play a part in causing or maintaining neurotic symptoms. For example, Lang *et al.* (1999) argue that phobias involve anxiety produced in response to some specific stimulus, such as a traumatic memory. In accordance with the New Theory of Disuse and the RIF phenomenon, Lang *et al.* argue that phobic responses may be strengthened by repeated retrieval, which would also suppress alternative memory responses to the same stimulus, responses which might have been less distressing. Lang *et al.* suggest that phobic patients might benefit from practising the retrieval of alternative (non-fearful) responses to the stimulus, in order to inhibit the phobic response. For example, a person who has acquired a spider phobia through some earlier bad experience with a spider should practise retrieving alternative memories of spiders which are less distressing. As you may have noticed, the treatments advocated by Lang *et al.* are basically similar to existing treatments such as cognitive behaviour therapy and progressive desensitisation (which have incidentally proved to be very effective treatments for phobia). However, Lang *et al.* emphasise the need to practise the retrieval of alternative memory traces, rather than just trying to extinguish a conditioned response by removing reinforcement.

It is possible that memory retrieval and inhibition could play a part in other neurotic disorders such as panic attacks and reactive depression, which may also in some cases be triggered by a memory of some past event.

Victims of severe traumatic events such as wars and earthquakes often suffer later on from intrusive memories which can cause great distress for many years (Horowitz, 1976; Brewin, 1998; Groome and Soureti, 2004). In fact intrusive memories are among the most important symptoms of PTSD (Post-Traumatic Stress Disorder), and it is possible that RIF phenomena could provide an explanation. The distressing intrusive memories may have been strengthened by repeated retrieval whilst other related memory traces may have been suppressed by RIF (Anderson, 2001). As before, the suggested therapy would involve repeated retrieval practice of neutral memories in response to the same stimulus.

The suggestion that anxiety disorders can be triggered by memories stored at an unconscious level is not of course new, as this idea lies at the heart of Freudian psychoanalytic theories of neurosis. However, the Freudian view was derived from theories about the dynamic interaction of hypothetical forces within the personality, and made no direct reference to memory mechanisms as such. Freud proposed that memories could be repressed into the unconscious because they were distressing or unacceptable, but no clear explanation was ever provided for the mechanism of repression. Anderson (2001) suggests that the phenomenon of repression (i.e. the selective forgetting of disturbing traumatic memories) could be explained by inhibitory mechanisms activated by the retrieval of competing memories. For example, he points out that victims of child abuse are often unable to recall the abusive event, especially if the abuser was a close relative rather than a stranger. Anderson argues that there would be many other memories of events involving the relative, which would be in competition with the memory for the abusive incident and thus likely to inhibit its retrieval.

The treatments advocated on the basis of RIF are as yet largely untested, but they do clearly offer some exciting alternatives to traditional therapy. In some ways they advocate an approach to neurosis which contrasts with the traditional psychoanalytical view. According to Freudian theory, it is necessary for the therapist to identify the repressed memories believed to underlie a neurotic condition, in order to bring them out into the open. It is assumed that uncovering a traumatic memory in this way will be somehow cathartic, and will help to release the patient from its effects. However, retrieval inhibition theory suggests that the traumatic memory needs to be inhibited in order to keep from being retrieved, a goal which is essentially the opposite of the Freudian approach, and one which has very different implications for therapy.

5.8 Memory in everyday life

Ecological validity

One major criticism which can be directed at the majority of memory research is that it tends to involve rather artificial situations which are unlikely to occur outside a laboratory. You might like to consider when was the last time you were asked during your normal day-to-day life to retain three letters in your short-term memory whilst counting backwards (Peterson and Peterson, 1959) or to complete word-stems whilst deliberately trying to exclude previously primed words (Jacoby *et al.*, 1993). Unless your life is very different from mine, I suspect that these will not have been common events. These are tasks that simply do not occur in everyday life. Of course, laboratory experiments do have an important function, as they enable us to isolate processes like implicit memory which are not otherwise seen in a pure form. Such processes probably do play a major part in everyday memory but usually in combination with other processes, hence the need for artificial experiments to isolate them. However, whilst accepting the value of laboratory experiments, Neisser (1976) has argued that memory should also be investigated in real-life settings where the conditions are completely natural. He describes this approach as seeking ecological validity. In recent years there has been an increasing amount of work on memory in real-life settings, including studies of autobiographical memory, **flashbulb memory**, and eyewitness testimony.

Autobiographical memory

How much can you remember about the events in your life up till now? How well can you remember your school-days? How many of your teachers and school-mates can you name? You might like to spend a few moments testing yourself on these questions. Better still, fish out an old school photograph (like the one in Figure 5.20), to provide a few retrieval cues. You will probably be surprised how much you can retrieve from the distant past, often about people and events you had not thought about for many years. Bahrick *et al.* (1975) investigated the ability of American adults to remember their old high school classmates from an old school photograph, and found that most of their subjects could still match up the names and photos of more than 80 per cent of their college classmates even 25 years after graduation. In fact there was no significant decline in their performance over the years since the actual period when they had graduated. Although scores did drop off slightly at longer retention intervals, they still remained above 70 per cent despite an average time lapse of 47 years. Bahrick *et al.* concluded that memory for real-life experiences tends to be far more accurate and durable than memory for items tested in a laboratory experiment. This is probably because autobiographical memories have far greater personal significance to the individual than do the test items in a lab experiment.

One problem with the study of autobiographical memory is that it is often difficult to check its accuracy. You may be quite sure that you remember the

Figure 5.20 An old school photograph
(The author is on the front row, second from the right, next to the boy wearing a tie)

events of your sixteenth birthday clearly and accurately, but this does not mean that your memories are correct. A number of investigators, notably Linton (1975) and Wagenaar (1986), deliberately kept very detailed diaries of their own daily experiences over a period of many years, which could later be used to check the accuracy of their retrieval. Linton (1975) found that items which had been tested previously were far more likely to be retrieved later on, presumably because retrieval provided reactivation of the item and kept retrieval routes open. Linton's results are thus consistent with laboratory findings showing that frequent retrieval strengthens a memory trace (Landauer and Bjork, 1978; Payne, 1987), and with the New Theory of Disuse (Bjork and Bjork, 1992) discussed in the previous section.

Wagenaar (1986) kept a detailed diary over many years, but he also took the trouble to record retrieval cues for later use. By this means he was able to establish that the likelihood of retrieval depended on the number of retrieval cues available. With suitable cues Wagenaar recalled about half of the events recorded over the previous six years. Wagenaar's findings are therefore in broad agreement with the usual laboratory finding that successful retrieval depends on the availability of suitable retrieval cues (Tulving, 1972).

Both Linton and Wagenaar noted that their recall of past events showed a strong bias towards the recall of pleasant events rather than unpleasant ones. There are several possible explanations for this retrieval bias. Psychoanalytic theory suggests that we tend to repress our more unpleasant memories as a means of self-protection (Freud, 1938). Another theory is that unpleasant memories have often been acquired in stressful situations, which may have inhibited memory input (Williams *et al.*, 1988). A third possibility is that pleasant memories are more frequently retrieved and rehearsed than unpleasant ones because people prefer to think about pleasant events when reminiscing about the past (Searleman and Herrmann, 1994).

Rubin *et al.* (1986) found that most subjects tend to recall more information from recent years than from the distant past, and these findings are consistent with decay and interference theory (see Section 5.2), both of which predict that memories will become less accessible with the passing of time. One exception to these general findings is that older subjects tend to recall relatively few recent events but an increased amount from their early adult years (Rubin *et al.*, 1998), a phenomenon known as the 'reminiscence bump'. For example, Rubin *et al.* found that people in their seventies tended to recall a large number of events from the period when they were aged 10–30 (see Figure 5.21). A possible explanation for this effect is that their earlier years may have been more memorable because they were more eventful or more pleasant. Since older people tend to enjoy remembering their younger days, this frequent retrieval might help to strengthen the retrieval routes to those early memories. Also, young adulthood is a period in life when an individual is often experiencing something for the very first time. Most people have vivid memories for their first trip abroad or their first date. Unfortunately subsequent dates and trips abroad tend to lose their novelty value and thus become less memorable.

Another interesting finding is that most people can remember virtually nothing of the first few years of their lives, a phenomenon known as 'infantile amnesia'. In fact most people appear to remember nothing at all from the first two or three years of their lives (Waldfogel, 1948; Pillemer and White, 1989). One possible explanation for infantile amnesia is that the brain may not have completed its physical development in early infancy and is not yet able to store memories. However, there is also a possibility that during infancy memories may be stored in a form that is not retrievable in adulthood. Nelson and Ross (1980) showed

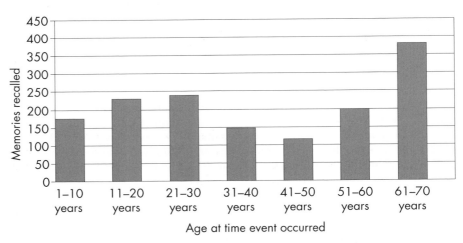

Figure 5.21 Retrieval scores for personal autobiographical events from different periods of an individual's life

Source: After Rubin *et al.* (1986)

that very young children are able to remember general facts (i.e. semantic memory) but not specific events (i.e. episodic memory). Their earliest memories thus tend to be based on schemas and scripts for general or typical events, but not for specific episodes of their own personal lives. This could explain why we do not remember actual events and incidents from early infancy. However, Newcombe *et al.* (2000) suggest that we may retain implicit memories from infancy which can affect our later behaviour, despite having no explicit conscious memory of the actual events concerned.

One finding that has emerged from studies of autobiographical memory is that events which are shocking or emotionally significant tend to leave a particularly vivid and lasting memory trace. The most extreme cases of emotionally significant events are not only memorable themselves, but may leave a lasting memory of trivial aspects of the context which happened to coincide with them. These are known as **flashbulb memories**.

Flashbulb memories

Can you remember where you were and what you were doing when you heard the news of the World Trade Center attack? If so then this is an example of 'flashbulb memory', so called because the shock of hearing such news seems to illuminate the relatively trivial events of our own lives and makes them highly memorable. The significance of flashbulb memory is not that the major news event itself was well remembered (which it fairly obviously would be), but that people are also able to remember trivial details of their own lives at the time of the event.

The first study of flashbulb memory was carried out by Brown and Kulik (1977), who decided to test out the widely held belief that all Americans could remember what they were doing when they heard the news of President Kennedy's assassination. Brown and Kulik found that all but one of their 80 subjects were indeed able to report some details of the circumstances and surroundings in which they heard the news of Kennedy's death, despite the passage of 14 years since that event. Similar findings have been reported for a range of other major news events, including the explosion of the space shuttle *Challenger* (Neisser and Harsch, 1992), the death of Princess Diana (Davidson and Glisky, 2002), and the terrorist attack on the World Trade Center (Talarico and Rubin, 2003).

In an effort to explain the occurrence of flashbulb memory, Brown and Kulik (1977) suggested that a special memory mechanism was involved, which could create a memory trace that was unusually accurate and immune to the normal processes of forgetting. This special mechanism was assumed to be brought into action only by events which were very emotionally shocking and which held great personal significance for the subject. It was argued that such a memory mechanism might have evolved because it would convey a survival advantage, by enabling an individual to remember vivid details of past catastrophes which would help them to avoid similar dangers in the future.

However, the notion of flashbulb memory as a special process has been challenged by subsequent studies showing that flashbulb memories are far from

Figure 5.22 The World Trade Center attack – where were you when you heard about it?
Source: Sean Adair/Reuters/CORBIS

infallible, and in fact seem to be no more accurate than any other type of memory. For example, Neisser and Harsch (1992) used a questionnaire to record details of the circumstances in which a group of American subjects first heard news of the *Challenger* disaster. They tested their subjects on the day after the disaster, and then tested them again three years later. In fact subjects showed a considerable amount of forgetting over the three years, and roughly half of the details recalled after three years disagreed with the information recalled the day after the crash. Talarico and Rubin (2003) also reported that flashbulb memories following the World Trade Center attack showed a decline in their accuracy over the months that followed, and were in fact no more accurate and lasting than the normal everyday memories of their subjects.

Whilst there is no doubt that flashbulb memory is unusually detailed and lasting, it can probably be adequately accounted for by the mechanisms underlying normal memory. Neisser (1982), for example, proposes that the memory for a very significant event would be likely to benefit from frequent recall and retelling of the memory. Another possible explanation for flashbulb memory is that the occurrence of a very dramatic event could serve as an exceptionally powerful contextual cue for otherwise trivial events (Groome, 1999; Davidson and Glisky, 2002). Although our surroundings and activities may not be very memorable in themselves, they could be made far more retrievable by their association with highly memorable contextual cues.

One intriguing possibility is that the mechanism underlying flashbulb memory could be partly responsible for certain clinical disorders. For example, one of the main symptoms of PTSD is the occurrence of intrusive memories, which are distressing memories of some horrifying experience. These memories are unusually vivid and intense, and so powerful that they cannot be kept out of consciousness. Sierra and Berrios (2000) suggest that the flashbulb mechanism could be involved in causing such intrusive memory effects, and possibly also those associated with phobia, depression, and drug-induced flashbacks. At present this view is entirely speculative, but if evidence is found to support it then the mechanism of flashbulb memory would acquire a new significance.

Eyewitness testimony

A courtroom is one place where memory can be of crucial importance. The testimony given by an eyewitness frequently provides the decisive evidence which determines whether the defendant is convicted, but there is a great deal of evidence to suggest that eyewitness testimony is fairly unreliable and does not justify the faith placed in it by the courts. Wells *et al.* (1998) describe 40 recent cases where DNA evidence has cleared a suspect who had been wrongly identified by eyewitnesses. In five of these cases the wrongly convicted person had been on death row awaiting execution. Yarmey (2001) concludes that mistaken eyewitness testimony has been responsible for more wrongful convictions than all of the other causes combined.

The pioneering work of Bartlett (1932) demonstrated that recall is extremely inaccurate (see Section 5.3), and particularly prone to distortion by the subject's prior knowledge and expectations. Research on eyewitness testimony has confirmed that eyewitnesses are indeed susceptible to reconstructive errors based on previous knowledge (Zaragoza and Lane, 1998). However, it has been found that eyewitness testimony is also prone to contamination from information acquired after the event, a phenomenon known as the '**misinformation effect**'. This effect was clearly demonstrated by Loftus and Palmer (1974), who showed subjects a film of a car accident. When subjects were later asked to estimate how fast the cars had been travelling, their responses were found to vary significantly according to how the question was worded. Subjects who were asked how fast the cars were travelling when they 'smashed into one another' gave a higher estimate of speed on average than did subjects who were asked how fast the cars were travelling when they 'hit one another'. They were also more likely to report having seen broken glass (although in fact none was shown) when tested a week later. Merely changing a single word in the question was sufficient to influence subjects, essentially by making an implicit suggestion to them about what they should have seen.

Post-event contamination is now known to be an important influence on eyewitness testimony, and it has been observed in real-life situations as well as in lab experiments. Following the Oklahoma City bombing of 1995 (in which 168 people were killed and over 600 injured by a massive car bomb) witnesses were found to have made errors in their description of events due to contamination from subsequent events. Timothy McVeigh, who was subsequently convicted of the bombing and executed in 2001, was described by three witnesses as having an accomplice when he hired the vehicle used for the bombing on the previous day. However, it was subsequently established that McVeigh had been alone. One of the witnesses had confused the memory of McVeigh's visit to the car-hire shop with that of two other men who came in to hire a vehicle later the same day, and that witness had later persuaded the other two that they had also seen two men rather than one. This case appears to demonstrate the occurrence of both post-event contamination and cross-witness contamination (Memon and Wright, 1999). Cross-witness contamination was also demonstrated in a laboratory experiment designed to simulate aspects of the McVeigh case. Wright *et al.* (2000) found that witnesses often changed their description of a crime after discussing it with another witness, especially if the other witness expressed confidence in what they had seen.

Like other forms of memory, eyewitness testimony becomes weaker and more fragmented with the passage of time, and consequently it becomes less reliable and more vulnerable to contamination from other sources. Flin *et al.* (1992) found that eyewitness reports became less accurate after a five-month delay, and although this applied to all age groups tested, small children were found to be particularly susceptible. Some studies have suggested that child witnesses may be generally more prone to suggestion and memory distortion (Loftus *et al.*, 1992). Children have also been found to be more likely to make a positive identification of the wrong person in an identity parade, though interestingly they are also more likely to make correct identifications (Dekle *et al.*, 1996), suggesting that children have a general tendency to make positive identifications more readily than do adults. Reviewing studies of child eyewitnesses, Gordon *et al.* (2001) concluded that whilst young children could provide accurate information under the right circumstances, they were particularly susceptible to suggestion and prone to reporting events which did not actually occur. Furthermore Gordon *et al.* reported that there was no reliable way that even experts could distinguish between true and false memories in the testimony of small children, so particular caution is required in cases involving child witnesses.

A number of recent studies have shown that the retrieval of a particular piece of information can be inhibited by omitting it from a subsequent presentation (Wright *et al.*, 2001), or simply by failing to ask about it during a post-event interview (Williams *et al.*, 2002). Again, children seem to be particularly susceptible to this effect. It is even possible to create entirely false memories in the mind of a witness by the use of suggestion effects, especially in small children (Hyman and Loftus, 2002). Instructions to create a detailed visual image of some imaginary scene or event were often sufficient to persuade subjects that they had a genuine personal recollection of events which never actually took place.

MacLeod (2002) has shown that eyewitness testimony can be affected by retrieval-induced forgetting (see Section 5.7), which could possibly play a part in causing the misinformation effect. Retrieval-induced forgetting could also be responsible for the tendency for witnesses to forget scenes which are omitted from a subsequent re-showing of the incident. In this case the strengthening of rival memory traces for items included in the re-showing would be likely to inhibit the memory traces of the items omitted from the re-showing.

From a consideration of these findings it is easy to see how easily a witness in a court case might be influenced by police questioning, or by information from other sources such as newspapers, lawyers, or other witnesses. There are obviously important lessons to be learned from these studies. In the first place, judges and juries should realise that witnesses cannot be expected to have infallible memories, and they should not place too much reliance on the evidence of eyewitness testimony alone. Statements should be taken from witnesses as soon as possible after the incident in question, and witnesses should be allowed to use notes when giving their evidence in court at a later date. Finally, police interviewers should be particularly careful about their methods of questioning, and should avoid the use of leading questions or suggestions which could implant misleading information in the witnesses' heads.

Crime reconstructions and cognitive interviews

The principle of context-dependent memory has recently been put to practical use in the field of crime detection. In an attempt to jog the memories of possible witnesses, crime reconstructions are often organised in which every effort is made to exactly replicate the original events and context of the crime as possible. Actors play out the roles of the people involved, usually in the setting where the actual crime took place. Such reconstructions are often shown on television in the hope that witnesses may be reminded of some relevant piece of information by the strong contextual cues.

Similar principles are used in a technique known as the **cognitive interview** ('**CI**'), introduced by Geiselman *et al.* (1985). Unlike the traditional police interview in which the witness is simply questioned about the actual crime, the witness undergoing a cognitive interview is also encouraged to recall various aspects of the context of the crime, and is wherever possible cued with contextual information. The witness may be reminded of various details of the crime setting, what the weather was like on the day in question, and even the newspaper headlines on that day. They may be shown photographs of the crime scene, or they may actually be taken back to it. There may also be an attempt to reinstate their mental state during the event, by asking them to try to remember how they felt at the time. An additional advantage of the CI is that it not only increases the amount of context reinstatement but also the variety of different retrieval cues, which may help to activate alternative retrieval routes. Geiselman *et al.* (1985) showed that the cognitive interview does in fact succeed in coaxing more information from the witness than does the traditional police interview (see Figure 5.23).

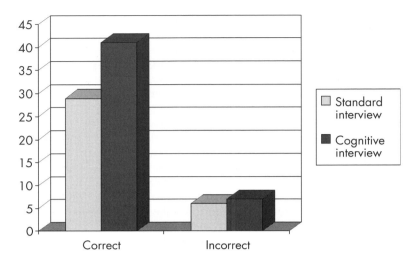

Figure 5.23 Recall performance with cognitive interview and standard interview procedures

Source: Geiselman *et al.* (1985)

Fisher *et al.* (1990) demonstrated that the CI procedure was also valuable in real-life police work. Police detectives interviewing real crime witnesses found that the CI produced a significant increase in the amount of information recalled. Many subsequent studies have confirmed the effectiveness of the CI in both laboratory and real-life settings. In a review of 42 CI studies, Koehnken *et al.* (1999) concluded that the CI consistently elicited more correct information than a standard interview, for both adult and child witnesses. There is also evidence that the CI procedure can reduce the witness's susceptibility to misinformation effects and post-event contamination (Milne and Bull, 2003). These effects are discussed further in Section 5.8.

In addition to the basic principle of context reinstatement (CR), an additional technique used in the CI is to instruct the witness to report everything (RE), regardless of how trivial or irrelevant it might seem. Studies have confirmed that both the CR and the RE techniques add to the effectiveness of the interview (Boon and Noone, 1994; Milne and Bull, 2002).

One limitation of the CI procedure is that it does not seem to be very suitable for use on very small children, who often have difficulty understanding the instructions (Geiselman, 1999). However, the CI has been found to be reasonably effective for children aged 8 years and above (Milne and Bull, 2003). Another problem with the CI procedure is that it becomes less effective when very long retention intervals are involved (Geiselman and Fisher, 1997), though Larsson *et al.* (2003) found that the CI could still produce a small but significant improvement in retrieval after a retention interval of six months. One further drawback of using the CI is that whilst it does elicit more correct information from witnesses it also elicits more incorrect information (Koehnken *et al.*, 1999). It has also been found that the CI procedure does not help with face recognition and person identification (Newlands *et al.*, 1999).

Although these limitations must be borne in mind when using the CI, research has shown that it is an extremely valuable procedure, and Kebbel *et al.* (1999) reported that most police officers had received formal CI training and that the CI procedure was widely used by police forces.

Repression and recovered memories

Freud (1915) suggested that very distressing memories can be pushed into the unconscious mind so that there is no longer any conscious access to them. He called this process repression. Although there is little evidence that repression plays a major role in forgetting, there have been claims that patients undergoing psychotherapy have in some cases been able to recover previously repressed memories. In some cases these memories have concerned traumatic experiences, such as the recall of being physically or sexually abused during childhood. Recovered memories of this kind obviously have important consequences, which might include accusations of abuse and even imprisonment of the alleged abuser, who may or may not be guilty. It is clearly of great importance to establish whether such recovered memories are accurate and reliable, and this issue has led to a fierce battle in recent years between those who are convinced that recovered memories are reliable and those who believe they may often be false.

A number of studies, mostly using the observations of psychotherapists, have provided support for the authenticity of recovered memories. For example, Andrews *et al.* (1999) collected information from over one hundred psychotherapists, many of whom had patients who reported recovered memories of childhood abuse. Some of these memories had been recovered during therapy, but the majority had actually been recovered at some earlier time before therapy had begun. Some of these patients were able to provide evidence from other people to corroborate their claims, which seemed to offer some support for their authenticity. It would therefore appear that some individuals probably do recover genuine memories of abuse. However, there remains a possibility that some recovered memories may be unreliable, and may even result from suggestions implanted during therapy. Some therapists have encouraged their patients to make a deliberate attempt to recover memories of abuse, and have made this the main goal of their therapy (Lindsay and Read, 1994), but this approach runs the risk of eliciting or even creating a false memory in the mind of the patient.

Recent studies have shown that recovered memories may, at least in some cases, involve events which never actually happened. For example, subjects who are asked to imagine certain fictitious events will often report them as actual experiences later on, especially after the passing of a long period of time (Manning, 2000; Lindsay *et al.*, 2004). These findings were obtained with adult subjects, but Ceci (1995) found that children have particular difficulty in distinguishing real from imaginary experiences. These studies demonstrate that normal people can come to believe that they have actually experienced events which were really just imagined. The possibility that such false memories do occur in actual cases of recovered memory is apparently confirmed by the finding that some of those who claim to have recovered memories of childhood abuse subsequently retract these claims and admit that their memories were not genuine (Kluft, 1999; Ost *et al.*, 2002).

Despite the intense heat generated by the recovered memories debate, most researchers have come to accept the existence of both valid recovered memories and false recovered memories, though there remains the problem of distinguishing between them. These issues have been the subject of extensive research, and for those of you who would like to know more there are a number of recent reviews which you may wish to read (Conway, 1997; Davies and Dalgleish, 2001).

Memory in the laboratory and memory in real life

In recent years there has been increasing interest in the study of memory in naturalistic settings, though these studies may in turn suggest scientific experiments to isolate certain key variables in controlled conditions. In some cases there has been a valuable interaction between laboratory studies and real-life applications, with a clear benefit to both approaches. One example is the interaction between experimental studies of context reinstatement and their application in police reconstructions and cognitive interviews. It is likely that in the future memory research will increasingly involve investigations of the same memory phenomena in both laboratory and real-life settings. For a more detailed review of applied aspects of memory in real-life settings, including autobiographical memory, flashbulb memory, and eyewitness testimony, see Groome (2005).

Summary

- Processing an input to a deep level, making use of schemas from past experience to analyse its meaningful content, will increase the likelihood of retrieving that input in the future.
- Retrieval cues have a major effect on the success of retrieval, and are especially effective if there is extensive feature overlap between retrieval cues and stored information.
- The reinstatement of the context in which a memory trace was acquired can be of great assistance in retrieving the trace.
- Retrieval involves both automatic processes (such as implicit memory and familiarity judgements) and controlled processes (such as explicit memory and context recollection).
- Retrieval-induced forgetting causes the inhibition of unwanted memories, which probably assists selective retrieval.
- Studies of memory phenomena in real-life settings, such as eyewitness testimony and the cognitive interview, provide an important complementary approach to laboratory studies because of their greater ecological validity.

Further reading

Esgate, A., Groome, D.H. *et al.* (2005). *An Introduction to Applied Cognitive Psychology*. Hove: Psychology Press. This book contains detailed chapters on most of the main areas of memory covered in the present chapter, but considered in the context of real-life applications.

Eysenck, M.W. and Keane, M.T. (2005). *Cognitive Psychology: A Student's Handbook*. Hove: Psychology Press. A well-established cognitive textbook, which covers many of the same areas as the present book. Normal cognition is dealt with in great detail, but there is not so much on disorders of cognition.

P.S. Familar faces (Fig. 5.14)

1. Monica Lewinsky
2. Michael Moore
3. J.K. Rowling
4. Bill Murray

Working memory

6.1 Multistore models of memory

The dual-store theory of memory

Early cognitive psychologists assumed that there was just one memory store. However, William James (1890) suggested that there were two separate memory stores, one for items being held in conscious awareness and the other for items held in unconscious storage. He called these two stores 'primary memory' and 'secondary memory' respectively, though they subsequently became known as **short-term memory (STM)** and **long-term memory (LTM)**. STM refers to the memories which are currently receiving our conscious attention, and it is a store of fairly brief duration and limited capacity. LTM refers to the memories which are *not* presently in conscious awareness, but which are held in storage ready to be recalled. The LTM store has a very large capacity and can hold information for a lifetime. Atkinson and Shiffrin (1968) used these ideas to develop a theoretical model of memory, which is shown in Figure 6.1.

According to the Atkinson and Shiffrin model, information is held in STM by continually rehearsing it, and without rehearsal it will be almost immediately forgotten. The LTM is seen as a more passive store of information which is available for retrieval but not kept in an activated form. Earlier models of memory storage had seen the STM as little more than a 'port of entry' into the LTM, but in the Atkinson and Shiffrin model the STM store is also used for retrieval of memories from storage. This notion of STM as a focus of both input and output of memories is of central importance to the more recent working memory model, which has developed the concept of the STM as a conscious workspace.

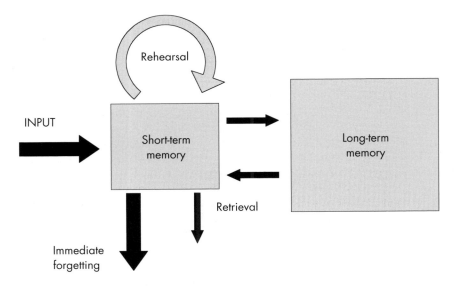

Figure 6.1 The dual-store model of memory
Source: Atkinson and Shiffrin (1968)

The distinction between STM and LTM is sometimes referred to as the 'dual-store' theory of memory, because it proposes two distinct forms of memory storage. It therefore constitutes one of the first 'multistore' theories of memory, describing memory as a number of related structures rather than as a single entity. In fact the Atkinson and Shiffrin model included a third store, which was seen as a very brief preliminary store for unprocessed sensory information, essentially an after-image occurring in the sense organ itself. There is some evidence for such a brief sensory store (Sperling, 1960), but the STM and LTM are of far greater importance to cognition.

James made the distinction between the STM and LTM stores essentially on the basis of subjective experience. He felt that conscious memory seemed different to storage memory, and seemed to have different characteristics. James was a psychologist of great intuitive genius, and like many of his theories the distinction between primary and secondary memory remains plausible to this day. However, it was left to later psychologists to provide scientific evidence for the existence of two separate memory stores.

Clinical evidence for the STM/LTM distinction

Over the years evidence has gradually accumulated in support of the dual-store theory, the most convincing evidence coming from the study of amnesic patients. Those suffering from organic amnesia (a memory impairment caused by physical damage to the brain), are characterised by their inability to form any new long-term memories. In contrast, their immediate short-term memory is usually unimpaired (Baddeley and Warrington, 1970). Such patients are able to remember what has been said to them during the previous few seconds, but not much else. The finding that STM can remain intact despite severe impairment of LTM suggests that they are separate and independent memory stores.

This view receives further support from the fact that a few patients have been studied who show the reverse of this dissociation, with an intact LTM but a severely impaired STM. For example, Warrington and Shallice (1969) described a patient known as KF who had suffered damage to the left parietal region of his brain in a motorcycle accident. KF had no LTM impairment but his STM was quite severely impaired. In fact he could only hold one or two digits in conscious STM at a particular moment in time, whereas most normal people can hold at least seven digits (this measure of STM is known as digit span, and it is further discussed in Section 6.2). Although this type of impairment is very rare, a few other patients have since been studied who show a similar pattern of impaired STM with an intact LTM (Basso *et al.*, 1982; Vallar and Baddeley, 1982) However, in recent years researchers have realised that these digit span impairments normally only affect one component of the STM, namely the phonological loop. This is explained more fully in Section 6.4.

Taking the two types of evidence together, it is apparent that both the STM and LTM can be separately impaired whilst the other store remains intact. A 'double dissociation' of this kind is regarded as being far more convincing than evidence of a single dissociation, and it is the main reason why most cognitive psychologists today accept that STM and LTM are separate memory stores.

The recency effect

The discovery of the STM/LTM distinction has provided a new explanation for the recency effect reported by Ebbinghaus (1885), which was described in the previous chapter. When a subject is tested for their recall of a list of items immediately after presentation, Ebbinghaus found that they usually tend to remember the last few items particularly well. Ebbinghaus explained the recency effect in terms of interference theory, but a more likely explanation is that the last few items are probably remembered because they are still in the STM at the time of recall. This theory received convincing support from the finding that the recency effect tends to disappear when a delay is introduced between learning a wordlist and recalling it (Glanzer and Cunitz, 1966). A delay of 30 seconds, filled with a simple task (counting backwards) to prevent subjects from rehearsing the wordlist, was found to be sufficient to entirely eliminate the recency effect. The results of this experiment are summarised in Figure 6.2. Glanzer and Cunitz concluded that the recency effect was caused by the last few items on the list being held in STM. Their findings add further support for the STM/LTM distinction, and they also suggest that information requires conscious rehearsal in order to maintain it in the STM store.

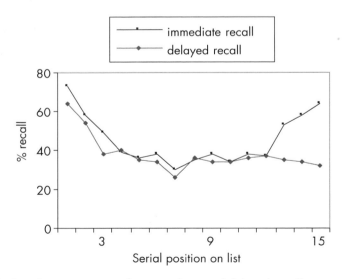

Figure 6.2 Serial position curves for immediate and delayed recall
Source: Glanzer and Cunitz (1966)

6.2 Measuring STM performance

STM capacity

Most traditional tests of memory, such as the recall of wordlists or stories, provide what is predominantly a measure of LTM. Tests of STM are harder to devise, but one of the most popular is the testing of immediate memory span. The subject is simply read a series of items (such as digits) and is then required to repeat them immediately, in the correct order. Since there is no time delay, immediate memory span is thought to depend largely on STM, and has become widely accepted as an approximate measure of STM performance.

If you wish to test your own digit span, you will find an example of the procedure in Figure 6.3. Read the five digits in the top row of the list, then cover up the list and try to write them down. If you get them all right, test yourself on to the next row, in which the number of digits is increased to six. Keep on going until you start getting some of the digits wrong. Your digit span is the largest number of digits you can get right in one trial.

Tests of this kind suggest that the average normal person has a maximum digit span of about seven digits, and in fact their maximum span for letters or words tends to be fairly similar (Miller, 1956). There is some variation among the general population, with scores varying typically from five to about nine items. However, immediate memory span is probably not a pure measure of STM, since there is evidence that LTM may make some contribution to span performance (Hulme *et al.*, 1991). This may explain why digit span tends to yield a higher estimate of STM capacity than other measures.

The recency effect offers another possible means of measuring STM capacity. Based on the number of items in the 'recency' section of the serial position curve, Craik (1970) estimated the capacity of STM to be about three or four items. This is rather less than the estimate obtained with the digit span method. For a review of recent approaches to the measurement of STM capacity see Cowan (2005).

```
71504
284936
8351609
25736184
940627135
2753180649
```

Figure 6.3 The digit span test

The first row of letters is read to the subject, who must repeat them immediately. If they get this row correct, move on to the next row, and so on until they make an error.

The duration of STM storage

The Brown–Peterson task (J. Brown, 1958; Peterson and Peterson, 1959) is a technique for measuring the duration of STM storage rather than its capacity, and more specifically its duration in the absence of rehearsal. The subject is presented with a test item which is well below maximum span (such as three letters), which they are required to repeat back after a short retention interval. However, during this retention interval the subject is required to perform a distraction task (such as counting backwards in threes) to prevent rehearsal of the test item. The results obtained by J. Brown and the Petersons showed that when rehearsal is prevented test items are forgotten very rapidly. In fact most items had been forgotten within 5–10 seconds of being presented (see Figure 6.4).

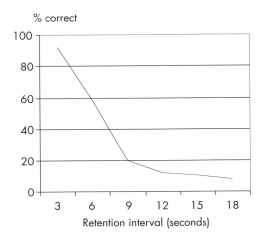

Figure 6.4 STM forgetting when rehearsal is prevented

Source: Peterson and Peterson (1959)

Two main conclusions can be drawn from these results. In the first place, STM storage apparently requires rehearsal of some kind, to keep the item in conscious attention. Secondly, when rehearsal is prevented items are lost from the STM very rapidly. In fact Muter (1980) has shown that most items are forgotten within three or four seconds if the subject is not expecting to be tested. Muter claims that this is probably a more accurate estimation of STM duration since the use of an unexpected test may help to eliminate the contribution of LTM.

6.3 The working memory model

Working memory

Early versions of the dual-store model tended to regard STM and LTM as two stores differing mainly in their duration. However, Baddeley and Hitch (1974) emphasised the different functions of these stores. They argued that the STM

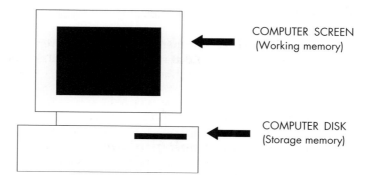

Figure 6.5
The computer as an
analogy for WM/SM
Source: Groome (1999)

was more than just a temporary store, suggesting that it functioned as an active 'working memory' ('WM' for short), a kind of mental workspace in which a variety of processing operations were carried out on both new and old memories. In contrast, the LTM was seen as a 'storage memory', maintaining information in a fairly passive state for possible future retrieval. A possible analogy (Groome, 1999) is to think of the working memory as resembling the screen of a computer, a space in which various tasks are performed on current data, whilst the storage memory serves a similar purpose to the computer's memory disks, holding large amounts of information in long-term storage (see Figure 6.5).

Baddeley and Hitch (1974) regarded the working memory (WM) as a work-space where analysis and processing of information would take place. They reasoned that such processing would require some means of storing information whilst it was being processed, but their research suggested that there were two short-term stores rather than just one. This research made use of the dual-task paradigm, in which the subject has to carry out two WM tasks at the same time. They found that two simultaneous WM tasks will disrupt one another severely if both tasks involve auditory input, or if both tasks involve visual input. This disruption is assumed to result from competition for the same storage space. However, a visual WM task and an auditory WM task can be carried out simultaneously without disrupting one another, suggesting that they are able to make use of two different stores. Baddeley and Hitch concluded that the working memory must have separate stores for visual and auditory information. They proposed a model of working memory (see Figure 6.6) comprising a **central executive** served by two short-term stores. These are the **'phonological loop'**, which holds auditory

Figure 6.6 The working memory model
Source: Baddeley and Hitch (1974)

and speech-based information, and the **'visuo-spatial sketchpad'**, which holds visual images.

The working memory model has been very influential over the last thirty years, and a great deal of research has been carried out on its components. Some of this research is described below.

6.4 The phonological loop

Evidence for the phonological loop

The phonological loop is assumed to provide brief storage for auditory input such as words, and it is assumed to be the mechanism underlying measures such as digit span. The main evidence for the existence of the phonological loop arises from the dual-task paradigm described above. For example, Baddeley and Lewis (1981) found that the immediate recall of a list of spoken words is severely disrupted by the simultaneous performance of a second verbal task, even one which requires no significant attention or processing. The second task in their experiment involved simply repeating 'the, the, the' over and over again, a procedure known as 'articulatory suppression' because, despite its simplicity, it uses up the subject's capacity for repetition of input. However, a task involving visual imagery does not disrupt the recall of spoken words. Baddeley and Lewis concluded that performing a second verbal task disrupts the first one because they are both competing for the limited storage space in the phonological loop.

Further evidence for the existence of two separate WM loops comes from the study of clinical patients with impaired STM. For example, Warrington and Shallice (1972) reported that their patient KF (referred to above) showed a severe impairment in the immediate recall of spoken items (e.g. digits, letters or words), but performed quite well when items were presented visually.

The word-length effect

The phonological loop is seen as being the mechanism underlying tasks such as digit span or word span, which was previously believed to have a limit of about seven items (Miller, 1956). However, Baddeley et al. (1975) found that the word span limit is greater for short words than for long words (a phenomenon known as the 'word-length effect'), which led them to suggest that the phonological loop was limited not by the number of items it could hold but by the length of time taken to speak them. In fact the word span was found to be limited to the number of words that could be spoken in about two seconds. The phonological loop thus seems to work in a rather similar way to a short loop of recording tape, which explains how it got its name. Some recent findings suggest that the word-length effect may primarily depend on the complexity and distinctiveness of the items rather than merely their length, since the word-length effect disappears when very distinct and complex items are used (Hulme et al., 2004).

Sub-components of the phonological loop

Baddeley (1986) suggested that the phonological loop contains two separate components. These are the *'phonological store'* which stores auditory information, and the *'articulatory control process'* which allows sub-vocal rehearsal of the information. The articulatory control process is seen as a kind of 'inner speech' mechanism linked to actual speech production, and it also helps to maintain verbal information in the phonological store.

These two sub-components were postulated because they offered an explanation for a number of unexpected findings. In the first place, it had been found that during articulatory suppression subjects were still able to make phonological judgements (Besner *et al.*, 1981), suggesting that there were separate systems to perform articulation and storage of auditory information. Another rather odd finding was that **articulatory suppression** eliminated the word-length effect for visually-presented words but not for spoken words (Baddeley *et al.*, 1984). In order to explain this finding Baddeley *et al.* suggested that the articulatory control process is required for registering visually presented words and transferring them into the phonological store, whereas auditorily presented words gain direct access to the phonological store since they are already in the appropriate format (see Figure 6.7). Thus articulatory suppression will affect the input of visually-presented words but not spoken ones. The word-length effect is seen as being a function of the limited space available in the articulatory rehearsal process, so this will also be eliminated by articulatory suppression.

The phonological store also offers a possible explanation for the 'irrelevant speech effect'. This is the finding that the retrieval of a sequence of visually presented items is disrupted by the simultaneous presentation of irrelevant spoken

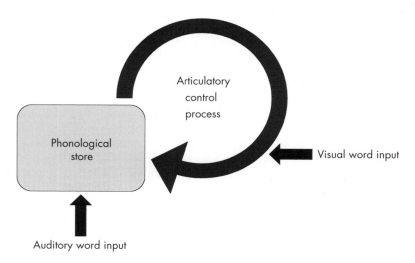

Figure 6.7 Access to the phonological loop
Source: Baddeley (1986)

material (Salame and Baddeley, 1982). Again this can be explained by hypothesising that all spoken material automatically enters the phonological store, even background speech which is not attended to.

The hypothesis that the phonological loop has two components receives some additional support from clinical findings, as certain brain-injured patients appear to show impairment of either the phonological store or the articulatory control process in isolation, whilst the other sub-component remains intact (Vallar *et al.*, 1997).

Non-speech sounds

Whilst the phonological loop is assumed to hold verbal items, there is some uncertainty about whether it also deals with non-speech sounds, such as the sound of a dog barking or a telephone ringing. Shallice and Warrington (1974) reported that their patient KF had a WM impairment which was restricted to verbal items, whereas his WM recall for non-speech sounds was fairly normal, which suggests that verbal material and non-verbal material appear to use different systems. In their study of the irrelevant speech effect (see previous section), Salame and Baddeley (1982) reported that background speech caused disruption of verbal memory, but non-speech sounds did not cause such disruption. They concluded from this that verbal material enters the phonological loop, but non-speech sounds do not. However, this view is disputed by Macken and Jones (1995), who found that unattended non-speech sounds did cause disruption in some circumstances. Groome and Levay (2003) found that the retrieval of non-speech sounds in normal subjects is impeded by articulatory suppression, which suggests that non-speech sounds require the use of the articulatory control process. However, the exact mechanism involved in storage and retrieval of non-speech sounds remains uncertain.

The phonological loop and language acquisition

Much research has been directed towards investigating the function performed by the phonological loop in real life, and studies have suggested that its main function may involve the use and development of language. Baddeley and Lewis (1981) found that articulatory suppression interfered with a subject's ability to detect errors of logic or word order in a sentence, suggesting that the function of the phonological loop may be to hold on to a sentence for long enough to analyse it for logic, word order, and overall meaning. This view is supported by clinical studies, which show that patients with severe impairment of the phonological loop (indicated by a very small memory span) often have difficulty in understanding long and complex sentences, but have no trouble with short and simple sentences (Vallar and Baddeley, 1984). It seems therefore that the problem is not one of basic comprehension, but an inability to retain and examine a long sentence. Other studies have found evidence of reduced phonological memory performance in children with language disorders (Raine *et al.*, 1992), and in normal children with poor linguistic ability (Gathercole and Baddeley, 1990).

Whilst these findings appear to suggest that the function of the phonological loop is concerned with language comprehension, in some cases patients with a severely impaired memory span have been found to exhibit normal language comprehension (Martin, 1993). This finding may suggest that the phonological loop is more important for the acquisition of language rather than for the subsequent use of that language (Baddeley *et al.*, 1998). Several studies offer support for this view. For example, children with specific language learning impairments have been found to have impaired phonological loop performance (Gathercole and Baddeley, 1989). It has also been found that a person's aptitude for learning a second language correlates with immediate memory span (Service, 1992; Gathercole *et al.*, 1999), and Baddeley *et al.* (1998) have reported a correlation between digit span and vocabulary.

6.5 The visuo-spatial sketchpad

Measuring the capacity of the visuo-spatial sketchpad

Just as the capacity of the phonological loop can be measured approximately by the number of spoken digits you can hold consciously at one moment, so the capacity of the **visuo-spatial sketchpad** can be measured by the number of visually-presented objects you can hold consciously at one moment. Try glancing briefly at the array of objects in Figure 6.8, then cover them up and try to

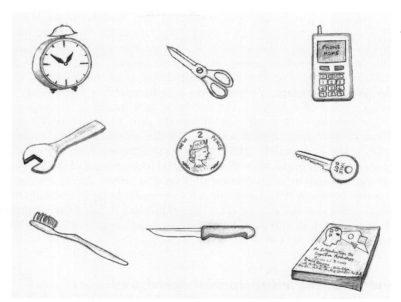

Figure 6.8 An array of items for testing the capacity of the visuo-spatial sketchpad
Source: Drawing by David Groome

remember the position of each one of the objects. Clearly there must be some short-term visual memory store which enables you to do this, and this store is referred to as the visuo-spatial sketchpad. Your ability to remember the identity of each of the items probably also involves the use of the visuo-spatial sketchpad, but this task will involve some input from the LTM as well, so testing the position of the objects is a purer measure of WM function.

There are several ways of testing the visuo-spatial sketchpad, most of which roughly follow the procedure described above. For example, one of the most widely-used measures is the Corsi Blocks test (Corsi, 1972), in which the experimenter touches the blocks in a certain sequential order which must then be copied by the subject. The Corsi Blocks test provides a means of measuring visuo-spatial WM span which is analogous to the use of digit span for the measurement of phonological WM capacity.

Evidence for the visuo-spatial sketchpad

As with the phonological loop, evidence for the existence of the visuo-spatial sketchpad comes from the dual task paradigm. Alan Baddeley (1995) describes an interesting real-life example of how difficult it can be to perform two visual WM tasks at the same time. Whilst driving his car down an American freeway, Baddeley noticed that his steering became hopelessly erratic when he attempted to visualise the details of an American football game he was listening to on the radio. Since his car was weaving from side to side he decided that it would be safer to switch over to a music programme.

Subsequent experiments have confirmed that short-term visual recall is severely disrupted by performing a second visual task at the same time, but is not disrupted by performing a non-visual task. For example, Logie (1986) found that the ability to learn words by using imagery was greatly disrupted by a second visual task but not by a speech task, and Robbins *et al.* (1996) found that the ability to recall positions on a chess board was disrupted by a secondary spatial task (manipulation of a keypad) but not by a task involving the repetition of words.

There is also some clinical evidence for the existence of the visuo-spatial sketchpad. There is a disorder called Williams syndrome where the main symptom appears to be an impairment of visuo-spatial processing and the visuo-spatial loop, but with normal verbal processing (Bellugi *et al.*, 1994). An interesting recent finding is that although Williams syndrome individuals perform normally on tests of grammar comprehension, they do in fact exhibit an impairment for grammatical structures which denote spatial position, such as 'above', 'below', or 'shorter' (Phillips *et al.*, 2004).

Sub-components of the visuo-spatial sketchpad

Logie (1995) suggests that, like the phonological loop, the visuo-spatial sketchpad also contains two sub-components. These are the visual cache, which stores information about shapes and colours, and the inner scribe, which holds spatial information and assists with the control of physical actions. Some evidence for this distinction comes from clinical studies which suggest that some brain-injured patients show impairment of the visual cache but not the inner scribe. For example, Farah *et al.* (1988) described a patient who showed very poor judgements based on visual imagery of objects, despite showing a fairly normal performance on spatial tasks.

6.6 The central executive

Investigating the central executive

The experiments described in the two preceding sections give some indication of the sort of tasks that make use of the phonological loop and the visuo-spatial sketchpad. Rather less is known about the central executive (CE), but it is thought to be concerned with the overall control of processing, and it is assumed to be in control of the two memory loops. The central executive is thought to be involved in many mental abilities, such as decision-making, problem-solving, making plans, selective attention, coordinating tasks, switching retrieval strategies, and manipulating information in long-term memory (Baddeley, 1996). The central executive also appears to be the main focus of conscious awareness, and thus probably represents the highest level of mental processing.

Testing the performance of the central executive is still at a relatively early stage. One widely used measure of CE performance is the random generation task (Baddeley, 1986), in which subjects are required to generate lists of items such as digits or letters in a random order, avoiding any non-random sequences such as runs of letters in alphabetical order or digits in ascending or descending order. A few other measures of CE function have been devised, but it appears that a variety of different tests may be required to assess different types of CE processing. Baddeley (1996) argues that the functions of the central executive can be fractionated into a number of separate and relatively independent components, such as focusing and switching attention, and accessing information from the LTM. These components may all require separate test procedures.

Impairment of central executive function

Certain brain lesions appear to cause an impairment of central executive function, such that patients tend to have difficulty in producing controlled and flexible responses and instead rely on automatic processing and stereotyped responses. This type of impairment is known as 'dysexecutive syndrome' (Baddeley and Wilson, 1988), and it has been found to be mainly associated with frontal lobe lesions (Shallice, 1988). Impaired executive function has been described in a wide variety of different conditions, including Alzheimer's disease (Baddeley, 1996), autism (Hill, 2004), and Tourette syndrome (Ozonoff *et al.*, 1994). Most of these conditions are known to involve damage to the frontal lobes (see Chapter 9 for further details of executive dysfunction relating to thinking disorders).

The occurrence of dysexecutive syndrome offers some support for the existence of the central executive. However, the central executive remains a rather unsatisfactory concept because so little is known about it. At present it merely provides a convenient repository for a collection of all those forms of processing which we do not fully understand, and thus in some ways resembles the traditional concept of 'the mind', with all the vagueness implied by that term. Further research is certainly needed before we can achieve a proper understanding of the functioning of the central executive.

6.7 Recent developments in working memory theory

The episodic buffer

Although the working memory model has been very influential, it has received a number of criticisms in recent years. One problem with the WM model is that, by fractionating the WM into a number of separate memory loops dedicated to specific sense modalities, it offers no clear explanation of how information from the visual and phonological loops can be combined and linked to multi-modular information in the LTM. Baddeley (2000) has therefore postulated an additional loop called the '**episodic buffer**', which integrates information from a variety of sense modalities and provides a link between the WM and the LTM.

The episodic buffer also helps to explain the finding that some amnesic patients are able to retain lengthy prose passages for a brief period of time, despite having very poor retention of prose over longer periods (Baddeley and Wilson, 2002). It is well known that normal subjects can remember lengthy prose passages over long or short retention periods, but it is assumed that they use LTM to achieve this performance. However, this is clearly not possible for amnesic subjects, whose LTM is severely impaired. Baddeley and Wilson suggest that both normal and amnesic subjects can use the episodic buffer to store such passages over a short period. Baddeley and Wilson (2002) note that this capacity for immediate prose recall is not found in Alzheimer patients, suggesting that these patients may have an impairment of the episodic buffer itself. Baddeley (2003) also suggests that the episodic buffer may be involved in conscious awareness, previously thought to reside primarily in the central executive. The latest version of the WM model, incorporating the episodic buffer, is illustrated in Figure 6.9.

Long-term working memory

An alternative view of working memory has been proposed which sees the WM not as a separate system from LTM, but as merely a subset of LTM memories which has been temporarily activated (Cowan, 1988; Ericsson and Kintsch, 1995; Buchner and Brandt, 2003). Ericsson and Kintsch have named this system the 'long-term working memory' (LTWM), and they suggest that this system can

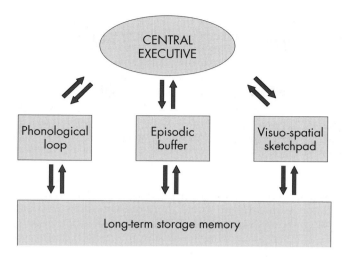

Figure 6.9 Revised version of the working memory model
Source: Adapted from Baddeley (2000)

retain processed items in a form that is rapidly accessible over long periods. In effect the LTWM represents a kind of 'short cut' to LTM, which bypasses the normal retrieval processes and can hold a large amount of LTM information in a state of activation. They point out that a mechanism of this kind could explain a number of phenomena, such as the finding that individuals possessing particular expertise (e.g. expert chess players) can hold large amounts of complex information in consciousness, which would overtax the normal retrieval routes connecting WM with LTM. It is suggested that by extensive practice experts are able to create special retrieval structures for a particular task.

Neuro-imaging studies and WM

The development of neuro-imaging technology (brain scans) has made it possible to investigate which parts of the brain are involved in the activities of the working memory and its various components. These techniques have confirmed that the phonological loop and the visuo-spatial sketchpad appear to involve activation in different parts of the brain, and their components also seem to involve activation of different brain areas.

Brain scan studies have revealed that use of the phonological store produces activation in a region at the edge of the left parietal lobe called the supra-marginal gyrus (Smith and Jonides, 1999; Henson *et al.* 2000), an area already known to be associated with language comprehension. In contrast, the same studies found that use of the articulatory control process produces activation of a part of Broca's area in the left frontal cortex, an area known to be involved in speech production.

Brain scans carried out during the performance of visuo-spatial tasks show activation of quite different brain areas. It has been found (Smith and Jonides, 1999; Wager and Smith, 2003) that WM tasks involving object recognition involve activation of the left parietal and inferotemporal zones, associated with the ventral pathway. However, spatial WM tasks involve activation of the right dorsal prefrontal, parietal, and occipital lobes, associated with the dorsal pathway. The ventral and dorsal pathways are known to be involved in 'what?' and 'where?' types of perceptual processing respectively, as explained in Chapter 2.

The central executive involves many different functions, so a variety of different brain areas are involved according to the task in question. However, brain scans suggest that most central executive tasks tend to involve activation of the prefrontal cortex, together with the parietal lobes in certain specific CE tasks (Collette and Van der Linden, 2002).

These brain scan findings would therefore appear to lend support to the WM model, in so far as they show that different areas of the brain are activated during the use of different components of WM. Figure 6.10 summarises the brain areas which are mainly associated with the various different types of WM task.

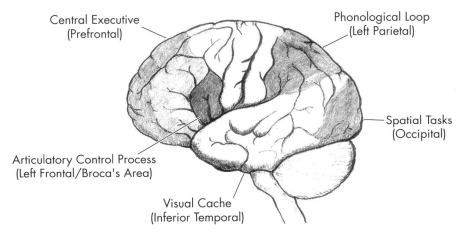

Figure 6.10 Brain areas involved in working memory
Source: Drawing by David Groome

Criticisms of the WM model

The WM model has now been in existence for over thirty years, and it has succeeded in accommodating almost all of the relevant research findings over that period. However, in order to do so it has had to change and adapt to fit each new challenge. Whenever a new finding is reported which cannot be explained by the existing version of the WM model, a modification is made to the model (such as the proposal of a new WM loop), which enables it to cope with the new findings. Some critics consider that this process of continuous modification and patching has perpetuated a model of working memory which is fundamentally flawed (Neath and Nairne, 1995; Nairne, 2002). They argue that each time a piece of evidence is found which fails to support the WM model, its supporters merely postulate another component to accommodate the new finding, thus making it impossible to falsify the model.

Neath and Nairne (1995) argue that there is no need to postulate multiple storage loops as assumed by the WM model, suggesting instead a model involving more general processing limitations which are partly modality-dependent but also partly modality-independent (i.e. a general representation of the actual item, rather than specific verbal or visual information). Neath and Nairne postulate that WM retrieval depends on matching the features of a WM trace with those of an SM trace, the main limitation being that the SM trace is degraded by interference. Nairne (2002) argues that this 'feature model' is able to explain many of the WM findings without requiring the existence of the various loops and components of WM, since the disruption caused by one task upon another similar task can be explained by interference phenomena. Nairne therefore concludes that the Baddeley and Hitch WM model can be replaced by a simpler model, without the need for a multitude of separate components. However, Baddeley (2003) insists that the WM model still provides the best available explanation of the data obtained, pointing out that it has been particularly useful in explaining clinical findings and various aspects of language learning.

The WM model has generated a vast amount of research over the last thirty years, and continues to do so. It remains to be seen whether it can survive in the face of future research, but if so it seems likely that it will be a rather different WM model which eventually emerges.

Summary

- There appear to be two separate and distinct memory stores, known as 'short-term memory' (or 'working memory') and 'long-term memory' (or 'storage memory').
- Evidence for the distinction between these two stores arises from clinical studies showing that amnesics may suffer damage to one store whilst the other remains intact.
- The short-term working memory is assumed to function as an active mental workspace in which a variety of processing operations are carried out. In contrast, the long-term storage memory is seen as a passive storage space.
- Baddeley and Hitch (1974) have proposed a widely accepted model of working memory which comprises a central executive served by two short-term stores, the 'phonological loop' and the 'visuo-spatial sketchpad'.
- Evidence for the existence of these memory systems has come from experiments showing that two tasks will interfere with one another if they make use of the same WM component.
- The phonological loop is assumed to provide brief storage for auditory input, and it is thought to play a major role in the use and development of language.

- The visuo-spatial sketchpad holds visual images, and it is also thought to be involved in visual pattern recognition, and in the perception and control of movement.
- The central executive is assumed to be the main focus of conscious awareness, and it appears to be involved in mental abilities such as decision-making, planning, and problem-solving.
- Recently an additional loop has been postulated called the 'episodic buffer', which integrates information from a variety of sense modalities, providing a link between the WM and the LTM.
- Impairment of the central executive is known as 'dysexecutive syndrome', and it has been found to be associated with frontal lobe lesions. It is considered to play a part in certain clinical disorders such as Alzheimer's disease, autism and schizophrenia.
- The development of neuro-imaging technology has made it possible to investigate which parts of the brain are involved in the activities of the working memory and its various components.
- The working memory model has been very influential, but in recent years it has received some criticism and alternative models have been proposed.

Further reading

Hitch, G.J. (2005). *Working Memory*. In Braisby, N. and Gellatly, A. (eds) *Cognitive Psychology*, Oxford: Oxford University Press. Graham Hitch was one of the originators of the working memory model, so you would expect him to write a good chapter on it, and he has.

Heathcote D. (2005). *Working Memory and Performance Limitations*. In Esgate, A. and Groome, D. (eds) *An Introduction to Applied Cognitive Psychology,* Hove: Psychology Press. This chapter deals with applied aspects of working memory and its performance limitations in real-life settings, such as language learning, industrial tasks and air-traffic control.

Disorders of
memory

7.1 Amnesia and its causes

The effects of amnesia

Amnesia is the name given to disorders of memory. Amnesia normally involves severe forgetfulness which goes beyond the everyday forgetting observed in normal people, to the extent that it may interfere with the activities of normal life. We are all prone to moments of forgetfulness, but most people with intact cognitive functioning can remember quite a lot about the events in their lives, especially their most recent experiences and events which are important to them. However, a person suffering from amnesia may be quite unable to remember any recent events in their lives, even the most important ones. You can probably recall quite easily where you were five minutes ago, or the person you just chatted with, or even what you did yesterday evening. Many amnesics would be unable to remember these simple things, and may have no idea of what they have done with their day so far. In severe cases they may be quite unable to commit any new experiences to memory, and this can be very disruptive to their lives. Without an intact memory it can become impossible to keep a job, to keep up relationships with family and friends, or even to look after oneself and maintain an independent existence. In fact it is clear from the study of severely amnesic patients that memory is quite crucial to our ability to function properly as human beings. Amnesia is a very disruptive and distressing condition. However, it is also a disorder from which a great deal can be learned about the nature of memory function.

Box 7.1 Case study: Alzheimer's disease (Ronald Reagan)

Ronald Reagan was probably one of the most successful and powerful people of all time. He first became famous as a film actor, appearing in many popular films. After retiring from the acting profession, Reagan began a new career in politics, and he was elected President of the United States in 1980. He remained in office until 1988, and during this eight-year period he was arguably the most powerful man in the world.

As President of the United States Ronald Reagan came to be regarded as an outstanding communicator, the skills from his acting days clearly standing him in good stead in his new career as a politician. But in 1994, a few years after he had left office, he was told that he had the early signs of Alzheimer's disease, a progressive dementia which first destroys the memory and then all other cognitive abilities.

Ronald Reagan announced the news in a brief handwritten letter to the American public. He wrote: 'I have recently been told that I am one of millions of Americans who will be afflicted with Alzheimer's disease. I now begin the journey that will lead me into the sunset of my life.' Within three years Ronald Reagan's memory had deteriorated so badly that he no longer remembered that he had once been the President of the United States. He was unable to understand why people waved at him in the street, and why strangers seemed to know him and wished to shake his hand. He was no longer able to recognise friends or former aides. In 1997 he received a visit from George Schultz, his former Secretary of State, but Mr Reagan did not seem to recognise his visitor despite their many years of working closely together. However, it is possible that some glimmer of recognition remained, perhaps a slight feeling of familiarity somewhere below the level of conscious recollection. At one point during the visit the former president had returned to the room where his wife Nancy was chatting with Mr Schultz. Mr Reagan turned to his nurse and asked, 'Who is that man sitting with Nancy on the couch? I know him. He is a very famous man.'

Source: Jacques M. Chenet/CORBIS

Ronald Reagan's dementia became increasingly severe over the next ten years, finally reaching a point where he no longer responded to any form of communication. In the spring of 2004 Nancy Reagan confirmed this, with the simple statement: 'Ronnie's long journey has taken him to a distant place where I can no longer reach him.' He died a few weeks later, on 5 June 2004.

Organic and psychogenic amnesias

Amnesia may arise from a number of different causes (also known as 'aetiologies'), which can be divided into two main groups, the **organic** amnesias and the **psychogenic** amnesias.

- **Organic amnesias** are caused by physical damage inflicted on the brain. This may arise from a variety of different causes, including brain infections, accidental injuries, and degenerative disorders such as Alzheimer's disease (see next section for a more detailed list). Organic amnesias tend to be severe and disabling, and they are also irreversible in the majority of cases because the brain lesion does not heal.
- **Psychogenic amnesias** are caused by psychological factors and usually involve the repression of disturbing memories which are unacceptable to the patient at some deep subconscious level. Psychogenic amnesias can be disorientating and disruptive to the patient, but they are rarely completely disabling, and as there is no actual brain damage they are reversible and in most cases will eventually disappear. The organic amnesias are far more serious, and since they are also particularly instructive in helping us to understand the nature of memory function they will provide the main substance of this chapter.

Causes of organic amnesia

There are many different ways in which the brain can be damaged, and any of these may cause amnesia if the relevant brain regions are involved. The main causes and origins (or 'aetiologies') of organic amnesia are listed below:

- **Alzheimer's disease (AD)** is the most common cause of amnesia. It is a degenerative brain disorder which first appears as an impairment of memory, but later develops into a more general dementia, affecting all aspects of cognition. AD occurs mostly in the elderly, and in fact it is the main cause of senile dementia, eventually affecting as many as 20 per cent of elderly people. Although seen mainly in people who are at least 60 or 70 years old, in rare cases AD may affect younger people, when it is referred to as pre-senile dementia. AD was first identified by Alois Alzheimer (1907), though the cases he described in fact concerned the pre-senile form. It was only later realised that the same basic degenerative disorder, with its characteristic pattern of tangled neural fibres, was also responsible for most senile dementias too. Since the amnesic symptoms of AD patients are usually complicated by additional symptoms of general dementia, they do not present a particularly pure form of amnesia and for this reason they are not the most widely researched amnesic group. See Box 7.1 for a case study of Alzheimer's disease (Ronald Reagan).
- **Korsakoff's syndrome** is a brain disease which usually results from chronic alcoholism, and it is mainly characterised by a memory impairment which

affects both recent memories and memories from the distant past. It was first described by Korsakoff (1887), and it has become one of the most frequently studied amnesic conditions, mainly because it presents as a relatively pure form of amnesia without the complication of extensive dementia or reduced intelligence. See Box 7.2 for a case study of Korsakoff's syndrome.

- **Herpes Simplex Encephalitis (HSE)** is a virus infection of the brain, which can leave the patient severely amnesic. Fortunately cases of HSE are very rare. One important characteristic of HSE amnesia is its relatively sudden onset, which means that in many cases the date of onset of amnesic symptoms is known fairly precisely, in contrast to the very gradual onset of degenerative disorders such as Korsakoff and Alzheimer cases. See Box 7.4 for a case study of HSE amnesia.

- **Temporal lobe surgery**. A very small number of patients have become amnesic as a result of brain lesions caused by deliberate surgical procedures, usually involving the temporal lobes. Such cases are fortunately very rare, but they have been extensively studied because they provide a particularly valuable source of knowledge about memory. This is because the precise moment of onset of their amnesia is known, and furthermore the location and extent of their lesions are also known fairly accurately. See Box 7.3 for a case study of Temporal Lobe amnesia.

- **Post-ECT amnesia**. ECT (electroconvulsive therapy) is a treatment used to alleviate depression, usually in patients who have failed to respond to any alternative form of therapy. ECT involves the administering of an electric shock across the front of the patient's head. It has been found that a period of amnesia may follow the administering of the shock, and in some cases this amnesia may persist over long periods or even permanently. ECT-induced amnesia has been extensively studied because it represents a serious side-effect of a deliberately administered treatment. It is therefore important to establish the severity and duration of post-ECT amnesia in order to evaluate the treatment.

- **Other causes of organic amnesia**. Since any condition which damages the appropriate areas of the brain can cause amnesia, there are many other possible causes, though none of them has been as widely studied as those listed above. For example, strokes and tumours can occasionally lead to amnesia, as can head injuries, brain damage caused by cardiac arrest, HIV infection, and degenerative conditions such as Huntington's Chorea and Parkinson's disease.

Amnesia as an impairment of long-term memory

The distinction between short-term memory (STM) and long-term memory (LTM) was explained in Chapter 6. The main characteristic of the organic amnesic syndrome is an impairment of *long-term memory*. Organic amnesics have difficulty in consolidating new information into their long-term memory store, and they often also have problems retrieving old memories from storage. However, despite this LTM impairment, organic amnesics usually have an intact short-term working

Box 7.2 Case study: Korsakoff's syndrome

Whitty and Zangwill (1976) describe the case of a pub manager who developed amnesic symptoms following many years of excessive alcohol consumption. He was brought into hospital at the age of 60, as his wife had noticed a severe deterioration in his memory and a number of other signs of neurological disorder. These included slurring of speech, unsteadiness when walking, periods of double vision and occasional fits.

Memory tests revealed that he was unable to learn any new material presented to him. For example, when a short story was read to him he was unable to recall any of it five minutes later, and when the story was read to him a second time he denied ever having heard it before. He also performed very poorly on several other memory tests, including tests of sentence recall and picture recognition. He was also unable to recollect any events or experiences from the previous seven or eight years. For example, he had no recollection at all of his recent work as a publican, which he had done for the previous five years. Instead he described himself as a newsagent, which he had in fact been several years earlier. He also gave his address as one from which he had moved many years before. He gave his age as 52 (in fact he was 60), and he gave the year as 1956 (in fact it was 1963). It was as though seven years had completely disappeared from his life. The patient also had no recollection of his second marriage, which had taken place two years earlier. However, when visited in hospital by his present wife he seemed to recognise her and he treated her as though she was familiar to him. In a similar way, he began to show a sense of familiarity with the nurses and clinicians in the hospital, although he claimed not to recognise them. Two further observations were made about this patient, both of which are characteristic of Korsakoff's syndrome. First, he had a strong tendency to confabulation, claiming to have experienced events and occurrences which had apparently not really taken place. Secondly, he showed no awareness or understanding of his condition, and in fact denied that he had any problems with his memory.

memory. One clear indication of their intact STM is the fact that most organic amnesics are able to carry on a fairly normal conversation. Their conversation will of course be somewhat limited by their inability to recall earlier events, but they are able to reply to questions, and they are able to complete sentences that they have started in a coherent fashion. This demonstrates that they are able to remember what has been said in the last few seconds, which is consistent with a normal short-term working memory. Their problem seems to lie primarily in consolidating these temporary memories into a permanent form for long-term storage.

Such observations have been confirmed by more objective measurements of STM function, such as digit span. Talland (1965) carried out a study involving no less than 29 Korsakoff patients, all of whom proved to be significantly impaired on a whole battery of long-term memory tests such as story recall, wordlist recall,

Box 7.3 Case study – temporal lobe surgery (HM)

On 23 August 1953 a 27-year-old man, referred to in the literature by his initials 'HM', underwent a surgical operation to remove both of the medial temporal lobes of his brain in an effort to alleviate his severe epilepsy. Although the surgeon did not realise it at the time, this operation was to have a devastating effect on HM's memory. Since that fateful day he has been unable to learn anything new, and consequently he has no intact memories for any of the events of his life since 1953.

Despite his inability to register any new experiences in his long-term memory, HM seems to have an intact short-term memory and his STM span is completely normal (Wickelgren, 1968). However, this only allows him to hold on to his experiences for a few seconds. HM is able to carry on a fairly normal conversation, but he can only remember the last sentence or so, which obviously limits his conversational range. He also has a tendency to repeat something he has just said a few moments earlier.

HM's inability to create new memories is known as anterograde amnesia. HM is virtually untestable on most measures of LTM, and it was reported that he 'forgets the events of his daily life as fast as they occur' (Scoville and Milner, 1957). Because of this HM will watch the same TV programme several times without recognising it, and he frequently does the same crossword puzzle many times without realising he has done it before. Even after several years of regular visits from clinicians such as Brenda Milner, he is still unable to recognise them.

Although HM remembers nothing that has happened to him since 1953, his memory is reasonably good for events preceding that date. This means that HM has severe anterograde amnesia, but has relatively little retrograde amnesia. Ogden and Corkin (1991) reported that HM actually has a fairly severe retrograde impairment for a period extending about three years before the date of his surgery, but has fairly good retrieval of events from earlier years.

However, a recent study of HM has shown that his retrograde amnesia is actually far more extensive for autobiographical events (Steinvorth *et al.*, 2005). HM is a particularly interesting case for the comparison of anterograde and retrograde amnesia, since the date of onset of his amnesia is known precisely. We can therefore be confident about estimating the extent of his anterograde and retrograde impairments.

Because of his severe amnesia HM is unable to live a normal life, and he requires continual care. However, he does retain some memory capabilities. Apart from his intact STM and childhood memories mentioned above, he also retains the ability to learn new motor skills such as mirror drawing, though he has no recollection of actually learning them. He also shows some learning on tests of implicit memory, such as completing the stems of previously primed words. In addition, HM shows some vague familiarity with a few major news events from the period since 1953, such as the assassination of President Kennedy (Ogden and Corkin, 1991). These studies indicate that HM's amnesia is actually quite selective, an observation which has important implications for our understanding of the modular nature of memory processes.

and picture recognition. However, their digit span scores were similar to those of normal subjects, averaging about seven items. Baddeley and Warrington (1970) again reported apparently normal STM span in Korsakoff patients, and in addition they found a normal recency effect in a test of free recall. As explained in the previous chapter, the recency effect is thought to reflect the STM component of free recall, so this provided further confirmation of the apparent preservation of STM. In a recent review, Pujol and Kopelman (2003) conclude that Korsakoffs show normal performance on tests of both verbal and non-verbal STM span.

HM, a patient whose amnesia was brought about by temporal lobe surgery, has been found to retain a normal digit span despite his extremely dense amnesia (Wickelgren, 1968). Patients suffering from HSE (Herpes Simplex Encephalitis) amnesia again tend to have normal STM function (including normal functioning of the WM loops and the central executive), in contrast to their severe LTM impairment (Starr and Phillips, 1970; Wilson and Wearing, 1995). Similar findings of preserved STM span have been obtained with patients in the early stages of Alzheimer's disease (Miller, 1977), though in the later stages Alzheimer patients do show a deterioration of STM performance reflecting the general dementia which eventually pervades all aspects of their cognitive functioning. Morris and Baddeley (1988) reported that Alzheimer patients usually have no impairment of the phonological and articulatory loops, but they show increasing impairment of central executive function. Becker and Overman (2004) confirm this executive dysfunction, which they suggest is a separate disorder which occurs in addition to LTM amnesia.

From a consideration of the studies reviewed in the present section, it would appear that in virtually every type of organic amnesia there is severe LTM impairment but a relatively unimpaired STM. This finding helps to explain the nature of organic amnesia, but it also tells us something about the structure of memory in normal individuals. It suggests that STM and LTM are essentially separate memory systems, since one can be impaired whilst the other is unaffected. Amnesic patients also provide us with an indication of the duration of STM storage, which has been estimated as approximately seven seconds, the length of time for which information can be retained by most severely amnesic patients. In fact Clive W, who is one of the most severely amnesic patients ever studied, was described in a recent TV documentary as 'the man with the seven-second memory'. The temporal lobe patient HM also exhibits this general pattern of severely impaired long-term memory with an apparently intact short-term memory.

7.2 Anterograde and retrograde amnesia

Distinguishing anterograde from retrograde amnesia

Korsakoff (1887) provided one of the first descriptions of organic amnesia. Having studied about thirty cases of severe amnesia associated with alcoholic abuse, Korsakoff concluded that the main impairment was an impairment of 'the memory of recent events'. However, he added that in many cases there was also an impairment of memory 'for the long past', which could extend back as far as thirty years.

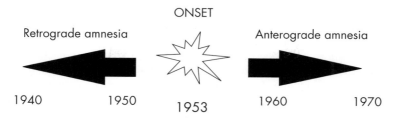

Figure 7.1 Anterograde and retrograde amnesia shown in relation to the moment of onset (in this case for patient HM)

These two types of amnesia roughly correspond to the definitions of 'anterograde' and 'retrograde' amnesia, which are the two main types of memory loss. They are defined as follows:

- **Anterograde amnesia (AA)**: impairment of memory for events occurring *since* onset of amnesia.
- **Retrograde amnesia (RA)**: impairment of memory for events occurring *before* onset of amnesia.

The relationship between anterograde and retrograde amnesia is illustrated in Figure 7.1. The distinction between AA and RA is most important, because it offers a possible means of distinguishing between learning disorders and retrieval disorders. A patient suffering from a disorder of learning would be expected to have AA but not RA, since they should have no difficulty in retrieving memories from the period before onset when their learning ability was unimpaired. On the other hand, a patient suffering from a disorder of retrieval would have difficulty in retrieving memories from any period in the past, and would thus be expected to have both AA and RA. It is possible that learning and retrieval disorders could occur together in the same patient, in which case both AA and RA would be expected but with the AA component probably being more severe.

A common observation, first noted by Ribot (1882), is that amnesic patients often have clear memories of childhood and early adulthood, despite being unable to remember more recent periods in their lives. Ribot concluded that their RA showed a 'temporal gradient', since the degree of impairment increased with the recency of the event. This observation has become known as 'Ribot's law', though more recent studies have shown that it does not apply universally since some amnesic patients have a uniformly dense RA without any obvious temporal gradient.

Testing anterograde and retrograde amnesia

AA is essentially an impairment of new learning, so testing for AA is fairly easy and straightforward. The patient can simply be asked to learn some form of test material (e.g. words, stories, pictures, etc.) and they are then tested for the retrieval of these items at some later time. However, tests of RA are more problematic, since they involve testing items learned prior to the onset of amnesia. The presentation of the test material is therefore beyond the control of the tester, who must instead try to think of test items that the patient is likely to have encountered earlier in their life. In practice this normally involves testing the patient's memory for events which happened many years before the test session, often referred to as 'remote memory', as opposed to the testing of 'recent memory' in more typical AA test procedures.

Remote memory tests can either involve the testing of past *public* events, which are likely to have been familiar to most people, or past *personal* events, which tend to be unique to each individual. Tests of past public events, such as major news events from the past, allow the same test items to be given to many different people. By choosing test materials which virtually everybody is likely to have been exposed to at some earlier time, it is possible to devise a standardised test with known performance norms, so that amnesic and control subjects can be compared on exactly the same test. Various different test materials have been used for this purpose, which usually attempt to sample different time periods by selecting items that were widely publicised at a particular period, but which have received no subsequent publicity. One widely used battery of tests for past public events is the Boston Remote Memory Test (Albert *et al.*, 1979), which includes tests of famous faces and news events from the past. More recently Steinvorth *et al.* (2005) have devised tests and interview procedures for the assessment of memory for public events and famous people.

Tests of past *personal* events tend to focus on autobiographical memory, for example asking the subject about events from their school-days. Because of the unique and personal nature of these items, the scores of different individuals are not so directly comparable, since they will be recalling different events. Another problem is that it is often difficult to check the accuracy of the responses given. Some refinement of this approach has been achieved by using a standard questionnaire to sample specific events in a typical person's life (Kopelman *et al.*, 1990), which are confirmed where possible by interviewing relatives. An autobiographical interview procedure has also recently been devised by Levine *et al.* (2002).

It is important to bear in mind that tests of past personal memory tend to involve specific events from an individual's autobiographical memory, which consist mainly of episodic memories. Past public memories on the other hand may sometimes involve semantic memory, in which items of general knowledge are retrieved without any specific episodic context (see Chapter 5 for the distinction between episodic and semantic memory). This distinction has not always been recognised in the past, and some earlier investigators made the mistake of comparing episodic measures of anterograde amnesia (e.g. 'Where did you go yesterday morning?') with semantic measures of retrograde amnesia (e.g. 'What was the name of your primary school?') without realising that they were not comparing like with like. In order to avoid such pitfalls, most recent studies have used the same test procedure (e.g. news events) to sample both anterograde and retrograde impairments. However, tests of personal and public events have both proved to be valuable measures of retrograde amnesia, offering the added possibility of assessing the relative impairment of episodic and semantic memory.

Anterograde and retrograde impairment in organic amnesia

Early studies such as those of Ribot (1882) and Korsakoff (1887) suggested that most amnesic patients suffer from both AA and RA, and more recent studies have generally confirmed this finding. A pattern of AA together with RA has been observed in dementing Alzheimer patients (Wilson *et al.*, 1981; Westmacott *et al.*, 2004), and in typical Korsakoff patients (Albert *et al.*, 1979; Kopelman *et al.*, 1999), and HSE patients usually show a similar pattern (Wilson and Wearing, 1995; McCarthy *et al.*, 2005). In many cases RA extends back over a very long time period. For example, in Korsakoff patients RA typically extends back over a period of thirty years or more before onset (Pujol and Kopelman, 2003), and usually shows a marked temporal gradient in accordance with Ribot's law. Some typical results are presented in Figure 7.2.

However, this general pattern of severe anterograde and retrograde amnesia is not found universally. Some patients show severe AA but their RA is limited to a very short time period. For example, the temporal lobe surgery patient HM has very severe AA, but his RA is mostly limited to events occurring during the three years or so before onset (Ogden and Corkin, 1991). However, his amnesia for specific autobiographical memories extends back over a far longer period (Steinvorth *et al.*, 2005). A few rather untypical Korsakoff patients have also been studied whose RA was limited to the few years before onset, and these patients have usually been found to lack the frontal lesions which are otherwise typical of Korsakoff patients (Mair *et al.*, 1979). Kopelman *et al.* (1999) also reported an RA period of only about three years in patients whose amnesia was caused by tumours or strokes affecting diencephalic structures such as the thalamus, but with no damage to other brain regions.

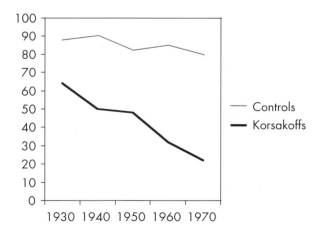

Figure 7.2
Memory performance for different time periods
Source: Albert *et al.* 1979

Focal retrograde and focal anterograde amnesia

Although most amnesics exhibit both AA and RA, a few cases have been studied who show either RA or AA in isolation. Examples of 'focal RA' (RA without AA) are extremely rare, but a few such cases have been reported in patients who have suffered head injuries (Kapur *et al.*, 1992; Sellal *et al.*, 2002), and in one case following HSE infection (O'Connor *et al.*, 1992). Mayes (2002) suggests that in some cases focal RA may be of psychogenic origin, but the existence of focal RA of organic origin also seems to be clearly established. Focal RA has been associated with lesions to various different brain areas, but most commonly it tends to involve lesions in the temporal cortex (Wheeler and McMillan, 2001).

In contrast, several studies have reported cases of 'focal AA' (AA without RA). Mair *et al.* (1979) studied two rather unusual Korsakoff patients with focal AA in the apparent absence of RA. Cohen and Squire (1981) also reported focal AA in their patient NA, who was injured in a freak accident. Whilst sitting at his desk, NA was accidentally stabbed with a fencing foil. A friend thrust the foil at NA as a joke, intending to stop short. Unfortunately the foil entered NA's nostril and penetrated his brain, with devastating effects. The area chiefly damaged was NA's thalamus, and it left him with severe AA but without any significant amount of RA. Other studies of focal AA have confirmed that damage is mostly restricted to the anterior thalamus (Kapur *et al.*, 1996).

From these admittedly somewhat unusual cases it would appear that deficits of learning and retrieval can occur separately, and thus appear to be largely independent disorders.

Brain lesions associated with anterograde and retrograde amnesia

The brains of amnesic patients have been extensively studied in an effort to identify the main sites where **lesions** (i.e. injuries) have occurred. The traditional method of doing this was by post-mortem examination, but in recent years a variety of brain imaging techniques have been developed which have made it possible to examine the brains of living patients. Brain scans of this kind have been able to detect a number of lesion sites which had not previously been identified by post-mortem studies. Such localisation techniques have identified several areas in the brain where lesions tend to be found in cases of organic amnesia. These include the *temporal lobes*, the **hippocampus** (which lies within the temporal lobes), the *thalamus*, and the *prefrontal lobes*. Their position is illustrated in Figure 7.3. The temporal lobes contain the hippocampus, and this structure is of particular importance to the creation of new memories. Surgical removal of the hippocampus and parts of the medial temporal lobes of the patient' HM was found to have a devastating effect on his memory, especially his ability to acquire and consolidate new memories (Scoville and Milner, 1957). More recently scanning techniques have confirmed HM's hippocampal lesions, but show that his lesions also extend into the temporal cortex (Corkin *et al.*, 1997).

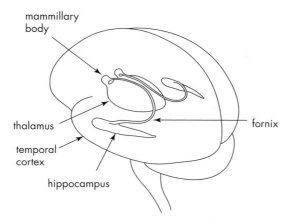

mammillary
body

thalamus

temporal
cortex

hippocampus

fornix

Figure 7.3 Brain structures involved in long-term memory storage

Source: Drawing by David Groome

The temporal lobes and hippocampus are also damaged in most cases of HSE (Damasio *et al.*, 1985; Colchester *et al.*, 2001), though their lesions are usually more extensive and may involve most of the temporal cortex. Similar temporal lobe lesions are found in the early stages of Alzheimer's disease (West *et al.*, 1994), though in the later stages of this progressive condition there are more extensive lesions, extending into the forebrain at first and later affecting most areas of the brain.

The other main area of the brain where lesions tend to produce AA is the **diencephalon**, a region which includes the *thalamus* and the *mammillary* bodies. These are the areas which are usually damaged in Korsakoff patients (Victor *et al.*, 1989), a finding confirmed by recent PET scan studies (Reed *et al.*, 2003). Although Korsakoff patients tend to suffer damage to much of the diencephalon, their amnesic symptoms are mainly associated with lesions in the *anterior thalamic nuclei* (Harding *et al.*, 2000).

Research on animal brains has shown that the hippocampus, anterior thalamus and mammillary bodies are interconnected, and appear to work as a single system (Aggleton and Saunders, 1997). This system is known as the *extended hippocampal complex*, and it appears to operate as a linked circuit which carries out the encoding and consolidation processes.

The retrieval of old memories seems to involve different regions of the brain, notably the temporal cortex and the prefrontal cortex. Some Korsakoff patients have prefrontal lesions in addition to their diencephalic lesions, and these patients are more likely to exhibit retrieval problems than those without such lesions (Victor *et al.*, 1989; Reed *et al.*, 2003). In fact Kopelman *et al.* (2001) established that in Korsakoff patients the severity of AA correlates with the extent of thalamic damage whereas the severity of RA correlates with the extent of prefrontal damage.

Lesions in the temporal cortex (i.e. the cortical area containing the hippocampus) are also associated with retrieval problems (Reed and Squire, 1998). HSE patients whose lesions extend beyond the hippocampus to include large areas of the temporal cortex are usually found to exhibit severe RA in addition to their dense AA (Cermak and O'Connor, 1983). Stefanacci *et al.* (2001) reported that in HSE patients AA correlated with the extent of hippocampal lesions whilst RA correlated with the extent of lateral temporal lobe lesions. Focal retrograde amnesia (i.e. severe RA without AA) is also associated with lesions in the temporal cortex but not in the hippocampus (Kapur *et al.*, 1992; Hokkanen *et al.*, 1995).

Encoding deficit theories of amnesia

The early studies of HM suggested that he suffered a profound AA but virtually no RA at all (Scoville and Milner, 1957). On the basis of this observation, Milner (1966) argued that HM's impairment was essentially an inability to learn new information and encode it into storage. More specifically Milner hypothesised that HM's amnesia reflected a failure to consolidate memories from a temporary STM trace into a permanent LTM trace, bearing in mind his intact STM.

This hypothesis raised the interesting possibility that other amnesias (such as Korsakoffs) might also be explained by the same underlying consolidation problem. It was argued that the apparent occurrence of RA in Korsakoff patients might actually be an anterograde (learning) impairment which had not been detected in earlier years (Piercy, 1977). Since the onset of Korsakoff's disease is slow and insidious, AA could well go undetected for many years and thus later be mistaken for retrograde amnesia. This would also provide an explanation for the temporal gradient of RA, since the increasing impairment would reflect the gradual onset of the condition.

However, the encoding-deficit theory lacks credibility as a general theory of amnesia. One problem for the theory is the finding that pronounced RA is often found in patients whose amnesia had a sudden onset, for example HSE patients (Wilson and Wearing, 1995; McCarthy *et al.*, 2005). Indeed HM is also now known to have fairly extensive retrograde amnesia (Ogden and Corkin, 1991; Steinvorth *et al.*, 2005). As the date of onset of amnesia is known with reasonable accuracy in these cases, it can be established beyond doubt that there is a genuine retrograde amnesia for events preceding that date.

There is also evidence of genuine RA in a Korsakoff patient, despite the fact that the date of onset is not precisely known. Butters and Cermak (1986) were able to test a Korsakoff patient PZ whose memory prior to the onset of amnesia had been objectively recorded, since PZ had been an eminent scientist and author before becoming amnesic and he had written his autobiography shortly before the onset of his disorder. Proof therefore existed that he had been able to remember many events and names of colleagues prior to onset, which he could no longer recall after onset. This demonstrated that in his case there was evidence of a genuine RA reflecting an impairment of retrieval.

Retrieval deficit theories of amnesia

In contrast to Milner's consolidation deficit theory, Warrington and Weiskrantz (1970) proposed retrieval impairment as the basis of organic amnesia. An impairment of retrieval could in theory explain both the anterograde and the retrograde components of amnesia, since a failure of the retrieval mechanism would be expected to affect all previous memories regardless of when they were acquired. However, a retrieval deficit theory would predict equally severe AA and RA, whereas most amnesics suffer far more AA than RA. This could possibly be explained by the fact that earlier memories are for some reason more durable, perhaps because they have benefited from many years of rehearsal. This hypothesis also offers a possible explanation for the occurrence of a temporal gradient in RA, since the earliest memories would be the most rehearsed (Squire *et al.*, 1984). Whilst this remains a possible explanation for the occurrence of temporal gradients, the retrieval deficit theory does not provide an adequate general explanation for all organic amnesias. It cannot readily explain the dramatic variations in the relative severity of AA and RA between different patients, and why some amnesics have virtually no RA at all. Nor can it explain how anterograde and retrograde impairments can sometimes occur in isolation, as in the case of focal AA and RA. These findings suggest that AA and RA are probably separate and independent impairments.

Separate disorders of encoding and retrieval

Attempts to explain both anterograde and retrograde amnesia in terms of a single mechanism have not been supported by research findings. It has become clear that there are impairments of encoding and impairments of retrieval which are essentially separate and independent of one another (Parkin, 1996). The finding that impairments of learning and retrieval are associated with lesions in different areas of the brain adds support to this view, as does the finding that both AA and RA can occur in isolation. The fact that most amnesics exhibit both AA and RA to some degree probably reflects the fact that the brain regions involved in learning and retrieval (the hippocampus and temporal cortex respectively) are actually quite close to one another and are extensively interconnected (see Figure 7.4), so that damage to one of these regions is likely to be accompanied by damage to the other. In summary it would appear that most amnesics suffer from both encoding and retrieval impairments, though their relative severity varies considerably from one patient to another.

The standard model of consolidation

One problem for theories of amnesia is that some amnesics (e.g. typical Korsakoffs) tend to have RA periods extending back thirty years or more, whilst others (e.g. temporal lobe patient HM) have RA periods of only about two or three years. Squire (1992) has put forward a theory to explain this finding, which is now known as the standard model of consolidation. Squire postulates that in addition to the normal consolidation process (which takes only a few seconds to create a LTM trace) there is also a slower form of consolidation which continues to strengthen the trace for two or three years after its initial acquisition. The trace

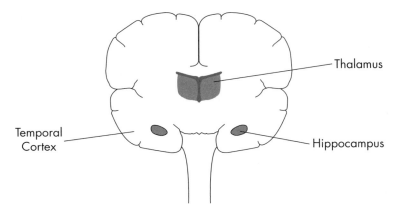

Thalamus

Temporal
Cortex

Hippocampus

Figure 7.4 A cross-section through the human brain, viewed from the front,
showing areas involved in memory function

would thus remain vulnerable for a few years after input, since it has still not been
fully consolidated. Squire argues that this long-term consolidation process probably involves the hippocampus, since patients with isolated hippocampal damage
(such as HM) appear to have a relatively short RA period. According to Squire's
theory, the hippocampus plays a role in both the initial encoding of a new trace
and in its subsequent strengthening over the next few years. The relatively limited
RA in patients such as HM may thus result from disruption of this slow consolidation process, whereas the far longer period of RA found in typical Korsakoff
patients may have a quite different cause, involving an impairment of the retrieval
mechanism.

Multiple trace theory

An alternative explanation is offered by the Multiple Trace Theory (Moscovitch
et al., 1999), which suggests that the hippocampus is involved in converting
episodic memories into semantic memories for the few years following their
acquisition. This is thought to involve the strengthening of connections with
other related episodic memories, which are bound together to create a semantic
memory. Once the construction of a semantic memory is complete, it becomes
independent of the hippocampus. However, it is hypothesised that the retrieval
of episodic memories always requires the hippocampus. This means that hippocampal lesions would be expected to disrupt episodic memories from all time
periods, but will only disrupt the most recently acquired semantic memories. The
model therefore predicts that hippocampal lesions will cause RA for all episodic
memories, but will only cause RA for recently acquired semantic memories.

Some evidence has been obtained which supports this model. In a recent
study of two amnesics (HM and WR) with temporal lobe lesions, Steinvorth *et al.*
(2005) found evidence of episodic RA extending back over the patients' entire life-
times, whereas semantic RA was limited to the few years prior to onset.

Explaining the temporal gradient in retrograde amnesia

Ribot (1882) noted that amnesics tend to retrieve older memories better than they can retrieve recent memories, and more recent studies have confirmed this temporal gradient in most types of organic amnesia. More recently A.S. Brown (2002) reviewed 61 separate studies of RA covering a wide range of aetiologies, and found that nearly all of them had reported a temporal gradient.

A number of possible explanations have been put forward for the occurrence of a temporal gradient in RA, some of which have already been mentioned above. One suggestion (Squire, 1982) is that older memories may be more durable than recent memories, possibly because they have developed more retrieval routes as a result of frequent retrieval over the years. Another explanation is based on the standard model of consolidation (Squire, 1992), discussed in the preceding section. According to this theory, the consolidation of a new memory takes several years to complete, and it becomes increasingly resilient during this time. Again, this means that older memories will be less vulnerable to disruption. The Multiple Trace Theory (Moscovitch *et al.*, 1999) suggests that memories for recent events remain vulnerable because they are still held as individual episodic memories. As time passes these episodic memories combine with others to produce a semantic memory, which is more lasting and does not depend on hippocampal activity. Older semantic memories will thus tend to be more robust than recent ones.

At present there is no clear evidence to support any one of these hypotheses over the others, and it is possible that all of these processes may contribute to the temporal gradient.

Box 7.4 Case study: Herpes Simplex Encephalitis (Clive W)

The case of Clive W is extremely well known, as he has been the subject of two television documentaries. Before his illness Clive was a professional musician, and his energy and brilliance had made him extremely successful. He was chorus master to the London Sinfonietta, and he worked as a music producer for the BBC. But in March 1985 Clive developed a flu-like illness, complaining of a severe headache and fever. The illness was eventually identified as Herpes Simplex Encephalitis (HSE), a rare viral infection of the brain. Unfortunately, by the time a diagnosis had been made Clive's brain had already sustained terrible damage, and he would never be able to return to his previous life.

Brain scans have subsequently revealed that Clive's left temporal lobe has been completely destroyed, together with some damage to his right temporal lobe and parts of his frontal lobes. These lesions have robbed Clive of his memory, in fact making him one of the most severely amnesic patients ever recorded. Clive suffers both anterograde and retrograde amnesia, and both are very severe. In fact his anterograde impairment is virtually total, so that he is completely unable to acquire any new memories. In the words of his wife, 'Clive's world now consists of just a moment. He sees what is right in front of him, but as soon as that information hits the brain it fades. Nothing registers.' This makes life extremely confusing for Clive. Any conversation he has with another person is immediately forgotten, as though it had never taken place. A visitor who leaves the room for a few minutes will be greeted afresh by Clive on re-entering the room, as if they were a new visitor. If Clive is allowed to go out into the street alone, he rapidly becomes lost. This is a risky situation for him, since he cannot find his way back and he cannot ask for assistance as he does not remember where he lives.

Unlike some amnesics, Clive also suffers from a very severe retrograde amnesia. He cannot remember any specific episodes from his life prior to the onset of his amnesia, and he no longer recognises most of his former friends. This retrograde impairment even extends to famous public figures. Clive says that he has never heard of John F. Kennedy or John Lennon. He was also unable to recognise a photo of the Queen and Prince Philip, though when pressed he suggested that they might have been singers. However, Clive's retrograde amnesia is not total. He does remember a few facts about his childhood (such as the fact that he grew up in Birmingham), though he cannot remember any specific events from that period. In contrast to these limited recollections, Clive still clearly recognises his wife and he treats her with the same familiarity and affection as in earlier times.

In addition to his episodic memory impairments Clive also shows clear evidence of a semantic memory disorder. He is unable to provide definitions of a number of common words such as 'tree' and 'eyelid'. He also has difficulty in recognising some common objects, for example jam and honey which he cannot distinguish from one another.

One aspect of Clive's memory which does seem to have remained surprisingly intact is his musical ability. He is still able to play the piano and sight-read music with great skill, despite the fact that he has virtually no memory of his previous career as a musician.

Before he became amnesic, Clive was a person of considerable intelligence, and he remains highly intelligent despite his lost memory. Perhaps this is why he is so acutely aware of the limitations of his present state. Clive does not know what has caused his problems, because when it is explained to him he immediately forgets. However, he is very well aware that there is something wrong with his ability to remember, and he has tried hard to find explanations for it. One of his conclusions is that he must have been unconscious until the last few seconds. At every moment of his life he feels as though he has just woken up, and his diary contains repeated entries of the same observation: 'I am now fully awake for the first time.' For most of us it is difficult to imagine what it must be like to experience such a state of mind, trapped in a few seconds of existence.

For a more detailed account of Clive's memory disorder see Wilson and Wearing (1995). Clive's wife Deborah has also recently written a book about their life together (Wearing, 2005), in which she reports that Clive's memory has actually improved slightly in recent years. From a neurological viewpoint this is a remarkable and unexpected turn of events.

7.3 Intact and impaired memory systems

Perhaps the most interesting feature of organic amnesia is that it does not involve a universal impairment of memory function. There are many aspects of memory which seem to remain largely unimpaired in organic amnesics, and these areas of intact memory functioning are of great interest because they not only tell us a great deal about the nature of the underlying memory disorder, but they also shed light on the mechanisms involved in normal memory.

Motor skills

They say you never forget how to ride a bike. Certainly motor skills tend to be very durable in normal people, and there is considerable evidence that motor skills are also preserved in organic amnesics. Not only do amnesics tend to retain their old skills from before onset, they also retain the ability to learn new skills and procedures, despite finding most other forms of learning impossible. This may indicate that skill learning is fundamentally different to other forms of learning, perhaps because skills are performed in an automatic way without any need for conscious recollection. For example, the HSE patient Clive W has been found to retain most of his ability as a musician, both in conducting and playing the piano (Wilson and Wearing, 1995), though he is totally unaware that he possesses this ability. Starr and Phillips (1970) also described a patient known as PQ, who had been a concert pianist before becoming amnesic as a result of an HSE infection. PQ not only retained his ability to play the piano, but proved to be quite capable of learning to play new pieces of music, though he remained quite unaware that he was able to play them.

Corkin (1968) reported that HM was able to learn a number of new motor skills such as mirror drawing. Mirror drawing involves drawing a shape on a piece of paper viewed through a mirror, which is a very difficult skill to learn since all of the normal visual feedback is reversed. HM succeeded in learning this new skill to a high level of competence and he retained this expertise over a long period of time, yet he remained unaware that he had learned it and he did not recognise the mirror apparatus when he was shown it on a later occasion. This ability to learn skills and procedures without being aware of having learned them seems to be a common finding in studies of amnesics.

A recent study by Cavaco et al. (2004) investigated the motor skills of ten amnesic patients, mostly with temporal lobe lesions caused by HSE. All of these patients displayed completely normal performance on a wide range of skills, including weaving, figure-tracing, and target-tracking. Glisky et al. (1986) reported that amnesics had been successfully trained to carry out simple computer tasks, though the training had required a great deal of time and patience. It was also noted that although these patients had been able to learn how to use several computer commands, this learning was only demonstrated whilst operating the computer program in question and showed no generalisation to other contexts. This suggests that skill learning in amnesics is highly inflexible, possibly because it takes place at an automatic and unconscious level.

In view of the many studies showing intact skill learning in amnesics, Cohen and Squire (1980) have suggested a distinction between **procedural memory**, which can be demonstrated by performing some skilled procedure, and **declarative memory**, which can actually be stated in a deliberate and conscious way. Cohen and Squire suggest that amnesics have an intact procedural memory, but an impaired declarative memory. This would explain the fact that they can learn new skills and procedures but reveal no conscious awareness of this expertise.

Implicit memory

In addition to motor skills there are a number of other types of behaviour which amnesics seem to be able to learn, though again without any conscious memory of the learning event. Such learning can sometimes be demonstrated by tests of implicit memory (see Chapter 5), in which the patient's behaviour is shown to have been influenced by some previous experience despite their inability to consciously recall it. An early demonstration of this phenomenon was reported by Claparede (1911), who carried out a rather bizarre experiment in which he greeted an amnesic patient with a handshake, made rather painful for them by the presence of a pin concealed in Claparede's hand. Claparede noted that the patient who had fallen foul of this trick refused to shake hands with him the following day, although she could not explain the reason for her unwillingness to do so. The cautious behaviour of the patient thus revealed evidence of learning without any conscious awareness of the learning episode.

Another demonstration of the preservation of implicit memory in amnesics was performed by Warrington and Weiskrantz (1968). They showed Korsakoff patients a series of degraded pictures of common objects or words (see Figure 7.5 for an example), starting with the most incomplete version and then showing increasingly complete versions until the word or object was correctly identified.

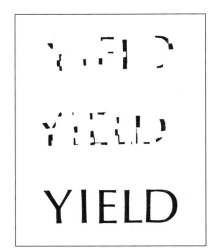

Figure 7.5
An example of a fragmented word stimulus

Source: Warrington and Weiskrantz (1968). Reproduced by permission of Macmillan

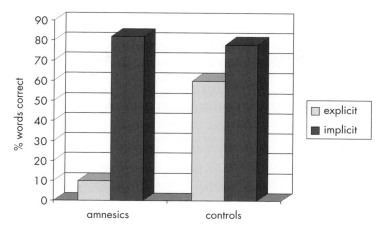

Figure 7.6 The performance of Korsakoff amnesics and normal control subjects on tests of implicit and explicit memory

Source: Graf *et al.* (1984)

When the same procedure was repeated at a later time, the Korsakoff patients showed a marked reduction in the number of trials required to identify the object, thus providing clear evidence of learning. A similar study was carried out on the patient HM, who also showed an improvement in the identification of degraded pictures following repetition priming (Milner *et al.*, 1968).

Graf *et al.* (1984) used the priming of verbal material to demonstrate intact implicit memory in Korsakoff patients. Following a word priming task, subjects were presented with word fragments and asked to complete them with the first word that came into their heads. In most cases the Korsakoff patients were found to respond with previously primed words, even though they revealed no conscious memory of those words in a test of explicit recall or recognition. In fact the Korsakoff patients achieved word-stem completion scores similar to those of the control subjects. Graf *et al.* concluded that implicit memory was unimpaired in Korsakoff patients, whereas explicit memory was severely impaired (see Figure 7.6). Several other studies have confirmed that implicit memory, but not explicit memory, appears to be preserved in amnesics (Graf and Schacter, 1985; Cermak *et al.*, 1985; Conroy *et al.*, 2005).

Although implicit memory is usually intact in organic amnesics, in occasional cases some impairment of implicit memory performance has been reported (Whitlow *et al.*, 1995). Brain scans suggest that impaired retrieval of implicit memory is associated with lesions in the occipital lobes (Schachter *et al.*, 1996) and in the left dorso-lateral area of the frontal lobes (Eskes *et al.*, 2003).

Familiarity and context recollection

As explained in Chapter 5, Mandler (1980) suggested that familiarity and recollection represent two alternative routes to recognition. An item may be judged familiar when we feel that we have seen it before, without necessarily remembering where or when. Recollection involves remembering the actual occasion in which the item was encountered. Recollection therefore involves the retrieval of context, whereas a familiarity judgement does not. Mandler argued that a familiarity judgement is an automatic process, which occurs without conscious effort or volition. Recollection on the other hand is considered to be a controlled process, which requires conscious effort and is carried out deliberately.

A number of studies have suggested that organic amnesics retain the ability to detect the familiarity of a previously encountered item, but have particular difficulty recollecting the context from which it is familiar. For example, the HSE patient Clive W clearly found his old friends and fellow-musicians familiar when he was reintroduced to them. He greeted them with warmth and happiness, even though he was unable to name them and had no idea where he had met them before (Wilson and Wearing, 1995).

Huppert and Piercy (1976) devised an experimental procedure to measure the accuracy of familiarity judgements. They showed Korsakoff and control subjects two sets of pictures, the first set being shown on day 1 of the experiment and the second set on day 2. Shortly after the presentation of the second set, the subjects were tested for their ability to recognise pictures they had seen before, by distinguishing between previously presented and unpresented pictures. They were then asked to indicate on which day they had seen each of the pictures. As Figure 7.7 shows, both the amnesics and the normal control subjects proved to be very good at identifying the pictures they had seen before. However, when asked to discriminate the pictures shown on day 1 from those shown on day 2, the performance of the amnesics fell to little more than chance level, whilst the control subjects still achieved a high level of accuracy. Most of us would have little difficulty in distinguishing between something we saw yesterday and something we saw today, but contextual judgements of this type seem to be particularly difficult for amnesics.

Huppert and Piercy (1978) carried out a follow-up experiment which showed that the recognition performance of the Korsakoff patients was mainly based on a judgement of the general familiarity of the pictures. The experiment was basically similar to their previous one, except that this time some of the pictures presented on day 1 were presented three times, in order to increase the strength of their familiarity. When requested on day 2 to pick out the recently presented (day 2) pictures, the amnesic subjects often chose pictures which had been presented three times on day 1, and in fact were just as likely to pick them as they were to pick out pictures presented once only on day 2. These results suggest that Korsakoff patients respond to a recognition test by making a judgement of the general familiarity of a test item, without knowing whether that familiarity arose from frequent presentation or from recent presentation.

One method of distinguishing familiarity-based responses from context recollection is the process dissociation procedure (Jacoby et al., 1993), which was described in Chapter 5. This procedure makes use of inclusion and exclusion tests, the former reflecting a conscious recollection of context and the latter an automatic familiarity judgement. Using this procedure, Verfaillie and Treadwell

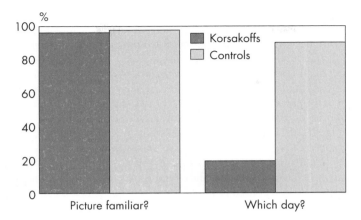

Figure 7.7 Familiarity judgements and context recollection for pictures in Korsakoff amnesics and normal control subjects

Source: Huppert and Piercy (1976)

Note: Scores shown are number of correct responses minus number of incorrect responses

(1993) confirmed the earlier findings that amnesics were largely restricted to familiarity-based recognition responses and were unable to recollect context.

A number of studies have suggested that familiarity-based recognition is relatively unimpaired in amnesics (Vargha-Khadem *et al.*, 1997; Mayes *et al.*, 2002), but others have reported impairment (Zola-Morgan and Squire, 2000). This discrepancy may reflect differences in the degree to which the stimulus facilitated the use of familiarity judgements. King *et al.* (2004) found unimpaired object recognition in amnesics, so long as the same stimulus was used for the learning and the test stages. However, any change in the viewpoint or even the background of the stimulus led to a significant impairment.

As with implicit memory it has been found that familiarity judgements can be impaired in some patients, and these individuals are found to have lesions in the perirhinal region of the temporal cortex (Simons *et al.*, 2001; Lee *et al.*, 2005), which is a small part of the temporal lobe lying beneath the brain. However, these studies found no such impairment in the more typical amnesias such as those caused by hippocampal lesions.

Episodic and semantic memory

The distinction between semantic and episodic memory (Tulving, 1972) was explained in Chapter 5. Episodic memory refers to memory for specific events in our lives, and it therefore involves the conscious retrieval of the event and its context (i.e. where and when the event took place). Semantic memory refers to the store of knowledge we possess (such as the meaning of a word), and requires no contextual retrieval and no conscious re-experiencing of an event.

Tulving (1989) suggested that amnesics exhibit a selective impairment of episodic memory, whilst their semantic memory remains intact. This theory is consistent with the general observation that amnesics usually retain a normal vocabulary despite their inability to remember any recent events in their lives (Warrington, 1979). However, although a person's vocabulary is certainly part of their semantic memory, it is mostly acquired in very early childhood, which could explain why it is preserved in amnesic patients. Language is also unlike most normal memories in that it is practised continually throughout life.

Certainly it has been found that episodic memory tends to be far more severely impaired than semantic memory in most organic amnesics (Spiers *et al.*, 2001), but semantic memory can also be impaired to some degree. Studies of Korsakoff patients have shown that they tend to show severely impaired episodic memory, but with some semantic impairment too, as shown by their poor ability to learn new vocabulary (Verfaillie and Roth, 1996). Studies of retrograde amnesia in Korsakoffs (Kopelman, 1989) have also revealed an impairment of semantic memory (e.g. identifying famous people) as well as episodic memory (e.g. retrieval of personal autobiographical events). Similar impairments of both semantic memory and episodic memory have been reported in HSE amnesics (Wilson *et al.*, 1995).

Alzheimer patients are generally found to show impairments of both episodic and semantic memory, though the episodic impairment is usually more severe. Addis and Tippett (2004) reported that Alzheimer patients tend to suffer impaired autobiographical memory extending back over their entire lifespan, but their semantic memory impairment is usually more limited. Indeed their relatively intact semantic memory has been successfully used in **rehabilitation strategies** (Clare *et al.*, 2003).

The temporal lobe patient HM has no recollection of any events of his life since onset, and in addition to this AA he also has RA for most autobiographical events from his earlier life too (Steinvorth *et al.*, 2005). HM retains a considerable amount of semantic knowledge acquired before onset, but he has difficulty in learning new words (Gabrieli *et al.*, 1988). For example, he is usually unable to define words and phrases introduced since the onset of his amnesia in 1953, such as 'Jacuzzi'. It has recently been reported that HM has learned some new semantic information since onset which he uses to solve crosswords, but this new learning seems to be restricted to items that he can relate to knowledge acquired before onset (Scotko *et al.*, 2004).

In view of these findings it would appear that both semantic and episodic memory are impaired in most organic amnesics, so there is no clear support for Tulving's original hypothesis that organic amnesia involves a selective impairment of episodic memory with a sparing of semantic memory. However, some individual patients have been studied who have focal episodic amnesia without any discernible semantic impairment. One example is the patient KC studied by Tulving and his colleagues (Tulving, 2001; Rosenbaum *et al.*. 2005). There are also a number of recorded cases of semantic amnesia, in which the meanings of words are often forgotten but no major episodic impairment occurs (Hodges *et al.*, 1994; Simons *et al.*, 2001). For example, Hodges *et al.* (1994) described a patient known as 'PP', who no longer knew the meanings of the word 'food' or 'the Queen'. Although episodic memory is usually unimpaired in such semantic dementia cases, Graham *et al.* (2003) report some impairment of early autobiographical memory in such patients.

Brain scan studies have generally suggested that the encoding of episodic memory is impaired by lesions to the hippocampus, whereas semantic memory impairment is associated with lesions in the temporal cortex (Vargha-Khadem *et al.*, 1997; Verfaillie *et al.*, 2000). Steinvorth *et al.* (2005) noted that HM (who has lesions restricted to the hippocampus and a small area of the temporal cortex) has extensive RA for episodic but not for semantic memory. On the other hand he has AA for both semantic and episodic memory. A similar pattern of amnesia has been reported in an HSE patient (McCarthy *et al.*, 2005), who again has very similar lesions to those found in HM. These cases suggest that semantic and episodic memory do show differential degrees of impairment, and for most amnesic patients episodic memory is more severely impaired than semantic memory.

Explaining preserved memory function in amnesia

The findings reported so far in this section suggest that amnesia is not usually an all-pervasive memory impairment, but tends to impair certain specific memory functions whilst leaving others intact. Figure 7.8 summarises the main memory systems, indicating those which are prone to severe impairment and those which are not.

As shown in the figure, there is evidence that procedural memory, implicit memory, and familiarity judgements all tend to remain largely unimpaired in typical cases of organic amnesia. The evidence for the preservation of semantic memory is not so clear-cut, but although semantic memory does often show some impairment it tends to be far less severe than that for episodic memory.

In view of the fact that several memory systems remain unimpaired in most amnesics, it is tempting to look for some common underlying factor uniting them which might explain all of these findings with a single overall theory. One

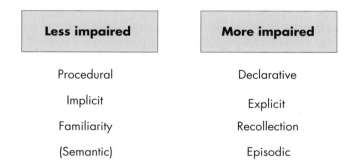

Figure 7.8 Memory mechanisms and their vulnerability to impairment in organic amnesia

such approach (Squire, 1992) argues that the three most frequently preserved functions (i.e. procedural memory, implicit memory and familiarity judgements) all involve memories which can be demonstrated without requiring any conscious declaration or verbal statement (e.g. performing a motor skill). Squire calls this type of memory 'non-declarative' memory. In fact it is normally demonstrated by some activity or behaviour which proves the presence of a memory even though the patient is not aware of it. Squire argues that amnesics suffer an impairment of 'declarative' memory, the type of memory which requires conscious retrieval and usually some kind of spoken response. Mandler (1989) emphasises that the impaired memory functions all require the use of consciously controlled processes, whereas the preserved functions all involve automatic processing. Mandler concludes that organic amnesia is essentially 'a disease of consciousness'. In his view amnesics have lost the ability to carry out consciously controlled retrieval and are thus left with only unconscious automatic memory processes.

In a further development of these theories, Cohen and Eichenbaum (1993) add that declarative memory may involve the creation of associative connections between memories (such as linking two memories together, or linking an item with its context). In contrast, non-declarative memory seems to be restricted to the strengthening of a single response mechanism (such as a motor skill or the level of activation and familiarity of a word). This could explain why declarative memory can be applied in a flexible way to fit novel situations, whereas non-declarative responses tend to occur in an inflexible manner in response to one particular stimulus situation. Cohen (1997) suggests that the hippocampus performs the associative binding function of declarative memory, whereas non-declarative memory involves the cortex and cerebellum. This view has received some support from MRI brain imaging studies (Cohen et al., 1994).

There is some disagreement about how the episodic/semantic distinction fits into this general theory of amnesia. Squire (1992) suggests that episodic and semantic memory should both be considered as sub-categories of declarative memory, since both episodic and semantic memory tend to be impaired in organic amnesics. However, Schacter et al. (2000) argue that episodic memory is a form of explicit memory whereas semantic memory is implicit (see Figure 5.17 in Chapter 5), since semantic memory is less severely impaired than episodic memory in most amnesics, and may sometimes remain completely intact. In fact the research suggests that episodic and semantic memory are separate memory systems, either of which can be independently impaired.

Baddeley (2004) argues that theories postulating a single underlying memory process to explain all aspects of amnesic impairment have not been supported by recent research findings. An alternative view is that all of the different memory mechanisms can suffer impairment in certain cases. Although procedural memory, implicit memory and familiarity remain intact in most typical cases of organic amnesia, each of these memory mechanisms can be impaired by a certain type of lesion. For example, implicit memory remains intact in most amnesics, but a few patients have been found to show impaired implicit memory (Whitlow et al., 1995). Similarly, in most amnesics familiarity judgements tend to be intact, but there are a few cases where they are not (Lee et al.,

2005). Perhaps the simplest theory to fit all of these findings might therefore be a 'multiple fractionation' theory of memory, which postulates a number of independent memory systems, any one of which may be separately and independently impaired.

7.4 Other types of memory disorder

Impairment of short-term memory

It was pointed out in Section 7.1 that organic amnesia normally involves an impairment of long-term memory, whereas the short-term memory of amnesics usually remains completely intact. Impairments of short-term memory do occasionally occur, but these are normally associated with a quite different pattern of brain lesions to those found in typical organic amnesia. In fact STM impairment was covered in Chapter 6, so it will not be reconsidered here.

Frontal lobe lesions

Patients with frontal lobe lesions often show some impairment of memory, though these tend to be rather different in nature to those associated with temporal lobe or thalamic lesions, and seem to mainly involve impaired retrieval. More specifically, patients with frontal lobe lesions tend to have particular difficulty in retrieving contextual information (Parkin *et al.*, 1995). Frontal patients also have difficulty in remembering temporal order. When presented with a series of test items, frontal lobe patients are usually able to recognise the items a short time later, but are unable to recall the order in which they were presented (Shimamura *et al.*, 1990; Swain *et al.*, 1998).

A related finding is that frontal lobe patients have difficulty in recalling the source of any information they recall. Impaired source memory in frontal lobe patients has been demonstrated by a number of studies in which subjects were provided with a list of facts that they were not previously familiar with. When tested a few days later frontal lobe patients showed no impairment in their recall of the facts, but unlike normal subjects they could not remember where or when they had learned them (Schacter *et al.*, 1984; Janowsky *et al.*, 1989). In some cases frontal patients would claim to have known the facts for many years, or to have learned them on some other occasion.

Overall it would seem that frontal lobe patients have a general inability to discriminate between the sources and origins of the memories they retrieve. They are usually able to retrieve memories in an adequate fashion, but they lack the normal ability to monitor and verify the source of their retrieved memories. One possible explanation (Shallice, 1988) for this defect of discrimination is that frontal lobe patients have an impairment in the central executive of their working memory. The central executive (which was discussed in Chapter 6) is assumed to be responsible for conscious decision-making processes. This might possibly include decisions about the source or accuracy of a retrieved memory. The central executive is also thought to control the conscious override of automatic processes, and this is also an ability which is thought to be impaired in frontal lobe patients. However, these impairments tend to have their main effect on thinking and problem-solving, so they will be taken up again in Chapter 9.

Another characteristic of patients with frontal lobe lesions is a tendency to **confabulation** (Moscovitch, 1989), which means that the patient describes memories for events which did not really take place and which are apparently invented. Recent studies have shown that confabulation is associated with impaired executive function, and more specifically with the loss of mental flexibility (Nys *et al.*, 2004). Confabulation often leads to misunderstandings, especially when other people believe what the patient tells them. For example, if a patient wrongly claims to have been attacked by another person this can have serious consequences. Alternatively confabulation may be mistakenly seen as deliberate lying. For example, a patient who claims to have spent the morning talking to the Queen may appear to be lying, at least to those who know that this is untrue. However, confabulation is not in fact lying, but merely an error of retrieval. Andrewes (2001) points out that patients with frontal lobe lesions have difficulty in judging the validity of their memories, as they are unable to verify the source or context of the remembered event. Consequently the patient may be unable to distinguish between memories for real and imagined events. This may partly explain the occurrence of confabulation, but impaired retrieval may also contribute. If a patient has difficulty in recalling something, they may attempt to fill the gap in their memory with the most likely possibility. Thus an elderly person who is unable to recall whether they have grandchildren may reply that they have, because this would seem likely for a person of their age. Confabulation could thus be seen as a tendency to use general knowledge from the semantic memory to fill in the gaps in their episodic or autobiographical memory. This is a mechanism which probably occurs to some extent even in perfectly normal people, but crucially they are usually able to distinguish between genuine events from their lives and their general knowledge of what is likely. Frontal lobe patients appear to have difficulty in making this distinction.

The impairments which have been described in this section are those which are associated with frontal lobe lesions, and the studies presented have all focused on patients with damaged frontal lobes. However, it is important to bear in mind that frontal lobe lesions can frequently co-exist with other types of lesion. For example, it has been found that many Korsakoff patients have frontal lobe lesions in addition to their diencephalic lesions (Shimamura *et al.*, 1988), and these particular individuals often exhibit a marked tendency to confabulation and retrieval problems in addition to the more usual amnesic symptoms found in Korsakoff's syndrome. On the other hand, Korsakoff patients without frontal lesions often show neither retrieval problems nor confabulation (Mair *et al.*, 1979; Pujol and Kopelman, 2003).

An impairment in frontal lobe functioning is also thought to occur in many otherwise normal elderly people, and this will be considered in the next section.

Memory loss in the normal elderly

It is widely accepted that memory tends to decline in older people. There is some evidence for such an age-related decline, but it is not readily detectable until the age of about 65 or 70. Even then the degree of impairment is not usually very great, at least not among the normal elderly. The popular view of old age leading to dementia is certainly not supported, and it is important to recognise the clear distinction between the dementing elderly (such as those with Alzheimer's disease), who suffer a severe memory impairment, and the normal elderly who show only a relatively small impairment.

Studies have indicated that the normal elderly tend to show a decline in recall ability though not in recognition (Craik and McDowd, 1987). Furthermore, elderly subjects tend to show a deterioration of explicit memory, but their implicit memory for previously primed items remains unimpaired (Parkin, 1993; Fleischman *et al.*, 2004). Elderly subjects seem to have particular problems in retrieving contextual information. For example, older subjects are found to have difficulty in remembering the temporal context of events (Parkin *et al.*, 1995), and also tend to have an impaired memory for the source of information (Craik *et al.*, 1990). Parkin and Walter (1992) used the 'R & K' (Remember and Know) procedure, as explained in Chapter 5, to demonstrate that elderly subjects (mean age 81) were able to recognise an item as familiar but had poor recall of context compared with younger subjects. An interesting feature of these results was that the amount of decline in context recollection correlated with measures of frontal lobe impairment, such as the Wisconsin card-sorting test. These findings are similar to those observed in patients with frontal lobe damage (see previous section), which is consistent with the finding that neural loss and degeneration in the elderly tends to be more extensive in the frontal lobes (Tisserand and Jolles, 2003).

One possible explanation of age-related memory decline consistent with the above findings is that the elderly lose some of their capacity for consciously controlled processing and attention, and have to rely more heavily on automatic processes (Craik and McDowd, 1987). Davis *et al.* (2003) have reported that the declining verbal recall performance in older subjects was correlated with their subjective organisation of the input. Another finding which may help to explain the observed cognitive decline in the elderly is a reduction in processing speed, which has been reported in many studies (Salthouse, 1994; Leonards *et al.*, 2002).

There is some evidence that the memory performance of elderly subjects can be improved by the use of an appropriate memory training programme (Wolters *et al.*, 1996; Troyer, 2001). Memory enhancement techniques are discussed further in Section 7.5.

Concussion amnesia

Concussion is one of the most common causes of amnesia, though fortunately the memory disturbance tends to be temporary. A person who is knocked unconscious by a blow on the head will typically suffer from both anterograde and retrograde amnesia, which may be extensive at first but which then usually shrinks to leave only a very limited period of time from which memory will never be recovered. For example, a footballer concussed by a collision with another player will probably be unable to remember the events immediately following the collision (e.g. being taken off the pitch and driven to hospital), and they are also frequently unable to remember the events immediately preceding the collision (such as the actual tackle or the play leading up to it). Typically, retrograde amnesia might extend backwards in time about a minute or two before the accident, and this brief gap in the player's memory would almost certainly be permanent.

Amnesias of this kind are known as concussion amnesias, and they fall within a broader category known as post-traumatic amnesias (PTA), which include any type of closed-head injury. Russell (1971) surveyed a large number of PTA victims and found that in most cases retrograde amnesia extended only a minute or two before the accident, though in a few cases it extended back over a period of days or even weeks. In all probability these cases of very extensive retrograde amnesia reflect some other form of memory disturbance in addition to the temporary effects of concussion, and either involve an organic brain lesion or alternatively a psychogenic amnesia.

In many respects the characteristics of concussion amnesia resemble a temporary version of the pattern found in organic amnesia. For example, during the period immediately following the concussive accident, the patient is likely to show an impairment in LTM tasks such as learning wordlists (Gasquoine, 1991), but will perform normally on tests of STM such as digit span (Regard and Landis, 1984). However, the very limited extent of retrograde amnesia suggests that there is usually no lasting impairment to the patient's retrieval. The most probable explanation of the pattern of amnesia associated with concussion is that the patient is temporarily unable to consolidate memories from the STM working memory into the LTM store. This would explain why events following the concussive injury are not stored, but it also explains why events held in STM immediately before the injury may also be lost. In all probability the contents of the STM working memory at the time of the accident are lost because they have not yet been transferred to the LTM, and the STM working memory (which depends on conscious awareness) is put out of action during the period of unconsciousness.

Although the effects of concussion on memory are usually temporary, a minority of mild to moderate head injuries may leave a more lasting impairment, referred to as post-concussive syndrome. However, lasting cognitive impairment rarely follows childhood concussive injuries, and rarely occurs after a single concussive injury (Teasdale and Engberg, 2003). There is some concern that sports involving frequent head impacts may produce a permanent cognitive impairment, and there is some evidence that this may occur in sports such as boxing (Haglund and Eriksson, 1993) and football (Kirdendall and Garrett, 2001). In cases of post-concussive syndrome brain lesions can often be detected by scanning techniques (Hofman et al., 2002). Specialised screening tests have recently been devised which provide a fairly accurate and reliable measure of the cognitive effects of mild traumatic brain injury (De Monte et al., 2005).

ECT and memory loss

ECT (electroconvulsive therapy) involves the passing of an electric current through the brain in an effort to alleviate depression. This treatment has been in fairly widespread use for over fifty years, though its value in the treatment of depression remains controversial. Although ECT has been shown to reduce depression in some patients, the benefits of ECT only last for a few weeks (Johnstone *et al.*, 1980; Buchan *et al.*, 1992). The benefits of ECT thus appear to be limited, and these benefits must be weighed up against the evidence that ECT may cause lasting brain damage.

The main evidence for such brain damage is the observation that ECT can apparently cause memory impairment. In the period immediately following the administration of an ECT shock, the patient typically shows a temporary amnesia rather similar to that seen following concussion. There is usually both antero-grade and retrograde amnesia (Squire *et al.*, 1981), which may be extensive at first but which usually then shrinks to leave only a fairly limited amnesia for the treatment period. It therefore appears that for most patients there is only a temporary impairment of memory. Follow-up tests of memory performance a few weeks after the completion of ECT treatment have usually failed to detect any lasting memory impairment (Weeks *et al.*, 1980; Warren and Groome, 1984), but these findings do not rule out the possibility of damage which the tests do not detect. In our study (Warren and Groome, 1984) patients showed a steady improvement in their memory scores over the period of their ECT treatment, which was probably a consequence of the alleviation of their depression over this period (see Figure 7.9). There is a slight dip in performance on verbal recogni-tion and story recall shortly after the administering of ECT, possibly resulting from the effects of the ECT shock. However, digit span and face recognition show

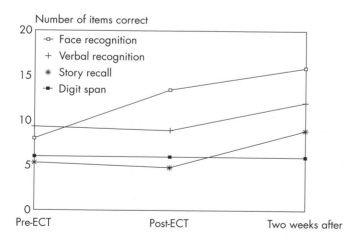

Figure 7.9 Performance on a battery of memory tests before, shortly after, and two weeks after the completion of a course of ECT treatment

Source: Warren and Groome (1984)

no such impairment. In the weeks following the shock there is a general improvement in memory performance. The overall effect, then, is that memory improves following the shock treatment, probably as a result of the lifting of depression. However, it remains possible that this general improvement may be masking an underlying memory impairment. This is difficult to assess because the patient's original level of memory performance is not accurately known, and there is no suitable control group to provide this baseline measure. Consequently it is not possible to separate the effects of ECT on memory from those of depression, and this has been a serious problem for such studies. For example, the control subjects used in ECT studies tend to differ from the experimental group not only in their freedom from ECT but also in their consequent level of depression.

Despite the fact that objective tests of memory usually fail to detect any lasting memory impairment following ECT treatment, patients often report that they still feel subjectively that their memories have been damaged (Freeman *et al.*, 1980; Rogers *et al.*, 1993). Although quantitative memory tests often fail to detect such impairment, this does not rule out the possibility of impairment for a number of reasons. In the first place, the memory tests available may not be sufficiently sensitive to subtle changes in real-life memory function. Secondly, as explained above, there are problems in finding a suitable control group or baseline measure to measure the memory performance of the patients prior to treatment. Testing the same patients prior to treatment is not an answer to this problem, since their memory will be affected by depression. Also, in many cases the patients will have received ECT on previous occasions.

McCall (2004) reports that, despite any possible memory impairment, most patients report an overall improvement in their quality of life following ECT treatment. However, it has been pointed out by Breggin (1997) that ECT, like any other brain trauma, produces a period of confusion and emotional flattening which may be mistakenly perceived as an improvement. In fact Breggin suggests that brain damage may actually be the basic mechanism of action which produces the benefits of ECT, since patients may derive temporary relief from the loss of painful memories.

In recent years there has been increasing concern about the use of ECT. Some researchers insist that ECT is valuable in the treatment of depression, since patients report an improvement in their quality of life following treatment (McCall, 2004). Other researchers argue that the limited benefits of ECT cannot be justified in the light of its possible effects on memory and cognition (Johnstone, 2003; Andre, 2005).

7.5 Rehabilitation

Helping patients to cope with amnesia

The effects of brain damage are normally irreversible, so it is not possible to restore memory function to those who suffer organic amnesia. However, this does not mean that nothing can be done to help them. There are a number of ways in which the lives of organic amnesics can be significantly improved, by helping them to cope with their impairment and to function as effectively as possible within the limitations it creates. This approach is known as rehabilitation. Some rehabilitation strategies involve the use of techniques for maximising the perform-ance of whatever memory function remains. Other strategies aim to bypass the impairment by finding alternative ways of carrying out a particular task. This may involve the use of some other type of memory process which remains intact, or alternatively makes use of external memory aids such as lists or electronic reminders.

Maximising memory performance

Most of the techniques used to maximise memory function in amnesia are based on methods which also help to improve normal memory. For example, it can be helpful to get amnesic patients to pay more attention to input, to repeat what is said to them, to organise items in memory, and to make meaningful associations between new input and the items already in memory. A group of amnesics taught these strategies achieved a significant improvement in memory performance compared with a control group of untaught amnesics (Milders *et al.*, 1995), though their advantage gradually disappeared over the next few years.

Wilson (2004) suggests a number of additional strategies. For example, it is helpful to ensure that an amnesic is only required to learn one thing at a time, and it is important to keep the input simple, avoiding jargon or long words. Amnesics also perform better if their learning is not context-specific. For example, a patient who has learned a memory technique in one setting may not use it in other settings, unless deliberately trained to do so. There is also evidence that amnesics can benefit from the use of 'spaced' rather than 'massed' learning sessions, especially when expanding retrieval practice intervals are employed (Broman, 2001). Mnemonic techniques have also proved to be helpful to many amnesics (Wilson, 1987; Clare *et al.*, 1999), and they can be devised specifically to suit the memory requirements of an individual patient.

One type of memory which usually remains intact in amnesic patients is procedural skill learning, and this type of learning can be used in amnesic patients who are otherwise unable to learn new information consciously. For example, Glisky *et al.* (1986) were able to teach amnesic patients to operate computer pack-ages which were previously unknown to them. Procedural skill learning can also be used to help amnesic patients to perform everyday skills despite their lack of conscious awareness of the procedures involved. These methods have been used to help amnesics carry out tasks such as washing, dressing, or making tea (Zanetti *et al.*, 2001).

Baddeley and Wilson (1994) demonstrated that amnesics derived particular benefit from 'errorless learning', a learning strategy which avoids the possibility of errors. For example, the patient's response can be restricted or guided in some way, or they may be told the correct information directly before testing or provided with a very strong retrieval cue. This contrasts with more normal learning situa-tions where responses are learned by trial and error. There are a number of possible reasons for the effectiveness of errorless learning. Baddeley and Wilson suggest that errorless learning may facilitate the retrieval of implicit or fragmented memory traces. However, an alternative explanation derives from the New Theory of Disuse and the phenomenon of **retrieval-induced forgetting** (see Chapter 5). According to this view, errorless learning ensures that only the correct response will be retrieved and strengthened, whilst rival responses are inhibited. If the patient is allowed to make an error, then this act of retrieval will strengthen the incorrect response and weaken the correct one.

External memory aids

In addition to these techniques for improving memory function in amnesics, external aids can be used to assist memory. One useful approach is to change the immediate environment and living conditions of the amnesic patient so as to minimise their dependence on memory, for example, putting big labels on cupboards, or labelling doors as a reminder of which is the kichen or the toilet. Environmental adaptations of this kind can help to make the amnesic's life easier and safer. For a more detailed discussion of environmental adaptations see Kapur *et al.* (2004).

External memory aids can also be used to support a failing memory by providing cues and reminders, and those in common use include lists, alarm clocks, and notices pinned to the wall. Electronic and computerised systems have also been devised which can be programmed to produce a reminder to carry out some action at a particular time, usually by emitting a warning 'beep' which draws attention to an instruction on screen. The first successful device of this kind was an electronic pager called the 'NeuroPage' (Hersh and Treadgold, 1994), which can be programmed to remind the user to perform a variety of tasks such as keeping appointments, taking medicine, or going to work. NeuroPage has been found to be of great assistance to most amnesics who have used it (Wilson, 2004). Another electronic memory aid has recently been developed, called 'SenseCam', which makes use of a digital camera attached to the user's belt to take photos of events experienced each day, in order to provide a reminder which can be viewed later on. The user can thus 'relive' each event many times until the memory begins to sink in, and because the camera is triggered automatically by a movement sensor they do not need to remember to take photos of key events. Preliminary studies suggest that this device can significantly enhance an amnesic's personal memories (Berry and Kapur, 2005).

A variety of memory strategies and aids are now in use, and most of them have been found to be of benefit to amnesic patients. Those amnesics who make use of a number of different memory aids and strategies have been found to derive the greatest benefit, and such patients are more likely to achieve independence in their daily lives (Evans *et al.*, 2003). Rehabilitation techniques have proved to be of great value in helping people to cope with amnesia, but this research is still in its infancy and we can expect to see major developments in the coming years. Unfortunately there is not space in this chapter to provide a detailed review of this specialised area, but those who wish to know more about rehabilitation techniques should see Wilson (1999, 2004).

Summary

- Organic amnesia is caused by brain damage of some sort, usually affecting the temporal lobes, hippocampus and anterior thalamic nuclei.
- Such brain lesions may arise from a variety of different causes, such as Alzheimer's disease, Korsakoff's syndrome, Herpes Simplex Encephalitis, strokes and tumours.
- Organic amnesia is characterised by an impairment of long-term memory, but the short-term working memory usually remains intact.
- Most amnesics suffer from an anterograde impairment, so that they have difficulty in learning new information from the time period subsequent to onset.
- Many amnesics also suffer from retrograde amnesia, in which memories are also lost from the period preceding onset. However, the retrograde impairment is often relatively mild, and memories for earlier time periods such as childhood frequently remain intact.
- The anterograde and retrograde components of amnesia appear to be fairly independent of one another, so that their relative severity can vary considerably from patient to patient. In rare cases either retrograde or anterograde amnesia may occur in isolation.
- Most amnesics suffer a severe impairment of conscious declarative and explicit memory processes such as recall or context recollection, but there is usually no impairment of non-declarative and implicit memory processes such as motor skill learning, priming and familiarity judgements.
- In addition to the amnesias which are characteristic of the organic amnesic syndrome, memory impairment may also be caused by other factors, such as ageing, frontal lobe lesions, concussion and ECT. However, these impairments tend to have their own distinct characteristics, and differ somewhat from the pattern of organic amnesic symptoms.
- Although brain lesions are usually irreversible, many rehabilitation strategies have been devised to help organic amnesics to cope with their memory impairment.

Further reading

Baddeley, A.D., Kopelman, M.D. and Wilson, B.A. (2004). *The Essential Handbook of Memory Disorders for Clinicians*. Chichester: Wiley. Offers detailed cover of all types and aspects of amnesia for the specialist. Aimed primarily at clinicians and researchers, but useful for undergraduate students as a reference book.

Campbell, R. and Conway, M.A. (1995). *Broken Memories*. Oxford: Blackwell. A book of individual case studies. Each chapter contains a detailed study of a single patient with some kind of memory disorder, including a detailed acount of the HSE patient Clive W (written by Barbara Wilson and Deborah Wearing).

Andrewes, D.G. (2001). *Neuropsychology: From Theory to Practice*. Hove: Psychology Press. This text covers most types of cognitive disorder, including amnesia. Unlike the present volume it contains a lot of detail on the biological bases of cognition. A useful source for students wishing to find out more about brain structure and function.

Chapter 8

Thinking: problem-solving and reasoning

8.1 Introduction

Most of us would suggest that 'thinking' covers a range of different mental activities, such as reflecting on ideas, having new ideas, theorising, arguing, making decisions and working out problems. An important feature common to all of these particular activities is that they are under our own control and we can run through actions symbolically in our minds. Also common to most of these activities is that our thinking is directed towards specific goals, for example solving crossword problems or composing the answers to questions. However, other types of thinking do not have these characteristics, for example with imaging, wishing and daydreaming there is often a feeling of an uncontrolled drifting of our thoughts.

This chapter will confine itself to providing a selective overview of the key findings of research into problem-solving and reasoning. It should be noted that whilst many have used problem-solving as an operational definition of thinking, such a narrow definition does restrict discussion to findings of research on goal-directed thought processes. However, problem-solving takes time, involves several cognitive processes and mental representations, and constructing a theory of problem-solving alone is comparable with trying to provide a theory of art broad enough to cover everything from ceramics to opera (Cohen, 1983).

8.2 Early research on problem-solving

Thought processes have been studied from many different theoretical points of view. Oswald Kulpe was one of the first to examine thought processes, such as the making of judgements, using specially trained adult human participants and the classical introspective report as his research methodology. Here, participants were asked to focus on the component sensations and this tended to lead to conflicting reports. Gilhooly (1996) comments that in particular the issue of thinking without images led to considerable controversy, with some introspectionists reporting imageless thought and others claiming that thought was always accompanied by imagery, albeit very faint images.

Frequently, we are conscious of the products of thinking rather than the processes themselves and the behaviourists offered a completely different approach, which of course focused on observable behaviour and 'learning' rather than 'thought'. Thorndike (1898) argued that the process of problem solution occurred through trial and error; in other words responses to the problem are simply random responses until one of them proves successful. A cat placed in a box with a trapdoor was not observed to show behaviour approximating thinking, but instead performed all kinds of behaviours until the appropriate responses were made accidentally, the trapdoor would then open and food was available as a reward. With practice, the cat would escape quite quickly by reproducing these learned responses. Whilst some problem-solving may indeed occur through trial and error, alternative means of arriving at problem solution were investigated by the Gestalt psychologists, who conducted a number of well-known and widely cited experiments in this field of research. Their research revealed some of the reasons why people can have difficulty in finding the correct solution to a problem.

The Gestalt approach to problem-solving

Research conducted by Wolfgang Köhler, one of the three founder members of the Gestalt school, took place on the island of Tenerife. He was trapped there during World War I and became the director of an animal research station. He founded a colony of chimpanzees and studied their problem-solving behaviour. For example, one chimp named Sultan was able to use a stick to obtain some bananas that were placed on the outside of his cage. When provided with two poles, neither of which was long enough to reach the bananas, the ape first 'sulked' then eventually put one pole inside the other to create a longer pole. Köhler (1925) used the term **insight** to refer to the ape's discovery. Other apes were observed when provided with bananas hanging from the ceiling out of their reach. Again, intense thinking typically preceded a flash of insight (the 'aha') and the apes would stack crates on top of each other to provide a staircase to the bananas. According to the Gestaltists, the process of some problem-solving requires the reorganising or restructuring of the elements of the problem situation in such a way as to provide a solution. This is known as productive thinking or insight. Reproductive thinking, on the other hand, relies on the rote application of past solutions to a problem.

The Gestalt ideas inspired the work of Maier, Duncker and Luchins. Maier (1930, 1931) investigated the 'two-string' problem. This involved human participants who were introduced to a room that had two strings hanging from the ceiling. Other objects in the room included pliers and poles. The participants were told to tie the two strings together, which was not easy as it was not possible to reach one string whilst holding the end of the other string. One solution is to attach the pliers to the end of one string so that it can swing like a pendulum. Maier waited until participants were obviously stuck and then brushed against the string to make it swing. Although not necessarily noticing his action, many went on to arrive at the pendulum solution and Maier claimed that his subtle hint resulted in a reorganisation or restructuring of the problem.

Some participants were unable to solve Maier's problem, even if he handed them the pair of pliers and explicitly told them that by using the pliers and no other object they could solve the problem. This was because they were unable to shift from seeing pliers as a tool for gripping things to seeing it as a weighty object. Duncker (1945) termed this **functional fixedness** and defined it as the inability to use an object appropriately in a given situation because of prior experience of using the object in a different way. Functional fixedness is a good example of stereotypical thinking and is a 'block' to problem solution.

A well-known study conducted by Duncker (1945) concerns a problem where individuals are handed a candle, a box of nails and other objects. The task is to fix the candle to a wall by a table, in such a way that it does not drip on the table. His observations revealed that few thought of using the box which contained the nails as a candle holder and were therefore considered to be 'fixated' on the usual function of the box, namely to hold the nails.

Another potential 'block' to problem-solving is referred to as 'set', which is the rote application of learned rules. Luchins (1942) asked participants to imagine that they had an unlimited supply of water and three jugs with which to measure

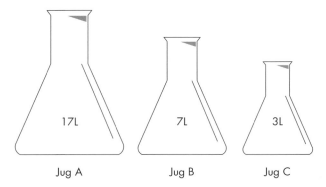

Jug A   Jug B   Jug C

Figure 8.1 An example of the water jug problem

Source: Adapted from Luchins (1942)

Note: The problem requires a quantity of water to be measured out. For example, to measure out four litres of water, you can either fill B and then pour three litres into C or follow a more complicated method, used in the set condition, which is to fill A, pour seven litres of water into B and then two lots of 3 litres into C.

out a certain quantity of water (see Figure 8.1). The volumes of the three jugs are specified for each separate problem. Participants were trained on a series of problems which either had the same complex solution method (the set condition) or on a series of problems that were solved using different methods (the control condition). Participants were then presented with critical problems, which could be solved either with the complex solution method or with a shorter, simpler method. To solve the critical problems, those in the control condition chose the simpler method. In contrast, those in the set condition used the complex method, providing evidence of reproductive thinking, even though in this case it hindered problem solution.

The nine-dot problem is another famous Gestalt problem. Scheerer (1963) presented participants with nine dots arranged in a 3×3 matrix. The task is to join all the dots in four straight lines without lifting the pencil from the paper, a task most participants could not do. The traditional Gestalt explanation is that this is a further example of a type of set effect, but this time produced by the way the task is arranged which means that participants attempt to keep their lines within the matrix or square created by the dots. The solution to the problem requires that they draw lines beyond the matrix (see Figure 8.2). However, explicitly informing participants of this does not necessarily lead to an improvement in performance (Weisberg and Alba, 1981).

The research inspired by the Gestalt ideas demonstrates that some problems cannot be solved through reproductive thinking (i.e. the rote application of past solutions to a problem) and that instead our past experience may hinder problem solution. However, this early research did not provide us with an explicit account of the processes underlying productive thinking, that is, insight; such attempts arose later with research conducted within the information-processing framework.

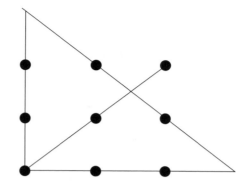

Figure 8.2
A solution to the nine-dot problem
Source: Adapted from Scheerer (1963)

8.3 The information processing approach to problem-solving

In the 1960s, Newell and Simon initiated research that resulted in the informa-tion processing view of problem-solving. Their work also involved creating a computer program called the General Problem Solver or GPS. They demonstrated that most simple problems consisted of a number of possible solutions and each of these solutions could be broken down into a series of discrete steps or stages. The stages they identified included:

1   Representing the problem – a **problem space** is constructed which includes both the initial state and the goal state, the instructions and the constraints on the problem and all relevant information retrieved from long-term memory. To assist such representation, symbols, lists, matrices, tree diagrams, graphs and visual imagery can all be used. This first stage reflects the assumption that problem-solving can be regarded as a form of search in a space consisting of all possible states of the problem.
2   Selection of operators – operators are actions that will achieve a goal, and are used for transforming the initial state.
3   Implementation of the selected operators – this results in a new current state within the problem space.
4   Evaluation of the current state – if it corresponds to the goal, a solution is reached.

Newell and Simon claimed that the key features of GPS were also characteristics of human problem-solving. They asked participants to solve problems whilst thinking out loud (a method known as 'protocol analysis') and when comparing the verbal protocols with the way GPS solved these same problems they found remarkable similarities.

Problem-solving strategies

According to Newell and Simon (1972) most problems are solved by the use of a small number of general purpose **heuristics**, which are basically 'rules of thumb'. Heuristics are methods or strategies which often lead to problem solution but are not guaranteed to succeed. They can be distinguished from algorithms, which are methods or procedures that will always produce a solution sooner or later. Our knowledge of the rules of arithmetic provides us with algorithms to solve problems such as 998 multiplied by 21. However, in certain situations we might estimate the solution to be in the region of 20,000. There are many situations in real life where we use heuristics, as either our memory constraints or other processing limitations do not allow us to use algorithms, or simply because there are no algorithms available.

Well-defined problems, where the initial state, the available operators and the goal state are clearly specified, could be solved by deciding which moves are possible, starting from that initial state, and thinking through the consequences of each of these moves. A diagram showing all the possible sequences of actions and intermediate states can be constructed and this is called a **state-action tree**. Such a tree will allow one to find a sequence of actions that leads from the initial state to the goal state. Applying such a 'check-every-state' algorithm would be very time-consuming and impossible for complex problem-solving activities such as playing chess. Instead, many problems can be solved through **problem reduction**, a sort of 'divide-and-conquer' approach. The problem is converted into a number of sub-problems and each of these is further subdivided unless it can be solved by the available operators.

Means–ends analysis is one method or heuristic for developing sub-problem structures. First, the difference between the current state and the goal state is noted and, by working backwards from the goal, a sub-goal is identified that will reduce this difference and a mental operator is selected to achieve the sub-goal. Choosing appropriate sub-goals to achieve the main goal is important to successful problem-solving and search processes are believed to involve the holding of these and any intermediate results in the limited-capacity working memory. An example of real-life means–ends analysis is making travel plans (Gilhooly, 1996). The desire to travel from London to New York will require one to note the large distance between the two and select air travel as the operator to reduce the difference. The initial sub-goal of 'ticket purchase' is then constructed which in turn leads to the sub-goal 'choose travel agent'. Clearly, a number of subsidiary problems have to be resolved in order to arrive at the desired destination.

Several well-defined problems that have been researched include the Tower of Hanoi and the Hobbits and Orcs; both are 'move' problems (problems of transformation). The GPS program, which incorporated means–ends analysis, was able to solve these problems. The Tower of Hanoi problem consists of three discs placed in order of size on the first of three pegs (see Figure 8.3). The goal state is for these three discs to be placed in the same order on the last peg. Only one disc can be moved at a time and a larger disc cannot be placed on top of a smaller disc. These two rules restrict which mental operator can be selected so that, for example, there are only two possible first moves: to place the smallest disc on the middle or on the last peg. According to means–ends analysis, a reasonable sub-goal is to place the largest disc on the last peg. Karat (1982) found that even though participants did not have a complete understanding of the problem before initiating their solution, they would solve this problem by using the heuristic of

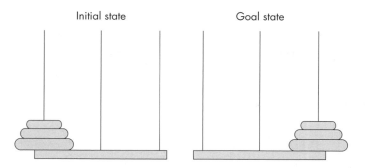

Initial state   Goal state

Figure 8.3 The Tower of Hanoi problem

Note: Only one disc can be removed at a time and a larger disc cannot be placed on top of a smaller disc

means–ends analysis. The Tower of London task is a very similar task and when Gilhooly *et al.*, 1999) asked individuals to solve this task whilst thinking aloud, they also found that generally the strategy of means–ends analysis was employed.

The difficulty that we humans face is being flexible in our choice of strategies and in being prepared to depart from strategies that entail moving towards closer approximations of the goal. This was demonstrated in the Hobbits and Orcs problem, where three hobbits and three orcs need to be transported across a river in a boat. The constraints are that the boat can only hold two creatures and the number of orcs on either bank of the river must never exceed the number of hobbits (as the orcs want to eat the hobbits). At one point the problem-solver has to transfer one orc and one hobbit back to the starting point (see Figure 8.4), and this move increases the difference between the current state and the goal state. Thomas (1974) found that participants experienced difficulty in making this move. However, participants also took longer and made more mistakes when there were a number of alternative moves that were possible. They were also observed to perform a sequence of moves quite rapidly, then pause for a while and then perform another sequence of moves, suggesting that to solve the problem several major planning decisions were required.

Simon and Reed (1976) asked their participants to solve a more complex version of the problem and, unlike Thomas (1974), they did not observe extensive forward planning. Participants were observed to make 'local' move-by-move decisions and to shift strategy. They found that initially a balancing strategy was employed, ensuring that there were equal numbers of the creatures being transported on each side of the river. Since this strategy could not result in successful problem solution, participants then switched to a means–ends strategy to move as many to the goal side of the river and, finally, to an anti-looping heuristic which involved avoiding any moves that reversed the immediately preceding move. Thus, to solve this complex version of the problem successfully, participants needed to be flexible and prepared to shift from one strategy to a different strategy.

Problem solution is not, however, simply dependent on our willingness to shift strategy. Asking individuals to verbalise their thoughts as they undertake

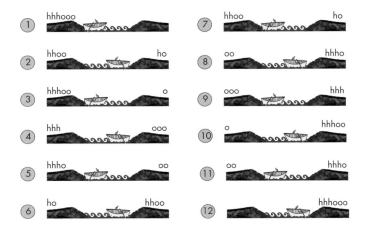

Figure 8.4 The Hobbits (h) and Orcs (o) problem

Note: Moving from step 6 to step 7 often causes difficulty for problem-solvers as this involves transferring one orc and one hobbit back to the starting point, hence moving away rather than towards the goal

such problem-solving tasks appears to have a positive effect, and different explanations for this have been put forward, including that it causes participants to 'stop and think' about the problem and that it focuses their attention on salient features of the problem. Davies (2000) found that unless directed at specific evaluation of moves, verbalisation *per se* did not lead to improvements in problem-solving performance (and such evaluation processes could take place non-verbally). Furthermore, explicitly asking participants to evaluate the success of a move immediately after making that move did not just enhance problem-solving performance (when the task was well-structured) but also appeared to help problem-solvers develop an explicit representation of the task. Next, the importance of problem representation is explored in more detail.

Problem representation

How individuals represent the problem initially is an important factor influencing solution. They are influenced by the language used to describe the problem as there is evidence suggesting that participants construct a representation of a problem that is very similar to the wording of the problem's instructions (Hayes and Simon, 1974).

Past experience will also bias the initial representation of a problem in particular ways and, in turn, this initial representation will activate potentially useful knowledge, for example about strategies, operators and constraints (Ohlsson, 1992). See Box 8.1 which looks at the influence of prior domain-relevant knowledge.

Box 8.1 Expertise

Summarised here are some of the key early studies looking at how experts and novices solve problems and these suggested that expertise was dependent upon the acquisition and organisation in long-term memory of domain-relevant knowledge. Research since has highlighted other factors such as individual differences.

Many studies have looked at chess and examined why grandmasters play chess better than others. DeGroot (1965) collected protocols from some of the best chess players and examined their memories for chess positions. DeGroot found that rather than spend time considering and discarding alternative moves, the grandmasters usually select the best move within the first five seconds of looking at the board, and then spend fifteen minutes checking the correctness of the move. Their prior knowledge allows them to avoid considering irrelevant moves. This contrasts with weaker players who select their best move after much thought, a move which is not as good as that of the grandmaster. It would appear that the two groups of players differ in the way they perceive the chess positions, as grandmasters were found to accurately reconstruct a chess position from memory after only five seconds of study. When doing so they repositioned the pieces in small groups, placing four or five pieces on the board, then pausing and then positioning another four or five pieces. In other words the grandmasters seemed to remember the chess board in chunks. Other research has shown that the grandmasters do not simply have better memories. If the pieces were arranged in a random way, in non-legal configurations of chess pieces, then the performance of the grandmasters and weaker players was comparable (Chase and Simon, 1973).

Studies of novices and experts solving physics problems have also demonstrated the importance of specific knowledge structures or schematic knowledge. Chi *et al.* (1981) gave expert physicists and novices the task of categorising problems in mechanics. They found that novices tended to group problems together that shared the same key words or objects, for example pulleys, springs, friction or ramps. Experts, on the other hand, classified problems according to the principles involved, for example the conservation of energy principle or Newton's laws. The experts would solve the problems four times faster than novices despite the fact that they would spend more time analysing and understanding the problems by drawing on their available knowledge. Larkin *et al.* (1980) found that experts used a different strategy to solve a problem and would work forwards to a solution, unlike novices who tended to work backwards (means–ends analysis).

If past experience is not helpful in relation to the problem that we are seeking to solve, then the initial problem representation, the problem space, will not permit a workable solution and an **impasse** will occur, a sort of mental 'blank' that is accompanied by a subjective feeling of not knowing what to do. This impasse can be broken by altering the representation of the problem – this may sound familiar as earlier it was noted that the Gestalt approach saw the process of some problem-solving as requiring the reorganising or restructuring of the elements of the problem situation, known as insight.

Ohlsson (1992) made several proposals regarding how restructuring might occur and these have been tested and developed further by Knoblich *et al.* (1999). For example, 'chunk decomposition' and 'constraint relaxation' are two processes by which problem representations can be changed. Familiarity with certain objects or events can result in the abstraction of a pattern or chunk of components or features, and to solve a problem we may need to change the way this information has been encoded. Knoblich *et al.* suggest that the probability of re-encoding a piece of information is an inverse function of how tightly the information is chunked in the current representation; if the chunks are loose then it is possible to decompose the inappropriate chunks into their component features. Familiarity with a task or event can also mean that constraints are inferred which may hinder problem solution. Knoblich *et al.* (1999: 1535) suggest that 'to understand a problem is, in part, to understand what does and does not count as a solution ... For example, opening a door is normally subject to the constraint that the door should not become damaged in the process.' Therefore, constraint relaxation can help overcome an impasse by making the requirements of the task less restrictive than initially assumed.

Knoblich *et al.* (1999) devised matchstick algebra problems to test their predictions. Each problem is presented in Roman numerals using matchsticks and these make up a numerical equation which can be made equal by moving a single matchstick. Some were predicted to be easier than others because they required the relaxation of fewer constraints and the decomposition of relatively loose chunks, and indeed the results were consistent with their predictions in terms of both solution times and rates. For example, one type of problem required a change to a number value and to a loose chunk:

$$VI = VII + I$$

This could be solved by moving one matchstick from VII to VI to produce VII = VI + I. Another type of problem required more than just a change to a number value:

$$I = II + II$$

This could be solved by removing one stick from the plus sign and hence changing addition into subtraction and then adding that stick to the first term to the right of the equal sign, thus producing I = III − II.

An account of insight problem-solving has also been offered (MacGregor *et al.*, 2001; Ormerod *et al.*, 2002; Chronicle *et al.*, 2004), which centres on the heuristics adopted to solve the problem. The authors suggest that for certain problems (e.g. the nine-dot problem) participants adopt a hill-climbing heuristic which means they select moves that appear to make progress towards the goal state. However, goal properties are inferred from the problem statement and these can then prevent problem-solvers from making moves that lie on the correct solution path. For example, in the nine-dot problem (see Figure 8.2) the goal inferred is that dots must be cancelled and individuals will evaluate potential moves according to the criterion that each line must cancel a number of dots given by ratio of dots remaining to lines available. This is easy for the first three moves as it is possible to cross out three dots with the first line and two with the next two lines, and because these criterion-meeting moves are available within the square shape of the dot array, solution attempts then stay within that square shape. Only by looking several moves ahead and realising that by the fourth move the criterion cannot be met, might problem-solvers realise alternative solutions where some lines extend beyond the nine-dot square.

8.4 Problem-solving by analogy

The discussion of problem-solving has so far focused on well-defined problems, where the problems are well specified and, like puzzles, the knowledge required to find the solution is present in the instructions given. The heuristics used to solve them have been termed *general-purpose* or *domain-independent* in that they can be applied to a wide range of situations or domains and do not involve specific knowledge of the domain. Frequently, in everyday life, the problems we face are either new or not well defined, but may resemble in some way a problem that we have previously encountered, and drawing on that by analogy may help us. The use of analogy in solving problems has been of considerable interest since the early 1980s.

Gentner and Gentner (1983) were among the first to consider how analogies might assist the way problems are solved. Participants learning how electricity flowed through the wires of an electrical circuit were taught either with a water flow analogy or with a moving crowd analogy. Then, they were presented with battery and resistor problems. In the water flow analogy, participants were told that the flow of electricity was like water flowing through pipes, with water pressure acting like voltage and flow rate like current. They were able to use this analogy to understand the effects of combining batteries, as separate batteries could be modelled by separate sources of water pressure. In the moving crowd analogy, participants were told that the flow of electricity was like a crowd of people moving through a passage and this group subsequently showed a better understanding when presented with resistor problems than with battery problems. They could see a resistor as analogous to a turnstile and the electric current as analogous to the rate of movement of people.

The processes of analogy or analogical mapping can be broken down into three phases (see Anolli *et al.*, 2001). First, the problem to be solved, the target problem, has to be interpreted and represented and here language comprehension plays a role. Secondly, a possibly useful source analogue has to be selected and retrieved from long-term memory. Thirdly, some similarity between source analogue and target problem has to be noted and the elements of the source analogue mapped onto the target problem. This mapping is most successful when the best set of correspondences is found between source analogue and target problem. The novel information provided by the source allows inferences to be drawn and transferred. It might be the case that the target problem is in an unfamiliar domain, so that the problem-solver will transfer as much as possible. Alternatively, the mapping may involve matching relationships rather than conveying new knowledge. A final phase in which schema induction takes place has also been hypothesised. Gick and Holyoak (1983) proposed that when we are provided with two examples of one type of problem, we will extract a schema based on their similarity or dissimilarity; this schema then assists analogical transfer and hence the successful solving of similar problems in the future.

One key finding to emerge is that providing source information is, in itself, not sufficient to induce participants to solve a new problem analogically. For example, Gick and Holyoak (1980) used Duncker's (1945) tumour problem. To solve the problem medical knowledge is not useful. The problem concerns a patient who has a malignant tumour that cannot be operated on. The tumour can only be removed by radiation, but radiation destroys healthy tissue at the same rate as diseased tissue. The solution is to direct a number of weaker rays towards the tumour so that they combine to destroy only the tumour. Gick and Holyoak (1980) found that presenting a completely different story, from a completely different domain of knowledge, could facilitate solution by analogy as both stories were structurally similar. In the General story, a General is attempting to attack a fortress which is well defended and can only be reached by a number of different roads. Each of these roads is mined and can only be crossed safely by a small group of men. The General splits his force into small groups, which approach simultaneously from different directions to converge at the fortress and win the battle. There was, however, little spontaneous use of the analogy; participants had to be provided with a cue as to how this different story was relevant. Similarly, Anolli *et al.* (2001) found in seven experiments that unless invited to relate the previously presented information to the target problem, by way of a 'hint', participants do not spontaneously transfer information from the source analogue to the target problem, even when this source has been activated. They conclude 'it seems that analogical problem-solving is not an automatic process, but it requires controlled attempts to relate the target to a prior source' (258).

Structural similarity, which refers to the underlying relations among the objects shared by the source and target problems (such as Duncker's tumour problem and the General story), has been contrasted with superficial similarity, which refers to objects and their properties, story protagonists or story lines that are common to both the source and target problems. Many laboratory studies have shown that participants tend to draw on source analogues that are superficially similar to the target and have difficulty when they are structurally similar. For example, Keane (1987) found that when presented with a problem about a stomach tumour, participants were more likely to benefit from a story about destroying a brain tumour than the General story. More recent findings, however, suggest that people can and do use analogical sources that do not have superficial features in common with the target. In a naturalistic study, Blanchette and Dunbar (2001) identified 234 analogies when looking in newspapers during the final week of a referendum campaign in Canada, suggesting that analogy is prevalent in political discourse. Over 75 per cent of the source analogues were based on higher-order relationships and structural features rather than on superficial features, and were taken from a range of source categories (including family, agriculture, sport and magic) with only 24 per cent from politics. As analogy appeared twice as many times in opinion articles than in news reports, they suggest analogies are often used in argumentative political discourse. Using a 'generation paradigm', Blanchette and Dunbar (2000) gave participants a target political problem (relating to cuts in public spending) and asked them to produce the source analogues themselves. They found that not only were most of the analogies generated (80 per cent) non-political or non-financial, but also relatively few were based on superficial similarities and instead had structural similarities. Asking people to generate analogies therefore appears to encourage participants to search their memory for relational, structurally similar sources.

Using a naturalistic context, Chen *et al.* (2004) found that people can use a source analogue even after a substantial time interval and that there was both explicit and implicit retrieval and use of the remote analogy. Their participants were able to draw on folk tales heard during their childhood to solve a target problem; even those participants who claimed that they were not reminded of the source tale outperformed a control group. They also noted that when a common solution tool is shared by both problems, then it was easier for participants to choose this tool to solve a target problem by mapping it to the source analogue. Other studies have shown that there are indeed pragmatic constraints which influence the use of a source analogue. For example, Keane (1990) provided participants with one of two versions of a story about a fire and then asked them to solve Maier's two-string problem. The story describes two ways in which a helicopter was used to save people trapped on the upper floors of a burning skyscraper. Which method failed and which was successful was reversed in the two versions. Participants typically used the successful method as a source analogue for the string problem, irrespective of its specific content, confirming the importance of pragmatic goals in problem-solving.

In summary, research on problem-solving has revealed that well-defined problems can be solved by using general-purpose, domain-independent heuristics. Our past experience can bias the initial representation of a problem which may activate potentially useful knowledge; however an impasse will occur if the initial problem presentation does not actually permit a solution. The importance of the role that knowledge may play for successful problem-solving in real life has come to light with research on the use of analogy.

8.5 Deductive and inductive reasoning

There appear to be three main criteria for deciding that an individual is engaging in problem-solving activities (Anderson, 1980), and a great variety of tasks meet these:

1   The activities must be goal-directed, i.e. the individual attempts to attain a particular end state.
2   The attainment of the goal or solution must involve a sequence of mental processes rather than just one.
3   These processes should be discernibly cognitive.

In many reasoning experiments, participants are asked to solve problems which have a well-defined structure in a system of formal logic. This qualifies as problem-solving, since the behaviour of anyone tackling this task is goal-directed and the task solution requires a number of intervening cognitive processes.

Research has involved tasks of both **deductive** and **inductive** reasoning. The distinction between these is that whereas with deductive reasoning the conclusion is certain, with inductive reasoning the conclusion is highly probable but not necessarily true. Deductive reasoning entails problems for which a normative solution is available, namely that required by the logical systems, and the participants' responses can be measured as either correct or incorrect against such a criterion. Certain statements or premises are provided and the task is to decide on whether the validity of the conclusion that follows is true. Inductive reasoning entails reaching conclusions which the participant cannot be certain are true, and in this sense the conclusion may be regarded as a hypothesis, the validity of which would have to be tested.

Much of the research that was conducted in the 1970s sought to examine whether individuals reason using formal rules such as logical calculus and to identify the particular rules that were used. In general, research found our reasoning to differ from that prescribed by a system of formal logic and that according to logic we make many errors, although not always if the content is drawn from everyday life. Before examining the key studies that were conducted and the type of errors that have been revealed, it is worth noting that the errors should not be considered to reflect unintelligent behaviour. Evans (1989) wrote that 'errors of thinking occur because of, rather than in spite of, the nature of our intelligence. In other words, they are an inevitable consequence of the way in which we think and a price to be paid for the extraordinary effectiveness with which we routinely deal with the massive information-processing requirements of everyday life' (111).

Deductive reasoning

Research on deductive reasoning involves presenting people with logically valid or invalid arguments where the truth of the conclusion or inference is dependent on the truth of certain premises. The information required to perform these reasoning tasks is provided and there is no need for the participant to draw on any stored information from long-term memory. An inference is made, and this simply entails making explicit something that was initially implicit in the premises. The following is one example of a valid deductive inference:

Premise 1	Hannah is older than Francesca;
Premise 2	Joseph is younger than Francesca;
Conclusion	Therefore, Hannah is older than Joseph.

This example simply requires us to know that the relation older–younger is *transitive*, which means that objects can be ordered in a single line (other transitive relations are smaller–larger, warmer–colder and darker–lighter). Another example of a valid deductive inference is:

Premise 1   The kettle will only work if it is switched on;

Premise 2   The kettle is not switched on,

Conclusion   Therefore, the kettle will not work.

This second example simply requires us to understand the connective 'only if' (there are other connectives, for example 'not' and 'and'). The point to note here is that in a logically valid argument, the truth of the premises will guarantee the truth of the conclusion – only the form of the argument and *not* the actual content is important.

With this sort of deductive reasoning, known as propositional logic, there are different rules of inference which are described in Box 8.2.

Box 8.2 Rules of inference

Two logically *valid* inferences:

1   *Modus ponens* (MP):

> *If p then q*   If the bell is ringing, then the dog is barking;
> *p*   The bell is ringing,
> *Therefore q*   Therefore, the dog is barking.

2   *Modus tollens* (MT):

> *If p then q*   If the bell is ringing, then the dog is barking;
> *Not q*   The dog is not barking,
> *Therefore not p* Therefore, the bell is not ringing.

Two logically *invalid* inference patterns:

1   Affirming the consequent (AC):

> *If p then q*   If the bell is ringing, then the dog is barking;
> *q*   The dog is barking,
> *Therefore p*   Therefore, the bell is ringing.

2   Denying the antecedent (DA):

> *If p then q*   If the bell is ringing, then the dog is barking;
> *Not p*   The bell is not ringing,
> *Therefore not q* Therefore, the dog is not barking.

So, how accurate are we at responding according to these rules of inference? Experiments have demonstrated that most of us do not make errors with MP; however, the error rate for MT can exceed 30 per cent, and participants frequently suggest that AC and DA are valid even though both are invalid (see Evans, 1989). In relation to AC, the bell does not have to be ringing for the dog to be barking; a letter might have been delivered instead. In relation to DA, equally, just because the bell is not ringing, does not mean the dog is not barking. Schroyens and Schaeken (2003) combined the data from a large number of experiments showing participants 'if p, then q' statements. They found that 97 per cent of participants endorsed the conclusion when the inference type was MP and 72 per cent when the inference type was MT. However, 63 per cent of participants erroneously endorsed the conclusion when the inference type was AC and 55 per cent when it was DA.

Newstead *et al.* (1997) presented conditional statements in the forms of either promises, tips, threats and warnings. For example:

> *Promise* (father to son): If you pass the exam, then I will buy you a bike.

> *Tip* (friend to friend): If you pass the exam, then your father will buy you a bike.

> *Threat* (boss to employee): If you are late for work again, then I will fire you.

> *Warning* (colleague to colleague): If you are late for work again, then the boss will fire you.

They then tested people's willingness to draw each of the four conditional types of inference outlined in Box 8.2. So, for the example of the 'promise' above, these would be:

> The son passed the exam, therefore his father bought him a bike. (MP)

> The father did not buy him a bike, therefore the son did not pass the exam. (MT)

> The father bought him a bike, therefore the son passed the exam. (AC)

> The son did not pass the exam, therefore his father did not buy him a bike. (DA)

They found that all four kinds of inference were significantly lower for tips than for promises, and for warnings than for threats.

Other research has also highlighted the importance of the content of the problem and how this is interpreted. For example, Evans *et al.* (1983) found that 71 per cent of participants accepted invalid arguments when the conclusion was believable, and Stevenson and Over (2001) found that when a premise was provided by an expert, it was perceived as more likely and as more believable than when provided by a novice. These findings suggest people do not reason according to formal rules; this issue is explored further in relation to research on inductive reasoning.

Inductive reasoning: hypothesis generation and testing

Inductive reasoning has been investigated by looking at the processes of hypothesis generation and hypothesis testing. One area of research relates to concept learning, which does not entail concept formation (how classes or categories are constructed) but concept attainment or identification, the search for attributes or qualities that are associated with a particular concept. In experiments, several stimuli will be identified as either positive or negative instances of the concept. The participant has to use the accumulating information from the positive and negative instances to decide what the concept is. Bruner *et al.* (1956) were the first to conduct research on concept learning, which demonstrated that we seem to select logical strategies when confronted with an inductive reasoning task. Which strategy is adopted, however, will depend on a range of factors, including the complexity of the problem and the cognitive skills of the person adopting the strategy. A tendency towards verifying rather than falsifying was observed in the way we seek to test the hypotheses we form and other research has provided evidence for this bias.

In a classic study, Wason (1960) informed participants that the three numbers '2 4 6' conformed to a simple relational rule (three numbers in increasing order of magnitude). Participants were then asked to generate sets of three numbers and to explain why they had chosen that set of three numbers. The experimenter in turn indicated whether each set conformed to the rule. Participants were told that when they thought they had discovered the correct rule, they were to reveal it. Wason found that most participants would generate a hypothesis, and then seek to generate sets of numbers that were consistent with the hypothesis. Only 21 per cent of participants guessed the rule correctly with their first attempt. Most participants did not attempt to disconfirm the hypothesis, which is actually the best way of testing its correctness. In a later study, Wason (1968) asked participants how they would determine whether or not their hypotheses were incorrect and only one quarter gave the correct answer. Wason went on to suggest that this confirmation bias is a very general tendency in human thought, and one possible explanation for why prejudices and false beliefs are maintained. Other research has shown that it is possible to encourage disconfirmation (e.g. Gorman and Gorman, 1984) and that when people reason together disconfirmation can be learned (Butera *et al.*, 2005).

Another very famous task devised by Wason (1960) is known as the four-card selection task (see Figure 8.5). This task has been intensively studied and requires participants to test hypotheses via deductive reasoning. Four cards are shown with A, K, 2 and 7 printed on them. The following rule is given: 'If there is an A on one side of the card, then there is a 2 on the other side of the card.' Participants are told to select only those cards that would need to be turned over in order to decide whether or not the rule is correct. The A card (*modus ponens*) and the 7 card (*modus tollens*) is the correct answer which was selected by very few. There is nothing to be gained by turning the 2 card over (affirmation of the consequent), since the rule does not claim that an A must be on the other side of a 2. The robustness of these findings has been demonstrated in subsequent work and typical results are that as few as 4 per cent of participants choose the

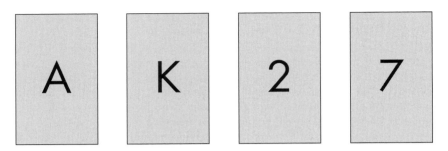

Figure 8.5 The Wason Selection Task

Source: Adapted from Wason (1960)

Note: The rule is 'If there is an A on one side of the card, then there is a 2 on the other side of the card.' Select only those cards that would need to be turned over in order to decide whether or not the rule is correct. Each card has a letter on one side and a number on the other.

correct answer, 46 per cent choose A and 2 cards, 33 per cent choose the A card only and 7 per cent choose A, 2 and 7 cards (Johnson-Laird and Wason, 1970). Originally, Wason explained the choice of cards in terms of a confirmation bias; that participants were trying to confirm rather than disconfirm the rule. However, alternative explanations have since emerged, one of these being that participants selected A and 2 because they were biased towards those items mentioned in the rule, i.e. there was a 'matching bias' (Evans and Lynch, 1973). Linguistic cues to relevance determine which cards the participants attend to and hence those they will consider for selection. Support for the explanation was offered by modifying the rule as follows: 'If there is an A on one side of the card, then there is NOT a 2 on the other side of the card.' Most participants would correctly select A and 2. They also incorrectly selected these cards when the rule was: 'If there is not an A on one side of the card, then there is a 2 on the other side of the card.' The correct response is K and 7.

However, the perceptual matching hypothesis cannot explain why more concrete everyday versions of the rule tend to elicit correct solutions. The ease with which people conform to logical principles when testing an hypothesis depends crucially on the content of the problem. One explanation is that reasoning is facilitated by the use of concrete and meaningful material (e.g. Wason and Shapiro, 1971; Johnson-Laird *et al.*, 1972). An alternative explanation, however, is that reasoning is facilitated when the problem relates directly to the participant's own experience (Griggs and Cox, 1982), although analogous rather than direct experience has also been found to assist performance on this task (Griggs and Cox, 1983).

Two conclusions can be drawn from research based on the card selection task devised by Wason. First, the original abstract version was not solved by thinking in a way that conformed to the logical rules of inference. Secondly, introducing a concrete version of the task that has thematic content, and associated prior knowledge, can sometimes produce more logical performance. Research by Evans (1996) has shown that participants actually spend little time thinking about

Box 8.3 Heuristics and human judgement

The experiments conducted by Daniel Kahneman and Amos Tversky in the late 1960s and early 1970s highlighted that people's assessments of likelihood and risk may not conform to the laws of probability but instead that judgement under uncertainty may rest on a limited number of simplifying heuristics. Their work has been highly influential and stimulated much research (see Koehler and Harvey, 2004, listed at the end of this chapter for further reading).

One important rule of thumb is the **availability heuristic**, whereby judgements are made on the basis of how available relevant examples are in our memory store, in other words the ease with which we can think of instances. Tversky and Kahneman (1973) asked participants whether the letters K, L, N, R and V occur more often in the first or the third position in English words. The common response was that each appears more often in the first position than the third, even though the reverse is the correct response, probably because it is easier to think of words starting with a certain letter. This heuristic is likely to make us overestimate the frequency of highly publicised events that are in fact comparatively rare, such as winning the lottery or dying in an air crash.

Other research has shown that we may make decisions between alternative possibilities on the basis of which appears more representative, regardless of other information; representative or typical instances of a category are judged to be more probable than unrepresentative ones. This **representativeness heuristic** can explain the *gambler's fallacy*, that after a run of losses there will be a good chance of a win. Similarly, when shown the following two sequences of coin tosses: (1) *HTHTTH*; (2) *TTTTTT* and asked which is more likely if the coin is fair, then the first sequence is usually picked. Although both are equally probable, the sample more representative of a larger run of coin tosses is preferred: namely the first sequence with equal numbers of 'heads' and 'tails'. Generally, we fail to acknowledge the random fluctuations observable in small samples.

This heuristic means that we make judgements on the basis of the extent to which the salient features of a person or object are representative of the features thought to be characteristic of some category. Kahneman and Tversky (1973) provided participants with brief descriptions of five people and told them that these descriptions had been chosen at random from a total of 100 descriptions. Half of the participants were told that this total consisted of descriptions of 70 engineers and 30 lawyers, whereas the others were told the opposite, that the descriptions were of 70 lawyers and 30 engineers – this is referred to as *base-rate* information or the *prior odds*. The participants' task was to decide the probability that the person written about in each description was an engineer or a lawyer. Some of the descriptions were similar to the stereotype we have of an engineer and dissimilar to that of a lawyer. In response to such a description, participants in both conditions would decide that there was approximately a 0.9 probability that the person was an engineer. The base-rate information about the sample composition was ignored – since

Jack resembles an engineer he is probably an engineer. This is known as the **base-rate fallacy**.

Alternatively, if they were provided with an uninformative description, which did not correspond to the stereotype of either an engineer or a lawyer, results showed that participants would typically rate the chance of Dick being an engineer or lawyer as equally likely, at 0.5 probability. However, if participants were asked to estimate the probability that an individual chosen at random was an engineer, and were provided with no information about the person, then they would estimate correctly either 0.7 or 0.3 probability depending on the base-rate data that had been given. This suggests that unless prior odds are the only relevant information, the representativeness heuristic guides our probability judgement. Tversky and Kahneman (1980) found that people were more inclined to take account of base-rate information when it seemed to be causally relevant.

the cards they do not select; cards with higher selection frequencies also had longer inspection times as if participants were taking the time to rationalise their choice. Therefore, although participants have selected the correct cards in some experiments using versions of Wason's task and hence showed evidence of logical reasoning, the findings of Evans (1996) suggests that their performance may not be the result of considering the consequences of alternative selections. Simply judging the correctness of our decisions according to a system of formal logic does not tell us whether the underlying process, our thinking, is logical.

8.6 Everyday reasoning

In our daily lives, we are required to draw conclusions or inferences and make decisions. Research on formal, well-defined reasoning problems has shown, as outlined above, that we make errors. The question then arises as to whether we perform as poorly with everyday, real-world problems.

Wagenaar (1994) reported on how the probability of guilt is determined in criminal courts and concluded that different heuristics are applied, with the availability heuristic being used most frequently (see Box 8.3). The confirmation bias is also apparent in that there is a preference for verification of guilt rather than falsification; for example, the positive identifications in a line-up by a few witnesses are likely to be believed even though the suspect was not recognised by a large number of other witnesses. Hill and Williamson (1998) reported on the decisions that players make when taking part in the National Lottery. They demonstrated that many of the heuristics and biases noted above are apparent in the Lottery number selections. For example, the tendency to choose numbers which have been least drawn can be explained in terms of the gambler's fallacy, whereas the tendency to choose numbers that appear 'random' rather than adjacent numbers can be explained in terms of the representativeness heuristic.

Research that has considered our ability to develop convincing arguments about everyday issues has also revealed shortcomings. Perkins *et al.* (1991) presented an overview of studies that asked participants questions of general social and political significance (e.g. would providing more money for state schools significantly improve the quality of teaching and learning?). Consistently, participants were found to perform poorly, with many providing only one-sided arguments or, worse still, biased arguments. Furthermore, education, maturation and life experience did not seem to improve the quality of the reasoning. Kuhn (1991) examined the effect of expertise on everyday reasoning skill. Participants were asked problems such as 'What causes unemployment?' Few presented alternative accounts or counter-arguments demonstrating a 'my-side' bias; 'my-side' arguments being those that support our initial judgements. Kuhn also selected participants who would be regarded as experts on the problems posed. However, again results showed that detailed knowledge of a topic is not necessarily linked to an improvement in their thinking. Sá *et al.* (2005) used a variant of the structured interview task introduced by Kuhn (1991) and looked at the generation of evidence and counter-evidence. They found many similarities between participants of high and low cognitive ability and both were more like to reiterate or elaborate on a previously stated theory than to provide a form of genuine evidence. The tendency to use the most sophisticated type of evidence in argument was not related to cognitive ability or thinking dispositions, but the tendency to use an unsophisticated form (i.e. reiterating or elaborating the original theory) was associated with both lower cognitive ability and lower actively open-minded thinking.

However, there is recent evidence that reasoning about real-life issues can involve a sophisticated chain of implicit inferences. Thompson *et al.* (2005) provided participants with conditional statements involving persuasions (e.g. 'If the Kyoto accord is ratified, greenhouse gas emissions will be reduced') and dissuasions (e.g. 'If the Kyoto accord is ratified, there will be a downturn in the economy'). Thus, the consequent event q, is presented as an incentive or disincentive for carrying out action p. Participants were then asked to reason about these statements from either the point of view of the writer or their own perspective. Their reasoning was found to rely on two main strategies which were: to assess the truth of the conditional statement or to argue the merits of carrying out action p. Furthermore, they were also more likely to adopt a deductive strategy when reasoning from a writer's point of view rather than from their own.

As with studies of formal reasoning, people's reasoning about general issues has been found to be error-prone or biased, but there is also some evidence of strategic reasoning. Although there are similarities between formal and everyday reasoning, there are, of course, differences. First, everyday reasoning requires us to generate premises, evaluate the premises we generate and take on board our existing emotions and beliefs attached to these premises or to the conclusions we reach. Secondly, in contrast to formal reasoning, we can revise or supplement the premises as we gain more information. Thirdly, whereas formal reasoning problems permit only one single conclusion, with everyday reasoning counter-arguments can be developed.

8.7 Theoretical approaches to reasoning

Mental logic theories

Mental logic theories (e.g. Braine and O'Brien, 1991; Rips, 1994), also known as formal rule theories, assume that our reasoning is underpinned by the use of mental rules even though we make errors and accept erroneous conclusions. These are similar to some of the rules of formal logic although we may not possess all the formal logical rules. Braine *et al.* (1984) have suggested that errors may also occur because of failures of comprehension; we expect to find all the information we need to know. If we are told, 'If the bell is ringing, then the dog is barking' then we will assume that it is just a bell ringing that makes the dog bark. Braine *et al.* (1984) showed that if we are provided with an additional premise, then we are less likely to consider the following affirmation of the consequent valid:

Premise 1	If the bell is ringing, then the dog is barking;
Premise 2	If the child is laughing, then the dog is barking;
Premise 3	The dog is barking,
Conclusion	Therefore, the bell is ringing.

These results provided further support for Braine's (1978) view that we use a natural logic; that we have a repertory of abstract rules that we will use unless tutored in standard logic. In the Wason selection task, participants will try to apply logical inference rules to the sides of the cards that are visible to predict what logically should be on the non-visible side. If they do not possess the *modus tollens* rule, then they would only select card A (and typically 33 per cent select just card A).

However, the findings of Byrne (1989) showed that information about additional requirements can *suppress* the valid inferences *modus ponens* and *modus tollens* (this is known as the suppression effect). For example, if provided with the following:

If she meets her boyfriend she will go to the cinema

She meets her boyfriend

many will conclude that she will go to the cinema. Yet if an additional premise is added:

If she has enough money she will go to the cinema

then, the number of participants concluding that she will go to the cinema is reduced. Although mental logic theories can provide explanations for such findings, it does not seem to be the case that our everyday conclusions are either endorsed or not. Instead, they appear to have a property which is known as 'non-monotonicity' – we constantly revise our everyday conclusions when we get new evidence.

Pragmatic reasoning schemata

Cheng and colleagues (Cheng and Holyoak, 1985; Cheng *et al.*, 1986) have argued that we develop abstract rules for reasoning from our experiences in many different domains, but these are not at a logical or syntactic level but at a pragmatic level. People often reason using **pragmatic reasoning schemata**, which are clusters of rules that are highly generalised and abstracted but defined with respect to different types of relationships and goals. For example, in our everyday lives we are exposed to situations involving permission (we need certain qualifications for certain professions), and these are situations in which some action A may be taken only if some precondition B is satisfied. Cheng *et al.* (1986) explain that if we encounter a problem where the semantic aspects suggest that this is a permission situation then all of the rules about permissions in general can be called on, including 'If action A is to be taken, then precondition B must be satisfied', 'Action A is to be taken only if precondition B is satisfied', 'If precondition B is not satisfied, then action A must not be taken', and so on. We are also exposed to situations involving obligation (if our child is ill for a while, we must inform the school they attend), and from these we note that the occurrence of some condition A incurs the necessity of taking some action B. Cheng *et al.* (1986) point out that rules about obligations are not quite the same but similar to rules about permissions. The rule 'If condition A occurs, then obligation B arises' implies 'If obligation B does not arise, then condition A must not have occurred', but not 'Condition A occurs only if obligation B arises'.

The rules of some of the pragmatic reasoning schemata will lead to the same solution as the rules of standard logic. Therefore, we will appear to provide responses that would be classified as logical. However, the underlying process has not entailed the application of logical rules, and errors will arise when the rules of the schemata differ from those that follow from standard logic. Of relevance here is that the 'abstract permission rule' will allow us to solve Wason's selection task, but this rule needs to be invoked by the rules stated in the task, and this is unlikely to occur with the standard abstract version of the task. Instead, we can solve versions of the task even if we do not have the direct experience of the rules, as long as the rules can be rationalised as giving permissions. Furthermore, pragmatic reasoning schemata account for why the content and context of the reasoning task is important.

Mental models

Rather than argue that our deductive reasoning is logical when we find the correct solution and illogical when we find the wrong one, Johnson-Laird (1983) suggested that we either use the appropriate **mental model** or an inappropriate one. We construct the mental model or representation according to what is described in the premises and this will depend on how these are interpreted. We can use imagery to create this representation. For example, according to the following set of premises:

> The milk is to the right of the margarine
> The yoghurt is to the left of the milk
> The cheese is in front of the milk
> The cream is to the left of the cheese

We could imagine the food on a shelf in a fridge laid out as:

margarine	yoghurt	milk
	cream	cheese

From this mental model we could conclude that the cream is in front of the yoghurt even though this is not explicitly stated in the premises. To test this we would need to search for an alternative model that would also fit these premises; if none is found then we can stick with that conclusion. However, a search would yield an alternative model, namely:

yoghurt	margarine	milk
	cream	cheese

We would have to conclude that we are not sure whether the margarine or the yoghurt is behind the cream.

This approach distinguishes between first comprehending the premises and secondly reasoning with the models. If we are not trained in logic, then we will find it difficult to reason with negation. Johnson-Laird *et al.* (1992) found that negation could either affect comprehension or it could affect reasoning. The statement 'It is not the case that there is no cream in the fridge' is difficult to comprehend and takes longer to comprehend than its logical equivalent 'There is cream in the fridge'. However, once the premises have been understood and represented as mental models, then reasoning will depend on whether you have searched for all possible models. For example, 'It is not the case there is cheese or there is yoghurt' only needs one mental model:

no cheese	no yoghurt

However, the statement: 'It is not the case that there is both cheese and yoghurt' actually yields three models:

no cheese yoghurt	cheese no yoghurt	no cheese no yoghurt

So although negation makes comprehension difficult, it is the number of mental models which have to be considered that makes reasoning more difficult. The limits of our working memory restrict the number of models that we can construct and hold in our working memory. Errors occur if more than one model has to be constructed to allow us to reach a valid conclusion and we shy away from doing so, providing instead a conclusion that is true according to our initial model.

The mental models theory has been found to have explanatory breadth, with many researchers applying it to different domains of reasoning and everyday reasoning, and the notion that we reason by constructing concrete internal representations of situations has intuitive plausibility. However, research investigating the claim that we search for alternative models (counter-examples) seems to suggest that we do not tend to do so spontaneously (e.g. Evans *et al.*, 1999).

The probabilistic approach

Oaksford and Chater (1994, 1998) proposed that logic does not provide us with an appropriate framework with which to understand people's everyday inferences. They argued that our everyday reasoning is probabilistic and we make errors when presented with logical tasks in the laboratory because we draw on the strategies we use in everyday life. For example, rather than use logical rules to ascertain an inference, we draw on our beliefs and prior experience and assess the likelihood, i.e. the conditional probability, that a certain conclusion is true. In relation to the following: If John has a runny nose then he has a cold, Oaksford (2005) explained that accepting this requires 'the belief that John's having a runny nose makes it very likely that he has a cold. This involves assessing the *conditional probability* that John has a cold given that he has a runny nose. So if you have noticed John having a runny nose on say 100 occasions, 95 of which involved him having a cold, then the relevant conditional probability is 0.95' (425).

Consistent with this approach are the findings of Evans *et al.* (2003). They conducted three experiments where they asked participants to judge the probability of 'if *p*, then *q*' conditional statements in order to explore the basis of their judgements. See Box 8.4 for an example of the type of problem they presented. They found that participants assessed the probability of conditional statements as a matter of degree and not according to what was implied by logic.

Oaksford and Chater have shown that probabilistic approach can account for participants' performances on deductive inference tasks as well as on Wason's selection task (see Oaksford and Chater, 2001). Importantly, this approach to reasoning departs from other explanations in the way it accounts for human rationality. Rather than define rationality as logical reasoning and explain departures from rationality (errors in our reasoning) in terms of performance limitations (e.g. the limited nature of short-term memory), the probabilistic approach defines rationality in terms of probabilistic reasoning.

> ## Box 8.4 Example of problem used by Evans et al. (2003)
>
> A pack contains cards that are either yellow or red and have either a circle or a diamond printed on them. In total there are:
>
> 1 yellow circle
> 4 yellow diamonds
> 16 red circles
> 16 red diamonds
>
> How likely are the following claims to be true of a card drawn at random from the pack?
>
> If the card is yellow then it has a circle printed on it.
> If a card has a diamond printed on it then it is red.

Dual process accounts

There have been attempts to integrate theories of reasoning by proposing a two-way partition in reasoning abilities. Dual process accounts have been applied to reasoning (Evans and Over, 1996; Stanovich and West, 2000) as well as to judgement and decision-making (Kahneman and Frederick, 2002). Most of these propose that we do have an (albeit limited) capacity for explicit logical reasoning which is embodied either in mental logic or in mental models. However, much of our reasoning takes place implicitly and is independent of such logical processes. For example, Evans and Over (1996) distinguished between two kinds of rationality; a personal rationality (rationality$_1$), when we are successful in achieving our goals, and an impersonal rationality (rationality$_2$), when we reason according to normative theory (formal logic or probability theory). They argued that whilst we have a considerable amount of the former, we have only a restricted capacity for the latter. Stanovich and West (2000) made a similar distinction between what they termed System 1 and System 2 reasoning processes. The former are automatic, unconscious and based on implicitly acquired world knowledge whereas the latter are controlled, analytic and based on explicitly acquired formal rules. Evans (2003) commented that although the notion of two distinct kinds of reasoning is not a new one, it is only in recent years that cognitive scientists have proposed two quite separate cognitive systems underlying thinking, which have distinct evolutionary histories. Using the terms introduced by Stanovich and West, he described System 1 as a form of universal cognition shared by humans and animals. In contrast, System 2 has evolved more recently and is considered to be uniquely human: 'System 2 provides the basis for hypothetical thinking that endows modern humans with unique potential for a higher level of rationality in their reasoning and decision-making' (458). Research needs to consider how these two systems interact, and how conflict and competition between the two systems might be resolved.

Summary

- The study of problem-solving has shown that we use a limited number of strategies and heuristics to solve a range of problems and these allow us to work within the limitations of our memory system.
- Successful problem-solving is dependent on how the problem is represented and on prior knowledge as well as the strategies used.
- Our existing knowledge may allow us to solve new problems through analogy; a source analogue is mapped onto the target problem.
- Naturalistic studies have shown that people will use structurally similar source analogues, although when tested in the laboratory analogical problem-solving may not be an automatic process.
- When assessed on formal logical tasks, participants do not appear to reason according to formal logic.
- Instead, the use of strategies and heuristics is also evident in how we solve reasoning tasks.
- Domain-specific rules such as pragmatic reasoning schemata may emerge with experience and explain why the content and the context of the problem is important.
- The theory of mental models provides us with a framework for understanding the processes underlying both formal and everyday reasoning.
- An alternative theoretical framework is the probabilistic approach, which provides a better account for performances on deductive tasks and avoids defining rationality in terms of logical rules.
- Dual process accounts also accept that much of our reasoning is independent of logical processes.

Further reading

Davidson, J.E. and Sternberg, R.J. (eds) (2003). *The Psychology of Problem Solving*. New York: Cambridge University Press. The edited book includes chapters by experts in the field and looks at problem-solving and the factors that influence problem solution.

Gilhooly, K.J. (1996). *Thinking: Directed, Undirected and Creative*. (3rd edn.) London: Academic Press. This book provides more detail on the research described here, as well as chapters on creativity and daydreaming, not covered here.

Evans, J.St.B.T. and Over, D.E. (1996). *Rationality and Reasoning*. Hove: Psychology Press. This book provides an overview of the research relevant to its title, and a full account of their view of rationality.

Koehler, D.J. and Harvey, N. (eds) (2004). *Blackwell Handbook of Judgment and Decision Making*. Oxford: Blackwell. This book provides an overview of this field, highlighting the major findings, current trends and practical applications as well as the different approaches that have been taken.

Chapter 9

Disorders of thinking: executive functions and the frontal lobes

9.1 Introduction

Many of our everyday tasks involve the implementation and monitoring of habitual well-established routines, such as making coffee and cleaning the bath, and these routines are considered to be established in memory requiring little of our attention. Many other tasks, including problem-solving activities, involve a series of operations such as searching, matching, deciding, evaluating and transforming, and established cognitive skills often have to be reorganised to allow novel patterns of behaviour to be implemented. Exactly how these mental processes are controlled is still open to debate, but increasingly, reference is made to the role of the frontal lobes in the **executive functions** of human cognition. Luria (1966) suggested that it was the responsibility of the frontal lobes to program and regulate behaviour and Baddeley (1986) saw the frontal lobes as having a coordinating, monitoring and organising role in working memory.

Although there is no single deficit of thinking equivalent to aphasia, agnosia or amnesia, damage to the frontal lobes and executive functions will affect the processes that are associated with problem-solving, the operational definition of thinking adopted in Chapter 8. Executive functions encompass meta-abilities necessary for appropriate social functioning and everyday problem-solving: the deployment of attention, the initiation of non-habitual action, goal-directed behaviour, planning, insight, foresight and self-regulation. A major part of this chapter will outline research looking at the effects of frontal lobe damage on tests involving attention, abstract and conceptual thinking, cognitive estimation and strategy formation. First, however, the chapter will look at the anatomy of the frontal lobes and consider the different behavioural deficits seen in patients with frontal lesions.

9.2 Anatomy and physiology of the frontal lobes

The frontal lobes constitute approximately one third of the mass of each cerebral hemisphere, encompassing all tissue anterior to the central sulcus. It is not surprising, therefore, that patients with damage to the frontal lobes area show a great diversity of impairments that may affect motor, emotional, social or cognitive processes. The lobes comprise a variety of areas which are functionally and anatomically distinct (see Figure 9.1) and which can be grouped into three broad categories (Kolb and Whishaw, 1996). The first category is the motor cortex, which was classified by Brodmann as area 4. The second category is the premotor cortex (area 6 and some of area 8), and in humans the lateral premotor area includes Broca's area (area 44). The motor and premotor areas play an important role in the control of limb, hand, foot and digit movements as well as influencing the control of face and eye movements.

The third category is the prefrontal cortex, which in primates can be subdivided into the dorsolateral prefrontal cortex (areas 9, 46); the ventral (or inferior) prefrontal cortex (areas 11, 12, 13, 14); and the medial frontal cortex (areas 25, 32). Studies conducted in the early decades of the twentieth century revealed rich and complex afferent and efferent connections to a variety of other areas of the

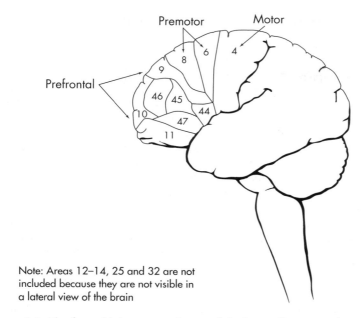

Note: Areas 12–14, 25 and 32 are not
included because they are not visible in
a lateral view of the brain

Figure 9.1 The frontal lobes. Lateral view of the brain illustrating the major
subdivisions of the frontal lobes

brain. The prefrontal cortex receives afferent pathways from the auditory, visual, gustatory, olfactory and somatosensory areas. There are connections to and from many subcortical areas including the limbic system (which plays an important role in arousal, motivation and affect), the caudate nucleus (the part of the basal ganglia involved in the integration, programming, inception and termination of motor activity) and the amygdala (which is implicated in the control of fear, rage and aggression).

9.3 The impact of frontal lobe damage on behaviour

Before looking at specific cognitive deficits that have been linked with frontal lobe functioning, this section provides an overview of the case histories of individuals who have sustained frontal damage and the range of behavioural deficits that have been observed. There is great variation in the functional results of frontal lobe damage, and this was apparent in studies conducted in the nineteenth and early twentieth centuries. Many of the changes in behaviour are actually related to lesions in the prefrontal cortex, and variation is hardly surprising given the size and complexity of the prefrontal cortex and its many connections to most brain areas. Some of these early studies will now be described and these serve to highlight how damage to the frontal lobes can impact on personality and bring about affective changes.

265

Early clinical studies

Early clinical work revealed wide-ranging changes in personality. Some found a pattern of aggression, bad temper and viciousness whereas others described a lack of concern and inappropriate cheerfulness. The most famous case concerning frontal lobe damage is that of Phineas Gage, described by Harlow (1848, 1868). Prior to injury, Phineas Gage was a conscientious and industrious railroad engineer, whose responsibilities included placing and detonating explosives. A fuse and a tamping iron, an iron bar 3.5 feet long and 13.25 pounds in weight, were used to set off the explosive. Accidentally, Gage placed the tamping iron on the explosive, prematurely detonating the explosive, and the result was that the tamping iron penetrated his skull. It entered through the side of his face, passed through the left frontal lobe and exited from the right frontal bone (see Figure 9.2 and Macmillan, 1986). Gage survived and the injury did not appear to have any major long-term effects, with the exception of a change in his personality. Following the accident he was no longer reliable or considerate and showed poor judgement and poor social skills. Harlow (1868) suggested that these changes in behaviour were a result of the frontal lobe's responsibility for planning and the maintenance of socially acceptable behaviour.

A change in personality was noted by Welt (1888) when reporting the case of a 37-year-old man, presumed drunk, who had fallen from a fourth-storey window. He suffered a severe penetrating frontal fracture. Five days after sustaining this injury he showed a change in personality. He went from being an honest,

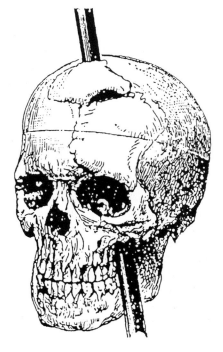

Figure 9.2
Phineas Gage's skull. The entry and exit of the tamping iron are shown here

Source: From Macmillan (1986), reproduced by permission of Academic Press

hard-working and cheerful man to being aggressive, malicious and prone to making bad jokes (the term 'Witzelsucht' was used to describe this addiction to joking). He teased other patients and played mean tricks on the hospital staff. After about a month of such objectionable behaviour, he became his old self, only to die some months later from an infection.

In contrast, Jastrowitz (1888) reported a form of dementia in patients with tumours of the frontal lobe, which was characterised by an oddly cheerful agitation. He used the term 'moria' (meaning stupidity) to describe this behaviour. Others, including Zacher (1901) and Campbell (1909), emphasised the lack of concern and apathy shown by their patients. Brickner (1936) described a patient whose prefrontal region was almost completely excised in an operation. The fundamental disability that emerged appeared to be a problem with synthesising essentially intact cognitive processes. Ackerly (1937) found no decline in 'general intelligence' in a 37-year-old woman whose entire right prefrontal region had been amputated and left prefrontal region damaged. She also continued to be the same sociable, likeable and kind-hearted person; instead the key change in her behaviour was that once she had started a task she had to complete it, reflecting an abnormal lack of distractibility.

Early animal studies

Early experimental work by physiologists on animals, investigating neural mechanisms, led to a variety of conclusions. Goltz (1892) experimented with dogs and, together with his assistant Loeb (1902), concluded that the prefrontal region did not contain the neural mechanisms underlying intelligence or personality traits. Ferrier (1876) found ablations of the prefrontal region in monkeys to result in changes that were difficult to describe precisely. Despite appearing normal, they seemed more apathetic and less attentive and intelligent. Bianchi (1922) conducted experimental studies on monkeys and dogs across three decades. He found unilateral prefrontal ablations to be without effect and whilst bilateral ablations did not result in any sensory or motor defects, they did result in marked changes in character. The animals became less affectionate and sociable and more fearful and agitated; furthermore, they tended to perform repetitive, aimless movements rather than purposeful actions. Bianchi suggested that these changes were linked to the disintegration of the total personality rather than to a loss of 'general intelligence' or of a specific ability.

With the rise of animal psychology, many other studies examining the effects of experimentally produced prefrontal lesions were conducted during the first half of the twentieth century. These confirmed that unilateral ablation had no significant effect. Bilateral lesions were found to impair animals on tasks where they were required to keep in mind an environmental event for a short period of time. Jacobsen et al. (1935) found in one female chimpanzee a change in personality and behaviour as a result of a bilateral prefrontal ablation. Behaviour suggestive of 'Witzelsucht' was observed alongside a change in her affective reactions. Like Bianchi, Jacobsen et al. found that prefrontally injured monkeys and dogs did show changes in personality, alongside certain cognitive deficits that were detectable but not easy to describe. Previously, the chimpanzee had become upset to the point of having temper tantrums when she made mistakes on complex tasks. After the bilateral lobectomy, she no longer showed such behaviour when making mistakes.

Later clinical studies

More recent clinical studies also describe changes to personality and, in addition, highlight that decision-making can be affected, despite the fact that there is no indication of any significant impairment in any specific cognitive skill. For example, Eslinger and Damasio (1985) described the case of an accountant who underwent an operation to remove part of his frontal lobes. Afterwards, he was very poor at organising his life, even though he performed extremely well on a wide range of neuropsychological tests and achieved an IQ of over 130. He was unable to hold down a job, went bankrupt and was twice divorced. He was frequently unable to make decisions over relatively simple matters such as which restaurants to dine in or which clothes to wear. A similar effect of frontal lobe damage was described by Schindler *et al.* (1995), when reporting on two cases. Both patients showed a change in personality and, despite having intact language, memory and perceptual skills, each showed impaired decisional capacity. Both patients were able to describe their medical problems and their need for treatment, and both felt they could provide adequate self-care. Neither patient wanted to give up their familiar surroundings and change their way of living. However, on several occasions one patient had been found in her house lying on the floor with inadequate heating and rubbish filling some of the rooms. The other patient had failed to prepare meals for herself, despite the fact that her son ensured that food was available in her apartment. The patients appeared to be competent,

---

Box 9.1 Three key aspects affected

Frontal lobe damage has been found to impact upon several different aspects of behaviour which are not necessarily mutually exclusive (Andrewes, 2001):

1. Drive: typically a patient fails to complete tasks on time, despite knowing that the task needs to be undertaken, she or he will not quite get round to doing it.

2. Impaired social skills: patients are frequently described as behaving inappropriately in social settings. In the more extreme cases, she or he may make inappropriate sexual advances and show aggressive behaviour. In less extreme cases, the patient may make inappropriate and hurtful comments.

3. Lack of insight: patients do not monitor their own behaviour or the reactions of others and this may hamper rehabilitation as they may not accept that they are performing poorly on tasks or in their social relationships.

demonstrating verbal fluency and intact memory, but in reality were unable to care for themselves.

The clinical and animal studies described in this section demonstrate that damage to the frontal lobes can result in a range of different behavioural deficits, pertaining to humour, affect and personality as well as aspects of decision-making behaviour. Della Sala *et al.* (1998) comment that although not all patients show personality change, certain recurring themes were observed, sometimes referred to as 'frontal lobishness' or 'frontal lobe syndrome'. One patient may show a higher level of apathy, another may display a contrasting picture of practical joking and disinhibited social behaviour, and a third may display, at different times, both of these patterns. Benton (1991) noted that the term frontal lobe syndrome 'was adopted to refer to this aggregation of deficits, perhaps as much as a convenient label as from any conviction that it represented a true syndrome, i.e., a conjunction of inherently related symptoms' (26). To avoid making assumptions about the area of the brain responsible, the term 'dysexecutive syndrome' is often used instead; alternatively some use the term 'executive dysfunction' to avoid the implications associated with the word 'syndrome'.

The case histories of those who have sustained frontal damage are rather perplexing in that any cognitive effects are often by no means immediately apparent and there is little or no obvious mental deterioration. In the past twenty years though, a considerable body of evidence has appeared which suggests that rather than being implicated in specific cognitive operations, such as memorising, the frontal lobes are concerned with the deployment and coordination of cognitive operation. Hence, as mentioned in the introduction, the frontal lobes have come to be regarded as being responsible for the highest forms of human thought, for the 'executive' or 'supervisory' functions of cognition, which refer to a range of related abilities, including our ability to plan and regulate goal-directed behaviour, to deploy attention and to use information flexibly.

The next section will review empirical findings concerning these executive functions. It will become apparent that there is no single test that will be failed by all frontal patients but instead a range of tests that appear to tap these so-called 'executive' tasks. It is also worth bearing in mind that although impairments on these tasks can be attributed to dysfunction of the frontal lobes, there are many different kinds of damage as the frontal lobes are large structures. Therefore, frontal patients are heterogeneous in terms of both the site of damage and their behavioural symptoms.

9.4 Impairments in the deployment of attention

Successful problem-solving requires both goal-directed thinking and an ability to correctly direct and sustain attention. The ability of brain-damaged patients to monitor what is happening in the environment, and their ability to sustain their concentration and not be distracted, has been examined using a variety of tests. Characteristically, patients with lesions to the frontal lobes show impaired performance.

Sustaining and concentrating attention

Salmaso and Denes (1982) asked participants to perform a vigilance task, namely to detect a target stimulus which was interspersed infrequently among repeated presentations of other stimuli (a signal detection task). The stimuli were either pairs of sloping lines or pairs of letters that were presented only briefly. Participants were required to respond on those occasional trials when the pairs of lines or letters were different. Some of the patients with bilateral frontal lobe damage could not reliably detect the targets. This suggests that their ability to sustain their attention was adversely affected.

An impairment in concentration in a simple counting task was observed in patients with right frontal lobe damage (Wilkins *et al.*, 1987). In particular, patients had difficulty in counting either auditory clicks or tactile pulse stimuli when they were presented at a rate of one per second. The involvement of the right frontal lobe in sustaining attention has also been reported in a more recent study. Rueckert and Grafman (1996) gave patients with left and right frontal lobe lesions three sustained attention tasks. The first was a simple reaction time task requiring participants to respond when they saw an X. The second was a Continuous Performance Test asking patients to respond to an X but not to any other letter. The third required them to respond to a specified target when reading a story. For all three tests, patients with right frontal lobe lesions missed more targets and showed longer reaction times compared with matched control participants. Furthermore, their performance on the Continuous Performance Test got worse with time.

Suppressing attention

The reduction in the ability of patients with frontal lobe damage to sustain their attention is complemented by evidence of their distractibility and their inability to inhibit automatic or habitual responses. During testing, their attention frequently wanders and they will often report irrelevant things. Frontal patients have been observed to grasp or use objects placed near them (Lhermitte, 1983), providing evidence that the patient's habitual responses are being triggered even in situations where they are not required. Lhermitte (1986) describes one incident when a patient was brought to an apartment and shown around. When introduced to the bedroom, where the bedspread had been removed from the bed and the top sheet turned back, the patient got undressed and climbed into bed. This behaviour is termed 'utilisation behaviour' and is dependent on external environmental cues which capture the attentional resources available to the patient. The patient is often conscious of this behavioural dependence but is unable to control it even when the patient has been instructed to do something else, such as complete a psychometric test. One patient, LE, was observed to pick up and deal out a pack of cards appropriately for the number of people present in the room (Shallice *et al.*, 1989). The pack of cards present in the clinical interview acted as an environmental trigger.

An inability to suppress the most salient response was observed when frontal patients were administered the Stroop Colour Word task. If shown the word 'red' written in 'blue', we usually have no trouble in saying what the word is, but find naming the colour of the ink more problematic because we need to suppress our habitual reading response (see Chapter 3 for further information). In one study, patients with left frontal lesions have been found to perform very poorly on the Stroop test (Perret, 1974) and in another only bilateral frontal damage was found to be associated with increased errors and slowness in response time for the incongruent condition (Stuss *et al.*, 2001). The involvement of the frontal structures in this task has been confirmed in an experiment using normal volunteers; activation of anterior right hemisphere and medial frontal structures were observed using positron emission tomography (Bench *et al.*, 1993).

Perret (1974) found that those patients performing poorly on the Stroop test also failed to perform well on a verbal fluency test (to search for words beginning with a certain initial letter). He suggested that this could be because the verbal fluency test makes similar cognitive processing demands, namely to suppress the habitual response of searching for words according to their meaning. Burgess and Shallice (1996a) considered this issue further, using a task which allowed them to examine both verbal response inhibition as well as response initiation. They presented a task involving sentences in which the last word was missing (the Hayling test). The missing word is strongly cued by the rest of the sentence, for example the word 'stamp' is cued by 'He mailed the letter without a . . .'. For the first half of these sentences, patients were asked to provide the word which they thought could fit at the end of the sentence (response initiation condition). For the second half they were asked to provide a word which made no sense at all in the context of the sentence (response suppression or inhibition condition). In comparison to patients with posterior lesions, patients with frontal lobe lesions took longer to complete the sentences in the response *initiation* condition. They also performed worse in the response *inhibition* condition, providing significantly more straightforward completions of the sentence. Even when the answers were not completions, the words they selected were more likely to be semantically related to the sentence. An inability to suppress a current response is also a possible reason for frontal lobe patients' failure on other tasks, for example the Wisconsin Card Sorting Test described in the next section.

9.5 Impairments in abstract and conceptual thinking

Successful problem-solving requires us to go beyond the information provided and engage in abstract thinking. One commonly used method of assessing abstraction involves classification or sorting tasks. Such tasks require participants to abstract the concept or rule used for sorting. These are similar to the inductive reasoning tasks described in Chapter 8. The ability of frontal patients to formulate and test hypotheses as to what the correct rule may be is usually impaired; however, the cognitive nature of this impairment has been linked to processes other than the inductive one.

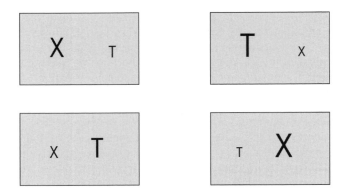

Figure 9.3 Card sorting task

Source: Adapted from Cicerone *et al.* (1983)

Note: The task is to abstract a single critical dimension from stimuli varying on four dimensions: size, colour, form and position

An early study by Halstead (1940) asked patients with bilateral frontal lesions to perform a fairly simple sorting task, namely to sort the items that were similar amongst 62 miscellaneous objects into separate groups. Some patients did not include all the items in their groupings, and the groupings themselves were not meaningful; there was no apparent coherent organising principle.

Other sorting tasks use an array of tokens which vary in dimensions such as shape and colour. In a study by Cicerone *et al.* (1983) patients with bilateral frontal lobe lesions were shown stimuli that varied on four dimensions, namely size, colour, form and position. The task was to abstract the critical dimension. On each trial, patients were shown four pairs of stimuli and asked to choose one according to what they thought the critical dimension might be (see Figure 9.3).

On specified trials, they were told if their choice was right or wrong, and negative feedback would require them to switch to a different hypothesis and select a different dimension. Results showed that patients with tumours of the frontal lobe were impaired on this task compared to participants with posterior tumours. Those with frontal lobe lesions used fewer hypotheses and frequently failed to shift from an irrelevant hypothesis, even when told their choice was incorrect. They continued to select the stimulus using the same dimension on subsequent trials despite negative feedback, as if they were failing to attend to all of the relevant dimensions.

Failure to make effective use of feedback was also noted in earlier research using the Wisconsin Card Sorting Test. Here, patients are presented with four cards, which can vary along three dimensions, namely number, colour and shape (see Figure 9.4). The number of items on the card ranges from 1–4, the shape of the items on the card is either a circle, triangle, cross or star and the colour of the items on the card is either red, green, yellow or blue. The task is to sort a stack of cards into four piles, with one pile below each card on the table.

Figure 9.4 Wisconsin Card Sorting Test

Note: The cards vary along three dimensions: number, colour and shape, and the task is to sort a stack of cards according to a rule

As with the previous test, the participant has to hypothesise the rule, for example sort according to colour, and the experimenter provides feedback as to whether each card is being placed correctly in one of the four piles. For example, if the card is red, the participant must sort the card with the pile that has red objects. After a specific number of cards have been correctly placed (for example ten consecutive correct responses), the experimenter changes the rule without warning and only sorts that accord with the new category will result in positive feedback. Neurologically intact individuals quickly detect such rule changes and switch to a new hypothesis accordingly. Patients with frontal lobe damage have been found to continue with their original rule despite the negative feedback they were receiving (Milner, 1964). This has been called a 'stuck-in-set' tendency; a change in rule involves a shift from the colour dimension to the number dimension but the patient still sticks with the colour dimension. They may continue to sort according to their first hypothesis for as many as 100 cards, showing an inability to shift response strategy, known as **perseveration**, and a lack of flexibility in their behaviour.

Perseverative responses were also observed in a recent study by Miller and Tippett (1996), when employing the Matchstick Test of Cognitive Flexibility. This test is a visual problem-solving task and therefore a very different task to the sorting tasks described previously. It requires the participant to show different ways of removing sticks from a two-dimensional geometric figure so that a particular shape emerges (see Figure 9.5). Their results showed that patients with damage to the right frontal lobe were impaired in their ability to shift strategy. Those with left frontal lobe damage displayed no significant difficulty. These results are consistent with earlier research that has found the right frontal lobe to be more important than the left when the tasks entail minimal verbal requirements.

Other research has attempted to identify the extent to which the perseveration observed in concept formation tasks is a result of not attending to the feedback provided. Findings have revealed that when a modified version of the Wisconsin Card Sorting Test is used, so that patients are warned and explicitly told of a change in the rule (Nelson, 1976), or are told explicitly which dimension to use to sort the cards (Delis *et al.*, 1992), a significant number of frontal

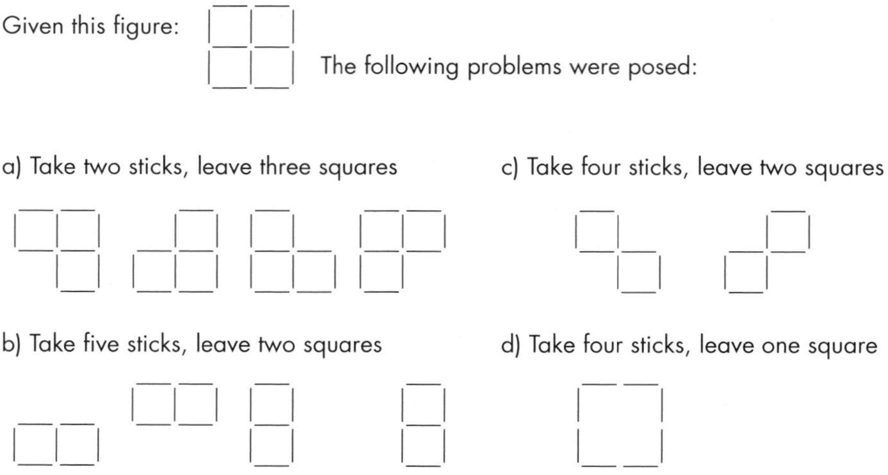

Given this figure: The following problems were posed:

a) Take two sticks, leave three squares

c) Take four sticks, leave two squares

b) Take five sticks, leave two squares

d) Take four sticks, leave one square

Figure 9.5 Matchstick Test of Cognitive Flexibility

Source: Adapted from Miller and Tippett (1996)

Note: The four problems associated with one of the geometric designs used in the Matchstick Test of Cognitive Flexibility are shown here

patients still continued to show perseveration. Although patients are able to abstract a rule or formulate an hypothesis when presented with the Wisconsin Card Sorting Test, they do not use the feedback they are given to modulate their behaviour and shift to a different rule. The results of Delis *et al.* suggest that patients are impaired both in their ability to use the feedback provided *and* in their ability to shift to a different rule. Delis *et al.* used a new sorting task requiring participants in one condition to sort six cards spontaneously and to report the rule they employed; in a second condition to report the rules for correct sorts performed by the examiner and in a third condition to sort the cards according to abstract cues or explicit information provided by the examiner. Their results revealed that no single deficit, such as perseveration, could account for their findings. The authors concluded that although impaired abstract thinking was not the primary deficit, it is one of several 'higher-level' functions that collectively disrupt the problem-solving ability of frontal patients.

Matters are complicated further by the findings of Owen *et al.* (1991). They found frontal patients were not impaired if the shift involved the same dimension. This is termed an intra-dimensional shift and occurs when a participant is required to transfer a rule involving a stimulus dimension such as colour or shape to a novel set of exemplars of that same stimulus dimension. Patients were impaired, however, when they were required to shift response set to an alternative, previously irrelevant dimension. This is termed an extradimensional shift and is a core component of the Wisconsin Card Sorting Test. The authors wrote that 'The behaviour of the frontal lobe group ... was observed to be characterized by a total disregard for the correct, previously irrelevant dimension' (1003). Barceló *et al.* (1997) suggested that frontal lobe patients may be impaired mostly in making extradimensional shifts because of their inability to suppress previous incorrect responses; thus the poor performance of frontal patients on the Wisconsin Card Sorting Test may be linked to problems in inhibitory control. Helmstaedter *et al.* (1996) found impaired response inhibition (known as **disinhibition**) to be one characteristic of patients with frontal lobe epilepsy that differentiated them from patients with temporal lobe epilepsy.

In order to understand better the cognitive nature of impairments in the Wisconsin Card Sorting Test, Barceló and Knight (2002) sought to analyse the nature of non-perseverative errors as these will reduce the total amount of achieved categories. Using a modified version of the Wisconsin Card Sorting Test, their earlier research had found that normal participants are forced to make non-perseverative errors early in the series in order to find the new sorting rule (e.g. Barceló, 1999); and this was because participants undertake a trial-and-error process whereby they keep track of past incorrect rules to obtain the correct new rule quickly. Barceló and Knight termed these 'efficient errors' as they entail the efficient use of recent contextual information to optimise set shifting, and one would expect someone to make these errors following a shift in the rule. Another type of non-perseverative errors are those that involve a shift in set but entail in-efficient use of past contextual information; these were termed 'random errors'. Compared to age-matched controls, their prefrontal patients made more perse-verative errors and this is in line with the studies outlined previously. However, their patients also made a larger number of random errors. Indeed, in 52 per cent of the series patients produced more random errors than perseverative errors. When describing their observations, Barceló and Knight wrote: 'Most patients described their problems sorting cards by saying that they were "confused" or "baffled" by the cards. One patient (WE) used to repeat aloud to himself the three categories when attempting a new shift in category. It appeared as if he had prob-lems in keeping online all the information needed to shift category. As a result of these difficulties, patients took an average of 2.6 seconds longer than controls to sort each card' (355).

Using a different rule-detection task, Burgess and Shallice (1996b) failed to find significant differences in the incidence of perseverative responses when comparing patients with different cerebral lesions. They designed the Brixton Spatial Anticipation Test which, unlike the Wisconsin Card Sorting Test, allows the amount of guessing to be estimated. Patients were presented with a booklet containing 56 pages, with each page showing a 2×5 array of circles numbered 1–10 (see Figure 9.6). Pages differed in terms of which circle was filled. The task was to predict which circle would be filled on the next page. The rule would apply to a certain number of pages, and this number would vary in an unsystematic way from 3 to 8. Therefore, changes in the rule could not be anticipated. The errors made by participants were scored either as perseverations, or as applications of other incorrect rules, or as bizarre responses and guesses. Patients with anterior lesions made more errors overall, with a significantly higher absolute number and proportion of the third type of errors. Also, having detected a correct rule, they were more likely to abandon it. However, their performance did not demonstrate a greater tendency to perseverate. These observations have been confirmed by

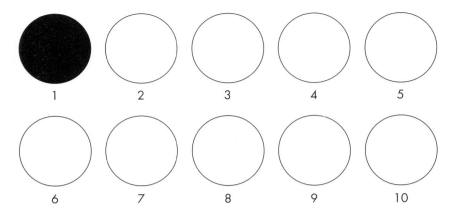

Figure 9.6 Brixton Spatial Anticipation Test

Source: Adapted from Burgess and Shallice (1996b)

Note: Each page of the test shows a 2 × 5 array of circles. The task is to predict which circle will be filled on the next page

Reverberi *et al.* (2005) who distinguished between two different types of perseveration responses and found that frontal patients did not show an increase in either type. However, they did find that only patients with left lateral frontal lesions and not those with right lateral frontal lesions were significantly impaired in their performance on the Brixton test.

Although the Brixton Spatial Anticipation Test resembles the Wisconsin Card Sorting Test in that the participant has to learn arbitrary rules which change, there are important differences. Relevant rules can be abstracted from the perceptual display in the sorting task, for instance sort by colour or sort by shape; this is not the case in the spatial anticipation test. One possible explanation for their results, one of the three offered by Burgess and Shallice, is that the creation of an appropriate rule is a more abstract process in the Brixton test. Alternatively, one of their other suggestions is consistent with findings from studies involving cognitive estimation which are described in the next section, namely that anterior patients are more willing to think of bizarre hypotheses which they do not disconfirm.

Reverberi *et al.* (2005) ruled out a number of different explanations for their findings and suggested that for their left frontal lateral group the fundamental process that is impaired is that of induction. They suggest that localised in the left frontal cortex is a key process necessary to carry out inductive inference, and point out that this proposal is in line with the findings of some of the recent imaging studies that have looked at brain activation whilst participants undertake inductive reasoning tasks (e.g. Parsons and Osherson, 2001).

A new clinical test of concept formation is the Twenty Questions Test which is based on a game where one player asks yes/no questions to identify which famous person or object the other player is thinking of. Like the Wisconsin Card

Sorting Test, it requires participants to abstract categories, utilise feedback to modify their responses as well as keep track of previous responses. They are shown an array of 30 lines drawings and told to ask examinees the fewest number of yes/no questions in order to identify a target from the array. The advantage of this test is that it measures concept-formation skills directly from the patients' verbal responses rather than inferring them from card sorting responses. Baldo *et al.* (2004) found frontal patients to perform poorly on this test compared with control participants, largely due to ineffective categorisation strategies; rather than narrowing down their search, patients predominantly asked single-item questions (e.g. 'Is it the owl?'). Baldo *et al.* conclude that the ability to abstract conceptual categories is supported by the frontal cortex.

9.6 Impaired strategy formation

Cognitive estimation tasks

A different kind of reasoning is employed in tasks involving cognitive estimates, where deductions or inferences about the world are drawn from known information. Shallice and Evans (1978) asked questions such as 'What is the largest object normally found in a house?', 'How fast do racehorses gallop?', 'What is the height of the Post Office Tower?' and 'What is the length of the average woman's spine?' – in other words questions that cannot be answered directly from information stored in memory. Instead, a realistic estimate can be inferred from other knowledge. For example, a reasonable answer to the last question can be arrived at by first using knowledge about the average height of a woman, then realising that the spine runs about one third to one half the length of the body, allowing one to judge the answer to be somewhere between 22 and 33 inches. Shallice and Evans found that patients with frontal lesions would perform worse than those with posterior lesions, sometimes providing absurd or outrageous values, for example that the spine is about '5 feet long' and that the largest object in the house is 'a ceramic toilet seat'. Shallice and Evans suggested that poor performance was a result of poor strategy formation – although the questions could be answered by drawing upon general knowledge, no immediate obvious strategy was available.

Poor cognitive estimation has also been observed in a task involving the price of goods. Smith and Milner (1984) showed individuals with frontal lobe damage miniature replicas of real-life products, such as a sewing machine and a car. Results showed that patients with right frontal lobectomies responded with bizarre estimates of price on about 25 per cent of trials. Again, poor performance is hypothesised to result from poor strategy formation.

In a later study, Smith and Milner (1988) asked patients to estimate the frequency of an event or item. A series of nonsense items was shown and some of the items appeared only once, whereas others appeared 3, 5, 7 or 9 times nonconsecutively. A series of test items followed and for each test item the patient had to state whether or not it was included in the initial sequence and furthermore, if this response was positive, they were asked to estimate how often it had

INTRODUCTION TO COGNITIVE PSYCHOLOGY

been shown. Whilst patients with lesions in both left and right frontal lobes were able to remember accurately the presence or absence of the test item in the initial sequence, they had difficulty estimating its frequency of occurrence. So, although these patients showed a normal ability to recognise an abstract design, they could not estimate accurately how many times they had seen that particular design. Closer inspection of the results reveals that their estimates were not significantly different at lower frequency levels; differences only emerged when the design had been shown at least seven times. Smith and Milner suggest that the patients' performance may reflect a difficulty in cognitive estimation; alternatively, frontal patients may find it difficult to carry out an orderly search for the representations of the designs in memory or in remembering information with a temporal component.

Goal-oriented problem-solving

Other tests have been developed to investigate how well frontal patients can formulate a strategy to obtain a goal, and performance on such tests is a good indication of how well the individual can produce a plan of action, which can involve subgoals, suited to the particular task presented. Shallice (1982) devised the 'Tower of London' task (a task related to the 'Tower of Hanoi' problem described in Chapter 8). The problem involves an apparatus with three beads and three pegs of varying heights so that each peg can hold one, two or all three beads. The task requires one to move the three beads which are placed on one part of the apparatus to a different position (for example, see Figure 9.7). These beads can only be moved one at a time and can only be moved to a different peg. The task is graded according to the number of moves necessary to achieve the solution. Frontal patients, specifically those with left frontal damage, were found to be both inefficient and ineffective at performing this task. In particular, they engaged in moves that only directly led towards their goal. Owen *et al.* (1990) used a computerised version of this task and found no differences between left and right frontal lobe patients. However, whereas normal participants and both groups of frontal patients spent the same amount of time planning their first move, the frontal patients spent considerably longer planning subsequent moves. Not only were they observed to have significantly longer thinking times overall, they needed more moves to solve the problem.

Morris *et al.* (1993) provided corroborative evidence of the involvement of the frontal regions in the Tower of London task by measuring regional blood flow in neurologically intact individuals. Participants performed a computerised touch-screen version of the task that entailed two conditions. In the first they were guided by the computer to solve the problem (a control task that requires no planning activity) whereas in the second they were asked to perform the task without guidance. Morris *et al.* found significantly higher levels of activation, i.e. a greater increase in regional cerebral blood flow, in the left frontal cortex in the second condition, when participants had to actively plan the moves. Furthermore, a relatively greater increase was shown by those participants who spent more time planning the solution and also in those who solved the problem in fewer moves.

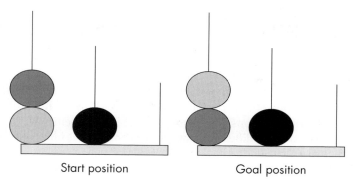

Start position   Goal position

Figure 9.7 An example of a problem from the Tower of London task
Source: Adapted from Shallice (1982)

The evidence presented so far implicates the frontal lobes in 'planning', at least in the case of the Tower of London task. Goel and Grafman (1995) presented twenty patients with lesions in the prefrontal cortex with a computerised five-disc version of the Tower of Hanoi puzzle and found them to be impaired on this task in comparison to normal controls. Their individual moves to solve the problems were analysed and both patients and controls were found to use the same strategy. However, the patients' poor performance could be attributed to a failure to spot and/or resolve the counterintuitive backward move. To achieve the goal, a move has to be made that takes you away from the goal and the conflict between the sub-goal and goal has to be acknowledged. This counterintuitive backward move was discussed in Chapter 8 in relation to the Hobbits and Orcs problem; many of us experience difficulty in implementing this move as it contravenes our favourite heuristic, to reduce the difference between the current state and the goal state. Goel and Grafman suggest that the patients are seeking to satisfy the goal rather than a conflicting sub-goal, and this is consistent with explanations of impaired performance on other tasks, namely that frontal patients have a particular problem with suppressing their current, salient or habitual response.

Goel and Grafman also stress that the Tower of Hanoi problem does not test planning ability in the sense of constructing and evaluating a particular plan, because unless the counterintuitive backward move is spotted the problem cannot be solved. The next section outlines research that considers planning ability in relation to real-life problems and, in line with the case studies described earlier, supports the notion that planning ability is impaired as a result of frontal lobe damage.

9.7 Deficits in everyday higher-order planning

It should be evident from the research outlined in the previous sections that a range of neuropsychological tests have been used to investigate the nature of the cognitive processes underlying the impaired performance of patients with frontal lobe damage. Failure on these is usually interpreted as suggesting that the cognitive processes involved in successfully completing the task are damaged. Burgess *et al.* (1998) make the point that with many of the tests, such as the Wisconsin Card Sorting Test, an assumption is made that the test itself taps into processes that are used to cope with many real-life situations. However, there may be little correspondence between the cognitive resources tapped by such a test and those tapped in real-world situations. For example, real-life problem-solving is usually open-ended in nature and different courses of action have to be considered and evaluated. It is rare that all the relevant pieces of information are available together and frequently solutions to real-life problems require a juggling of priorities which differ in importance according to the specific context. Therefore, there is a need to assess performance using tests that involve formalised versions of real-world activities and hence are more ecologically valid.

Shallice and Burgess (1991a) have developed tests that specifically explore higher-order planning deficits, and these mimic everyday problem-solving. The 'Six Element Test' is undertaken in a standard hospital office. It requires the patient to complete three different but not difficult tasks, each with two components, within a specified time period of fifteen minutes. The tasks are: dictating a route into a recorder; carrying out arithmetic problems and writing down the names of approximately one hundred pictures of objects. One key aspect of the instructions given to participants is that all the tasks should be completed and that the important thing is to do a little of each of the components of each of the tasks.

The 'Multiple Errands Test' requires the patient to carry out certain tasks in situations where minor unforeseen events can arise. The patient is given a card with eight tasks written on it and then sent to a shopping precinct to carry out these tasks. There are six simple requests (for example, buy a lettuce), the seventh tasks requires the patient to be somewhere in fifteen minutes and the eighth task requires the recording of four pieces of information during the errands (for example, the price of a pound of tomatoes or the rate of exchange of the French franc yesterday). Patients are instructed to spend as little money as possible (within reason) and take as little time as possible (without rushing excessively). They are told to enter a shop only when wanting to buy something, and to tell the experimenter when they leave the shop what they have bought. They are informed that they cannot use anything not bought on the street, other than a watch, to help them. Finally, they are told that they can do the tasks in any order.

These tests were used in a study of three frontal head-injury patients (AP, DN and FS) described in Box 9.2. All three had Wechsler Adult Intelligence Scale (WAIS) IQs between 120 and 130, and on thirteen tests considered to be sensitive to frontal lobe damage, for instance the Wisconsin Card-Sorting, Stroop and Cognitive Estimation tests, the performance of two of the patients (AP and DN) fell within the normal range. The performance of the third patient FS was impaired on four of these tests. In daily life, the three patients planned few activities and showed little spontaneous organisation; two had lost jobs because of gross oversights. When asked to complete the Six Element Test, all three patients

Box 9.2 The case histories of AP, DN and FS

In a paper by Shallice and Burgess (1991a), three patients with traumatic injuries to the prefrontal structures are described. All three found the organisation and planning of everyday life activities problematic and their specific difficulties are described here.

AP was 23 years of age when he was involved in a road traffic accident. A CT scan revealed considerable bifrontal damage. He was unable to return to his job and a year later he attended a hospital as a day patient for rehabilitation. Although he was well-motivated and keen, he was unable to complete the simplest of activities as he was unable to maintain his concentration on the task at hand. For example, instead of returning to the therapy room after fetching coffee, he was found on the local golf course. Shopping was impossible because he was unable to buy more than one item before returning to his car. As soon as three months later he was transferred to a different rehabilitation clinic as an in-patient, where he remained for a year. Although there was some improvement in his ability to organise daily activities, he went home to live with his parents. He later reported in a clinical interview that he was unable to keep his room tidy, to file his magazines or to carry out shopping, cleaning and laundry duties. He was not able to plan ahead for his social life or provide any example of organising something in advance.

DN was 26 years of age when he was involved in a road traffic accident. Six months after sustaining his injuries, he found that he was unable to continue with his previous employment. Despite some success at studying and obtaining a teacher's certificate, he spent five years doing a variety of jobs and being dismissed from most of them. A CT scan performed 22 years later, when he was 48 years of age, revealed considerable damage to the right frontal lobe and some to the left frontal lobe. It emerged in a clinical interview that he was untidy and shaved, washed his hair and changed his clothes only when told to do so by his wife, bathing only if going out somewhere special. Domestic chores were rarely undertaken spontaneously and if his wife went out he would usually leave the food preparation to his 10-year-old son. When asked to do something by his wife, she had to give specific instructions and even then he might only complete some aspects of the task. The organisation of their social life was left to his wife. He was rarely successful at buying items needed, despite his wife's preparing a shopping list and she reported that he was occasionally irresponsible with money.

FS sustained injuries in two separate incidents. She suffered a skull fracture when thrown from a horse in her twenties and then at the age of 53 years she was knocked off her bicycle by a car, hitting her head on the road. A CT scan conducted two years later revealed a large lesion to the left frontal lobe and some atrophy to the left temporal lobe. It was revealed that she had kept the same job for the previous 25 years and lived by herself in a single room. In a clinical interview she reported that she was very untidy, that she shopped every day to buy just a few things and never visited the supermarket. She seldom went out in the evenings and almost never travelled away from her home town. She generally did not undertake inessential or novel activities and in the interview reported no plans for the following weekend. She could not recall an incident where someone relied on her to do something, and reported leaving the organising of any joint activity to others.

performed at below the normal range; not only were their scores quantitatively lower, their performance was qualitatively different also when compared to that of control participants. AP started by making notes for four minutes, which were then never used. DN spent ten minutes on one task and did not even attempt a second task that was very similar. FS only tackled three of the six subtasks.

The three patients performed equally poorly on the Multiple Errands Test. They made more than three times as many inefficient actions and broke three times as many rules in comparison with normal controls. Again, their behaviour was qualitatively different. Two of the patients experienced difficulties with shop-keepers. AP asked for the previous day's newspaper and on obtaining it angered the shopkeeper by leaving the shop without paying for it, breaking the rule that only bought items can be used. DN asked a shop assistant to give him a birthday card free, breaking the buying rule and resulting in a heated argument. FS broke the rule that no shop should be entered other than to buy something because the shop, a chemist, did not stock the soap she especially liked. She would not buy other cheap soap even though this would have been adequate for the task.

Shallice and Burgess proposed that these patients were able to generate intentions but not reactivate these intentions later on, when these were not directly signalled or primed by the stimulus situation. The patients lost the facility to activate or trigger markers. Normally, when intentions are created or rules are temporarily created, markers are activated which are then triggered if a relevant situation occurs. This triggering will interrupt ongoing behaviour to ensure that the intention or rule is realised. They explain that 'a marker is basically a message that some future behaviour or event should not be treated as routine and instead, some particular aspect of the situation should be viewed as especially relevant for action' (737). The patients performed poorly on the Six Elements and the Multiple Errands Tests, not because of motivational or retrospective memory impairments, but because of processes that bridge these; processes which assist the realisation of goals and intentions.

These findings shed light on why patients with frontal lobe damage can perform well in many laboratory tests that supposedly tap frontal lobe function and yet fail in everyday activities. The situations where these patients have problems are those that can be approached in a number of different ways and require decisions about how to allocate resources, and that tap subtle planning and prospective memory. Duncan *et al.* (1996) wrote, 'In the laboratory it is often the rule to give strong verbal prompts to task requirements, to repeat these until performance is correct, to gather data over a long series of stereotyped trials, and to have only a modest set of concurrent task requirements. In all these respects, the activities of daily life may often be different: there are no explicit verbal prompts, no stereotyped repetition of closely similar 'trials', and sometimes multiple, concurrent concerns' (296).

Research since has confirmed the value of a simplified version of the Multiple Errands Test for use in clinical practice. Alderman *et al.* (2003) found that although many patients passed the traditional tests of executive frontal lobe function, they made more and different types of errors than control participants on the new test, and patients' performance was characterised either by rule breaking because they failed to act upon the information they received or misunderstood the instructions or by failure to achieve tasks, usually because the tasks were not initiated.

9.8 Conceptual issues

It is apparent from the earlier sections of this chapter that a number of distinct processes have been related to the frontal lobes, including abstract/conceptual thinking and planning, which can be classified as 'supervisory' or 'executive' functions. Apart from cognitive processes, damage to the frontal lobes can influence behaviour, emotion and motivation as well as impact on personality. The twenty most commonly reported symptoms of the 'frontal lobe' or 'dysexecutive' syndrome are reported in Box 9.3.

Box 9.3 Characteristics of the dysexecutive syndrome (taken from Burgess et al. 1998)

1   Abstract thinking problems
2   Impulsivity
3   Confabulation
4   Planning problems
5   Euphoria
6   Temporal sequencing deficits
7   Lack of insight and social awareness
8   Apathy and lack of drive
9   Disinhibition
10 Variable motivation
11 Shallowing of affective responses
12 Aggression
13 Lack of concern
14 Perseveration
15 Restlessness–hyperkinesis
16 Inability to inhibit responses
17 Knowing–doing dissociation
18 Distractibility
19 Poor decision-making ability
20 No concern for social rules

The development of a model of executive functioning is still in its infancy (Andrewes, 2001); however the most influential also happens to be one of the oldest and most developed models and this will be described next.

Supervisory attentional system

Norman and Shallice (1986) adopted an information processing approach to explain these deficits of executive function. Complex but well-established patterns of behaviour are controlled by hierarchically organised schemas or memory representations. High-level schemas can call up subordinate programmes or subroutines, so, for example, 'making dinner' will have component schemas containing at the lowest level instructions on how to use the oven and at higher levels how to make a cheese cake. Fundamental to their approach is the distinction between habitual and novel action routines. They suggested that each of these are selected and integrated in different ways.

Norman and Shallice suggested that we frequently function on 'auto pilot', selecting and integrating cognitive or behavioural skills on the basis of established schemas. Environmental cues trigger certain responses which in turn trigger specific schemas, for instance a kettle may trigger your 'make a cup of tea' schema. Once triggered, a schema competes for dominance and control of action by inhibiting other schemas which might conflict with it. When there is a clash between two routine activities, an operation they call *contention scheduling* prevents two competing activated schemas from being selected through lateral inhibition. However, it is not always desirable to select schemas on the basis of the strength of their initial activation. Norman and Shallice argued that coping with novelty involves the selection of schemas that are modulated by the operation of a **supervisory attentional system** (similar to Baddeley's concept of a central executive, see Chapter 6). This system can heighten a schema's level of activation, allowing it to be in a better position to compete with other schemas for dominance and thus increasing its probability of being selected in contention scheduling (see Figure 9.8).

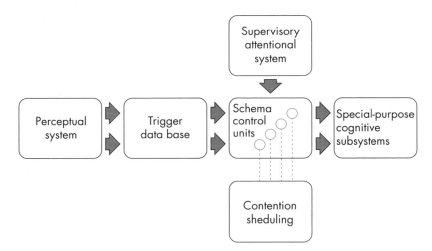

Figure 9.8 A diagram of the Norman and Shallice model
Source: Adapted from Shallice (1982)

Norman and Shallice indicated five types of situations that would involve the operation of this system:

1   Situations that involve planning or decision-making (e.g. Tower of London test).
2   Situations that involve error-correction or trouble shooting (e.g. Wisconsin Card Sorting Test).
3   Situations that require less well-learned responses or require the involvement of a new pattern of actions (e.g. tasks involving cognitive estimates).
4   Situations that are considered to be dangerous or technically difficult.
5   Situations that require us not to suppress a strong habitual response or to resist temptation (e.g. Stroop test).

Their approach assumes that we might operate in one mode where potentially demanding but routine action or thought processes are selected by well-learned triggering procedures. When these routine operations will not allow us to achieve our goal then some form of explicit modulation or novel activity must take place, involving higher-level processes – the supervisory system. The notion that our cognitive processes might operate on different levels or modes (routine versus non-routine processing) is also contained in artificial intelligence models of problem-solving, e.g. SOAR (Laird et al., 1987). Their use of the concept of 'schema' is also apparent in other explanations of cognitive behaviour (see Chapter 5).

Shallice (1988) explains how this approach can account for impairments of problem-solving. Lesions to the frontal lobes impair the functioning of the super-visory system so that contention scheduling operates unmodulated. The deficits in sustained attention and distractibility described earlier arise because unless strong trigger-schema contingencies are present, the patient is unable to inhibit irrelevant input. Observations of utilisation behaviour, the tendency to pick up and use objects in close proximity, are consistent with this. Perseveration will be observed when the situation triggers a well-learned set of responses. One schema would gain abnormal levels of dominance over others and it would be difficult to switch to a different set of responses. Perseveration has been observed in the performance of frontal patients on the Wisconsin Card Sorting Test. Tasks or situations that require a 'novel' response, for example those involving cognitive estimates, will be problematic as there is no routine procedure that allows the patient to produce an appropriate response.

Alternative approaches

Others have proposed accounts of frontal lobe dysfunction that do not specify a damaged central executive mechanism. Goldman-Rakic (1987) conducted extensive research with non-human primates and proposed that the dorsolateral prefrontal cortex is crucial for the working memory, called 'representational memory' by that author. This framework has been extended by Kimberg and Farah (1993) to account for the range of human cognitive impairments following frontal lobe damage. They proposed that the strength of associations among working memory representations are weakened, specifically those representations of goals, environmental stimuli and stored declarative knowledge. The representations themselves are unaffected; instead the associations among these different working memory representations are deficient. Kimberg and Farah went on to simulate the weakening of working memory associations using a computer model. They selected four tasks that frontal patients had been found to fail, and found that their 'damaged' model also failed all four tasks in the same ways as frontal-damaged patients.

Duncan *et al.* (1996) argued that there is considerable overlap between the functions reflected in Spearman's concept of general intelligence ('*g*') and the executive functioning of the frontal lobes. This is based partly on the finding that some tests providing good estimates of overall intelligence also tap executive function. However, Crinella and Yu (2000) failed to replicate the findings of Duncan *et al.*; their results did not show that frontal lobe lesions affected fluid intelligence, a measure of *g*, although performance on tests of executive functions was affected.

Fractionation of the executive functions of the frontal lobes

More recent theoretical developments have sought to clarify the extent to which the executive functions are unitary in nature. Shallice and Burgess (1991b) suggested that the supervisory system should not be considered to act as a single resource and this view is supported by Stuss and Alexander (2000: 289), who wrote that 'there is no unitary executive function. Rather, distinct processes related to the frontal lobes can be differentiated which converge on a general concept of control functions'.

Burgess *et al.* (1998) performed factor analysis on patients' dysexecutive symptoms and reported that these twenty symptoms (see Box 9.3) could be grouped into five orthogonal factors; two of these relate to the emotional and personality changes that can be seen in patients with frontal lobe damage. The remaining three are:

- Inhibition or the ability to suppress a habitual response, assuming that impulsivity and disinhibition are the behavioural consequences of such a cognitive problem.
- Intentionality which is related to the creation and maintenance of goal-related behaviour.
- Executive memory, which is related to confabulation and inability to recall the correct order of events.

These findings provide support that at the behavioural level the dysexecutive syndrome can be fractionated.

By fractionating the supervisory processes, it is possible to account for dissociations of deficits in problem-solving, and explain why a patient may be impaired on a scheduling test such as the Multiple Errands Test and not on other more standard tests of frontal lobe functioning. For example, Bamdad *et al.* (2003) found only a weak relationship between traditional measures of executive function and a newly developed measure of real-world planning/problem-solving abilities. Rueckert and Grafman (1996) failed to find significant correlations between any of the three measures of sustained attention and performance on the Tower of Hanoi or the Wisconsin Card Sorting Test. The authors suggest that the regions of the frontal lobe subserving sustained attention may not be the same regions involved in the problem-solving tasks. In the Burgess and Shallice (1996a) study that employed the Hayling Sentence Completion Test, analysis revealed extremely low correlations between the patients' performance in the response initiation and response inhibition conditions. Such results suggest that initiation and inhibition may be impaired singly and that the two processes are separable. Burgess and Shallice (1994) also reported low correlations between patients' performance on the Hayling Test and the Brixton Spatial Anticipation Test and concluded that the two tests are tapping either differing executive processes or dedicated supervisory resources.

However, although the finding of low correlations among executive tasks seems to be robust, Miyake *et al.* (2000) point out that it is not completely clear that these are indeed a reflection of distinct dissociable underlying executive functions. Non-executive processing requirements may instead obscure the existence of underlying commonalities among the different executive tasks. In their study, Miyake *et al.* sought to extract what might be common among different tasks of executive function and then used this extracted factor to explore how different executive functions related to each other. They chose three executive functions: shifting between tasks, updating and monitoring working memory representations, and inhibition of dominant responses. They then selected a number of simple tasks that are believed to tap each function and a more complex, conventional executive task that is thought to tap several of these three functions. One hundred and thirty-seven college students performed each task. Miyake *et al.* concluded that their results 'suggest that the three often postulated executive functions of Shifting, Updating, and Inhibition are separable but moderately correlated constructs, thus indicating both unity and diversity of executive functions' (87). They also found that each function contributed differently to participants' performance on the more complex executive test, highlighting the multi-factorial nature of certain executive tasks that are often used in cognitive and neuropsychological studies.

The challenge faced by theorists is to understand the executive functions in terms of their psychological processes, how they are organised and the roles they play in complex cognition. However, future research needs to clarify the relation of these functions to the frontal lobes; when tested with complex tasks such as the Wisconsin Card Sorting Test the frontal lobes appear functionally homogeneous yet there is some evidence to suggest that distinct processes might be related to different brain regions (see Stuss and Alexander, 2000). To explore this relationship further, we need to know more about the individual processes that are tapped by these executive tasks, in particular those that are complex. Identifying associations as well as disassociations between tasks sensitive to frontal lobe damage should further our understanding of both the unity and diversity of executive functions.

Summary

- Executive functions encompass the deployment of attention, the initiation of non-habitual action, goal-directed behaviour, planning, insight, foresight and self-regulation, and hence processes that are associated with problem-solving, an operational definition of thinking.
- There is no single deficit of thinking equivalent to aphasia, agnosia or amnesia; however, frontal lobe damage can affect performance on a wide range of tasks that are thought to tap executive functions.
- Case histories show that frontal damage may also result in changes to personality and affective behaviour.
- Neuropsychological studies have shown that impairments in the deployment of attention, in abstract and conceptual thinking and in strategy formation can follow frontal lobe damage.
- Recent findings suggest that laboratory tests may not be suitable for tapping those social problem-solving activities that frontal patients find difficult to perform in everyday life.
- Norman and Shallice have provided a theory of frontal lobe function that specifies damage to the central executive of working memory.
- The executive functions appear separable but they also seem to share some underlying commonality.
- Research in this area is problematic, partly because many tests of executive functions are complex tasks which make demands on a variety of cognitive skills.

Further reading

Hommel, B., Daum, I. and Kluwe, R.H. (eds) (2004). Executive Control of Human Action, *Acta Psychologica*, 115 (2–3), 99–292. A special issue that considers cognitive control and where control comes from.

Andrewes, D. (2001). *Neuropsychology: From Theory to Practice*. Hove: Psychology Press. This book will provide you with information on the physiology, ontogeny and neurochemistry of the brain and includes a chapter devoted to executive dysfunction.

Norman, D.A. and Shallice, T. (1986). Attention to action: Willed and automatic control of behaviour. In R.J. Davidson, G.E. Schwartz and D.E. Shapiro (eds), *Consciousness and Self-Regulation* (vol. 4). New York: Plenum Press. This chapter provides a full description of an information processing account of executive function.

Stuss, D.T. and Knight, R.T. (2002). *Principles of Frontal Lobe Function*. New York: Oxford University Press. This book includes chapters from key researchers in the area.

Language

10.1 Introduction

For the cognitive psychologist, perhaps the most remarkable and intriguing of human abilities is our capacity to use language. Why should this be so? After all, activities involving language are commonplace in our everyday lives. We talk to our families, listen to the news, read the newspaper, chat on the phone, all without conscious effort or obvious premeditation. These activities, however, rely on an ability which, on reflection, is exceptionally clever and impressive. In the words of Steven Pinker (1994), 'Simply by making noises with our mouths, we can reliably cause precise new combinations of ideas to arise in each other's minds' (15). So, by varying those sounds, each of us can tell someone the plot of a film seen last night, ask what they had for breakfast or tell them to 'go and take a running jump'. In the same way each of us can follow that film plot, provide information about what our breakfast consisted of or react to the injunction to take a running jump (without, it should be noted, taking its words literally).

What cognitive processes are involved in such an ability? Language undoubtedly has interconnections with other cognitive capacities discussed elsewhere in this book. For example, in listening to people talking and in reading text, working-memory processes may be involved in holding the input long enough for it to be analysed and understood (Gathercole and Baddeley, 1993). Information gained through language becomes part of our long-term memory system and helps us make sense of future messages. Thinking and reasoning processes are also closely intertwined with language. However, many cognitive scientists hold that language processing cannot be understood simply in terms of aspects of memory, reasoning and other cognitive processes that help us make sense of the world. They argue that language must rely on a relatively autonomous set of abilities, each having its own knowledge base and the whole affair functioning, to a large extent, independently of other cognitive processes (Fodor, 1983; Chomsky, 1986).

This chapter will consider the nature of language as a system and review research which has looked at how language is understood, how it is produced, and how it functions in interactional contexts such as conversations. Much of the evidence concerning the language system has come from the study of how language can break down in people who have language disorders resulting from brain injury. Evidence from disorders of language will be reviewed in Chapter 11.

10.2 The language system

Psychologists' main concern is in working out what processes are involved, on the one hand, in understanding speech and in reading and, on the other hand, in producing language when we talk or write. 'The goal is to discover how speakers turn ideas into words and how listeners turn words into ideas' (Clark and Clark, 1977: 10). In understanding language (or language comprehension), we can think of the process as beginning with hearing sounds, attaching meaning to the sounds in the form of words, combining the words into a sentence and working out what thought or intention the speaker was trying to convey. In communicating our own thoughts through language (language production), we start with a

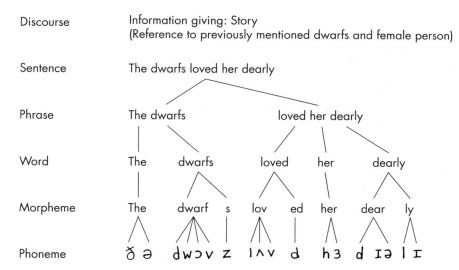

Figure 10.1 Levels of linguistic structure
Source: After Gleitman (1995)

proposition (a thought), translate this thought into a sentence and produce the speech sounds that express that sentence. A number of levels seem to be involved: speech sounds, words and sentences at the very least.

The discipline of linguistics has provided further insight into the levels of language and the systematic and rule-governed way in which each operates. These levels consist of the sounds of speech (known in linguistics as **phonetics**), the sound system of any particular language (**phonology**), word formation (**morphology**), the combination of words into phrases and sentences (**syntax**), the meanings of words, phrases and sentences (**semantics**) and activities using language which extend beyond individual sentences, such as stories, speeches, newspaper articles and conversations (**discourse**). A diagram showing the different levels is shown in Figure 10.1.

Speech sounds

When we speak we use the lips, tongue, mouth and vocal cords to fashion a column of air from the lungs in such a way as to produce a variety of physical sounds. The field of phonetics investigates this process of the articulation of speech and the physical characteristics of speech as sound waves. Not all of the differences between speech sounds are perceived as making a difference to meaning within a language. For example, the sound of the first letter in 'pin' and the second letter in 'spin' actually differ from one another in that there is a small puff of air (called aspiration) that accompanies the *p* in 'pin' but not in 'spin'. However, in the English language, this is not a distinction that is critical to a difference in meaning. In contrast, the difference between *p* and *b*, actually a difference in voicing, does affect meaning so that we know that 'pin' is not the same word as 'bin'. In English the /p/ and /b/ sounds are two **phonemes**, whereas the two variants of /p/ are not. Every language, then, has a different set of phonemes (English has 40), and learning to pronounce and discriminate them is one of the challenges we face when we try to learn a foreign language.

Phonemes combine to form words. Each language has its own rules about which phonemes can follow others and, although we conform to these rules every time we talk, most of us would have difficulty explaining the rules to someone else. Like many aspects of language they rely on tacit, rather than explicit, knowledge. So, for example, we know implicitly that in English the sound /p/ cannot be followed by the sound /b/ at the beginning of a word and so we would be unlikely to choose a word like 'PBLITZ' if we had to create a brand name for a new product. We make a different sound to form the plural 'cats' (the phoneme /s/) from that for 'dogs' (the phoneme /z/), since /s/ cannot follow 'g' at the end of a word.

Word level

At the level of words, language makes contact with items in the non-linguistic world. Words, sometimes known as **lexical items**, designate things and people, abstract concepts, actions, events and properties of objects. In addition to analysing words into their component speech sounds, we can also consider units of meaning within words. Take the following sets of words:

> Speak, speaks, speaker, speaking, spoke
> Ease, easy, easily, easier, easiest, unease

The need to have meaningful units of language that are larger than the phoneme but smaller than the word becomes apparent. The word 'speaks' can be divided into the component 'speak', which it shares with 'speaker', speaking' and 'speaker', and the component '-s', the third person singular ending. Linguists call these units **morphemes**, the smallest linguistic units that carry meaning. Many morphemes, known as *free morphemes*, can be used on their own as words, for example, 'speak', 'ease', 'cat', 'book'. Others, like '-s', '-ing', '-est' and 'un-' cannot occur on their own and are known as *bound morphemes*. Bound morphemes can occur at the beginning of a word (**prefixes**) or at the end (**suffixes**) where they are also known as **inflectional endings**.

There is a particular set of free morphemes which cannot have bound morphemes attached to them, are mostly short common words and function mainly to indicate sentence structure. These include determiners ('the', 'a', 'an'), prepositions ('in', 'by', 'to'), conjunctions ('and', 'but', 'because') and relative pronouns ('who', 'which'). Psychologists have termed these **grammatical function words** (or just 'function words') and contrast them with **content words** which are the words conveying the main semantic content of the message. Content words can be regarded as open-class items since new ones, such as 'eco-warrior' are always being added, whereas function words belong to a relatively fixed, closed-class (about 360 items in English). While the distinction between function and content words is not a strictly linguistic one, psychologists have been interested in whether there may be differences in the way these two sets of words are processed.

A native speaker of a language has a knowledge of words, a vocabulary which in terms of words that are recognised may extend to several hundred thousand items. When a word, say 'dinosaur', has been learned, the person will have knowledge of how the word is pronounced, how it can function in a sentence (for example, as a noun) and its meaning. This knowledge appears very like the information that would appear in a dictionary entry for 'dinosaur' and this has led to the mental store of words being referred to as a **mental lexicon** in which each word has a *lexical entry*. The way words are organised in such a mental lexicon and how they are accessed when needed has been a major topic in the psychology of language.

Sentence level

Words are not uttered one at a time but are combined in phrases and sentences, allowing us flexibility in expressing our thoughts, not having to learn a new word for each thought. Sentences express propositions that convey aspects of events in the world. They may convey to the listener 'who? did what? and to whom?' These basic components of the meaning of a sentence (or *thematic roles*) are conveyed through syntax. Take the sentence:

(1)   The journalist vexed the drunken politician.

Linguistic intuition tells us that this sentence follows the grammatical rules of the English language, whereas the following does not:

(2)   Vexed the drunken the journalist politician.

In (1) we know from the word order that 'the journalist' is the person doing the vexing (the subject of the verb) and 'the drunken politician' is the person being vexed (the object). Syntax includes rules for combining words in certain orders and for adding appropriate inflectional endings such as the 'ed' ending on 'vex'. The nature of the linguistic rules which can best characterise the syntactic structures of a language such as English is the focus of much of the endeavours of academic linguists. Psychologists' interest is in the processes by which the brain can crack this complex system of rules efficiently and at great speed.

The level of discourse

We do not speak in individual sentences as isolated units. One sentence links with the last and together they build up a connected discourse. Nor do we talk in monologues. Language is a social activity that allows us to interact and share our thoughts with other people. We relate to other people by linking what we say with what they have just said. Through this process we participate in conversation. To be able to converse effectively with other people we need to know more than just the sounds, words and sentence structures of a language. We have to make subtle adjustments to what we say and make complex inferences about what other speakers are getting at for conversation to proceed smoothly. Cognitive psychologists are becoming aware of the sophisticated cognitive processing involved in such a process.

10.3 Psychology and linguistics

The psychological study of language is often known as **psycholinguistics**. As this name implies, psycholinguistics sprang from an attempt at an integration of the fields of psychology and linguistics, though their differing intellectual traditions have made the relationship between the two a somewhat uneasy one.

The person most responsible for providing insight into the intricacy of language as a system is Noam Chomsky, the linguist who revolutionised the study of language and who has been making major theoretical contributions to linguistics over the last forty years (Chomsky, 1957, 1965, 1981, 1986). Although Chomsky's thinking has evolved over the years and aspects of his linguistic theories have changed considerably, certain aspects of his theoretical position have been maintained. A crucial insight was that people routinely produce and understand utterances that are completely new to them, ones they have never said before or had said to them. This *creativity* that characterises language must imply that language users have a set of rules which allow them to tackle any sentence that comes along. It is this set of rules, known as the **grammar**, that linguists like Chomsky set out to discover. This set of rules will be powerful enough to create (or 'generate') grammatical sentences in a particular language and, importantly, not generate ungrammatical sentences.

How do linguists go about establishing the laws or 'rules' of language? One way would be to record people talking as they go about their everyday business, transcribe what they say and then attempt to analyse the transcripts for underlying regularities of some sort. Chomsky argues that such an attempt would come to nothing because people's talk is liable to contain grammatical errors along with all sorts of false starts, self-corrections, hesitations and unfinished sentences. He compares this messy and contaminated language **performance** with the more pure and unadulterated language **competence**, the tacit knowledge people have which underpins their performance. Linguists gain access to language competence by asking speakers to judge whether strings of words are grammatical or not. Often, in actual fact, they themselves make these *grammaticality judgements*, a source of some criticism from cognitive psychologists who consider themselves to be more methodologically rigorous.

Chomsky pointed out that certain sentences seem intuitively to be related to one another, despite being very different in structure. A set of such sentences would be:

(3)   Chomsky analysed this sentence.

(4)   This sentence was analysed by Chomsky.

(5)   It was Chomsky who analysed this sentence.

(6)   It was this sentence that was analysed by Chomsky.

By contrast, two sentences may be identical in form but seem very different, like the two below:

(7)   Chomsky is easy to please.

(8)   Chomsky is eager to please.

To capture such relationships, Chomsky (1965) argued that every sentence could be given two grammatical descriptions, one a surface structure and the other a deep or underlying structure. Two sentences could have very different structures at surface level but be the same or very similar at a deep structure level of syntax. Similarly, two sentences could be very similar in the surface form of words but have quite different descriptions at deep structure level. Chomsky's notion of an underlying level of structure has had a strong influence on psychologists' models of language processing, though in Chomsky's own linguistic theory it has diminished in significance in later versions (1981).

Psychologists have been interested in the grammars developed by linguists because of the possibility that they will help in understanding what goes on in speaking and listening. Chomsky (1965), however, believes that there is no direct relation between the rules of grammar (competence) and the way people proceed to produce and understand speech (performance). He says the relation is only indirect and it is up to psychologists of language to discover what it is.

Early psycholinguistic research tried to incorporate linguistic theoretical constructs directly and test out whether empirical research could validate their role in psychological processing, what was referred to as their 'psychological reality'. Indeed, some early work seemed to show some success in demonstrating a link between syntactic complexity and processing difficulty (Mehler, 1963; Miller and McKean, 1964; Savin and Perchonock, 1965) (for a review see Harley, 2001). So, for example, passive voice sentences such as

(9)   The policeman was shot by the robber.

would take longer to process and be more difficult to recall than active voice sentences such as

(10)   The robber shot the policeman.

However, a classic study by Slobin (1966) demonstrated that the situation was not so straightforward. He presented participants with sentences which had to be judged true or false with respect to a picture, known as a sentence verification task. For example, he presented a sentence such as

(11)   The cat is being chased by the dog.

and showed a picture of a dog chasing a cat. He confirmed that more complex sentences such as passive voice sentences took longer to verify than syntactically simpler ones. However, this was only the case for sentences like (11), which are said to be **reversible** because the subject and object could be reversed and still result in a sensible sentence. Other sentences were non-reversible, such as

(12)   The flowers are being watered by the girl.

To reverse subject and object in (12) results in a semantically implausible sentence. Slobin found that the non-reversible sentences could be verified more quickly than reversible ones, suggesting that semantic cues facilitated comprehension. In addition, he found that when the sentences were non-reversible, participants took no longer to judge a passive sentence such as (12) than the equivalent active voice sentence:

(13)   The girl is watering the flowers.

It seems that any extra syntactic difficulty associated with the passive voice over the active does not hold when semantic plausibility can be used to work out who is doing what, to whom.

Slobin's study not only cast doubt on the idea that sentence processing mirrored syntactic complexity, it also raised questions about the way syntactic and semantic information interacted in sentence processing. This point will be discussed further below.

The psycholinguistic study of language had its roots in the testing of linguistic concepts for plausibility as psychological constructs. However, as it has developed as a key element of cognitive psychology, the focus has been more on testing psychological models of language processing. There has been a strong focus on methods that measure reaction time on experimental tasks involving single words or single sentences. For example, a widely used task is the lexical decision task where a set of letters is displayed (e.g. 'FLOT' or 'FLAT') and the participant has to decide whether it is a word or not. Time taken to read a sentence may be measured by participant-controlled presentation of text where the participant sees a word or phrase on a screen and presses a key for the next word or phrase to be exposed. You might think that such methods are fairly far removed from our everyday experiences of communication and in recent years psycholinguists have developed techniques that focus more on spoken language and have begun to tackle how we deal with the hesitations and revisions we encounter in what people say to us. The new electrophysiological methods of measuring brain activity while engaged in language tasks using scalp-recorded event-related brain potentials (Event-Related Potentials (ERPs) and the involving of PET scans and fMRI have also made a major impact on the psychology of language. For example,

Coulson and Wu (2005) were able to find differences in ERPs as participants read probe words such as *CRAZY* which had been preceded by jokes such as 'Everyone had so much fun jumping into the swimming pool, we decided to put in a little *water*' as opposed to non-funny controls such as 'Everyone had so much fun jumping into the swimming pool, we decided to put in a little *platform*' (jokes elicited less negative ERPs 300–700 millisec. post onset (N400)).

10.4 Recognising spoken and written words

Crucial to understanding what people say to us is the ability to recognise the individual words that make up the message. We can usually do this very efficiently, regardless of whether we are familiar with the speaker and regardless of variations in regional accent. The process is very rapid. In one study participants identified a target word in a spoken passage and pressed a button to indicate that they had done so, on average 275 millisec. after the start of the word, even though the average duration of the words in the passage was 370 millisec. (Marslen-Wilson and Tyler, 1980). Similarly impressive is the ability of the reader to recognise written words at tremendous speed, sometimes as fast as 150 millisec. per word (Rayner and Pollatsek, 1989) and despite variations in font and styles of handwriting. Cognitive psychologists have been particularly interested in the question of what mental processes make such efficient word recognition possible.

Processes involved in spoken word and written word recognition may operate in similar ways but, as will be seen in Chapter 11, there is evidence from patients with disorders of language for separate systems for spoken and written word recognition. It cannot be assumed that conclusions based on lexical access in one domain can necessarily be applied in the other (Connine *et al.*, 1990).

What factors influence the efficiency of word recognition? One clearly established finding is that the time it takes to recognise a word depends on the frequency with which that word is encountered in the language. Frequency can be established by referring to counts that have been undertaken of the frequency of occurrence of each word in a sample of books, magazines and other printed material, amounting to some 20 million words in the case of the Thorndike–Lorge Word Frequency Count (Thorndike and Lorge, 1944) and one million words in the case of the more recent Kucera and Francis listing (1967). Words can be selected for experiments that differ in frequency but do not differ in word length, e.g. 'catch' and 'cache'. In a phoneme monitoring task participants listen to a spoken passage with instructions to understand the passage and to listen out for a target phoneme such as /t/. In a classic study by Foss (1969) the target phoneme sometimes followed a high-frequency word and sometimes a low-frequency word. Results showed that on average it took longer to identify the target phoneme after low-frequency words, suggesting an increased processing load for accessing them. Rayner and Duffy (1986) investigated the effect of word frequency on reading. By measuring eye fixations during reading they were able to show that low-frequency words were fixated on average for about 100 millisec. longer than high-frequency words.

Another factor found to affect visual word recognition is known as the neighbourhood effect, first demonstrated by Coltheart *et al.* (1977). This refers to the influence of a word's orthographic neighbourhood. The number of orthographic neighbours a word has is defined as the number of other words of the same length that have the same letters in the same position, apart from one. For example, the word 'list' has several orthographic neighbours that include 'last', 'lisp' and 'fist'. On experimental tasks, participants respond more rapidly to words with many such neighbours than to words with fewer neighbours, though this finding applies only to words with relatively low frequencies (Andrews, 1989, 1992; Sears *et al.*, 1995; Forster and Shen, 1996; Grainger *et al.*, 2005).

Could the recognition of printed words be affected by factors related to the sound of words, even when only silent reading is required? The answer seems to be yes. When spoken, a word like MAID sounds the same as the word MADE. They are known as heterographic homophones in that they sound the same but are spelled differently. Such words are generally harder to recognise than words which do not have any other words that sound the same, known as non-homophonic (Ferrand and Grainger, 2003). Ziegler *et al.* (1997) reported a study where participants were asked to press a key when a visually presented word contained a particular letter. They found that participants made more errors identifying the target letter when it wasn't actually there (e.g. A in LEEK) when the word was one that had a homophone mate which did contain the target letter, e.g. LEAK).

An important issue has been whether word recognition is affected by the context in which the word occurs, that is, is it recognised less quickly and accurately in isolation than when it follows a preceding word or is part of a sentence? Many findings in cognitive psychology support the notion that stimuli are recognised better in context. The issue involves the question of the extent to which the processing of 'bottom-up' information such as the component sounds or letters of words is influenced by 'top-down' information, in this case from semantic, syntactic and pragmatic aspects of what is being said.

One way of investigating the effect of context has been to ask whether the meaning of a preceding word or sentence can affect the recognition of a succeeding word, an effect known as semantic priming. Word reading times have been shown to be influenced by sentence context. Zola (1984) measured eye fixations while participants read pairs of sentences like (14) and (15):

(14)   Movie theatres must have buttered popcorn to serve their patrons.

(15)   Movie theatres must have adequate popcorn to serve their patrons.

Participants fixated longer on the target word 'popcorn' in sentence (15) than in (14), probably because in (14) the word 'buttered' limits the range of possible succeeding nouns to a greater extent than the word 'adequate' does in (15) and thus 'popcorn' can be recognised faster in (14) than in (15).

Many studies of semantic priming have used the lexical decision task where the participant is presented with a string of letters and has to decide whether or not they form a word. Meyer and Schvaneveldt (1971) presented words in pairs and showed that participants were faster at making lexical decisions for each member of the pair when the words were related (e.g. 'cat–dog') than when they were unrelated (e.g. 'cat–pen') and many other studies have supported this finding (for a review see Balota, 1992).

A variant on the lexical decision task uses a cross-modal paradigm where the participant receives input from both auditory and visual modalities. A word or sentence is heard through earphones immediately prior to a target string appearing on a screen for a lexical decision to be made. Swinney (1979) presented context sentences that produced a bias towards one of the meanings of an ambiguous target word. For example, immediately following sentence (16) the participant might see either the word ANT, SPY or SEW.

(16) Because he was afraid of electronic surveillance, the burglar carefully searched the room for bugs.

Swinney found that reaction times were faster for words like SPY, which fit with the context, than for neutral words such as SEW. However, he found that words like ANT which do not fit with the context sentence but are semantically related to the final word in the sentence, were also faster relative to neutral words. Swinney's finding has been taken to show that both senses of the ambiguous word are activated simultaneously and can lead to semantic priming effects but that these effects are relatively independent of broader contextual knowledge coming, in this case, from the remainder of the sentence.

Fewer studies have investigated semantic priming in spoken word recognition. Although auditory lexical decision tasks have been used (Blumstein *et al.*, 1982), there are problems with the use of this technique because a non-word, when spoken, can often sound like a variation in the pronunciation of some real word. Liu *et al.* (1997) have proposed the use of a single-word shadowing task to investigate semantic priming in lexical access for spoken words. This task involved participants listening to word pairs or to sentences and repeating a target word. The target word was signalled by a shift in voice from a male to a female speaker (or vice versa). They found evidence of priming effects, with responses being faster when target words followed related words (e.g. water–DRINK) than unrelated words (e.g. fruit–SILVER) and when target words were more predictable from the sentence context (e.g. 'The gambler had a streak of bad LUCK') than when they were less predictable (e.g. 'The kind old man asked us to RACE').

Explaining lexical access

A central concept in explanations of word recognition has been the notion of the mental lexicon, the body of knowledge we hold about words, including their pronunciation, spelling, meaning and typical syntactic roles. Listeners and readers access the lexicon each time they encounter a word in reading or when listening to someone talking. How do we access the appropriate word so efficiently? Do we search right through the lexicon on each occasion? Do other comprehension processes interact with lexical access or is lexical access independent of them, i.e. modular? A number of models of how the lexicon is accessed have been put forward.

There are two main types of model of lexical access: direct access models and serial search models. Direct access models assume that the lexicon contains a detection device for each lexical item within it. Features of words, such as letters or component sounds, activate detectors for many possible candidate lexical entries simultaneously until one becomes pre-eminent. Serial search models, on the other hand, hold that lexical entries are examined one by one to match to features of the input.

Forster (1976, 1979) proposed an autonomous serial search model. In this model the lexicon is seen as containing a master file of words, rather like the way books are organised in a library. This master file links with a series of access files, in the way a library might have online files in which books are organised by author, title, subject and date. There are orthographic access files, phonological access files and syntactic-semantic access files. When a word is perceived, a search is carried out through the access files until a match is made and directions given to the master file in the lexicon which holds all the information to do with the word, including its meaning. To make the process more efficient, the access files are organised into separate 'bins' on the basis of the initial sound or letter of a word. Items within each of the 'bins' are then ordered by frequency, so that the more frequent items can be examined first. The model is modular in the sense that the search process is independent of other possible sources of information such as sentence context.

One of the most influential models has been the logogen model of lexical access developed by John Morton (Morton 1969, 1970, 1979; Morton and Patterson, 1980). This model is a direct access model and is based on the concept of thresholds. In the model, each word in the lexicon is represented as a 'logogen'. A logogen acts as a feature counter and passively accumulates evidence. Evidence can be from sensory sources, so that hearing the phoneme /t/ increases the activation levels of all words containing this sound, including, for example, the word 'cat'. Evidence can also be from contextual sources so that hearing the word 'pet' may increase the activation level of the logogens associated with the names of a range of animals including the one for 'cat'. The logogen builds up evidence until its individual threshold level is reached, when it 'fires' and the word is recognised. Each time a word is encountered, the threshold for that word is temporarily lowered and less sensory information would be needed to recognise it. Word frequency has long-term effects which lower the logogen's resting activation level.

The logogen model can be seen as an important precursor of connectionist models of word recognition. As discussed in Chapter 12, connectionist models of reading single words (Seidenberg and McClelland, 1989; Plaut et al., 1996) are highly interactive models with input and output layers representing written (orthographic) and spoken (phonological) elements and one or more hidden layers. Each unit in these layers has an activation level and each unit is connected to the units in the next layer by a complex web of weighted connections, which can be either excitatory or inhibitory. By being exposed to word-pronunciation pairs, such models are 'trained' to associate spellings with pronunciations and 'tested' on novel letter strings. Seidenberg and McClelland (1989) and Plaut et al. (1996) have shown that such models can mimic human performance in a number of ways. For example, written words such as 'gave' whose pronunciation is regular, following the pattern of other words ending in 'ave', such as 'brave', 'save' and 'rave', were processed more accurately than exception words such as 'have'. The models can also be damaged or 'lesioned' in ways that give rise to performance similar to that of people who have brain injury (Plaut *et al.*, 1996). The success of such models in mimicking human patterns of performance tends to suggest the pre-eminence of interactive models of word processing. Such models have exciting implications for cognitive psychology but, as pointed out by Forster (1994), showing that a network model can successfully learn a complex task like reading does not necessarily mean that the model corresponds to the way that humans actually do it.

The cohort model (Marslen-Wilson, 1973, 1975, 1987, 1989) was devised to explain the process of spoken word recognition, in a way that captures the sequential on-line nature of speech recognition. According to this model, once the first two phonemes of a word have been heard, listeners develop a set of likely candidates for the word, known as the 'word initial cohort'. Thus, recognition units for all the words that begin in the same way as that word are activated. As successive phonemes are perceived, recognition units for words that no longer fit decline in activation and are eliminated until the cohort becomes smaller and smaller and finally one word is left, the one whose recognition unit has a much higher activation level than the others and the target word is identified. Like the logogen model, the cohort model allows direct, parallel access to the lexicon. However, unlike the passive process of accumulation of positive evidence in the logogen model, the cohorts actively seek to eliminate themselves.

O'Rourke and Holcomb (2002) carried out an electrophysiological investigation of predictions of the Marslen-Wilson (1987) cohort model. While ERPs were being measured, participants carried out a timed lexical decision task on spoken words and non-words. The experimenter manipulated the recognition point, the point in the word at which no other lexical item was consistent with the acoustic signal. Similarly for the non-words, the deviation point, the point at which no real word is consistent with the acoustic signal, was manipulated. An event-related potentials negativity in the region of the N400 component and reaction time (RT) was found to occur sooner for items with early than late recognition/deviation points. This study illustrates the type of evidence that is becoming available to test out predictions of language processing models.

10.5 Sentence comprehension

Understanding language involves considerably more than just recognising the words. We have to bring to bear syntactic and semantic knowledge as to what each word means in context and work out how the meanings are combined. When we hear on the news a sequence like:

(17)   In a shooting incident in Basra today, a British soldier was shot dead
       by a gunman

we need to be able to use syntactic knowledge of the passive voice to find out who did the shooting, the soldier or the gunman, and which of the two died. Moreover, knowledge of the world may have to be employed too, for example, in making sense of newspaper headlines, such as the following one:

'NOW WE'VE ALL BEEN SCREWED BY THE CABINET'

In grasping what this 1993 headline meant, newspaper readers could bring to bear knowledge that it appeared on the day after an announcement of tax changes and in the wake of a sex scandal involving a government minister. Pragmatic knowledge too would be involved in appreciating that this headline is to be regarded as figurative rather than literal in meaning.

There are many challenges in finding methods to investigate sentence comprehension, since the processes involved occur so rapidly and automatically, often while the sentence is still unfolding.

Just as ambiguous stimuli have been used to help us understand visual perceptual processes (Chapter 2), psycholinguists have made considerable use of sentences whose meaning is ambiguous in order to help gain insight into processes involved in sentence interpretation. A sentence such as 'They are racing cars' has a **structural ambiguity** and in one like 'Jane went up the steps to the bank' there is a **lexical ambiguity** since the noun 'bank' can refer to both a river bank and a financial institution. Ambiguities in language are more numerous than most people realise. Advertisers often make use of ambiguous phrases because they may require some extra processing and engage the curiosity of the reader, alerting attention to the product. Sometimes the ambiguity is inadvertent as in the following which appeared on a newspaper hoarding:

```
FORGIVE
ME
QUEEN
BEGS
FERGIE
```

Now consider the following sentence:

(18)   The horse raced past the barn fell.

If you have the same difficulty as most psychology students who have read this sentence since Bever (1970) first quoted it, you will be stumped by that final word 'fell' until you realise the sentence could be paraphrased as

(19)   The horse that had been raced past the barn fell.

Such sentences are known as **garden-path sentences** for the obvious reason that they lead you astray in your initial syntactic parsing.

It is important to consider whether sentences are processed as they are heard or read, on a word-by-word basis over time, or whether we wait until a whole clause or sentence has been completed before processing takes place all in one go. A 'wait and see' approach might be most appropriate because, although we receive words one at a time, sentences are more than just chains of words. The interpretation of one word may depend on other words at some distance within the sentence, known as 'long-distance dependencies'. An example would be the referent of the word 'it' in (20):

(20) If the point of what I am trying to say is obscure, let me assure you that I am going to clarify *it* in a minute.

However, the 'wait and see' approach would place heavy demands on the working memory system. It seems more likely that we follow an 'immediacy principle', making decisions about how each word functions in the sentence as we go along (Just and Carpenter, 1980, 1992). In sentences like (18) we take the first verb we encounter to be the main verb for that sentence and carry on with this assumption until we subsequently come across the second verb and have to revise our strategy. The surprise we experience at encountering the second verb is some indication in itself of the immediacy principle being followed. The immediacy principle is also supported by studies of the duration of people's eye fixations while they read sentences like (18) and (19) which show that longer is spent fixating on the second verb in sentences like (18) than in sentences like (19) (Just and Carpenter, 1992).

The way each type of knowledge, syntactic, semantic and pragmatic, is used in sentence processing, and their roles relative to one another, has been the basis for considerable research and debate in the psychology of language. There are two points of view on the way syntactic, semantic and pragmatic information apply in the interpretation of a sentence. One view is that the syntactic analysis of the sentence operates independently of, and is not influenced by, semantic and pragmatic knowledge (Frazier, 1989). Such a view is in line with Chomsky's linguistic theory (1986) which sees syntax as an autonomous module and Fodor's (1983) modular approach to cognition. The other point of view is an interactive one which holds that semantic information can guide syntactic analysis (Taraban and McClelland, 1988; Trueswell *et al.*, 1994).

Syntactic processing

When we hear a sentence, we have to work out how the incoming words relate together to form a representation in our minds of the syntactic structure of the sentence, a process known as **parsing**. In conceptualising the mental representation of syntactic structure, many psycholinguists have drawn on linguists' proposals for a set of formal rules for creating sentences out of groups of words, the **phrase structure rules** and, in particular, linguists' way of depicting these rules diagramatically in the form of phrase structure trees (see Figure 10.2 for a phrase structure tree diagram). A phrase structure tree is a useful way of

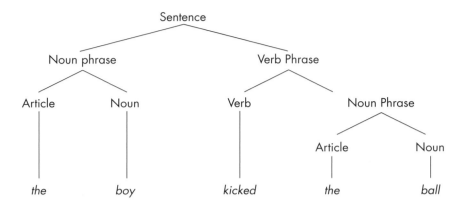

Figure 10.2 A phrase structure tree diagram

expressing the hierarchical structure of the phrase groupings that make up a sentence. Each point at which the tree branches is known as a 'node' and the more syntactically complex the sentence is, the more nodes will be present in the tree diagram.

How might the process of parsing work? Early psycholinguistic research (e.g. Sachs, 1967; Slobin, 1966) had shown that we do not use processes that mirror linguistic rules when interpreting sentences (see Section 10.3). Fodor *et al.* (1974) argued that although linguistic rule systems were not blueprints for psychological processing (i.e. were not 'psychologically real'), the end-product of parsing was a syntactic representation and this representation was the deep structure of the sentence as described by Chomsky (1965). They proposed that to recover the syntactic structure of sentences, rather than following systematic rules, we use a number of heuristic strategies, essentially rules of thumb, which generally allow us to arrive at the appropriate structure but are not foolproof and may sometimes fail and lead us astray.

One strategy, proposed by Bever (1970), was that, since in English sequences of noun-verb-noun often correspond to active voice sentences, parsing might in the first instance proceed by taking the initial noun in a noun-verb-noun sequence to be the participant (and agent of the action) and the second noun to be the object (and acted-upon element) in the sentence. He argued that young children are sometimes misled by this strategy into misinterpreting passive voice sentences, where the first noun corresponds to the acted-upon and not the actor. Kimball (1973) extended the strategy approach and proposed seven principles of parsing. Frazier (1987) argued that our initial attempt to parse a sentence follows the principle: use the simplest, easiest to construct phrase structure tree possible.

Frazier combined a number of the previously proposed strategies for recovering underlying syntax into two basic strategies which people were said to use to keep their initial syntactic parsing as simple as possible. These are the 'late closure strategy' and the 'minimal attachment strategy'. The late closure strategy is stated as:

If grammatically permissible, each new incoming term is attached to the clause or phrase currently being processed.

The operation of the late closure strategy can be detected in reading a sentence like (21):

(21)   Since Jay always jogs a mile seems like a short distance.

A garden path is created in (21) because the new noun phrase 'a mile' gets attached to the verb phrase 'jogs' and is assumed to be its object, whereas it is, in fact, the subject of the main verb 'seems'. Eye movement studies of people reading sentences like (21) show that after the point of ambiguity people's fixations increase in duration and regressive eye movements show that people backtrack to the area at which ambiguity arises, in this case, to 'jogs' (Frazier and Rayner, 1982).

The minimal attachment strategy is stated as:

Each new incoming item is added to the phrase structure in a way that requires the minimum of additional nodes.

The operation of the minimal attachment strategy is shown in the way a garden path is created in sentence (22):

(22)   The performer sent the flowers was very pleased.

When the word 'sent' is encountered, the reader using the minimal attachment strategy parses it as a verb, attaching a verb phrase to the sentence node in the phrase marker. However, the word 'sent' actually denotes the beginning of a relative clause which involves a more complex parsing with three additional nodes having to be formed. The parsing of sentence (22), therefore, violates the minimal attachment strategy and this is demonstrated in the element of surprise experienced as we read to the end of such a sentence.

Frazier holds the position that syntactic analysis is autonomous and proceeds independently of semantic and pragmatic considerations. A study by Rayner *et al.* (1983) compared sentences like (22) with (23):

(23)   The florist sent the flowers was very pleased.

If semantic knowledge influences syntactic analysis, then sentences like (23) should be more susceptible to the garden-path effect, since florists usually send flowers, rather than receive them. In fact, eye movements were very similar for each of the sentences, in terms of the time participants spent inspecting the words 'was very' in each. These findings appear to show that the garden-path effect was equally strong in both types of sentence thus supporting the independence of syntactic processing and semantic knowledge, rather than an interactive view.

This conclusion has been controversial and other psycholinguists argue for a model of parsing that allows for interaction between processing of sentence structure and processing based on semantic knowledge, such as knowledge of the objects and actions referred to by the words in the sentence.

Taraban and McClelland (1988) devised pairs of sentences like (24) and (25):

(24) The couple admired the house with a friend but knew that it was overpriced.

(25) The couple admired the house with a garden but knew that it was overpriced.

Here (25) violates the minimal attachment strategy but follows the semantic expectation set up by the use of the definite article 'the', that some further information about 'the' house may be provided. Taraban and McClelland (1988) found that sentences like (25) were read faster than ones like (24), supporting the idea that semantic expectations influenced readers' behaviour more than the minimal attachment strategy. Based on such findings, Taraban and McClelland have argued for a parallel interactional model of sentence parsing based on connectionist principles.

Much of the research on sentence processing has been based on ambiguous sentences or carefully constructed 'garden-path' sentences, presented in isolation from any context of ongoing discourse. Because processing takes place extremely swiftly, the use of ambiguous sentences, which take longer, has helped obtain measurable response times. Concentration on single sentences in psycholinguistics has probably to some extent reflected a similar focus in the science of linguistics. However, more recently a wider range of sentence types and a wider range of discourse settings has been brought into play in psycholinguistic research (e.g. Ferreira *et al.*, 2003; Grodner *et al.*, 2005).

Grodner *et al.* (2005) have investigated the impact of discourse context on sentence comprehension. They refer to research by Crain and Steedman (1985) who found that the interpretation of ambiguous sentences can be affected by presenting them in the context of a short ongoing discourse:

(26) The psychologist told the woman that he was having trouble with ...
   a.   ... her husband
   b.   ... to leave.

Read in isolation, sentences ending like (26 b) take longer to process than sentences ending like (26 a). However, if a context like (27) is read first, the difference is lessened (Crain and Steedman, 1985).

(27) A psychologist was counselling two women. He was worried about one of them but not the other.

Grodner *et al.* (2005) have queried why semantic and contextual effects should be thought to apply only to parsing of sentences that are ambiguous. They hypothesised that in comprehension of any sentence, both syntactic and discourse analyses are in progress and influence one another throughout. They asked participants to read sentences that are unambiguous such as (28) and (29):

(28) 'The postman that the dog bit on the leg needed seventeen stitches and had a permanent scar from the injury.'

(29) 'The postman, who the dog bit on the leg, needed seventeen stitches and had a permanent scar from the injury.'

These sentences both contain relative clauses and there is no ambiguity about the syntactic structure. However, from the point of view of the discourse function the relative clauses operate differently. With (28) there is an implication that there is a wider group of one or more postmen who did *not* get bitten on the leg. Working out this implication may take more time, reflecting more cognitive resources being required. Grodner *et al.* (2005) found that participants were indeed slower at reading sentences like (28) than sentences like (29). However, Grodner *et al.* were able to reverse this difference when they provided each of the sentences with a supportive discourse statement, e.g.:

(30) 'A vicious guard dog bit a postman on the leg and another postman on the arm.'

'The postman that the dog bit on the leg needed seventeen stitches and had a permanent scar from the injury.'

(31) 'A vicious guard dog bit a postman and a garbage man.'

'The postman, who the dog bit on the leg, needed seventeen stitches and had a permanent scar from the injury.'

When the supportive statement was provided, (30) was read more quickly than (31), suggesting that discourse processing and syntactic processing interact with one another and that this may apply generally in language comprehension.

In the speech of those around us, disfluencies such as 'uh' and 'um' are common, as well as revisions, rewordings and repetitions. Yet we are able to understand such sentences with apparent ease, often not even noticing that a disfluency has occurred (Lickley and Bard, 1998). Psycholinguists are just beginning to look at how such disfluencies may be dealt with during language comprehension (Ferreira *et al.*, 2003). Ferreira and her colleagues have used sentences such as:

(32) Simon says you should drop the frog.

(33) Simon says you should put-uh drop the frog.

(34) Simon says you should put the frog.

(35) Simon says you should drop-uh put the frog.

Participants were asked to listen to sentences such as these and to make button-press judgements as to whether each one was grammatical or not. They were instructed not to base their judgements simply on the presence or absence of disfluencies. A verb like 'put' normally requires a location to be specified, such as 'put the ball into the box', whereas for a verb like 'drop', stating a location is optional. Overall, participants preferred sentences where the verb, or the replacement verb, was one like 'drop' (preferring sentences like (32) and (33) to (34) and (35)). However, participants were more likely to judge sentences like (32) as grammatical than those like (33), while they were more likely to judge as grammatical sentences like (35) which contain a disfluency than those like (34) which do not. These findings seem to demonstrate that the verb that was replaced still had some ongoing impact on the processing of the sentence and thus on the grammaticality judgements.

Research on language comprehension is currently developing in interesting ways as it opens up to encompass spoken as well as written input, unambiguous as well as ambiguous constructions, language embedded in discourse and stimuli that reflect more natural phenomena of everyday speech such as disfluencies.

10.6 Language production

When we talk we convert thoughts into language. How do we match the elements of thought to the words by which they can be expressed? The elements of thought are usually referred to as 'concepts'. Concepts divide the world into units, some of which may correspond to words. If a speaker wishes to convey the information that, for example, a lorry has crashed into a car, the speaker has to match the elements of the thought with the linguistic units, words in English or whatever language is being used. As well as a semantic match with the underlying concepts the speaker has to take syntax into account. The word to be selected will have to be of a particular grammatical category, such as a noun, verb or adjective, in order to fit into the sentence frame that is being constructed. Choice of word is also influenced by such factors as whether the word has already been mentioned in the discourse, thus allowing a pronoun to stand in for it. Different words may even be selected when addressing different listeners, for example, for children as opposed to adults or for close family as opposed to strangers. Despite the range of factors that have to be taken into account in accessing words, the process is accomplished extremely accurately. Estimates suggest that a typical speaker has a production vocabulary of around 20,000 words, yet error data suggest that the wrong word is chosen only about once per million words.

Lexicalisation is the name given to this process by which the thought that underlies a word is turned into the sound of the word. Lexicalisation has been widely thought to be a two-stage process (Levelt 1989, 1992). In the first stage the concept makes contact with an abstract form which includes the semantic representation of the word and the syntactic information associated with it, but does not include the phonological form of the word. This abstract level of representation is known as the *lemma* and the process of making contacting with it is known as lemma selection. The second stage of lexicalisation involves specifying the actual phonological form of the word, known as the *lexeme*, by a process known as lexeme selection.

This two-stage model of lexicalisation can help us understand a common experience which psychologists refer to as the *'tip-of-the-tongue state'*. This is the experience of being unable to retrieve a particular word despite strong feelings of knowing it. The tip-of-the-tongue state can be seen as the result of success at the stage of lexicalisation that involves contacting the lemma but failure at the stage of making contact with the lexeme (see Harley, 2001).

Evidence to support the distinction between the two stages of lexicalisation comes from research that has used a priming paradigm. Wheeldon and Monsell (1992) investigated lexical priming in lexicalisation. They found that participants were faster at naming pictures when they had recently produced the name of the picture while reading aloud or giving a definition but not if they had produced a word that sounds the same (a homophone such as 'weight' for 'wait'). Thus the effect came about when the priming was semantically and phonologically generated but not when the priming was solely phonological. Whether or not the two stages are independent of one another or whether they interact has been the subject of some debate. An interactive model based on connectionist principles which proposes that processing during speech planning occurs at several levels at once (Dell, 1986; Dell and O'Seaghdha, 1991; Dell *et al.* 1997) is described later.

Language production differs from the understanding of language in that understanding begins with a spoken or written message which has to be interpreted to determine the underlying thoughts, whereas, when we talk, we start with a thought for which we have to find the appropriate words. It has been relatively difficult to find research strategies for studying this process because its starting point is a thought or idea which cannot be readily detected and observed. The final product, the spoken word, can, however, be observed and one of the most fruitful strategies has been to study speech output for **slips of the tongue**, the errors people make when they talk. Fromkin (1973) said these errors 'provide a window into linguistic processes' (43–4).

When psycholinguists began to make detailed records of the speech errors made by their friends and acquaintances (Fromkin, 1971; Garrett, 1975) and to make detailed analyses of them, they found that the errors people make are not just random substitutions, omissions or insertions. In fact slips of the tongue are quite systematic. Figure 10.3 shows some examples of types of slips of the tongue based on errors reported by Fromkin (1973), Garrett (1975), Dell (1986) and Harvey (2001). Slips of the tongue generally involve one word, one morpheme or one phoneme being substituted for another word, morpheme or phoneme. Garrett (1975, 1984) studied several thousand such errors and developed a model of speech production based on the most frequent types encountered. Four types which he thought to be particularly important for an understanding of speech production processes were:

Word substitutions such as 'boy' for 'girl' and 'black' for 'white', which only occur with content words and certain prepositions, e.g. 'At low speeds it's too light (heavy)'.

Word exchanges such as 'Fancy getting your model renosed' for 'Fancy getting your nose remodelled'. In these errors words from the same categories exchange with one another e.g. nouns with nouns, adjectives with adjectives and verbs with verbs.

Sound exchange errors such as 'shinking ships' for 'sinking ships' These usually affect adjacent words.

Morpheme exchange or 'stranding' errors such as 'slicely thinned' for 'thinly sliced', 'He is schooling to go' for 'He is going to school' where the 'ing' ending has been stranded in its original position and the verb stem to which it was originally attached ('go' in this example) has been moved elsewhere in the sentence.

The production of a sentence according to Garrett's model (Garrett, 1975, 1984) involves a series of levels of processing which operate independently of one another (see Figure 10.4). The basic ideas the speaker wants to talk about are conceptualised at the 'message level'. At the 'functional level', concepts are matched up with semantic representations of lexical items and with the thematic roles, such as agent or object, which those lexical items will take. At the 'positional level', information about the phonological form of words and about the syntactic form the sentence will take is specified and lexical items are ordered in terms of particular syntactic structures, such as the active or the passive voice.

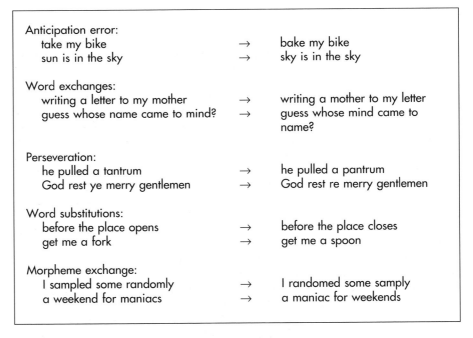

Figure 10.3 Examples of types of slips of the tongue

Source: From Fromkin (1973), Harvey (2001), Dell (1986), Garrett (1975)

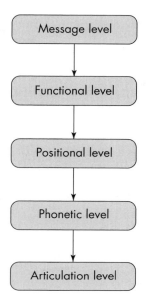

Figure 10.4 Garrett's model of speech production
Source: Adapted from Garrett (1984)

At the 'phonetic level', the phonological form of the words is specified in greater detail to yield a phonetic level of representation and, finally, at the 'articulation level', commands to the vocal apparatus to speak the sentence are put in place.

Garrett suggested an important difference between the way function words and bound morphemes on the one hand, and content words on the other hand, are introduced into the sentence plan. According to his formulation, at the functional level only semantic representations associated with content words are involved. At the positional level, when the syntactic form of the sentence is selected, it comes with the phonological form of the grammatical function words and bound morphemes already specified and they are already in position. The phonological forms of the content words, however, are not yet specified and in position. The phonological form of each content word has to be specified and inserted into the syntactic form of the sentence within the positional level of sentence generation.

This distinction helps explain some of the types of slips of the tongue that have been documented. Word substitutions, for example, are thought to arise at the functional level, explaining why they occur only with content words and at the stage of lexicalisation when lemmas are being identified. Sound exchange errors, according to this model, are thought to arise during the positional level when content words are being inserted into syntactic structures and do not apply to function words because these are already in position in the syntactic structure when it is specified. Stranding errors also occur while content words are being positioned in the sentence structure. The wrong position may be selected for the content word but the grammatical ending does not move with the remainder of the word. It is 'stranded' because it was already in position when the syntactic form was selected.

Whether planning during speech production proceeds in a serial fashion, along the lines set out by Garrett and in the later model proposed by Levelt (Levelt, 1989; Bock and Levelt, 1994; Levelt *et al.*, 1999), or whether planning involves interaction between different levels is a matter for debate. Dell (1986), Dell and O'Seaghdha (1991) and Dell *et al.* (1997) propose an interactive model based on connectionist principles by which processing during speech planning occurs at the same time as semantic, syntactic, morphological and phonological levels. This *spreading activation* model allows feedback from later levels such as phonological levels to earlier levels of planning. When at a certain point in a sentence frame a verb, say, is to be inserted, activation is set up within the lexicon, which takes the form of a connectionist network of interconnected nodes. There are nodes for concepts, words, morphemes and phonemes. When a node within the lexicon becomes activated, activation spreads to all the nodes connected to it. So, for example, when the node for the verb 'opens' becomes activated, there will also be some activation of the node for 'closes'. The most highly activated node that belongs to the verb category is chosen. Once a word has been selected, its activation reduces to zero for a time, preventing it from being selected repeatedly. Sometimes an incorrect word will have a higher level of activation than the correct one and this would give rise to a speech error such as a word substitution. Categorical rules constrain the types of items that are activated at each level within the model, explaining why errors usually occur within one category with, for example, nouns replacing nouns. Exchange errors can be explained by the idea that once an item has been selected its activation reduces to zero. Thus, because all the elements of the sentence will have become activated during planning, a word (or a phonological element) may be spoken earlier in a sentence than is appropriate. The activation level for that word (or phonological element) will reduce to zero so it is unlikely to be repeated in its intended slot and one of the other words (or phonological elements) which were highly activated takes its place.

Dell (1995) points out that some speech errors, such as 'The competition is a little strougher', appear to reflect both semantic and phonological processes. These 'mixed errors' may be best explained by an interactive model of speech production allowing simultaneous activation of different levels. Such a conclusion, however, is contested by those like Levelt and colleagues (Levelt, 1989; Bock and Levelt, 1994; Levelt *et al.*, 1999) who hold to a more sequential approach. Levelt and colleagues have developed a model of the processes involved in producing individual words in speech which is called WEAVER++ (Word-form Encoding by Activation and VERification). This is a complex model with six stages: conceptual preparation, lexical selection during which the lemma is selected, morphological encoding, phonological encoding, phonetic encoding and articulation. This is also a spreading activation model but the critical difference from that of Dell is that activation feeds forward through the stages in the network from selecting the meaning to articulating the word but not backwards. Each stage is completed before the next begins.

Critical of the heavy reliance on spontaneous error data in studies of speech production, investigators have been attempting to devise experimental paradigms that will help test the predictions of the theoretical approaches of Dell and his colleagues (Dell *et al.*, 1997) and of Levelt and colleagues (Levelt *et al.*, 1999). Levelt *et al.* (1991) developed an experimental method to induce speech errors whereby people were asked to name pictures as quickly as possible, while also listening to a spoken word through earphones and pressing a button as soon as they recognised this word. Some of the words they heard were semantically related to the picture, some were phonologically related, some were unrelated and some were 'mediated', linked through a semantic and phonological connection. For example, given the picture of a sheep, the word heard was 'goal' which is phonologically related to 'goat' which in turn is semantically related to 'sheep'. Levelt *et al.* (1991) argued that an interactive model of lexicalisation would predict that naming of the sheep picture would be facilitated by the presentation of the mediated stimulus 'goal'. However, such facilitation did not occur. The findings seemed to support a sequential model since semantically related words facilitated naming only when presented after a very short delay (less than 100 millisec.) and phonologically related words had an effect only after a longer delay (more than 600 millisec.). These timings appeared to support the idea of a sequence of stages in the production of words, from the selection of meaning to phonological encoding and articulation.

Another experimental approach, however, has provided findings that appear to go against predictions from the Levelt *et al.* (1999) model. Participants in a study by Morsella and Miozzo (2002) were asked to name pictures in one colour while being shown pictures in that colour and distractor pictures in a different colour. When distractor pictures had names that were related phonetically to the names of the target pictures, the target pictures were named more rapidly. The findings suggest that there was an influence of phonological encoding on stages that come earlier in Levelt's sequential feed-forward model.

10.7 Discourse level

Discourse is the term for a set of sentences related to one another in a meaningful way. In investigating language processing at discourse level, we go beyond the study of word and sentence processing to the level at which speakers and listeners integrate the thoughts and ideas expressed in sentences into topics and follow the flow of ideas from one topic to the next. Topics can be negotiated and developed across speakers, the process normally referred to as 'having a conversation' or 'chatting'.

At discourse level, the processes of sentence comprehension and production which we have been discussing still come into play but the picture becomes more complex. The speaker has to present what he or she has to say in a way that allows the listener to work out the purpose intended. This purpose, known as the communicative intention, may be, for example, to provide information, to request the listener to do something or to request information. There is no one-to-one matching between linguistic structure and communicative intention.

For instance, a listener has to infer that an utterance in the form of a question may be intended to convey information, as in 'Would you believe that England have just won/lost two more wickets?' or to request that an action is carried out, as in 'Can you pass me the newspaper?', or one of a range of other communicative intentions which can be conveyed in the form of a question.

If the intention is to convey information as, for example, for an item in a news bulletin, the propositions expressed must be presented in an organised way, rather than as a random list of statements. The listener has to be able to do the work of understanding each proposition, relating it to the broader topic.

Cues that help us connect ideas from different sentences together are known as *cohesive devices*. Halliday and Hasan (1976) have outlined a range of such devices in English. A commonly used one is that of pronominal reference, where pronouns such as 'she' 'her' 'it' 'their' refer to items mentioned earlier:

(36)   The little girl opened her present. *She* became very excited.

Another cohesive device is that of demonstrative reference where 'the', 'that', 'those' may be used to refer to back to something that has gone before as in (37):

(37)   Once there was a handsome prince. *The* prince was lonely.

Psychologists have made a distinction between *given* and *new* information. Given information refers to information that the speaker assumes the listener already knows while new information is information the listener is assumed not to know as yet. Often given information is introduced by the definite article 'the' and new information by the indefinite article 'a' (Haviland and Clark, 1974). Clark and Haviland (1977) suggested a model of sentence integration known as the 'given/new strategy' by which the given and new information in each incoming sentence is identified, an antecedent in memory is found for the given information and the new information is attached to that antecedent. They measured the time taken to read pairs of sentences like (38) and (39):

(38)   We got some beer out of the car.
       The beer was warm.

(39)   We got some picnic supplies out of the car.
       The beer was warm.

The use of 'the' in the second sentence of each pair establishes that 'the beer' is given information. Establishing the antecedent for 'the beer' is more straightforward in (38) than in (39) because it can be easily matched with the beer mentioned in the first sentence. In pairs like (39), Haviland and Clark suggest that we have to make a 'bridging inference' that since beer is sometimes included in picnic supplies, 'the beer' referred to must have been part of those picnic supplies. Time taken to read the pairs of sentences was indeed longer for pairs like (39) than for those like (38).

Many other complex inferences are involved when two or more people are involved in conversation. For communication to proceed smoothly, a speaker needs to make relatively accurate inferences about what the other person already knows about the topic and what needs to be explained. The partner in the conversation needs to have a working model in mind of the speaker's line of thought to be able to determine what the speaker 'is getting at' and to work out 'why she is telling me this'. Speakers and listeners cooperate in *grounding* their communication, establishing and building on knowledge and beliefs that they can share to make interactions efficient and effective.

In a laboratory study of these processes, Clark and Krych (2004) observed the way speakers monitor addressees for understanding and, when necessary, alter their utterances as they go along. In their study one person directed another in constructing models from building blocks. When the two participants were able to talk freely and observe one another, the person directing the activity would adjust what they said to support the other person's ongoing activity and non-verbal signals which included showing, poising, pointing at, placing, and orienting the building blocks, and eye-gaze, head-nods, and head-shakes, all timed with precision. Similarly the person doing the building would make moment-by-moment adjustments to what they said and did, to link with the verbal and non-verbal behaviour of the person who was directing. These sorts of adjustments occur all the time in everyday interactions but we are usually unaware of them unless something goes wrong.

Complex knowledge of the world may also have to be brought to bear in conversational interaction, as in this telling example from Pinker (1994) who asks us to imagine having to programme a computer to understand an exchange like the following:

Woman: I'm leaving you.
Man: Who is he?

There is enormous potential for confusion and misunderstandings in conversational exchanges, as another exchange quoted by Pinker (1994) indicates:

First guy: I didn't sleep with my wife before we were married, did you?
Second guy: I don't know. What was her maiden name?

Yet, for the most part, conversations proceed smoothly. In order for this to be the case, people must have some implicit, shared assumptions about the way each will contribute to the joint conversational enterprise. Grice (1975) identified four such shared assumptions which he called 'maxims':

1   **The maxim of quantity**: say as much as is needed to be informative but no more than is needed.
2   **The maxim of quality**: only say what you believe to be true.
3   **The maxim of relation**: make your contribution relevant to what has gone before and the aims of the conversation.
4   **The maxim of manner**: be clear, brief and to the point.

Of course, speakers do not always conform to all these conventions but they do provide one way of conceptualising the basic ground rules for being able to participate with others in conversational interaction. It is when conversation becomes awkward that we become aware that some convention has been violated, that someone is being too long-winded, too terse or is frequently straying from the point. The possibilities for characterising difficulties that may arise at the level of discourse for people with brain injury, with dementia, schizophrenia or with autism is now an active area of investigation.

Summary

- The use of language provides us with a subtle and sophisticated tool for communicating with other people. The relative independence of cognitive processes involved in language from other aspects of cognition is a matter of debate.
- Language involves a complex system operating at a number of levels from the basic sounds of speech, through word, sentence and discourse levels.
- Linguists focus their study on language competence, the knowledge of the grammar of language that is thought to underlie our ability to use language creatively. Psycholinguists are more interested in studying aspects of language performance, how we produce language and the way we understand and remember what is said to us.
- A number of variables have been identified which can affect the speed with which a word is recognised, including frequency and context effects and a number of models of lexical access have been proposed.
- The process of lexicalisation by which the thought underlying a word is turned into the sound of the word appears likely to involve both semantic and phonological activation but the extent to which they interact is a matter of some dispute.
- The study of sentence comprehension has been heavily based on studies of processing of visually presented ambiguous and 'garden-path' sentences but there are now more studies of the understanding of spoken language in a wider range of experimental paradigms, some involving electrophysiological measures taken during on-line processing.
- There is evidence for an 'immediacy principle' and two major processing strategies have emerged from research: the 'late closure' strategy and the 'minimal attachment' strategy. However, the extent to which semantic and other types of contextual information interact with syntactic processing in sentence comprehension is still in dispute.
- Much of the research on language production has involved studies of the characteristics of typical spontaneous slips of the tongue but experiments in which errors are induced can allow models of speech production processes to be tested out.
- Psycholinguistic research is beginning to unravel some of the processes involved in managing the production and comprehension of connected discourse. These are particularly complex where interaction between conversational partners is involved.

Further reading

Berko-Gleason, J. and Ratner, N. (1998). *Psycholinguistics* (2nd edn). Orlando, FA: Harcourt Brace College Publishers. An excellent introductory text very well presented.

Carroll, D.W. (2003). *Psychology of Language* (3rd edn). Belmont, CA: Brooks/Cole. This is a good introductory textbook covering a wide range of topics in an accessible way.

Clark, H.H. (1996). *Using Language*. New York: Cambridge University Press. A stimulating account of the way people cooperate together in speaking and listening, participating in the joint enterprise of using language for conversational interaction.

Harley, T.A. (2001). *The Psychology of Language: From Data to Theory* (2nd edn). Hove: Psychology Press. This is very comprehensive textbook on the psychology of language, more advanced than the Carroll or Whitney texts and with more coverage of UK-based research. Highly recommended.

Pinker, S. (1994). *The Language Instinct: The New Science of Language and Mind*. Harmondsworth: Penguin. A fascinating and exceptionally well-written exploration of the nature of language and its role in our mental makeup. A really good read.

Whitney, P. (1997). *The Psychology of Language*. Boston, MA: Houghton Mifflin. A good introductory text.

Disorders of language

11.1 Introduction

In Chapter 10 it was stressed that, though talking and listening to others are natural, effortless activities for most people, analysis from a psychological point of view reveals a complexity and diversity of component processes. These include sound and word identification, production of complex sound patterns, accessing intricate networks of word meanings, comprehension processes and, in addition, personal–social considerations. Language is closely involved in problem-solving and thought as well as in communicating with others.

For some people, neurological disease or traumatic injury to the brain causes this natural, effortless use of language to be disturbed and to become effortful and fraught with difficulties. In this chapter we will consider the ways in which the ability to use language can be impaired, focusing on what can be learned about language processes in the brain by studying the patterns of difficulty demonstrated by people with **aphasia**, impairment of language ability caused by brain injury. Evidence about brain–language relations from neuro-imaging studies using PET and fMRI techniques will also be drawn upon.

Early work on language impairment was largely concerned with neurological issues, identifying which parts of the brain were most involved in language function, and these issues remain an enduring interest. However, much of the recent work on language disorder has been concerned with what such language disturbances can tell us about brain function, about what processes are involved in using language and how these processes interrelate. Again the issue of modularity is central to the debates in this area: Is language separate from the central system that performs non-linguistic cognitive processing? And are components of the language processing system modular in the sense that they function separately and can be selectively impaired?

11.2 Historical perspective

Since ancient times it was known that damage to the brain could affect language functioning but a major breakthrough occurred in 1861 when Paul Broca, a surgeon and anthropologist in Paris, reported on an autopsy he had carried out on the brain of a man who had had severe loss of language for more than twenty years. The man's nickname was 'Tan' because, although he could answer some questions with gestures, all he could say were a few swear words and the syllable 'tan'. Broca found that an infection had left Tan's brain with a large abscess in the left frontal lobe. Based on this case and on others he subsequently studied, Broca concluded that the two hemispheres of the brain were not identical in function and that the left hemisphere was the one involved in language. Loss of speech was localised in the left frontal lobe, more specifically in the posterior portion of the lower frontal lobe, the area now known as Broca's area. While Tan's language impairment appears to have been a very severe one, the language of patients with **Broca's** aphasia is usually described as being slow, laborious and lacking in fluency; speech is produced in short phrases with little variation in intonation and with frequent mispronunciations. People with this disorder often seem to grope for words but the words they do manage to come out with are usually meaningful. Here is an example of a brief exchange with a man with Broca's aphasia reported by Gardner (1977):

'What happened to make you lose your speech ?'
'Head, fall, Jesus Christ, me no good, str ... str ... Oh Jesus ... stroke.'
'I see. Could you tell me, Mr Ford, what you've been doing in the hospital?'
'Yes, sure. Me go, er, uh, P.T. nine o'cot, speech ... two times ... read ... wr ... ripe, er, write ... practice ... getting better.'
'And have you been going home on weekends?'
'Why yes ... Thursday, er, er, er, no, er, Friday ... Barbara ... wife ... and, oh, car, ... drive ... purnpike ... you know ... rest and ... tee-vee.'
'Are you able to understand everything on television?'
'Oh, yes, yes, ... well ... almost.' [Ford grinned a bit.]

Within a few years Carl Wernicke had noticed that some forms of language disturbance present a different picture and not all involve Broca's area. He described a form of aphasia now known as **Wernicke's** aphasia in which the person's speech is fluent but has little informational value and in which there is poor comprehension of language. This form of aphasia is associated with damage in the upper part of the left temporal lobe. The following excerpt (again from Gardner, 1977) demonstrates why this form of language disorder is sometimes known as 'fluent aphasia':

'What brings you to the hospital?' I asked the 72-year-old retired butcher four weeks after his admission to the hospital.
'Boy, I'm sweating, I'm awful nervous, you know, once in a while I get caught up, I can't mention the tarripoi, a month ago, quite a little, I've done a lot well, I impose a lot, while, on the other hand, you know what I mean, I have to run around, look it over, trebbin and all that sort of stuff.'
I attempted several times to break in, but was unable to do so against this relentlessly steady and rapid outflow.

Difficulties with comprehension of language cannot be assumed just because questions are not answered meaningfully but when comprehension is assessed on tasks which require non-verbal responses to verbal requests and instructions, people with Wernicke's aphasia do indeed show poor comprehension.

Wernicke (1874) also theorised about the neurological organisation for language, basing his ideas on a model in which Broca's area contained motor memories, memories of the sequences of motor movements needed to articulate words, and thus was responsible for speech output. Wernicke suggested that the area that now bears his name recognises the sounds of words, being the location that holds memories of the sound patterns of words. Wernicke also speculated about what might happen if the connecting pathways between Broca's area and

Wernicke's area should be damaged, but the areas themselves intact. He suggested that comprehension of language and production of speech would not be impaired but there would be a difficulty in repeating what had just been heard, because sound images received by Wernicke's area could not be transmitted forward to Broca's area to be produced. More recently it has been established that some people with aphasia do fit this picture, a pattern of aphasia which is referred to as **conduction aphasia** (Geschwind, 1965). When asked to repeat a sentence, these people often make phonological errors, leave out words, substitute other words or may have extreme difficulty in saying anything. A large tract of fibres, known as the *arcuate fasciculus*, does connect Broca's area with Wernicke's area and damage to this tract and surrounding tissues is indeed found in cases of conduction aphasia.

Wernicke's model was elaborated on by Lichtheim (1885), who argued that there was a third centre for language processing, a 'concept centre' which stores the mental representations of objects and associates them with words. Geschwind (1972) more recently postulated the location of such a centre in an area of the parietal lobe known as the angular gyrus. The three-centre Lichtheim–Geschwind model, underlies the classic approach to the categorisation of the different types of aphasia. Because the model is based on ideas about connections between language centres it became known as the 'Connectionist model of language' but it should be noted that this is not the same type of connectionist model as is now current in cognitive psychology (see Chapter 12).

Disruption could occur not only because of damage to Broca's and Wernicke's areas and to the fibres linking them, but also, it was thought, to the fibres linking the concept centre with Broca's and Wernicke's areas. It was postulated that if there was disruption to the connections between the concept centre and Broca's area then the person's speech would be very disrupted. However, they should still be able to repeat language they have heard if the connection from Wernicke's to Broca's area is still intact. Such a pattern of language disorder has been found and is known as transcortical motor aphasia. The person has the same impairment of speech as in Broca's aphasia but is able to repeat what has just been said, in fact often seems to have a compulsion to repeat what is heard, a characteristic known as **echolalia**. Using similar reasoning, if there was disruption to the links between Wernicke's area, where the sounds of words are processed, and the concept centre but the links from Wernicke's area to Broca's area were intact, then the effect might be that the person could not interpret the meaning of words but could still repeat what had been said. Again such a pattern of language disorder has been observed and is known as transcortical sensory aphasia. The person with this type of disorder has a similar disruption to the ability to understand language as someone with Wernicke's aphasia, but is able to repeat language and shows echolalia.

Another particularly striking pattern of language disruption in aphasia is one that has been found to occur in rare cases where Broca's area, Wernicke's area and the connection between them are intact, but they are essentially cut off from the rest of the brain. In these cases the 'ring' of tissue that surrounds those areas becomes starved of oxygen, being relatively far from the main artery which supplies it. Lung disease and some toxins, including carbon monoxide poisoning, can cause this loss of oxygen and other nutrients in turn, causing the ring of tissue to become permanently damaged. The effect of such 'isolation of the language zone' (Geschwind *et al.*, 1968; Caplan, 1992) is that the person loses the ability both to understand and to produce speech beyond a few stereotyped expressions but has some preservation of the ability to repeat sentences verbatim. Some ability to recognise words must therefore be preserved but the person is unable to understand the meaning of what they hear and repeat.

It is sometimes overlooked in accounts of relatively rare aphasic syndromes that a common type of aphasia is where damage extends to a number of parts of the system and the ability to understand and to produce language is very greatly disrupted. This global aphasia results from extensive damage to the language areas of the left hemisphere. The various syndromes of aphasia, according to the classic syndrome approach are shown in Figure 11.1.

Syndrome	Symptoms	Deficit	Lesion site
Broca's aphasia	Sparse halting speech misarticulations, understanding relatively intact, function words and inflections omitted	In speech planning and production	Posterior portion of left frontal lobe
Wernicke's aphasia	Poor auditory comprehension. Fluent speech but phonetic morphological and semantic errors	In representations of sound patterns of words	Posterior half of temporal cortex
Global aphasia	Major disturbance in all language functions	Disruption of all language processing components	Large portion of frontal and temporal lobes
Conduction aphasia	Disturbance of repetition and spontaneous speech	Disconnection: sound patterns of words from speech production mechanism	Arcuate fasciculus
Isolation of the language zone	Disturbance of speech production and comprehension with some preservation of repetition	Disconnection: concepts from word sounds and from speech production mechanism	Ring of cortical tissue around language areas

Figure 11.1 Major aphasic syndromes according to the classic view
Source: Adapted from Caplan (1992)

Other important types of language disorder are those of **acquired dyslexia** (also known as 'alexia') where the person experiences loss of the ability to read after brain injury and **acquired dysgraphia** (also known as 'agraphia') where the person loses the ability to write. According to the classic Lichtheim–Geschwind model, what occurs in these disorders is essentially that the visual areas of the brain become disconnected from the language areas because of damage to the angular gyrus, an association area in the brain that is important for the association of visual stimuli with linguistic symbols. Often dyslexia and dysgraphia co-occur but in some cases individuals have one without the other (Geschwind, 1965). A person with dyslexia without dysgraphia can write with little difficulty but is unable to read what he or she has written. Clearly the implication is that the neural systems for reading and writing are separable to some extent and do not critically rely on each other. We do not have one single module in the brain for both interpreting written language and producing it.

Alongside disturbances to language production and comprehension, many patients with aphasia have additional difficulties with reading. Patients with Wernicke's aphasia often have difficulties with both auditory and reading comprehension. Such a co-occurrence could be expected on the basis of the Lichtheim–Geschwind model since Wernicke's area is thought to control phonological access, a process important to most reading (see Chapter 10). However, difficulties with reading also occur in patients with Broca's aphasia, a finding less easy to explain in terms of the classic model according to which Broca's area is the speech centre.

Although the classic Lichtheim model, and its close relative the Lichtheim–Geschwind model, have been very influential in the study of aphasia, known as 'aphasiology', they have not been without their critics. The idea that there are language centres that function relatively independently of one another has been criticised, notably in an early commentary by Sigmund Freud in 1891. Freud wrote that many clinical cases did not neatly fit the pattern expected and argued that, despite Broca's and Wernicke's findings, language processes could be distributed widely throughout the cortex. Broca's and Wernicke's areas might not so much control certain functions but rather be areas where several cortical interconnections involved with language happen to cross. The English neurologist Henry Head (1926), who studied language disorders resulting from gunshot wounds to the head inflicted during the World War I, also argued that similar injuries could lead to different types of aphasic symptoms. He, too, argued against a one-to-one correspondence between brain regions and language operations and proposed that the language system operated as an integrated whole.

The main evidence in favour of the classic language circuit model is said to be that lesions in the language centres and to the connections between them do typically result in the occurrence of the classic aphasic syndromes described above (Benson and Geschwind, 1971; Geschwind, 1972). However, it has been pointed out by Caplan (1992) and others that groups of patients with the same syndrome, even groups carefully selected for research purposes, may actually show considerable variation in the extent to which particular components of language are disrupted.

It is a major drawback to the classic view of brain–language relations that there is a considerable amount of variation in the brain lesion sites that produce a particular set of deficits. Lesions in Broca's area do not of necessity give rise to the classic symptoms of Broca's aphasia (Mohr *et al.*, 1978; Dronkers, 1996) and Broca's type aphasias can result from lesions outside Broca's area (Caplan and Hildebrandt, 1988; Dronkers *et al.*, 2000). Wernicke's aphasia too can result from a range of different lesions (Kertesz *et al.*, 1993). Dronkers *et al.* (1995) reported two cases of Wernicke's aphasia having no damage to Wernicke's area at all and seven cases with damage to Wernicke's area but without having the typical features of Wernicke's aphasia. Data from PET and fMRI scanning of patients with aphasia are broadly consistent with the classic syndromes so that patients with Broca's aphasia show abnormally low activity in the lower-left frontal lobe and patients with Wernicke's aphasia show low activity in the temporal/parietal area (Metter *et al.*, 1990; Bates *et al.*, 2003). However, PET and fMRI scanning in normally functioning people has not always supported the classic language circuit model with the inferior parietal lobe, a crucial language area according to the theory, showing no activation on language tests (Petersen *et al.*, 1988; Posner *et al.*, 1988). Another type of neuroanatomical study involving electrocortical stimulation during neurosurgical operations has shown considerable individual variation in the localisation of language processes (Ojemann, 1983).

The language circuit approach provides information about the localisation of damage giving rise to the classic syndromes, not about the localisation of the individual language processing components. As research into the cognitive processes involved in language has developed, those working in the area of aphasiology have become very aware of the complexity of each of the components of the system that processes language. So, for example, Wernicke's area has been traditionally associated with processing speech input but, as described in the previous chapter, such processing involves many components. These components include word identification and word recognition, parsing, and determining the structure of discourse. Questions arise as to whether all are disrupted or whether some may be disrupted and not others. It has also been recognised that it is important to approach aphasia with a detailed model of language and language processing in mind, rather than lumping together many different aspects. Such thinking has given rise to the psycholinguistic approach to the study of language disorders.

11.3 The psycholinguistic perspective

The psycholinguistic approach to aphasia attempts to identify for each patient which components of the language processing system are disrupted and to describe how those components are disrupted (Caplan, 1992). The approach is closely allied with the cognitive neuropsychological approach described elsewhere in this book, and indeed language is one of the main areas in which cognitive neuropsychology was developed (Ellis and Young, 1996). In practice, the psycholinguistic approach involves setting a number of language-related tasks for the patient, tasks chosen on the basis of what is known of normal language functioning, to tap different aspects of the operation of the language processing system, and then identifying which tasks can be accomplished effectively and which cause difficulty. If it is found that a patient is able to accomplish one task but is impaired in performance of another task, then this pattern is taken to point towards that person having a selective deficit in one language processing operation and not in another. In addition, analysis of the types of errors made can provide evidence of the nature of a person's disorder. Insight into the particular pattern of disorder for that individual may help focus strategies for treatment or approaches to help the individual cope with or compensate for the impairment.

As well as providing insight for work with individual patients, the psycholinguistic approach can provide insights into the workings of the language system, in particular about which components of the system can be selectively impaired and, therefore, which components seem to operate as separate modules from one another. Instances are sought where performance on two language tasks is such that one patient performs relatively well on task 1 but poorly on task 2, whereas another patient performs relatively well on task 2 but poorly on task 1. This is known as the method of **double dissociation** (see Chapter 1) (Shallice, 1988). The search for such dissociations has been a major focus of activity of psycholinguistic/cognitive neuropsychological approach to the study of language disorder (Ellis and Young, 1996; see Parkin, 1996 for a discussion of this approach).

It should be clear from this account of the psycholinguistic approach that its orientation is towards dealing with each patient with language disorder as a single case who may show an individual pattern of language impairment, rather than as a representative of a particular syndrome. In fact, some cognitive neuropsychologists with a particular interest in language suggest that very little can be gained from conducting research based on group studies of patients with aphasia, since syndrome-based groups often show marked individual variation in symptoms. In a series of papers debating the issue, Caramazza has argued that psycholinguists should abandon the syndrome approach and only consider data from single-case studies (e.g. Caramazza, 1984; Caramazza and Badecker, 1991). Other psychologists have argued that single-case studies raise problems of generalisation and replication and that, with strict criteria for subject inclusion, group studies can still be valuable. The dynamic nature of this debate can be seen in Caramazza's title for one of his articles: 'Clinical syndromes are not God's gift to cognitive neuropsychology: A reply to a rebuttal to an answer to a response to the case against syndrome-based research' (Caramazza and Badecker, 1991). Group studies continue to be published in journals alongside reports of single-case studies.

The following sections will consider disruptions to three levels of language processing and the insights gained from the viewpoint of a psycholinguistic approach.

11.4 Disruptions to language processing at word level

Processing spoken words

Just as there are many different aspects of language processing at word level (see Sections 10.4 and 10.5), detailed psycholinguistic analysis shows that there are many different ways in which word level processing may break down. Deficits may occur in recognising spoken words or in speaking words. They may occur in reading words or in spelling words. They may occur in repeating a word-like string of sounds or they may occur in grasping the meaning of a spoken word or in finding the appropriate word to name an object. Various combinations of such deficits may occur and some deficits may be even more specific and apply to only one type of word.

Cognitive neuropsychological models have been developed which help provide a systematic way of conceptualising such diverse patterns of impairments. Based, to a large extent, on psycholinguistic research on recognising and producing single words (as reviewed in Chapter 10), models of the component processes involved in recognising, understanding, and repeating spoken words and in reading and spelling words, can help us understand in what ways processes can be impaired because of brain injury. Figures 11.2 and 11.3 present versions of these models based on those presented by Ellis and Young (1996).

In Figure 11.2 there are three routes between hearing a word and saying it. One route goes from the auditory analysis system, where the speech signal is converted into a phonemic code to the auditory input lexicon, where that code may be matched with one of the items in our store of how all the words we know sound, then through the semantic system, where its meaning may be identified, and then on through the speech output lexicon, to link up with the relevant item from our store of information about how to say all the words we know. From there it goes to the phonemic response buffer where the information about how to say the word is held until we are ready to say it. The second major route is directly from the auditory analysis system to the phonemic response buffer, allowing us to repeat words we have never heard before and nonsense words. A third route, from the auditory input lexicon to the phonemic output lexicon, has also been hypothesised.

This model can be used to investigate and explain the pattern of symptoms of patients. A person's ability to name pictures and objects may be tested under a number of conditions, for example with familiar words and less familiar words and with and without phonological cues from the first sound in the target word. The pattern of errors, phonological or semantic, is observed. An intriguing example is the case described by Atkinson *et al.* (2004) of 'Charles', a deaf man who used British Sign Language and who developed sign language aphasia following a stroke. He had a marked difficulty in retrieving signs and made a range of types of error, sometimes coming up with a sign that was similar in meaning to the target and sometimes one that was similar in the way the sign is formed. Just like many people with difficulties in retrieving spoken words, he had more difficulty with less familiar signs and was helped by cueing. The difficulty in retrieving signs could be demonstrated to be linguistically based, rooted in his

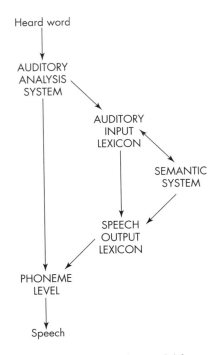

Figure 11.2 Diagrammatic representation of a model for recognising, understanding and repeating spoken words

Source: Ellis and Young (1996), reproduced with permission

sign language, since he could produce gestures quite well, even ones that were similar to signs that caused him difficulty.

The psycholinguistic model of Ellis and Young (1996) is the basis for an approach to assessment of people with aphasia known as Psycholinguistic Assessments of Language Processing in Aphasia (PALPA: Kay *et al.*, 1992), which involves a systematic testing of one aspect of language functioning as against another so that an evaluation can be made of where in the processing model the individual's deficits might lie.

An example of the way the model can be applied is in understanding a pattern of symptoms that has come to be known as **pure word deafness**. Patients who show this pattern of symptoms can talk and read fluently but are unable to repeat words they cannot understand and are unable to understand speech addressed to them. This disability occurs despite relatively normal hearing. Ellis and Young (1996) cite the case of a Scottish sheep farmer who said he could 'hear everything, even a leaf falling' but of listening to speech, 'It sounds far away. You think you can catch it and it fades away ... jumbled together like foreign folk speaking in the distance.' The specific problem appears to be in the ability to perceive speech-like sounds and thus appears to lie in phonemic processing in the auditory analysis system of the language processing model.

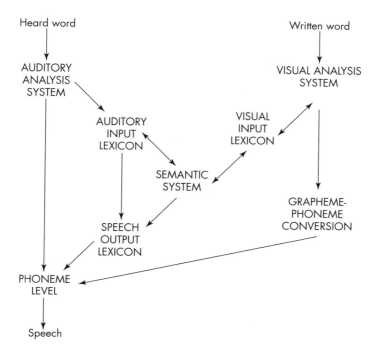

Figure 11.3 Diagrammatic representation of a model for recognising, understanding and naming written words in reading

Source: Ellis and Young (1996), reproduced with permission

Another pattern of symptoms related to word processing is known as **pure word meaning deafness**. The patient is unable to understand what words mean even though those words can be repeated and written accurately to dictation (Ellis, 1984; Schacter *et al.*, 1993). Franklin *et al.* (1994) describe an attempt to understand the word 'slow': 'Slow, slow, slow, I know what it is but I can't get it, slow, slow – you'll have to write it down for me . . . [after word is written] . . . Oh slow, well slow is the opposite of fast.' A person with pure word meaning deafness may be unimpaired on a lexical decision task (requiring discrimination between real words and non-words), suggesting that the representation of words in the auditory input lexicon is intact. Understanding of written material may be unimpaired, so that the semantic system may also be intact and the deficit may therefore lie in the connection between the auditory input lexicon and the semantic system. The case study provides an example of the psycholinguistic investigation of an individual's language processing in practice.

Other patients have been described who can read aloud and write well but on closer investigation have difficulties with repetition of non-words. Their pattern of symptoms has been called auditory phonological agnosia. Beauvois and Dérouesné (1981) report on a patient who could read and write but who had noticed difficulty with understanding place names and scientific terms which he had not encountered before. Subsequent testing revealed that words which he knew could be repeated correctly, indicating that the route via the auditory input lexicon was in order, but that non-words could not be repeated, suggesting that the direct route for repetition via the auditory analysis system and the phonemic response buffer was impaired. The problem was not simply in the pronunciation of non-words, since he was able to read them accurately.

A very common group of symptoms of patients with aphasia are difficulties in finding the right word, a problem known as **anomia**. Attempts have been made to explore whether these difficulties relate to those models of word production developed by psycholinguists involving at least two stages: lexical selection and phonological encoding (e.g. Dell, 1986; Levelt *et al.*, 1999); see Chapter 10). Wilshire and Saffran (2005) gave two patients with selective deficits in word production a task where they had to name a target picture after hearing an auditory prime. The prime was either begin-related to the target word (e.g. *ferry-feather*) or end-related (e.g. bro*ther*-fea*ther*). One of the patients benefited only from begin-related primes and one only from the end-related primes. This finding suggests that the two patients have deficits involving different stages of the word production process, in one the lexical selection stage and in the other the phonological encoding stage.

When responding to picture-naming tasks, aphasics often indicate that they don't know and make no response, known as omission errors. Dell *et al.* (2004) analysed the pattern of omission errors in 14 aphasics and suggested that models of lexical access need to include a lexical-threshold, a threshold that may not always be crossed on naming tasks, particularly by people with aphasic naming difficulties.

Sometimes brain injury affects the processing of certain types of words more so than others. Such cases, known as *category specific semantic deficits*, raise particularly intriguing questions about the representation of words and their meanings in the brain. For example, dissociations may be found between concrete and abstract words (Breedin *et al.*, 1994; Tyler *et al.*, 1995, Warrington, 1981). Dissociation between knowledge of living things compared with non-living was described by Warrington and Shallice (1984), where knowledge of living things is impaired, relative to non-living things. However, a few patients have also been found who have more difficulty with non-living things in comparison with relatively preserved knowledge of living things (e.g. Warrington and McCarthy, 1983; Damasio *et al.*, 2004). Sacchett and Humphreys (1992) called their paper on this subject, 'Calling a squirrel a squirrel but a canoe a wigwam'. In some cases the deficit may be even more specific, for example affecting the naming of fruit and vegetables (Hart *et al.*, 1985).

Findings from patients with category-specific semantic deficits have led to investigations of whether living and non-living concepts are represented in different brain regions or even in different hemispheres, with deficits for non-living things tending to be associated with damage to left hemisphere brain regions (Tranel *et al.*, 1997). Pilgrim *et al.* (2005) carried out an experimental study in which they presented words for living and non-living concepts at short durations to the right or left visual fields of healthy volunteers, and thus to left and right hemispheres respectively, and asked them to decide whether the word referred to a living or non-living concept. They found that responses were slower and more error prone for non-living things when presented to the right hemisphere than to the left but found no differences between the hemispheres for living concepts. Responses were slower to non-living than to living things in both the left hemisphere and the right but the difference was much more pronounced in the right. These findings supported the neuropsychological data.

Mirroring our everyday experiences of difficulty in coming up with the names of people whom we feel we should know, some patients with anomia seem to have marked difficulty in producing people's names and other proper nouns (Hittmair-Delazer *et al.*, 1994). If proper nouns and common nouns are represented differently, it should be possible to find the opposite pattern and, indeed, McKenna and Warrington (1980) were able to identify a patient with a selective preservation of geographic names while other investigators have described the relative preservation of proper nouns (Semenza and Sgarmella, 1993; McNeil *et al.*, 1994).

A rare, but very interesting, pattern of symptoms is that of **deep dysphasia**. In deep dysphasia the patient is unable to repeat non-words and is likely to make semantic errors when repeating real words, so that, for example, he or she might say 'yellow' for 'red' or 'kite' for 'balloon' (Morton, 1980). Abstract words are more difficult to repeat than concrete words. In terms of the model of single-word processing in Figure 11.2, Ellis and Young (1996) suggest that the most likely account of deep dysphasia is in terms of impaired access to semantics from the auditory input lexicon. Additionally, since non-words cannot be repeated, there is also impairment to both the route from the auditory analysis system to the phonemic response buffer and to the third route, the one going from the auditory input lexicon to the phonological output lexicon.

Processing words in reading and writing

Psycholinguistic investigations of disorders of reading and spelling have, to a large extent, been based on the sort of model of reading single words described in Chapter 10. A version of such a model, which was developed partly in the light of research on patients with reading and writing difficulties and which shows some of the ways in which reading can be disrupted, is shown in Figure 11.3.

Acquired dyslexia refers to the sudden loss of some aspect of reading ability due to a brain lesion and *acquired dysgraphia* refers to the sudden loss of the ability to spell words. Detailed psycholinguistic investigation of processes involved in reading and writing in such patients have revealed a number of different patterns of symptoms (Ellis and Young, 1996). The investigations centre around the patients' abilities to read and spell invented, but pronounceable, non-words, as compared with real words, and to read and spell words that are regular in their reading and spelling patterns, such as HINT or TOAD, or irregular, such as PINT or BROAD. Patients are also often tested on sets of words that vary in their frequency in the language, in their imageability and in whether they are content words (such as 'hound' or 'walk') or function words (such as 'and', 'that' or 'to').

Some patients can read many words correctly, provided those words are regular in their spelling, in the sense that they obey English grapheme-to-phoneme (or spelling-to-sound) correspondence rules. In addition, non-words can be read. However, words which are irregular and thus do not follow those rules (such as 'ache' and 'yacht') cause difficulty and a word like 'pint' may be pronounced as if it rhymed with 'hint'. This form of dyslexia, known as surface dyslexia, was first described by Marshall and Newcombe in 1973. Only when the patient has pronounced the word does he or she seem to know the word's meaning. This form of dyslexia seems to be associated with temporal lobe damage (Deloche *et al.*, 1982). The damage seems to in some way have interfered with the connections between the visual word forms and the semantic network so that the patient is not able to use the lexical-semantic route (sometimes known as the whole-word route) but has to work out the pronunciation of each word by using grapheme-to-phoneme correspondence rules.

Other patients are able to read real, familiar words but have difficulty with non-words (Shallice and Warrington, 1980; Ellis and Young, 1996). Patterson (1982) described a patient who in one testing session was able to read aloud 95 per cent of a list of content words including uncommon words such as 'decree' and 'phrase' but only 8 per cent of a list of non-words. He frequently read non-words as a visually similar real word, e.g. he read 'soof' as 'soot'. This pattern suggests that patients with this pattern of reading difficulty, known as phonological dyslexia, cannot apply grapheme–phoneme conversion procedures but have retained the ability to pronounce words that are known to them because the lexical-semantic route is spared.

Sometimes the difficulty with reading non-words is very marked and is associated with a number of other features. The most striking of these is the **semantic error**, where a word is read aloud as another word, not similar in the way it looks or sounds to the target word but similar in meaning. So, for example, 'cost' might be read as 'money', 'city' as 'town' and 'duel' as 'sword'. The presence of such errors alongside difficulty with non-words signals that the disorder may be a case of deep dyslexia (Marshall and Newcombe, 1973; Coltheart, 1980a). Other features commonly associated with deep dyslexia include a strong tendency for concrete imageable words to be easier to read than abstract words and for grammatical function words to be particularly problematic. As well as the occurrence of semantic errors, visual errors tend to occur, such as the misreading of 'signal' as 'single' and 'decree' as degree' and even what are known as 'visual-then-semantic' errors, where 'sympathy' may be read as 'orchestra', presumably because a visual error has led to it being interpreted as 'symphony' and then a semantic error has led to 'symphony' being read as 'orchestra'.

Deep dyslexia is associated with damage to the temporal lobe of the left hemisphere and one approach to explaining its pattern of features is to assume that there is impairment to the normal left hemisphere reading system. It has been argued (Morton and Patterson, 1987) that a number of components of the system become damaged in parallel. Not only has the grapheme-to-phoneme route been lost, as in phonological dyslexia, but there must also be some form of lexical deficit to explain why function words are so problematic and impairment to the semantic system to explain semantic errors, not to mention impairments affecting visual analysis to explain visual errors. It is not easy to explain why such a range of deficits should occur together, yet deep dyslexia is a consistently reoccurring pattern of symptoms.

A quite different approach to explaining the pattern of features of deep dyslexia was proposed by Coltheart (1980a; 1987) and by Saffran *et al.* (1987). It was argued that patients with deep dyslexia are reading with the right rather than the left hemisphere. According to this 'right hemisphere hypothesis', in deep dyslexia a lesion has disrupted visual access to the reading system in the left hemisphere but the right hemisphere is able to identify the word and assign semantics to it. This semantic information is then transferred to the intact left hemisphere speech output system which then allows the word to be spoken. The hypothesis explains the occurrence of semantic errors by arguing that the right hemisphere may generate a range of associates of the word and one of these other semantic representations may get transmitted to the left hemisphere. Abstract words and function words may be less well-represented in the right hemisphere, where meaning is hypothesised to be more image-based, and therefore these words would be read less well by that hemisphere. Similarly non-words, not having meaning, could not be accessed by this postulated system.

The idea that word identification and semantic access can occur in the right hemisphere is a far cry from the classic language circuit of the left hemisphere as presented by Geschwind (1965). However, there has been growing evidence that the right hemisphere can read, even if it cannot speak. In split-brain studies (Sperry and Gazzaniga, 1975), when a word was flashed to the right hemisphere, some patients could pick out from an array of objects the one that the word represented. In studies of people with intact brains using the split-field method, there is evidence that words can be recognised in the right hemisphere and that, when presented to the right hemisphere, words high in imagery are reported better than those lower in imagery, but this difference does not apply when the words are presented to the left hemisphere (e.g. Ellis and Shepherd, 1974). This finding, though controversial (Patterson and Besner, 1984), is in line with the notion that the right hemisphere can process concrete, imageable words but is relatively poor at processing other types of words. Studies of semantic priming with healthy participants have also provided evidence which may suggest differences in semantic processing between the right and left hemispheres (Beeman *et al.*, 1994). They concluded that words presented to the right hemisphere result in weaker levels of activation of semantic associates over a wider range than those presented to the left hemisphere.

Deep dyslexia provides an excellent demonstration of a number of aspects of the psycholinguistic approach: it has been recognised through a detailed analysis of the types of reading task that each patient can and cannot do and of the types of errors made. The pattern of symptoms has, however, been difficult to explain in a parsimonious way by the sorts of model based on a modular approach. The right hemisphere hypothesis may prove to be the most appropriate model or eventually a connectionist network account may be able to simulate the impact of a brain lesion that will result in the pattern of deficits characteristic of deep dyslexia and indeed the other dyslexias (Hinton and Shallice, 1991; Plaut and Shallice, 1993). More recently Colangelo *et al.* (2004) have rejected modularity and developed a different type of explanation for the impact of brain injury, citing deep dyslexia as an example. They hypothesise that human behaviour is a self-organising mechanism and that brain injury causes destabilisation of this mechanism, which can lead to a reduction of constraints that support naming and give rise to qualitative changes such as the production of semantic errors.

11.5 Disruption to processing of syntax

Impairments of syntactic aspects of language production have traditionally been associated with Broca's aphasia and the incidence of such impairments has been termed **agrammatism** by neuropsychologists. For many years people with Broca's aphasia were described as having difficulties with producing language but having the ability to understand what is said to them essentially intact. Clinical observations and performance on language tests often backed up this view. However, since the 1970s when psycholinguists began to use more sophisticated tests of language comprehension, the traditional view has had to be reassessed.

In 1976 Carramazza and Zurif published a paper in which language comprehension of patients with aphasia was examined. Patients heard sentences that were either non-reversible such as (1) or reversible such as (2) and had to choose a picture to match the sentence. (See Section 10.3 for discussion of reversible and non-reversible sentences.)

(1)   The bicycle that the boy is holding is broken.

(2)   The man whom the woman is hugging is happy.

In line with their known comprehension difficulties, patients with Wernicke's aphasia did poorly on both types of sentence. Patients with Broca's aphasia performed well on non-reversible sentences but their performance on reversible sentences fell to chance levels. These findings suggest that patients with Broca's aphasia make use of semantic cues when they are available, as they are in most everyday situations. When semantic cues are eliminated, as in the reversible sentences, patients with Broca's aphasia can be seen to have difficulties that suggest subtle deficits in parsing, the process of computing the syntactic structure of sentences (see Section 10.6). Backing up this proposal was the finding that even simple reversible sentences such as (3) were liable to be misinterpreted (Schwartz *et al.*, 1980).

(3)   The policeman shot the robber.

It appeared that Broca's aphasia might result in virtually complete loss of syntactic ability, with agrammatism characterising comprehension as well as production of language (Berndt and Caramazza, 1980). Such a view might imply that the language module that controls syntax is located in Broca's area and is put out of commission when damage occurs in that area.

However, subsequent research has complicated such a picture. One such complication arises from research carried out by Linebarger *et al.* (1983) who investigated the ability of patients with Broca's aphasia to make judgements about whether sentences were grammatical or not. On the whole the patients performed surprisingly well. Their performance was particularly good on sentences in which the structure was distorted as in (4).

(4)   How many did you see birds in the park?

They were not so good at judging sentences where an inappropriate pronoun had been used such as (5).

(5)   The little boy fell down, didn't it?

It may be that patients with Broca's aphasia have knowledge of syntax that they can employ in the making of grammaticality judgements when sufficient time is available to them, but may not be able to access this knowledge quickly enough in comprehension of ongoing speech.

Further complications arise from growing evidence that individual patients may show some of the symptoms of agrammatism without showing others, and so any search for a single underlying deficit may be fruitless. For example, while many patients have difficulty both with ordering words into sentences and with using function words and inflections, Saffran *et al.* (1980) described a patient who used function words and inflections but had great difficulty in arranging words into grammatical sentences. Kolk *et al.* (1985) reported on two patients whose speech production was severely agrammatic but whose comprehension was at, or near, normal levels. Miceli *et al.* (1983) described how some of Broca's patients could have comprehension of complex reversible sentences that was flawless. Even the tendency to omit function words and inflections does not apply across the board to all such elements, with some elements more likely to be omitted than others. For instance, detailed analysis of speech output indicates that the -s ending on nouns is much more likely to be omitted when it is a possessive -s than when it is a plural -s (Goodglass and Berko, 1960; Kean, 1977; Caplan, 1992).

The complex picture that has emerged from recent research has led to debate about whether the terms Broca's aphasia and agrammatism should be abandoned as, it is argued, they no longer describe a meaningful syndrome. As has been indicated, single-case studies have shown dissociations between the three main symptoms of agrammatism: sentence construction deficit, grammatical element loss and syntactic comprehension deficit (Saffran *et al.* 1980; Howard, 1985; Berndt, 1987). Other patients show a pattern of impairment similar to that of Broca's aphasia, even though their lesions are outside Broca's area (Caplan and Hildebrandt, 1988).

Caramazza and Badecker's arguments about the non-viability of the syndrome approach have particular relevance to the concept of agrammatism. He proposes that, if there is no one syndrome of agrammatism, the methodological implication is that it is no longer meaningful to carry out research that involves

335

groups of patientswith this clinical diagnosis (Badecker and Caramazza, 1985). In a review of what Ellis and Young (1996) call 'the saga of agrammatism', Howard (1985) argued that a fundamental mistake was made in taking a cluster of symptoms and creating the notion of a 'syndrome' of agrammatism, a process of reification by which patients are seen as exemplars of the syndrome rather than as individuals with qualitatively different patterns of impairment. Such arguments led to a debate among aphasiologists, many of whom believe that, even if single-case studies show dissociations among symptoms of a classic syndrome such as Broca's aphasia, it is still convenient to use the classic syndrome labels (Caplan, 1986, 1992) and that group studies should not be rejected entirely (Shallice, 1988).

In recent times there has been an added dimension to the debate about the nature and generalisability of the symptoms of Broca's aphasia. Grodzinsky (2000) argued that Broca's area is not responsible for most human language abilities but only for certain highly specific syntactic operations. According to an influential theory in linguistics called the Trace-Deletion Hypothesis, these operations are involved in the construction of higher parts of the syntactic tree in the understanding and production of certain types of sentences such as passive voice sentences. These sentences are thought to have a constituent, a phrase, which has moved from one position to another in the process of sentence generation. Grodzinsky's hypothesis is based on the claim that Broca's aphasics can understand sentences in the active voice, which according to the Trace-Deletion theory do not involve any movement of constituents in their generation, but perform at chance level on passive voice sentences. Carramazza and colleagues have taken issue with this hypothesis, particularly its assumption that all aphasics essentially perform in the same way in comprehension tasks, quoting the evidence outlined above that there have been many different patterns of comprehension performance seen in Broca's aphasic patients (Caramazza et al., 2001).

Carramazza et al. (2001) reanalysed the scores in the same dataset that Grodzinsky had employed (Grodinsky et al., 1999) but analysed them on an individual-by-individual statistical basis. They found statistical evidence that different patients showed different patterns of sentence comprehension performance. They concluded that, contrary to Grodzinsky's claim (Grodinsky, 2000), Broca's aphasia is not associated with one particular pattern of sentence comprehension performance. Their findings seem to undermine Grodzinsky's assertion that Broca's area is the 'neural home' to certain specific aspects of linguistic ability.

Research and theorising centred on the concept of agrammatism continues despite Badecker and Caramazza's (1985) and Howard's (1985) arguments that the concept has long outlived its usefulness.

11.6 Disruption to processing of pragmatics and discourse

Can we find patients whose brain injury leads them to have particular difficulty at the level of processing of pragmatics, the use of language in context? An aspect of pragmatics is the use of language in discourse, the level of language that is concerned with making inferences, going beyond literal meanings, drawing on knowledge of the listener and social conventions (see Section 10.7).

In fact, many patients with aphasia perform surprisingly well on tasks that involve aspects of pragmatics, including tasks that require comprehending and retaining aspects of discourse, relative to their problems at lexical and syntactic levels (Caplan, 1992). For example, Soroker *et al.* (2005) point out that aphasics often produce pragmatically appropriate responses to commands, questions and requests, though in their study people with brain damage were impaired relative to controls on language tests involving this ability. In another example of relative competence with aspects of language use, Armus *et al.* (1989) found evidence that knowledge of scripts can be preserved in patients with aphasia. Scripts are abstract descriptions of events, such as the knowledge that eating a meal in a restaurant involves ordering, being served with food, eating and paying the bill. Aphasic patients in their study performed as well as control participants in discriminating events that would occur in a script from those that would not be expected to occur and in ordering words to form sentences.

However, some patients have difficulties affecting the comprehension of discourse but do not have other significant language impairments and they are of particular interest from a neuropsychological point of view. These patients tend to have lesions in the right hemisphere (Joanette and Brownell, 1990). Although these patients may be able to tell coherent stories and to show knowledge of scripts, some subtle disturbances of discourse processes can be found. In a study by Heath and Blonder (2005), patients with right hemisphere damage and their spouses reported a significant decline in the patients' orientation to humour post-stroke and the investigators observed less spontaneous conversational humour than was the case for controls. One aspect of humour that appears to be affected is the ability to appreciate punchlines in jokes. In a study by Brownell *et al.* (1983), patients with right hemisphere lesions heard and read the start of a joke and then had to choose a humorous continuation for it from three possibilities: the real punchline, a non-sequitur and a non-humorous but coherent ending. One joke went as follows:

> The quack was selling a potion which he claimed would make men live to a great age. He claimed he himself was hale and hearty and over 300 years old.
>
> > 'Is he really as old as that?' asked a listener of the youthful assistant. 'I can't say,' said the assistant:
>
> *Correct punchline*: 'I've only worked with him for 100 years.'
>
> *Non-sequitur*: 'There are over 300 days in the year.'
>
> *Coherent non-humorous ending*: 'I don't know how old he is.'

Patients with right hemisphere lesions made more errors than controls and were more likely to choose non-sequitur endings, implying that they knew there should be an element of surprise in the ending but not how to make it coherent with the rest of the joke.

In a study by Hough (1990) two types of stories were read to patients with right hemisphere lesions and to a non-brain-injured control group and questions about the stories asked. In one set of stories the theme of the story was stated at the outset and in the other the statement of the theme was delayed until the end. Patients with right hemisphere lesions performed very much worse when the theme was not stated till the end, suggesting they had particular difficulty in integrating the information in the sentences into a coherent theme.

In their own conversation too, patients with right hemisphere lesions show evidence of impairments at discourse level. They tend to mention specific information without giving the setting or theme for what they are talking about (Myers, 1993). They do not appear sensitive to other speakers' mood or intonation cues and their own intonation is very flat, leading sometimes to a misdiagnosis of depression (Brownell *et al.*, 1995). They have difficulties in picking up on ambiguities, metaphor, irony and may interpret familiar idioms such as 'pull your socks up' literally (Winner and Gardner, 1977). Such a pattern of symptoms has come to be termed the 'right hemisphere syndrome'. It remains to be seen whether this so-called syndrome will turn out to be caused by a single underlying deficit or whether, as with agrammatism, detailed single-case studies will demonstrate dissociations between component processes.

Summary

- The way we view localisation of language functions has changed considerably from the earlier notion of the classic language circuit. Rather than classifying processes at the level of speech input and speech output, we now have considerably more sophisticated models of language processing which allow psycholinguists to investigate impairment of quite specific aspects of phonological, semantic, syntactic and discourse processes.
- Methods have also evolved, with increased focus on detailed analysis of single cases rather than group studies. Methods such as PET scans and fMRI scans are making a considerable impact on our understanding of language processing in both the intact brain and people with disorders of language.
- There is substantial evidence that the components of the classic language circuitry are important in language functioning. However, the picture is considerably more complex than early theorists believed.
- The cognitive neuropsychological approach has provided useful models of the components and processes of language functioning allowing systematic investigation of where in the system an individual's impairment in language functioning may lie.
- There is increasing indication from patterns of dissociation of language functions in people with brain injury that many components of the language processing system, though richly interconnected, are to some extent modular in their organisation.

Further reading

Behrmann, M. and Patterson, K. (2004). *Words and Things.* Hove: Psychology Press. This edited book contains interesting chapters on language processing by patients with language disorders.

Ellis, A.W. and Young, A.W. (1996). *Human Cognitive Neuropsychology.* Hove: Psychology Press. In this book the authors provide a careful rationale for a model of the processes involved in speaking, understanding, reading and writing words, a model that has been widely adopted in neuropsychological research and approaches to intervention.

Gardner, H. (1977). *The Shattered Mind.* Hove: Psychology Press. Although written some time ago, the sections on language in this book have not been equalled as a colourful and gripping introduction to patients with aphasia and the challenges they provide for an understanding of language function in the brain.

Martin, G.N. (2006). *Human Neuropsychology* (2nd edn). Englewood Cliffs, NJ: Prentice Hall. This textbook contains a good introduction to the neuropsychology of language.

Parkin, A. (2000). *Explorations in Cognitive Psychology.* Hove: Psychology Press. The sections on disorders of language provide a clear overview of the cognitive neuropsychological approach.

Chapter 12

Computational models of cognition

12.1 Theories of cognition: from metaphors to computational models

The computer allows the development and exploration of theories beyond the horizon of an individual's reason and intuition. Formal, computational, models have been used in cognitive psychology in many different ways, for many different purposes. Rather than present a disconnected list of techniques and examples, this chapter emphasises the fundamental principles which should give the student some familiarity with the different major classes of model.

What constitutes a theory of cognition? What does it mean to build a model of a cognitive process? We will use the term 'theory' in a fairly liberal way; any body of concepts, ideas or hypothetical structures which enable us to understand, explain or predict some of the experimental data relating to an aspect of cognition will be deemed to be a theory.

Why do we need theories of cognition? A collection of experimental data does not, of itself, constitute a science of cognition. Science proceeds by developing theories that explain a body of data and make predictions for the outcome of new experiments. If the theory doesn't match the data then we either have to modify the theory or abandon it for one that does. The most interesting experiments are those which provide data that either can't be explained by existing theories or which distinguish between two competing theories.

Theories come in all sizes and levels of detail. Take, for example, the 'zoom-lens' theory of visual attention proposed by Eriksen (1990). This claims that visual attention is restricted to a disc-like area much like that in the field of a camera lens. However, as in the case of a zoom-lens, the area of attention may be altered to encompass more or less of the visual field. The theory then predicts that when a target (for example, in a letter recognition task) is placed within the attentional area, it will be recognised more rapidly than one which is placed outside this area. Although there is evidence both for and against this outcome, the point to emphasise here is that it is a perfectly good theory in that it posits a model of visual attention which has testable predictions. Note, however, that it is just a theory of one aspect of visual attention, and only really describes *how* visual attention operates, not *why* it works like that. It is really an analogy, which does not make any quantative predictions (e.g. *how much* more rapidly are objects perceived within the attentional 'zoom-lens'?).

Another type of theory goes one step further and describes the mechanisms which are supposed to be responsible for the thing to be explained. Consider the multiple store models of memory (e.g. Atkinson and Shiffrin, 1968) of which a typical example is shown in Figure 12.1 (see also Chapter 6). Three mechanisms are postulated together with their interrelationships. The arrows are supposed to indicate the flow of information and this example is typical of models which conform to this view of cognition as the result of information processing.

It is often the case that the terms 'theory' and 'model' are used interchangeably. After all, models are kinds of theories, and theories often imply a model. However, for the purposes of this chapter let us be a little more careful. The word 'model' will be used to refer to a computational model – in other words

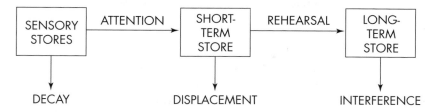

Figure 12.1 Typical multistore model of memory

a formally defined structure or system which embodies a theory about how some-thing behaves (which is typically implemented on a computer). Because a computational model is formally defined it is possible to say exactly what it predicts, and what it doesn't predict.

The multistore 'model' of memory isn't actually a model under this defini-tion because it doesn't precisely state what information is processed and stored, and how it is processed and stored. There is insufficient detail specified to allow us to build this model as a computer program. This doesn't mean it can't be useful for understanding data, just that all the predictions will be qualitative, addressing the nature of trends and ordering within data. For example, this model implies that more rehearsal will assist the laying down of long-term memories but we can say nothing about any mathematical laws relating the degree of rehearsal to memory.

To make this a computational model we would need to articulate and make precise aspects of the theory which were previously unspecified. For example, how exactly would a visual scene be encoded as input and how would the infor-mation at each stage be represented in the model? Possible representations may make use of numbers, symbols or a mix of both; in any case we have to flesh out the details of how this is to be done. As we will see, the theme of representation is one which is central to the whole enterprise of model construction. Having instantiated a model as a computer program we can now simulate the process of storing memories and derive quantitative predictions which are testable in the laboratory and may be compared directly with the data. This process is not, however, risk-free; we must be sure that we understand which low-level details are part of the cognitive model and which are by-products of having to implement it in a particular computer language.

Building computational models of our theories allows us to make precise predictions. When theories are complex, as when multiple interacting processes are involved, models allow us to explore the implications of those theories – some-thing a single individual's intuition or reason may not be sufficient for. Often, building a model gives insight into the general nature of the problem, not just into the specific theory being modelled. Computational models also bring the benefit that their behaviour is always consistent with the theory on which they are based and logical at each step of the process involved. With complex theories we cannot be sure that our beliefs about what a theory predicts are logical and consistent in the same way. A final benefit is that a sufficiently detailed model allows you to actually build a machine that does the cognitive task being modelled. What better way to show that your theory works than to use it to make a machine that does the task you have a theory about?

Computational modelling also has disadvantages and dangers. It is important to avoid the temptation to judge a model solely according to how well it fits the data (Pitt and Myung, 2002). A complex model may be able to fit any conceivable data, not just the true data, so it is not a good indication of worth if it does fit the experimental data. What results the model cannot predict and which results the model predicts cannot occur are equally important for judging the value of a model (Roberts and Pashler, 2000). In other words, it is not just what the model does that we are interested in, but how it does it. A working model provides an existence proof that a task *can* be done in a certain way; more careful testing is required, however, to demonstrate that the task *is* done in that way by the human mind.

The relationship between the model and the theory it is supposed to be testing can be unclear. It is possible to build a complex model which performs some task but which is a 'black box' telling you nothing about which psychological theories are correct (McClosky, 1991). That said, there is no reason why a complex model cannot be investigated after it has been built, and its relationship to theory understood. In fact, most of the work in modelling is not in the actual building of the model, but in investigating how and why it works after it has been built.

In summary, theories of cognition come in several flavours ranging from high-level metaphors and analogies, to full simulation models in which low-level details are articulated and which generate quantitative prediction. The transition from metaphor to simulation is a process of refinement. Thus, we might imagine endowing the zoom-lens model with systemic mechanism and, subsequently, implementing this in a full simulation. A single metaphor could lead to many different computational models. Once built, the value of a model needs to be investigated – it is not enough to simply look and see if it does the task it was supposed to do.

Paradigms and frameworks

Psychology has always borrowed metaphors from technology to understand the mind. Plato thought of the mind as a chariot pulled by two horses, Reason and Emotion (which didn't always pull the same way!). Descartes thought that it was like a complex hydraulic system, controlled via the passage of fluid in the supposed 'nerve tubes'. Since then, as new technologies have emerged, the brain has been likened to a telephone exchange, or memory likened to a hologram. Inspired by the advent of the digital computer, cognitive psychology marks the ascent of the 'information processing' metaphor of mind, which is still common currency today.

The term **paradigm** was introduced by Kuhn (1970) to denote the overarching framework within which a branch of science operates. It does not necessarily refer to a specific theory in isolation (although one or more of these

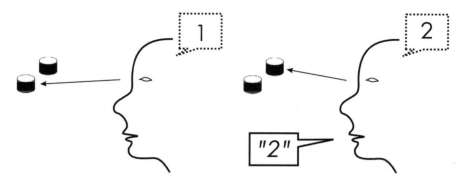

Figure 12.2 Possible inputs (two cylinders), outputs (the spoken number, shown in solid speech box) and representations (in dotted thought boxes) during counting

may be crucial) but rather the set of general assumptions, ideas, and the accepted techniques and problems that mark out that arena of investigation. A characteristic hallmark of all information processing theories, and therefore of the information processing paradigm, is that they make use of internal **representations** of the outside world upon which manipulations are carried out that allow the cognitive system to draw conclusions about its environment. For example, suppose we are given two collections of objects and are asked how many objects there are altogether. One way would be simply to count serially through both sets and announce the answer. Another way would be to count the items in each set and then add them together. In this method, we internalise (encode) the numbers in each set, representing them in some way 'in our heads', and then perform a manipulation (the process of addition) on these representations. Finally we decode the result by transforming the internal representation of the answer to a speech utterance or written token. These concepts are illustrated in Figure 12.2.

Information processing is the underlying metaphor of much of cognitive psychology, so it is entirely natural that cognitive theories should be tested by building computational models. The style of information processing that is assumed to underlie cognition defines various subdisciplines, or frameworks for computational model of cognition. One approach assumes that information processing is the manipulation of symbols according to a set of rules embodied in a program running on a conventional digital computer. This is the symbolic approach of classical cognitivism or simply **cognitivism** (Clark, 1990). In contrast there is the processing done on signals (or other continuous numerical values) that is done by **neural networks** or **connectionist systems**. These are interconnected systems of simple units which are supposed to represent more closely the circuits of neurons found in the brain. The extent to which this is the case will warrant further discussion later. It is also possible to construct hybrids which make use of both symbolic and connectionist techniques.

Artificial Intelligence is a related discipline, which involves attempting to build intelligent machines, but not necessarily machines that are intelligent in the same way that humans are. It used to be the case that most work in artificial intelligence was based on symbol-manipulating approaches – '**Classical AI**' – but now a variety of approaches flourish (see, e.g., Franklin, 1995 for an introduction). Refining connectionist models with details of the anatomical circuits in the brain has produced the field of **computational cognitive neuroscience**. O'Reilly and Munakata (2000) is a good introductory text on this.

All these variants share the assumption that cognition is information processing. Some in the field of **situated robotics**, or behaviour-based robotics (Brooks, 1991; Hallam and Malcolm, 1994), challenge this view. It is possible to build small autonomous machines which by interacting directly with an environment display simple, 'intelligent', ecologically relevant, behaviours such as wall avoidance, coping with movement on rough terrain, and seeking out the source of simple stimuli. The assumption here is that true intelligence is an emergent property of the intimate relation between the agent and environment rather than something intrinsic to the agent itself – the dynamical systems view of cognition (Clark, 1997, 1999). In pursuing this line the workers in this field have abandoned any attempt to build a representational model of the world and rely on direct processing of the environmental stimuli. Although, this framework circumvents many of the problems that are encountered in the process of building complex representations, it appears to echo some of the claims of the behaviourists in their emphasis on the study of stimulus-response associations at the expense of mental states. As in the case of behaviourism, it is not clear how this approach will scale up to capture the full richness and diversity of human cognition. Nevertheless, the agent–environment interaction stressed by the workers in situated robotics may prove to be a key aspect in understanding the nature of intelligence.

Whatever theoretical stance we take, there is another question that is worthy of our attention here. Is it possible to build a general theory of cognition in which a uniform model architecture and set of operational principles can account for all cognitive processes? The alternative is that, within a given paradigm, we may have to construct several discrete models whose structures differ and which make use of different representations. This point is taken up by Newell (1990) who argues for unified models, two examples of which (Soar and ACT* – pronounced ACT-star) are discussed later. The alternative, that mind is a collection of specialised processors, or 'modules', is the view held by the so-called 'Evolutionary Psychologists' (such as Steven Pinker, 1997).

Studying cognition as computation

In his book *Vision* David Marr (1982) formalised a hierarchical scheme for categorising which questions can and should be asked of a perceptual or cognitive process. The first-level question is: *What* is the goal of the computation? *Why* is it being carried out, what assumptions can be made, what information is provided and what information needs to be produced by the process? At the next level we ask *how* the computation is to be performed. This is the specification of an algorithm or procedure which will do the computation, and usually entails invoking the kind of representation to be used. Finally we want to know what hardware will implement the computation. For artificial intelligence this question of implementation requires recourse to engineering, for cognitive psychology it will involve physiology and neuroscience.

Marr illustrated his scheme using an example of computing the bill in a supermarket with a cash register. In answer to the top-level question of *what* is being computed here, it is the arithmetical operation of addition. As to *why* this is being done, it is simply that the laws of addition reflect the way we should accumulate prices from piles of goods in a trolley; it is incorrect, for example, to multiply the prices together. Next we wish to know how we do this arithmetic and the answer is that it is done by the normal procedure taught at school where we add individual digits in columns and carry to the next column if required. Note that the question of representation rears its head here and we assume one in which numbers are denoted using the Arabic numerals $(0, 1, 2 \ldots 8, 9)$.[1] As for the implementation, this occurs using logic gates made out of silicon, silicon-oxide and metal. Alternative implementations might make use of an older mechanical machine (e.g. an abacus?) or pencil and paper. Notice that, as presented, the three levels are independent. In particular the type of algorithm used is quite independent of the particular implementation and, for any given computation, we may choose from a variety of algorithms to achieve the same final result.

The picture outlined by Marr with clearly defined boundaries between levels of the hierarchy is not always satisfied in practice. However, it is often useful to keep the scheme in mind when tackling a problem in cognitive science and to step back to look at the wood (computational level) rather than the trees (algorithm/ implementation) that threaten to obscure the fundamental principles at work. Much modelling work rests on the assumption that you can discover something important about the algorithms of cognition without necessarily mimicking all the implementational details of the biological machinery (Dror and Gallogly, 1999). The opinion of exactly how much implementational detail you do need to include often defines the difference between various frameworks.

A major division between schools of thought is between those approaches which involve manipulation of symbols and those which involve the manipulation of signals (principally connectionism). We will proceed by outlining both approaches followed by a 'compare and contrast' exercise, at the end of which it should be apparent that some synthesis is possible and both have a role to play.

12.2 Symbol-based systems

In this paradigm we attempt to capture knowledge as a set of irreducible objects which have a transparent and unchanging meaning – symbols – and to model cognition as a series of processes that manipulate these symbols according to a set of well-defined rules which may be broken combined into a set of 'recipes' or **algorithms**. The symbols stand for, or represent, things, ideas or concepts with which the cognitive process is supposed to be dealing. The mapping between symbols and things in the world then defines a representation of the problem. Note the similarity here to systems of formal logic (including computer languages). The formal articulation of the symbolic paradigm has been made most vigorously by Newell and Simon (1976). They believe that symbol-based systems are necessary and sufficient for the instantiation of intelligence and, assuming the symbols are brought into existence in a computer implementation, this stance becomes their so-called **physical symbol hypothesis**.

An example: playing chess

A simple game-playing example will serve to illustrate the main characteristics of the symbolic approach. Games like chess were one of the early targets of researches in AI, with the ability to play chess seeming at the time to reflect the true and highest incarnation of human intelligence. Years later chess-playing computers can defeat any human, but we're still having trouble getting machines to walk on two feet like humans, which goes to show that true intelligence is not always where you think it is.

The details of the example here have been chosen for pedagogical reasons rather than for any relation to genuine chess programs. The first ingredient is a method of describing the state of the board at any time. This might easily be represented by assigning symbolic tokens to the pieces and using a grid system for the squares in which board columns are labelled (symbolised) by letters (a–h) and board rows by numbers (1–8). It then makes sense to say, for example, that 'white_pawn(2) is on square(d3)'. Any position or state of the game is then represented by a suitably ordered array of piece and grid symbols. Notice that the symbolic token for 'white_pawn(2)' does not contain within it any know-ledge of white pawns in relation to the game (such as legal moves and intrinsic value, etc.). Rather, the symbolic token is simply a marker which designates (or points to) the fact that this knowledge is pertinent and may then be accessed when needed. This illustrates the power of the symbolic approach which stems from the way in which symbols 'stand for' something else and their meaning is implicit in their interrelationships. Thus, the fact that white_pawn(2) is on square (d3) is encoded by some data structure in which both symbols are participants.

Next the system must have knowledge of what constitutes a valid move. This might consist of a series of rules of the form: 'IF there is a white pawn at square(d2) AND square(d3) is empty THEN the pawn can move to square(d3).' Of course, higher-level abstractions of rules like this (which don't require specific square labels, etc.) will almost certainly be used. The use of legal moves should then guarantee that only legal board positions are obtained. Rules of the form: 'IF C_1 AND C_2 AND . . . THEN R' are known as **production rules** or simply produc-tions since they produce a result R if the conditions C_1, C_2, . . . prevail. They are one form of knowledge representation in symbolic systems – others will be described later.

So far we have laid the foundations, but how is the program to 'know' how to play chess? This is done by formalising the idea of the game as a sequence of board positions – *states* – and that play consists of a series of moves – *state tran-sitions* – each of which generates a new position. Thus, the game starts in an initial state and the goal is to arrive at some final state in which the machine's pieces have achieved check-mate. In between we need some controlling strategy which tells the system how to find goal states. This will take the form of a search through the set of board states (the *state-space*) for a path from the initial to a final, winning state. In fact, of course, this is not a realistic strategy as it stands since to each machine move there are a great many opponent moves, in reply to which there are an even greater number of machine responses, etc. We therefore have a so-called *combinatorial explosion* of possibilities and we need to be more cunning in our search strategy. To this end, we might allow the machine to look a fixed number of moves ahead, evaluate the board positions there and play to ensure that the new position is more advantageous to it than the one where it started. This will necessitate assigning a value to board states which measures the 'goodness' or utility of the position. For example, moves which result in loss of pieces will (usually) score poorly. The search may be guided by more rules or heuristics which embody further knowledge of the game, e.g. 'IF your Queen is placed under attack THEN score poorly' or 'IF material loss is incurred THEN this should be done only if mate can be guaranteed in 2 moves.'

To summarise the main ingredients in our approach: symbolic descriptions are all-pervasive in helping to internalise the game of chess and its rules. The game is conceived of as a search through a state-space of board positions (starting with the conventional opening state) for final states that correspond to check-mate. In the case of chess this space is very large and the search must proceed piecemeal by using a utility function for each legal board state. Knowledge about the game is represented as a series of production rules; this includes knowledge to ensure legal moves, together with heuristics that aid the search. Symbols, production rules, searching in state-space, and heuristics are all characteristic features of symbolic systems. Knowledge representations other than production rules are used but these will nevertheless be subject to manipulation by procedures or algorithms that are implemented in some high-level computer language.

Symbols and computers

The rise of the symbolic modelling approach was driven to a large extent by work in AI which, in turn, had many of its ideas channelled by the nature of general purpose computers. There is an intimate relationship between the two.

The computers we use today work in the same fundamental way as those of fifty years ago (albeit much, much, faster). They utilise something called a 'Von Neumann architecture', named after one of the early pioneers of machine computation. This involves a Central Processing Unit (CPU) and a memory. The memory contains instructions and data, while the CPU is capable of performing very simple operations on the data according to a stored program, which is also contained in the memory. The following cycle of events is endlessly repeated:

1   fetch an instruction from memory
2   fetch any data required by the instruction from memory
3   execute the instruction (process the data)
4   store results in memory
5   go back to step 1.

The first computers were designed to perform numerical calculations, but it was immediately apparent to those who worked on them that the machines they had built could also be thought of as manipulating symbols. The numbers which the computer dealt with could be taken to represent objects and the calculations could be the implementation of rules. This ability of a machine to do calculation, and therefore, logic is what first inspired the idea of artificial intelligence, so it is not surprising that many of the first models of intelligence were based on a process of formal, algorithmic symbol manipulation.

Knowledge representation

We have seen (in the chess example) how knowledge may be represented in a symbolic system as a set of production rules. This method will be fleshed out a little further later but, in the meantime, we look at alternative ways of knowledge representation. The problem of representation is crucial to any cognitive model and its description must occur prior to elucidating any associated processing or dynamics.

Semantic nets

Semantic networks are a class of systems for representing knowledge that have been used for models of memory, concept storage and sentence understanding. They consist of a set of nodes, which represent objects or concepts, and links between nodes that indicate inter-node relationships. For example, the network shown in Figure 12.3 represents knowledge about a small subset of the bird family considered as sub-class of all animals. Thus, a canary is a bird because it is connected to the *bird* node via a link labelled with the relation 'is-a'; the bird named *Canny* is an instance of the class of canaries because it is connected to the *canary* node via a link indicating this. It is apparent that the example network represents a hierarchy of ever more specific objects, from animals in general through birds and species to particular instances of birds. This is not necessarily the case but, where it applies, the implication is that knowledge about a general class is held at the node representing it and is not repeated at nodes which are more specific (but for which the knowledge applies). This property is known as inheritance and holds, say, for the *canary* node which inherits all the information supplied about birds (because it 'is-a' bird). Thus we infer that a canary's main locomotion is flying and that it is an animal. On the other hand, knowledge which is specific to a node overrides any contradictory inheritance so that, while an *ostrich* is a bird and, by inheritance, has flying as its main locomotion, it also has the node-specific main-locomotion link to *running* which therefore prevails.

The example above is similar to that of Collins and Quillian (1969) which attempted to model the way categories were stored and accessed in human memory. Accessing knowledge in the network is done by starting at the node we wish to enquire about and moving along links (applying inheritance) until we reach a node that supplies the required information. Thus, according to the model,

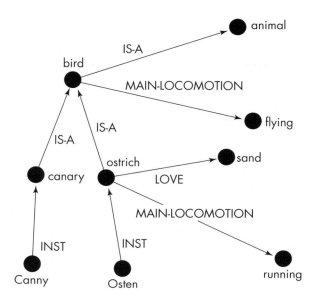

Figure 12.3 Semantic network

if someone is asked if the bird named 'Canny' can fly, they should take longer to answer than if they are asked if canaries (in general) can fly since the former question requires traversing two links in the net whereas the latter only uses one. A similar argument would be made about asking if Canny is a bird. Collins and Quillian conducted experimental work based on this type of query and found their predictions were, indeed, borne out by their data.

A slightly different type of network was used by Collins and Loftus (1975) to model similarity relations in memory. These nets had no special relationships along their links but worked by spreading activity from the initial nodes and noting if the activity traces intersected at any time, thereby signifying a relationship. For example, in order to answer the previous query 'Can Canny fly', the nodes for flying and Canny would be initialised and activity spread outwards along all links emanating from them. The resulting paths or traces of activity would intersect at the *canary* and *bird* nodes, signifying a semantic link between the two nodes and indicating an affirmative response to the question.

Schemata, frames and scripts

Semantic nets with their item-attribute structure provide a limited framework for knowledge representation. This is particularly evident in respect of much of our so-called common sense knowledge, each part of which consists of a complex mesh of ideas, objects, concepts and attributes which does not easily avail itself of a simple graphical (network) description with strict hierarchical inheritance.

Two features of this type of knowledge supply clues as to how we might go about representing it. First, it often refers to a stereotypical situation or **schema** (plural *schemata*) in which the constituent elements may change but their relations are constant and, second, there is the possibility of hierarchical *chunking* where a new schema may have elements consisting of entire schemata in themselves. As an example, consider the schema implied by a trip to eat out at a restaurant. Thus, a group of friends drive to a restaurant and wait to be seated. They are given menus, give orders for drinks and each person chooses from the menu. The meal arrives, people eat, order sweets and coffee and pay the bill. Note that there are many variations on this theme which are provided by changing the values of variables in a number of *slots*. Thus, instead of a group of friends, we might have a family group; instead of driving to the restaurant they may take a taxi or use public transport; instead of waiting to be seated they may go straight to a table or have a drink at the bar first, etc. In spite of these variations the temporal sequence of events remains the same as does the relation between the slots. In this way schemata encode generic knowledge that may be applied to many situations. Further, each slot may consist of its own schema. For example, taking a taxi (to get to the restaurant) may be broken down into: wait at kerb, hail taxi, give directions, pay driver. Finally, in the absence of information to the contrary we assume that each slot is filled with some default value (if you see a group of people in a restaurant you assume they are friends; if you don't know how they got there you assume they drove, etc.).

There have been several similar theories that have refined the schemata representation in its form outlined above. Schank and Abelson (1977) coined the term script for their version of schema used to account for knowledge of everyday situations (indeed their famous restaurant script is the inspiration for the above example). Rumelhart (1975) introduced story grammars to help explain the comprehension of stories and Minsky (1975) invoked structure called frames for visual perception.

Production systems

These embody the archetypal representation technique for symbolic systems introduced earlier. Recall that they consist of a set of conditional rules of the form 'IF C_1 AND C_2 AND ... THEN R' where the C_i are conditions to be met and R the result or consequence implied by these conditions. Psychologically we are supposed to think of a collection of items (the conditions C_i) existing in a working memory. Each production rule is supposed to be constantly looking out for a match between its preconditions and items in working memory and, if a match is obtained, the rule 'fires' and the result of the production is transferred into working memory. This new item may then be able to complete the precondition set for another production which is now allowed to fire and send its result into working memory. This iterative process is supposed to continue until no further production firings occur. This view of a production system makes it look like a pattern-matching, content-addressable memory whose operation is shown in Figure 12.4. Allen Newell was the main champion of this view of production

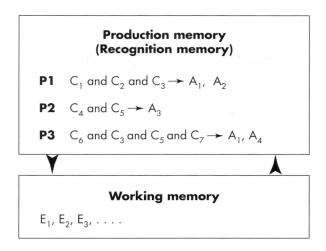

Figure 12.4 Production system as content addressable memory

systems as models of human knowledge. The view finds its fullest articulation in the system known as *Soar* (Laird *et al.*, 1984; Newell, 1990). This uses a working memory of the type outlined above with the productions constituting the long-term memory store. As with the chess example discussed previously, solutions to problems take place in a state- or search-space, and goals (final states) are achieved by moving from state to state under a series of state transition-inducing operators. Soar is, however, a large system and this simple scheme is supplemented by several additional features. The result is that Soar is supposed to be a unified theory of cognition. That is, it is to be thought of as a generic architecture (and accompanying computational processes) into which specific tasks can be mapped. As Newell (1990) notes, this allows for the possibility that existing cognitive theories may be taken and reframed in the language of Soar. In this way it should be possible to build on existing knowledge while embedding it within a common framework. Soar has successfully been applied to toy puzzles such as tic-tac-toe, Tower of Hanoi, etc., to problems in reasoning such as the Wason verification task, and to the implementation of large-scale expert systems, one of which (NEOMYCIN) is able to assist in the diagnosis of infectious diseases. For the most up-to-date review of its accomplishments readers should visit the official Soar webpage (http://sitemaker.umich.edu/soar).

Shortcomings of the symbolic approach

Mainstream AI, which is not necessarily psychologically motivated, has proved successful in many areas and indeed, with the advent of expert systems that can aid medical diagnosis or oil exploration, it has become big business. For a history of the field see McCorduck (2004). However, AI has not fulfilled much of the early promise that was conjectured by the pioneers in the field. Dreyfus, in his book *What Computers Can't Do* (Dreyfus, 1972, 1979) criticises the early extravagant claims of the AI practitioners and outlines the assumptions they made. Principal among these is the belief that all knowledge or information can be formalised, and that the mind can be viewed as a device that operates on information according to formal rules.

In game-playing, puzzle-solving, mathematics, etc., it is often clear how to formulate much of the knowledge representation, although the higher-level heuristics may be less apparent. In less artificial domains even the 'ground rules' (as it were) may be less apparent, as illustrated in the following example given by Minsky concerning the representation of the concept 'bird':

> Let's take a very simple fact like all birds can fly. Well that's true in a certain dictionary context but it's not true of all birds, so if you try to put this information in a rule based system you'd have a little trouble. First you'd have to say if Tweetie is a bird it can fly unless it is an ostrich or unless it's a penguin so now you're starting to get exceptions. Then somebody might say 'What if you clipped its feathers?' and you'd say 'If something is a bird and it has normal feathers and it is not an ostrich or a penguin then it can fly'. Then someone might say 'Well what if it's dead?' so you'd reply 'If it's . . . and it's not dead then it can fly.' Someone else might say 'What if it's in a cage?', 'What if it got its feet stuck in concrete?'. You can quickly see that it's almost impossible to think of any fact about the real world that is always true regardless of exceptions and context.

This example characterises the kind of difficulty we typically get into using the symbol-based approach. It may be summarised in the notion that the rules appear 'brittle' and are easily broken. Thus, it has proven very difficult to formalise large areas of human perceptual and non-intellectual cognitive ability. These are principally the kind of things that most of us take for granted and they consist of natural language understanding, fine motor control (e.g. in sport and music), visual navigation and scene understanding, and some of the intuitive knowledge of experts in narrow domains that are non-technical in nature. Connectionist systems promise to offer an alternative that may be more suited to modelling these areas of human competence.

12.3 Connectionist systems

It is not the intention here to give a detailed description of the training and operation of connectionist systems (also known as 'artificial neural networks'). Several introductory accounts are readily available (Gurney, 1997; Ellis and Humphreys, 1999). Rather, the intention here is to sketch some basic principles, focus on the nature of knowledge representation and to give a flavour of the type of models that have been constructed to account for human cognition.

A connectionist system or neural network is an interconnected assembly of simple processing elements, units or **nodes**, whose functionality is loosely based on the animal neuron. The processing ability of the network is stored in the inter-unit connection strengths, or **weights**, usually obtained by a process of learning from a set of training patterns. The latter represent input from the external world and may range from, for example, digitised pictures, as in a visual recognition task, to phonological representations of speech for natural language understanding. We may put some flesh on the bones of this definition by examining some of the key components of biological networks and comparing this with their artificial counterparts.

Real and artificial neurons

Real neurons communicate by voltage spikes known as action potentials. It is believed that the most important information is communicated via the frequency of spike production. In artificial nets, this is approximated by using signals which are a single continuous value which in turn represents the total amount of activity. Each real neuron combines the effect of incoming signals from other neurons by first passing each one of them through a synaptic contact. Synapses may be excitatory or inhibitory and have differing modulatory strengths. Thus a strong excitatory synapse may make a significant contribution to the elicitation of action potentials in the neuron while weaker ones have little effect. Similarly, inhibitory synapses tend to prevent firing to an extent commensurate with their strength. The rate of firing of a real neuron depends therefore on the summed value of all its synapse-modulated inputs. This story is, of course, extremely simplified (so much so that some neuroscientists still balk at the appellation 'neural' in the context of connectionism). However, this simple version of events is a good starting point.

Connectionist networks model the synapse as a single number that acts to multiply the incoming signal before sending the result to be summed with others. Thus a connectionist node performs a linear weighted sum of its inputs with positive and negative weights corresponding to excitatory and inhibitory synapses respectively. This total input is then often converted, by 'squashing', into an output (typically this squashing involves putting all possible input values somewhere in the range 0 to 1). A typical artificial neuron or connectionist node is shown in Figure 12.5. We now move from individual nodes to consider networks as a whole.

Feed-forward networks

One type of arrangement of nodes in a network is shown in Figure 12.6. Here, information is presented from an external source at the bottom of the diagram and each node in the net evaluates its output. Conceptually, each node is supposed to be working independently of all the others in the net. That is, if we conceive of each node as a separate processor, it works continuously and in parallel with all the others. This means that the evaluation of the first layer of output begins to take form immediately some input is presented, and is complete in the time it

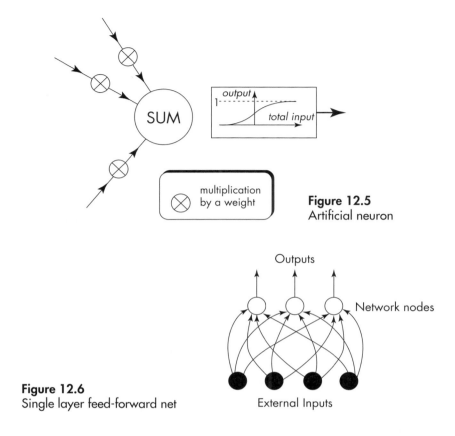

Figure 12.5
Artificial neuron

Figure 12.6
Single layer feed-forward net

takes for one model neuron to adjust to that input (because, by the time one model neuron has adjusted, so will all the others). Of course, when a network is run in simulation on a conventional computer, this parallelism is lost but it should still be regarded as inherent in the connectionist architecture.

The task that the net is supposed to perform is encapsulated in a set of training examples. Each example consists of a pattern of inputs and a corresponding pattern of target outputs. In order for the net to implement the task, it must produce an output that is a close approximation, in each instance, to the target. To bring this situation about, the weights in the net must be adjusted to force each node to respond in the correct way across all exemplars. Thus, the net learns, or is trained, by a process of adaptation to the set of training patterns.

The use of target outputs means that the net undergoes **supervised learning** since the targets are thought of in the context of a supervisory teacher supplying the desired network response to each input pattern. The general method in this case is to iteratively repeat the following sequence of steps: apply a training input pattern; find the net's output response; compare this with the target pattern; make small weight adjustments according to some **learning rule**. In contrast to this, it is possible to let the network discover regularities (clusters) in the training set for itself in which case it is said to undergo a process of **self-organisation**. We shall not be concerned a great deal with this type of learning here but there is a sense in which it is more biologically plausible.

There are many supervised learning rules but they all work by making weight changes that depend on the size of the difference or error between the network output and the corresponding target.

What happens when a network like that in Figure 12.6 is presented with a pattern that it has not seen during training? The network must give some kind of output, and ideally it will be one that is sensible in the context of the task to be learned. One way in which this happens automatically occurs because a single artificial neuron will respond in a similar way to input patterns that are close to each other. What constitutes 'close' here is illustrated in Figure 12.7 with an example taken from the domain of visual pattern recognition. Three versions of a letter X are supposed to be displayed on a grid of small black and white squares or pixels – it is this grid that provides the inputs to the network. Suppose the X on the left-hand side is the one presented during training and that some node in the network has developed large positive weights on those inputs from the dark pixels in this pattern and negative weights to the rest. The result is that when this pattern is given as the input to the network, the total input to the node will be large and positive and, given a suitable output function, it will produce an output close to its maximum value (usually 1). In effect the network is signaling that it has recognised the X pattern from training. Consider now the X in the centre of the figure. Many of its pixels share a common value with the training pattern on the left and it is in this sense that the patterns are said to be close to each other. The total input to the node from the two patterns will then be approximately the same and so the final output will also be similar, i.e. close to maximum. The network is signalling X just as it did to the training X. The node is said to have **generalised** to give the correct output in response to the previously unseen X in the centre.

Consider now the X on the extreme right-hand side of the figure. There are no pixels in common between this and the training pattern on the left, resulting in an output which is almost zero. The node therefore fails to generalise to the X on the right-hand side. The only way for a node to have similar outputs across all three patterns is for it to have large positive weights to *any* pixels

Figure 12.7 Concept of pattern proximity in network generalisation

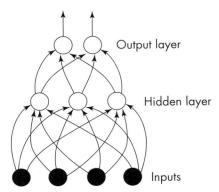

Output layer

Hidden layer

Inputs

Figure 12.8
Multilayer feed-forward net

that are dark in any of the patterns. However, this would result in the node being entirely indiscriminate in its response – it would respond to any larger letter – which is clearly not useful.

Linguistically, all the patterns in the figure are equivalent. They are all examples of the third from last letter in the Roman alphabet, and so we would normally require them all to elicit the same network response. The way to facilitate this is to re-represent the letters in such a way that, in the new representation, all the cognitively similar patterns (the Xs for example) have similar pattern representations. This requires (at least) another layer of nodes whose role is then to transform the original input into a form suitable for a final output layer to act on (Figure 12.8; Rumelhart and Todd, 1993).

These intermediate layers consist of **hidden nodes** because they take no part in the interaction of the net with the external environment. In particular, we do not directly influence their output during training via a set of target values. Instead, the hidden nodes have to learn their own internal representation of the input so as to help minimise the error at the output. However, unlike the output nodes, where there is a direct causal relationship between the error and the weight, it is not clear initially how we should assign 'blame' to the hidden nodes for any target-output discrepancy. Thus, an error may be due to incorrect weight values on an output node or it may be due to the hidden nodes providing the outputs with poor information to work on. This is the so-called *credit assignment problem* and was a serious impediment to progress within connectionist modelling until the mid 1980s. Prior to this, training algorithms were known only for single-layer nets. This severely restricted the class of problems that could be solved, a point made forcibly by Minsky and Papert (1969) in their book *Perceptrons*. This work appeared to deal a serious blow to the field of neural networks but a renaissance of interest was assisted when it was shown that the credit assignment problem had an exact solution. The training algorithm that implements this is known as **backpropagation** and is claimed by a multiple authorship. Thus it was discovered by Werbos (1974), rediscovered by Parker (1982), but was discovered again and made popular by Rumelhart *et al.* (1986a).

Learning to read

We now describe a network which illustrates the kind of issues that may be addressed by connectionist systems and shows the power of these models for explaining patterns of human cognitive behaviour.

Reading aloud involves at least two cognitive activities. One is concerned with translating the graphical structure (or orthography) of the written language into its spoken equivalent (the phonology). Another is concerned with interpreting the semantic content of the text. There is doubtless considerable interaction between the two processes. One piece of evidence for this is that some of the mistakes that patients with 'acquired dyslexia' make when reading aloud are influenced by what the words mean rather than just how they sound. However, as a first simplification it is useful to consider the problem of going from orthography to phonology in isolation.

The problem may be characterised as quasi-regular since, though the pronunciation of many words follows some simple rules (e.g. the vowel sounds in *gave, mint)*, there are often exceptions to the rules so that words with similar orthography to these, such as *have, pint*, have quite a different sound. Indeed, there are some letter patterns which have no dominant pronunciation, as with the appearance of *-ough* in *cough, rough, bough, though, through*. This has led to the dual-route theory of language processing in which two separate mechanisms are used: one rule-based system for the regular cases and another which takes the form of a look-up table for the exceptions.

Plaut *et al.* (1996), building on earlier work of Seidenburg and McClelland (1989), have developed a series of connectionist models which can learn the pronunciation of a subset of English text with a single, unified network which does not appear to contain two separate routes for pronunciation of words and non-words. The simplest of these is a feed-forward net containing a single hidden layer in which the input and output nodes represent orthographical and phonological primitives respectively. The network contained 105 inputs, 61 output nodes, 100 hidden units, and the training data consisted of nearly 3,000 monosyllabic words.

The net successfully learned the training set which contained both regular and rule-exception words. This appears to refute the dual-route theories but Plaut *et al.* admitted the possibility that, in the process of training, the net may have divided itself into two sub-networks, one which processed the regular words and the other the exceptions. To test this they cut away or 'lesioned' individual hidden nodes and measured the change in the error in the pronunciation of each type of word. It was found that hidden nodes were responsible for error in both word classes to roughly the same degree although some nodes made a more significant overall change than others. They concluded that both regular and exceptional words were processed by the same mechanisms, thereby showing that it is not necessary to resort to a dual-route theory.

There are two points to be made from the net-lesioning exercise above. First, we now know that a dual-route structure is not a necessary prerequisite for human competence in reading aloud; the model demonstrates the existence of a solution to the problem which avoids this mechanism. A more general point emerges from the way in which the net fails. Thus, it is not the case that the net suddenly fails to give the correct output in all instances. Rather, as the severity of the lesion increases, so does the number of errors made. This ability of the net to show a gradual change in performance as damage is incurred is known as **graceful degradation** and is a characteristic of all connectionist systems. It comes about because a node's output is a continuous function of its total input which is a sum of contributions from many other nodes, each of which can only have a limited effect. This effect is further enhanced by the non-linear nature of the output function since, if the activity is very large (positive or negative), the node is operating at a point on the function where the gradient is rather shallow and small changes in total input can have little influence on the output activity. This gradual decline in performance is analogous to the deterioration seen in dementias such as Alzheimer's and the late stages of Parkinson's disease. We might surmise therefore that similar mechanisms are at work as when we lesion individual nodes in a neural network.

Under some circumstances we may go further and use net lesioning to provide a direct way of testing the validity of a model, or a class of related models, against results from the neurospsychology of cognitive disorders (Mayall, 1998). Thus, suppose a particular layer or group of nodes corresponds to an anatomically identified brain region and that this group of nodes is removed from the net. If the resulting performance of the net is similar to that observed when the brain has been damaged by a lesion to the area in question, then this may be interpreted as supporting evidence for the model. This type of study is exemplified in the network of Hinton and Shallice (1991), which is discussed later.

One of the key tests of a network, is how well it generalises to input patterns it has not seen during training. If it gives the correct output here it is a sign that the net has truly discovered the underlying regularities in the training set and has not merely established a complex look-up table for each input–output pair. One way of testing the reading network is to present it with non-words that are, nevertheless, pronounceable such as *hean, brane, frane*, etc. The Plaut *et al.* (1996) network was able to mimic human behaviour in this task accurately as it correctly applied the rules of pronunciation where they were clear and often came up with exceptions where they were ambiguous. Finally, the net was able to emulate human performance in terms of the latency effects for naming various types of words: for example, when frequently encountered regular words are named rather more quickly than infrequent irregular words. The network, of course, processes all words at the same speed but Plaut *et al.* interpreted the network error as an indication of duration to response in a full system that would have to take the output and articulate it in a speech motor system. This interpretation is somewhat unsatisfactory and becomes unnecessary in other, so-called, relaxation models which will be discussed next and in which temporal effects arise naturally within the net.

The nature of representation in connectionist systems

At the end of training a network, any knowledge or long-term memory is stored in the weights or connection strengths – hence the term 'connectionism'. In one sense then, knowledge is stored in the weights of the net but there is an additional and more significant way in which knowledge representation occurs in networks. On applying an external input and allowing it to be processed, a characteristic pattern of activity will develop across the net. This may be thought of as representing knowledge about the current input. For feed-forward nets it is the intermediate hidden layers that provide the focus of interest here for it is across these nodes that an internal representation of the training set occurs. These are then operated on, or decoded by, the output layer into a form which is to be interpreted as the 'answer' or response to the input. As noted above, the role of the hidden layer(s) may be thought of as ensuring that cognitively similar inputs are re-represented so as to be close together in the pattern-matching sense. Another, related perspective conceives of hidden units as feature detectors that extract the underlying aspects of the training set while ignoring irrelevant clutter or noise.

In any event, there are two essentially different types of activity profile that can occur. In the **localist representation**, each semantically discrete item, concept or idea is associated with the activity of a single node. For example, in a letter recognition task, the occurrence of a particular letter may be signalled within a layer by a single node of that layer being active while all others are inactive. In contrast, in a **distributed representation**, each node within the layer plays a role in the activity profile representation of each semantic object. Thus, all nodes may be active to some extent for every pattern and so act as *micro-features* or *sub-symbolic* entities. In the letter-recognition task, each node may encode small orthographic features such as line segments, curves or particular groupings of these. The emphasis on distributed representations and parallel processing has sometimes led to the acronym PDP (for Parallel Distributed Processing) being applied to connectionist systems.

Rumelhart and Todd (1993) provide an example which explores the nature of connectionist representations. It is based on the idea of capturing the knowledge embedded in a semantic net. While the inputs are encoded using a localist representation of nodes in the semantic net, an intermediate layer learns a distributed representation of these inputs which gets passed to the hidden layer proper.

Networks with feedback

Consider the small network shown in Figure 12.9. Each node is connected to every other node by a weighted link in such a way that the weight values between two nodes in either direction are the same. There is no separate input and output in this net and so its operation is not governed by a simple flow of information from one end to another. Instead, we start the net in some state defined by a set of output values and then update the outputs gradually until the net 'relaxes' into a state of equilibrium. In this condition the output of each node is consistent with the input it receives from its neighbours. The dynamics of coming to equilibrium must be allowed to happen gradually because the effect of any node update has to be allowed to diffuse throughout the net. This flow of information includes feedback paths from each node, around the net, and back to itself, leading to the description of these nets as **recurrent**.

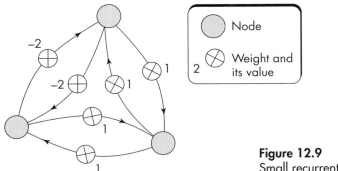

Figure 12.9
Small recurrent network

A detailed description of the network dynamics, from an arbitrary initial state to one of equilibrium, is not usually available *a priori* and so we concern ourselves with the general behaviour and the nature of the stable states at equilibrium. Hopfield (1982, 1984) showed how nets such these could be described in terms of an 'energy' function which always decreases as the net progresses through its state-space. Since the energy is bounded below by some minimum value, this formulation demonstrates that a stable state is indeed always found. This perspective leads to nets of this type being thought of as associative memories in which the stable states correspond to the stored memories. In this framework, if the net is started in an initial state which is close to some stable state then this state will be recalled as the associated pattern in memory. The set of initial states that produce recall of a particular memory is known as its **basin of attraction**, or simply **attractor**, since these states are all ultimately drawn to the given memory state. The entire state-space of the net is then divided into a series of mutually exclusive attractors.

At equilibrium, there will be an overall tendency for each weighted connection to support the current state. If a particular node has an output very close to 1 (implying a large total input) then this will most likely be due to a preponderance of positive weights with associated inputs which are also close to 1. In this way, each weight may be thought of as helping to constrain the network state by helping to force the activity across its link to take on a preferred value. This process is symmetrical because the weights between two nodes are the same in either direction and so the constraints take the form of node–pair activity correlation.

The constraint satisfaction perspective is demonstrated effectively in a network developed by Rumelhart *et al.* (1986b) which deals with knowledge about rooms in a domestic-house setting. Each node stands for an item or attribute associated with one or more of the rooms envisaged: kitchen, bathroom, office, living room and bedroom. All nodes are connected to each other by symmetric weights which capture the degree of correlation to be expected in a typical room setting. Although the item-attribute representation is localist, higher-level schema-like qualities which define the rooms are defined by the distributed pattern of activity across the network, both in terms of its weight encoding and its activity profiles.

Thinking of the weights in a recurrent net as capturing correlations or constraints between pattern components suggests a way that the net may be trained: choose a training pattern and *clamp* it to the net, that is, force the outputs to take on the values implied by the pattern components. Next, if there is a correlation between the output on two nodes, increment the weight by a small amount, otherwise make a small weight decrement. If we were to allow only positive increments then this is essentially the learning mechanism postulated by Hebb in 1949 for the way that biological neurons learn and which may have similarities with what we now call long-term potentiation (LTP) at synaptic contacts.

A model of deep dyslexia

Previously we considered a model of reading aloud that addressed the process of transforming the orthographic (visual) appearance of a word directly into its acoustic or phonological representation. In this section we consider a model of reading due to Hinton and Shallice (1991) which is concerned with the translation of orthography into semantics.[2]

People with deep dyslexia make three types of error when reading aloud. The first consists of semantic errors where a word is confused with another which has a similar or related meaning (e.g. *cat* becomes *mice*). Another type consists of visual errors in which words are confused with others which appear to be similar (e.g. *patent* becomes *patient*). Finally, it is possible for errors to occur which mix both semantics and appearance (e.g. *last* becomes *late*).

Hinton and Shallice constructed a network which learned to encode semantics in a distributed fashion as a series of basins of attraction. They then proceeded to lesion the network by severing or corrupting groups of connections and to see what result this had on the network's performance. The network architecture is shown in Figure 12.10.

It consists of two sub-networks. The first is a feed-forward net which contains the input layer of orthographic encoding *grapheme units* and a single hidden layer. This output of this net is then used to drive the input of a recurrent network capable of supporting stable-state attractors. Conceptually this is broken down, in turn, into a set of *sememe* units over which there is a distributed representation of the word semantics, and a set of *clean-up* units. This division highlights an alternative view of the function of recurrent nets in which an approximately correct output pattern is passed on to another layer to be refined or 'cleaned-up'. The improved pattern is then fed back to the original units for still further processing. This iterative refinement continues until no further change is possible, at which point the net has reached equilibrium.

The training set consisted of forty short words divided into five categories: indoor objects; animals; body parts; foods; and outdoor objects. The semantic representation occurs by activating the sememe units which have micro-features pertinent to the current word. For example, 'cat' (a member of the animal category) would activate units for 'mammal', 'has legs', 'soft' and 'fierce'. Of course, the recurrent-net still operates as an associative memory store and, since the sememe units play an intimate role in its construction, the dynamics may be

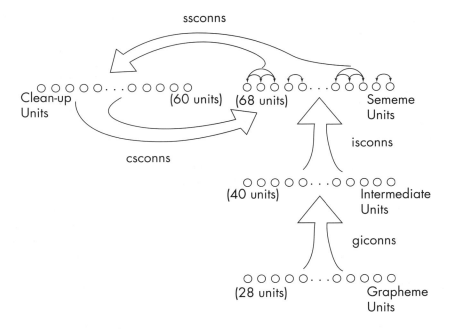

Figure 12.10 The semantic route network for reading and modelling dyslexia

thought of as occurring in a semantic state-space in which words with similar meanings are encoded by nearby attractors.

The net was trained using a variant of backpropagation adapted for use with recurrent nets and it successfully learned the training set. The net was then lesioned in various ways, either by removing whole units, a random selection of connections, or by corrupting a group of weights with noise. No matter which inter-layer group of connections or method of lesioning was chosen, the effects were qualitatively similar in that both semantic and visual errors occurred. It is clear that, if connections in the recurrent sub-net are lesioned, then the attractor for some words may be diminished or removed entirely. Thus, a word whose semantic representation was previously closest to its correct attractor is now drawn into a neighbouring basin which, by virtue of its proximity in state-space, will most likely have related semantic content. However, damage in the feed-forward sub-net will have a similar effect since incorrect semantic encoding will now result and be passed on to the recurrent net where it proceeds to initiate the dynamics in the wrong (but nearby) attractor. This is in accordance with the experimental data that semantic errors are obtained in dyslexia in spite of alternative lesion sites nominally associated with visual processing and semantic storage.

The origin of visual errors can be explained by the network's tendency to generalise over its input. Thus, although an undamaged net will be able to differentiate *cat* and *cot*, having managed to encode these in the intermediate units in such a way as to pull their representations apart, a damaged net may resort to the default behaviour of categorising orthographically similar inputs together. This explanation holds good for the feed-forward sub-net but is less convincing in the recurrent part. To see how damage here may play a part in visual errors, we need to consider the role of the clean-up units. These work to continually refine the representation delivered by the sememe units on a first pass through the feed-forward sub-net. Thus, the sememe units need not necessarily have to produce the optimal encodings that would be expected in a feed-forward-only net and so orthographically similar inputs may not be separated by as much as they might otherwise have to be. Damage to the attractors will then expose any short-comings in the robustness of the initial encoding and produce erroneous results. In summary, the co-occurrence of semantic and visual errors over a wide range of lesion sites is accounted for by the network.

Another phenomenon in deep dyslexia occurs when a patient has a lesion so extensive that semantic identification is severely impaired. In this case, rather than make an incorrect identification of the word, all that can be done is to say which category the word is in, say, 'animal' rather than 'food'. If the network is made to suffer substantial damage, then the equilibrium patterns in the sememe units are no longer close to those of any of the words in the training set. However, the equilibria are close to the centres of the regions that were occupied by items in a particular group. Thus, it makes sense to say that the net is delivering a category rather than an individual item as output in accordance with the neuro-physiological finding.

To what extent are the details of this particular network architecture responsible for the observed behaviour? Conversely, what are the key structural components in this respect? Hinton and Shallice tried variations in which there were connections within the sememe layer; in which there were sparse and fully interconnected layers; and in which the recurrent sub-net was placed closer to the input in the processing hierarchy. They also experimented with different ortho-graphic representations at the input. The finding was that these features are all largely irrelevant; the behaviour appears to stem from the existence of a recurrent sub-net which can support basins of attraction.

The dyslexia network of Hinton and Shallice illustrates how several psycho-logical phenomena (in this case, types of error) can be considered to be emergent phenomena resulting from a single-system model; it is not necessarily the case that multiple patterns of behaviour require multiple paths or subsystems. The model accounts for many aspects of deep dyslexia and the experiments with structural modifications have managed to highlight the possibly key role played by attractor networks in processing semantic information.

Shortcomings of the connectionist approach

While neural network models appear to have many attractive explanatory features for modelling certain types of cognitive behaviour, attempts to use them to model tasks that are clearly algorithmically based can appear cumbersome and irrelevant. For example, does the number 1010111010010011 have an odd or an even number of 1s? It is possible to build a network that can classify patterns such as this as having and odd or an even number (although, incidentally, it can be proved that such a network must have more than one layer) but is it psychologically interesting? The network would produce a classification (the output) immediately upon the input being presented. But a normal person asked the same question would have to count the number of 1s, remembering the running total and the next item to be counted. It seems natural to describe this process in terms of internal symbolic representations and rule-following, so why build a connectionist model that does the same task, but not in the same way? It might be best to focus on the higher descriptive level of a symbolic, algorithmic explanation in terms of counting, rather than on a sub-symbolic connectionist model.

Another criticism sometimes levelled against connectionism is that sensible explanations of cognition are obscured because the network is a 'black-box' whose operation is difficult to understand (McCloskey, 1991). This attack is based on the nature of distributed representations which, by their very nature, are composed of micro-features which may not be semantically transparent. We have seen, however, that it is quite possible to understand the mechanisms at work in a network without having to have an intimate knowledge of the minutiae of each representation. General principles, such as the role of attractors, pattern-space-distance measures, graceful degradation, and the like can be invoked that have powerful high-level explanatory power.

Although it is claimed that connectionist models process information in a brain-like way, it is clear that the units of these models are like the neurons of the brain only in the most superficial way. The attempt to build models out of units which incorporate some of the wealth of physiological details known about biological neurons is called **computational neuroscience** (Churchland and Sejnowski, 1994).

12.4 Symbols and neurons compared

As noted previously, the symbolic approach is good for modelling areas of cognition that can easily be formulated as a series of rule-based procedures, or which lend themselves to a fairly rigid knowledge representation. These areas include many high-level intellectual activities that require logical inference such as problem-solving, theorem-proving in mathematics, game-playing, and the enactment of some types of technical and scientific expertise; these are just the areas within which it is difficult to formulate connectionist models and which we intuitively expect a psychological account to be in terms of rules and symbols. On the other hand, symbolic systems often perform poorly at (for example) perceptual and motor tasks (including both low-level and high-level vision and visuomotor coordination) and some aspects of natural language understanding; these are just the areas at which connectionist models excel. So it seems that, depending on the psychological problem to be understood, either a symbolic approach or a connectionist approach may be the natural choice.

It is instructive to draw up a series of points for comparison between the two approaches.

Learning

Connectionist: Gradual learning is implicit in connectionist models – nets start with some random weight set and adapt these by repeatedly being shown examples from the problem to be solved or task to be done.

Symbolic: Learning in these systems is possible but is not inherent. Further, what is learnt is more rules and symbols, i.e. more of the same; if a problem does not lend itself to the symbolic approach then no amount of learning will help.

Knowledge representation

Connectionist: Knowledge is stored as a pattern of weighted connections. In one type of representation this knowledge then manifests itself in distributed patterns of activity. There is then no simple correspondence between nodes and high-level semantic objects. Rather, the representation of a 'concept' or 'idea' within the net is via the complete pattern of unit activities, being distributed over the net as a whole. In this way, any given node may partake in many semantic representations. In contrast, localist representations imply a one-to-one mapping between nodes and features or ideas. However, even in this case, higher-level structures may be implicitly distributed over the entire net (as in the schema network model, for instance).

Symbolic: There is a clear correspondence between the semantic objects being dealt with (numbers, words, concepts, etc.) and both the model structures (symbols) and the physical hardware of an implementation. Thus, each object can be 'pointed to' in a block of computer memory.

Style of processing

Connectionist: Is more akin to signal processing than computation *per se*; networks combine and process numerical signals rather than symbols. Further, they sometimes behave like physical, dynamical systems in that they relax to some equilibrium state.

Symbolic: Executes a program stored in memory on a von Neumann machine (computer architecture invented by John von Neumann). The program results in the processing of objects with symbolic value rather than simple numerical values.

Parallel/serial computation

Connectionist: Inherently parallel where many nodes may work at the same time.[3]

Symbolic: Usually serial, in which each instruction or stage in the algorithm has to be executed before the next one can be performed.

Mode of failure under damage

Connectionist: Nets are robust under hardware failure; altering or even destroying a few connections may still allow the net to work and performance gradually declines rather than catastrophically collapsing.

Symbolic: Altering or destroying a few memory locations in a computer running a symbolic algorithm may prevent the machine from working altogether, resulting in a so-called machine 'crash'.

Plausibility

Connectionist: Biological plausibility – although unlike real neurons, connectionist models do process information in the same way (i.e. as signals).

Symbolic: Psychological plausibility – symbolic processing is a natural way of understanding much of cognition.

12.5 Towards a synthesis

In spite of the differences outlined in the above list, we started our comparison by noting that the symbolic and connectionist paradigms can reasonably lay claim to non-overlapping domains of competence. It would appear therefore that there is room in the cognitive modeller's tool-bag for both symbolic and connectionist systems. However, it is not satisfactory to simply ignore the fundamental difference in approach and try to live uneasily with two very different paradigms. If we are to embrace them both it is vital that we understand how they may be reconciled.

One important step in this direction was taken by Smolensky (1988) who attempted to clarify some of the issues surrounding the nature of connectionist and symbolic modelling. Smolensky advocated what he called the *Proper Treatment of Connectionism* (PTC), which embraced many aspects of the modelling problem in a lengthy argument that is, in places, rather subtle. One of the main aspects of PTC, however, is that it argues for the use of distributed (rather than localist) representations acting at what he calls the *sub-symbolic* level (the level of *micro-features*). Smolensky then claims that any rule-based description constitutes an emergent property of the sub-symbolic model. To illustrate what is meant here consider the behaviour of the stock market. During a rapid rise in share prices, individual investors may be buying or selling according to their own predispositions. However, the overall (emergent) pattern is that of people buying the most significant shares. The investors or brokers are not 'obeying a law' that says they will buy to increase the market-index with a positive linear trend; rather the linear increase is an emergent property of many contributions from individuals acting independently. We can now see that, on occasion, symbolic models may be appropriate, although Smolensky conceives of these as secondary to an underlying sub-symbolic system from which it springs.

A rather different stance has been adopted by Clark (1990) who posits the ability of the brain (and hence connectionist architectures) to simulate or emulate a von Neumann machine directly. In this way the sub-symbolic description may be subservient in certain instances to the emulation of a serial, algorithmic processor. In defence of this stance, it would be appear to be almost a truism, for example, that when we perform mental arithmetic we are simulating a suite of well-defined algorithms. The point here is that, while processing within neural networks is done on signals, it is sometimes possible to understand the overall behaviour of the net as the manipulation of a high-level symbolic data structure. For example, if a particular output unit, Y, only fires if both of a pair of input units, A and B, are active then the network can be understood as implementing a classic logic rule : 'IF A is on AND B is on THEN Y'.

It is also possible to construct models which contain elements of both approaches. The logic of symbolic networks can implement 'soft' rather than 'hard' rules using 'uncertain reasoning', or 'fuzzy logic' (Kosko, 1992; Pearl, 1995). There are hybrid models which incorporate both symbol manipulation and connectionist-style memory activitations, such as the ACT* model (Anderson, 1983).

Summary

- Theories vary in their degree of specification, from metaphors, through structural descriptions, to fully implemented computational models that generate quantitative predictions.
- A paradigm is a general framework of (sometimes tacit) assumptions, methods and theories that underpin an area of scientific investigation. The information processing paradigm in cognitive science views cognition as the effective manipulation and transformation of information about the environment which makes extensive use of internal representations of the world. There is a major division within this paradigm between symbolic (AI-based) and connectionist (neural network) approaches. The study of situated robotics is an attempt to break free from this representational stance.
- The task performed by a computational model may be described using the three-level hierarchy proposed by Marr; the computational level describes what is being computed and why; the algorithmic level describes the way this is to be carried out in the abstract; and the implementation level describes the hardware that runs the algorithm.
- Cognitive science has drawn heavily from the study of Artificial Intelligence (AI) but, while AI programs may perform a task well, they may not necessarily provide a good description of the corresponding human cognitive process.
- The symbolic paradigm assumes that knowledge can be captured in a set of basic, semantically transparent objects (symbols) and that cognition may be described by supplying the rules according to which these objects are manipulated. There is a close parallel between models built in this paradigm and their implementation on von Neumann computing engines (conventional computers).

- One of the key features in a model is the way in which knowledge is represented. Within the symbolic paradigm several methods have been developed. In a semantic net, nodes in a graph represent concepts, or objects, and links between nodes denote inter-object/concept relationships. A schemata, frame or script describes a stereotypical situation whose specifics are fleshed out by assigning values to its slots or variables. A production system consists of a collection of rules and an information database to which the rules may be applied to obtain new rules or answers to queries.
- While the symbolic approach has proven very powerful, its dependence on semantically transparent, well-articulated rules and objects means that it can be rather 'brittle' when it is applied to perceptual problems or non-intellectual domains that make use of 'common-sense' reasoning.
- Connectionism is the main alternative to the symbolic approach in psychology. Networks are constructed using simplified artificial neurons whose interconnection strengths or weights are adapted under a training regime. The network learns by being exposed to a set of examples of the problem to be solved.
- Simple feed-forward networks tend to undergo supervised learning in which each input pattern is also supplied with a desired output. However, with some modifications a network may undergo self-organisation and learn to extract information about clusters of patterns.
- Neural networks can generalise their ability to classify information from training examples to patterns previously unseen.
- Multilayer nets contain one or more layers of hidden nodes which are not subject to intervention by supervision and, instead, learn their own internal representation of the training data.
- The work of Plaut *et al.* (1996) uses a feed-forward net to model the process of reading aloud. The network processed regular and irregular words in the same way, thus not supporting the dual-route theory of reading
- Networks exhibit graceful degradation when lesioned. The precise way in which this occurs may correspond to the way in which certain cognitive deficits arise in the ability being modelled. This is sometimes used as evidence in support of a model but is more conservatively able to support a class of models which share some general architectural features.
- Information is represented in connectionist nets in the instantaneous pattern of activity over the node outputs and (long-term) knowledge via the weights. Patterns of activity may correspond to either a localist or distributed representation.
- Feedback or recurrent nets may be used as dynamic systems to store memories as foci within basins of attraction.
- The work of Hinton and Shallice used a combination of feed-forward and recurrent nets to encode word semantics as a series of basins of attraction. Lesioning the net led to behaviour comparable with that of deep dyslexia.
- While networks work well for modelling many types of cognitive behaviour, they are poor at tasks that are clearly governed by well-defined rules. A network's operation may be difficult to understand if it uses a distributed representation of node activity.

- Symbolic systems are fundamentally static (not adaptable), semantically transparent, serial models which have a natural implementation in von Neumann hardware leading to catastrophic failure under damage. Networks are fundamentally adaptable, semantically opaque (under a distributed representation), parallel models which exhibit graceful degradation under hardware failure.
- While the symbolic and connectionist approaches may appear quite different, points of contact and comparison have been made by Smolensky ('the proper treatment of connectionism') and Clark (von Neumann emulation) and by those who construct hybrid systems.

Notes

1 Machines for the manipulation of financial quantities often work with decimal representations rather than binary because of the possibility of incurring rounding errors when converting to and from binary.
2 A precis of this work has also appeared in *Scientific American* (Hinton *et al.*, 1993).
3 In simulating networks on conventional computers we are limited by the serial computer architecture and not by the network itself.

Further reading

Ellis, R. and Humphreys, G.W. (1999). *Connectionist Psychology: A Text with Readings*. Hove: Psychology Press. The major models in all areas of cognitive psychology are covered. Key influential papers are provided as readings.

Franklin, S. (1995). *Artificial Minds*. Cambridge, MA: MIT Press. This is an engaging and good-humoured tour of the 'interdisciplinary matrix' that makes up the cognitive sciences. Franklin discusses the basis for the different approaches and the philosophical implications of constructing 'thinking machines'.

Gurney, K. (1997). *An Introduction to Neural Networks*. London: UCL Press. A short introduction to the technical aspects of connectionism with as little mathematics as possible.

O'Reilly, R.C. and Munakata, Y. (2000). *Computational Explorations in Cognitive Neuroscience: Understanding the Mind by Simulating the Brain*. Cambridge, MA: MIT Press. A textbook which emphasises how assemblies of biologically realistic units can perform cognitive functions, thus allowing cognitive models to make contact with neuroscientific data.

Glossary

Acquired dysgraphia A specific difficulty with writing words, caused by brain damage.

Acquired dyslexia Impairment of the ability to read caused by brain damage.

Active perception Perception as a function of interaction with the world.

Affordances Represent the interaction of the individual with the environment. Objects afford the use to which the individual can put them.

Agnosia The failure to recognise or interpret stimuli despite adequate sensory function. Usually classified by sensory modality, so visual agnosia is the failure to recognise objects that are seen.

Agrammatism A pattern of aphasic symptoms characterised by a lack of grammatical structure in speech, with a tendency for grammatical function words and inflections to be omitted.

Algorithm A well-defined procedure or recipe for processing information.

Alzheimer's disease (AD) A degenerative brain disorder usually (but not always) afflicting the elderly, which first appears as an impairment of memory but later develops into a more general dementia.

Amnesia A pathological impairment of memory function.

Anomia An impaired ability to name objects.

Anterograde amnesia (AA) Impaired memory for events which have occurred since the onset of the disorder (contrasts with retrograde amnesia).

Aphasia Loss or impairment of one or more aspects of language abilities caused by brain damage.

Articulatory suppression   A task used to occupy the articulatory control process of the working memory, normally involving the repetition of a sound (such as 'the') which requires articulation but little processing.

Attention   Focusing cognitive resources on a single input or distributing them across multiple tasks.

Attention conspicuity   The interaction of aspects of a stimulus (such as colour, luminance, form) with aspects of an individual (such as attention, knowledge, pre-conceptions) that determine how likely a stimulus is to be consciously perceived. *See also* **sensory conspicuity**.

Attentional engagement theory (AET)   Modification of feature integration theory (FIT) proposed by Duncan and Humphries in which relationship between distracters in visual search tasks is also important.

Attenuation   Amount of processing a stimulus receives being variable depending upon the task and the personal significance of the stimulus.

Attractor see *basin of attraction*.

Automatic processing   Processing that is not under conscious control, and which is rapid, inevitable and involuntary (contrasts with **controlled processing**).

Availability heuristic   Making judgements on the basis of how available relevant examples are in our memory store.

Backpropagation   'Backpropagation of error'. A supervised learning algorithm for training multilayer feed-forward networks.

Base-rate fallacy   Ignoring information about the base rate in light of other information.

Basin of attraction   In a recurrent net with stable states, the set of states which eventually lead to a particular stable state.

Behaviourism   An approach to psychology which constrains psychologists to the investigation of externally observable behaviour, and which rejects any consideration of inner mental processes.

Binaural cues   Cues to, for example, sound direction that rely on comparing the input to both ears.

Blindsight   The ability of some functionally blind patients to detect visual stimuli at an unconscious level, despite having no conscious awareness of seeing them. Usually observed in patients with occipital lobe lesions.

Bottom-up (or stimulus-driven) processing   Processing which is directed by information contained within the stimulus (contrasts with **top-down processing**).

Broca's area   A region of the brain normally located in the left frontal region, which controls motor speech production.

Capacity   A fixed limit on the information processing ability of the human cognitive system.

Cell assembly   A group of cells which have become linked to one another to form a single functional network. Proposed by Hebb as a possible biological mechanism underlying the representation and storage of a memory trace.

Central executive   A hypothetical mechanism which is believed to be in overall control of the working memory. It is assumed to control a variety of tasks, such as decision-making, problem-solving and selective attention.

Channels   In dichotic listening (q.v.), refers to the subjects' ears.

Classical AI   Artificial intelligence which relies on algorithmic symbol manipulation.

Cocktail-party phenomenon   Situation of attending to a single conversation against a background of many other conversations. Modelled by dichotic listening (q.v.).

Cognitive interview   An approach to interviewing eyewitnesses which makes use of the findings of cognitive psychology, such as context reinstatement.

Cognitive neuropsychology   The study of the brain activities underlying cognitive processes, often by investigating cognitive impairment in brain-damaged patients.

Cognitive neuroscience   The investigation of human cognition by relating it to brain structure and function, normally based on brain imaging techniques.

Cognitive psychology   The study of the way in which the brain processes information. It includes the mental processes involved in perception, learning and memory storage, thinking and language.

Cognitivism   A paradigm for cognitive science that holds that cognition may be adequately explained using symbol-based models.

Cohesive devices   Ways of indicating within a text that an item such as a word or sentence is linked with what has gone before.

Competence   The linguistic knowledge hypothesised to underlie the ability to use language.

Computational cognitive neuroscience   Using a neural network-style model which is structured by what we know about the circuits in the brain responsible for that particular cognitive task.

Computational neuroscience   Building neural network models which incorporate anatomical and physiological data about the artificial neurons.

Computer modelling   The simulation of human cognitive processes by computer. Often used as a method of testing the feasibility of an information-processing mechanism.

Conduction aphasia   An impairment of language in which the most obvious symptom is an inability to repeat what was just heard.

Confabulation   The reporting of memories which are incorrect and apparently fabricated, but which the patient believes to be true.

Conjoint search   Visual search for a target defined by a combination of characteristics.

Connectionist system   A neural network which attempts to model some aspect of perception or cognition.

Consistent mapping   In Shiffrin and Schneider's (1977) visual search tasks, a situation in which the memory set of to-be-detected items is consistent across trials.

Constancy   Ability to perceive constant objects in the world despite continual changes in viewing conditions.

Constructivist approach   Building up our perception of the world from incomplete sensory input. *See also* **perceptual hypotheses**.

Content word   A word such as a noun, verb or adjective that carries meaning beyond its grammatical role in the sentence.

Contention Scheduling A term used by Norman and Shallice to describe an operation which prevents two competing activated schemas from being selected on the basis of the strength of their initial activation.

Controlled processing Processing that is under conscious control, and which is a relatively slow, voluntary process (contrasts with **automatic processing**).

Covert attending Visual attending without moving the eyes or head.

Data-limited Processes that are limited by stimulus quality rather than by investment of cognitive resources.

Declarative memory Memory which can be reported in a deliberate and conscious way (contrasts with **procedural memory**).

Deductive reasoning task A problem that has a well-defined structure in a system of formal logic where the conclusion is certain.

Deep dyslexia A specific pattern of dyslexic symptoms characterised by semantic errors, visual errors, difficulty reading non-words and function words.

Deep dysphasia A specific pattern of aphasic symptoms in which the person is likely to make semantic errors when repeating words back, has more difficulty repeating abstract words than concrete words and is unable to repeat non-words.

Dichotic listening Experimental simulation of cocktail-party phenomenon (q.v.) in which separate messages are presented to the two ears simultaneously via headphones.

Diencephalon A brain structure which includes the thalamus and hypothalamus. Parts of the diencephalon are involved in processing and retrieving memories, and damage to these structures can cause amnesia.

Digit span A measure of the largest number of digits which an individual can recall when tested immediately after their presentation. Widely used as a test of the capacity of the phonological component of the working memory.

Direct perception Perception without the need for top-down processing.

Discourse A set of sentences that are related to one another in a meaningful way.

Disinhibition Impaired response inhibition, an inability to suppress previous incorrect responses observed in patients with frontal lobe epilepsy.

'Distracters' In visual search, the background array in which a target (q.v.) is embedded.

Distributed representation A representation in connectionist models in which each node may partake in the encoding of many features, objects, or ideas.

Divided attention Dividing cognitive resources over two or more tasks simultaneously. Contrasts with **focused attention** (q.v.).

Dorsal stream Projection from primary visual cortex to the posterior parietal cortex thought to underlie perception of spatial location.

Double dissociation A method of establishing that two systems are separate, by showing that either system can be impaired whilst the other remains intact.

Dysexecutive syndrome A collection of deficits observed in frontal lobe patients which may include impaired concentration, impaired concept formation, disinhibition, inflexibility, perseveration, impaired cognitive estimation and impaired strategy formation.

Early selection Idea that selection in attention occurs before semantic analysis and at the level of physical characteristics of stimuli.

Echolalia A marked tendency to repeat what has just been said.

Ecological validity The extent to which the conditions of a research experiment resemble those encountered in real-life settings.

Electroconvulsive therapy (ECT) A treatment used to alleviate depression which involves passing an electric current through the front of the patient's head.

Encoding The process of transforming a sensory stimulus into a memory trace.

Encoding specificity principle (ESP) The theory that retrieval cues will only be successful in accessing a memory trace if they contain some of the same items of information which were stored with the original trace.

Episodic buffer A hypothetical component of working memory which integrates information from different sense modalities, and provides a link with the LTM.

Episodic memory Memory for specific episodes and events from personal experience, occurring in a particular context of time and place (contrasts with **semantic memory**).

Executive functions Meta-abilities necessary for appropriate social functioning and everyday problem-solving, for example the deployment of attention, self-regulation, insight, planning and goal-directed behaviour.

Exhaustive search In visual search (q.v.), a search over all items in the array. Contrasts with **self-terminating search** (q.v.).

Experimental cognitive psychology An approach which involves the use of psychological experiments on human subjects to investigate the ways in which they perceive, learn, remember or think.

Experimental psychology The scientific testing of psychological processes in human and animal subjects.

Explicit memory Memory which a subject is able to report consciously and deliberately (contrasts with **implicit memory**).

Extended hippocampal complex A system of interconnected structures within the brain, incorporating the hippocampus, anterior thalamus and mammillary bodies, which is involved in the encoding and storage of new memory traces.

Facilitatory Something that speeds up subsequent processing.

Familiarity The recognition of an item as one that has been encountered on some previous occasion.

Feature analysis Analysis of visual stimuli in terms of simple visual features such as lines, corners and curves. Occurs fairly early on in visual processing.

Feature detectors Mechanisms in an information processing device (such as a brain or a computer) which respond to specific features in a pattern of stimulation, such as lines or corners.

Feature integration theory (FIT) Idea due to Triesman that attention is necessary to re-bind stimulus features into coherent perceptual units after pre-attentive feature analysis has occurred.

Feature overlap The extent to which features of the memory trace stored at input match those available in the retrieval cues. According to the encoding specificity theory (q.v.) successful retrieval requires extensive feature overlap.

Features   Elements of a scene that can be extracted and then used to build up a perception of the scene as a whole. *See also* **geons**.

Flanker effect   Processing of a word affected by flanking words.

Flashbulb memory   A subject's recollection of details of what they were doing at the time of some major news event or dramatic incident.

fMRI (functional magnetic resonance imaging)   A medical imaging technology that uses very strong magnetic fields to measure changes in the oxygenation of the blood in the brain and thus map levels of activity in the brain.

Focused attention   Focusing cognitive resources on a single source of stimulation.

Functional fixedness   The inability to use an object appropriately in a given situation because of prior experience of using the object in a different way.

Garden-path sentence   A sentence that initially gives rise to an incorrect interpretation, necessitating backtracking and reinterpretation.

Generalisation   Occurs in a neural network when a net correctly classifies examples it has not seen during training.

Geons   Basically features, but conceived explicitly as being 3-D features.

Gestalt psychology   An approach to psychology which emphasised the way in which the components of perceptual input became grouped and integrated into patterns and whole figures.

Global   Information in a visual scene relating to gross outline or configuration. Contrasts with **local** information (q.v.).

Graceful degradation   The way in which the performance of a neural network gradually breaks down as its connections are damaged.

Grammar   In linguistics, a set of hypotheses about how language is organised.

Grammatical function word   A word such as an article, preposition or conjuction which serves a grammatical function in a sentence rather than carrying meaning in itself.

Haptic perception (or **haptic information**)   Tactile (touch) and kinesthetic (awareness of position and movement of joints and muscles) perception.

Herpes Simplex Encephalitis (HSE)   A virus infection of the brain, which in some cases leaves the patient severely amnesic.

Heuristic   A loosely defined rule of thumb for helping symbolic systems search for solutions to a task.

Hidden nodes   Those units in a neural network which provide neither input nor output signals and whose activities may not be determined during training.

Hippocampus   A structure lying within the temporal lobes which is involved in the creation of new memories. Hippocampal lesions usually cause impairment of memory, especially the storage of new memories.

Illusions   Cases in which perception of the world is distorted in some way.

Illusory conjunctions   Novel prediction of FIT borne out by experimentation. Involves elementary features being re-bound together resulting in perception of stimuli that were not actually presented.

Impasse   A sort of mental 'blank' experienced when trying to solve a problem, that is accompanied by a subjective feeling of not knowing what to do.

Implicit memory   Memory whose influence can be detected by some indirect test of task performance, but which the subject is unable to report deliberately and consciously (contrasts with **explicit memory**).

Individuation   Recognising one specific item from other members of that class of item (e.g. recognising the face of a particular individual).

Inductive reasoning task   A problem that has a well-defined structure in a system of formal logic where the conclusion is highly probable but not necessarily true.

Inflectional endings   An ending on a word stem that expresses a grammatical relation, such as the past tense -ed ending or the plural -s ending.

Inhibitory   Something which tends to slow down subsequent processing. Contrasts with **facilitatory** (q.v.).

Insight   The reorganising or restructuring of the elements of the problem situation in such a way as to provide a solution. Also known as productive thinking.

Interpolation   Using computerised image processing systems to construct images that are intermediate between two other images.

Knowledge   Information that is not contained within the sensory stimulus.

Korsakoff's syndrome   A brain disease which usually results from chronic alcoholism, and which is mainly characterised by a memory impairment.

Lapses   A type of human error.

Late selection   Idea that selection in attention can occur fairly late on, after **semantic** (q.v.) processing has occurred. Can explain **subliminal perception** (q.v.).

Laws of perceptual organisation   Principles (such as proximity) by which parts of a visual scene can be resolved into different objects.

Learning rule   The formula for changing the weights in a **neural network**.

Lesions   Injuries or damage of some kind.

Lexical ambiguity   Ambiguity caused by a word that has more than one meaning (for example 'bank').

Lexical item   A word (*see also* **mental lexicon**).

Lexicalisation   The process by which a thought that underlies a word is turned into the spoken form of that word.

Local   Information in a visual scene relating to fine detail (contrasts with **global** information).

Localist representation   A representation in connectionist models in which each node stands for a particular (semantically transparent) feature.

Long-term memory   Memory held in permanent storage, available for retrieval at some time in the future (contrasts with **short-term memory**).

Long-term potentiation (LTP)   A lasting change in synaptic resistance following the application of electrical stimulation to living brain tissue. Possibly one of the biological mechanisms underlying the learning process.

Means–ends analysis   A general heuristic where a sub-problem is selected that will reduce the difference between the current state and the goal state.

Mental lexicon   The store in memory of information about words.

Mental model   A representation that we construct according to what is described in the premises of a reasoning problem, which will depend on how we interpret these premises.

Messages   In dichotic listening, information presented on channels (q.v.).

Misinformation effect   The contamination of eyewitness testimony by information acquired after the witnessed event.

Mnemonic   A technique or strategy used for improving the memorability of items (e.g. adding meaningful associations).

Modular system   A system in which different types of processing are carried out by separate and relatively independent sub-systems.

Modules   Discrete information processing units dedicated to particular functions.

Morphemes   The smallest meaningful units into which words can be divided. Some words such as 'cat' may consist of one morpheme whilst others may be analysed into units that recur in other words. For example, 'unthinkable' may be analysed into: un + think + able.

Morphology   The study of the internal structure of words.

Neural network   A network of interconnected processing elements, loosely based on the networks of neurons found in the animal brain.

Neurotransmitter   A chemical substance which is secreted across the synapse between two neurons, enabling one neuron to stimulate another.

Node   A processing element in a **neural network**.

Numena   The world as it really is. *See also* **phenomena**.

Organic amnesia   An impairment of memory function caused by physical damage to the brain.

Orienting   In the spotlight model of visual attention this is attention to regions of space that does not depend upon eye movements.

Orienting task   A set of instructions used to influence the type of cognitive processing employed.

Pandemonium   A theoretical model of a feature extraction process.

Paradigm   An overarching framework of ideas, assumptions, methods and theories that underpins an area of scientific investigation.

Parallel distributed processing (PDP) approaches   Stimuli are represented in the brain, not by single neurons, but by networks of neurons. An approach sometimes used to model cognitive processes.

Parallel processing   Processing of multiple objects (or their attributes) simultaneously. Contrasts with **serial processing** (q.v.).

Parsing   The process of analysing a string of words into grammatical constituents.

Perception   The subjective experience of sensory information after having been processed by the cognitive processes (e.g. attention), as compared to 'sensation'.

Perceptual hypotheses   An element of the constructivist approach in which hypotheses as to the nature of a stimulus object are tested against incoming sensory information.

Performance   The psychological processes involved in language use, as opposed to competence; the knowledge of language said to underlie that use.

Perseveration   An inability to shift response strategy, characteristic of frontal lobe patients.

PET (positron emission tomography)   A medical imaging technique which uses harmless radioactive tracers injected into the patient to reveal areas of metabolic activity in the brain and other organs.

Phantom word illusion   What we hear may be influenced by what we expect to hear.

Phenomena   Numena as we perceive them.

Phenomenological experience   Our conscious experience of the world.

Phoneme   The smallest unit of sound that has an effect on meaning. For example, the initial phonemes differ between 'bin' and 'pin' and the two words differ in meaning.

Phonetics   The study of speech sounds, especially their articulation and acoustic properties.

Phonological loop   A hypothetical component of working memory that is assumed to provide brief storage for verbally presented items.

Phonology   The study of the sound system of a language, especially the pattern of combinations of sounds in that language.

Phrase structure rules   Rules that describe the hierarchical organisation of sentences into grammatical elements.

Physical symbol hypothesis   The stance that holds that an intelligent agent must be equivalent to a symbol-based system capable of direct implementation on von Neumann (conventional) computer architecture.

Pragmatic reasoning schemata   Clusters of rules that are highly generalised and abstracted but defined with respect to different types of relationships and goals.

Prefixes   A bound morpheme that is added to the beginning of a word (for example, -pre, -un and -dis).

Primal sketch   First stage in Marr's model of vision. Results in computation of edges and other details from retinal images.

Problem reduction   An approach to problem-solving that converts the problem into a number of sub-problems, each of which can be solved separately.

Problem space   A term introduced by Newell and Simon to describe the first stage in problem-solving; represented in the problem space are the initial state, the goal state, the instructions, the constraints on the problem and all relevant information retrieved from long-term memory.

Procedural memory   Memory which can be demonstrated by performing some skilled procedure such as a motor task, but which the subject is not necessarily able to report consciously (contrasts with **declarative memory**).

Production rule   A conditional rule used in a symbol-based system for combining data to produce a new result.

Proprioception   Knowledge of the position of the body and its parts (arms, fingers, etc.). *See also* **haptic perception**.

Prosopagnosia   An inability to recognise faces despite adequate visual acuity.

Prototypes   Representations of objects in terms of fairly abstract properties. More flexible than templates.

Psychogenic amnesia A form of amnesia caused by psychological factors (such as the repression of disturbing memories) rather than brain damage.

Psycholinguistics The study of the comprehension, production and acquisition of language.

Psychological refractory period (PRP) Delay in responding when a stimulus is presented shortly after a preceding one.

Pure word deafness A type of aphasia in which the person is unable to understand spoken language, despite their speaking and reading being relatively unaffected.

Pure word meaning deafness A type of aphasia in which the person is unable to understand what words mean even though those words can be repeated and written accurately to dictation.

Recency effect The tendency for subjects to show particularly good recall for items presented towards the end of a list.

Recollection Remembering a specific event or occasion on which an item was previously encountered.

Recurrent Used to describe networks with feedback loops within their interconnections.

Re-entrant processing Information flow between brain regions is bi-directional.

Rehabilitation strategies Used to help patients to cope with an impairment or disability, enabling them to function as effectively as possible within the limitations created by the impairment.

Representation An internal coding of certain aspects of the information dealt with in a computational model of cognition.

Representativeness heuristic Making judgements on the basis of the extent to which the salient features of an object or person are representative of the features thought to be characteristic of some category.

Resource-limited Processes which are improved by the investment of additional cognitive resources. Contrasts with **data-limited** processes (q.v.).

Resources Cognitive resources, including discrete processing modules, capacity limitations and central executive (q.v.).

Retrieval-induced forgetting (RIF) The phenomenon whereby the successful retrieval of a memory trace inhibits the retrieval of rival memory traces.

Retrograde amnesia (RA) Impaired memory for events which occurred prior to the onset of amnesia (contrasts with **anterograde amnesia**).

Reversible figure A figure in which the object perceived depends on what is designated as 'figure' and what is designated as '(back)ground'.

Saccadic eye movements Small eye movements which are automatic and involuntary.

Schema A mental pattern, usually derived from past experience, which is used to assist with the interpretation of subsequent cognitions, for example by identifying familiar shapes and sounds in a new perceptual input.

Scotoma A blind area within the visual field, resulting from damage to the visual system (plural 'scotomata').

Selective attention Focusing on a single source of stimulation. Contrasts with **divided attention** (q.v.).

Self-organisation   The process whereby a neural network may learn about the structure of the training examples without being shown target responses (contrasts with **supervised learning**).

Self-terminating search   Visual search that terminates once a target is located. Contrasts with **exhaustive search** (q.v.).

Semantic   Concerned with meanings, especially of words.

Semantic error   A semantically related word is substituted for another word in speaking or in reading, for example 'yellow' for 'red' or 'sleep' for 'night'.

Semantic memory   Memory for general knowledge, such as the meanings associated with particular words and shapes, without reference to any specific contextual episode (contrasts with **episodic memory**).

Semantics   The study of the meaning of words and sentences.

Sensation   The 'raw' sensory input as compared to 'perception'.

Sensory conspicuity   The extent to which aspects of a stimulus (such as colour and luminance) influence how easily it can be registered by the senses. *See also* **attention conspicuity**.

Sensory overload   A situation in which there is too much incoming sensory information to be adequately processed.

Serial processing   Processing of objects or attributes one at a time in sequence. Contrasts with **parallel processing** (q.v.).

Set-size function   In visual search, relationship between number of elements in an array and the time taken to locate the target.

Shadowing   Dichotic listening with repeating message heard on one channel.

Short-term memory   Memory held in conscious awareness, and currently receiving attention (contrasts with **long-term memory**).

Simulation (simulated)   Construction of a working model of an aspect of information processing, usually implemented on a computer.

Situated robotics   Building robots which display complex behaviours, but which (it is claimed) do not make explicit use of internal representations.

Size constancy   The perceived size of objects is adjusted to allow for perceived distance.

Slip of the tongue   Errors people make when they talk.

Slips   Type of human error.

Spectral cues   Auditory cues to, for example, distance provided by the distortion of the incoming stimulus by (e.g.) the pinnae (ear lobes).

Spotlight   Model of visual attention due to Posner in which a small but variable part of the visual field is selected for analysis.

State-action tree   A diagram showing all the possible sequences of actions and intermediate states which can be constructed if the problem is well defined.

Streaming   Separation of auditory input into separate streams to enable concurrent tasks to be performed.

Structural ambiguity   Ambiguity that arises from the possibility of parsing a phrase or sentence in more than one way.

Subliminal perception   Perception outside awareness.

Suffix   A bound morpheme that is added to the end of a word stem (for example -ing, -ly and -s).

Supervised learning Learning in a neural network that proceeds by providing the network with a desired or target response to each input.

Supervisory attentional system A term used by Norman and Shallice to describe a system that can heighten a schema's level of activation, allowing it to be in a better position to compete with other schemas for dominance and thus increasing its probability of being selected in contention scheduling.

Synaesthesia A condition in which individuals presented with sensory input of one modality consistently and automatically experience a sensory event in a different modality (for example seeing colour on hearing musical notes).

Synaesthete A person who has the condition synaesthesia.

Synapse The gap between the axon of one neuron and the dendrite of another neuron.

Syntax The study of the rules governing the combinations of words in sentences.

Target Item to be located in visual search.

Templates Stored representations of objects enabling object recognition.

Three-dimensional (3-D) model Third stage in Marr's model of vision. This is a viewer-independent representation of the object which has achieved perceptual constancy or classification.

Time-share Strategy of combining two activities involving dividing resources between the two activities such that the appearance may be created that both are being undertaken simultaneously.

Top-down (or schema-driven) processing Processing which makes use of stored knowledge and schemas to interpret an incoming stimulus (contrasts with **bottom-up processing**).

Two-and-a-half-dimensional (2.5-D) representation Second stage in Marr's theory of vision. Aligns details in primal sketch into a viewer-centred representation of the object.

Varied mapping In Shiffrin and Schneider's (1977) experiment a memory set of to-be-detected items that varied across trials.

Ventral stream Projection from the primary visual cortex to the inferotemporal cortex thought to underlie object perception.

Vigilance task Task requiring sustained attention.

Visual glue In feature integration theory, idea that attention is required to glue, or re-bind, separate visual features into a perceived object.

Visual masking Experimental procedure of following a briefly presented stimulus by random visual noise or fragments of other stimuli. Interferes with or interrupts visual processing.

Visual search Experimental procedure of searching through a field of objects ('distractors') for a desired object ('target').

Visuo-spatial sketchpad A hypothetical component of working memory, which is assumed to provide brief storage for visually-presented items.

Weight The strength of a connection between two nodes in a neural network.

Wernicke's area A region of the brain, normally located in the left temporal region, which is concerned with the perception and comprehension of speech.

Word-length effect The finding that word span in immediate recall is greater for short words than for long words.

Working memory (WM) A hypothetical short-term memory system which serves as a mental workspace in which a variety of processing operations are carried out on both new input and retrieved memories.

References

Ackerly, S. (1937). Instinctive, emotional and mental changes following prefrontal lobe extirpation. *American Journal of Psychiatry*, 92, 717–729.

Addis, D.R. and Tippett, L.J. (2004). Memory of myself: Autobiographical memory and identity in Alzheimer's disease. *Memory*, 12, 56–74.

Adolphs, R. Tranel, D. Damasio, H. and Damasio, A. (1994). Impaired recognition of emotion in facial expressions following bilateral damage to the human amygdala. *Nature*, 372, 669–672.

Aggleton, J.P. and Saunders, R.C. (1997). Anatomical basis of anterograde amnesia. *Memory*, 5, 49–71.

Aglioti, S. DeSouza, J.F.X. and Goodale, M.A. (1995). Size-contrast illusions deceive the eye but not the hand. *Current Biology*, 5, 679–685.

Albert, M.S. Butters, N. and Levin, J. (1979). Temporal gradients in the retrograde amnesia of patients with alcoholic Korsakoff's disease. *Archives of Neurology*, 36, 211–216.

Alderman, N. Burgess, P.W. Knight, C. and Henman, C. (2003). Ecological validity of a simplified version of the multiple errands shopping test. *Journal of the International Neuropsychological Society*, 9, 31–44.

Allport, D.A. (1977). On knowing the meaning of words we are unable to report: The effects of visual masking. In S. Dornic (ed.) *Attention* and *Performance VI*, Hillsdale, NJ: LEA.

Allport, D.A. Antonis , B. and Reynolds P. (1972). On the division of attention: A disproof of the single channel hypothesis. *Quarterly Journal of Experimental Psychology*, 24, 225–235.

Alm, H. and Nilsson, L. (1994). Changes in driver behaviour as a function of hands-free mobile phones: A simulator study. *Accident Analysis and Prevention*, 26, 441–451.

Alzheimer, A. (1907). Über eine eigenartige Erkrankung der Hirnrinde. *Allgemeine Zeitschrift für Psychiatrie Psychoisch-Gerichliche Medicin*, 64, 146–148.

Anderson, J.R. (1980). *Cognitive Psychology and its Implications*. San Francisco: W.H. Freeman.

Anderson, J.R. (1983). *The Architecture of Cognition*. Cambridge, MA: Harvard University Press.

Anderson, J.R. and Bower, G.H. (1972). *Human Associative Memory*. Washington DC: Winston.

Anderson, M.C. (2001). Active forgetting: Evidence for functional inhibition as a source of memory failure. *Journal of Aggression, Maltreatment, and Trauma*, 4, 185–210.

Anderson, M.C. (2003). Rethinking interference theory: Executive control and the mechanisms of forgetting. *Journal of Memory and Language*, 49, 415–445.

Anderson, M.C. Bjork, R.A. and Bjork, E.L. (1994). Remembering can cause forgetting: Retrieval dynamics in long-term memory. *Journal of Experimental Psychology: Learning, Memory, and Cognition*, 20, 1063–1087.

Anderson, M.C. Bjork, R.A. and Bjork, E.L. (2000). Retrieval-induced forgetting: Evidence for a recall-specific mechanism. *Journal of Experimental Psychology: Learning, Memory, and Cognition*, 7, 522–530.

Anderson, M.C. and Neely, J.H. (1996). Interference and inhibition in memory retrieval. In E.L. Bjork and R.A. Bjork (eds), *Memory: Handbook of Perception and Cognition*. New York: Academic Press.

Andrade, J. and Meudell, P.R. (1993). Is spatial information encoded automatically in memory? *Quarterly Journal of Experimental Psychology*, 46A, 365–375.

Andre, L. (2005). Quality of life and ECT. *British Journal of Psychiatry*, 186, 264.

Andrewes, D.G. (2001). *Neuropsychology: From Theory to Practice*. Hove: Psychology Press.

Andrews, B. Brewin, C.R. Ochera, J. Morton, J. Bekerian, D.A. Davies, G.M. and Mollon, P. (1999). The timing, triggers and qualities of recovered memories in therapy. *British Journal of Clinical Psychology*, 39, 11–26.

Andrews, S. (1989). Frequency and neighborhood size effects on lexical access: Activation or search? *Journal of Experimental Psychology: Learning, Memory, and Cognition*, 15, 802–814.

Andrews, S. (1992). Frequency and neighborhood effects on lexical access: Lexical similarity or orthographic redundancy? *Journal of Experimental Psychology: Learning, Memory, and Cognition*, 18, 234–254.

Anolli, L. Antonietti, A. Crisafulli, L. and Cantoia, M. (2001). Accessing source information in analogical problem solving. *The Quarterly Journal of Experimental Psychology*, 54A, 237–261.

Anstis, S. (1998). Picturing peripheral acuity. *Perception*, 27, 817–825.

Armus, S.R. Brookshire, R.H. and Nicholas, L.E. (1989). Aphasic and non-brain-damaged adults' knowledge of scripts for common situations. *Brain and Language*, 36, 518–528.

Assal, G. Favre, C. and Anders, J.P. (1984). Non-reconnaissance d'animaux familièrs chez un paysan: Zooagnosie ou prosopagnosie pour les animaux. *Revue Neurologique*, 140, 580–584.

Atkinson, J. Marshall, J. Smulovitch E. and Woll, B. (2004). Aphasia in a user of British Sign Language. *Cognitive Neuropsychology*, 21, 5, 537–554.

Atkinson, R.C. and Shiffrin, R.M. (1968). Human memory: A proposed system and its control processes. In K.W. Spence and J.T. Spence (eds) *The Psychology of Learning and Motivation* (vol. 2). London: Academic Press.

Baddeley, A.D. (1986). *Working Memory*. Oxford: Clarendon Press.

Baddeley, A.D. (1995). Memory. In C.C. French and A.M. Colman (eds) *Cognitive Psychology*. New York: Longman.

Baddeley, A.D. (1996). Exploring the central executive. *Quarterly Journal of Experimental Psychology*, 49A, 5–28.

Baddeley, A.D. (1997). *Human Memory: Theory and Practice*. Hove: Erlbaum.

Baddeley, A.D. (2000). The episodic buffer: A new component of working memory? *Trends in Cognitive Sciences*, 4, 417–423.

Baddeley, A.D. (2003). Working memory and language: An overview. *Journal of Communication Disorders*, 36, 189–208.

Baddeley, A.D. (2004). The psychology of memory. In A.D. Baddeley, M.D. Kopelman and B.A. Wilson (eds) *The Essential Handbook of Memory Disorders for Clinicians*, Chichester: Wiley.

Baddeley, A.D. Gathercole, S. and Papagno, C. (1998). The phonological loop as a language learning device. *Psychological Review*, 105, 158–173.

Baddeley, A.D. and Hitch, G.J. (1974). Working memory. In G.H. Bower (ed.) *The Psychology of Learning and Motivation* (vol. 8). London: Academic Press.

Baddeley, A.D. Kopelman, M.D. and Wilson B.A. (2004). *The Essential Handbook of Memory Disorders for Clinicians*. Chichester: Wiley.

Baddeley, A.D. and Lewis, V.J. (1981). Inner active processes in reading: The inner voice, the inner ear, and the inner eye. In A.M. Lesgold and C.A. Perfetti (eds) *Interactive Processes in Reading*. Hillsdale, NJ: Lawrence Erlbaum Associates Inc.

Baddeley, A.D. Lewis, V.J. and Vallar, G. (1984). Exploring the articulatory loop. *Quarterly Journal of Experimental Psychology*, 36A, 233–252.

Baddeley, A.D. Thomson, N. and Buchanan, M. (1975). Word length and the structure of short-term memory. *Journal of Verbal Learning and Verbal Behaviour*, 14, 575–589.

Baddeley, A.D. and Warrington, E.K. (1970). Amnesia and the distinction between long- and short-term memory. *Journal of Verbal Learning and Verbal Behaviour*, 9, 176–189.

Baddeley, A.D. and Wilson, B.A. (1988). Frontal amnesia and the dysexecutive syndrome. *Brain and Cognition*, 7, 212–230.

Baddeley, A.D. and Wilson, B.A. (1994). When implicit learning fails: Amnesia and the problem of error elimination. *Neuropsychologia*, 32, 53–68.

Baddeley, A.D. and Wilson, B.A. (2002). Prose recall and amnesia: Implications for the structure of working memory. *Neuropsychologia*, 40, 1737–1743.

Badecker, W. and Caramazza, A. (1985). On considerations of method and theory governing the use of clinical categories in neurolinguistics and cognitive neuropsychology: The case against agrammatism. *Cognition*, 20, 97–125.

Bahrick, H.P. Bahrick, P.O. and Wittlinger, R.P. (1975). Fifty years of memory for names and faces: A cross-sectional approach. *Journal of Experimental Psychology: General*, 104, 54–75.

Bailey, C.H. and Kandel, E.R. (2004). The synaptic growth and persistence of long-term memory: A molecular perspective. In M.S. Gazzaniga (ed.) *The Cognitive Neurosciences* (3rd edition). Cambridge Mass: MIT Press.

Baizer, J.S. Ungerleider, L.G. and Desimone, R. (1991). Organization of visual inputs to the inferior temporal and posterior parietal cortex in macaques. *Journal of Neuroscience*, 11, 1, 168–190.

Baldo, J.V. Delis, D.C. Wilkins, D.P. and Shimamura, A.P. (2004). Is it bigger than a breadbox? Performance of patients with prefrontal lesions on a new executive function test. *Archives of Clinical Neuropsychology*, 19, 407–419.

Balota, D.A. (1992). Visual word recognition: The journey from feature to meaning. In M. Gernsbacher (ed.) *Handbook of Psycholinguistics*. New York: Academic Press.

Bamdad, M.J. Ryan, L.M. and Warden, D.L. (2003). Functional assessment of executive abilities following traumatic brain injury. *Brain Injury*, 17, 1011–1020.

Banich, M.T. (2004). *Cognitive Neuroscience and Neuropsychology*. Boston, MA: Houghton Mifflin.

Barceló, F. (1999). Electrophysiological evidence of two different types of error in the Wisconsin card sorting test. *Neuroreport*, 10, 1299–1303.

Barceló, F. and Knight, R.T. (2002). Both random and perseverative errors underlie WCST deficits in prefrontal patients. *Neuropsychologia*, 40, 349–356.

Barceló, F. Sanz, M. Molina, V. and Rubia, F.J. (1997). The Wisconsin Card Sorting Test and the assessment of frontal function: A validation study with event-related potentials. *Neuropsychologia*, 35, 399–408.

Baron-Cohen, S. (1992). The theory of mind hypothesis of autism: History and prospects of the idea. *The Psychologist*, 5, 9–12.

Baron-Cohen, S. Burt, L. Smith-Laittan, F. and Harrison, J.(1996). Synaesthesia: Prevalence and familiarity. *Perception*, 25, 1073–1080.

Baron-Cohen, S. Harrison, J. Goldstein, L.H. and Wyke, M. (1993). Coloured speech perception: Is synaesthesia what happens when modularity breaks down? *Perception*, 22, 419–426.

Baron-Cohen, S. Wyke, M.A. and Binnie, C. (1987). Hearing words and seeing colours: An experimental investigation of a case of synaesthesia. *Perception*, 16, 761–767.

Bartlett, F.C. (1932). *Remembering*. Cambridge: Cambridge University Press.

Barton, J.J.S. Cherkasova, M.V. and O'Connor, M. (2001). Covert recognition in acquired and developmental prosopagnosia. *Neurology*, 57, 1161–1168.

Barton, J.J.S. Cherkasova, M.V. Press, D.Z. Intriligator, J.M. and O'Connor, M. (2003). Developmental prosopagnosia: A study of three patients. *Brain and Cognition*, 51, 12–30.

Basso, A. Spinnler, H. Vallar, G. and Zanobio, M.E. (1982). Left hemisphere damage and selective impairment of auditory-verbal short-term memory. *Neuropsychologia*, 20, 263–274.

Bates, E. Wilson, S.E. Saygin, A.P. Dick, F. Sereno, M.I. Knight, R.T. and Dronkers, N.F. (2003). Voxel-based lesion symptom mapping. *Nature Neuroscience*, 6, 448–450.

Bay, E. (1953). Disturbances of visual perception and their examination. *Brain*, 76, 515–551.

Baylis, G.C. Driver, J. and Rafal, R.D. (1993). Visual extinction and stimulus repetition. *Journal of Cognitive Neuroscience*, 5, 453–466.

Beauvois, M.F. and Dérouesné, J. (1981). Lexical or orthographic agraphia. *Brain*, 104, 21–42.

Beck, A.T. Rush, A.J. Shaw, B.F. and Emery, G. (1979). *Cognitive Therapy of Depression*. New York: Wiley.

Beck, D.M. Muggleton, N. Walsh, V. and Lavie, N. (2005). Right parietal cortex plays a critical role in change blindness. *Cerebral Cortex*, 15, 1736–1741.

Beck, D.M. Rees, G. Frith, C.D. and Lavie, N. (2001). Neural correlates of change detection and change blindness. *Nature Neuroscience*, 4, 6, 645–650.

Becker, J.T. and Overman, A.A. (2004). The memory deficit in Alzheimer's disease. In A.D. Baddeley, M.D. Kopelman, and B.A.Wilson (eds) *The Essential Handbook of Memory Disorders for Clinicians*. Chichester: Wiley.

Beeman, M. Friedman, R.B. Grafman, J. Perez, E. Diamond, S. and Beadle Lindsay, M.B. (1994). Summation priming and coarse semantic coding in the right hemisphere. *Journal of Cognitive Neuroscience*, 6, 26–45.

Bellugi, U. Wang, P.P. and Jernigan, T.L. (1994). Williams syndrome: An unusual neuropsychological profile. In S.H. Broman and J.Grafman (eds) *Atypical Cognitive Deficits in Developmental Disorders: Implications for Brain Function*. Hillsdale, NJ: Laurence Erlbaum.

Bench, C.J. Frith, C.D. Grasby, P.M. Friston, K.J. Paulesu, E. Frackowiak, R.S.J. and Dolan, R.J. (1993). Investigations of the functional anatomy of attention using the stroop test. *Neuropsychologia*, 31, 907–922.

Benson, D.F. and Geschwind, N. (1971). Aphasia and related cortical disturbances. In A.B. Baker and L.H. Baker (eds) *Clinical Neurology*. New York: Harper and Row.

Benton, A.L. (1991). The prefrontal region: Its early history. In H.S. Levin, H.M. Eisenberg and A.L. Benton (eds) *Frontal Lobe Function and Dysfunction*. Oxford: Oxford University Press.

Beranek, L.L. (1996). *Concert and Opera Halls: How They Sound*. Woodbury, NY: Acoustical Society of America.

Berndt, R.S. (1987). Symptom co-occurrence and dissociation in the interpretation of agrammatism. In M. Coltheart, G. Sartori and P. Job (eds) *The Cognitive Neuropsychology of Language* (pp. 221–233). London: Erlbaum.

Berndt, R.S. and Caramazza, A. (1980). A redefinition of the syndrome of Broca's aphasia: Implications for a neuropsychological model of language. *Applied Psycholinguistics*, 1, 225–278.

Berry, E. and Kapur, N. (2005). Unpublished research cited in *The Psychologist*, 18, 529.

Berti, A. (2002) Unconscious processing in neglect. In H. Karnath, D. Milner and G. Vallar (eds) *The Cognitive and Neural Bases of Spatial Neglect* (pp. 313–326). New York: Oxford University Press.

Berti, A. Rizzolatti, G. (1992). Visual processing without awareness: Evidence from unilateral neglect. *Journal of Cognitive Neuroscience*, 4, 345–351.

Besner, D. Davies, J. and Daniels, S. (1981). Reading for meaning: The effects of concurrent articulation. *Quarterly Journal of Experimental Psychology*, 33A, 415–437.

Bever, T.G. (1970). The cognitive basis for linguistic structures. In J.R. Hayes (ed.) *Cognition and the Development of Language*. New York: Wiley.

Bianchi, L. (1922). *The Mechanisms of the Brain and the Functions of the Frontal Lobes* (trans. J.H. Macdonald). Edinburgh: Livingstone.

Biederman, I. (1987). Recognition-by-components: A theory of human image understanding. *Psychological Review*, 94, 115–147.

Bisiach, E. and Luzzatti, C. (1978). Unilateral neglect of representational space. *Cortex*, 14, 129–133.

Bjork, R.A. and Bjork, E.L. (1992). A new theory of disuse and an old theory of stimulus fluctuation. In A.F. Healy, S.M. Kosslyn, and R.M. Shiffrin (eds) *From Learning Processes to Cognitive Processes: Essays in Honour of William K. Estes* (vol. 2, pp. 35–67). Hillsdale, NJ: Erlbaum.

Blackmore, S. (2001). Consciousness. *The Psychologist*, 14, 522–525.

Blackmore, S. (2003). *Consciousness: An Introduction*. London: Hodder & Stoughton.

Blanchette, I. and Dunbar, K. (2000). How analogies are generated: The roles of structural and superficial similarity. *Memory and Cognition*, 28, 108–124.

Blanchette, I. and Dunbar, K. (2001). Analogy use in naturalistic settings: The influence of audience, emotion, and goals. *Memory and Cognition*, 29, 730–735.

Bliss, T.V.P. and Lomo, T. (1973). Long-lasting potentiation of synaptic transmission in the dentate area of the anaesthetised rabbit following stimulation of the perforant path. *Journal of Physiology*, 232, 331–356.

Blumstein S. Milberg, W. and Shrier, R. (1982). Semantic processing in aphasia: Evidence from an auditory lexical decision task. *Brain and Language*, 17, 301–315.

Bock, J.K. and Levelt, W.J.M. (1994). Language production: Grammatical encoding. In M.A. Gernsbacher (ed.) *Handbook of Psycholinguistics*. London: Academic Press.

Bodamer, J. (1947). Die Prosopa-Agnosie. *Archiv für Psychiatrie und Nervenkrankheiten*, 179, 6–53.

Boon, J.C. and Noone, E. (1994). Changing perspectives in cognitive interviewing. *Psychology, Crime, and Law*, 1, 59–69.

Bornstein, B. Sroka, M. and Munitz, H. (1969). Prosopagnosia with animal face agnosia. *Cortex*, 5, 164–169.

Boucart, M. and Humphreys, G.W. (1992). Global shape cannot be attended without object identification. *Journal of Experimental Psychology: Human Perception and Performance* 18, 3, 785–806.

Boucart, M. and Humphreys, G.W. (1994). Attention to orientation, size, luminance, and colour: Attentional failure within the form domain. *Journal of Experimental Psychology: Human Perception and Performance*, 20, 61–80.

Bower, G.H. (1981). Mood and memory. *The American Psychologist*, 36, 129–220.

Bower, G.H. and Mayer, J.D. (1989). In search of mood-dependent memory: Theory, research, and applications. *Journal of Social Behaviour and Personality*, 4, 121–156.

Bower, G.H. Monteiro, K.P. and Gilligan, S.G. (1978). Emotional mood as a context for learning and recall. *Journal of Verbal Learning and Verbal Behaviour*, 17, 573–585.

Braine, M.D.S. (1978). On the relation between the natural logic of reasoning and standard logic. *Psychological Review*, 85, 1–21.

Braine, M.D.S. and O'Brien, D.P. (1991). A theory of *if*: a lexical entry, reasoning program, and pragmatic principles. *Psychological Review*, 98, 182–203.

Braine, M.D.S. Reiser, B.J. and Rumain, B. (1984). Some empirical justification for a theory of natural propositional logic. In G.H. Bower (ed.) *The Psychology of Learning and Motivation* (vol. 18, pp. 313–371). New York: Academic Press.

Bransford, J.D. and Johnson, M.K. (1972). Contextual prerequisites for understanding: Some investigations of comprehension and recall. *Journal of Verbal Learning and Verbal Behaviour*, 11, 717–726.

Breedin, S.D. Saffran E.M. and Coslett, H.B. (1994). Reversal of the concreteness effect in a patient with semantic dementia. *Cognitive Neuropsychology*, 11, 617–660.

Breggin, P. (1997). *Brain-Disabling Treatments in Psychiatry*. New York: Springer.

Brewin, C.R. (1998). Intrusive memories, depression, and PTSD. *The Psychologist*, 11, 281–283.

Brickner, R.M. (1936). *The Intellectual Functions of the Frontal Lobes*. New York: Macmillan.

Bridgeman, B. (1992). Conscious vs unconscious processing: The case of vision. *Theory and Psychology*, 2, 1, 73–88.

Bridgeman, B. Peery, S. and Anand, S. (1997). Interaction of cognitive and sensorimotor maps of visual space. *Perception and Psychophysics*, 59, 3, 456–469.

Broadbent, D.E. (1958). *Perception and Communication*. Oxford: Pergamon.

Broadbent, D.E. (1982). Task combination and the selective intake of information. *Acta Psychologica*, 50, 253–290.

Broadbent, D.E. Cooper, P.E. Fitzgerald, P. and Parkes, K.R. (1982). The Cognitive Failures Questionnaire (CFQ) and its correlates. *British Journal of Clinical Psychology*, 21, 1–16.

Broca, P. (1861). Perte de la parole: Ramollissement chronique et destruction partielle du lobe antérieur gauche du cerveau. *Bulletin de la Société d'anthropologie* (Paris), 2, 235–238.

Broman, M. (2001). Spaced retrieval: A behavioural approach to memory improvement in Alzheimer's and related dementias. *NYS Psychologist*, 13, 35–40.

Brooks, R.A. (1991). New approaches to robotics. *Science*, 253, 5025, 1227–1232.

Brown, A.S. (2002). Consolidation theory and retrograde amnesia in humans. *Psychonomic Bulletin and Review*, 9, 403–425.

Brown, A.S. (2004). *The Déjà Vu Experience*. Hove: Psychology Press.

Brown, A.S. and Murphy, D.R. (1989). Cryptomnesia: Delineating inadvertent plagiarism. *Journal of Experimental Psychology: Learning, Memory, and Cognition*, 15, 432–442.

Brown, J. (1958). Some tests of the decay theory of immediate memory. *Quarterly Journal of Experimental Psychology*, 10, 12–21.

Brown, R. and Kulik, J. (1977). Flashbulb memories. *Cognition*, 5, 73–99.

Brown, R. and McNeill, D. (1966). The 'tip-of-the-tongue' phenomenon. *Journal of Verbal Learning and Verbal Behaviour*, 5, 325–337.

Brownell, H. Gardner, H. Prather, P. and Martino, G. (1995). Language, communication, and the right hemisphere. In H.S. Kirshner (ed.) *Handbook of Neurological Speech and Language Disorders: Neurological Disease and Therapy* (vol. 33, pp. 325–350). New York: Marcel Dekker.

Brownell, H.H. Michel, D. Powelson, J.A. and Gardner, H. (1983). Surprise but not coherence: Sensitivity to verbal humor in right hemisphere patients. *Brain and Language*, 18, 20–27.

Bruce, V. Green, P.R. and Georgeson, M.A. (1996). *Visual Perception, Physiology, Psychology and Ecology* (3rd edn). Hove: Psychology Press.

Bruce, V. and Humphreys, G.W. (1994). Recognizing objects and faces. *Visual Cognition*, 1, 141–180.

Bruce, V. and Young, A. (1986). Understanding face recognition. *British Journal of Psychology*, 77, 305–327.

Bruner, J.S. Goodnow, J.J. and Austin, G.A. (1956). *A Study of Thinking*. New York: Wiley.

Bruner, J.S. and Postman, L. (1947). Tension and tension-release as organising factors in perception. *Journal of Personality*, 15, 300–308.

Bruyer, R. (1991). Covert face recognition in prosopagnosia — A review. *Brain and Cognition*, 15, 2, 223–335.

Bruyer, R. Laterre, C. Seron, X. Feyereisen, P. Strypstein, E. Pierrard, E. and Rectem, D. (1983). A case of prosopagnosia with some preserved covert remembrance of familiar faces. *Brain and Cognition*, 2, 257–284.

Buchan, H. Johnstone, E. McPherson, K. Palmer, R.L. Crow, T.J. and Brandon, S. (1992). Who benefits from electroconvulsive therapy? *British Journal of Psychiatry*, 160, 345–349.

Buchner, A. and Brandt, M. (2003). The principle of multiple memory systems. In R.H. Kluwe and G. Lueer (eds) *Principles of Learning and Memory*. Cambridge, MA: Birkhaeuser.

Buckner, R.L. (2000). Neuroimaging of memory. In M.S. Gazzaniga (ed.) *The New Cognitive Neurosciences* (2nd edn). Cambridge, MA: MIT Press.

Bullier, J. and Nowak, L.G. (1995). Parallel versus serial processing: New vistas on the distributed organization of the visual system. *Current Opinion in Neurobiology*, 5, 4, 497–503.

Burgess, P.W. Alderman, N. Evans, J. Emslie, H. and Wilson, B.A. (1998). The ecological validity of tests of executive function. *Journal of the International Neuropsychological Society*, 4, 547–558.

Burgess, P.W. and Shallice, T. (1994). Fractionation of the frontal-lobe syndrome. *Revue de Neuropsychologie*, 4, 345–370.

Burgess, P.W. and Shallice, T. (1996a). Response suppression, initiation and strategy use following frontal lobe lesions. *Neuropsychologia*, 34, 263–273.

Burgess, P.W. and Shallice, T. (1996b). Bizarre responses, rule detection and frontal lobe lesions. *Cortex*, 32, 241–259.

Butera, F. Caverni, J.-P. and Rossi, S. (2005). Interaction with a high- versus low-competence influence source in inductive reasoning. *Journal of Social Psychology*, 145, 173–190.

Butters, N. and Cermak, L.S. (1986). A case study of the forgetting of autobiographical knowledge: Implications for the study of retrograde amnesia. In D.C. Rubin (ed.) *Autobiographical Memory*. Cambridge: Cambridge University Press.

Byrne, R.M.J. (1989). Suppressing valid inferences with conditionals. *Cognition*, 31, 61–83.

Calder, A.J. Young, A.W. Rowland, D. Perrett, D.I. Hodges, J.R. and Etcoff, N.L. (1996). Facial emotion recognition after bilateral amydala damage: Differentially severe impairment of fear. *Cognitive Neuropsychology*, 13, 699–745.

Campbell, D. (1909). Störungen der Merkfähigkeit und fehlenders Krankheitsgefühl bei einem Fall von Stirnhirntumor. *Monatsschrift für Psychiatrie*, 26, 33–41.

Campbell, R. and Conway, M.A. (1995). *Broken Memories*. Oxford: Blackwell.

Campbell, R. Landis, T. and Regard, M. (1986). Face recognition and lip reading: A neurological dissociation. *Brain*, 109, 509–521.

Campion, J. and Latto, R. (1985). Apperceptive agnosia due to carbon monoxide poisoning: An interpretation based on critical band masking from disseminated lesions. *Behavioural Brain Research*, 15, 227–240.

Campion, J. Latto, R. and Smith, Y.M. (1983). Is blindsight an effect of scattered light, spared cortex, and near-threshold vision? *Behavioural and Brain Sciences*, 6, 423–428.

Caplan, D. (1986). In defense of agrammatism. *Cognition*, 24, 263–276.

Caplan, D. (1992). *Language: Structure, Processing and Disorders*. Cambridge, MA: MIT Press.

Caplan, D. and Hildebrandt, N. (1988). *Disorders of Syntactic Comprehension*. Cambridge, MA: MIT Press.

Caramazza, A. (1984). The logic of neuropsychological research and the problem of patient classification of aphasia. *Brain and Language*, 21, 9–20.

Caramazza, A. and Badecker, W. (1991). Clinical syndromes are not God's gift to cognitive neuropsychology: A reply to a rebuttal to an answer to a response to the case against syndrome-based research. *Brain and Cognition*, 16, 211–227.

Caramazza, A. Capitani, E. Rey A. and Berndt, R.S. (2001). Agrammatic Broca's aphasia is not associated with a single pattern of comprehension performance. *Brain and Language*, 76, 158–184.

Caramazza, A. and Zurif, E.B. (1976). Dissociation of algorithmic and heuristic processes in language comprehension. *Brain and Language*, 3, 572–582.

Carpenter, S. (2001). Everyday fantasia: The world of synaesthesia. *Monitor on Psychology*, 32.

Cavaco, S. Anderson, S.W. Allen, J.S. Castro-Caldas, A. and Damasio, H. (2004). The scope of preserved procedural memory in amnesia. *Brain*, 127, 1853–1867.

Ceci, S.J. (1995). False beliefs: Some developmental and clinical considerations. In D.L. Schacter (ed.) *Memory Distortions*. Cambridge, MA: Harvard University Press.

Cermak, L.S. and O'Connor, M. (1983). The anterograde and retrograde retrieval ability of a patient with amnesia due to encephalitis. *Neuropsychologia*, 21, 213–234.

Cermak, L.S. Talbot, N. Chandler, K. and Woolbarst, L.R. (1985). The perceptual priming phenomenon in amnesia. *Neuropsychologia*, 23, 615–622.

Chalmers, D.J. (1995). The puzzle of conscious experience. *Scientific American*, 62–68.

Chase, W.G. and Simon, H.A. (1973). Perception in Chess. *Cognitive Psychology*, 4, 55–81.

Cheesman, J. and Merikle, P.M. (1986). Distinguishing conscious from unconscious perceptual processes. *Canadian Journal of Psychology*, 40, 343–367.

Chen, Z. Mo, L. and Honomichl, R. (2004). Having the memory of an elephant: Long-term retrieval and the use of analogues in problem solving. *Journal of Experimental Psychology: General*, 133, 415–433.

Cheng, P.W. and Holyoak, K.J. (1985). Pragmatic reasoning schemas. *Cognitive Psychology*, 17, 391–416.

Cheng, P.W. Holyoak, K.J. Nisbett, R.E. and Oliver, L.M. (1986). Pragmatic versus syntactic approaches to training deductive reasoning. *Cognitive Psychology*, 18, 293–328.

Cherry, E.C. (1953). Some experiments on the recognition of speech with one and two ears. *Journal of the Acoustical Society of America*, 25, 975–979.

Cherry, K.E. Park, D.C. Frieske, D.A. and Rowley, R.L. (1993). The effect of verbal elaborations on memory in young and older adults. *Memory* and *Cognition*, 21, 725–738.

Chi, M.T.H. Feltovich, P.J. and Glaser, R. (1981). Categorization and representation of physics problems by experts and novices. *Cognitive Science*, 5, 121–152.

Chomsky, N. (1957). *Syntactic Structures*. The Hague: Mouton.

Chomsky, N. (1965). *Aspects of the Theory of Syntax*. Cambridge, MA: MIT Press.

Chomsky, N. (1981). *Lectures on Government and Binding*. Dordrecht: Foris.

Chomsky, N. (1986). *Knowledge of Language*. New York: Praeger Special Studies.

Chronicle, E.P. MacGregor, J.N. and Ormerod, T.C. (2004). What makes an insight problem? The roles of heuristics, goal conception, and solution recording in knowledge-lean problems. *Journal of Experimental Psychology: Learning, Memory, and Cognition*, 30, 14–27.

Chu, S. and Downes, J.J. (2000). Long live Proust: The odour-cued autobiographical memory bump. *Cognition*, 75, 41–50.

Churchland, P. and Sejnowski, T. (1994). *The Computational Brain*. Cambridge, MA: MIT Press (Bradford Books).

Cicerone, K. Lazar, R. and Shapiro, W. (1983). Effects of frontal lobe lesions on hypothesis sampling during concept formation. *Neuropsychologia*, 21, 513–524.

Claparede, E. (1911). Recognition et moité. *Archives Psychologiques Geneve*, 11, 79–90.

Clare, L. Baddeley, A.D. Moniz-Cook, E. and Woods, R. (2003). A quiet revolution. *The Psychologist*, 16, 250–254.

Clare, L. Wilson, B.A. Breen, E.K. and Hodges, J.R. (1999). Errorless learning of face-name associations in early Alzheimer's disease. *Neurocase*, 5, 37–46.

Claret, P.L. Castillob, J.d.D.L.d. Moleónc, J.J.J. Cavanillasc, A.B. Martínc, M.G. and Vargasc, R.G. (2003). Age and sex differences in the risk of causing vehicle collisions in Spain, 1990 to 1999. *Accident Analysis and Prevention*, 35, 2, 261–272.

Clark, A. (1990). *Microcognition: Philosophy, Cognitive Science and Parallel Distributed Processing*. Cambridge, MA: MIT Press (Bradford Books).

Clark, A. (1997). *Being There: Putting Brain, Body, and World Together Again*. Cambridge, MA: The MIT Press.

Clark, A. (1999). An embodied cognitive science? *Trends in Cognitive Sciences*, 3, 9, 345–351.

Clark, H.H. and Clark, E.V. (1977). *Psychology and Language: An Introduction to Psycholinguistics*. New York: Harcourt Brace Jovanovich.

Clark, H.H. and Haviland, S.E. (1977). Comprehension and the given-new contract. In R. Freedle (ed.) *Discourse Processes: Advances in Research and Theory*. Norwood, NJ: Ablex.

Clark, H.H. and Krych, M.A. (2004). Speaking while monitoring addressees for understanding. *Journal of Memory and Language*, 50, 62–81.

Claxton, G. (1998). Knowing without knowing why. *The Psychologist*, 11, 217–220.

Cohen, G. (1983). *The Psychology of Cognition* (2nd edn). London: Academic Press.

Cohen, N.J. (1997). Memory. In M.T. Banich (ed.) *Neuropsychology*, Boston, MA: Houghton Mifflin.

Cohen, N.J. and Eichenbaum, H.E. (1993). *Memory, Amnesia, and the Hippocampal System*. Cambridge, MA: MIT Press.

Cohen, N.J. Ramzy, C. Hu, Z. Tomaso, H. Strupp, J. Erhard, P. Anderson, P. and Ugurbil, K. (1994). Hippocampal activation in fMRI evoked by demand for declarative memory-based binding of multiple streams of information. *Society for Neuroscience Abstracts*, 20, 1290.

Cohen, N.J. and Squire, L.R. (1980). Preserved learning and retention of pattern-analysing skill in amnesia: Dissociation of knowing how and knowing that. *Science*, 210, 207–210.

Cohen, N.J. and Squire, L.R. (1981). Retrograde amnesia and remote memory impairment. *Neuropsychologia*, 19, 337–356.

Colangelo, A. Holden, J.G. Buchanan, L. and Van Orden G.C. (2004). Speculation about behavior, brain damage, and self-organisation: The other way to herd a cat. *Brain and Language*, 90, 151–159.

Colchester, A. Kingsley, D. Lasserson, D. Kendell, B. Bello, F. Rush, C. Stevens, T. Goodman, G. Heilpern, G. Stanhope, N. and Kopelman, M.D. (2001). Structural MRI volumetric analysis in patients with organic amnesia, 1: methods and findings, comparative findings across diagnostic groups. *Journal of Neurology, Neurosurgery, and Psychiatry*, 71, 13–22.

Cole, B.L. and Hughes, P.K. (1984). A field trial of attention and search conspicuity. *Human Factors*, 26, 3, 299–313.

Collette, F. and Van der Linden, M. (2002). Brain imaging of the central executive component of working memory. *Neuroscience and Biobehavioural Reviews*, 26, 105–125.

Collins, A. and Loftus, E. (1975). A spreading activation theory of semantic processing. *Psychological Review*, 82, 407–428.

Collins, A. and Quillian, M. (1969). Retrieval time from semantic memory. *Journal of Verbal Learning and Verbal Behaviour*, 8, 240–248.

Coltheart, M. (1980a). Deep dyslexia: A review of the syndrome. In M. Coltheart, K.E. Patterson and J.C. Marshall (eds.) *Deep Dyslexia* (pp. 22–47). London: Routledge and Kegan Paul.

Coltheart, M. (1980b). Iconic memory and visible persistence. *Perception and Psychophysics*, 27, 183–228.

Coltheart, M. (1987). Reading, phonological recoding and deep dyslexia. In M. Coltheart, K.E. Patterson and J.C. Marshall (eds) *Deep Dyslexia*. London: Routledge and Kegan Paul.

Coltheart, M. Davelaar, E. Jonasson, J.T. and Besner, D. (1977). Access to the internal lexicon. In S. Dornic (ed.) *Attention and Performance VI* (pp. 535–555). London: Academic Press.

Connine, C.M. Mullennix, J. Shernoff, E. and Yelen, J. (1990). Word familiarity and frequency in visual and auditory word recognition. *Journal of Experimental Psychology: Learning, Memory, and Cognition*, 16, 1084–1096.

Conroy, M.A. Hopkins, R.O. and Squire, L.R. (2005). On the contribution of perceptual fluency and priming to recognition memory. *Cognitive, Affective, and Behavioural Neuroscience*, 5, 14–20.

Conway, M.A. (1997). *Recovered Memories and False Memories*. Oxford: Oxford University Press.

Corkin, S. (1968). Acquisition of motor skill after bilateral medial temporal-lobe excision. *Neuropsychologia*, 6, 255–265.

Corkin, S. Amaral, D.G. Gonzalez, R.G. Johnson, K.A. and Hyman, B.T. (1997). H.M.'s medial temporal lobe lesion: Findings from magnetic resonance imaging. *Journal of Neuroscience*, 17, 3964–3979.

Corsi, P.M. (1972). Human memory and the medial temporal region of the brain. Unpublished thesis, cited in S. Della Sala, C. Gray, A.D. Baddeley, N. Allamano and N. Wilson (1999). Pattern span: A tool for unwelding visuo-spatial memory. *Neuropsychologia*, 37, 1189–1199.

Coulson, S. and Wu, Y.C. (2005). Right Hemisphere activation of joke-related information: An event-related brain potential study. *Journal of Cognitive Neuroscience*, 17, 3, 494–506.

Cowan, N. (1988). Evolving conceptions of memory storage, selective attention, and their mutual constraints within the human information processing system. *Psychological Bulletin*, 96, 341–370.

Cowan, N. (2005). *Working Memory Capacity.* Hove: Psychology Press.

Cowey, A. (2004). The 30th Sir Frederick Bartlett lecture. Fact, artefact, and myth about blindsight. *The Quarterly Journal of Experimental Psychology*, 57A, 577–609.

Cowey, A. and Azzopardi, P. (2001). Is blindsight motion blind? In B. de Gelder, E. de Haan and C.A. Heywood (eds) *Out of Mind* (pp. 87–103). Oxford: Oxford University Press.

Cowey, A. Small, M. and Ellis, S. (1994). Left visuo-spatial neglect can be worse in far than in near space. *Neurospychologia*, 32, 1059–1066.

Craik, F.I.M. (1970). The fate of items in primary memory. *Journal of Verbal Learning and Verbal Behaviour*, 9, 143–148.

Craik, F.I.M. (1977). Depth of processing in recall and recognition. In S. Dornik (ed.) *Attention and Performance* (vol. 6, pp. 679–698). New York: Raven Press.

Craik, F.I.M. (2002). Levels of processing: Past, present . . . and future? *Memory*, 10, 305–318.

Craik, F.I.M. and Lockhart, R.S. (1972). Levels of processing: A framework for memory research. *Journal of Verbal Learning and Verbal Behaviour*, 11, 671–684.

Craik, F.I.M. and McDowd, J.M. (1987). Age differences in recall and recognition. *Journal of Experimental Psychology: Learning, Memory, and Cognition*, 13, 474–479.

Craik, F.I.M. Morris, L.W. Morris, R.G. and Loewen, E.R. (1990). Relations between source amnesia and frontal functioning in older patients. *Psychology of Ageing*, 5, 148–151.

Craik, F.I.M. and Tulving, E. (1975). Depth of processing and the retention of words in episodic memory. *Journal of Experimental Psychology, General*, 104, 268–294.

Crain, S. and Steedman, M.J. (1985). On not being led up the garden path: The use of context by the psychological parser. In D. Dowty, L. Karttunen and A. Zwicky (eds) *Natural Language Parsing* (pp. 320–358). Cambridge: Cambridge University Press.

Creem, S.H. and Proffitt, D.R. (1998). Two memories for geographical slant: Separation and interdependence of action and awareness. *Psychonomic Bulletin and Review*, 5, 1, 22–36.

Crick, F. (1994). *The Astonishing Hypothesis.* London: Simon and Schuster.

Crick, F. and Koch, C. (1990). Towards a neurobiological theory of consciousness. *Seminars in the Neurosciences*, 2, 263–275.

Crinella, F.M. and Yu, J. (2000). Brain mechanisms and intelligence. Psychometric *g* and executive function. *Intelligence*, 27, 299–327.

Dallenbach, K.M. (1951). A puzzle-picture with a new principle of concealment. *American Journal of Psychology*, 64, 431–433.

Damasio, A. Eslinger, P.J. Damasio, H. Van Hoesen, G.W. and Cornell, S. (1985). Multi-modal amnesic syndrome following bilateral temporal and basal forebrain lesions. *Archives of Neuropsychology*, 42, 252–259.

Damasio, H. Tranel, D. Grabowski, T. Adolphs, R. and Damasio, A. (2004). Neural systems behind word and concept retrieval. *Cognition*, 92, 179–229.

Davidson, P.S.R. and Glisky, E.L. (2002). Is flashbulb memory a special instance of source memory? Evidence from older adults. *Memory*, 10, 99–111.

Davies, G.M. and Dalgleish, T. (2001). *Recovered Memories: Seeking the Middle Ground.* Chichester: Wiley.

Davies, G.M. and Thomson, D.M. (1988). *Memory in Context: Context in Memory.* Chichester: Wiley.

Davies, S.P. (2000). Move evaluation as a predictor and moderator of success in solutions to well-structured problems. *The Quarterly Journal of Experimental Psychology*, 53A, 1186–1201.

Davis, H.P. Small, S.A. Stern, Y. Mayeux, R. Feldstein, S.N. and Keller, F.R. (2003). Acquisition, recall, and forgetting of verbal information in long-term memory by young, middle-aged, and elderly individuals. *Cortex*, 39, 1063–1091.

REFERENCES

Day, R.H. (1989). Natural and artificial cues, perceptual compromise and the basis of veridical and illusory perception. In D. Vickers and P.L. Smith (eds) *Human Information Processing: Measures and Mechanisms* (pp. 107–109). Amsterdam: Elsevier.

Dayhoff, J. (1990). *Neural Network Architectures: An Introduction*. New York: Van Nostrand Reinhold.

De Gelder, B. de Haan, E.H.F. and Heywood, C.A. (2001). *Out of Mind: Varieties of Unconscious Processes*. Oxford: Oxford University Press.

De Haan, E.H.F. (1999). A familial factor in the development of face recognition deficits. *Journal of Clinical and Experimental Neuropsychology*, 21, 312–315.

De Haan, E.H.F. Young, A.W. and Newcombe, F. (1987). Face recognition without awareness. *Cognitive Neuropsychology*, 4, 385–415.

De Monte, V.E. Geffen, G.M. Kwapil, K. (2005). Test-retest reliability and practice effects of a rapid screen test of mild traumatic brain injury. *Journal of Clinical and Experimental Neuropsychology*, 27, 624–632.

De Renzi, E. Faglioni, P. Grossi, D. and Nichelli, P. (1991). Apperceptive and associative forms of prosopagnosia. *Cortex*, 27, 213–221.

DeGroot, A.D. (1965). *Thought and Choice in Chess*. The Hague: Mouton.

Dekle, D.J. Beal, C.R. Elliott, R. and Huneycutt, D. (1996). Children as witnesses: A comparison of lineup versus showup identification methods. *Applied Cognitive Psychology*, 10, 1–12.

Delis, D.C. Squire, L.R. Bihrle, A. and Massman, P. (1992). Componental analysis of problem-solving ability: Performance of patients with frontal lobe damage and amnesic patients on a new sorting test. *Neuropsychologia*, 30, 683–697.

Dell, G.S. (1986). A spreading-activation theory of retrieval in sentence production. *Psychological Review*, 93, 283–321.

Dell, G.S. (1995). Speaking and misspeaking. In L.R. Gleitman and M. Liberman (eds) *Language: An Invitation to Cognitive Science* (vol. 1, 2nd edn). Cambridge, MA: MIT Press.

Dell, G.S. Burger, L.K. and Svec, W.R. (1997). Language production and serial order: A functional analysis and a model. *Psychological Review*, 104, 123–147.

Dell, G.S. Gordon, J.K. Harris, H.D. and Lawler, E.N. (2004). Models of errors of omission in aphasic naming. *Cognitive Neuropsychology*, 21, 125–145.

Dell, G.S. and O'Seaghdha, P.G. (1991). Mediated and convergent lexical priming in language production: A comment on Levelt *et al.* (1991). *Psychological Review*, 98, 604–614.

Della Sala, S. Gray, C. Spinnler, H. and Trivelli, C. (1998). Frontal lobe functioning in man. *Archives of Clinical Neuropsychology*, 13, 663–682.

Deloche, G. Andreewsky, E. and Desi, M. (1982). Surface dyslexia: A case report and some theoretical implications for reading models. *Brain and Language*, 15, 12–31.

Denes, G. and Semenza, C. (1975). Auditory modality-specific anomia: Evidence from a case of pure word deafness. *Cortex*, 11, 401–411.

Deutsch, D. (2003). *Phantom Worlds and Other Curiosities*. Philomel Records (CD-ROM).

Deutsch, J.A. and Deutsch, D. (1967). Comments on 'Selective attention: perception or response?' *Quarterly Journal of Experimental Psychology*, 19, 362–363.

Di Lollo, V. Enns, J.T. and Rensink, R.A. (2000). Competition for consciousness among visual events: The psychophysics of reentrant visual processes. *Journal of Experimental Psychology: General*, 129, 4, 481–507.

Dixon, M.J. Smilek, C.C. and Merikle, P.M. (2000). Five plus two equals yellow: Mental arithmetic in people with synaesthesia is not coloured by visual experience. *Nature*, 406, 365.

Dixon, M.J. Smilek, D. and Merikle, M. (2004).Not all synaesthetes are created equal: Projector versus associator synaesthetes. *Cognitive, Affective, and Behavioral Neuroscience*, 4, 335–343.

Dixon, N.F. (1981). *Preconscious Processing*. Chichester: Wiley.

Dixon, N.F. and Henley, S.H.A. (1974). Without awareness. In M. Jeeves (ed.) *Psychology Survey No. 3*. London: George Allen & Unwin.

Dreyfus, H. (1972). *What Computers Can't Do – The Limits of Artificial Intelligence*. New York: Harper and Row.

Dreyfus, H. (1979). *What Computers Still Can't Do: A Critique of Artificial Reason*. Cambridge, MA: MIT Press.

Driver, J. (1996). Attention and segmentation. *The Psychologist*, 9, 3, 119–124.

Driver, J. and Baylis, G.C. (1989). Movement and visual attention: The spotlight metaphor breaks down. *Journal of Experimental Psychology: Human Perception and Performance*, 15, 448–456.

Dronkers, N. (1996). A new brain region for coordinating speech articulation. *Nature*, 384, 159–161.

Dronkers, N.F. Redfern, B.B. and Knight, R.T. (2000). The neural architecture of language disorders. In M.S. Gazzaniga (ed.) *The New Cognitive Neurosciences* (pp. 949–958). Cambridge, MA: MIT Press.

Dronkers, N.F. Redfern B.B. and Ludy, C.A. (1995). Lesion localization in chronic Wernicke's aphasia. *Brain and Language*, 51, 1, 62–65.

Dror, I.E. and Gallogly, D.P. (1999). Computational analyses in cognitive neuroscience: In defense of biological implausibility. *Psychonomic Bulletin and Review*, 6, 2, 173–182.

Drosopoulos, S. Wagner, U. and Born, J. (2005). Sleep enhances explicit recollection in recognition memory. *Learning and Memory*, 12, 44–51.

Duchaine, B.C. and Nakayama, K. (2004). Developmental prosopagnosia and the Benton Facial Recognition test. *Neurology*, 62, 1219–1220.

Duffy, P.L. (2001). *Blue Cats and Chartreuse Kittens: How Synaesthetes Colour Their World*. New York: W.H. Freeman.

Duncan, J. Emslie, H. and Williams, P. (1996). Intelligence and the frontal lobe: The organization of goal-directed behavior. *Cognitive Psychology*, 30, 257–303.

Duncan, J. and Humphreys, G.W. (1992). Beyond the search surface: Visual search and attentional engagement. *Journal of Experimental Psychology: Human Perception and Performance*, 18, 578–588.

Duncker, K. (1945). On problem solving. *Psychological Monographs*, 58 (Whole No. 270).

Durie, B. (2005). Doors of perception. *New Scientist*, 185, 2484, 34–36.

Ebbinghaus, H. (1885). *Über das Gedächtnis: Untersuchugen zur experimentellen Psychologie*. Leipzig: Dunker & Humbolt.

Edgar, G.K. Edgar, H.E. and Curry, M.B. (2003). 'Using signal detection theory to measure situation awareness in command and control'. Paper presented at the Human Factors and Ergonomics Society 47th Annual Meeting, Denver, Colorado.

Edworthy, J. Hellier, E.J. Walters, K. Clift-Matthews, W. and Crowther, M. (2003). Acoustic, semantic and phonetic influences in spoken warning signal words. *Applied Cognitive Psychology*, 17, 915–933.

Egeth, H.E. and Yantis, S. (1997). Visual attention: Control, representation, and time course. *Annual Review of Psychology*, 48, 269–297.

Eich, E. (1985). Context memory, and integrated item/context imagery. *Journal of Experimental Psychology: Learning, Memory, and Cognition*, 11, 764–770.

Ekman, P. and Friesen, W.V. (1976). *Pictures of Facial Affect*. Palo Alto, CA: Consulting Psychologists Press.

Ellis, A.W. (1984). Introduction to Bramwell's (1887) case of word-meaning deafness. *Cognitive Neuropsychology*, 1, 245–248.

Ellis, A.W. and Young, A.W. (1996). *Human Cognitive Neuropsychology* (augmented edn with readings). Hove: Lawrence Erlbaum Associates.

Ellis, H.D. and Shepherd, J.W. (1974). Recognition of abstract and concrete words presented in left and right visual fields. *Journal of Experimental Psychology*, 103, 1035–1036.

Ellis, R. and Humphreys, G.W. (1999). *Connectionist Psychology: A Text with Readings*. Hove: Psychology Press.

Enns, J.T. and Di Lollo, V. (2000). What's new in visual masking? *Trends in Cognitive Sciences*, 4, 9, 345–352.

Erdelyi, M.H. (1974). A new look at the New Look: Perceptual defense and vigilance. *Psychological Review*, 81, 1–25.

Ericsson, K.A. and Kintsch, W. (1995). Long-term working memory. *Psychological Review*, 102, 211–245.

Eriksen, C.W. (1990). Attentional search of the visual field. In D. Brogan (ed.) *Visual Search*. London: Taylor & Francis.

Esgate, A. and Groome, D.H. (2005). *An Introduction to Applied Cognitive Psychology*. Hove: Psychology Press.

Eskes, G.A. Szostak, C. and Stuss, D.T. (2003). Role of the frontal lobes in implicit and explicit retrieval tasks. *Cortex*, 39, 847–869.

Eslinger, P.J. and Damasio, A.R. (1985). Severe disturbance of higher cognition after bilateral frontal lobe ablation: Patient E.V.R. *Neurology, Cleveland*, 35, 1731–1741.

Evans, J.J. Graham, K.S. Pratt, K.H. and Hodges, J.R. (2003). The impact of disrupted cortico-cortico connectivity: A long-term follow-up of a case of focal retrograde amnesia. *Cortex*, 39, 767–790.

Evans, J.St.B.T. (1989). *Bias in Human Reasoning: Causes and Consequences*. Hove: Erlbaum.

Evans, J.St.B.T. (1996). Deciding before you think: Relevance and reasoning in the selection task. *British Journal of Psychology*, 87, 223–240.

Evans, J.St.B.T. (2003). In two minds: dual process accounts of reasoning. *Trends in Cognitive Science*, 7, 454–459.

Evans, J.St.B.T. Barston, J.L. and Pollard, P. (1983). On the conflict between logic and belief in syllogistic reasoning. *Memory and Cognition*, 11, 295–306.

Evans, J.St.B.T. Handley, S.J. Harper, C.M.J. and Johnson-Laird, P.N. (1999). Reasoning about necessity and possibility: A test of the mental model theory of deduction. *Journal of Experimental Psychology: Learning, Memory, and Cognition*, 25, 1495–1513.

Evans, J.St.B.T. and Lynch, J.S. (1973). Matching bias in the selection task. *British Journal of Psychology*, 64, 391–397.

Evans, J.St.B.T. and Over, D.E. (1996). *Rationality and Reasoning*. Hove: Psychology Press.

Eysenck, M.W. (1979). Depth, elaboration, and distinctiveness. In L.S. Cermak and F.I.M. Craik (eds.) *Levels of Processing in Human Memory*. Hillsdale, NJ: Lawrence Erlbaum Associates Inc.

Eysenck, M.W. and Keane, M.T. (2005). *Cognitive Psychology: A Student's Handbook*. Hove: Psychology Press.

Farah, M.J. (1990). *Visual Agnosia: Disorders of Object Recognition and What They Can Tell Us about Normal Vision*. Cambridge, MA: MIT Press.

Farah, M.J. (1991). Patterns of co-occurence among the associative agnosias: Implications for visual object representation. *Cognitive Neuropsychology*, 8, 1–19.

Farah, M.J. (2004). *Visual Agnosia* (2nd edn). Cambridge, MA: MIT Press.

Farah, M.J. Hammond, K.M. Levind, D.N. and Calvanio, R. (1988). Visual and spatial mental imagery: Dissociable systems of representation. *Cognitive Psychology*, 20, 439–462.

Farah, M.J. Hammond, K.M. Mehta, Z. and Ratcliff, G. (1989). Category-specificity and modality-specificity in semantic memory. *Neuropsychologia*, 27, 193–200.

Farah, M.J. Levinson, K.L. and Klein, K.L. (1995). Face perception and within-category discrimination in prosopagnosia. *Neuropsychologica*, 33, 661–674.

Farah, M.J. McMullen, P.A. and Meyer, M.M. (1991). Can recognition of living things be selectively impaired? *Neuropsychologia*, 29, 185–193.

Felleman, D.J. and Van Essen, D.C. (1991). Distributed hierarchical processing in primate visual cortex. *Cerebral Cortex*, 1, 1–47.

Ferrand, L. and Grainger, J. (2003). Homophonic interference effects in visual word recognition. *Quarterly Journal of Experimental Psychology*, 56A, 403–419.

Ferreira, F. Lau, E.F. and Bailey, K.G.D. (2003). Disfluencies, language comprehension, and tree adjoining grammars. *Cognitive Science*, 28, 721–749.

Ferrier, D. (1876). *The Functions of the Brain*. London: Smith, Elder.

Fisher, R.P. and Craik, F.I.M. (1977). Interaction between encoding and retrieval operations in cued recall. *Journal of Experimental Psychology: Human Learning and Memory*, 3, 701–711.

Fisher, R.P. Geiselman, R.E. and Amador, M. (1990). A field test of the cognitive interview: Enhancing the recollections of actual victims and witnesses of crime. *Journal of Applied Psychology*, 74, 722–727.

Fleischman, D.A. Wilson, R.S. Gabrieli, J.D.E. Bienias, J.L. and Bennett, D.A. (2004). A longitudinal study of implicit and explicit memory loss in old persons. *Psychology and Ageing*, 19, 617–625.

Flin, R. Boon, J. Knox, A. and Bull, R. (1992). The effect of a five-month delay on children's and adult's eyewitness memory. *British Journal of Psychology*, 83, 323–336.

Fodor, J.A. (1983). *The Modularity of Mind*. Cambridge, MA: MIT Press.

Fodor, J. Bever, T.G. and Garrett, M.F. (1974). *The Psychology of Language*. New York: McGraw-Hill.

Forster, K.I. (1976). Accessing the mental lexicon. In R.J. Wales and E.C.T. Walker (eds) *New Approaches to Language Mechanisms*. Amsterdam: North Holland.

Forster, K.I. (1979). Levels of processing and the structure of the language processor. In W.E. Cooper and E.C.T. Walker (eds) *Sentence Processing: Psycholinguistic Studies Presented to Merrill Garrett*. Hillsdale: NJ: Lawrence Erlbaum Associates.

Forster, K.I. (1994). Computational modeling and elementary process analysis on visual word recognition. *Journal of Experimental Psychology: Human Perception and Performance*, 20, 1292–1310.

Forster, K.I. and Shen, D. (1996). Neighborhood frequency and density effects in visual word recognition. *Journal of Experimental Psychology: Learning, Memory, and Cognition*, 22, 696–713.

Foss, D.J. (1969). Decision processes during sentence comprehension: Effects of lexical item difficulty and position upon reaction times. *Journal of Verbal Learning and Verbal Behavior*, 8, 457–462.

Franklin, S. (1995). *Artificial Minds*. Cambridge, MA: MIT Press.

Franklin, S. Howard, D. and Patterson, K. (1994). Abstract word meaning deafness. *Cognitive Neuropsychology*, 11, 1–34.

Frazier, L. (1987). Theories of sentence processing. In J.L. Garfield (ed.) *Modularity in Knowledge Representation and Natural Language Understanding*. Cambridge, MA: MIT Press.

Frazier, L. (1989). Against lexical generation of syntax. In W.D. Marslen-Wilson (ed.) *Lexical Representation and Process*. Cambridge, MA: MIT Press.

Frazier, L. and Rayner, K. (1982). Making and correcting errors during sentence comprehension: Eye movements in the analysis of structurally ambiguous sentences. *Cognitive Psychology*, 14, 178–210.

Freeman, C.P.L. Weeks, D. and Kendell, R.E. (1980). ECT: Patients who complain. *British Journal of Psychiatry*, 137, 17–25.

Freud, S. (1891). *On Aphasia: A Critical Study*. New York: International Universities Press (trans. E. Stengel, reprinted 1953).

Freud, S. (1915). Repression. In *Freud's Collected Papers, Vol. IV*. London: Hogarth.

Freud, S. (1938). Psychopathology of everyday life. In A.A. Brill (ed.) *The Writings of Sigmund Freud*. New York: Modern Library.

Fromkin, V.A. (1971). The non-anomalous nature of anomalous utterances. *Language*, 47, 27–52.

Fromkin, V.A. (ed.) (1973). *Speech Errors as Linguistic Evidence*. The Hague: Mouton.

Funell, E. and Sheridan, J. (1992). Categories of knowledge? Unfamiliar aspects of living and nonliving things. *Cognitive Neuropsychology*, 9, 135–153.

Funk, M. Shiffar, M. and Brugger, P. (2004). Hand movement observation by individuals born without hands: Phantom limb experience constrains visual limb perception. *Experimental Brain Research*, 164, 341–346.

Gabrieli, J.D.E. Cohen, N.J. and Corkin, S. (1988). The acquisition of lexical and semantic knowledge in amnesia. *Society for Neuroscience Abstracts*, 9, 328.

Gallace, A. and Spence, C. (2005). Examining the crossmodal consequences of viewing the Muller-Lyer illusion. *Experimental Brain Research*, 162, 4, 490–496.

Galton, F. (1883). *Inquiries into the Human Faculty*. London: Dent.

Garcia-Larrea, L. Perchet, C. Perren, F. and Amendo, E. (2001). Interface of cellular phone conversations with visuomotor tasks: An ERP study. *Journal of Psychophysiology*, 15, 14–21.

Gardiner, J.M. (2002). Episodic memory and autonoetic consciousness: A first person approach. In A. Baddeley, M. Conway, and J. Aggleton (eds) *Episodic Memory: New Directions in Research*. Oxford: Oxford University Press.

Gardiner, J.M. and Java, R.I. (1993) Recognising and remembering. In R.F. Collins, S.E. Gathercole, M.A. Conway, and P.E. Morris (eds) *Theories of Memory*. Hove: Lawrence Erlbaum Associates Ltd.

Gardiner, J.M. and Parkin, A.J. (1990). Attention and recollective experience in recognition. *Memory and Cognition*, 18, 579–583.

Gardner, H. (1977). *The Shattered Mind*. Hove: Psychology Press.

Gardner, H. (1985). *The Mind's New Science*. New York: Basic Books Inc.

Gardner, M.B. and Gardner, R.S. (1973). Problem of localization in the median plane: Effect of pinnae cavity. *Journal of the Acoustical Society of America*, 53, 400–408.

Garrett, M.F. (1975). The analysis of sentence production. In G. Bower (ed.) *Psychology of Learning and Motivation, Vol 9*. New York: Academic Press.

Garrett, M.F. (1984). The organisation of processing structure for language production: Applications to aphasic speech. In D. Caplan, A.R. Lecours and A. Smith (eds) *Biological Perspectives of Language*. Cambridge, MA: MIT Press.

Gasquoine, P.J. (1991). Learning in post-traumatic amnesia following extremely severe closed-head injury. *Brain Injury*, 5, 169–175.

Gathercole, S.E. and Baddeley, A.D. (1989). Development of vocabulary in children and short-term phonological memory. *Journal of Memory and Language*, 28, 200–213.

Gathercole, S.E. and Baddeley, A.D. (1990). Phonological memory deficits in language disordered children: Is there a causal connection? *Journal of Memory and Language*, 29, 336–360.

Gathercole, S.E. and Baddeley, A.D. (1993). *Working Memory and Language*. Hove: Lawrence Erlbaum Associates.

Gathercole, S.E. Service, E. Hitch, G. Adams, A.M. and Martin, A.J. (1999). Phonological short-term memory and vocabulary development: Further evidence on the nature of the relationship. *Applied Cognitive Psychology*, 13, 65–77.

Gazzaniga, M.S. Ivry, R.B. and Mangun, G.R. (1998). *Cognitive Neuroscience: The Biology of the Mind*. New York: W.W. Norton and Co.

Geiselman, R.E. (1999). Commentary on recent research with the cognitive interview. *Psychology, Crime, and Law*, 5, 197–202.

Geiselman, R.E. and Fisher, R.P. (1997). Ten years of cognitive interviewing. In D.G. Payne and F.G. Conrad (eds) *Intersections in Basic Memory Research*. Mahwah, NJ: Erlbaum.

Geiselman, R.E. Fisher, R.P. MacKinnon, D.P. and Holland, H.L. (1985). Eyewitness memory enhancement in police interview: Cognitive retrieval mnemonics versus hypnosis. *Journal of Applied Psychology*, 70, 401–412.

Gentner, D. and Gentner, D.R. (1983). Flowing waters and teeming crowds: Mental models of electricity. In D. Genter and A.L. Stevens (eds) *Mental Models*. Hillsdale, NJ: Lawrence Erlbaum Associates.

Geschwind, N. (1965). Disconnection syndromes in animals and man. *Brain*, 88, 237–294, 585–644.

Geschwind, N. (1972). Language and the brain. *Scientific American*, 76–83.

Geschwind, N. Quadfasel, F.A. and Segarra, J.M. (1968). Isolation of the speech area. *Neuropsychologia*, 6, 327–340.

Gibson, J.J. (1950). *The Perception of the Visual World*. Boston, MA: Houghton Mifflin.

Gibson, J.J. (1966). *The Senses Considered as Perceptual Systems*. Boston, MA: Houghton Mifflin.

Gibson, J.J. (1979). *The Ecological Approach to Visual Perception*. Hillsdale, NJ: Lawrence Erlbaum Associates.

Gick, M.L. and Holyoak, K.J. (1980). Analogical problem solving. *Cognitive Psychology*, 12, 306–355.

Gick, M.L. and Holyoak, K.J. (1983). Schema induction and analogical transfer. *Cognitive Psychology*, 15, 1–38.

Gilhooly, K.J. (1996). *Thinking: Directed, Undirected and Creative* (3rd edn). London: Academic Press.

Gilhooly, K.J. Phillips, L.H. Wynn, V. Logie, R.H. and Della Sala, S. (1999). Planning processes and age in the 5 disk Tower of London task. *Thinking and Reasoning*, 5, 339–361.

Glanzer, M. and Cunitz, A.R. (1966). Two storage mechanisms in free recall. *Journal of Verbal Learning and Verbal Behaviour*, 5, 351–360.

Gleitman, H. (1995). *Pyschology*. New York: W.W. Norton & Co.

Glenberg, A.M. Smith, S.M. and Green, C. (1977). Type 1 rehearsal: Maintenance and more. *Journal of Verbal Learning and Verbal Behaviour*, 16, 339–352.

Glisky, E.L. Schacter, D.L. and Tulving, E. (1986). Computer learning by memory-impaired patients: Acquisition and retention of complex knowledge. *Neuropsychologia*, 24, 313–328.

Godden, D.R. and Baddeley, A.D. (1975). Context-dependent memory in two natural environments: On land and under water. *British Journal of Psychology*, 66, 325–331.

Godden, D.R. and Baddeley, A.D. (1980). When does context influence recognition memory? *British Journal of Psychology*, 71, 99–104.

Goel, V. and Grafman, J. (1995). Are the frontal lobes implicated in 'planning' functions? Interpreting data from the Tower of Hanoi. *Neuropsychologia*, 33, 623–642.

Goldman-Rakic, P.S. (1987). Circuitry of primate prefrontal cortex and regulation of behavior by representational knowledge. In F. Plum and V. Mountcastle (eds) *Handbook of Physiology* (vol. 5, pp. 373–417). Bethesda, MD: American Physiological Society.

Goldstein, E.B. (2002). *Sensation and Perception*. Pacific Grove, CA: Wadsworth.

Goltz, F. (1892). Der Hund ohne Grosshirn: Siebente Abteilung über die Verrichtungen des Grosshirns. *Pfuger's Archiv für die gesamte Physiologie 51*, 570–614.

Goodale, M.A. and Milner, A.D. (1992). Separate visual pathways for perception and action. *Trends in Neurosciences*, 15, 1, 20–25.

Goodale, M.A. and Milner, A.D. (2004). *Sight Unseen: An Exploration of Conscious and Unconscious Vision*. Oxford: Oxford University Press.

Goodglass, H. and Berko, J. (1960). Agrammatism and inflectional morphology in English. *Journal of Speech and Hearing Research*, 3, 257–267.

Goodwin, D.W. Powell, B. Bremer, D. Hoine, H. and Stern, J. (1969). Alcohol and recall: State dependent effects in man. *Science*, 163, 1358.

Gordon, B.N. Baker-Ward, L. and Ornstein, P.A. (2001). Children's testimony: A review of research on memory for past experiences. *Clinical Child and Family Psychology Review*, 4, 157–181.

Gorman, Michael E. and Gorman, Margaret E. (1984). A comparison of disconfirmation, confirmation and control strategy on Wason's 2–4–6 task. *Quarterly Journal of Experimental Psychology*, 36A, 629–648.

Govier, E. and Pitts, M. (1982). The contextual disambiguation of a polysemous word in an unattended message. *British Journal of Psychology*, 73, 537–545.

Graf, P. and Komatsu, S. (1994). Process dissociation procedure: Handle with caution. *European Journal of Cognitive Psychology*, 6, 113–129.

Graf, P. and Schacter, D.L. (1985). Implicit and explicit memory for novel associations in normal and amnesic subjects. *Journal of Experimental Psychology: Learning, Memory, and Cognition*, 11, 501–518.

Graf, P. Squire, L.R. and Mandler, G. (1984). The information that amnesic patients do not forget. *Journal of Experimental Psychology: Learning, Memory, and Cognition*, 10, 164–178.

Graham, K.S. Kropelnicki, A. Goldman, W.P. and Hodges, J.R. (2003). Two further investigations of autobiographical memory in semantic dementia. *Cortex*, 39, 729–750.

Grainger, J. Muneaux, M. Farioli, F. and Ziegler, J.C. (2005). Effects of phonological and orthographic neighbourhood density interact in visual word recognition. *Quarterly Journal of Experimental Psychology*, 58A, 6, 981–998.

Grainger, J. and Whitney, C. (2004). Does the huamn mnid raed wrods as a wlohe? *Trends in Cognitive Sciences*, 8, 58–59.

Greenough, W.T. (1987). Experience effects on the developing and the mature brain: Dendritic branching and synaptogenesis. In N.A. Krasnegor, E. Blass, M. Hofer, and W.P. Smotherman (eds) *Perinatal Development: A Psychobiological Perspective*. New York: Academic Press.

Greenspoon, J. and Ranyard, R. (1957). Stimulus conditions and retroactive inhibition. *Journal of Experimental Psychology*, 53, 55–59.

Greenwald, A.G. (1992). New Look 3: Unconscious cognition reclaimed. *American Psychologist* 47, 6, 766–779.

Gregory, R. (1966). *Eye and Brain*. London: Weidenfeld & Nicolson.

Gregory, R. (1970). *The Intelligent Eye*. London: Weidenfeld & Nicolson.

Gregory, R.L. (1980). Perceptions as hypotheses. *Philosophical Transactions of the Royal Society of London B*, B290, 181–197.

Gregory, R.L. (1997). Knowledge in perception and illusion. *Philosophical Transactions of the Royal Society London B*, 352, 1121–1128.

Grice, H.P. (1975). Logic and conversation. In P. Cole and J.L. Morgan (eds) *Syntax and Semantics: Vol 3. Speech Acts*. New York: Seminar Press.

Griggs, R.A. and Cox, J.R. (1982). The elusive thematic materials effect in the Wason selection task. *British Journal of Psychology*, 73, 407–420.

Griggs, R.A. and Cox, J.R. (1983). The effects of problem content and negation on Wason's selection task. *Quarterly Journal of Experimental Psychology*, 35A, 519–533.

Grimm, J.L.C. and Grimm, W.C. (1909). *Grimm's Fairy Tales* (trans. E. Lucas). London: Constable and Co. Ltd.

Grodner, D. Gibson, E. and Wilson, D. (2005). The influence of contextual contrast on syntactic processing: Evidence for strong-interaction in sentence comprehension. *Cognition*, 95, 275–296.

Grodzinsky, Y. (2000). The neurology of syntax: Language use without Broca's area. *Behavioural and Brain Sciences*, 23, 1–21.

Grodzinsky, Y. Pinango, M.M. Zurif, E. and Drai, D. (1999). The critical role of group studies in neuropsychology: Comprehension regularities in Broca's aphasia. *Brain and Language*, 67, 134–147.

Groeger, J.A. (1984). Qualitatively different effects of undetected and unidentified auditory primes. *Quarterly Journal of Experimental Psychology*, 40(A), 323–329.

Groome, D. (1999). Memory. In D. Groome (ed.)*An Introduction to Cognitive Psychology: Processes and Disorders*. Hove: Psychology Press.

Groome, D. (2005). Everyday memory. In A. Esgate and D. Groome (eds) *An Introduction to Applied Cognitive Psychology*. Hove: Psychology Press.

Groome, D. and Grant N. (2005). Retrieval-induced forgetting is inversely related to everyday cognitive failures. *British Journal of Psychology*, 96, 313–319.

Groome, D.H. and Levay, L. (2003). The effect of articulatory suppression on free recall of auditory images, visual images, written words, and spoken words. *Proceedings of the Annual Conference of the British Psychological Society*. Leicester: BPS.

Groome, D. and Soureti, A. (2004). PTSD and anxiety symptoms in children exposed to the 1999 Greek earthquake. *British Journal of Psychology*, 95, 387–397.

Grossenbacher, P.G. and Lovelace C.T. (2001). Mechanisms of synaesthesia: Cognitive and physiological constraints. *Trends in Cognitive Sciences*, 5, 36–41.

Gurney, K. (1997). *An Introduction to Neural Networks*. London: UCL Press Ltd.

Gurney, K. and Wright, M. (1996). A biologically plausible model of early visual motion processing: Theory and implementation. *Biological Cybernetics*, 74, 339–348.

Habib, R. McIntosh, A.R. Wheeler, M.A. and Tulving, E. (2003). Memory encoding and hippocampally-based novelty/familiarity discrimination networks. *Neuropsychologia*, 41, 271–279.

Haglund, Y. and Eriksson, E. (1993). Does amateur boxing lead to chronic brain damage? A review of some recent investigations. *American Journal of Sports Medicine*, 21, 97–109.

Hallam, J. and Malcolm, C. (1994). Behaviour: Perception, action and intelligence – the view from situated robotics. *Philosophical Transactions of the Royal Society* A, 349, 29–42.

Halliday, M.A.K. and Hasan, R. (1976). *Cohesion in English*. London: Longman.

Halligan, P.W. (2002). Phantom limbs: The body in mind. *Cognitive Neuropsychiatry*, 7, 251–268.

Halligan, P.W. and Marshall, J.C. (1991). Left neglect for near but not far space in man. *Nature*, 350, 498–500.

Halstead, W.C. (1940). Preliminary analysis of grouping behaviour in patients with cerebral injury by the method of equivalent and non-equivalent stimuli. *American Journal of Psychiatry*, 96, 1263–1294.

Handy, T.C. Grafton, S.T. Shroff, N.M. Ketay, S. and Gazzaniga, M.S. (2003). Graspable objects grab attention when the potential for action is recognized. *Nature Neuroscience*, 6, 421–427.

Harding, A. Halliday, G. Caine, D. and Kril, J. (2000). Degeneration of anterior thalamic nuclei differentiates alcoholics with amnesia. *Brain*, 123, 141–154.

Harley, T.A. (2001). *The Psychology of Language: From Data to Theory* (2nd edn). Hove: Psychology Press.

Harlow, J.M. (1848). Passage of an iron bar through the head. *Boston Medican and Surgical Journal*, 39, 389–393.

Harlow, J.M. (1868). Recovery from the passage of an iron bar through the head. *Publications of the Massachusetts Medical Society*, 2, 327–347.

Harrison, J. (2001). *Synaesthesia: The Strangest Thing*. Oxford: Oxford University Press.

Hart, J. Berndt, R.S. and Caramazza, A. (1985). Category-specific naming deficit following cerebral infarction. *Nature*, 316, 439–440.

Hasher, L. and Zacks, R.T. (1979). Automatic and effortful processes in memory. *Journal of Experimental Psychology: General*, 108, 356–388.

Hastorf, A.H. and Cantril, H. (1954). They saw a game: A case study. *Journal of Abnormal and Social Psychology*, 49, 129–134.

Haviland, S.E. and Clark, H.H. (1974). What's new? Acquiring new information as a process in comprehension. *Journal of Verbal Learning and Verbal Behavior*, 13, 512–521.

Hay, J.F. and Jacoby, L.L. (1996). Separating habit and recollection: Memory slips, process dissociations, and probability matching. *Journal of Experimental Psychology: Learning, Memory, and Cognition*, 22, 1233–1335.

Hayes, J.R. and Simon, H.A. (1974). Understanding written problem instructions. In L.W. Gregg (ed.) *Knowledge and Cognition*. Hillsdale, NJ: Lawrence Erlbaum Associates.

Hayman, C.A.G. and Tulving, E. (1989). Is priming in fragment completion based on a 'trace-less' memory system? *Journal of Experimental Psychology: Learning, Memory, and Cognition*, 15, 941–956.

Haynes, J.D. and Rees, G. (2005). Predicting the orientation of invisible stimuli from activity in human primary visual cortex. *Nature Neuroscience*, 8, 686–691.

Head, H. (1926). *Aphasia and Kindred Disorders of Speech*. Cambridge: Cambridge University Press.

Heath, R.L. and Blonder, L.X. (2005). Spontaneous humor among right hemisphere stroke survivors. *Brain and Language*, 93, 3, 267–276.

Heathcote D. (2005). Working memory and performance limitations. In A. Esgate and D.H. Groome (eds) *An Introduction to Applied Cognitive Psychology*. Hove: Psychology Press.

Hebb, D. (1949). *The Organization of Behaviour*. Chichester: John Wiley.

Heliman, K.M. Watson, R.T. and Valenstein, E. (2002). Spatial Neglect. In H. Karnath, D. Milner and G. Vallar (eds) *The Cognitive and Neural Bases of Spatial Neglect* (pp. 3–30). New York: Oxford University Press.

Heller, M.A. Brackett, D.D. Wilson, K. Yoneyama, K. and Boyer, A. (2002). The haptic Muller-Lyer illusion in sighted and blind people. *Perception*, 31, 1263–1274.

Helmstaedter, C. Kemper, B. and Elger, C.E. (1996). Neuropsychological aspects of frontal lobe epilepsy. *Neuropsychologia*, 34, 399–406.

Henriques, D.Y. and Soechting, J.F. (2003). Bias and sensitivity in the haptic perception of geometry. *Experimental Brain Research*, 150, 95–108.

Henson, R.N.A. Burgess, N. and Frith, C.D. (2000). Recoding, storage, rehearsal, and grouping in verbal short-term memory: An fMRI study. *Neuropsychologia*, 38, 426–440.

Herrmann, D. Raybeck, D. and Gruneberg, M. (2002). *Improving Memory and Study Skills: Advances in Theory and Practice*. Ashland, OH: Hogrefe & Huber.

Hersh, N. and Treadgold, L. (1994). Neuropage: The rehabilitation of memory dysfunction by prosthetic memory and cueing. *NeuroRehabilitation*, 4, 187–197.

Hill, E. (2004). Executive dysfunction in autism. *Trends in Cognitive Sciences*, 8, 26–32.

Hill, E. and Williamson, J. (1998). Choose six numbers, any numbers. *The Psychologist*, 11, 17–21.

Hinton, G. Plaut, D. and Shallice, T. (1993). Simulating brain damage. *Scientific American*, pp. 59–65.

Hinton, G.E. and Shallice, T. (1991). Lesioning an attractor network: Investigations of acquired dyslexia. *Psychological Review*, 98, 74–95.

Hitch, G.J. (2005). Working memory. In N. Braisby and A. Gellatly (eds) *Cognitive Psychology*. Oxford: Oxford University Press.

Hittmair-Delazer, M. Denes, G. Semenza, C. and Mantovan, M.C. (1994). Anomia for people's names. *Neuropsychologia*, 32, 465–476.

Ho, C.E. (1998). Letter recognition reveals pathways of second-order and third-order motion. *Proceedings of the National Academy of Sciences of the United States of America*, 95, 1, 400–404.

Hodges, J.R. Patterson, K. and Tyler, L.K. (1994). Loss of semantic memory: Implications for the modularity of mind. *Cognitive Neuropsychology*, 11, 505–542.

Hofman, P.A.M. Verhay, F.R.J. Wilmink, J.T. Rozandaal, N. and Jolles, J. (2002). Brain lesions in patients visiting a memory clinic with postconcussional sequelae after mild to moderate brain injury. *Journal of Neuropsychiatry and Clinical Neurosciences*, 14, 176–184.

Hokkanen, L. Launes, R. and Vataja, L. (1995). Isolated retrograde amnesia for autobiographical memory associated with acute left temporal lobe encephalitis. *Psychological Medicine*, 25, 203–208.

Hopfield, J. (1982). Neural networks and physical systems with emergent collective computational properties. *Proceedings of the National Academy of Sciences of the USA*, 79, 2554–2588.

Hopfield, J. (1984). Neurons with graded response have collective computational properties like those of two-state neurons. *Proceedings of the National Academy of Sciences of the USA*, 81, 3088–3092.

Horowitz, M.J. (1976). *Stress Response Syndromes*. New York: Aronson.

Hough, M.S. (1990). Narrative comprehension in adults with right and left hemisphere brain-damage: Theme organisation. *Brain and Language*, 38, 253–277.

Howard, D. (1985). Introduction to 'On agrammatism' (Ueber Agrammatismus). *Cognitive Neuropsychology*, 2, 303–307. (Original work published in 1922 by M. Isserlin.)

Hu, Y. and Goodale, M.A. (2000). Grasping after a delay shifts size-scaling from absolute to relative metrics. *Journal of Cognitive Neuroscience*, 12, 856–868.

Hubel, D.H. and Weisel, T.N. (1959). Receptive fields of single neurons in the cat's striate cortex. *Journal of Physiology*, 148, 574–591.

Hulme, C. Maughan, S. and Brown, G.D.A. (1991). Memory for familiar and unfamiliar words: Evidence for a long-term memory contribution to short-term memory span. *Journal of Memory and Language*, 30, 685–701.

Hulme, C. Suprenant, A.M. Bireta, T.J. Stuart, G. and Neath, I. (2004). Abolishing the word-length effect. *Journal of Experimental Psychology: Learning, Memory, and Cognition*, 30, 98–106.

Humphreys, G.W. and Riddoch, M.J. (1987). *To See or Not to See: A Case Study of Visual Agnosia*. London: Lawrence Earlbaum Associates.

Hunt, R.R. and McDaniel, M.A. (1993). The enigma of organisation and distinctiveness. *Journal of Memory and Language*, 32, 421–445.

Hunt, R.R. and Smith, R.E. (1996). Accessing the particular from the general: The power of distinctiveness in the content of organization. *Memory and Cognition*, 24, 217–225.

Hupe, J.M. James, A.C. Payne, B.R. Lomber, S.G. Girard, P. and Bullier, J. (1998). Cortical feedback improves discrimination between figure and ground by V1, V2 and V3 neurons. *Nature*, 394, 784–787.

Huppert, F.A. and Piercy, M. (1976). Recognition memory in amnesic patients: Effect of temporal context and familiarity of material. *Cortex*, 4, 3–20.

Huppert, F.A. and Piercy, M. (1978). The role of trace strength in recency and frequency judgements by amnesic and control subjects. *Quarterly Journal of Experimental Psychology*, 30, 346–354.

Husserl, E. (1931). *Ideas: General Introduction to Pure Phenomenology* (vol. 1). New York: Macmillan.

Hyde, T.S. and Jenkins, J.J. (1973). Recall for words as a function of semantic, graphic, and syntactic orienting tasks. *Journal of Verbal Learning and Verbal Behaviour*, 12, 471–480.

Hyden, H. (1967). Biochemical and molecular aspects of learning and memory. *Proceedings of the American Philosophical Society*, 111, 347–351.

Hyman, I.E. and Loftus, E.F. (2002). False childhood memories and eyewitness memory errors. In M.L. Eisen (ed.) *Memory and Suggestibility in the Forensic Interview*. Mahwah, NJ: Erlbaum.

Intraub, H. and Richardson, M. (1989). Wide-angle memories of close-up scenes. *Journal of Experimental Psychology: Learning, Memory, and Cognition*, 15, 2, 179–187.

Jacobsen, C.F. Wolfe, J.B. and Jackson, T.A. (1935). An experimental analysis of the functions of the frontal association areas in primates. *Journal of Nervous and Mental Disease*, 82, 1–14.

Jacoby, L.L. (1991). A process dissociation framework: Separating automatic from intentional uses of memory. *Journal of Memory and Language*, 30, 513–541.

Jacoby, L.L. and Dallas, M. (1981). On the relationship between autobiographical memory and perceptual learning. *Journal of Experimental Psychology: General*, 3, 3006–3340.

Jacoby, L.L. Toth, J.P. and Yonelinas, A.P. (1993). Separating conscious and unconscious influences of memory: Measuring recollection. *Journal of Experimental Psychology: General*, 122, 139–154.

James, W. (1890). *Principles of Psychology*. New York: Holt.

Janowsky, J.S. Shimamura, A.P. and Squire, L.R. (1989). Source memory impairment in patients with frontal lobe lesions. *Neuropsychologia*, 27, 1043–1056.

Jastrowitz, M. (1888). Beiträge zur Localisation im Grosshirn und über deren praktische Verwertung. *Deutsche Medizinische Wochenschrift*, 14, 81–83, 108–112, 125–128, 151–153, 172–175, 188–192, 209–211.

Jenkins, R. Burton, A.M. Ellis, A.W. (2002). Long-term effects of covert face recognition. *Cognition*, 86, 43–52.

Jerabek, I. and Standing, L. (1992). Imagined test situations produce contextual memory enhancement. *Perceptual and Motor Skills*, 75, 400.

Joanette, Y. and Brownell, H. (eds.) (1990). *Discourse Ability and Brain Damage*. New York: Springer-Verlag.

Johnson-Laird, P. (1983). *Mental Models*. Cambridge: Cambridge University Press.

Johnson-Laird, P.N. Byrne, R.M.J. and Schaeken, W. (1992). Propositional reasoning by model. *Psychological Review*, 99, 418–439.

Johnson-Laird, P.N. Legrenzi, P. and Legrenzi, M.S. (1972). Reasoning and a sense of reality. *British Journal of Psychology*, 63, 395–400.

Johnson-Laird, P.N. and Wason, P.C. (1970). Insight into a logical relation. *Quarterly Journal of Experimental Psychology*, 22, 49–61.

Johnston, W.A. and Heinz, S.P. (1978). Flexibility and capacity demands of attention. *Journal of Experimental Psychology: General*, 107, 420–435.

Johnstone, E.C. Deakin, J.F.W. Lawler, P. Frith, C.D. Stevens, M. McPherson, K. *et al.* (1980). The Northwick Park ECT trial. *The Lancet*, 1317–1320.

Johnstone, L. (2003). A shocking treatment? *The Psychologist*, 16, 236–239.

Jones, D.M. Alford, D. Bridges, A. Tremblay, S. and Macken, B. (1999). Organisational factors in selective attention: The interplay of acoustic distinctiveness and auditory streaming in the irrelevant sound effect. *Journal of Experimental Psychology: Learning, Memory, and Cognition*, 25, 464–473.

Juola, J.F. Bowhuis D.G. Cooper E.E. and Warner C.B. (1991). Control of attention around the fovea. *Journal of Experimental Psychology: Human Perception and Performance*, 15, 315–330.

Just, M.A. and Carpenter, P.A. (1980). A theory of reading: From eye fixations to comprehension. *Psychological Review*, 87, 329–354.

Just, M.A. and Carpenter, P.A. (1992). A capacity theory of comprehension: Individual differences in working memory. *Psychological Review*, 99, 122–149.

Kahneman, D. (1973). *Attention and Effort*. Englewood Cliffs, NJ: Prentice-Hall.

Kahneman, D. and Frederick, S. (2002). Representativeness revisited: Attribute substitution in intuitive judgment. In T. Gilovich, D. Griffin and D. Kahneman (eds.) *Heuristics and Biases: The Psychology of Intuitive Judgment*. Cambridge: Cambridge University Press.

Kahneman, D. Slovic, P. and Tversky A. (eds) (1982). *Judgement under Uncertainty: Heuristics and Biases*. Cambridge: Cambridge University Press.

Kahneman, D. and Tversky, A. (1973). On the psychology of prediction. *Psychological Review*, 80, 237–251.

Kanwisher, N. and Driver, J. (1992). Objects, attributes and visual attention: Which, what and where. *Current Directions in Psychological Science*, 1, 26–31.

Kapur, N. Ellison, D. Smith, M. McLellan, D.L. and Burrows, E.H. (1992). Focal retrograde amnesia following bilateral temporal lobe pathology. *Brain*, 115, 73–85.

Kapur, N. Glisky, E.L. and Wilson, B.A. (2004). External memory aids and computers in memory rehabilitation. In A.D. Baddeley, M.D. Kopelman, and B.A. Wilson (eds) *The Essential Handbook of Memory Disorders for Clinicians*. Chichester: Wiley.

Kapur, N. Thompson, C. Cook, P. Lang, D. and Brice, J. (1996). Anterograde but not retrograde memory loss following combined mammilary body and medial thalamic lesions. *Neuropsychologia*, 34, 2–8.

Karat, J. (1982). A model of problem-solving with incomplete constraint knowledge. *Cognitive Psychology*, 14, 538–559.

Karbe, H. Szelies, B. Herholz, K. and Heiss, W.D. (1990). Impairment of language is related to left parieto-temporal glucose metabolism in aphasic stroke patients. *Journal of Neurology*, 2327, 19–23.

Karnath, H.O. Milner, A.D. and Vallar, G. (2002). *The Cognitive and Neural Bases of Spatial Neglect*. Oxford: Oxford University Press.

Kay, J. Lesser, R. and Coltheart, M. (1992). *Psycholinguistic Assessments of Language Processing in Aphasia*. Hove: Psychology Press.

Kean, M.L. (1977). The linguistic interpretation of aphasic syndromes: Agrammatism in Broca's aphasia, an example. *Cognition*, 5, 9–46.

Keane, M.T.G. (1987). On retrieving analogues when solving problems. *Quarterly Journal of Experimental Psychology*, 39A, 29–41.

Keane, M.T.G. (1990). Incremental analogizing: Theory and model. In K.J. Gilhooly, M.T.G. Keane, R.H. Logie and G. Erdos (eds) *Lines of Thinking: Reflections on the Psychology of Thought, Vol. 1: Representation, Reasoning, Analogy and Decision Making*. Chichester: John Wiley.

Kebbel, M.R. Milne, R. and Wagstaff, G.F. (1999). The cognitive interview: A survey of its forensic effectiveness. *Psychology, Crime, and Law*, 5, 101–115.

Kentridge, R.W. Heywood, C.A. Weiskrantz, L. (1997). Residual vision in multiple retinal locations within a scotoma: Implications for blindsight. *Journal of Cognitive Neuroscience*, 9, 191–202.

Kertesz, A. Lau, W.K. and Polk, M. (1993). The structural determinants of recovery in Wernicke's aphasia. *Brain and Language*, 44, 153–164.

Kimball, J. (1973). Seven principles of surface structure parsing in natural language. *Cognition*, 2, 15–47.

Kimberg, D.Y. and Farah, M.J. (1993). A unified account of cognitive impairments following frontal lobe damage: The role of working memory in complex, organized behavior. *Journal of Experimental Psychology: General*, 122, 411–428.

King, J.A. Trinkler, I. Hartley, T. Vargha-Khadem, F. and Burgess, N. (2004). The hippocampal role in spatial memory and the familiarity-recollection distinction: A case study. *Neuropsychology*, 18, 405–417.

Kintsch, W. (1968). Recognition and free recall of organised lists. *Journal of Experimental Psychology*, 78, 481–487.

Kirdendall, D.T. and Garrett, W.E. (2001). Heading in soccer: Integral skill or grounds for cognitive dysfunction? *Journal of Athletic Training*, 36, 328–333.

Klatzky, R.L. Lederman, S.J. and Metzger, V. (1987). Identifying objects by touch: An 'expert' system. *Perception and Psychophysics*, 37, 299–302.

Klein, D.E. and Murphy, G.L. (2001). The representation of polysemous words. *Journal of Memory and Language*, 45, 259–282.

Kluft, R.P. (1999). True lies, false truths, and naturalistic raw data: Applying clinical research findings to the false memory debate. In L.M. Williams and V.L. Banyard (eds) *Trauma and Memory*. Thousand Oaks, CA: Sage.

Knoblich, G. Ohlsson, S. Haider, H. and Rhenius, D. (1999). Constraint relaxation and chunk decomposition in insight problem solving. *Journal of Experimental Psychology: Learning, Memory, and Cognition*, 25, 1534–1556.

Koehnken, G. Milne, R. Memon, A. and Bull, R. (1999). The cognitive interview: A meta-analysis. *Psychology, Crime, and Law*, 5, 3–27.

Koffka, K. (1935). *Principles of Gestalt Psychology*. New York: Harcourt Brace.

Köhler, W. (1925). *The Mentality of Apes*. New York: Harcourt Brace, and World.

Kolb, B. and Whishaw, I.Q. (1996). *Fundamentals of Human Neuropsychology* (4th edn). New York: Freeman.

Kolk, H.H.J. van Grunsven, M.J.F. and Keyser, A. (1985). On parallelism between production and comprehension in agrammatism. In M.L. Kean (ed.) *Agrammatism*. New York: Academic Press.

Kopelman, M.D. (1989). Remote and autobiographical memory, temporal context memory and frontal atrophy in Korsakoff and Alzheimer patients. *Neuropsychologia*, 27, 437–460.

Kopelman, M.D. Lasserson, D. Kingsley, D. Bello, F. Rush, C. *et al.* (2001). Structural MRI volumetric analysis in patients with organic amnesia, 2: Correlations with anterograde memory and executive tests in 40 patients. *Journal of Neurology, Neurosurgery, and Psychiatry*, 71, 23–28.

Kopelman, M.D. Stanhope, N. and Kingsley, D. (1999). Retrograde amnesia in patients with diencephalic, temporal lobe, or frontal lesions. *Neuropsychologia*, 35, 1533–1545.

Kopelman, M.D. Wilson, B.A. and Baddeley, A.D. (1990). *The Autobiographical Memory Interview*. Bury St Edmunds: Thames Valley Test Company.

Koriat, A. Goldsmith, M. and Panksy, A. (2001). Towards a psychology of memory accuracy. *Annual Review of Psychology*, 51, 481–537.

Korsakoff, S.S. (1887). Troubles de l'activité psychique dans la paralysie alcoolique et leurs rapports avec les troubles de la sphère psychique dans la vévrité multiple d'origine non alcoolique. *Vestnik Psychiatrii*, 4, 2.

Kosko, B. (1992). *Neural Networks and Fuzzy Systems*. Princeton, NJ: Prentice Hall.

Kosslyn, S.M. Thompson, W.L. Kim, I.J. and Alpert, N.M. (1995). Topographical representations of mental images in primary visual cortex. *Nature*, 378, 496–498.

Kucera, H. and Francis, W.N. (1967). *Computational Analysis of Present-Day American English*. Providence, RI: Brown University Press.

Kuffler, S.W. (1953). Discharge patterns and functional organisation of mammalian retina. *Journal of Neurophysiology*, 16, 37–68.

Kuhn, D. (1991). *The Skills of Argument*. Cambridge: Cambridge University Press.

Kuhn, T. (1970). *The Structure of Scientific Revolutions*. Chicago: Chicago University Press.

Kurucz, J. Feldmar, G. and Werner, W. (1979). Prosopo-affective agnosia associated with chronic organic brain syndrome. *Journal of the American Geriatrics Society*, 27, 91–95.

LaBerge, D. (1983). Spatial extent of attention to letters and words. *Journal of Experimental Psychology: Human Perception and Performance*, 9, 371–379.

Laird, J. Newell, A. and Rosenbloom, P. (1987). SOAR: An architecture for general intelligence. *Artificial Intelligence*, 33, 1–64.

Laird, J. Rosenbloom, P. and Newell, A. (1984). Towards chunking as a general learning mechanism. In *Proceedings of the AAAI '84: National Conference on Artificial Intelligence*, Menlo Park, CA: American Association for Artificial Intelligence.

Lamble, D. Kauranen, T. Laasko, M. and Summala, H. (1999). Cognitive load and detection thresholds in car following situations: Safety implications for using mobile (cellular) telephones while driving. *Accident Analysis and Prevention*, 31, 617–623.

Landauer, T.K. and Bjork, R.A. (1978). Optimal rehearsal patterns and name learning. In M.M. Gruneberg, P.E. Morris, and R.N Sykes (eds) *Practical Aspects of Memory*. London: Academic Press.

Lang, A.J. Craske, M.J. and Bjork, R.A. (1999). Implications of a new theory of disuse for the treatment of emotional disorders. *Clinical Psychology: Science and Practice*, 6, 80–94.

Langham, M. Hole, G. Edwards, J. and O'Neil, C. (2002). An analysis of 'looked but failed to see' accidents involving parked police vehicles. *Ergonomics*, 45, 3, 167–185.

Larkin, J.H. McDermott, J. Simon, D. and Simon, H.A. (1980). Expert and novice performance in solving physics problems. *Science*, 208, 1335–1342.

Larsson, A.S. Granhag, P.A. and Spjut, E. (2003). Children's recall and the cognitive interview: Do the positive effects hold over time? *Applied Cognitive Psychology*, 17, 203–214.

Lashley, K.S. (1950). In search of the engram. *Symposium of the Society of Experimental Biology*, 4, 454–482.

Lederman, S.J. and Klatzky, R.L. (1990). Haptic classification of common objects: Knowledge-driven exploration. *Cognitive Psychology*, 22, 421–459.

Lee, A.C.H. Bussey, T.J. Murray, E.A. Saksida, L.M. Epstein, R.A. Kapur, N. Hodges, J.R. and Graham, K.S. (2005). Perceptual deficits in amnesia: Challenging the medial temporal lobe mnemonic view. *Neuropsychologia*, 43, 1–11.

Leonards, U. Ibanez, V. and Giannakopoulos, P. (2002). The role of stimulus type in age-related changes of visual working memory. *Experimental Brain Research*, 146, 172–183.

Levelt, W.J.M. (1989). *Speaking: From Intention to Articulation*. Cambridge, MA: MIT Press.

Levelt, W.J.M. (1992). Accessing words in speech production: Stages, processes and representations. *Cognition*, 42, 1–22.

Levelt, W.J.M. Roelofs, A. and Meyer, A.S. (1999). A theory of lexical access in speech production. *Behavioural and Brain Sciences*, 22, 1–38.

Levelt, W.J.M. Schriefers, H.. Vorberg, D. Meyer, A.S. Pechmann, T. and Havinga, J. (1991). The time course of lexical access in speech production: A study of picture naming. *Psychological Review*, 98, 122–142.

Levine, B. Svoboda, E. Hay, J.F. Winocur, G. and Moscovitch, M. (2002). Ageing and autobiographical memory: Dissociating episodic from semantic retrieval. *Psychology and Ageing*, 17, 677–689.

Lhermitte, F. (1983). 'Utilization behaviour' and its relation to lesions of the frontal lobes. *Brain*, 106, 237–255.

Lhermitte, F. (1986). Human autonomy and the frontal lobes. Part II: patient behaviour in complex and social situations: the 'environmental dependency syndrome'. *Annals of Neurology*, 19, 335–343.

Libet, B. (1985). Unconscious cerebral initiative and the role of conscious will in voluntary action. *Behavioural and Brain Sciences*, 8, 529–539.

Lichtheim, L. (1885). On aphasia. *Brain*, 7, 433–484.

Lickley, R.J. and Bard, E.G. (1998). When can listeners detect disfluency in spontaneous speech? *Language and Speech*, 41, 2, 203–226.

Lindsay, D.S. and Read, J.D. (1994). Psychotherapy and memories of childhood sexual abuse: A cognitive perspective. *Applied Cognitive Psychology*, 8, 281–338.

Lindsay, D.S. Hagen, L. Read, J.D. Wade, K.A. and Garry, M. (2004). True photographs and false memories. *Psychological Science*, 15, 149–154.

Lindsay, P.H. and Norman, D.A. (1972). *Human Information Processing*. New York: Academic Press.

Linebarger, M.C. Schwarz, M.F. and Saffran, E.M. (1983). Sensitivity to grammatical structure in so called agrammatic aphasics. *Cognition*, 13, 361–392.

Linton, M. (1975). Memory for real-world events. In D.A. Norman and D.E. Rumelhart (eds) *Explorations in Cognition*. San Francisco: Freeman.

Lissauer, H. (1890). Ein Fall von Seelenblindheitnebst einem Beitrage zur Theorie Derselben. *Archiv für Psychiatrie und Nervenkrankheit*, 21, 222–270.

Liu, H. Bates, E. Powell, T. and Wulfeck, B. (1997). Single-word shadowing and the study of lexical access. *Applied Psycholinguistics*, 18, 157–180.

Lockhart, R.S. (2002). Levels of processing, transfer-appropriate processing, and the concept of robust encoding. *Memory*, 10, 397–403.

Lockhart, R.S. and Craik, F.I.M. (1990). Levels of processing: A retrospective commentary on a framework for memory research. *Canadian Journal of Psychology*, 44, 87–112.

Loeb, J. (1902). *Comparative Physiology of the Brain and Comparative Psychology*. New York: Putnam.

Loftus, E.F. and Klinger, M.R. (1992). Is the unconscious smart or dumb? *American Psychologist*, 47, 6, 761–765.

Loftus, E.L. Levidow, B. and Duensing, S. (1992). Who remembers best? Individual differences in memory for events that occurred in a science museum. *Applied Cognitive Psychology*, 6, 93–107.

Loftus, E.L. and Palmer, J.C. (1974). Reconstruction of automobile destruction: An example of the interaction between language and memory. *Journal of Verbal Learning and Verbal Behaviour*, 13, 585–589.

Logie, R.H. (1986). Visuo-spatial processes in working memory. *Quarterly Journal of Experimental Psychology*, 38A, 229–247.

Logie, R.H. (1995). *Visuo-spatial Working Memory*. Hove: Erlbaum.

Logothesis, N.K. (1994). Physiological studies of motion inputs. In A.T. Smith (ed.) *Visual Detection of Motion* (pp. 177–216). London: Academic Press.

Lorayne, H. and Lucas, J. (1974). *The Memory Book*. London: W.H. Allen.

Luchins, A.S. (1942). Mechanization in problem solving. *Psychological Monographs*, 54, 6, Whole No. 248.

Luria, A.R. (1966). *Higher Cortical Functions in Man*. London: Tavistock.

Luria, A.R. (1973). *The Working Brain: An Introduction to Neuropsychology*. Harmondsworth: Penguin Books.

MacGregor, J.N. Ormerod, T.C. and Chronicle, E.P. (2001). Information processing and insight: A process model of performance on the nine-dot and related problems. *Journal of Experimental Psychology: Learning, Memory, and Cognition*, 27, 176–201.

Macken, W.J. and Jones, D.M. (1995). Functional characteristics of the 'inner voice' and the 'inner ear': Single or double agency? *Journal of Experimental Psychology: Learning, Memory, and Cognition*, 21, 436–448.

MacLeod, C.M. (1998). Training on integrated versus separated stroop tasks: The progression of interference and facilitation. *Memory and Cognition*, 26, 201–211.

MacLeod, M.D. (2002). Retrieval-induced forgetting in eyewitness memory: Forgetting as a consequence of remembering. *Applied Cognitive Psychology*, 16, 135–149.

MacLeod, M.D. and Macrae, C.N. (2001). Gone today but here tomorrow: The transient nature of retrieval-induced forgetting. *Psychological Science*, 12, 148–152.

Macmillan, M.B. (1986). A wonderful journey through the skull and brains: The travels of Mr Gage's tamping iron. *Brain and Cognition*, 5, 67–107.

Macrae, C.N. and MacLeod, M.D. (1999). On recollections lost: When practice makes imperfect. *Journal of Personality and Social Psychology*, 77, 463–473.

Maier, N.R.F. (1930). Reasoning in humans I: On direction. *Journal of Comparative Psychology*, 10, 115–143.

Maier, N.R.F. (1931). Reasoning in humans II: The solution of a problem and its appearance in consciousness. *Journal of Comparative Psychology*, 12, 181–194.

Mair, W.G.P. Warrington, E.K. and Weiskrantz, L. (1979). Memory disorders in Korsakoff's psychosis: A neuropathological and neuropsychological investigation of two cases. *Brain*, 102, 749–783.

Mandler, G. (1980). Recognising: The judgement of a previous occurrence. *Psychological Review*, 27, 252–271.

Mandler, G. (1989). Memory: Conscious and unconscious. In P.R. Soloman, G.R. Goethals, C.M. Kelley and B.R. Stephens (eds) *Memory: Interdisciplinary Approaches*. New York: Springer-Verlag.

Mandler, G. Pearlstone, Z. and Koopmans, H.S. (1969). Effects of organisation and semantic similarity on a recall and recognition task. *Journal of Verbal Learning and Verbal Behaviour*, 8, 410–423.

Manning, C.G. (2000). Imagining inflation with posttest delays: How long will it last? Unpublished doctoral dissertation, University of Washington.

Mantyla, T. (1986). Optimising cue effectiveness: Recall of 500 and 600 incidentally learned words. *Journal of Experimental Psychology: Learning, Memory, and Cognition*, 12, 66–71.

Marcel, A.J. (1983). Conscious and unconscious perception: An approach to the relations between phenomenal experience and perceptual processes. *Cognitive Psychology*, 15, 238–300.

Marr, D. (1982). *Vision: A Computational Investigation into the Human Representation and Processing of Visual Information*. San Francisco: Freeman.

Marr, D. and Nishihara, K. (1978). Representation and recognition of the spatial organisation of three-dimensional shapes. *Philosophical Transactions of the Royal Society, Series B*, 269–294.

Marshall, J.C. and Halligan, P.W. (1988). Blindsight and insight in visuo-spatial neglect. *Nature*, 336, 766–767.

Marshall, J.C. and Halligan, P.W. (1993). Visuo-spatial neglect: A new copying test to assess perceptual parsing. *Journal of Neurology*, 240, 37–40.

Marshall, J.C. and Newcombe, F. (1973). Patterns of paralexia: A psycholinguistic approach. *Journal of Psycholinguistic Research*, 2, 175–199.

Marslen-Wilson, W. (1973). Linguistic structure and speech shadowing at very short latencies. *Nature*, 244, 522–523.

Marslen-Wilson, W. (1975). Sentence perception as an interactive parallel process. *Science*, 189, 226–228.

Marslen-Wilson, W. (1987). Functional parallelism in spoken word recognition. *Cognition*, 25, 71–102.

Marslen-Wilson, W. (ed.) (1989). *Lexical Representation and Process*. Cambridge, MA: MIT Press.

Marslen-Wilson, W. and Tyler, L. (1980). The temporal struture of spoken language understanding. *Cognition*, 8, 1–71.

Martin, R.C. (1993). Short-term memory and sentence processing: Evidence from neuropsychology. *Memory and Cognition*, 21, 176–183.

Massie, D.L. Campbell, K.L. and Williams, A.F. (1995). Traffic accident involvement rates by driver age and gender. *Accident Analysis and Prevention*, 27, 1, 73–87.

Mattingley, J.B. Rich, A.N. Yelland, G. and Bradshaw, J.L. (2001). Unconscious priming eliminates automatic binding of colour and alphanumeric form in synaesthesia. *Nature*, 410, 580–582.

Mayall, K. (1998). Methodology and validity in the construction of computational models of cognitive deficits following brain damage. *Artificial Intelligence in Medicine*, 13, 1–2, 13–35.

Mayes, A.R. (2002). Does focal retrograde amnesia exist and if so, what causes it? *Cortex*, 38, 670–673.

McCall, W.V. (2004). Quality of life and function after electroconvulsive therapy. *British Journal of Psychiatry*, 185, 405–409.

McCarthy, R.A. Kopelman, M.D. and Warrington, E.K. (2005). Remembering and forgetting of semantic knowledge in amnesia: A 16-year follow-up investigation of RFR. *Neuropsychologia*, 43, 356–372.

McClelland, J.L. and Rumelhart, D.E. (1986). *Parallel Distributed Processing: Explorations in the Microstructure of Cognition* (Vols 1 and 2). Cambridge, MA: MIT Press.

McCloskey, M. (1991). Networks and theories – the place of connectionism in cognitive science. *Psychological Science*, 2, 6, 387–395.

McCorduck, P. (2004). *Machines Who Think: A Personal Inquiry into the History and Prospects of Artificial Intelligence*. Wellesley, MA: A.K. Peters.

McGeoch, J.A. (1932). Forgetting and the law of disuse. *Psychological Review*, 39, 352–370.

McGinn, C. (1999). *The Mysterious Flame: Conscious Minds in a Material World*. New York: Basic Books.

McGurk, H. and MacDonald, J. (1976). Hearing lips and seeing voices. *Nature*, 264, 746–748.

McKenna, P. and Warrington E.K. (1980). Testing for nominal dysphasia, *Journal of Neurology, Neurosurgery and Psychiatry*, 43, 781–788.

McLeod P. (1977). A dual-task response modality effect: Support for multiprocessor models of attention. *Quarterly Journal of Experimental Psychology*, 29, 651–667.

McNeil, J.E. Cipolotti, L. and Warrington, E.K. (1994). The accessibility of proper names. *Neuropsychologia*, 32, 193–208.

McNeil, J.E. and Warrington, E.K. (1993). Prosopagnosia: A face-specific disorder. *Quarterly Journal of Experimental Psychology*, 46A, 1–10.

Mehler, J. (1963). Some effects of grammatical transformations on the recall of English sentences. *Journal of Verbal Learning and Verbal Behavior*, 2, 346–351.

Memon, A. and Wright, D.B. (1999). Eyewitness testimony and the Oklahoma bombing. *The Psychologist*, 12, 292–295.

Mendez, M.F. Tomsak, R.L. and Remler, B. (1990). Disorders of the visual system in Alzheimer's disease. *Journal of Clinical Neuro-Ophthalmology*, 10, 62–69.

Meredith, C. and Edworthy, J. (1994). Sources of confusion in intensive care unit alarms. In N. Stanton (ed.) *Human Factors in Alarm Design* (pp. 238). London: Taylor & Francis.

Metter, E.J. (1995). PET in aphasia and language. In H.S. Kirsner (ed.) *Handbook of Neurological Speech and Language Disorders: Neurological Disease and Therapy* (vol. 33). New York: Marcel Dekker.

Metter, E.J. Hanson, W.R. Jackson, C.A. Kempler, D. Van Lanker, D. Mazziotta, J.C. and Phelps, M.E. (1990). Temporopariatal cortex in aphasia: Evidence from positron emission tomography. *Archives of Neurology*, 47, 1235–1238.

Meyer, D.E. and Schvaneveldt, R.W. (1971). Facilitation in recognising pairs of words: Evidence of a dependence between retrieval operations. *Journal of Experimental Psychology*, 90, 227–234.

Miceli, G. Mazzucchi, A. Menn, L. and Goodglass, H. (1983). Contrasting cases of Italian agrammatic aphasia without comprehension disorder. *Brain and Language*, 19, 65–97.

Middlebrooks, C.J. (1992). Narrow-band sound localisation related to external ear acoustics. *Journal of the Acoustical Society of America*, 92, 5, 2607–2624.

Milchmann, M.S. (2003). 'Implicit memory' cannot explain dissociated traumatic memory: A theoretical critique. *Journal of Trauma and Dissociation*, 4, 27–49.

Milders, M.V. Berg, I.J. and Deelman, B.G. (1995). Four year follow-up of a controlled memory training study in closed head injured patients. *Neuropsychological Rehabilitation*, 5, 223–238.

Miller, E. (1977). *Abnormal Ageing: The Psychology of Senile and Presenile Dementia*. Chichester: Wiley.

Miller, G.A. (1956). The magic number seven, plus or minus two: Some limits on our capacity for processing information. *Psychological Review*, 63, 81–93.

Miller, G.A. and McKean, K.E. (1964). A chronometric study of some relations between sentences. *Quarterly Journal of Experimental Psychology*, 16, 297–308.

Miller, L.A. and Tippett, L.J. (1996). Effects of focal brain lesions on visual problem-solving. *Neuropsychologia*, 34, 387–398.

Mills, C.B. Boteler, E.H. Oliver, G.K. (1999). Digit synaesthesia: A case study using a stroop-type test. *Cognitive Neuropsychology*, 16, 181–191.

Milne, R. and Bull, R. (2002). Back to basics: A componential analysis of the original cognitive interview mnemonics with three age groups. *Applied Cognitive Psychology*, 16, 743–753.

Milne, R. and Bull, R. (2003). Does the cognitive interview help children to resist the effects of suggestive questioning? *Legal and Criminological Psychology*, 8, 21–38.

Milner, A.D. and Goodale, M.A. (1995). *The Visual Brain in Action*. Oxford: Oxford University Press.

Milner, A.D. and McIntosh, R.D. (2002). Perceptual and visuomotor processing in spatial neglect. In H. Karnath, D. Milner and G. Vallar (eds) *The Cognitive and Neural Bases of Spatial Neglect* (pp. 153–166). New York: Oxford University Press.

Milner, B. (1964). Some effects of frontal lobectomy in man. In J.M. Warren and K. Akert (eds) *The Frontal Granular Cortex and Behavior*. New York: McGraw-Hill.

Milner, B. (1966). Amnesia following operation on the temporal lobes. In C.W.M. Whitty and O.L. Zangwill (eds) *Amnesia*. London: Butterworth.

Milner, B. Corkin, S. and Teuber, H.L. (1968). Further analysis of hippocampal amnesia – 14-year follow-up of H.M. *Neuropsychologia*, 6, 215–234.

Minsky, M. (1975). A framework for representing knowledge. In Winston, P. (ed.) *The Psychology of Computer Vision*. New York: McGraw-Hill.

Minsky, M. and Papert, S. (1969). *Perceptrons*. Cambridge, MA: MIT Press.

REFERENCES

Miyake, A. Friedman, N.P. Emerson, M.J. Witzki, A.H. and Howerter, A. (2000). The unity and diversity of executive functions and their contributions to complex 'frontal lobe' tasks: A latent variable analysis. *Cognitive Psychology*, 41, 49–100.

Mohr, J.P. Pessin, M.S. Finkelstein, S. Funkenstein, H.H. Duncan, G.W. and Davis, K.R. (1978). Broca's aphasia: Pathologic and clinical. *Neurology*, 28, 311–324.

Moray, N. (1959). *Attention: Selective Processes in Vision and Hearing.* London: Hutchinson.

Morris, C.D. Bransford, J.D. and Franks, J.J. (1977). Levels of processing versus transfer appropriate processing. *Journal of Verbal Learning and Verbal Behaviour*, 16, 519–533.

Morris, J.S. Frith, C.D. Perrett, D.I. Rowland, D. Young, A.W. Calder, A.J. and Dolan, R.J. (1996). A differential neural response in the human amygdala to fearful and happy facial expressions. *Nature*, 383, 812–815.

Morris, P.E. Gruneberg, M.M. Sykes, R.M. and Merrick, A. (1981). Football knowledge and the acquisition of new results. *British Journal of Psychology*, 72, 479–484.

Morris, R.D. and Baddeley, A.D. (1988). Primary and working memory functioning in Alzheimer-type dementia. *Journal of Clinical and Experimental Neuropsychology*, 10, 279–296.

Morris, R.G. Ahmed, S. Syed, G.M. and Toone, B.K. (1993). Neural correlates of planning ability: Frontal lobe activation during the Tower of London test. *Neuropsychologia*, 31, 1367–1378.

Morsella, E. and Miozzo, M. (2002). Evidence for a cascade model of lexical access in speech production. *Journal of Experimental Psychology: Learning, Memory, and Cognition*, 28, 555–563.

Morton, J. (1969). The interaction of information in word recognition. *Psychological Review*, 76, 165–178.

Morton, J. (1970). A functional model of memory. In D.A. Norman (ed.) *Models of Human Memory.* New York: Academic Press.

Morton, J. (1979). Word recognition. In J. Morton and J.C. Marshall (eds) *Psycholinguistics (Series 2).* London: Elek.

Morton, J. (1980). Two auditory parallels to deep dyslexia. In M. Coltheart, K.E. Patterson and J.C. Marshall (eds) *Deep Dyslexia* (2nd edn). London: Routledge.

Morton, J. and Patterson, K.E. (1980). A new attempt at an interpretation or, an attempt at a new interpretation. In M. Coltheart, K.E. Patterson and J.C. Marshall (eds.) *Deep Dyslexia.* London: Routledge.

Morton, J. and Patterson, K.E. (1987). A new attempt at an interpretation, or, an attempt at a new interpretation. In M. Coltheart, K.E. Patterson and J.C. Marshall (eds) *Deep Dyslexia* (2nd edn). London: Routledge.

Moscovitch, M. (1989). Confabulation and the frontal system: Strategic versus associative retrieval in neuropsychological theories of memory. In H.L. Roediger and F.I.M. Craik (eds) *Variety of Memory and Consciousness: Essays in Honour of Endel Tulving.* Hillsdale, NJ: Lawrence Erlbaum Associates.

Moscovitch, M. Yaschyshyn, M. Ziegler, M. and Nadel, L. (1999). Remote episodic memory and retrograde amnesia: Was Endel Tulving right all along? In E. Tulving (ed.) *Memory, Consciousness, and the Brain: The Tallin Conference.* New York: Psychology Press.

Muter, P. (1980). Very rapid forgetting. *Memory and Cognition*, 8, 174–179.

Myers, P.S. (1993). Narrative expressive deficits associated with right-hemisphere damage. In H.H. Brownell and Y. Joanette (eds) *Narrative Discourse in Neurologically Impaired and Normal Aging Adults.* San Diego: Singular Publishing.

Myles, K.M. Dixon, M.J. Smilek, D. Merikle, P.M. (2003). Seeing double: The role of meaning in alphanumeric-colour synaesthesia. *Brain and Cognition*, 53, 342–345.

Nairne, J.S. (2002). Remembering over the short term: The case against the standard model. *Annual Review of Psychology*, 53, 53–81.

Naish, P. (2005). Attention. In N. Braisby and A. Gellatly (eds) *Cognitive Psychology*. Oxford: Oxford University Press.

Navon, D. (1977). Forest before trees: The precedence of global features in visual perception. *Cognitive Psychology*, 9, 353–383.

Navon, D. and Gopher, D. (1979). On the economy of the human information processing system. *Psychological Review*, 86, 214–255.

Neath, I. and Nairne, J.S. (1995). Word-length effects in immediate memory: Overwriting the trace decay theory. *Psychonomic Bulletin and Review*, 2, 429–441.

Neisser, U. (1964). Visual Search. *Scientific American*, 210, 94–102.

Neisser, U. (1967). *Cognitive Psychology*. New York: Appleton-Century-Crofts.

Neisser, U. (1976). *Cognition and Reality*. San Francisco: Freeman.

Neisser, U. (1982). *Memory Observed*. San Francisco: Freeman.

Neisser, U. (1994). Multiple systems: A new approach to cognitive theory. *European Journal of Cognitive Psychology*, 6, 3, 225–241.

Neisser, U. and Becklin, P. (1975). Selective looking: Attending to visually superimposed events. *Cognitive Psychology*, 7, 480–494.

Neisser, U. and Harsch, N. (1992). Phantom flashbulbs: False connections of hearing the news about Challenger. In E. Winograd and U. Neisser (eds) *Affect and Accuracy in Recall: Studies of 'Flashbulb' Memories*. New York: Cambridge University Press.

Nelson, H.E. (1976). A modified card sorting test sensitive to frontal lobe defects. *Cortex*, 12, 313–324.

Nelson, K. and Ross, G. (1980). The generalities and specifics of long-term memory in infants and younger children. In M. Perlmutter (ed.) *Children's Memory: New Directions for Child Development*. San Francisco, CA: Jossey-Bass.

Newcombe, N.S. Drummey, A.B. Fox, N.A. Lye, E. and Ottinger-Alberts, W. (2000). Remembering early childhood: How much, how, and why (or why not). *Current Directions in Psychological Science*, 9, 55–58.

Newell, A. (1990). *Unified Theories of Cognition*. Cambridge, MA: Harvard University Press.

Newell, A. Shaw, J.C. and Simon, H.A. (1958). Elements of a theory of human problem solving. *Psychological Review*, 65, 151–166.

Newell, A. and Simon, H. (1972). *Human Problem Solving*. Englewood Cliffs, NJ: Prentice-Hall.

Newell, A. and Simon, H. (1976). Computer science as empirical enquiry: Symbols and search. *Communications of the ACM*, 19, 113–126.

Newlands, P.J. George, R.C. Towell, N.A. Kemp, R.I. and Clifford, B.R. (1999). An investigation of description quality from real-life interviews. *Psychology, Crime, and Law*, 5, 145–166.

Newstead, S.E. Ellis, M.C. Evans, J.St.B.T. and Dennis, I. (1997). Conditional reasoning with realistic material. *Thinking and Reasoning*, 3, 49–76.

Nilsson, L.G. and Gardiner, J.M. (1993). Identifying exceptions in a database of recognition failure studies from 1973 to 1992. *Memory and Cognition*, 21, 397–410.

Norman, D.A. (1981). Categorisation of action slips. *Psychological Review*, 88, 1–15.

Norman, D.A. and Shallice, T. (1986). Attention to action: Willed and automatic control of behaviour. In R.J. Davidson, G.E. Schwartz, and D.E. Shapiro (eds) *Consciousness and Self-regulation*. New York: Plenum Press.

Norman, J. (2001). Ecological psychology and the two visual systems: Not to worry. *Ecological Psychology*, 13, 2, 135–145.

Norman, J. (2002). Two visual systems and two theories of perception: An attempt to reconcile the constructivist and ecological approaches. *Behavioral and Brain Sciences*, 25, 1, 73–96.

Nunn, J.A. Gregory, L.J. Brammer, M. Williams, S.C.R. Parslow, D.M. Morgan, M.J. Morris, R.G. Bullmore, E.T. Baron-Cohen, S. and Gray, J.A. (2002). Functional magnetic resonance imaging of synesthesia: Activation of V4/V8 by spoken words. *Nature Neuroscience*, 5, 371–375.

Nyberg, L. (2002). Levels of processing: A view from functional brain imaging. *Memory*, 10, 345–348.

Nys, G.M. van Zandvoort, M.J.E. Roks, G. Kappelle, L.J. de Kort, P.L. and de Haan, E.H. (2004).The role of executive functioning in spontaneous confabulation. *Cognitive and Behavioural Neurology*, 17, 213–218.

Oaksford, M. (2005). Reasoning. In N. Braisby and A. Gellatly (eds) *Cognitive Psychology*. Oxford: Oxford University Press.

Oaksford, M. and Chater, N. (1994). A rational analysis of the selection task as optimal data selection. *Psychological Review*, 101, 608–631.

Oaksford, M. and Chater, N. (1998). *Rationality in an Uncertain World: Essays on the Cognitive Science of Human Reasoning*. Hove: Psychology Press.

Oaksford, M. and Chater, N. (2001). The probabilistic approach to human reasoning. *Trends in Cognitive Sciences*, 5, 349–357.

Oberauer, K. (2003). Understanding serial position curves in short-term recognition and recall. *Journal of Memory and Language*, 4, 469–483.

O'Connor, M. Butters, N. Miliotis, P. Eslinger, P. and Cermak, L.S. (1992). The dissociation of retrograde and anterograde amnesia in a patient with herpes encephalitis. *Journal of Clinical and Experimental Neuropsychology*, 14, 159–178.

Ogden, J.A. and Corkin, S. (1991). Memories of H.M. In W.C. Abraham, M.C. Corballis, and K.G. White (eds) *Memory Mechanisms: A Tribute to G.V. Goddard*. Hillsdale, NJ: Erlbaum.

Ohlsson, S. (1992). Information processing explanations of insight and related phenomena. In M.T. Keane and K.J. Gilhooly (eds) *Advances in the Psychology of Thinking* (pp. 1–44). London: Harvester Wheatsheaf.

Ojemann, G.A. (1983). Brain organisation for language from the perspective of electrical stimulation mapping. *Behavioral and Brain Sciences*, 6, 189–230.

Oldfield, S.R. and Parker, S.P.A. (1984a). Acuity of sound localization: A topography of auditory space. I. Normal conditions. *Perception*, 13, 581–600.

Oldfield, S.R. and Parker, S.P.A. (1984b). Acuity of sound localization: A topography of auditory space. II. Pinna cues absent. *Perception*, 13, 601–617.

O'Regan, J.K. (1992). Solving the 'real' mysteries of visual perception: The world as an outside memory. *Canadian Journal of Psychology*, 46, 3, 461–488.

O'Reilly, R.C. and Munakata, Y. (2000). *Computational Explorations in Cognitive Neuroscience: Understanding the Mind by Simulating the Brain*. Cambridge, MA: MIT Press.

Ormerod, T.C. MacGregor, J.N. and Chronicle, E.P. (2002). Dynamics and constraints in insight problem solving. *Journal of Experimental Psychology: Learning, Memory, and Cognition*, 28, 791–799.

O'Rourke, T.B. and Holcomb, P.J. (2002). Electrophysiological evidence for the efficiency of spoken word processing. *Biological Psychology*, 60, 121–150.

Ost, J. Costall, A. and Bull, R. (2002). A perfect symmetry? Retractors' experiences of recovering and retracting abuse memories. *Psychology, Crime, and Law*, 8, 155–181.

Otten, L.J. and Rugg, M.D. (2001). Task-dependency of the neural correlates of episodic encoding as measured by fMRI. *Cerebral Cortex*, 11, 1150–1160.

Owen, A.M. Downes, J.J. Sahakian, B.J. Polkey, C.E. and Robbins, T.W. (1990). Planning and spatial working memory following frontal lobe lesions in man. *Neuropsychologia*, 28, 1021–1034.

Owen, A.M. Roberts, A.C. Polkey, C.E. Sahakian, B.J. and Robbins, T.W. (1991). Extra-dimension versus intra-dimensional shifting performance following frontal lobe excisions, temporal lobe excisions or amygdalo-hippocampectomy in man. *Neuropsychologia*, 29, 993–1006.

Owen, D.H. (1990). Lexicon of terms for the perception and control of self-motion and orientation. In R. Warren and A.H. Wertheim (eds) *Perception and Control of Self-Motion* (pp. 33–50). Hillsdale, NJ: Lawrence Erlbaum.

Ozonoff, S. Strayer, D. McMahon, W. and Filoux, F. (1994). Executive function abilities in autism and Tourette syndrome: An information-processing approach. *Journal of Child Psychology and Psychiatry*, 35, 1015–1032.

Parker, D. (1982). Learning-logic. Technical Report 581–64, Office of Technology Licensing, Stanford University.

Parkin, A.J. (1983). The relationship between orienting tasks and the structure of memory traces: Evidence from false recognition. *British Journal of Psychology*, 74, 61–69.

Parkin, A.J. (1993). *Memory: Phenomena, Experiment, and Theory*. Oxford: Blackwell.

Parkin, A.J. (1996). *Explorations in Cognitive Neuropsychology*. Oxford: Blackwell.

Parkin, A.J. (1997). *Memory and Amnesia*. Oxford: Blackwell.

Parkin, A.J. (2000). *Essential Cognitive Psychology*. Hove: Psychology Press.

Parkin, A.J. Gardiner, J.M. and Rosser, R. (1995). Functional aspects of recollective experience in face recognition. *Consciousness and Cognition*, 4, 387–398.

Parkin, A.J. Reid, T. and Russo, R. (1990). On the differential nature of implicit and explicit memory. *Memory and Cognition*, 18, 507–514.

Parkin, A.J. and Walter, B. (1992). Ageing, conscious recollection, and frontal lobe dysfunction. *Psychology and Ageing*, 7, 290–298.

Parkin, A.J. Walter, B.M. and Hunkin, N.M. (1995). Relationships between normal ageing, frontal lobe function, and memory for temporal and spatial information. *Neuropsychology*, 9, 304–312.

Parsons, L.M. and Osherson, D. (2001). New evidence for distinct right and left brain systems for deductive versus probabilistic reasoning. *Cerebral Cortex*, 11, 954–965.

Pashler, H. (1990). Do response modality effects support multiprocessor models of divided attention? *Journal of Experimental Psychology: Human Perception and Performance*, 16, 826–842.

Patterson, K.E. (1982). The relation between reading and phonological coding: Further neuropsychological observations. In A.W. Ellis (ed.) *Normality and Pathology in Cognitive Functions*. London: Academic Press.

Patterson, K.E. and Besner, D. (1984). Is the right hemisphere literate? *Cognitive Neuropsychology*, 1, 315–341.

Paulesu, E. *et al.* (1995). The physiology of coloured hearing: A PET activation study of colour-word synaesthesia. *Brain*, 118, 661–676.

Payne, D.G. (1987). Hyperamnesia and reminiscence in recall: A historical and empirical review. *Psychological Bulletin*, 101, 5–27.

Payne, D.G. Peters, L.J. Birkmire, D.P. Bonto, M.A. Anastasi, J.S. and Wenger, M.J. (1994). Effects of speech intelligibility level on concurrent visual task performance. *Human Factors*, 36, 441–475.

Pearl, J. (1995). Bayesian networks. In M. Arbib, (ed.) *The Handbook of Brain Theory and Neural Networks* (pp. 149–153). Cambridge, MA: MIT Press.

Perkins, D.N. Farady, M. and Bushey, B. (1991). Everyday reasoning and the roots of intelligence. In J.F. Voss, D.N. Perkins and J.W. Segal (eds) *Informal Reasoning and Education* (pp. 83–105). Hillsdale, NJ: Lawrence Erlbaum Associates; Ann Arbor: University of Michigan Press.

Perret, E. (1974). The left frontal lobe of man and the suppression of habitual responses in verbal categorical behavior. *Neuropsychologica*, 12, 323–330.

Petersen, S.E. Fox, P.T. Posner, M.I. Mintun, M. and Raichle, M.E. (1988). Positron emission tomographic studies of the cortical anatomy of single-word processing. *Nature*, 331, 585–589.

Peterson, L.R. and Peterson, M.J. (1959). Short-term retention of individual items. *Journal of Experimental Psychology*, 58, 193–198.

Phillips, C.E. Jarrold, C. Baddeley, A.D. Grant, J. and Karmiloff-Smith, A. (2004). Comprehension of spatial language terms in Williams syndrome: Evidence for an interaction between domains of strength and weakness. *Cortex*, 40, 85–101.

Piercy, M.F. (1977). Experimental studies of the organic amnesic syndrome. In C.W.M. Whitty and O.L. Zangwill (eds) *Amnesia*. London: Butterworth.

Pilgrim, L.K. Moss, H.E. and Tyler, L.K. (2005). Semantic processing of living and nonliving concepts across the cerebral hemispheres. *Brain and Language*, 94, 86–93.

Pillemer, D.B. and White, S.H. (1989). Childhood events recalled by children and adults. In H.W. Reese (ed.) *Advances in Child Development and Behaviour*. San Diego, CA: Academic Press.

Pinker, S. (1994). *The Language Instinct: The New Science of Language and Mind*. London: Penguin.

Pinker, S. (1997). *How the Mind Works*. London: Penguin.

Pitt, M.A. and Myung, I.J. (2002). When a good fit can be bad. *Trends in Cognitive Sciences*, 6, 10, 421–425.

Plaut, D.C. McClelland, J.L. Seidenberg, M.S. and Patterson, K.E. (1996). Understanding normal and impaired word reading: Computational principles in quasi-regular domains. *Psychological Review*, 103, 56–115.

Plaut, D.C. and Shallice, T. (1993). Deep dyslexia: A case study of connectionist neuropsychology. *Cognitive Neuropsychology*, 10, 377–500.

Poppel, E. Held, R. and Frost, D. (1973). Residual visual function after brain wounds involving the central visual pathways in man. *Nature*, 243, 295–296.

Posner, M.I. (1980). Orienting of attention. *Quarterly Journal of Experimental Psychology*, 32, 3–25.

Posner, M.I. and Cohen, Y. (1984). Components of visual orienting. In H. Bouma and D.G. Bouwhuis (eds) *Attention and Performance X*. Hove: LEA.

Posner, M.I. and Petersen, S.E. (1990). The attention system of the human brain. *Annual Review of Neuroscience*, 13, 25–42.

Posner, M.I. Peterson, S.E. Fox, P.T. and Raichle, M.E. (1988). Localization of cognitive operations in the human brain. *Science*, 240, 1627–1632.

Posner, M.I. Rafal, R.D. Choate, L.S. and Vaughan J. (1985). Inhibition of return: Neural bias and function. *Cognitive Neuropsychology*, 2, 211–228.

Posner, M.I. Walker, J.A. Friedrich, F.J. and Rafal, R.D. (1984). Effects of parietal lobe injury on covert orienting of visual attention. *Journal of Neuroscience*, 4, 1863–1874.

Pujol, M. and Kopelman M.D. (2003). Korsakoff's syndrome. *Advances in Clinical Neuroscience and Rehabilitation*, 3, 14–17.

Rafal, R.D. and Posner, M.I. (1987). Deficits in human visual spatial attention following thalamic lesions. *Proceedings of the National Academy of Science*, 84, 7349–7353.

Raine, A. Hulme, C. Chadderton, H. and Bailey, P. (1992). Verbal short-term memory span in speech-disordered children: Implications for articulatory coding in short-term memory. *Child Development*, 62, 415–423.

Ramachandran, V.S. and Hubbard, E.M. (2002). Synaesthesia – A window into perception, thought and language. *Journal of Consciousness Studies*, 8, 3–34.

Rao, S.C. Rainer, G. and Miller, E.K. (1997). Integration of what and where in the primate prefrontal cortex. *Science*, 276, 821–824.

Rayner, K. Carlson, M. and Frazier, L. (1983). The interaction of syntax and semantics during sentence processing: Eye movements in the analysis of semantically biased sentences. *Journal of Verbal Learning and Verbal Behavior*, 22, 358–374.

Rayner, K. and Duffy, S.A. (1986). Lexical complexity and fixation times in reading: Effects of word frequency, verb complexity, and lexical ambiguity. *Memory and Cognition*, 14, 191–201.

Rayner, K. and Pollatsek, A. (1989). *The Psychology of Reading.* Hove: Psychology Press.

Reason, J. (1979). Actions not as planned: The price of automaticity. In G. Underwood and R. Stevens (eds) *Aspects of Consciousness Vol. 1: Psychological Issues.* Chichester: Wiley.

Reason, J. (1984). Absent-mindedness. In J. Nicholson and H. Beloff (eds) *Psychology Survey 5.* Leicester: BPS.

Reason, J. (1990). *Human Error.* Cambridge: Cambridge University Press.

Reason, J. (1992). Cognitive underspecification: Its variety and consequences. In B.J. Baars (ed.) *Experimental Slips and Human Error: Exploring the Architecture of Volition.* New York: Plenum.

Reason, J. and Mycielska, K. (1982). *Absent-Minded? The Psychology of Mental Lapses and Everyday Errors.* Englewood Cliffs, NJ: Prentice-Hall.

Reed, J.M. and Squire, L.R. (1998). Retrograde amnesia for facts and events: Findings from four new cases. *Journal of Neuroscience*, 18, 3943–3954.

Reed, L.J. Lasserson, D. Marsden, P. Stanhope, N. Stevens, T. Bello, F. Kingsley, D. Colchester, A. and Kopelman, M.D. (2003). FDG-PET findings in the Wernicke–Korsakoff syndrome. *Cortex*, 39, 1027–1045.

Reeve, D.K. and Aggleton, J.P. (1998). On the specificity of expert knowledge about a soap opera: An everyday story of farming folk. *Applied Cognitive Psychology*, 12, 35–42.

Regard, M. and Landis, T. (1984). Transient global amnesia: Neuropsychological dysfunction during attack and recovery of two 'pure' cases. *Journal of Neurology, Neurosurgery, and Psychiatry*, 47, 668–672.

Renault, B.S. Signoret, J. Debruille, B. Breton, F. Bolgert, F. (1989). Brain potentials reveal covert facial recognition in prosopagnosia. *Neuropsychologia*, 27, 905–912.

Reverberi, C. Lavaroni, A. Gigli, G.L. Skrap, M. and Shallice, T. (2005). Specific impairments of rule induction in different frontal lobe subgroups. *Neuropsychologia*, 43, 460–472.

Ribot, T. (1882). *Diseases of Memory.* New York: Appleton.

Riccio, G.E. and McDonald, P.V. (1998). *Multimodal Perception and Multicriterion Control of Nested Systems, 1, Coordination of Postural Control and Vehicular Control* (Technical Report No. NASA/TP-3703): NASA.

Richardson-Klavehn, A. and Gardiner, J.M. (1995). Retrieval volition and memorial awareness in stem completion: An empirical analysis. *Psychological Research*, 57, 166–178.

Rips, L.J. (1994). *The Psychology of Proof.* Cambridge, MA: MIT Press.

Robbins, T.W. Anderson, E.J. Barker, D.R. Bradley, A.C. Fearnyhough, C. Henson, R. Hudson, S.R. and Baddeley, A.D. (1996). Working memory in chess. *Memory and Cognition*, 24, 83–93.

Roberts, S. and Pashler, H. (2000). How persuasive is a good fit? A comment on theory testing. *Psychological Review*, 107, 2, 358–367.

Rock, I. (1977). In defense of unconscious inference. In W. Epstein (ed.) *Stability and Constancy in Visual Perception: Mechanisms and Processes* (pp. 321–377). New York: Wiley.

Rock, I. (1983). *The Logic of Perception.* Cambridge, MA: MIT Press.

Rogers, A. Pilgrim, D. and Lacey, R. (1993). *Experiencing Psychiatry: Users' Views of Services.* London: Macmillan.

Rogers, T.B. Kuiper, N.A. and Kirker, W.S. (1977). Self-reference and the encoding of personal information. *Journal of Personality and Social Psychology*, 35, 677–688.

Rose, D. (1996). Guest editorial: Some reflections on (or by?) grandmother cells. *Perception*, 25, 8.

Rosenbaum, R.S. Kohler, S. Schacter, D.L. Moscovitch, M. Westmacott, R. Black, S.E. Gao, F. and Tulving, E. (2005). The case of K.C.: Contributions of a memory-impaired person to memory theory. *Neuropsychologia*, 43, 989–1021.

Rubin, D.C. Rahal, T.A. and Poon, L.W. (1998). Things learned in early adulthood are remembered best. *Memory and Cognition*, 26, 3–19.

Rubin, D.C. and Wenzel, A. (1996). One hundred years of forgetting: A quantitative description of retention. *Psychological Review*, 103, 734–760.

Rubin, D.C. Wetzler, S.E. and Nebes, R.D. (1986). Autobiographical memory across the life span. In D.C. Rubin (ed.) *Autobiographical Memory*. Cambridge: Cambridge University Press.

Rubin, E. (1915). *Synoplevde Figurer*. Copenhagen: Gyldendalske.

Rueckert, L. and Grafman, J. (1996). Sustained attention deficits in patients with right frontal lesions. *Neuropsychologia*, 34, 953–963.

Rumelhart, D. (1975). Notes on a schema for stories. In D. Bobrow and A. Collins (eds) *Representation and Understanding: Studies in Cognitive Science*. New York: Academic Press.

Rumelhart, D. Hinton, G. and Williams, R. (1986a). Learning representations by back-propagating errors. *Nature*, 323, 533–536.

Rumelhart, D.E. and McClelland, J.L. (eds). (1986). *Parallel-Distributed Processing: Explorations in the Microstructure of Cognition* (vol. 1). Cambridge, MA: MIT Press.

Rumelhart, D. Smolensky, P. McClelland, J. and Hinton, G. (1986b). Schemata and sequential thought processes in PDP models. In *Parallel Distributed Processing* (vol. 2, pp. 7–57). Cambridge, MA: MIT Press.

Rumelhart, D. and Todd, P. (1993). Learning and connectionist representations. In D. Meyer and S. Kornblum (eds) *Attention and Performance* (vol. XIV, pp. 3–31). Cambridge, MA: MIT Press.

Russell, W.R. (1971). *The Traumatic Amnesias*. London: Oxford University Press.

Sá, W.C. Kelley, C.N. Ho, C. and Stanovich, K.E. (2005). Thinking about personal theories: Individual differences in the coordination of theory and evidence. *Personality and Individual Differences*, 38, 1149–1161.

Sabey, B. and Staughton, G.C. (1975). 'Interacting roles of road environment, vehicle and road user'. Paper presented at the 5th International Conference of the International Association for Accident Traffic Medicine, London.

Sacchett, C. and Humphreys, G.W. (1992). Calling a squirrel a squirrel but a canoe a wigwam – a category specific deficit for artifactual objects and body parts. *Cognitive Neuropsychology*, 9, 73–86.

Sachs, J.S. (1967). Recognition memory for syntactic and semantic aspects of connnected discourse. *Perception and Psychophysics*, 2, 437–442.

Saffran, E.M. Bogyo, L.C. Schwartz, M.F. and Marin, O.S.M. (1987). Does deep dyslexia reflect right hemisphere reading? In M. Coltheart, K.E. Patterson and J.C. Marshall (eds) *Deep Dyslexia* (2nd edn). London: Routledge and Kegan Paul.

Saffran, E.M. Schwartz, M.F. and Marin, O.S.M. (1980). Evidence from aphasia: Isolating the components of a production model. In B. Butterworth (ed.) *Language Production: Speech and Talk* (vol. 1). London: Academic Press.

Salame, P. and Baddeley, A.D. (1982). Disruption of short-term memory by unattended speech: Implications for the structure of working memory. *Journal of Verbal Learning and Verbal Behaviour*, 21, 150–164.

Saliba, A. (2001). 'Auditory-visual integration in sound localisation'. University of Essex, Colchester.

Salmaso, D. and Denes, G. (1982). The frontal lobes on an attention task: A signal detection analysis. *Pereptual and Motor Skills*, 45, 1147–1152.

Salthouse, T.A. (1994). Ageing associations: Influence of speed on adult age differences in associative learning. *Journal of Experimental Psychology: Learning, Memory, and Cognition*, 20, 1486–1503.

Savin, H.B. and Perchonock, E. (1965). Grammatical structure and the immediate recall of English sentences. *Journal of Verbal Learning and Verbal Behavior*, 4, 348–353.

Schacter, D.L. Harbluk, J.L. and McLachlan, D.R. (1984). Retrieval without recollection: An experimental analysis of source amnesia. *Journal of Verbal Learning and Verbal Behaviour*, 23, 593–611.

Schacter, D.L. McGlynn, S.M. Milberg, W.P. and Church, B.A. (1993). Spared priming despite impaired comprehension: Implicit memory in a case of word-meaning deafness. *Neuropsychology*, 7, 107–118.

Schacter, D.L. Savage, C. and Rauch, S. (1996). Conscious recollection and the human hippocampal formation: Evidence from PET. *Proceedings of the National Academy of Science*, 93, 321–325.

Schacter, D.L. Wagner, A.D. and Buckner, R.L. (2000). Memory systems of 1999. In E. Tulving and F.I.M. Craik (eds) *The Oxford Handbook of Memory*. New York: Oxford University Press.

Schank, R.C. (1982). *Dynamic Memory*. Cambridge: Cambridge University Press.

Schank, R. and Abelson, R. (1977). *Scripts, Plans, Goals and Understanding*. Hillsdale, NJ: Lawrence Erlbaum Associates Inc.

Scheerer, M. (1963). Problem solving. *Scientific American*, 208, 118–128.

Schindler, B.A. Ramchandani, D. Matthews M.K. and Podell, K. (1995). Competency and the frontal lobe. *Psychosomatics*, 36, 400–404.

Schneider, G.E. (1967). Contrasting visuomotor functions of tectum and cortex in the golden hamster. *Psychologische Forschung*, 31, 52–62.

Schneider, G.E. (1969). Two visual systems. *Science*, 163, 895–902.

Schneider, W. and Shiffrin, R.M. (1977). Controlled and automatic human information processing: 1. Detection, search, and attention. *Psychological Review*, 84, 1–66.

Schroyens, W. and Schaeken, W. (2003). A critique of Oaksford, Chater, and Larkin's (2000) conditional probability model of conditional reasoning. *Journal of Experimental Psychology: Learning, Memory, and Cognition*, 29, 140–149.

Schwartz, M.F. Saffran, E. and Marin, O. (1980). The word order problem in agrammatism I: Comprehension. *Brain and Language*, 10, 249–262.

Scotko, B.G. Kensinger, E.A. Locascio, J.J. Einstein, G. Rubin, D.C. Tupler, L.A. Krendl, A. and Corkin, S. (2004). Puzzling thoughts for H.M.: Can new semantic information be anchored in old semantic memories? *Neuropsychology*, 18, 756–769.

Scoville, W.B. and Milner, B. (1957). Loss of recent memory after bilateral hippocampal lesions. *Journal of Neurology, Neurosurgery, and Psychiatry*, 20, 11–21.

Searleman, A. and Herrmann, D. (1994). *Memory from a Broader Perspective*. New York: McGraw-Hill.

Sears, C.R. Hino, Y. and Lupker, S.J. (1995). Neighborhood size and neighborhood frequency effects in word recognition. *Journal of Experimental Psychology: Human Perception and Performance*, 21, 876–900.

Segall, M.H. Campbell, D.T. and Herskovits, M.J. (1963). Cultural differences in the perception of geometrical illusions. *Science*, 139, 769–771.

Seidenberg, M.S. and McClelland, J.L. (1989). A distributed developmental model of word recognition. *Psychological Review*, 96, 523–568.

Selfridge, O.G. (1959). Pandemonium: A paradigm for learning. In *Symposium on the Mechanisation of Thought Processes*. London: HMSO.

Selfridge, O.G. and Neisser, U. (1960). Pattern recognition by machine. *Scientific American*, 203, 60–68.

Sellal, F. Manning, L. Seegmuller, C. Scheiber, C. and Schoenfelder, P. (2002). Pure retrograde amnesia following a mild head trauma: A neuropsychological and metabolic study. *Cortex*, 38, 499–509.

Semenza, C. and Sgarmella, T. (1993). Proper names production: A clinical case study of the effects of phonemic cueing. *Memory*, 1, 265–280.

Sergent, J. and Signoret, J.L. (1992). Varietirs of functional deficits in prosopagnosia. *Cerebral Cortex*, 2, 375–388.

Service, E. (1992). Phonology, working memory, and foreign language learning. *Quarterly Journal of Experimental Psychology*, 45A, 21–50.

Shaffer, L.S. (1975). Multiple attention in continuous verbal tasks. In P.M.A. Rabbitt and S. Dornic (eds) *Attention and Performance V*. London: Academic.

Shaffer, W.O. and LaBerge, D. (1979). Automatic semantic activation of unattended words. *Journal of Verbal Learning and Verbal Behaviour*, 18, 413–426.

Shallice, T. (1982). Specific impairments of planning. *Philosophical Transactions of the Royal Society of London, B298*, 199–209.

Shallice, T. (1988). *From Neuropsychology to Mental Structure*. Cambridge: Cambridge University Press.

Shallice, T. and Burgess, P.W. (1991a). Deficits in strategy application following frontal lobe damage in man. *Brain*, 114, 727–741.

Shallice, T. Burgess, P.W. Schon, F. and Baxter, D.M. (1989). The origins of utilization behaviour. *Brain*, 112, 1587–1598.

Shallice, T. and Burgess, P.W. (1991b). Higher-order cognitive impairments and frontal lobe lesions. In H.S. Levin, H.M. Eisenberg and A.L. Benton (eds) *Frontal Lobe Function and Dysfunction*. Oxford: Oxford University Press.

Shallice, T. and Evans, M.E. (1978). The involvement of frontal lobes in cognitive estimation. *Cortex*, 13, 294–303.

Shallice, T. and Warrington, E.K. (1974). The dissociation between long-term retention of meaningful sounds and verbal material. *Neuropsychologia*, 12, 553–555.

Shallice, T. and Warrington, E.K. (1980). Single and multiple component central dyslexic syndromes. In M. Coltheart, K.E. Patterson, and J.C. Marshall (eds) *Deep Dyslexia*. London: Routledge and Kegan Paul.

Shapley, R. (1995). Parallel neural pathways and visual function. In M.S. Gazzaniga (ed.) *The Cognitive Neurosciences* (pp. 315–324). Cambridge, MA: MIT Press.

Shaw, J.S. Bjork, R.A. and Handal, A. (1995). Retrieval-induced forgetting in an eyewitness-memory paradigm. *Psychonomic Bulletin and Review*, 2, 249–253.

Shepard, R.N. and Metzler, J. (1971). Mental rotation of three-dimensional objects. *Science*, 171, 701–703.

Shiffrin, R.M. and Schneider, W. (1977). Controlled and automatic human information processing: II. Perceptual learning, automatic attending, and a general theory. *Psychological Review*, 84, 127–190.

Shimamura, A.P. Janowsky, J. and Squire, L.R. (1990). Memory for temporal order of events in patients with frontal lobe lesions and amnesic patients. *Neuropsychologia*, 28, 803–813.

Shimamura, A.P. Jernigan, T.L. and Squire, L.R. (1988). Korsakoff's syndrome: Radiological (CT) findings and neuropsychological correlates. *Journal of Neuroscience*, 8, 4400–4410.

Sierra, M. and Berrios, G.E. (2000). Flashbulb and flashback memories. In G.E. Berrios and J.R. Hodges (eds) *Memory Disorders in Psychiatric Practice*. New York: Cambridge University Press.

Simon, H.A. and Reed, S.K. (1976). Modelling strategy shifts on a problem solving task. *Cognitive Psychology*, 8, 86–97.

Simons, J.S. Graham, K.S. Galton, C.J. Patterson, K. and Hodges, J.R. (2001). Semantic knowledge and episodic memory for faces in semantic dementia. *Neuropsychology*, 15, 101–114.

Skinner, B.F. (1938). *The Behaviour of Organisms*. New York: Appleton-Century-Crofts.

Slamecka, N.J. and Graf, P. (1978). The generation effect: Delineation of a phenomenon. *Journal of Experimental Psychology: Human Learning and Memory*, 4, 592–604.

Slobin, D. (1966). Grammatical transformations and sentence comprehension in childhood and adulthood. *Journal of Verbal Learning and Verbal Behavior*, 5, 219–227.

Smilek, D. Dixon, M.J. Merikle, P.M. (2005). Synaesthesia: Discordant male monozygotic twins. *Neurocase*, 11, 363–370.

Smith, E.E. and Jonides, J. (1999). Working memory: A view from neuroimaging. *Cognitive Psychology*, 33, 5–42.

Smith, M.L. and Milner, B. (1984). Differential effects of frontal-lobe lesions on cognitive estimation and spatial memory. *Neuropsychologia*, 19, 781–793.

Smith, M.L. and Milner, B. (1988). Estimation of frequency of occurrence of abstract designs after frontal or temporal lobectomy. *Neuropsychologia*, 26, 297–306.

Smith, R.W. and Healy, A.F. (1998). The time-course of the generation effect. *Memory and Cognition*, 26, 135–142.

Smith, S.M. (1986). Environmental context-dependent memory: Recognition memory using a short-term memory task for input. *Memory and Cognition*, 14, 347–354.

Smith, S.M. and Vela, E. (2001). Environmental context-dependent memory: A review and meta-analysis. *Psychonomic Bulletin and Review*, 8, 203–220.

Smolensky, P. (1988). On the proper treatment of connectionism. *Behavioural and Brain Sciences*, 11, 1–74.

Soroker, N. Kasher, A. Giora, R. Batori, Corn, C. Gil, M. and Zaidel, E. (2005). Processing of basic speech acts following localized brain damage: A new light on the neuroanatomy of language. *Brain and Cognition*, 57, 214–217.

Spelke, E.S. Hirst, W.C. and Neisser, U. (1976). Skills of divided attention. *Cognition*, 4, 215–330.

Sperling, G. (1960). The information available in brief visual presentations. *Psychological Monographs*, 74, 1–29.

Sperry, R.W. and Gazzaniga, M.S. (1975). Dichotic testing of partial and complete split-brain subjects. *Neuropsychologia*, 13, 341–346.

Spiers, H.J. Maguire, E.A. and Burgess, N. (2001). Hippocampal amnesia. *Neurocase*, 7, 357–382.

Sprengelmeyer, R. Schroeder, U. Young, A.W. Epplen, J.T. (2006). Disgust in pre-clinical Huntington's disease: A longitudinal study. *Neuropsychologia*, 44, 518–533.

Sprengelmeyer, R. Young, A.W. Calder, A.J. Karnat, A. Lange, H.W. Hömberg, V. Perrett, D.I. and Rowland, D. (1996). Loss of disgust: Perception of faces and emotions in Huntington's disease. *Brain*, 119, 1647–1665.

Squire, L.R. (1982). Comparisons between forms of amnesia: Some deficits are unique to Korsakoff's syndrome. *Journal of Experimental Psychology: Learning, Memory, and Cognition*, 8, 560–571.

Squire, L.R. (1992). Declarative and nondeclarative memory: Multiple brain systems supporting learning and memory. *Journal of Cognitive Neuroscience*, 4, 232–243.

Squire, L.R. Cohen, N.J. and Nadel, L. (1984). The medial temporal region and memory consolidation: A new hypothesis. In H. Weingartner and E. Parker (eds) *Memory Consolidation*. Hillsdale, NJ: Erlbaum.

Squire, L.R. Ojeman, J.G. Miezin, F.M. Petersen, S.E. Videen, T.O. and Raichle, M.E. (1992). Activation of the hippocampus in normal humans: A functional anatomical study of memory. *Proceedings of the National Academy of Science*, USA, 89, 1837–1841.

Squire, L.R. Slater, P.C. and Miller, P.L. (1981). Retrograde amnesia and bilateral electro-convulsive therapy. *Archives of General Psychiatry*, 38, 89–95.

Starr, A. and Phillips, L. (1970). Verbal and motor memory in the amnestic syndrome. *Neuropsychologia*, 8, 75–88.

Stavonich, K.E. and West, R.F. (2000). Individual differences in reasoning: Implications for the rationality debate? *Behavioural and Brain Sciences*, 23, 654–664.

Stefanacci, L. Buffalo, E.A. Schmolk, H. and Squire, L.R. (2001). Profound amnesia after damage to the medial temporal lobe: A neuroanatomical and neuropsychological profile of patient E.P. *Journal of Neuroscience*, 20, 7024–7036.

Steinvorth, S. Levine, B. and Corkin, S. (2005). Medial temporal lobe structures are needed to re-experience remote autobiographical memories: Evidence from H.M. and W.R. *Neuropsychologia*, 43, 479–496.

Steven, M.S. Blakemore, C. (2004). Visual synaesthesia in the blind. *Perception*, 33, 855–868.

Stevenson, R.J. and Over, D.E. (2001). Reasoning from uncertain premises: Effects of exper-tise and conversational context. *Thinking and Reasoning*, 7, 367–390.

Stewart, F. Parkin, A.J. and Hunkin, N.M. (1992). Naming impairments following recovery from Herpes Simplex Encephalitis: Category specific? *The Quarterly Journal of Experimental Psychology*, 44A, 261–284.

Stroop, J.R. (1935). Studies of interference in serial verbal reactions. *Journal of Experimental Psychology*, 18, 643–662.

Stuss, D.T. and Alexander, M.P. (2000). Executive functions and the frontal lobes: A concep-tual view. *Psychological Research*, 63, 289–298.

Stuss, D.T. Floden, D. Alexander, M.P. Levine, B. and Katz, D. (2001). Stroop performance in focal lesion patients: Dissociation of processes and frontal lobe lesion location. *Neuropsychologia*, 39, 771–786.

Styles, E.A. (1997). *The Psychology of Attention*. Hove: Psychology Press.

Sutherland, S. (1989). *The International Dictionary of Psychology*. London: Macmillan.

Swain, S.A. Polkey, C.E. Bullock, P. and Morris, R.B. (1998). Recognition memory and memory for order in script-based stories following frontal lobe excisions. *Cortex*, 34, 25–45.

Swinney, D. (1979). Lexical access during sentence comprehension: (Re) consideration of context effects. *Journal of Verbal Learning and Verbal Behavior*, 18, 645–712.

Talarico, J.M. and Rubin, D.C. (2003). Confidence, not consistency, characterises flashbulb memories. *Psychological Science*, 14, 455–461.

Talland, G.A. (1965). *Deranged Memory*. New York: Academic Press.

Taraban, R. and McClelland, J.L. (1988). Constituent attachment and thematic role assign-ment in sentence processing: Influences of content-based expectations. *Journal of Memory and Language*, 27, 597–632.

Taylor, F.K. (1965). Cryptomnesia and plagiarism. *British Journal of Psychiatry*, 111, 1111–1118.

Teasdale, T.W. and Engberg, A.W. (2003). Cognitive dysfunction in young men following head injury in childhood and adolescence: A population study. *Journal of Neurology, Neurosurgery, and Psychiatry*, 74, 933–936.

Teuber, H.L. (1968). Alteration of perception and memory in man. In L. Weiskrantz (ed.) *Analysis of Behavioural Change.* New York: Harper and Row.

Thomas, J.C. (1974). An analysis of behaviour in the hobbits–orcs problems. *Cognitive Psychology*, 6, 257–269.

Thomas, N.J.T. (1999). Are theories of imagery theories of imagination? An active perception approach to conscious mental content. *Cognitive Science*, 23, 2, 207–245.

Thompson, L.A. Williams, K.L. L'Esperance, P.R. and Cornelius, J. (2001). Context-dependent memory under stressful conditions: The case of skydiving. *Human Factors*, 43, 611–619.

Thompson, V.A. Evans, J.St.B.T. and Handley, S.J. (2005). Persuading and dissuading by conditional argument. *Journal of Memory and Language*, 53, 238–257.

Thorndike, E.L. (1898). Animal intelligence: An experimental study of the associative processes in animals. *Psychological Monographs*, 2, No. 8.

Thorndike, E.L. (1914). *The Psychology of Learning.* New York: Teachers College.

Thorndike, E.L. and Lorge, I. (1944). *The Teacher's Word Book of 30,000 Words.* New York: Teachers College, Columbia University.

Tipper, S.P. (1985). The negative priming effect: Inhibitory priming by ignored objects. *Quarterly Journal of Experimental Psychology*, 37A, 571–590.

Tipper, S.P. and Behrmann, M. (1996). Object-centred not scene-based visual neglect. *Journal of Experimental Psychology: Human Perception and Performance*, 22, 1261–1278.

Tipper, S.P. and Driver, J. (1988). Negative priming between pictures and words: Evidence for semantic analysis of ignored stimuli. *Memory and Cognition*, 16, 64–70.

Tipper, S.P. Weaver, B. Jerreat, L.M. and Burak, A.L. (1994). Object-based and environment-based inhibition of return of visual attention. *Journal of Experimental Psychology: Human Perception and Performance*, 20, 3, 478–499.

Tippett, L.J. Miller, L.A. and Farah, M.J. (2000). Prosopamnesia: A selective impairment in face learning. *Cognitive Neuropsychology*, 17, 241–255.

Tisserand, D.J. and Jolles, J. (2003). On the involvement of prefrontal networks in cognitive ageing. *Cortex*, 39, 1107–1128.

Toth, J.P. Reingold, E.M. and Jacoby, L.L. (1995). A response to Graf and Komatsu's critique of the process dissociation procedure: When is caution necessary? *European Journal of Cognitive Psychology*, 7, 113–130.

Tranel, D. Damasio, H. and Damasio, A.R. (1997). A neural basis for the retrieval of conceptual knowledge. *Neuropsychologia*, 35, 10, 1319–1327.

Treisman, A.M. (1964). Verbal cues, language and meaning in selective attention. *American Journal of Psychology*, 77, 206–219.

Treisman, A.M. (1988). Features and objects: The fourteenth Bartlett Memorial Lecture. *Quarterly Journal of Experimental Psychology*, 40A, 201–237.

Treisman, A.M. and Geffen, G. (1967). Selective attention: Perception or response? *Quarterly Journal of Experimental Psychology*, 12, 1–18.

Treisman, A.M. and Gelade, G. (1980). A feature integration theory of attention. *Cognitive Psychology*, 12, 97–136.

Troyer, A.K. (2001). Improving memory, knowledge, satisfaction, and functioning via an educational and intervention program for older adults. *Ageing, Neuropsychology, and Cognition*, 8, 256–268.

Trueswell, J.C. Tanenhaus, M. and Garnsey, S. (1994). Semantic influences on parsing: Use of thematic role information on syntactic ambiguity resolution. *Journal of Memory and Language*, 33, 285–318.

Tuckey, M.R. and Brewer, N. (2003). How schemas affect eyewitness memory over repeated retrieval attempts. *Applied Cognitive Psychology*, 17, 785–800.

Tulving, E. (1972). Episodic and semantic memory. In E. Tulving and W. Donaldson (eds) *The Organisation of Memory*. New York: Academic Press.

Tulving, E. (1976). Ecphoric processes in recall and recognition. In J. Brown (ed.) *Recall and Recognition*. New York: Wiley.

Tulving, E. (1983). *Elements of Episodic Memory*. Oxford: Clarendon Press.

Tulving, E. (1985). How many memory systems are there? *American Psychologist*, 40, 385–398.

Tulving, E. (1987). Multiple memory systems and consciousness. *Human Neurobiology*, 6, 67–80.

Tulving, E. (1989). Memory: Performance, knowledge, and experience. *The European Journal of Cognitive Psychology*, 1, 3–26.

Tulving, E. (2001). The origin of autonoesis in episodic memory. In H.L. Roedigger and J.S. Nairne (eds) *The Nature of Remembering: Essays in Honour of Robert G. Crowder*. Washington, DC: American Psychological Association.

Tulving, E. Schacter, D.L. and Stark, H.A. (1982). Priming effects in word fragment completion are independent of recognition memory. *Journal of Experimental Psychology: Learning, Memory, and Cognition*, 17, 595–617.

Tulving, E. and Thomson, D.M. (1971). Retrieval processes in recognition memory: Effects of associative context. *Journal of Experimental Psychology*, 87, 116–124.

Tulving, E. and Thomson, D.M. (1973). Encoding specificity and retrieval processes in episodic memory. *Psychological Review*, 80, 352–373.

Turvey, M.T. (1973). On peripheral and central processes in vision: Inferences from information processing analysis of masking with patterned stimuli. *Psychological Review*, 80, 1–52.

Tversky, A. and Kahneman, D. (1973). Availability: A heuristic for judging frequency and probability. *Cognitive Psychology*, 5, 207–232.

Tversky, A. and Kahneman, D. (1980). Causal schemas in judgements under uncertainty. In M. Fishbein (ed.) *Progress in Social Psychology*. Hillsdale, NJ: Erlbaum Inc.

Tyler, L.K. Moss, H.E.and Jennings, F. (1995). Abstract word deficits in aphasia – evidence from semantic priming. *Neuropsychology*, 9, 354–363.

Underwood, B.J. and Postman, L. (1960). Extra-experimental sources of interference in forgetting. *Psychological Review*, 67, 73–95.

Underwood, G. (1974). Moray vs. the rest: The effects of extended shadowing practice. *Quarterly Journal of Experimental Psychology*, 67, 73–95.

Ungerleider, L.G. and Mishkin, M. (1982). Two cortical visual sysems. In D.J. Ingle, M.A. Goodale and R.J.W. Mansfield (eds) *Analysis of Visual Behaviour*. Cambridge, MA: MIT Press.

Vallar, G. and Baddeley, A.D. (1982). Short-term forgetting and the articulatory loop. *Quarterly Journal of Experimental Psychology*, 34A, 53–60.

Vallar, G. and Baddeley, A.D. (1984). Fractionation of working memory: Neuropsychological evidence for a phonological short-term store. *Journal of Verbal Learning and Verbal Behaviour*, 23, 151–161.

Vallar, G. Di Betta, A.M. and Silveri, M.C. (1997). The phonological short-term store rehearsal system: Patterns of impairment and neural correlates. *Neuropsychologia*, 35, 795–812.

Vargha-Khadem, F. Gadian, D.G. Watkins, K.E. *et al.* (1997). Differential effects of early hippocampal pathology on episodic and semantic memory. *Science*, 277, 376–380.

Verfaillie, M. Koseff, P. and Alexander, M.P. (2000). Acquisition of novel semantic information in amnesia: Effects of lesion location. *Neuropsychologia*, 38, 484–492.

Verfaillie, M. and Roth, H.L. (1996). Knowledge of English vocabulary in amnesia: An examination of premorbidly acquired semantic memory. *Journal of the International Neuropsychology Society*, 5, 443–453.

Verfaillie, M. and Treadwell, J.R. (1993). Studies of recognition memory in amnesia. *Neuropsychology*, 7, 5–13.

Victor, M. Adams, R.D. and Collings, G.H. (1989). *The Wernicke–Korsakoff Syndrome and Related Neurologic Disorders due to Alcoholism and Malnutrition* (2nd edn). Philadelphia: Davis.

Von Wright, J.M. Anderson, K. and Stenman, U. (1975). Generalisation of conditioned GSRs in dichotic listening. In P.M.A. Rabbitt and S. Dornic (eds) *Attention and Performance V*. London: Academic Press.

Vroomen, J. Bertelson, P. and Gelder, B.D. (2001). The ventriloquist effect does not depend on the direction of automatic visual attention. *Perception and Psychophysics*, 63, 4, 651–659.

Vroomen, J. and de Gelder, B.D. (2000). Sound enhances visual perception: Cross-modal effects of auditory organization on vision. *Journal of Experimental Psychology: Human Perception and Performance*, 26, 5, 1583–1590.

Wagenaar, W.A. (1986). My memory: A study of autobiographical memory over six years. *Cognitive Psychology*, 18, 225–252.

Wagenaar, W.A. (1994). The subjective probability of guilt. In G. Wright and P. Ayton (eds) *Subjective Probability*. Chichester: John Wiley and Sons Ltd.

Wager, T. and Smith, E.E. (2003). Neuroimaging studies of working memory: A meta-analysis. *Cognitive, Affective, and Behavioural Neuroscience*, 3, 255–274.

Waldfogel, S. (1948). The frequency and affective character of childhood memories. *Psychological Monographs: General and Applied*, 62 (whole issue).

Walker, B.N. and Kramer, G. (2004). Ecological psychoacoustics and auditory displays: Hearing, grouping and meaning making. In J.G. Neuhoff (ed.) *Ecological Psychoacoustics*: San Diego, CA: Academic Press; London: Elsevier.

Ward, R. Goodrich, S. and Driver J. (1994). Grouping reduces visual extinction: Neuropsychological evidence for weight-linkage in visual selection. *Visual Cognition*, 1, 101–129.

Warren, E.W. and Groome, D.H. (1984). Memory test performance under three different waveforms of ECT for depression. *British Journal of Psychiatry*, 144, 370–375.

Warrington, E.K. (1979). Neuropsychological evidence for multiple memory systems. In *Brain and Mind: Ciba Foundation Symposium 69 (new series)*. Amsterdam: Excerpta Medica, 153–166.

Warrington, E.K. (1981). Concrete word dyslexia. *British Journal of Psychology*, 72, 175–196.

Warrington, E.K. (1982). Neuropsychological studies of object recognition. *Philosophical Transactions of the Royal Society of London, Series B*, 298, 15–33.

Warrington, E.K. (1985). Agnosia: The impairment of object recognition. In P.J. Vinken, G.W. Gruyen and H.L. Klawans (eds) *Handbook of Clinical Neurology*. Amsterdam: Elsevier.

Warrington, E.K. (1986). Memory for facts and memory for events. *British Journal of Clinical Psychology*, 25, 1–12.

Warrington, E.K. and McCarthy, R.A. (1983). Category specific access dysphasia. *Brain*, 106, 859–878.

Warrington, E.K. and Shallice, T. (1969). The selective impairment of auditory-verbal short-term memory. *Brain*, 92, 885–896.

Warrington, E.K. and Shallice, T. (1972). Neuropsychological evidence of visual storage in short-term memory tasks. *Quarterly Journal of Experimental Psychology*, 24, 30–40.

Warrington, E.K. and Shallice, T. (1984). Category specific semantic impairments. *Brain*, 107, 829–853.

Warrington, E.K. and Weiskrantz, L. (1968). A new method of testing long-term retention with special reference to amnesic patients. *Nature*, 217, 972–974.

Warrington, E.K. and Weiskrantz, L. (1970). Amnesic syndrome: Consolidation or retrieval? *Nature*, 228, 628–630.

Wason, P.C. (1960). On the failure to eliminate hypotheses in a conceptual task. *Quarterly Journal of Experimental Psychology*, 12, 129–140.

Wason, P.C. (1968). Reasoning about a rule. *Quarterly Journal of Experimental Psychology*, 23, 63–71.

Wason, P.C. and Shapiro, D. (1971). Natural and contrived experience in a reasoning problem. *Quarterly Journal of Experimental Psychology*, 23, 63–71.

Watson, J.B. (1913). Psychology as the behaviourist views it. *Psychological Review*, 20, 158–177.

Wearing, D. (2005). *Forever Today*. London: Transworld.

Weeks, D. Freeman, C.P.L. and Kendell, R.E. (1980). ECT: II. Enduring cognitive deficits? *British Journal of Psychiatry*, 137, 26–37.

Wegner, D.M. and Wheatley, T.P. (1999). Apparent mental causation: Sources of the experience of will. *American Psychologist*, 54, 480–492.

Weisberg, R.W. and Alba, J.W. (1981). An examination of the alleged role of 'fixation' in the solution of several 'insight' problems. *Journal of Experimental Psychology: General*, 110, 169–192.

Weiskrantz, L. (1986). *Blindsight: A Case Study and Implications*. Oxford: Oxford University Press.

Weiskrantz, L. Warrington, E.K. Sanders, M.D. and Marshall, J. (1974). Visual capacity of the hemianopic field following a restricted occipital ablation. *Brain*, 97, 709–728.

Welford, A.T. (1952). The psychological refractory period and the timing of high speed performance. *British Journal of Psychology*, 43, 2–19.

Wells, G.L. Small, M. Penrod, S. *et al.* (1998). Eyewitness identification procedures: Recommendations for lineups and photospreads. *Law and Human Behaviour*, 22, 603–647.

Welt, L. (1888). Über Charakterveränderungen des Menschen infolge von Läsionen des Stirnhirns. *Deutsche Archiv für Klinische Medizin*, 42, 339–390.

Werbos, P. (1974). Beyond regression: New tools for prediction and analysis in the behavioural sciences. Ph.D. thesis, Harvard University, Cambridge, MA.

Wernicke, C. (1874). Der Aphasische Symptomen Komplex. Breslau: Cohn and Weigert. Reprinted in G. Eggert (ed.) *Wernicke's Works on Aphasia: A Source Book and Review* (vol. 1). The Hague: Mouton, 1977.

Wertheimer, M. (1912). Experimentelle studien uber das sehen von bewegung. *Zeitschrift für Psychologie*, 61, 161–265.

Wertheimer, M. (1923). Untersuchungen zur Lehre von der Gestalt. *Zeitschrift Forschung*, 4, 301–350.

Wessinger, C.M. Fendrich, R. and Gazzaniga, M.S. (1997). Islands of residual vision in hemianopic patients. *Journal of Cognitive Neuroscience*, 9, 203–221.

West, M.J. Coleman, P.D. Flood, D.G. and Troncoso, J.C. (1994). Differences in the pattern of hippocampal neuronal loss in normal ageing and Alzheimer's disease. *The Lancet*, 344, 769–772.

Westmacott, R. Freedman, M. Black, S.E. Stokes, K.A. and Moscovitch, M. (2004). Temporally graded semantic memory loss in Alzheimer's disease: Cross-sectional and longitudinal studies. *Cognitive Neuropsychology*, 21, 353–378.

Westwood, D.A. and Goodale, M.A. (2003). Perceptual illusion and the realtime control of action. *Spat Vis*, 16, 243–254.

Wheeldon, L.R. and Monsell, S. (1992). The locus of repetition priming of spoken word production. *Quarterly Journal of Experimental Psychology*, 44A, 723–761.

Wheeler, M.A. and McMillan, C.T. (2001). Focal retrograde amnesia and the episodic-semantic distinction. *Cognitive, Affective, and Behavioural Neuroscience*, 1, 22–36.

Whitlow, S.D. Althoff, R.R. and Cohen, N.J. (1995). Deficit in relational (declarative) memory in amnesia. *Society for Neuroscience Abstracts*, 21, 754.

Whitty, C.W.M. and Zangwill, O.L. (1976). *Amnesia*. London: Butterworths.

Wickelgren, W.A. (1968). Sparing of short-term memory in an amnesic patient: Implications for strength theory of memory. *Neuropsychologia*, 6, 235–244.

Wickens, C.D. (1992). *Engineering Psychology and Human Performance* (2nd edn). New York: Harper Collins.

Wilkins A.J. Shallice, T. and McCarthy, R. (1987). Frontal lesions and sustained attention. *Neuropsychologia*, 25, 259–365.

Williams, J.M.G. Watts, F.N. MacLeod, C. and Mathews, A. (1988). *Cognitive Psychology and Emotional Disorders*. New York: Wiley.

Williams, S.J. Wright, D.B. and Freeman, N.H. (2002). Inhibiting children's memory of an interactive event: The effectiveness of a cover-up. *Applied Cognitive Psychology*, 16, 651–664.

Wilshire, C.E. and Saffran, E.M. (2005). Contrasting effects of phonological priming in aphasic word production. *Cognition*, 95, 31–71.

Wilson, B.A. (1987). *Rehabilitation of Memory*. New York: Guilford.

Wilson, B.A. (1999). *Case Studies in Neuropsychological Rehabilitation*. New York: Oxford University Press.

Wilson, B.A. (2004). Management and rehabilitation of memory problems in brain-injured adults. In A.D. Baddeley, M.D. Kopelman, and B.A.Wilson (eds) *The Essential Handbook of Memory Disorders for Clinicians*. Chichester: Wiley.

Wilson, B.A. Baddeley, A.D. and Kapur, N. (1995). Dense amnesia in a professional musician following herpes simplex virus encephalitis. *Journal of Clinical and Experimental Neuropsychology*, 17, 668–681.

Wilson, B.A. Kazniak, A.W. and Fox, J.H. (1981). Remote memory in senile dementia. *Cortex*, 17, 41–48.

Wilson, B.A. and Wearing, D. (1995). Amnesia in a musician. In R. Campbell and M. Conway (eds) *Broken Memories*. Oxford: Blackwell.

Winner, E. and Gardner, H. (1977). The comprehension of metaphor in brain damaged patients. *Brain*, 100, 717–729.

Winograd, E. (1976). Recognition memory for faces following nine different judgements. *Bulletin of the Psychonomic Society*, 8, 419–421.

Wolters, G. Theunisen, I. Bemelmans, K.J. van der Does, A.J.W. and Spinhoven, P. (1996). Immediate and intermediate-term effectiveness of a memory training program for the elderly. *Journal of Cognitive Rehabilitation*, 14, 16–22.

Wright, D.B. Loftus, E.F. and Hall, M. (2001). Now you see it, now you don't: Inhibiting recall in the recognition of scenes. *Applied Cognitive Psychology*, 15, 471–482.

Wright, D.B. Self, G. and Justice, C. (2000). Memory conformity: Exploring misinformation effects when presented by another person. *British Journal of Psychology*, 91, 189–202.

Yarmey, A.D. (2001). Does eyewitness memory research have any probative value for the courts? *Canadian Psychology*, 42, 92–100.

Yonelinas, A.P. (2002). Components of episodic memory: The contribution of recollection and familiarity. In A. Baddeley, M. Conway, and J. Aggleton (eds) *Episodic Memory: New Directions in Research*. Oxford: Oxford University Press.

Young, A.W. (ed.) (1998). *Face and Mind*. Oxford: Oxford University Press.

Young, A.W. Newcombe, F. de Haan, E.H.F. Small, M. and Hay, D.C. (1993). Face perception after brain injury: Selective impairments affecting identity and expression. *Brain*, 116, 941–959.

Zacher, W. (1901). Über ein Fall von doppelseitigem, symmetrisch gelegenem Erweich-ungsherd im Stirnhirn und Neuritis optica. *Neurologisches Zentralblatt*, 20, 1074–1083.

Zanetti, O. Zanieri, G. Giovanni, G.D. de Vreese, L.P. Pezzini, A. Metitieri, T. *et al.* (2001). Effectiveness of procedural memory stimulation in mild Alzheimer's disease patients. In L. Clare and R.T. Woods (eds) *Cognitive Rehabilitation in Dementia: A Special Issue of Neuropsychological Rehabilitation*. Hove: Psychology Press.

Zaragoza, M.S. and Lane, S.M. (1998). Processing resources and eyewitness suggestibility. *Legal and Criminological Psychology*, 3, 294–300.

Zeki, S. (2003). The disunity of consciousness. *Trends in Cognitive Sciences*, 7, 214–218.

Ziegler, J.C. Van Orden, G.C. and Jacobs, A.M. (1997). Phonology can help or hurt the perception of print. *Journal of Experimental Psychology: Human Perception and Performance*, 23, 845–860.

Zola, D. (1984). Redundancy and word perception during reading. *Perception and Psycho-physics*, 36, 277–284.

Zola-Morgan, S. and Squire, L.R. (2000). The medial temporal lobe and the hippocampus. In E. Tulving and F.I.M. Craik (eds) *The Oxford Handbook of Memory*. Oxford: Oxford University Press.

Author index

Subject index